ROUTLEDGE HANDBOOK OF POLITICAL ADVERTISING

This Handbook provides the most comprehensive overview of the role of electoral advertising on television and new forms of advertising in countries from all parts of the world currently available. Thematic chapters address advertising effects, negative ads, the perspective of practitioners and gender role. Country chapters summarize research on issues including political and electoral systems; history of ads; the content of ads; reception and effects of ads; regulation of political advertising on television and the Internet; financing political advertising; and prospects for the future. The Handbook confirms that candidates spend the major part of their campaign budget on television advertising. The US enjoys a special situation with almost no restrictions on electoral advertising whereas other countries have regulation for the time, amount and sometimes even the content of electoral advertising or they do not allow television advertising at all. The role that television advertising plays in elections is dependent on the political, the electoral and the media context and can generally be regarded as a reflection of the political culture of a country. The Internet is relatively unregulated and is the channel of the future for political advertising in many countries.

Christina Holtz-Bacha is Professor of Communication at Friedrich-Alexander University Erlangen-Nürnberg, Germany. She was a visiting scholar at the University of Minnesota in Minneapolis, a Research Fellow at the Shorenstein Center, Harvard University and a guest researcher at the University of Gothenburg, Sweden. She is presently the Chair of the Political Communication Research Section of IAMCR. Her research interests are political communication, media systems and media policy.

Marion R. Just is Professor of Political Science at Wellesley College and an Associate of the Shorenstein Center on Media, Politics and Public Policy at Harvard's Kennedy School of Government. Her research in political science focuses on elections, politics and the media. She has published several co-authored books and articles in professional journals.

"Holtz-Bacha and Just have compiled a comprehensive handbook on political advertising in many countries around the world. It has first-rate writers who concisely and effectively convey the latest in ad messaging and impact. If you want to know what works and why, this is the book for you. Both practitioners and researchers will benefit from this handbook."

Darrell West, *Vice President and Director – Governance Studies and Founding Director – Center for Technology Innovation, Brookings Institute, USA*

ROUTLEDGE HANDBOOK OF POLITICAL ADVERTISING

Edited by Christina Holtz-Bacha and Marion R. Just

Routledge
Taylor & Francis Group

NEW YORK AND LONDON

First published 2017
by Routledge
711 Third Avenue, New York, NY 10017

and by Routledge
2 Park Square, Milton Park, Abingdon, Oxon, OX14 4RN

Routledge is an imprint of the Taylor & Francis Group, an informa business

Library of Congress Cataloging in Publication Data
Names: Holtz-Bacha, Christina, editor. | Just, Marion R., editor.
Title: Routledge handbook of political advertising / edited by Christina Holtz-Bacha and Marion R. Just.
Other titles: Handbook of political advertising
Description: New York, NY: Routledge, 2017. | Includes bibliographical references and index.
Identifiers: LCCN 2016040025 | ISBN 9781138908307 (hbk) | ISBN 9781315694504 (ebk)
Subjects: LCSH: Advertising, Political. | Advertising, Political–Case studies.
Classification: LCC JF2112.A4 R68 2017 | DDC 324.7/3–dc23
LC record available at https://lccn.loc.gov/2016040025

ISBN: 978-1-138-90830-7 (hbk)
ISBN: 978-1-315-69450-4 (ebk)

Typeset in Bembo
by Out of House Publishing

Printed and bound in the United States of America by
Edwards Brothers Malloy on sustainably sourced paper

CONTENTS

FIGURES

TABLES

NOTES ON CONTRIBUTORS

Alessandra Aldé is a professor and researcher at the postgraduate program of Communication Studies of Rio de Janeiro State University (UERJ), Brazil. Her main interests are citizens' political attitudes and the role of the Internet; political propaganda and persuasion strategies; and newspaper coverage of elections. She has been founder and president (2013–15) of the Brazilian Association of Political Communication Researchers (Compolítica), and is Editor of the *Compolítica* journal. She directed, with Vicente Ferraz, the documentary *Arquitetos do Poder* (2010), on Brazilian media and politics.

Jair Alberto Arciniegas is a research analyst at the National Department of Statistics of Colombia. He holds a master's degree in Political Science from Universidad de los Andes. His research focuses on mass media and political economy.

Marco Arellano-Toledo holds a Ph.D. in Political Science, Universidad Nacional Autónoma de México (UNAM). He is a professor in the Department of Political Science at UNAM and co-author of the book *Negative campaigns, how it affects the vote* (PNUD/IBERO, 2012).

Mary C. Banwart is Professor of Communication at the University of Kansas. Her research focuses on political campaign communication and the influence of gender in political campaigns. She co-authored the book *Gender and political candidate communication: Videostyle, webstyle, and newsstyle*. Dr. Banwart was a co-recipient of the 2003 Central States Communication Association Federation Prize for research analyzing gender in US Senate, House, and gubernatorial mixed-gender debates, and a co-recipient of the 2000 Carrie Chapman Catt Prize for Research on Women and Politics.

Todd L. Belt is Professor of Political Science at the University of Hawai'i at Hilo. His research and writing focuses on the mass media, public opinion, the presidency, campaigns and elections. He is the co-author of four books and has published over a dozen chapters in edited scholarly books, and over two dozen scholarly articles. Dr. Belt received his B.A. in Economics and Political Science at the University of California, Irvine, and his M.A. and Ph.D. in Political Science at the University of Southern California. He has worked as a consultant doing public opinion research for interest groups and media market research for think tanks and media corporations. Dr. Belt has been a lecturer or instructor at numerous universities and held a Visiting Scholar position at Kyungpook University in Daegu, South Korea. He is a frequent contributor to media reporting on politics and is the recipient of two teaching awards.

Felipe Borba is Professor of Political Science and head of the Department of Political Studies at the Federal University of the State of Rio de Janeiro – Unirio (Brazil). His main lines of research are elections, Brazilian politics, public opinion, political communication, negative campaign, campaign effect and electoral behavior. Felipe Borba is also the coordinator of the Electoral Research Group at Unirio and director of the "Local Politics in the State of Rio de Janeiro" project.

Alexandre Borrell holds a Ph.D. in contemporary history and is associate editor-in-chief of *Parlement[s], Revue d'histoire politique*. He is an associate researcher at LCP (UMR Irisso 7170, CNRS/Université Paris-Dauphine, PSL Research University), at POLEN (EA 4710, Université of Orléans), where he teaches contemporary and visual history, and an associate member of the team Cultura mediática (Universidad de Chili). He works on political communication, news media coverage of political campaigns, media coverage of French suburbs in television news, and pictures of the French society in media and political communication. These themes brought him to work on the regulation, the production and the content of French political spots. He was part of the "European Election Campaign 2014" research project and has written several chapters about the content of the spots of the French presidential campaigns from 1988 to 2012 in *Médias et élections* (2011), *Nottingham French Studies* (2013) and *Sous les images, la politique* (2014).

Steve Bouchard has over 25 years of experience in local, state, national and international campaigns, and has worked for candidates across the US, including Senator Mark Warner (D-VA), Governor Ted Strickland (D-OH), former Senators Bob Graham (D-FL) and Bob Kerrey (D-NE), then-Senator Hillary Clinton and others. He is a founding partner at SJB Strategies, International, an international consulting firm, and he is a partner at Bouchard Gold Communications, an award-winning political communications firm. He has guest lectured at numerous colleges and universities including Georgetown and Cornell and for the past several years has served as a judge at the Harvard Kennedy School's Mock Presidential Debates.

Dianne Bystrom (Ph.D., University of Oklahoma, 1995) has served as the director of the Carrie Chapman Catt Center for Women and Politics at Iowa State University since 1996. A frequent commentator about political and women's issues for state, national and international media, her current research focuses on the styles and strategies used by female and male political candidates in their television advertising, websites and speeches and the coverage of women candidates and political leaders by the media. Dr. Bystrom is a contributor, co-author or co-editor of 21 books on women and politics, political communication, and campaigns and elections and has written journal articles on the Iowa caucus, youth voters and the media coverage of female political candidates.

Baki Can is a lecturer in the Department of Public Relations at Ege University in İzmir, Turkey. He holds a doctorate in using reasoning and emotion in persuasive communication from İstanbul University. He specializes in the study of political communication, especially in political propaganda, voter persuasion, political advertising and public speaking. He has taught at his department and written about these issues, which have been published in Turkey, the US and other countries. In addition to his academic duties, he has been a consultant for numerous members of parliament and mayoral candidates during election campaigns. He served as a consultant to the mayor of İzmir and as adviser to the Speaker of the Grand National Assembly of Turkey. Currently he works as the İzmir Coordinator of the Presidency for Turks of Abroad, of the Republic of Turkey Prime Ministry.

Ann Crigler is Professor of Political Science with appointments in the Price School of Public Policy and the Annenberg School for Communications at the University of Southern California. She has published numerous books, articles and essays on political communication, elections, emotions and political behavior. Her co-authored and edited books include: *Common knowledge: News* *and the construction of political meaning* (University of Chicago Press, 1992); the award-winning *Crosstalk: Citizens, candidates and the media in a presidential campaign* (University of Chicago Press, 1996); *The psychology of political communication* (University of Michigan Press, 1996); *Rethinking the vote: The politics and prospects of American election reform* (Oxford University Press, 2004); and *The affect effect: Dynamics of emotion in political thinking and behavior* (University of Chicago Press, 2007). Her current research examines the role of social media in US elections, emotions and political decision-making and youth civic engagement. She and her students are currently working with elementary schools in Los Angeles to conduct research and increase children's civic skills, involvement and community networks through the USC Penny Harvest.

Simon Cross is Senior Lecturer in the Department of English and Media at Nottingham Trent University. He has published widely on the history of media and various policy and political matters relating to young people, the representation of political leadership and local news reporting practices. This also includes related work on news coverage of drugs and journalistic coverage of highly sensitive topics. His various others works reflect his long-standing interest in understanding the past and include *Mediating madness* (Palgrave Macmillan, 2010) and assorted other publications exploring the interaction between media representation and mental illness.

Jamil Dakhlia is Professor in Media Studies at the Sorbonne Nouvelle University (Paris 3- USPC), where he is also Dean of the Faculty of Arts and Media (UFR Arts & Médias). He is a researcher at the CIM-MCPN (Paris 3) and an associate researcher at the LCP (UMR Irisso 7170, CNRS/ Université Paris-Dauphine, PSL Research University). His main research topics are media history and sociology, especially of magazines and popular media, celebrity culture, political communication, and in particular celebrity politics. Among his publications in French are *Politique people* (2008, new edition in 2015) and *Mythologie de la peopolisation* (2010), and in English, "Humour as a means of popular empowerment: The discourse of the French gossip magazines," in J. Chovanec and I. Ermida (Eds.), *Language and humour in the media* (Cambridge Scholars Publishing, 2012); "From the Olympians to the ordinary heroes: Stars in the French popular press," *History of Stardom Reconsidered*, University of Turku (Finland): http://iipc.utu.fi/reconsidered/Dakhlia.pdf.

Martín D'Alessandro holds a B.A. in Political Science (Universidad de Buenos Aires), M.A. in Research in Social Sciences (Universidad de Buenos Aires) and Ph.D. in Social Sciences (Universidad de Buenos Aires). He is Professor of Political Science at the Universidad de Buenos Aires, and has also taught graduate and undergraduate courses at Universidad de San Andrés (Argentina), Facultad Latinoamericana de Ciencias Sociales, Flacso (Argentina), Universidad Torcuato Di Tella (Argentina) and Universidad Nacional de San Martín (Argentina). He is a researcher of the Consejo Nacional de Investigaciones Científicas y Técnicas, Conicet (Argentina) and of the Instituto de Investigaciones "Gino Germani," Facultad de Ciencias Sociales of the Universidad de Buenos Aires (Argentina). Currently, he is the editor of *POSTData* political science journal, and President of the Sociedad Argentina de Análisis Político (SAAP).

Bogusława Dobek-Ostrowska, Ph.D., is a professor of communication and a chair of the Department of Communication and Journalism at the University of Wrocław in Poland. She was a founder and the first President of the Polish Communication Association. She is a founder and editor of the *Central European Journal of Communication*, an official journal of the PCA. She was the President of the International Federation of Communication Associations (2010–12). She was a member of the Editorial Board of *Communication Theory* (2012–16), a journal of the International Communication Association. She is co-editor of the series Studies in Communication and Politics (Peter Lang Edition) and editor of the series Communication and Media (University of Wrocław Press). She has published several books and articles and she is one of the most highly cited Polish communication scholars. Her research interests include political communication and the transformation of the media system after the collapse of communism in Central and Eastern Europe.

Elina Erzikova is an associate professor of public relations in the Department of Journalism at Central Michigan University. Her research interests include the role of power in the state – media relations, professional ethics, cultural aspects of journalism and public relations. She has published in *Political Communication, Mass Communication and Society, International Communication Gazette, Journalism Studies, Public Relations Review* and *Public Relations Journal*.

Miguel García-Sánchez is Associate Professor of Political Science and Associate Director of Observatorio de la Democracia at Universidad de los Andes. He holds a Ph.D. in Political Science from the University of Pittsburgh. His research focuses on public opinion, and the relationship between social contexts and political behavior. His work has appeared in various peer-reviewed outlets and he has published a book on democratization and citizenship in Colombia.

Ian Glenn is Emeritus Professor of Media Studies at the University of Cape Town. He received his Ph.D. in English and American Literature from the University of Pennsylvania after studies at the University of Kwa-Zulu Natal and York University in the UK. After joining the Department of English at the University of Cape Town, he helped found the Centre for Film and Media Studies at the university and served as director for much of its first decade. His research interests include nature and travel media and political communication. He is currently working on a history of wildlife documentary in Southern Africa and on communication strategies linked to the prevention of rhino poaching. Recent publications include an analysis of framing in the Oscar Pistorius trial (co-author Kelly Phelps) in the *Journal of African Media Studies* and an analysis of the role of media in student protests in South Africa in the *Bulletin of the National Library of South Africa*.

Justin Hartley is a US political strategist, public policy analyst, campaign manager and scholar in leadership and persuasive communications. Justin is currently a research fellow at the Center for Public Leadership, Harvard University. Prior to that he held the position of Visiting Scholar in Media, Politics and Public Policy at the Shorenstein Center, also at Harvard. A Harvard graduate, he completed a master's in Public Administration at the John F. Kennedy School of Government, where he graduated in the top 1% in his class. Justin also has the distinction of being both a John F. Kennedy Fellow at Harvard and a 2014 Fulbright Scholar (Australia).

Jenny L. Holland is Assistant Professor of Politics and Government at Ohio Wesleyan University. She has worked as a research associate for the Wesleyan Media Project, and her research focuses on political campaigns, voter choice and political advertising. Holland received her Ph.D. in political science from Washington State University in 2013. Her work has been published in *Presidential Studies Quarterly* and in several book chapters.

Christina Holtz-Bacha is Professor of Communication at Friedrich-Alexander Universität Erlangen-Nürnberg, Germany. She was a visiting scholar at the University of Minnesota in Minneapolis, a research fellow at the Shorenstein Center, Harvard University and a guest researcher at the University of Gothenburg, Sweden. She is currently the Chair of the Political Communication Research Section of IAMCR. She is a co-editor of the German communication journal *Publizistik* and a member of the editorial boards of several international journals. Her research interests are political communication, media systems and media policy. Recent publications include *Europawahlkampf 2014* (Springer VS, 2016), *Die Massenmedien im Wahlkampf. Die Bundestagswahl 2013* (Springer VS, 2015); *Opinion polls and the media: Reflecting and shaping public opinion* (Palgrave 2012, with J. Strömbäck).

Steve Jarding currently teaches at the John F. Kennedy School of Government at Harvard University, where he has taught since 2004. His course on campaign management has twice been nominated for the "Most Influential Course Award" and in 2016 he was voted by the student body as "Teacher of the Year." He also teaches at the IESE Business School in Madrid, Spain and annually to educational groups in Brazil and Romania, and has taught at the University of Oklahoma, George Mason University and American University. He is the founding partner and CEO of the international consulting company, SJB Strategies International which advises candidates and causes around the world. He has lectured or consulted internationally for campaigns and causes in over 20 countries in Asia, Africa, India, South America and Europe. Jarding is the co-author of the political book, *Foxes in the henhouse*, which was Simon & Schuster's lead political book in 2006.

Jan Jirák, Ph.D., is Professor and Chair of the Department of Media Studies at Metropolitan University Prague and member of the Department of Media Studies, Faculty of Social Sciences, Charles University, Prague. He became a professor in the field of Media Studies in 2008. He is the author of texts on the transformation of the Czech media and a co-author of *Introduction to media studies* (2001), *Media and society* (2003), *Mass media* (2009, 2015) and *The history of Czech media* (2011), and co-editor of *Political Communication and Media* (2000). From 1997 to 2000, he chaired the Council of Czech Public Television. He translates novels (Updike, Vonnegut, Le Carré, Auster) as well as media-related texts (McQuail, DeFleur-Ball-Rokeach, Thompson, Curran).

Bengt Johansson, Ph.D., is Professor in Journalism and Mass Communication at the Department of Journalism, Media and Communication, University of Gothenburg. His research is mainly focused on different aspects of political communication, where political advertising is one of the key areas of interest. Among the most recent publications are *Election posters around the globe* (in press, Springer, co-edited with Christina Holtz-Bacha), "Negativity in the public space: Comparing 100 years of election posters in Sweden" (in Voltmer and Canel (Eds.), *Political communication across time and space* (Palgrave, 2014)) and "Through the party lens: How citizens evaluate TV electoral spots" (*Journal of Political Marketing*, 2014, with Christina Holtz-Bacha).

Matias Jove has a Ph.D. in Communication from the University Complutense of Madrid, Spain. He combines academia with communication practice at political institutions. He has lectured at the School of Communication at the University CEU San Pablo. Currently he works as Chief of Staff of the Ministry of Employment and Social Security of Spain.

Julio Juárez-Gámiz is a research associate at the Centre for Interdisciplinary Research for Sciences and Humanities (CEIICH) at the National Autonomous University of Mexico (UNAM). He holds a B.A. in Psychology from UNAM and an M.A. and Ph.D. in Political Communication from the University of Sheffield, England. He recently published the book *The other digital gap: The information and knowledge societies* (UNAM, 2015) and the paper "Organized crime and news treatment in Mexico: A longitudinal analysis of three news television programs" (2015) in the *Journal of Latin American Communication Research*. He has conducted electoral observation projects funded by the United Nations Development Program regarding political advertising in two federal elections in Mexico (2009, 2012).

Marion R. Just is Professor of Political Science at Wellesley College and an associate of the Shorenstein Center on Media, Politics and Public Policy at Harvard's Kennedy School of Government. Her research in political science focuses on elections, politics and the media. Her co-authored books include *We interrupt this newscast: How to improve local news and win ratings, too; Crosstalk: Citizens, candidates and the media in a presidential campaign* and *Common knowledge: News and the construction of political meaning*. She is a co-editor of *Twitter and elections around the world: Campaigning in 140 characters or less, Framing terrorism: The news media, the government and the public* and *Rethinking the vote:*

Politics and prospects of election reform. She has published numerous articles in professional journals and book chapters. Just is a past chair of the Political Communication Section of the American Political Science Association. She received the Section's Edelman Distinguished Career Award in 2007. Her current research focuses on new media.

Michael W. Kearney is a doctoral candidate in communication studies at the University of Kansas. His research examines political polarization in an era of digital and social media. He has authored work on advanced topics in quantitative research methods and published experimental research examining political campaign communication via social media.

Sanne Kruikemeier is Assistant Professor of Political Communication at the Amsterdam School of Communication Research, University of Amsterdam. Her research focuses on the content and effects of online communication in a political context. She is currently co-chair of the political communication division of the Netherlands-Flanders Communication Association.

Guy Lachapelle is Professor in the Department of Political Science at Concordia University since 1984. He obtained his Ph.D. in Political Science from Northwestern University (1986). He was president of the Société québécoise de science politique (1996–7). He was the co-chairperson of the organizing Committee for the XVIIIth World Congress of the International Political Science Association in Quebec City in the year 2000 (August 1–5, 2000), and was director of the MPPA program (1990–1). He has been the Secretary General of the International Political Science Association (IPSA) since 2000. His latest publications include: *Political parties in the digital age* (De Gruyter, 2015); *L'analyse des politiques publiques* (PUM, 2011); *Le destin américain du Québec: Américanité, américanisation et anti-américanisme* (PUL, 2010); *Le Bloc Québécois – 20 ans au nom du Québec* (Richard Vézina Éditeur, 2010); *Diversité culturelle, identités et mondialisation – De la ratification à la mise en œuvre de la Convention sur la diversité culturelle* (PUL, 2008); *Claude Ryan et la violence du pouvoir* (PUL, 2005); *Mastering globalization: New sub-states' governance and strategy* (Routledge, 2005); *Globalización, gobernanza e identidades* (Estudis 12, Fundació Carles PI i Sunyer, 2004); *Mondialisation, gouvernance et nouvelle stratégies subétatiques* (PUL, 2004); *Robert Bourassa: un bâtisseur tranquille* (PUL, 2002); *Globalization, governance and identity* (PUM, 2002). His publications include contributions to *Revue française de science politique*, *Publius*, *Canadian Journal of Political Science*, *Revue québécoise de science politique*, *Québec Studies*, *Canadian Journal of Program Evaluation*, *Éthique publique* and *Politique et sociétés*. He is often solicited by the media. His recent work has focused on public policy, public opinion theory, and US and Quebec politics.

Jinah Lee is a professor in the Communication Department at Tokyo Woman's Christian University in Japan. She received her Ph.D. in Sociology from Keio University in 2001. She has been a visiting professor at the Institute of Asian Research, College for Interdisciplinary Studies, The University of British Columbia in 2011. Her research interests include political communication, advertising, gender and transnational media consumption. She has published widely on political advertising, women politicians and the media, and advertising and consumer psychology. She is a co-translator of the Japanese version of *Mass communication theory: Foundations, ferment, and future*, 3rd ed. (2007). She is the author of the book *The content and reception of political advertising in Japan* (2011, in Japanese). She was the 2009 recipient of the Yoshida Award for Grant Research from the Yoshida Hideo Memorial Foundation of Dentsu, which supported the research in her book. The book has been published with the aid of a grant from the Academic Society of Tokyo Woman's Christian University.

Alberto Pedro López-Hermida Russo is Professor of Communication Theory, Public Opinion and Political Communication at the School of Communication at the Universidad de los Andes (Chile). He holds a Ph.D. in Public Communication and a Master in Government and Cultural Organization from Universidad de Navarra (Spain). He recently developed lines of research on storytelling and new narrative transmedia in the political and institutional environment, the image of women in political campaigns, the analysis of electoral advertising, new technologies and the relationship between fiction and political communication. Besides Chile, he has been invited to lecture and conduct workshops on these topics in Uruguay, Paraguay, Colombia, Mexico and other countries, where he has been a consultant.

Tristan Masson is a second-year undergraduate student at Concordia University enrolled in the Political Science – Honours and Co-operative Education, and Sustainability Studies programs. Together with Prof. Guy Lachapelle, he is conducting research in Canadian-Québec politics and political communication. He also has a research interest in sustainable development and, to this end, has presented research and policy proposals at international conferences. Tristan Masson is also an active member in his community, volunteering for various organizations. He is socially engaged and his goal is to contribute to the academic dialogue and policy debates.

Robert Mattes is Professor of Political Studies and Director of the Democracy in Africa Research Unit in the Centre for Social Science Research at the University of Cape Town. He is also Senior Adviser to, and co-founder of, Afrobarometer, a ground-breaking regular survey of public opinion in 34 African countries. He has also helped to launch and run other major research projects such as the African Legislatures Project (Co-Principal Investigator) and the South African National Election Study (Principal Investigator). His research has focused on the development of democratic attitudes and practices in South Africa and across the continent. He is the co-author (with Michael Bratton and E. Gyimah-Boadi) of *Public opinion, democracy and markets in Africa* (Cambridge University Press, 2005) and has authored or co-authored articles in journals such as the *American Journal of Political Science*, *British Journal of Political Science*, *World Development*, *Journal of Democracy*, *Democratization* and *Party Politics*. He holds a Ph.D. in Political Science from the University of Illinois, Urbana-Champaign (1992).

Stephen Mills is a lecturer in the Graduate School of Government, University of Sydney. He has written widely on Australian campaign management and political parties. His 2014 book *The professionals: Strategy, money and the rise of the political campaigner in Australia* was awarded the Australian Political Studies Association's Henry Mayer Book Prize in 2015. He is a former newspaper journalist and editor, corporate public affairs practitioner and political adviser, serving as speechwriter to former Australian Prime Minister Bob Hawke.

Aida Mokhtar is a lecturer in the Department of Communication of the IIUM. She obtained her Ph.D. from the University of Stirling, United Kingdom (UK) in 2011. Her Ph.D. research study was a case study of PETRONAS corporate television advertisements that were supervised and created by the late Creative Director, Yasmin Ahmad. Her research interests are social advertising, advertising regulations, television advertising, corporate advertising, Islamic advertising and Integrated Marketing Communication (IMC). She is a member of the International Communication Association and American Academy of Advertising.

Tom Moring (Dr.Pol.Sc., Swedish School of Social Science, University of Helsinki) is Professor of Communication and Journalism. His research interests include political communication, election campaign studies and broadcasting. Together with the Finnish TNS Gallup he has since 1992 systematically conducted a time series survey covering all nation-wide selections in Finland. He has worked as a leader and grant-holding partner in international projects, and published comparative research on political communication culture, professionalization of journalism, politics, and election campaigns, political advertising, mediatization, and broadcasting. He started his career as a journalist, and later as Director of Radio Programs of the Swedish radio programs in the Finnish Broadcasting Company (Yle), and has served as Chair of the Board of the newspaper publishing house HSS Media in Ostrobotnia in Finland.

Edoardo Novelli is Associate Professor at the University of Roma Tre. His research interests focus on evolution of political communication, the history of propaganda, electoral campaigns and on the relationship between politics, media and images. He promoted international research on 2009 and 2014 European Election Campaigns, is a member of the editorial board of the journal *Comunicazione Politica*, and is head of the digital archive of Italian political spots: www.archivispotpolitici.it. He has published articles in the *Journal of Italian Cinema & Media Studies*, *Studi Culturali* and *Comunicazione Politica*, and collaborated with newspapers La Stampa, Il Venerdì di Repubblica and television stations RAI Tre, RAI International, La7. His most recent publications are *La democrazia del talk show: Storia di un genere che ha cambiato la televisione, la politica l'Italia [The talk-show democracy: History of a genre that has changed television, politics, Italy]* (Carocci, 2016); *Political advertising in the 2014 European Parliament elections* (Palgrave Macmillan, forthcoming; with C. Holtz-Bacha and Kevin Rafter); and "Selling Europe before and after the economic crisis: Themes and styles of the last two European election campaigns" (in Holtz-Bacha and Johansson (Eds.), *Election posters around the globe* (Springer, forthcoming)).

Lilia Raycheva is Professor at the Department of Communication and Audio-Visual Production of the Faculty of Journalism and Mass Communication at the St. Kliment Ohridski University of Sofia. She has served as Vice-Dean for Scientific Research and International Affairs (1998–2001) and Head of Radio and Television (1999–2001). For seven years she also served (elected by the National Assembly) as a member of the Council for Electronic Media – the regulatory authority for radio and television broadcasting in Bulgaria (2001–8) and as such – for three years – as a member of the Standing Committee on Transfrontier Television at the Council of Europe (2005–8). She has lectured at home and abroad, and has been extensively published. Her professional authorship portfolio includes a number of television programs (one of which has been airing since 1980). She has also participated in a number of international projects and networks on various mass media issues. Her scientific interests relate to the impacts of information and communication technologies, media developments and political advertising.

Travis N. Ridout is Thomas S. Foley Distinguished Professor of Government and Public Policy in the School of Politics, Philosophy and Public Affairs at Washington State University. He is also co-director of the Wesleyan Media Project and served as chair of the Political Communication section of the American Political Science Association. He received his Ph.D. in political science from the University of Wisconsin-Madison in 2003, and his research on political campaigns, political advertising and campaign finance has appeared in the *American Journal of Political Science*, *British Journal of Political Science*, *Journal of Politics*, *Political Communication*, *Political Behavior*, *Political Psychology*, *Annual Review of Political Science* and in several book chapters. His most recent book, *Political Advertising in the United States*, was published in 2016.

Jolán Róka, CSc (equivalent to Ph.D.) has been appointed Professor, Head of B.A. and M.A. programs in Communication and Media Studies and Associate Rector for International Relations at the Budapest College of Communication and Business since September 2001. She was previously an associate professor at Eötvös Loránd University between 1978 and 2012. Currently she is Professor of Communication and Media Studies, and also the editor-in-chief of the yearbook *Annales* and of the journal *Communication, Media, Business* at the Budapest Metropolitan University. In addition, she is a guest lecturer at the European McDaniel College, Budapest. She lectures on the history of mass media, theory of communication, cross-cultural communication, nonverbal and visual communication, interpersonal communication, and political communication. She is the grantee of the Széchényi Professor Award. She is the author or editor of 12 books and more than 80 journal articles and book chapters, and has been awarded several national and international grants, including an IREX Grant to the University of Pennsylvania, Annenberg School of Communications and a Fulbright Grant to Texas A&M University, Faculty of Journalism. For decades, she has been the member of several international research teams on political communication and marketing and journalism.

Teresa Sádaba is Associate Professor at the University of Navarra, Spain, and a member of the faculty at George Washington University, US. She is a Fulbright fellow and holds a Ph.D. in communication and a B.A. in journalism and political science. Her research interests and publications are focused on framing theory and strategic communication.

Sergei A. Samoilenko is a public relations instructor in the Department of Communication at George Mason University. He is the past president of the Eurasian Communication Association of North America (https://eurasianresearchers.com/). His professional service is focused on bridging academic and professional communities in the areas of crisis communication, public relations and Eurasian studies. He developed and held numerous workshops and webinars on strategic communication in the US and internationally. His new research focuses on issues in character assassination and reputation management in public relations.

Anna Shavit holds a Ph.D. in political science and works as Assistant Professor at Charles University in Prague, Department of Marketing Communication and PR. Her research fields are political marketing (with focus on relations to political parties, citizen participations and democratic process), government communication (especially covering the Czech environment) and electoral campaigns (campaign professionalization, the role of political consultants, etc.). She combines her academic career with actual experience from campaigning (she worked as a chief strategist on the 2013 presidential campaign and as an adviser in the parliamentary elections in 2013). She is currently editing a book on Czech presidential elections in 2013. She is a former Fulbright scholar (Columbia University New York 2007/8).

Rodney Smith is Professor of Australian Politics in the Department of Government and International Relations at the University of Sydney, where he has taught since 2001. His recent research on elections includes articles on confidence in different types of voting channels in Australia (in *The Australian Journal of Political Science*) and on the sources of voter information in Australian constitutional referendums (in *The UNSW Law Journal*). His books include *Contemporary Australian political party organisations* (co-edited, 2015), *Contemporary Australian politics* (co-edited, 2012) and *From Carr to Keneally: Labor in office in NSW 1995–2011* (co-edited, 2012).

Rens Vliegenthart is Professor of Media and Society at the Amsterdam School of Communication Research, University of Amsterdam. His research focuses on media–politics relations, media coverage of social movements and businesses, election campaigns and economic news coverage. He is currently chair of the Young Academy of the Royal Netherlands Academy of Arts and Sciences.

Dominic Wring is Professor of Political Communication at Loughborough University. He has previously written on the history and development of election campaigning in the UK including, most recently, "Framing politics: The enduring appeal of the poster in British elections" (with Chris Burgess) in Christina Holtz-Bacha and Bengt Johansson (Eds.), *Election posters around the globe: Political campaigning in the public space* (Springer, forthcoming). Previously he co-founded the *Journal of Political Marketing* and served as its first European editor. Currently he is the lead editor of the Political Communications series of studies, one of which has appeared after every UK general election since 1979. The latest volume (co-edited with Roger Mortimore and Simon Atkinson) is *Political communication in Britain: Polling, campaigning and media in the 2015 general election* (Palgrave, 2016).

PART I

General Perspectives

1

AMPLE OPPORTUNITIES – MOSTLY REGULATED

Political Advertising Across the World

Christina Holtz-Bacha

With the spread of television in the 1950s and its growing importance in society, the new medium also became attractive for electoral communication. From the outset in 1949, US television was held in private hands and survived on revenues from advertising. Campaigners in the US were quick to incorporate television into their strategic repertoire. The 1952 presidential campaign saw the advent of electoral ads on television.

Whereas Republican candidate Dwight D. Eisenhower and his strategists from Madison Avenue readily embraced the new campaign instrument, the Democratic contender Adlai Stevenson had difficulty adapting to television and openly expressed his reservations against television advertising: "I think the American people will be shocked by such contempt for their intelligence. This isn't Ivory Soap versus Palmolive" (Museum of the Moving Image, 2012).

In the US, television ads developed into the most important means for directly speaking to the voters. With each race, campaigners spent more and more money on television advertising. Even after the introduction of the Internet and social network sites, which also allow candidates to address voters directly and with more individualized messages, more than half of the campaign budgets still go into television advertising (see e.g., Bachman, 2011; Kurtzleben, 2015).

Even though the use of television spots started in other parts of the world at about the same time or soon after, they did not acquire the same relevance as in the US. Reservations about promoting politics in commercials, just as Adlai Stevenson expressed them, were common and are still reflected today in the restrictions for electoral advertising in most parts of the world. The "anything goes" principle also led to the emergence of a specific culture of political advertising in the US. This culture is first of all influenced by the fact that there are no restrictions on political commercials. Political actors can purchase as much broadcast time as they can afford. There is no limit to a certain time period, as for instance the last weeks of a campaign. In addition, the political and the electoral system have contributed to the specifics of US electoral advertising. The candidate-focused electoral system together with long campaigns, primaries and fierce competition even within the same party leads to material battles fought over the media and swallowing enormous amounts of money. The personal competition is also a reason for the vital role of negative advertising in the electoral race. Finally, the commercial media system and the fact that broadcast time had to be paid for from the beginning, brought about a dominance of very short ads.

In Western Europe, where in some countries electoral advertising on television was introduced at about the same time as in the US, the development was different. Skepticism toward promoting politics just like soap persisted and is one reason for the more or less extensive regulation of political advertising on television in European countries. Most of the West European countries featured a monopoly of public service broadcasting until the introduction of commercial broadcasting in the 1980s. The public service philosophy has also left an imprint on the conditions for electoral broadcasts in radio and television and the substantial, if not dominant, role of the public service broadcasters in many West European countries still shapes the handling of political advertising in the region. In contrast to the US and with the exception of France, these countries have parliamentary systems making parliamentary elections the most important race in most of Western Europe. The electoral systems focuses on parties, which nevertheless does not preclude a prominent role for the party leaders in the campaign.

For instance, in the UK, Party Election Broadcasts (PEBs) first appeared on television during the 1951 parliamentary election campaign. Lasting 15 and in the next elections even 20 minutes these first party broadcasts were lengthy presentations and do not bear much relation to today's political advertising (Padmanabhan, 2015). The term, that is still used for the parties' electoral advertising on radio and television today, reflects the different approach to campaign broadcasts taken in the UK. From the beginning, first on radio and later on television, broadcast time for PEBs had to be provided free of charge and could not be purchased. Parties using the broadcast media to present themselves to the electorate was seen as part of the media's information function rather than as disdainful advertising.

The same was true for Germany, which actually derives its public service broadcasting from the British who, together with the Americans, introduced the model during the occupation after World War II. Electoral spots first appeared on television in the 1957 parliamentary election campaign and the only television channel existing at that time had to provide free airtime for the parties (Holtz-Bacha, 2000). Early on, the German Federal Constitutional Court got involved in disputes over the right of parties to advertise on television. From the beginning, the Court emphasized the opportunity for parties to present themselves to the electorate in order to provide voters with the information they needed to make up their minds.

In fact, protecting political advertising from commercial interests has often been the reason for not allowing the purchase of broadcast time on commercial television once most West European countries opened their markets to private broadcasters. In those countries that still do not allow advertising time to be purchased, political advertising is viewed differently from commercials promoting products and services.

The dominance of party-oriented systems in Western Europe also plays a part in the emergence of a different culture of electoral advertising in these countries, particularly where coalition governments are the rule. Parties coming out of a coalition government or envisaging going into a coalition after Election Day will think twice about criticizing a former or future partner. Parties do not want to risk being seen as unreliable. In general, where airtime is given to parties and not to candidates it is up to the parties and their campaign advisers to decide about the advertising strategy, and that may or may not involve the party leader. In addition to parliamentary elections, some of the West European countries hold direct elections for the head of state whose influence on the government and day-to-day politics, however, is different and often reduced to a ceremonial function.

The situation is somewhat different in the countries of Central and Eastern Europe where political changes around the fall of the Berlin Wall in 1989 led to a democratization process and free elections. Until then, the media and specifically broadcasting had been in the hands of, and under the strict control of, the state. The transformation of the former state-controlled media into public service institutions has mostly not yet brought about independent broadcasting similar to West European systems. In some cases, the development of an independent broadcasting system has even regressed and government intervention has returned.

In contrast to Europe, the Latin American countries mostly feature presidential systems where the head of state is also the head of the government. Until recently, several of these countries were under dictatorial regimes and re-introduced free elections only a short time ago. Whereas the political systems are mostly classified as democratic, independence of the media cannot be taken for granted. In some countries there is a close connection between media ownership and political power as well as, in some cases, a high degree of media concentration. As in the US, the presidential systems in Latin America result in candidate-oriented campaigns.

Negative advertising is a characteristic of US campaign culture (see Chapters 5 and 23, this volume). Attacking opponents has become a necessity in US campaigns and in the most recent presidential races negative ads greatly outnumbered positive ads. The prominence of attack advertising is also a consequence of the involvement of the political action committees (PACs) and super-PACs that spend millions to support candidates on television or the Internet. Because of the risk of a backlash effect on the sponsor, candidates prefer not to appear in negative ads themselves. Candidates do not have to take responsibility for ads they do not produce. In contrast to the US, negativity and attacks, especially on the personal character of an opponent, are not accepted everywhere. As a result, some countries ban negative advertising altogether.

Regulatory Aspects

Regulation of political advertising takes many different forms. In democratic systems with electoral competition, political advertising in newspapers, on radio, television and more recently the Internet is usually regarded as a legitimate instrument for parties and candidates to promote themselves. Nevertheless, even in established democracies, political advertising, particularly on television, is regulated in one way or the other. Some countries such as Denmark, Norway and Switzerland, though scoring high on democracy or freedom indexes (e.g., Puddington & Roylance, 2016, pp. 20–24), do not allow political advertising on television at all. Other countries make a distinction between political advertising in general and electoral advertising, only permitting the latter to give contenders the opportunity to present themselves to the electorate but keeping political or any kind of ideological advertising off television.

In fact, one reason for not allowing political advertising on television are reservations of the same kind, as Adlai Stevenson argued. "Selling" politics just as any other commercial product and submitting it to marketing is regarded as inappropriate and therefore harmful to the image of politics. In particular, negative advertising and attacks on opponents are often seen as detrimental to the world of politics. Such concerns first and foremost apply to television because of the presumed effectiveness of the audiovisual medium.

With reference to freedom of expression as laid down in the European Convention on Human Rights, the Council of Europe (CoE) has repeatedly made political advertising an issue of its recommendations on free and fair elections for its 47 member states. For instance, in its "Code of good practice in electoral matters" the CoE's European Commission for Democracy through Law (often called the Venice Commission) emphasized the importance of providing all electoral contenders with equal opportunities for advertising. The Commission also recommended promoting legal provisions to ensure minimum access to advertising on privately owned audiovisual media as well as airtime on public or state-owned broadcasting. In addition, the Venice Commission mentioned the possibility of limiting party spending, particularly on advertising, on the grounds of equal opportunity (European Commission for Democracy through Law, 2002, pp. 7, 18). The Venice Commissions' guidelines take up the recommendations made earlier by the CoE's Committee of Ministers (1999) which suggested the provision of free airtime during election campaigns and balanced conditions for paid advertising, if permitted.

Against this background, equal opportunities for all parties and candidates with respect to advertising on radio and television can also be regarded as an indicator of fair elections. If the airwaves are opened for electoral advertising, provision of airtime should be guided by the equal opportunity principle.

Table 1.1 gives an overview of regulation of electoral advertising on television in 57 countries[1] all over the world (for previous studies see Holtz-Bacha, 2014, forthcoming). These are findings from an online survey among experts of political communication.[2] To take account of different

Table 1.1 Availability of airtime in most important election

	System of government	Most important election	
		Free airtime on public or commercial television	Airtime can be purchased on public or commercial television
Argentina	Pres.	Yes (p+c)	No
Australia	CM	Yes (p)	Yes (c)
Austria	Parl.	No	Yes (p+c)
Belgium – Flanders	CM	No television advertising	
Belgium – Wallonia	CM	Yes (p)	No
Bolivia	Pres.	Yes (p)	Yes (c)
Brazil	Pres.	Yes (p+c)	No
Bulgaria	Parl.	No	Yes (p+c)
Canada	CM	Yes (p)	Yes (c)
Chile	Pres.	Yes (c)	No
Colombia	Pres.	Yes (c)	Yes (c)
Croatia	Parl.	No	Yes (p+c)
Cyprus	Pres.	Yes (p+c)	Yes (p+c)
Czech Republic	Parl.	Yes (p)	No
Denmark	CM	No television advertising	
El Salvador	Pres.	Yes (p)	Yes (c)
Estonia	Parl.	No	Yes (c)
Finland	Parl.	No	Yes (c)
France	SemiPres.	Yes (p)	No
Germany	Parl.	Yes (p)	Yes (c)
Greece	Parl.	Yes (p+c)	Yes (p+c)
Hungary	Parl.	Yes (p)	No
India	Parl.	No	Yes (p+c)
Ireland	Parl.	Yes (p+c)	No
Israel	Parl.	Yes (c)	No
Italy	Parl.	Yes (p)	No
Japan	CM	Yes (p+c)	Yes (c)
Kenya	Pres.	No	Yes (p)
Latvia	Parl.	Yes (p)	Yes (p+c)
Lithuania	SemiPres.	Yes (p)	Yes (c)
Luxembourg	CM	Yes (c)	No
Malaysia	CM	Yes (p)	No
Malta	Parl.	Yes (c)	No
Mexico	Pres.	Yes (c)	No
Morocco	CM	Yes (p)	No
Netherlands	CM	Yes (p)	Yes (c)
New Zealand	CM	Yes (p)	Yes (p+c)
Norway	CM	No television advertising	
Peru	Pres.	Yes (c)	Yes (c)
Poland	Parl.	Yes (p)	Yes (p+c)
Portugal	SemiPres.	Yes (p+c)	No
Romania	Parl.	Yes (p+c)	No
Russia	SemiPres.	No	Yes (p+c)
Singapore	Parl.	Yes (p)	No
Slovakia	Parl.	No	Yes (c)
Slovenia	Parl.	Yes (p)	Yes (c)
South Africa	Parl.	Yes (p)	Yes (p+c)
South Korea	Pres.	No	Yes (c)

	System of government	Most important election	
		Free airtime on public or commercial television	*Airtime can be purchased on public or commercial television*
Spain	CM	Yes (p)	No
Sweden	CM	No	Yes (c)
Switzerland	Dir.	No television advertising	
Taiwan	SemiPres.	Yes (p+c)	Yes (p+c)
Turkey	Parl.	Yes (p)	No
UK	CM	Yes (p+c)	No
Uruguay	Pres.	Yes (c)	Yes (p+c)
US	Pres.	No	Yes (c)

Abbreviations: Parl.=parliamentary system; (Semi)Pres.=(semi)presidential system; CM=constitutional monarchy; Dir.=directorial; p=public or state-owned broadcasting; c=commercial/private broadcasting.

Sources: Information on availability of airtime taken from own surveys (see footnote 2); information on the government systems: www.auswaertiges-amt.de/sid_18E4E0569EF9266B66AB8ED45C53584D/DE/Aussenpolitik/Laender/Laender_Uebersicht_node.html.

political systems, respondents were asked to refer their answers to the most important election in their country.

The provision of airtime for electoral advertising on television with no charge is quite common all over the world and is by no means restricted to public or state-owned broadcasting. Even though there is a tendency to allocate free airtime in countries where public broadcasting has a long tradition, such as the UK, France, Italy or Germany, Table 1.1 does not show any consistent pattern.

In fact, over the years, there have been some remarkable changes in political advertising policies. One of the major turning points was the opening of the European broadcasting market for private companies. With the adoption of legal regulation for private broadcasters, some countries also cleared the way for political advertising on commercial channels and thus increased the number of outlets for advertising by political actors. In some cases, the commercial broadcasters were obliged to make free airtime available, in others, airtime can be purchased. In Sweden, for instance, political advertising had been prohibited until 2005. Digitization finally led to a liberation of the broadcasting market and television ads were first broadcast during the European election campaign in 2009 and, one year later, for the Swedish parliamentary election (Chapter 22, this volume; see also Grusell & Nord, 2010; Holtz-Bacha, Johansson, Leidenberger, Maarek, & Merkle, 2012). Sweden's neighbor Norway, on the other hand, decided in 2006 to keep the ban on political and religious advertising on television contrary to a proposal of an earlier government. The major arguments against lifting the ban referred to the equal opportunities principle and raised the common reservations against subjecting politics to commercial thinking: "allowing political advertising would favour powerful financial groups and … such advertising could have a negative impact on the political debate by simplifying the information available to the voters using commercial language" (Conradi Andersen, 2006). After some wavering in earlier decisions, the European Court of Human Rights in 2013 confirmed admissibility of blanket bans on political advertising on television and their compatibility with freedom of expression as laid down in Article 8 of the European Convention on Human Rights (Vorhoof, 2013).

South Africa was also late in introducing political advertising. In 2009, political ads were permitted only in election periods (Independent Communications Authority of South Africa, 2009). The ruling distinguished PEBs, for which airtime is allocated, from political advertisements. Parties could employ the new campaign instrument for the first time in the parliamentary elections in 2009. The regulation was changed again for the election in 2014, limiting the allocated time slots for PEBs to one minute (Independent Communications Authority of South Africa, 2014).

Austria is another case. The country abolished the obligation of providing airtime to parties, professional interest groups, trade unions and industrial unions for their advertising in 2001. When the new law on the public service ORF (Österreichischer Rundfunk=Austrian Broadcasting) was presented, then Vice-Chancellor Riess-Passer said this step would be a "great relief" for people because the political broadcasts had been among "the most superfluous parts of the program" (as cited in Ministerrat beschließt Medienpaket, 2001). At the same time, and with the introduction of private broadcasting, Austria allowed airtime to be purchased for ideational advertising, which is not restricted to election campaigns.

In Flanders, the Flemish part of Belgium, electoral ads on television that formerly had been provided for no charge by the public broadcaster, were also abolished a couple of years ago. In contrast with Austria, Flanders did not open commercial television for purchase of airtime.

There is considerable variance in the amount of time provided for campaign advertising on television. In particular, where broadcast time is allocated with no charge, the number of time slots for the advertising and the length of individual broadcasts is usually restricted. Several countries have opted for a spot length of less than one minute and thus for a format that resembles commercial advertising the most. The UK has distinctive provisions, allowing parties to choose a length of 2 minutes and 40 seconds, 3 minutes and 40 seconds, or 4 minutes and 40 seconds. Greece requires parties to produce a 10-minute broadcast which is aired at least once. Excerpts from this broadcast are used for the production of short spots. Some countries provide time in spot length and give additional time that is apportioned among the electoral contenders. For instance, Brazil allocates 15-, 30- or 60-second time slots and also 25 minutes to be divided among the parties (see Chapter 8, this volume).

Many countries determine at which time during the day electoral spots can be broadcast. It may be an indicator of the role assigned to this kind of electoral advertising that they are often scheduled during prime time and thus have a chance at reaching the largest audience.

Even where electoral advertising is bound to equal treatment of all parties and candidates running for election, this does not necessarily mean giving all of them access to the same amount of broadcast time. Many countries practice a graded allocation of airtime, usually according to "relevance" determined by criteria such as representation in the parliament, votes in the previous election, and standing in the polls. Proportional allocation that favors bigger parties over smaller ones is common. Some Latin American countries such as Argentina, Brazil, Mexico and Uruguay divide the time given for electoral advertising by reserving a certain percentage for equal allocation to all contenders leaving the other part to proportional allocation according to certain criteria of relevance (see Chapters 7, 8 and 15, this volume). The UK, for instance, differentiates between major or large parties and other registered parties, which must fulfill minimum qualifying requirements to be allocated airtime.

Restricting the allocation of airtime to parties that are already represented in the parliament as it is done in Wallonia/Belgium or in Peru represents a hurdle for new parties that are dependent on making themselves known to the electorate. The allocation practice in Chile imposes similar restrictions on independent candidates and candidates from parties that are currently not represented in Congress – they receive the same time as the smallest parties in Congress, leaving them with only a few seconds for their electoral promotion (Chapter 9, this volume).

Any kind of electoral advertising allows political actors to present themselves to the electorate and to promote their platform. Whether time is provided free of charge or whether it has to be paid for, parties and candidates should make their case without any interference from the broadcasters or authorities. Electoral advertising has therefore also been linked to freedom of expression. Referring to the Council of Europe's European Convention on Human Rights and the European Union's legal framework for television, Jones (2004) for instance argued that a ban on political advertising or restrictions on content as found in some European countries are disputable and may even be illegal. However, in several cases the European Court of Human Rights (2003, 2008, 2013) ruled that even a blanket ban on ideological (political, religious) advertising does not violate freedom of expression as guaranteed by the European Convention on Human Rights (Article 10).

In order to point out who is responsible for the ideas presented in the advertising, broadcasters make announcements emphasizing that the spots have been produced by the parties or candidates and are their sole responsibility. In Argentina, for instance, electoral broadcasts must include subtitles and point out at the beginning that time is allocated without charge by the National Electoral Office (Chapter 7, this volume). German broadcasters also make announcements before the spots are aired, pointing out that the parties are responsible for the content. In addition, the spots are often put into a frame that carry an insert telling viewers that they are watching electoral advertising (Chapter 27, this volume). Some countries, such as France (Chapter 11, this volume), stipulate that the candidate must appear in the broadcast and thus link the contents directly to the advertised politician. In the US, regulation requires sponsoring candidates to appear in a visual and explicitly declare that they approve the ad (Chapter 5, this volume). Australian electoral law also prescribes that the spots must contain the name and address of the individual authorizing the advertisement (Chapter 24, this volume). The requirement of a clear assignment of responsibility is also linked to reservations against negative campaigning. In the US, in order to avoid a possible backlash for attack ads, super-PACs rather than the candidates themselves produce many of the negative ads.

Most countries do not explicitly regulate the contents of electoral advertising and thus follow the principle of letting political actors present themselves to the electorate in the way they see fit. However, usually electoral messages fall under criminal law and its prohibition of instigation to hatred and racism, but, for instance, that does not apply to the US.

If restrictions for the contents of electoral advertising apply, they often aim at the prevention of negativity. Electoral regulation in Brazil prohibits messages that are intended to degrade or ridicule a party, candidate or coalition (Chapter 8, this volume). Similarly, Cyprus, France and Kenya prohibit attacks against the opponent. In South Africa, too, the advertising may not be derogatory, racist, or slanderous (Chapter 31, this volume). In Mexico, parties can lodge a complaint against defamatory attacks with the National Electoral Institute, which takes the message off air while investigating the complaint.

In addition to references to different kinds of negativity, there are only a few other restrictions on the audio and the visuals of electoral advertising. Several countries, such as Colombia (Chapter 26, this volume) and France, do not allow the use of national symbols in the electoral advertising.

France is a country with unusually far-reaching restrictions on advertising, even though those rules have been relaxed in recent years. In addition to prohibiting the denigration of opponents and fundraising appeals, the electoral spots that are broadcast on public television with no charge are not allowed to use the national anthem, national or European symbols such as the flag or national allegories, the combination of the national colors and pictures of official buildings. Leaving out the flag was particularly problematic because they often appeared in material that was filmed in party conventions, etc. and therefore the prescription has been modified (Chapter 11, this volume). In earlier years, the spots had to be filmed by the French audiovisual authority but recently parties were allowed to produce their own broadcasts.

India is another example of detailed regulation of the provision of broadcast time for parties and its content. Airtime on public radio and television is given to national parties and state parties with no charge. In addition, parties can purchase advertising time on other channels. The broadcasts on public television are not allowed to criticize other countries, attack religions, contain obscene or defamatory contents, incite violence, denigrate the president or the judiciary, affect the unity, sovereignty and integrity of the nation, or criticize any persons by name (see Election Commission of India, 2014, p. 27).

Transcripts of the broadcasts have to be submitted in advance to the public broadcaster. Advertising on other channels must be pre-certified by a commission before they can air.

Tunisia, a country that is undergoing democratic transformation, prohibited electoral advertising for the first election after the revolution in order to ensure equal opportunities for all contestants (Holtz-Bacha, 2014, p. 556). For the legislative and the presidential elections in 2014 the Tunisian public television channel Al Wataniya broadcast short campaign messages with a maximum length of three minutes. Again, to make sure that all electoral contenders produced their messages under the same conditions, the technical equipment for filming, the lighting and the camera angle were prescribed. No special effects were allowed. The candidates were bound to respect human dignity and privacy, freedom of belief, protection of children, national security, public order and public health (HAICA, 2014a, 2014b; see also National Democratic Institute, 2014, p. 42).

Israel prohibits pictures of children and the army in the electoral advertising. Morocco restricts the broadcasts to the presentation of the electoral program and does not allow a comparison of parties. El Salvador prohibits the use of symbols of other parties or candidates and Uruguay, similarly, forbids the use of pictures and the voice of opponents. Allowing one speech only, regulation in Singapore restricts electoral appearances on television to the talking head format.

Conclusion

Across the world, political actors have ample possibilities to present themselves to voters on television. Electoral or media laws regulate how electoral contenders get on the air. With these rules, the lawmakers act in their own interest and create opportunities for themselves to promote their ideas, work on their images and garner votes. In fact, many countries oblige public and/or commercial broadcasters to allocate airtime free of charge during election campaigns.

Against this background, it comes as a surprise that regulation of electoral advertising comprises diverse restrictions on the amount, the form and the content of the broadcasts. In particular, where airtime is allocated without charge, the time when political advertising is allowed, the number of spots and their length are restricted. Equal opportunities for all campaigners is often practiced as proportional allocation thus giving an advantage to bigger parties. Small as well as new parties get less time than their bigger competitors and therefore have less chances to make themselves known in the electorate and get the attention of the voters.

In those countries where airtime can be purchased, broadcasters are often obliged to provide for equal conditions for all electoral contenders. However, equal opportunities have their limits in the different financial capacities of the competitors. Even though parties and candidates often do not have to pay regular rates for acquiring airtime, newcomers, minor parties and candidates have difficulties in meeting the challenge of their financially stronger competitors. Thus, the availability of airtime for electoral advertising mostly plays out in favor of the major parties and candidates with their well-filled war chests. This disadvantage adds to the media hurdle that often exists for smaller parties, which have to struggle to get the attention of the media.

Taken together, in addition to production costs which usually have to be borne by the parties or candidates, proportional allocation of airtime and/or having to pay for advertising time on television make for inequalities that work to the disadvantage of newcomers and minor electoral contenders. One way of countering the equality problem is practiced by New Zealand. The country's Electoral Commission allocates money to the parties registered for election which they can use either for purchasing airtime or for the production of electoral broadcasts. Once again, however, the allocation of money is carried out proportionally according to certain criteria such as votes in previous elections and members in parliament (Broadcasting Act, 1989).

The formal features and the content of the advertising are first of all influenced by the political and electoral system of a country. It is obvious that presidential systems and those where the head of state is directly elected by the people tend to focus advertising on candidates. In some countries, the appearance of candidates in electoral broadcasts is mandatory for reasons of transparency. The personalization of political communication in parliamentary systems, in the sense of focusing the self-presentation of parties on their leading candidates, has been discussed for a long time. Because the conception of electoral advertising lies in the hands of the political actors and thus reflects their strategies, advertising lends itself to the analysis of personalization on the part of the parties. Comparisons across countries and systems would allow for assessing the influential factors for personalization and whether it is indeed a general trend or whether there are different developments in different countries.

Blanket bans on political advertising, the common limitation to the period of election campaigns and the exclusion of third parties (interest groups), blackouts during the last days before Election Day and different kinds of restrictions concerning the content, all reflect reservations about political advertising in general and negative advertising in particular and both can be regarded as indicators of political culture and its impact on political communication. Whereas personal attacks and aggressive campaigning are common in the US, negative advertising is not equally accepted in other countries. In fact, the regulations in some countries explicitly prohibit appeals that are intended to denigrate the electoral competitors. By prohibiting the use of the national anthem, emblems or the flag, others want to keep the national symbols out of the electoral struggle.

The country chapters in this volume describe regulations in more detail. How they play out and what the effects are on the actual design of advertising, let alone systematic international comparisons of different cultures of electoral advertising, have not yet been a major topic of research and remain a task for future studies.

Notes

1   Due to different regulation for the two parts of Belgium, Wallonia and Flanders appear separately.
2   The author thanks numerous colleagues from all over the world who helped with information on the regulation of political advertising in their countries and answered patiently to further questions. The most recent survey was conducted in winter 2015/16. In addition, findings from a previous survey done in connection with the 2014 European Election Project (Holtz-Bacha, forthcoming; Holtz-Bacha, Novelli, & Rafter, forthcoming) are included. Thanks also to Raphael Brendel (University of Erlangen-Nürnberg) for compiling background data for the countries included in Table 1.1.

References

Bachman, K. (2011, June 22). Digital losing out on campaign ad billions: Politicians love the web for outreach, but television's far ahead in the race for their ad dollars. *Adweek*. Retrieved from www.adweek.com/news/advertising-branding/digital-losing-out-campaign-ad-billions-132676.

Broadcasting Act 1989. Reprint as at April 30, 2016. (2016). Retrieved from www.legislation.govt.nz/act/public/1989/0025/latest/096be8ed812fdfe9.pdf.

Conradi Andersen, I. (2006). Ban on political advertising on TV upheld. Retrieved from http://merlin.obs.coe.int/iris/2006/7/article30.en.html.

Election Commission of India. (2014). *General election to the 16th Lok Sabha 2014. Handbook for media.* Retrieved from http://eci.nic.in/eci_main/ElectoralLaws/HandBooks/Handbook%20for%20Media%202014.pdf.

European Commission for Democracy through Law. (2002). *Code of good practice in electoral matters. Guidelines and explanatory report.* [CDL-AD (2002) 23 rev]. Retrieved from www.venice.coe.int/webforms/documents/default.aspx?pdffile=CDL-AD(2002)023rev-e.

European Court of Human Rights. (2003, July 10). Case of Murphy v. Ireland. Judgment. Retrieved from http://hudoc.echr.coe.int/eng?i=001-61207#{%22itemid%22:[%22001-61207%22]}.

European Court of Human Rights. (2008, December 11). Case of TV Vest As & Rogaland Pensjonistparti v. Norway. Judgment. Retrieved from http://hudoc.echr.coe.int/app/conversion/docx/pdf?library=ECHR&id=001-90235&filename=CASE%20OF%20TV%20VEST%20AS%20AND%20ROGALAND%20PENSJONISTPARTI%20v.%20NORWAY.pdf.

European Court of Human Rights. (2013, April 22). Case of Animal Defenders International v. The United Kingdom. Judgment. Retrieved from http://hudoc.echr.coe.int/eng?i=001-119244#{%22itemid%22:[%22001-119244%22]}.

Grusell, M., & Nord, L. (2010). More cold case than hot spot: A study of public opinion on political advertising in Swedish television. *Nordicom Review*, 31, 95–111.

HAICA. (2014a). Cahier de charge fixant les conditions de production, de programmation et de diffusion des émissions d'expression directe de la campagne officielle télévisée prévue sur les antennes de la Télévision Tunisienne candidats aux élections législatives pour l'année 2014. Retrieved from http://haica.tn/media/Cahiers-des-charges-expression-directe-V3-1.pdf.

HAICA. (2014b). Note relative aux conditions de production et de diffusion des émissions d'expression directe des candidats aux élections législatives 2014. Retrieved from http://haica.tn/fr/2014/09/note-relative-aux-conditions-de-production-et-de-diffusion-des-emissions-dexpression-directe/.

Holtz-Bacha, C. (2000). *Wahlwerbung als politische Kultur. Parteienspots im Fernsehen 1957–1998*. Wiesbaden: Westdeutscher Verlag.

Holtz-Bacha, C. (2014). Political advertising in international comparison. In H. Cheng (Ed.), *The handbook of international advertising research* (pp. 554–574). Malden, MA: Wiley-Blackwell.

Holtz-Bacha, C. (forthcoming). Regulation of electoral advertising in Europe. In C. Holtz-Bacha, E. Novelli & K. Rafter (Eds.), *Political advertising in the 2014 European Parliament elections*. Basingstoke: Palgrave.

Holtz-Bacha, C., Johansson, B., Leidenberger, J., Maarek, P., & Merkle, S. (2012). Advertising for Europe: TV ads during the 2009 European election campaign in four countries. *Nordicom Review*, 33, 77–92.

Holtz-Bacha, C., Novelli, E., & Rafter, K. (Eds.). (forthcoming). *Political advertising in the 2014 European Parliament elections*. Basingstoke: Palgrave.

Independent Communications Authority of South Africa. (2009, March 3). Regulations on party elections broadcasts, political advertisements, the equitable treatment of political parties by broadcasting licensees and related matters. *Government Gazette*, 31980, 3–11. Retrieved from www.icasa.org.za/LegislationRegulations/FinalRegulations/BroadcastingRegulations/Partyelectionbroadcastspoliticaladvertisement/tabid/150/ctl/ItemDetails/mid/865/ItemID/791/Default.aspx.

Independent Communications Authority of South Africa. (2014, February 14). Regulations on party elections broadcasts, political advertisements, the equitable treatment of political parties by broadcasting licensees and related matters. *Government Gazette*, 37350, 3–17. Retrieved from www.icasa.org.za/LegislationRegulations/FinalRegulations/BroadcastingRegulations/Partyelectionbroadcastspoliticaladvertisement/tabid/150/ctl/ItemDetails/mid/865/ItemID/1819/Default.aspx.

Jones, C. A. (2004). Regulating political advertising in the EU and the USA: A human rights perspective. *Journal of Public Affairs*, 4, 244–255.

Kurtzleben, D. (2015, August 19). 2016 campaigns will spend $4.4 billion on TV ads, but why? *NPR*. Retrieved from www.npr.org/sections/itsallpolitics/2015/08/19/432759311/2016-campaign-tv-ad-spending.

Ministerrat beschließt Medienpaket. (2001, May 29). *Der Standard*. Retrieved from http://derstandard.at/596029/Ministerrat-beschliesst-Medienpaket.

Museum of the Moving Image. (2012). Presidential campaign commercials 1952–2012. 1952 Eisenhower vs. Stevenson. Retrieved from www.livingroomcandidate.org/commercials/1952.

National Democratic Institute. (2014). Final report on the 2014 legislative and presidential elections in Tunisia. Retrieved from www.ndi.org/files/Tunisia%20Election%20Report%202014_EN_SOFT%20(1).pdf.

Padmanabhan, L. (2015, April 21). The story of the party election broadcast. Retrieved from www.bbc.com/news/election-2015-31711345.

Puddington, A., & Roylance, T. (2016). Anxious dictators, wavering democracies: Global freedom under pressure. In Freedom House (Ed.), *Freedom in the world 2016* (pp. 1–24). Retrieved from https://freedomhouse.org/report/freedom-world/freedom-world-2016.

Vorhoof, D. (2013). Europäischer Gerichtshof für Menschenrechte: *Animal Defenders International* gegen das Vereinigte Königreich. *Iris*, 6, 3–4.

2

MODERN POLITICAL ADVERTISING AND PERSUASION

Steve Jarding, Steve Bouchard and Justin Hartley

Introduction

Politicians have been utilizing various persuasion techniques to attract voters' support for centuries. These skills are sometimes seen as unsavory and some political philosophers have postulated that they should have no place in politics whatsoever. Plato was one of the first to denounce the use of persuasion techniques some 2,500 years ago (as cited in Turan, 2014) when he warned "The ruler who is good for anything ought not to beg his subjects to be ruled by him."

Plato's thought-provoking notion on public service implies that no leader *worthy of being leader* should have to use persuasive communication or self-promotion to garner favor from would-be supporters. Indeed, in the US, early presidents and presidential contenders went to great lengths to avoid the appearance of seeking the office, seemingly heeding Plato's advice. Instead they opted to appear as statesman reluctant to step into the spotlight, but willing to serve their country "if called upon" by the people.

This practice was actually a ruse because through much of America's history, presidential candidates were selected by party elites, not the public, and as such did not need to employ mass voter persuasion techniques. The advent of television and the opening of party nominating procedures in the 1950s and 1960s changed all of that.

Even the early persuasion techniques used in US political campaigns – leaflets, political cartoons, campaign buttons and town square soapboxes – certainly would have been frowned upon by Plato. Persuasion techniques in electronic communications, beginning with the telegraph in the 1830s, then radio, before culminating in today's blitzkrieg of video on television and an ever-growing plethora of social media platforms, would probably set Plato spinning in his grave.

Yet, for all of the changes in technology and its ability to reach, connect and persuade voters through various delivery systems, no tool of persuasion has consistently proved more powerful than video. And historically there has been one method of delivering video that has had a far greater impact than any other – television. It has trumped all others – until now – for the advent of social media platforms is changing the persuasive communication landscape entirely.

This chapter will explore the traditional power of video as a voter persuasion technique – delivered through television signals – to the passing of the torch where video images are delivered through social media platforms. It will also illustrate why demand for video, in light of exciting new technologies, is stronger than ever.

But let's begin with a brief history of the delivery of political messages through television.

The Advent of Political Advertising on Television

Prior to 1952, when presidential candidates in the US wanted to court voters, they routinely did so with leaflets, campaign buttons and whistle-stop tours from the caboose of a slow moving train.

Then came Dwight D. Eisenhower.

War hero Eisenhower was well known and respected for his use of state-of-the-art tactics and weaponry to win World War II, but he proved he could be just as creative and cunning with the new weapon of political persuasion – television.

In his first run for political office, Eisenhower became the first American presidential candidate to use television to persuade voters. In all, the Eisenhower campaign created 40 20-second commercials titled, "Eisenhower Answers America" in which Eisenhower answered a different question in each commercial posited by an ordinary American citizen.

Over a three-week period in October 1952, the Eisenhower campaign spent $2 million to run these commercials across 12 key states. Eisenhower's opponent, Adlai Stevenson, refused to appear in television ads and his campaign manager even condemned the Eisenhower commercials for attempting to sell Eisenhower like "soap." (Even without Stevenson appearing in any ads, Democrats did spend money on television advertising – but only $77,000 in the entire 1952 campaign.) The lack of understanding of the power of television proved to be a critical error for Stevenson, and Eisenhower never looked back. He won the election in a landslide and, in doing so, forever changed the face of political persuasion techniques in the US. Stevenson, meanwhile, became the first and last presidential candidate to decline to appear in television ads.

Fast forward 60 years to the 2012 presidential election where Democrats' spending on advertising increased from $77,000 in 1952 to $404 million, while the Republicans increased their spending to $492 million. Even after adjusting for inflation over this time, the Democratic Party had increased its political advertising spending by more than 600 times.

It is also important to consider that, in 1948, less than 3% of American homes owned a television. In 1952 – only four years later – that figure was fast approaching 50%. Today the ownership level hovers around 98% of all households (Lepore, 2012, para. 54).

Following the 1952 campaign, candidates learned that the power of video did not reside solely in paid television commercials. Instead, candidates and their campaign teams soon realized that getting a candidate on television in almost any fashion could have significant and quantifiable results.

This first occurred in dramatic fashion in the 1960 presidential campaign, when underdog presidential hopeful Democrat John F. Kennedy saw television as the key to raising his stature and image. In an attempt to make his candidacy more compelling, Kennedy challenged his Republican opponent, frontrunner Vice President Richard M. Nixon to a series of debates on live television. Nixon accepted and the debates transformed the 1960 election.

What made television so powerful was that by 1960 it clearly had become the vehicle of choice for Americans to receive information and messaging whether that information and those messages came in the form of paid commercials or in news programming.

Webley (2010) notes that by 1960, 88% of American households had televisions. Further, Webley highlights that the 60-minute opening debate between Kennedy and Nixon was seen by 74 million Americans out of a population of slightly more than 179 million people – a stunning 41% of all Americans.

The Kennedy–Nixon Debates (A&E Television Networks, 2016, The Kennedy-Nixon Debates, para. 3) proved pivotal for Kennedy. Surveys following the debate showed that those who watched the debate on television (it was also broadcast live on radio) thought that Kennedy was the big winner. In fact, Kennedy looked so tanned and fit in the debate and Nixon so pale and pasty that Nixon's mother famously called her son immediately following the debate to ask if he was ill.

In the election just weeks later, which Kennedy won by the slimmest of margins, 49.7% to 49.5%, polls indicated that more than half of all voters had been influenced by the debates while a full 6% of all voters claimed the debates alone had decided their choice – and Kennedy was the choice of most of the viewers (The Kennedy-Nixon Debates, para. 5).

So why had television become such a powerful new medium?

There is overwhelming empirical evidence that voters or consumers of messaging are influenced in a far greater manner by video stimulation than by messaging in other platforms (such as billboards, leaflets, newspaper or radio). With video, the audio could be supplemented with strong visual images such as physical appearance, style, emotion, passion, wardrobe, mannerisms and body language – face and hand gesturing. These additional factors greatly stimulated the viewers' senses as no other medium had ever done. Thus, it did not take marketers and politicians long to realize that visual images and messages on television advertising increased sales and increased voter support (Xoto, 2013, p. 9).

Since 1960, television indeed had grown to become the most powerful medium to persuade and cajole consumers, audiences and voters. In 1968, Roger Ailes (the television producer and Nixon campaign consultant) prognosticated, "Television is no gimmick, and nobody will ever be elected to major office again without presenting themselves well on it" (Kaushik, 2011, para. 1). Ailes was prescient.

Reporter Derek Willis who covers the media for the *New York Times* noted that by 2015, television was reaching 87% of people over 18 years of age – with no other single medium coming close (Willis, 2015, para. 2).

Willis sees television as still the most powerful medium in helping candidates with name recognition, particularly early after announcing their candidacy. His research shows that dollar for dollar, television is still extremely effective in boosting lesser-known candidates.

In today's information age, data and news abound, saturating the public's senses 24 hours a day. In the world of politics, advertising is a requisite means of "selling" a candidate, whether the selling of their values and beliefs, their stance on issues or how they differ from their rivals. US politics has now become a fast-moving aggressive beast where the Republican and Democratic parties battle each other for votes within a multi-billion-dollar campaign industry. Political advertising is their major weapon of choice and video is their silver bullet.

Legal and Regulatory Framework

Over the first 60 years of television, laws governing the production, broadcasting and funding of political advertisements in federal races – US Congress, US Senate or the presidency – have gone through substantial changes that have impacted the nature of ads, the timing of ads and most importantly the method of paying for political ads and the disclosure of the group paying for them.

Media firms still must produce ads with compelling sounds, images and information. But they must also now allocate space for disclosures of who has paid for – and who has authorized the ad. They must now sort through sophisticated viewing research to determine where best to place the ads on which of the multitudes of television networks and shows, in what time slots, and to what target audiences.

To get a message to voters, then, it has become much more difficult and expensive to place ads on the proper platforms and numerous shows to reach and persuade voters. It is the expense of doing this that rapidly transformed the nature of political advertising on television.

Without delving too deeply into the arcane weeds of US campaign finance laws, it can simply be said that as the nature of the funding of political campaigns evolved, the advertising industry and the campaigns themselves responded deftly. To deal with the mushrooming costs of television advertising, there have been many efforts to drastically reduce the amount of money spent on them. These efforts have largely backfired and simply caused campaigns and elected officials to develop creative ways to achieve the same goals – more often increasing campaign spending not reducing it.

Although campaign finance reforms aim to increase accountability and decrease the likelihood of corruption, they have instead led to a proliferation of spending by independent organizations not officially affiliated with a political candidate or even a political party. In addition, several US Supreme Court decisions starting in 2010 largely ruled that controls on big money were unconstitutional. These decisions proved catalysts for a large proportional shift in campaign spending away from direct candidate and party spending to that from outside and largely unregulated groups. The result has been a dramatic and sustained shift in who was spending advertising dollars and in what amount in American presidential politics. As Dunbar (2015) implies, these new outside groups could now spend money on advertisements in a way that legally circumvented limits intended for parties and candidates.

Chief among these new political players were Political Action Committees (PACs) and their even less-regulated cousin, super-PACs. The new groups had access to money outside of the limits imposed on candidates ($5,000 limit for PACs and effectively no limits on super-PACs) and as a rule had to be run independent of guidance or direction from any candidate or candidate's campaign. This was particularly true of super-PACs where wealthy donors could now write unlimited checks to those super-PACs that supported their candidate. In short, these organizations could spend vast amounts of money advocating for their candidate or discrediting their candidate's opponent, as long as there was no coordination with the campaign.

One interesting development stemming from these new groups was that candidates began putting video footage of themselves onto public sites such as YouTube. These sites provided an arm's-length mechanism through which candidates could feed preferred campaign footage to outside groups and those outside groups could capture it and use it in their own video advertising without having to deal with the campaign in any way.

By 2014 there were approximately 4,600 registered PACs in the US. In 1990, all registered PACs raised approximately $50 million. By 2014, that amount had ballooned to nearly $1.7 billion. Moreover, because PACs tend to be mere shell organizations with minimal staff and little overhead, most PAC spending is earmarked for paid advertising for candidates – and television is by far the biggest beneficiary of PAC largess (Center for Responsive Politics, 2016).

Another consequence of these changes was that while campaigns and their political consultants/advertising agencies still determined the messages in their television advertising – now because so much more spending on television advertising was being run through these outside PACs – the majority of decisions on what ads to run were now being made by PAC directors not campaigns.

To underscore the profound impact unregulated super-PACs are having, consider this: According to Murray (2015, para. 1), of all the money spent through the first three-quarters of 2015 on the 2016 Republican presidential race, super-PACs had spent 95% of the total compared to just 5% by the candidates themselves.

Super-PACs' massive spending has led to a seismic shift in the traditional dynamics of presidential elections. Historically, candidate's campaigns paid for their own advertising, particularly in primary nominating contests (in the general election, political parties are allowed to supplement candidate spending). But because federal law capped the amount individuals could give to a candidate – in the low thousands of dollars per election – candidates needed thousands and even tens or hundreds of thousands of individual donors to raise the necessary funds to remain politically viable. With the advent of super-PACs, a candidate now only needs to have a wealthy donor to fund a sympathetic super-PAC in order to keep his or her campaign hopes alive, with or without broad public support.

Another trend that is developing and becoming more commonplace is that campaigns are largely producing biographical ads and positive ads, leaving the dirty work of negative spots to the super-PACs – giving the campaign an arm's-length distance from negative ads that, while effective, can often offend voters.

Craig Varoga, founder of the progressive group Patriot Majority PAC, describes the impact this way:

"Citizens United (the Supreme Court ruling equating political contributions with speech, thus allowing for the emergence of unregulated Super PACs) has made election seasons longer, more expensive and more negative, especially paid advertising on TV…"

(Varoga, 2015)

In effect, the introduction of super-PACs has resulted in the injection of sizeable sums of money early into the system, with the aim to discredit opponents with negative messaging.

How Political Ads Are Produced

The fundamentals of political ad production have not changed all that much since the first political ads hit the airwaves in 1952. First, media consulting firms along with key campaign staffers script the ads. Then the media firm films, edits and produces the ads before shipping them to stations from which they will air. This entire process can take several days or, if need be, a single ad can be produced and aired within a 24-hour period.

Within each area of ad production, finance laws, technology and the very nature of broadcast television and mass communications have made significant changes to the finer details of the process.

The following are the key steps in political ad production and are normally completed by senior campaign officials in consultation with media consultants:

- Define the media budget for ads and the timing of spending.
- Define the strategic objectives of the ad and the target audience of persuadable voters. The landscape of the race, the news cycle and internal campaign polling all instruct this process.
- Draft the scripts (media firm) and present to the campaign team for edits, fact-checking, legal compliance and approval to proceed.
- Film, edit and produce the ad, with any graphics, voiceover and music added.
- Circulate the rough-cut of the ad to the campaign team for edits and approval.
- In some cases, the ad is tested through either focus groups or online.
- Final tweaks are made as necessary before the ad is sent to the campaign team for final approval.
- Once approved, the media team determines exact contours of the ad buy – that is they determine during what time slots, programs and networks on television to buy, depending on which audience they want to impact.
- The ad is shipped to stations (historically truly shipped, now this is done digitally).
- The ad begins airing.
- Once sufficient exposure points are behind the ad – budget permitting – additional polling/testing is performed to see if the message is breaking through.

In addition, there are more technical steps in the process that media firms will either do in-house or will sub-contract to vendors, these include:

- hiring of camera crews (unless the firm has in-house crews);
- professional lighting and sound;
- hiring of talent and/or recruiting of volunteers to appear in the ads;
- professional editing;
- licensing of music or images;
- legal liability and releases from liability for any individuals appearing in the footage;
- permits for use of locations;
- site security for ads of a more sensitive nature.

These are all core functions of great importance and, without utilizing the services of professionals, can suffer or even get overlooked by those hoping to keep costs down by producing "in-house" ads.

However, the barriers to entry to ad production in many respects have been lowered by technological improvements that are cheaper and easier to use. For example, cell phones are affordable and can produce good quality hand-held video, distributable quite effortlessly on a multitude of platforms. The process is relatively quick and easy, however hurdles remain.

Video production of the sort an amateur can create with a cell phone camera and some editing software will not necessarily hold up well across all formats and is still lower quality than professional production. Most televisions on the market today are high-definition televisions of increasingly large size – making the need for extremely high quality/professional grade video a requisite and urgent one, if an ad is to be used on television.

In the early days of political advertising, these production steps were often the most difficult, for equipment was not as compact and maneuverable as today's equipment and digital compression – which increases the quality of the video – was not even available. Reels of film had to be shipped or flown from production facilities to networks. Advances in technology have rendered many of those problems moot or, at worst, reduced them to the level of minor annoyance. The more challenging tasks today are often around placement of ads, for the days of three networks have gone. There is now potential to place ads on literally dozens or even hundreds of networks. As such, "Ad Buyers," the professionals who pore over Nielsen ratings, demographic data, cost-per-point analyses as well as the campaign's budget, have become increasingly critical players in a campaign's success or failure.

Political Advertising Costs

The cost of political advertising on television is largely a function of two variables: (1) the arrangement made with the media consultant for production and airing of the ad; and (2) the cost of placing the ads in the markets in which they are to air.

Media firms are often compensated in a combination of ways, including a monthly retainer – often tens of thousands of dollars a month depending on the size and budget of the campaign. While campaigns obviously have to pay media firms the production costs of making the ads, they historically have had to pay media firms a percentage of their overall television buy. The industry standard for decades was 15% of the actual ad buys – meaning the media firm took 15% off the top of the cost of the purchased ad time from the networks/stations on which the ad was to air. Or to put it another way, if a campaign decided it needed $1 million in television ad buys, the campaign would actually have to come up with $1,150,000 to get $1 million in actual advertising buys, because the media firm was contracted to receive a 15% commission on the actual television buy. Over the course of time, increased competition has driven that percentage cost down, with firms being paid closer to 10–11% of the ad buy or even lower.

Finally, it is not uncommon for other members of the campaign team, including campaign managers, to receive a percentage of the television buy. This has not only raised the cost of television advertising; it has incentivized campaigns to keep spending on television (Johnson, 2015).

The cost of actually placing the ad is more complex and somewhat arcane. Television ad time is purchased in Gross Ratings Points or GRPs, which represent reach and frequency within a given market. In essence, it is the percentage of the market you aim to reach multiplied by the number of impressions (views of a given ad by a person in the target audience). So if a campaign is aiming to reach 80% of an audience five times, that would require an estimated 400 GRPs or "400 points" in industry speak. Campaign research consistently indicates that for a single ad to impact a voter's decision in a campaign, it should be seen as many as 10–12 times by an individual voter – which often means putting 1,000 to 1,200 points or more behind just one ad. That is why it is not uncommon in the latter stages of a campaign for campaigns – when more people are paying attention and making up their minds as to how they will vote – to run 1,600 or even 2,000 points behind a given television ad. These point levels are then normally spread over a 7–10-day period.

The Cost Per Point (CPP) varies greatly from market to market and fluctuates throughout the year. The low end for CPP is somewhere in the $50–100 range in television markets with small viewership, while the high end would be in dense cities like Los Angeles and New York City where the CPP can be as much as $1,200.

Supply and demand impacts the CPP as well. In Ohio, which is a traditionally heavily contested "battleground state" in US presidential elections, the larger media markets tend to sell out their inventory during presidential cycles, causing the CPP in these markets to soar, for example as high as $700 in the Cleveland market and $500 in the Columbus market during the 2012 presidential election. Using the 1,600 points per ad example above, this means that running 1,600 points per week in the Cleveland media market for the final month of a campaign would cost approximately $3.2 million dollars. And remember that cost is just one month, in one market and in one state. Historically there have been anywhere from 12–18 battleground states, albeit not all of them with CPPs as high as they are in Cleveland or Columbus, Ohio.

Also bear in mind that the number of weeks in a campaign that campaigns advertise has been inching steadily upward for decades and, at least in presidential elections, the primary nominating contests are also normally very competitive and require extensive and earlier advertising.

A Look to the Future

Current evidence suggests four noticeable trends that are likely to continue to shape political advertising in the future:

(1) A Sizeable Increase in Overall Spending

Experts forecast that overall spending on political advertising will continue to increase, at least in the short term. For the 2016 presidential elections, Cassino (2015) noted that political advertising was expected to hit a record $11.4 billion – 20% more than the last comparable 2012 presidential election year, while Kurtzleben (2015) references Elizabeth Wilner, senior vice president at Kantar's Campaign Media and Analysis Group who noted that in 2016 – for federal races alone (US House, US Senate and presidential races) – television spending would rise from $3.8 billion in 2012 to top $4.4 billion.

Citing just one more of many examples of this trend – Kurtzleben denotes that by August 2015, there had been seven times more political ads for the 2016 presidential race than at the same stage for the 2012 race.

(2) The Majority of Growth in Advertising Will Be Due to Online Media Platforms With – at Best – Only Moderate Growth in Television Advertising, With That Growth Eventually Flattening Out and Declining

Data shows that online advertising has been growing rapidly – far more so than television advertising – and this pattern is likely to continue with the gap widening (Figure 2.1). Digital/online spending in 2016 is expected to top $1 billion for the first time. Kurtzleben elucidates further noting that market research firm Borrell and Associates calculates this represents growth from 2012 to 2016 of a whopping 576%. By comparison the firm estimated that cable spending would grow by only 28% and broadcast television by a comparably lowly 7%. Looking at the forecast growth in online political advertising from 2008 to 2020, the number is even more staggering. Borrell and Associates data shows "About $1 billion will be spent on digital media, a nearly 5,000 percent increase from the measly $22.25 million spent on digital ads in 2008. And that's only the beginning" (Lapowsky, 2015, para. 2).

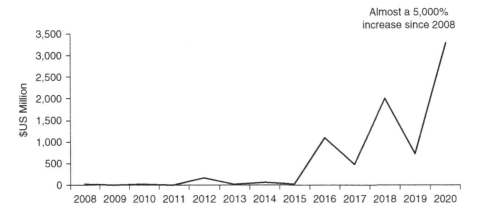

Figure 2.1 Forecast growth in online political advertising (2016–20)
Source: Original graph constructed from data taken from Borrell and Associates.

Assuming the forecasts in Figure 2.1 are correct, it could be expected that television spending will subsequently flatten before actually starting to fall off around 2024. In fact, there is strong evidence to conclude that television as a vehicle to move video messaging is already less effective.

(i) More Advertising Is Required for Less Return

There is evidence to contend that as more and more voters are turned off to politics in the US and are either not voting or making up their minds late in the process, more advertising dollars are required to chase fewer voters in general elections. Political researchers Michael M. Franz and Travis N. Ridout found that while advertising had meaningful effects on voting in the 2008 election, it required a candidate running many more ads than their opponent for just a little gain. They declared that, "Having a 1,000-ad advantage across the entire campaign, for instance, resulted in about a 0.5 percentage point improvement in a candidate's share of the vote in 2008" (Franz & Ridout, 2010, p. 21).

(ii) Increased Advertising Has Only a Short-term Effect

There is also a growing body of evidence that suggests campaigns are spending a lot of money to gain only a short-term effect on a small group of voters. When studying the outcomes of the 2012 presidential election, researchers John Sides and Lynn Vavreck found that while ads had a measurable effect on voter attitudes, that effect was small and remarkably short-lived – it disappeared within a week (Sides & Vavreck, 2013, p. 22).

(iii) People More Readily Avoid Watching Ads

There is much research to support this notion. For example, Donald Green, a professor of political science at Columbia University, says, "Television ads are not as effective as they once were" because "once upon a time, people had to get up to change channels or turn down the volume to avoid ads." Obviously, advances in technology long ago changed that (Johnson, 2015, p. 23). However, notwithstanding the above, campaigns will still buy ads and spend big on television in the short term.

For so long, television was the sole or dominant medium for advertising, and as such campaigns have been slow to abandon the medium. Rather than switch political advertising spending from television to digital/online media, campaigns instead began spending heavily on digital *in addition to* their television spending.

In this new multi-platform world using both television and digital, campaigns are less likely to really know how effective their ads are. And while that is alarming, determining the effectiveness of advertising has always been difficult. Department store magnate and advertising pioneer John Wanamaker is reported to have said in the late 1800s, "Half my advertising is wasted. I just don't know which half" (Chapman, 2014). Campaigns have tended to continue to spend money on both television and digital advertising merely to cover all bases because of uncertainty – they just do not know how effective their spending is in today's explosion of video options.

There is further evidence to question the effectiveness of spending on television today. Research by Professor Travis Ridout from Washington State University suggests that "In a highly competitive race where candidates are well-known, ads aren't going to make more than a 2–3 percentage point difference, but obviously, some races are decided by 2–3 percentage points … you just don't want to give up on that" (Kurtzleben, 2015, para. 24). Gregg Phillips, who ran Newt Gingrich's super-PAC, Winning Our Future, in 2012, forecasted different viewing habits for younger viewers. Phillips suggested there was some evidence that more people are turning off these ads to instead be moved by a different type of ad – those placed on social media.

Yet interestingly, he notes that campaign teams often do not really know their return on investment, so are reluctant to drop one form of advertising in place of another – for fear that changing may risk losing a vote. One vote lost may risk losing overall, so spending, which he likens to an "arms race," just keeps on increasing (Kurtzleben, 2015, para. 22).

(3) In an Unchanged Regulatory Framework, Spending by PACs/Super-PACs Will Continue to Increase and Far Outweigh Campaign Spending

The August 2015 super-PAC mid-year filing deadline gave clear perspective into the influence of independent expenditure groups on the 2016 US presidential race. Kahloon (2015) demonstrates this point with figures showing such groups had already raised $301.8 million – more than six times the rate seen in the contentious 2014 cycle and 11 times more than the 2012 cycle. He also showed that, at that point in the 2016 presidential cycle, of the 15 individuals/groups that had surpassed $20 million in fundraising, 10 were PACs or super-PACs, not candidate or political party organizations. Of the next 11 individuals or groups that raised between $10 million and $20 million, 10 were PACs or super-PACs.

We think Figure 2.2 aptly depicts the current state of play and likelihood of future influence by the super-PACs. It shows the truly incredible growth in the presence of these groups on the political landscape.

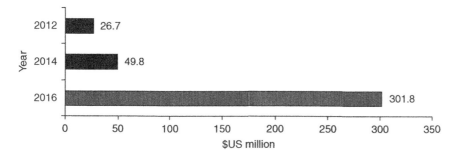

Figure 2.2 Super-PACs: outside money raised in first six months of cycle
Source: Original data from Federal Election Commission displayed by the Sunlight Foundation.

(4) *Advertising and Testing Will Become More Ingenious and Innovative*

Political campaigns are working much harder to find innovative ways to gain advantage over their competition. Due to the rapidity of technological change, it would be risky, if not foolhardy, to make specific predictions as to what the future holds for political advertising. However, if history is any guide, campaigns will be using technologies and advertising strategies within the next decade that have not even yet been imagined. One thing we can be certain of, however, is that regardless of the new technologies or platforms, video and digital imaging will remain as the most powerful tool to move voters.

In today's competitive political world, adapting to fast developing technology and platforms is critical to electoral success. Adopting new technologies enables campaigns to reach large segments of voters more affordably while speeding up the news cycle. Digital tools are now replacing traditional physical events. For example, a campaign launch can be broadcast on YouTube, rather than at a physical rally. Michael Slaby, former chief integration and innovation officer for the 2012 Obama campaign, suggests that utilization of digital tools is now a political way of life, "I think that's mostly a reflection of the deeper, smarter understanding of the landscape…" (Ingham, 2015, para. 29).

Perhaps the most foreboding comments for television's future came from Kip Cassino, the vice president of research at Borrell Associates, when he predicted that by 2020, the political spending that was once on television will move online and be within a billion dollars of television by the 2020 election. If Cassino is correct, we can expect online political advertising spending to surpass television spending for the first time by the 2024 election.

Most experts are not surprised in the shift. Scott Kozar from New Media Firm, a Democratic aligned media firm, said that "Innovation is not new to politics … The challenge political ad-makers face is to produce better, more emotionally compelling ads that hold a viewer's attention no matter the platform" (Kozar, 2015, Interview). Despite our above caveats, we further explore below some technology areas that are likely to play a larger role in the future of political advertising. They are:

(a) Social Media "Trust Filters," "Civic Engagement" and "Nudge Effect";
(b) Micro-targeted Advertising;
(c) Neuropolitics;
(d) Drones;
(e) Video Gaming;
(f) Virtual Reality Campaigning; and
(g) Holographic Campaigning.

Let us expand on each and explain why they are areas to watch.

(a) Social Media "Trust Filters," "Civic Engagement" and "Nudge Effect"

In the future, political advertising will focus more on social media and its networks. Furthermore, social media "network effects" will play an integral part in helping persuade voters. Three such effects are:

(i) *"Trust Filter" Effect*

In a world where people are inundated with vast quantities of information and 24-hour news, they must be more discerning in what they choose to read, listen to and believe. The "trust filter" effect occurs when people use their close personal social media networks to help them evaluate or "filter" the accuracy and importance of information.

The trust filter can help persuade or dissuade allegiance to a person or political party. Lee Rainie, director of the Pew Internet & American Life Project, supports this assertion and says these developments "act like broadcasters and publishers" allowing individuals and their networks to transform the nature of political communications (West, 2011, p. 50). It should be noted too that the 2012 Obama campaign used trust filters with great success to recruit supporters, move video, build crowds and even enhance voter turnout.

(ii) *"Civic Engagement" Effect*

Many citizens today are apathetic toward politics and are disengaged during election time. Social media offers an outlet for citizens and leaders to connect and establishes an environment that can encourage a sense of public responsiveness and accountability. This is the "civic engagement" effect. President Obama's former White House Director of Digital Strategy, Macon Phillips, argued that social media creates a new model of civic engagement. He noted that reporters also follow social media and incorporate the voices of ordinary people in news reporting. This enhances democratic conversation and gives citizens more of a voice in national debates (West, 2011, p. 51).

(iii) *"Nudge" Effect*

Nudge theory originated in the US through Professor Richard Thaler and involves encouraging or "nudging" people subtly down a particular choice path by altering the environment. It provides people with easier judgments and choices while protecting freedom of choice. Corbyn (2012) references the Facebook experiment that is credited as being the first to demonstrate that the online world can affect real-world behavior on a large scale. In this experiment, on the day of the 2010 US congressional elections, Facebook sent 61 million US account owners messages at the top of their news feeds. The messages in part, showed photos of friends who had voted and provided a link to click "I voted." This small encouragement to get-out-the-vote is attributed to indirectly nudging 280,000 more people to the polls.

(b) Micro-targeted Advertising

Micro-targeted advertising is another fast arriving technology that has shown significant results. This type of advertising begins by collecting a vast array of (big) data using digital and social media platforms and uses the results to better target voters. It is based on a myriad of factors, including tastes, preferences, location and spending habits.

If "Social Data" and its multitude of communication platforms drove the 2008 US presidential election, "Big Data" drove the 2012 election, allowing voters exhibiting certain characteristics or behaviors to be targeted with specific messages.

What campaigns did in 2012 – for the first time – was to gather volumes of personal information on individual voters, including what they ate, what they read, what they drank, drove, watched, listened to and literally scores of additional pieces of information on tens of millions of voters. They then tested how people who read certain newspapers or magazines, who ate certain foods, who drank certain drinks, who drove certain cars, etc., would vote and what issues were most important to them. The predictability was uncanny and when the campaigns compared this data with state-by-state election data, they wove all the pieces into a comprehensive candidate political campaign-messaging platform.

Statistical analysts were then able to develop the reams of campaign data at their fingertips into actionable targeted messages to persuade prospective voters across the nation.

Yet, to be clear, while both parties used this technology, the Obama campaign took it to a new level of success. The online site, Wired, summed that race up as follows:

> "…Barack Obama has cemented the role of Big Data in every aspect of the campaigning process. His ultimate success came from the work of historic get-out-the-vote efforts dominated by targeted messaging and digital behavioral tracking."
>
> (Chahal, 2013, para. 39)

Micro-targeted advertising will build off such success and continually improve the accumulation and dissemination of data in the future.

Comparing micro-targeted advertising to the blanket advertising broadcast on commercial television is like comparing a surgeon's scalpel to a hacksaw. Micro-targeted advertising has considerable potential to make a big difference in political advertising and in impacting the outcome of elections. The beauty and power of micro-targeted advertising is its ability to target individual voters with specific messages.

In another instance of the usage of big data, in 2015 D2Media Sales, a strategic relationship between DIRECTV and DISH, began working with Clarity Campaign Labs and TargetSmart Communications (using the Democratic National Committee voter file database) to make addressable advertising a reality for campaigns and voters. The combined reach of this technology exceeded 20 million DIRECTV and DISH households across the country and allowed campaigns to target specific households and deliver specific ads that were relevant to voters residing there. Warren Schlichting, DISH senior vice president of media sales, captured the power of the technology with his simple definition of it, "The more the message resonates with the voter, the more efficient and effective the campaign can be" (Clarity Campaign Labs, 2014, para. 38).

This data-centric shift in advertising has enabled political parties to hone campaign approaches toward predicting outcomes. Undeniably, it is this elegant blend of social data, big data and targeting that will help determine US presidential elections for the foreseeable future. According to the Center for Responsive Politics, the advent of Big Data and Social Data did not rein in campaign spending across all media. In the 2012 US presidential election, they note, total spending for all media topped $6 billion (Chahal, 2013, para. 40).

(c) Neuropolitics

While the technology is relatively new, neuropolitics (also known as neuromarketing) has been used already in political campaigns with some positive outcomes. Neuropolitics involves facial coding, biofeedback and brain imaging. Cameras capture viewers' facial expressions and emotional reactions to videos (surprise, anger, disgust, happiness, sadness, etc.) and feed the results through an algorithm. As Randall (2015) posits, it is spontaneous, unwitting feedback (unlike focus groups, surveys and dial testing) and so campaigns can tweak an ad almost instantly – adjusting the images, sounds or words – to come up with an improved visual message that resonates more with voters.

Neuroconsultants contend that political interest in their work is growing although in many quarters it is still largely considered taboo. Chief Executive of Neuro Discover, Kilinc Orhan Erdemir, believes that "Citizens don't know what neuromarketing is … they see it as a mind manipulation technique. So politicians fear talking about it" (Randall, 2015, para. 33).

There has been successful employment of neuropolitics internationally too. For instance in Mexico, President Enrique Peña Nieto's campaign and his party, the Institutional Revolutionary Party (PRI), employed such tools to measure voters' brain waves, skin arousal, heart rates and facial expressions during the 2012 presidential campaign. Francisco Olvera Ruiz, the governor of the Mexican state of Hidalgo and a governing party member, said that neuroscience research is "especially valuable because it has allowed us to discover with more precision and objectivity what people think, perceive and feel" (Randall, 2015, para. 35).

In Colombia, President Juan Manuel Santos' 2014 re-election team hired a neuropolitical consultancy (they won) (Randall, 2015, para. 36).

In Turkey, Prime Minister Ahmet Davutoglu and his Justice and Development Party hired a Turkish neuromarketing company for their June 2015 election. Testing revealed the Prime Minister needed to connect more with voters emotionally. His campaign team adjusted his approach and appeal – he won the election (Randall, 2015, para. 37).

(d) Drones

Another technological advance that continues to improve video usage, regardless of the platform, is the use of drones (a remote-controlled aircraft equipped with video equipment) to gather video footage never before so easily attainable. Veteran GOP ad-maker Fred Davis is a pioneer of using drones to film campaign ads and believes the camera-equipped aerial vehicles, many of which are very small, offer some exciting opportunities. Davis said that drones "can do things that even a helicopter can't do, and … at an unbelievably reasonable price." Because the cost of using drones has fallen dramatically, ad makers expect their use to increase in political campaigns (Lippman, 2015, para. 46).

Colin Hoffman from Sandlot Strategies (a full service advertising agency), alludes to some of the benefits of using drones. He states that advertisers must tell compelling stories and drones are an effective way to enhance that. Candidates get to stand out, be more memorable and the aerial footage provides a unique way to give a "birds-eye-view" of a desired setting. It also gives the impression the candidate is modern, in touch and embracing change (Hoffman, 2015, para. 47).

(e) Video Gaming

This is an already massive area and one often underestimated. While the gaming industry might seem like an unlikely source for political advertising, consider that it already generates more revenue than Hollywood. Entertainment writer, Stuart McGurk, suggests that the gaming market is simply too large for advertisers to neglect, "Games are fast becoming the dominant culture medium" and that "It's now bigger than Hollywood" (McGurk, 2014, para. 41). That being the case, there are real opportunities for political advertisers to explore this realm further into the future. Tamara Gaffney, principal analyst and director at Adobe Analytics, echoed that sentiment: "The gaming industry is a lot bigger than most marketers realize." She added "These games get more social buzz on opening day than most movies do…" As further evidence, Gaffney noted that revenue from the release of one of the top games nearly doubled that of the opening of the highest grossing movie (Harry Potter and the Deathly Hallows Part 2) (Tim, 2015, para. 42).

The majority of older voters in the US in 2012 likely knew nothing about the use of gaming to move messages to voters. But it was used with great impact and effect by the Obama campaign to reach younger voters – a critical group of voters Obama needed if he hoped to be re-elected. Because the Obama campaign knew that younger voters were less likely to watch television they had to reach these voters with what they did watch – in this case, video games.

Michael Turk, who was former eCampaign director for the Bush/Cheney 2004 presidential race was impressed with the Obama campaign's ingenuity, "They [Obama campaign] were actually running ads in Xbox games, so when you were in a racing game as you were racing down the street, there would be a billboard … 'Vote for Barack Obama' … in the game" (Ingham 2015, para. 43).

(f) Virtual Reality Campaigning

Another new technology that has sprung onto the video communications field is that of Virtual Reality campaigning. This technology allows campaigns to provide images and pictures of actual events that give viewers a 360-degree perspective of an event that can be watched on various platforms, most notably smartphones. It gives viewers the sensation of being at an event without them actually being there.

Political content in Virtual Reality began appearing in the US in the 2016 presidential campaign. A speech by Democratic candidate Sen. Bernie Sanders, for example, was available as a VR video through YouTube, although his team did not even produce it. VR has the potential to play a larger role, giving voters unprecedented virtual access to candidates, whose events might be taking place thousands of miles away (Ingham, 2015, para. 45).

(g) Holographic Campaigning

A hologram is a free-standing, three-dimensional image that is projected by a laser or other light source onto a backdrop. Holograms provide the capability for candidates to be seen and heard at multiple locations simultaneously – in high quality imaging. In the 2014 Indian national election, prime ministerial candidate Narendra Modi illustrated this potential with impressive results. Modi's team displayed his image at over 100 different rallies across the country – simultaneously – giving literally hundreds of thousands of citizens a sense of personal attention, including those in rural areas with access to only poor digital infrastructure (Ingham, 2015, para. 49).

It remains to be seen whether this would be successful in other countries but the technology is promising.

Conclusion

Political advertising has evolved and is evolving at great speed as the battle to win office becomes more competitive and more expensive. With the expansion of television options for viewers and the technological advances in video quality and in social media platforms to move video images, political advertising will have to be moved in vastly different ways. For while video images on television dominated the political persuasion and advertising landscape for 60 years, that medium is rapidly giving way to new technological platforms largely – but not exclusively – surrounding social media.

But as we have also seen, while the platforms for delivering political messages are changing, the power of video as a tool to persuade and capture audiences has not and in fact arguably has never been stronger. The challenge then for political advertisers in the future is not whether video advertising has run its course but rather in what new and exciting ways can they use the power of video to persuade voters. The campaigns that do this the best are likely to be the most successful electorally.

Finally, we have seen that blanket advertising effectiveness is giving way to big data and more targeted strategies and overall, the advertising "scalpel," even if reluctantly, is replacing the "hacksaw." It is hard to determine the limits of this powerful new tool in voter persuasion but it is fair to say that those limits have not yet been envisioned.

In short, this chapter concludes with the following summary of what Americans can expect with respect to trends in political advertising in the future:

- Spending on political advertising will continue to rise overall.
- More participants will enter the market with super-PACs and vested organizations outspending campaign teams.
- Platform options for advertising will continue to evolve and increase.
- Television as a medium will give ground to the online platform with the latter growing at a much faster rate. Television advertising growth will flatten and inevitably decline with online becoming the largest medium, overtaking television by 2024.
- There will be a greater focus on micro-targeted advertising – collection of big data via both digital and online platforms and using those results and same platforms to micro-target voters more effectively.
- The virtual world will play a bigger role in advertising with video gaming, Virtual Reality and perhaps even holograms improving messaging effectiveness and connection with younger voters.
- Use of new innovations such as neuropolitics and drones will increase their role in ad creation and testing.

- Social media and "close friend networks" will play an even larger role in establishing "trust filters," "civic engagement" and contribute to the "nudge effect" with respect to formation of political opinions, activity and get-out-the-vote turnout.
- Technological innovations will expand accessibility and lower barriers to entry for members of the public to influence campaigns.

References

Cassino, K. (2015, August). 2015–2016 Political Advertising Outlook. Retrieved from www.borrellassociates. com/industry-papers/papers/2015-to-2016-political-advertising-outlook-august-15-detail.

Center for Responsive Politics. (2016). Political action committees. Retrieved from www.opensecrets.org/pacs/.

Chahal, G. (2013, May 14). Election 2016: Marriage of big data, social data will determine the next president. Retrieved from www.wired.com/insights/2013/05/election-2016-marriage-of-big-data-social-data-will-determine-the-next-president/.

Chapman, S. (2014, May 29). "Half my advertising is wasted; I just don't know which half" – or is it asks new research. Retrieved from www.prolificnorth.co.uk/2014/05/half-my-advertising-is-wasted-i-just-dont-know-which-half-or-is-it-asks-new-research/.

Clarity + Campaign Labs (2014, August 11). Democratic candidates step into the future of political advertising with D2Media Sales. Retrieved from http://www.claritycampaigns.com/news/2014/8/11/d2media-sales.

Corbyn, Z. (2012, September 12). Facebook experiment boosts US voter turnout. Retrieved from http://www.nature.com/news/facebook-experiment-boosts-us-voter-turnout-1.11401.

Dunbar, J. (2015). The "Citizens United" decision and why it matters. Retrieved from www.publicintegrity.org/2012/10/18/11527/citizens-united-decision-and-why-it-matters.

Franz, M., & Ridout, T. (2010). Political advertising and persuasion in the 2004 and 2008 presidential elections. *American Politics Research*, 38(2), 303–329.

Hoffman, C. (2015, May 15). 6 ways drone cinematography can help your campaign. Retrieved from www.campaignsandelections.com/campaign-insider/2452/6-ways-drone-cinematography-can-help-your-campaign.

Ingham, L. (2015, September 7). Holograms, VR and in-game ads: Meet the future of the political campaign. Retrieved from http://factor-tech.com/feature/holograms-vr-and-in-game-ads-meet-the-future-of-the-political-campaign/.

Johnson, L. P. (2015, November 20). Long campaigns grueling – for voters. Retrieved from www.mysanantonio.com/opinion/commentary/article/Long-campaigns-grueling-for-voters-6647008.php.

Kahloon, I. (2015, August 3). Outside groups' influence on 2016 election grows, super PAC filings show. Retrieved from https://sunlightfoundation.com/blog/2015/08/03/outside-groups-influence-on-2016-election-grows-super-pac-filings-show/.

Kaushik, P. (2011). Attention politicians: "Keep your eyes on social media." Retrieved from www.businessinsider.com/attention-politicians-keep-your-eyes-on-social-media-2011-10.

Kozar, S. (2015, December 8). Interview.

Kurtzleben, D. (2015, August 19). 2016 campaigns will spend $4.4 billion on TV ads, but why? Retrieved from www.npr.org/sections/itsallpolitics/2015/08/19/432759311/2016-campaign-tv-ad-spending.

Lapowsky, I. (2015, August 8). Political ad spending online is about to explode. Retrieved from http://www.wired.com/2015/08/digital-politcal-ads-2016/.

Lepore, J. (2012). The lie factory: How politics became a business. Retrieved from www.newyorker.com/magazine/2012/09/24/the-lie-factory.

Lippman, D. (2015, February 7). Drones fly into the political ad wars. Retrieved from www.politico.com/story/2015/02/political-ads-drones-114980#ixzz3u9BmTlN0.

McGurk, D. (2014, February 19). Gaming special: Welcome to the world of grown up gaming. Retrieved from www.gq-magazine.co.uk/entertainment/articles/2014-02-/19/video-game-industry-evolution-2014.

Murray, M. (2015, November 4). Super PACs, outside groups dominate '16 ad spending. Retrieved from www.nbcnews.com/meet-the-press/super-pacs-outside-groups-dominate-gop-16-ad-spending-n457351.

Randall, K. (2015, November 3). Neuropolitics. Where campaigns try to read your mind. Retrieved from www.nytimes.com/2015/11/04/world/americas/neuropolitics-where-campaigns-try-to-read-your-mind.html?_r=0.

Sides, J., & Vavreck, L. (2013). *The gamble: Choice and chance in the 2012 presidential election*. Princeton, NJ: Princeton University Press.

The Kennedy-Nixon Debates. History. Retrieved from http://www.history.com/topics/us-presidents/kennedy-nixon-debates.

The Sunlight Foundation. (2012, April 11). Fundraising and spending by political leaning, 2011–2012. Retrieved from www.reporting.sunlightfoundation.com/outside-spending-2012/by-affiliation/.

Tim, G. (2015, October 15). The video game industry continues to outperform Hollywood. Retrieved from www.lazygamer.net/industry-2/the-video-game-industry-continues-to-outperform-hollywood/.

Turan, S. (2014, May 20). Plato Books 6–7. Retrieved from https://prezi.com/j17nlw5qlhlc/may-21-plato-books-6-7/.

Varoga, C. (2015, December 8). Interview.

Webley, K. (2010, September 23). How the Nixon-Kennedy debate changed the world. *Time Magazine.* Retrieved from http://content.time.com/time/nation/article/0,8599,2021078,00.html.

West, D. (2011, June 28). Ten ways social media can improve campaign engagement and reinvigorate American democracy. Retrieved from www.brookings.edu/research/opinions/2011/06/28-social-media-west.

Willis, D. (2015, June 30). Why television is still king for campaign spending. Retrieved from www.nytimes.com/2015/07/01/upshot/why-television-is-still-king-for-campaign-spending.html?_r=0.

Xoto, J. (2013). Video persuasion manifesto. Smart video persuasion (p. 9). Retrieved from http://rtwtutorials.s3.amazon.com/video%20persuastion%20manifesto.pdf.

3

METHODOLOGICAL APPROACHES

Michael W. Kearney and Mary C. Banwart

Political ads have become a fixture of modern political campaigns. Accordingly, political advertising has been studied from a variety of perspectives and methodological approaches. Even a cursory review of political advertising literature is likely to produce evidence of methodological diversity. The majority of studies examining political advertising deploy empirical methods, but researchers have also used rhetorical and interpretive methods (e.g., Gronbeck, 1992; Kates, 1998; Parmelee, Perkins, & Sayre, 2007; Reyes, 2006; Richardson, 2000; Sheckels, 2002). Researchers often use rhetorical and interpretive methods to examine specific themes or case studies, but this research informs much of the empirical research on political advertising as well.

Use of focus groups is one of the most common methods of qualitative research on political advertising. Focus groups are facilitated and/or organized discussions among small groups of recruited participants about a well-known issue or study-specific stimulus. Focus groups are particularly well suited for in-depth investigations concerning the ways in which participants perceive certain phenomena. Compared to the traditional survey and experimental methods discussed throughout the rest of this chapter, focus groups allow researchers to avoid over-simplifications of the communicative processes that take place within political advertising (Delli Carpini & Williams, 1994). Focus groups are frequently used to better understand how political ads are received by overlooked, time-sensitive, or difficult-to-access populations (e.g., Parmelee, Perkins, & Sayre, 2007; Sparrow & Turner, 2001).

In the following sections, we provide an overview, along with several examples, of popular empirical research methods used in political advertising research, including content analysis, surveys and experiments. Research methods in the literature can generally be divided into three categories – content analysis, experimental and survey. We therefore organized this chapter to reflect these categories. First, we define content analysis and describe several examples of its use in the literature. Second, we discuss independent and dependent variables used in experimental research. In this section we also discuss the pros and cons of several types of experiments. In the third section we review advantages and disadvantages of survey methods and discuss developments related to the rise of digital media and "big data." In each of these sections, we review methodological trends and issues in political advertising research.

Empirical Research

Before describing different empirical approaches to the study of political advertising, we feel it necessary to first reflect on some fundamental assumptions of empirical research. Empirical approaches to the study of political advertising predominantly reflect assumptions associated with null hypothesis significance testing, a hybrid of Fisher's significance testing and Neyman-Pearson's model comparison approach to statistical inference. In contrast to these frequentist approaches to statistical inference, recent advances in software and computational efficiency have made alternative methods, i.e., Bayesian approaches to statistical inference, increasingly popular as well. Despite growth of Bayesian methods, however, frequentist approaches continue to dominate the literature. The focus of this chapter is on the different empirical approaches to the study of political advertising.

Content Analysis Research

Content analysis refers to the systematic categorization, or *coding*, of one or more communication artifacts via numeric assignment. Content analysis is perhaps the most common quantitative method used to explore and describe political advertisements. Unlike historical, critical and interpretive methods, which have also been used to identify themes and analyze political ads (Kaid, 2004), content analysis attempts to quantify distinguishing elements of the content in question. This systematic categorization often referred to as coding is applied to each unit of analysis, which is defined by the researchers given the topic and purpose of study. Each unit of analysis is coded (i.e., counted) in one or more categories as theorized by the researchers. Categories are typically defined prior to data analysis, though some exploratory research creates and uses categories derived from patterns observed in the data exploration process. Many researchers rely on one or (preferably) more human coders – frequently undergraduate or graduate students – though computerized content analysis has become increasingly more common over the past few decades. Scholars using content analysis methods have employed numerous types of categories (e.g., valence, or whether political ads are positive or negative, frames, e.g., whether ads focus on issues or candidate image (Meirick, 2002), emotion, language, verbal style and tone).

One of the systematic content analysis methods by which political candidates' televised advertisements have been studied is that of videostyle (e.g., Banwart, Bystrom, & Robertson, 2003; Bystrom, Robertson, Banwart, & Kaid, 2004; Johnston & Kaid, 2002). Videostyle as a method (Kaid & Davidson, 1986) is in part grounded in Goffman's (1959) work on self-presentation and is the study of "the way candidates present themselves to voters through the television medium" (Johnston & Kaid, 2002, p. 285). The broadcast ad in its entirety – whether it is 15 seconds, 30 seconds, or one minute in length, with most samples including ads that are 30 seconds in length – serves as the unit of analysis. Coders then search for items that represent three major categories of study: verbal content, nonverbal content and production techniques (Kaid & Davidson, 1986).

The first category, verbal content, of videostyle focuses on the "semantic characteristics" of the advertisement's message (Kaid & Tedesco, 1999). The variables coded, which represent the spot ad's verbal content, include the positive or negative tone of the message, whether issues or candidate image is discussed and the content of both issues and candidate images presented, language choice, appeals (e.g., ethos, logos, pathos, fear), and the presence of incumbent or challenger strategies. The second category, nonverbal content, examines "visual elements and audio elements that do not have specific semantic meaning" (Kaid & Davidson, 1986, p. 187). Variables such as personal appearance, kinesics, paralanguage, body language of the candidate, and facial expressions are analyzed. The third category of analysis is the film/video production techniques. Such techniques are central to the design content of an ad as they aid in the delivery of the verbal and nonverbal messages by setting the mood and directing the focus of the viewer. Variables in this category include music, camera angles, special effects, cutting techniques and setting.

Videostyle has been widely used to analyze broadcast advertising in presidential elections (e.g., Bystrom et al., 2004; Johnston & Kaid, 2002) and in comparing US presidential and Korean presidential advertising (Tak, Kaid, & Khang, 2007). Scholars have also advanced videostyle analysis to account for the influence of gender. For instance, Bystrom (1995) introduced new items identified by scholars as distinct to female and male communication styles. For example, variables included candidate posture, use of touch, language intensifiers, traits identified with female communication styles (i.e., sensitive/understanding, cooperation with others, etc.), and an expanded list of issues that are analyzed within feminine, masculine and neutral categories.

Another approach to content analysis categorizes political ads using Benoit's (1999) functional analysis theory. According to functional analysis political campaign messages can attack (criticism, negative association, etc.), acclaim (praise), and/or defend (explain, respond, etc.). This method has been used to examine broadcast ads during US presidential elections (e.g., Benoit, 1999; Benoit & Glantz, 2015; Henson & Benoit, 2016), to draw a comparison with web-only ads and broadcast ads from US presidential campaigns (Roberts, 2013), congressional broadcast ads (Brazeal & Benoit, 2001, 2006), and comparisons between broadcast advertising in US presidential and Taiwanese presidential (Wen, Benoit, & Yu, 2004) and Korean presidential races (Lee & Benoit, 2004).

In much of the content analysis approaches to studying campaign advertising, persuasion theory and media effects research guides category selections. Granted, researchers have incorporated more applied approaches to content analysis as well. For example, Atkin and Heald (1976) interviewed campaign media directors to identify the key communication messages in order to examine voter opinions.

Content analysis is a flexible method that also extends to effects-focused research. When combined with experimental or observational data, content analysis can be used to make claims about potential effects of certain political advertising media. In response to medium-to-small effect sizes commonly found in political communication research and the limitations associated with participant recall, scholars have introduced new techniques designed to increase the validity of this kind of content analysis. For example, researchers analyzed political ads and then matched the results with levels of exposure to different geographical areas or different populations (e.g., Slater, 2016). It is also possible to specify procedures in content analysis to systematically alter the results from the analysis. This is especially useful when dealing with sampling limitations. For example, Prior (2001) proposed using *weighted* content analysis in order to distinguish between aired versus watched political ads. In his study, political ad buy data were used as weights in a model examining differences between major parties in advertising tone.

Experimental Research

Scholars have taken a number of different approaches in examining the effects of political advertising, but experimental methods, in particular, are favored in the literature. Advancements in software have also made it easier to conduct experiments entirely online (Fridkin, Kenney, & Wintersieck, 2015; Iyengar & Vavreck, 2012). Experiments allow researchers to examine the unique effects of political advertising. Researchers have explored a wide range of possible effects including voting, candidate image, knowledge, cynicism, polarization and efficacy, among others. Political advertising experiments can be further broken down into different study designs and stimuli.

Experimental designs in political advertising research include pretest/post-test designs (e.g., Kaid, Postelnicu, Landreville, Yun, & LeGrange, 2007) using control or comparison groups (e.g., Broockman & Green, 2014; Valentino, Hutchings, & Williams, 2004), or post-test only, factorial designs (Phillips, Urbany, & Reynolds, 2008). Many of these experiments use political advertisements from real political campaigns (e.g., Kahn & Geer, 1994; Meirick, 2002; Phillips et al., 2008). Participants in experiments include general populations, variety of targeted populations and, most commonly, college students. Although experimental methods offer greater external validity compared to cross-sectional surveys, though it may not be enough to correct for potential shortcomings associated with student samples. For example, some research suggests the effects of political advertising may be larger on students (Benoit, Leshner, & Chattopadhyay, 2007). This makes sense as college students are more likely to be politically engaged later in life than non-college students (Klofstad, 2015). Student samples are thus not necessarily representative. College students tend to be more engaged with public affairs than the general population, making them more sensitive to experimental manipulations involving politics. In short, experimental methods avoid some of the problems associated with observational research methods, but results may still be shaped by the nature of the sample.

Experimental methods in political advertising research typically treat political advertisements as independent variables, though some derivatives do examine contingencies which frame political ads – e.g., fact-checking following a negative ad experiment (Fridkin et al., 2015). In many of these experiments, participants are randomly assigned to media containing different political ads or different levels (or types) of exposure to political ads. For instance, participants could be assigned to groups to watch positive ads or negative ads, or they could be assigned to groups to watch several ads or only one ad. By using political ads as stimuli, experiments provide direct evaluations of their effects. Researchers have used experiments to compare one or more political ads from radio (e.g., Shapiro & Rieger, 1992), print (e.g., Pinkleton, 1998), television (Garramone, Atkin, Pinkleton, & Cole, 1990; Roddy & Garramone, 1988), or the Internet (Broockman & Green, 2014), with a control group or with different (comparison) ads. When using a control group, often researchers will display non-political entertainment or informational media content in order to control for medium-specific effects. When using comparison group, researchers will often maximize systematic differences by displaying several examples of each type of ad. For example, one group may be exposed to ten different image-focused political ads while a second group is exposed to ten different candidate-focused political ads. Control groups allow researchers to isolate effects of *exposure* to political ads. Comparison groups allow researchers to isolate the effects of *types* of political ads.

In terms of the stimulus being tested, some experiments focus on individual elements of advertisements – e.g., voice-over announcers (Strach, Zuber, Fowler, Ridout, & Searles, 2015), background music and images (Brader, 2005), etc. – with some experiments examining audio and video separately. Most lab experiments expose participants to several ads in succession (Kaid et al., 2007) or within other types of programming (Roddy & Garramone, 1988). Participants are typically exposed to multiple advertisements, though media environments and whether advertisements are embedded in other programming tends to vary with the study. In other words, researchers almost always expose participants to multiple ads, but, depending on the context and purpose of the study, researchers may also decide to replicate different physical environments (e.g., private versus public television exposure or personal versus laboratory computer use) sandwich political ads between entertainment or news programming – like one might imagine exposure to political ads occurs in real life.

Researchers also take multiple approaches to measuring the effects, or dependent variables. Common dependent variables include voter turnout, vote choice, political participation, perceptions of candidates, recall, affect and others. Many studies rely on self-reports from participants, though researchers employ other measurement techniques as well, such as thought-listing techniques (e.g., Phillips et al., 2008; Pinkleton, Um, & Austin, 2002; Schenck-Hamlin, Procter, & Rumsey, 2000; Shen, 2004) or asking participants to report on the perceived effects on other people (Cohen & Davis, 1991). More recently, advancements in technology have made other methods such as computer-assisted self-interviews and dials more popular as well (e.g., Iyengar & Simon, 2000; Iyengar & Vavreck, 2012; Schenck-Hamlin et al., 2000). Many of these alternatives to self-report are used not only to produce more reliable data but also to improve the reliability of self-report measurement strategies.

The major advantage of using experimental methods is relatively straightforward. Experiments give researchers unparalleled ability to ensure that manipulation only occurs on the independent variable of interest. This makes experiments uniquely suited for tests of causality. However, some scholars consider the external validity of these kinds of lab experiments to be in question (Goldstein & Ridout, 2004). Lab settings allow researchers to maximize control over experiments but they are not necessarily realistic. This raises several questions. Are advertisements presented in isolation or embedded in other media programming? Does the experiment capture the intensity or frequency of ad exposure that happens in the real world? These questions and concerns over ecological validity have caused many scholars to pursue field experiments (Goldstein & Ridout, 2004). For example, researchers have used field experiments to exposure to political advertising on the Internet (Broockman & Green, 2014) and on television (Phillips et al., 2008).

In one particularly interesting use of field experiments, researchers worked with campaigns to randomly assign different television ad buys to different television markets during the 2006 gubernatorial campaign in Texas (Gerber, Gimpel, Green, & Shaw, 2011). Although concerns of campaign strategy led to the exclusion of two of the largest markets from random assignment, researchers were still able to manipulate levels of exposure by cooperating with campaigns to systematically vary ad buys by geographical area and population. Given the degree of control and influence their design had on the actual election, the researchers were able to leverage short, low-cost surveys to voter populations at relatively high frequencies (e.g., weekly). As this study demonstrates, the collection of time series data during large-scale field experiments makes it possible to trace things such as the persistence of advertising effects. Thus, while meaningful insights can still be gained from laboratory experiments, field experiments offer much needed evidence of the effects of political advertising in real media environments.

Survey Research

In addition to experimental methods, literature describing the effects of political advertising comes from survey research as well. Less resource intensive and easier to distribute than experiments, surveys enable the collection of observational data. Survey research methods offer researchers several advantages. Surveys are relatively easy to access. Respondents can therefore complete surveys in more natural (and more familiar) settings. Ease of access even makes it feasible for many researchers to use longitudinal research designs. Longitudinal data can be used to track naturally occurring exposure to political ads over time. When longitudinal research consists of collecting panel data, or repeated observations over multiple points of time, researchers can isolate the directional effects, or temporal sequences, of political advertisements. For example, Shah et al. (2007) used panel data to analyze the influence of exposure to political advertisements on information-seeking behaviors. In this study, researchers used panel data to examine lagged effects and time-sensitive mediation models – relationships that are not directly testable when analyzing cross-sectional data.

Although surveys are relatively low-cost and easily accessible for numerous populations, they are not without disadvantages. One notable problem with survey methods concerns the endogeneity of political ad exposure. Researchers in this area of research often assume exposure to political advertisements is exogenous (i.e., the independent variable) when, in reality, exposure is likely influenced by media diet, political interest, geographical location, etc.

The problem of endogeneity potentially confounds all of the identified effects of political advertising. Survey designs that rely on self-report, for example, are likely bias due to endogeneity between respondent recall and political interest. That is, people who are more interested in politics are more likely to remember seeing political ads, while people who are less interested are more likely to forget, or under-report, ad exposure. For another example, consider one of the more reliable effects of political ads found in the literature, the effect of negative ads on negativity toward campaigns. Rather than concluding that negative ads influence the minds of voters to be more negative toward campaigns, it could be that people who are not as cynical about politics often forget (i.e., under-report) the degree to which they were exposed to negative political ads. Conversely, people who are more cynical about politics, on the other hand, might over-report their exposure to negative ads since they likely pay more attention when negative political ads get played. To address this problem, several studies on media effects have leveraged Nielson ratings and media tracking technology, but these alternative approaches are not without their own problems as well. Nielson estimates are still susceptible to sampling error, and they do not reflect the degree to which people paid attention to the media. Media tracking devices have potential to record large amounts of rich data, but the use of tracking devices for the purpose of research is largely not feasibile due to technological hurdles and prohibitive costs.

In addition to inherent limitations on a researcher's ability to control for other variables, one of the biggest obstacles to survey research is measuring *exposure*, or the amount of contact with communication messages, to political advertising. Recall problems, in particular, plague the measurement of media exposure (Iyengar & Vavreck, 2012; Prior, 2009, 2013). To minimize participant memory problems, scholars recommend increasing specificity in choices (Dilliplane, Goldman, & Mutz, 2013) and including population values or other specific referents (Prior, 2009). Despite proposed alternatives to traditional approaches to measurement, however, research suggests recall problems remain in media effects research (Prior, 2013). Proposed alternatives, such as measuring proxies for political advertising such as campaign spending or ad buys, offer imperfect solutions (Goldstein & Ridout, 2004). For example, several studies have used data on political ad buys as a proxy for political advertising (Goldstein & Ridout, 2004; Prior, 2001) even though ad buys do not necessarily translate into direct measurements of ad exposure. Ads are likely more expensive in New York than they are in Montana, but, as Goldstein and Ridout (2004) note, researchers rarely apply weights to ad buys to account for these differences in baseline costs in different markets.

Problems associated with measurements of political ad exposure remain, but new types of data do offer some potential. The rise of digital media, for example, has made it possible to track when and where political advertisements are played (Fowler & Ridout, 2013). In addition, the use of media tracking technology (Goldstein & Ridout, 2004; Iyengar & Vavreck, 2012) appear promising as well. These advancements may still suffer from similar limitations associated with traditional observational methods (e.g., ad buys), but they also create new possibilities for researchers as well. For example, technological advancements in the tracking of political advertising exposure make it easier to merge content analysis with survey methods (Iyengar & Simon, 2000). For example, in a study analyzing US Senate races in 1988 and 1992, Iyengar and Simon (2000) were able to replicate a data set of newspapers during that time in only six weeks. Researchers today have unprecedented access to news archives as nearly all news organizations now organize and maintain their archives electronically.

Technological advances continue to drive innovations in research. Many scholars are currently exploring numerous ways to access huge amounts of digital data generated from millions of online users. Future studies attempting to track the effects of political advertisements on voters will likely benefit from data made publicly available via application programming interface (API). APIs refer to sets of software routines and procedures that allow individuals to make requests for information created or maintained by a source. The *New York Times*, for example, allows users to request API keys associated with different sections of content. API keys function like a digital password in API requests sent to the *New York Times*. APIs enable users to make requests for information in much the same way that browsers make requests of a news organization's website. API documentation typically describes the procedures that can produce a specific call – like entering a specific URL – and response – like the loading of the webpage associated with that URL address. One promising source of online, digital-trace data made available via APIs comes from social media platforms, such as Facebook and Twitter. Millions of users, young and old, frequently use social media platforms to communicate with others about politics and current events. Many users use these platforms to share links, videos and news articles with other users in their networks. This method of message transmission is particularly effective as it also serves as a social validating function. Results from a nationwide Facebook experiment during the 2010 US congressional elections found that exposure to social-validating political messages had a positive effect on voter turnout (Bond et al., 2012). Political campaigns have taken note, and they will likely continue to design ads in ways to maximize their potential shareability on social media sites. In fact, campaigns have already started running ads specifically designed for social media sites like Facebook and Twitter. Facebook's API offers developers some access to user ad experiences, though much of the data require permission from users via third party applications. Future research will likely use these applications as a means of data collection, particularly for panel or experimental studies.

Although political campaigns cannot track individual users, Facebook does allow targeted political messaging. At the time of writing this, Facebook offers a feature that allows political advertising to target "political influencers," or very politically active Facebook users (Lapowsky, 2015). As of 2016, political campaigns can match voter files with Facebook user accounts in order to target certain users via Facebook for political advertisements (Davies & Yadron, 2016). In other words, campaigns can purchase ads, identify users also found in their voter files, and then track how those users interact with the purchased advertising. As a result, studies that measure ad exposure on Facebook may also be measuring strategic, empirically driven advertising decisions made by campaigns. For example, if over time ad exposure concentrated on rural users, one might reasonably infer the campaign in question decided to specifically target that group of rural voters. Even without voter files, campaigns can still purchase advertising plans that target certain demographics and even use Facebook's algorithm to identify liberal versus conservative users (Lapowsky, 2015).

Summary and Conclusion

Grounded in frequentist assumptions and informed by rhetorical and interpretive research, empirical research methods can be used in a variety of ways in the study of political advertising. Content analysis can be used to identify trends or claims in political ads. Experimental research can be used to isolate causal relationships – i.e., effects – related to political advertising and other political behaviors. Survey research can be used to describe and track these relationships nationwide and/or over time. In this chapter we reviewed advantages and disadvantages to each of these methodological approaches. Given the shifting nature of media technology and political communication, we can expect certain aspects of these methods, along with their advantages and disadvantages, to change over time. Although we have outlined several future directions for research methods in the study of political advertising, scholars should continue to adapt to the evolving political climate and, most importantly, the ever-changing media environment.

References

Atkin, C., & Heald, G. (1976). Effects of political advertising. *Public Opinion Quarterly*, 40(2), 216–228.

Banwart, M. C., Bystrom, D. G., & Robertson, T. (2003). From the primary to the general election a comparative analysis of candidate media coverage in mixed-gender 2000 races for governor and US Senate. *American Behavioral Scientist*, 46(5), 658–676.

Benoit, W. L. (1999). *Seeing spots: A functional analysis of presidential television advertisements, 1952–1996*. Westport, CT: Greenwood Publishing Group.

Benoit, W. L., & Glantz, M. (2015). A functional analysis of 2008 general election presidential TV spots. *Speaker & Gavel*, 49(1), 2.

Benoit, W. L., Leshner, G. M., & Chattopadhyay, S. (2007). A meta-analysis of political advertising. *Human Communication*. Retrieved from http://epublications.marquette.edu/comm_fac/9/.

Bond, R. M., Fariss, C. J., Jones, J. J., Kramer, A. D., Marlow, C., Settle, J. E., & Fowler, J. H. (2012). A 61-million-person experiment in social influence and political mobilization. *Nature*, 489(7415), 295–298.

Brader, T. (2005). Striking a responsive chord: How political ads motivate and persuade voters by appealing to emotions. *American Journal of Political Science*, 49(2), 388–405. doi:10.2307/3647684.

Brazeal, L. M., & Benoit, W. L. (2001). A functional analysis of congressional television spots, 1986–2000. *Communication Quarterly*, 49, 436–454. doi:10.1080/01463370109385640.

Brazeal, L. M., & Benoit, W. L. (2006). A functional analysis of congressional television spots, 1980–2004. *Communication Studies*, 57, 401–420. doi:10.1080/10510970600945972.

Broockman, D. E., & Green, D. P. (2014). Do online advertisements increase political candidates' name recognition or favorability? Evidence from randomized field experiments. *Political Behavior*, 36(2), 263–289.

Bystrom, Dianne G. (1995). Candidate gender and the presentation of self: The videostyles of men and women in US senate campaigns. Unpublished Doctoral Dissertation, University of Oklahoma.

Bystrom, D. G., Robertson, T., Banwart, M. C., & Kaid, L. L. (Eds.). (2004). *Gender and candidate communication: Videostyle, webstyle, newstyle.* New York, NY: Routledge.

Cohen, J., & Davis, R. G. (1991). Third-person effects and the differential impact in negative political advertising. *Journalism & Mass Communication Quarterly,* 68(4), 680–688. doi:10.1177/107769909106800409.

Davies, H., & Yadron, D. (2016, January 28). How Facebook tracks and profits from voters in a $10bn US election. Retrieved from www.theguardian.com/us-news/2016/jan/28/facebook-voters-us-election-ted-cruz-targeted-ads-trump.

Delli Carpini, M. X., & Williams, B. (1994). The method is the message: Focus groups as a method of social, psychological, and political inquiry. In M. X. Delli-Carpini, L. Huddy, & R.Y. Shapiro (Eds.), *Research in micropolitics: New directions in political psychology* (Vol. 4, pp. 57–85). Greenwhich, CT: JAI Press.

Dilliplane, S., Goldman, S. K., & Mutz, D. C. (2013). Televised exposure to politics: New measures for a fragmented media environment. *American Journal of Political Science,* 57(1), 236–248.

Fowler, E. F., & Ridout, T. N. (2013). Negative, angry, and ubiquitous: Political advertising in 2012. In *The Forum* (Vol. 10, pp. 51–61). Retrieved from www.degruyter.com/view/j/for.2012.10.issue-4/forum-2013-0004/forum-2013-0004.xml.

Fridkin, K., Kenney, P. J., & Wintersieck, A. (2015). Liar, liar, pants on fire: How fact-checking influences citizens' reactions to negative advertising. *Political Communication,* 32(1), 127–151.

Garramone, G. M., Atkin, C. K., Pinkleton, B. E., & Cole, R.T. (1990). Effects of negative political advertising on the political process. *Journal of Broadcasting & Electronic Media,* 34(3), 299–311. doi:10.1080/08838159009386744.

Gerber, A. S., Gimpel, J. G., Green, D. P., & Shaw, D. R. (2011). How large and long-lasting are the persuasive effects of televised campaign ads? Results from a randomized field experiment. *American Political Science Review,* 105(1), 135–150.

Goffman, E. (1959). *The presentation of self in everyday life.* Garden City, NY: Anchor.

Goldstein, K., & Ridout, T. N. (2004). Measuring the effects of televised political advertising in the United States. *Annual Review of Political Science,* 7, 205–226.

Gronbeck, B. E. (1992). Negative narratives in 1988 presidential campaign ads. *Quarterly Journal of Speech,* 78(3), 333–346.

Henson, J. R., & Benoit, W. L. (2016). Because I said so: A functional theory analysis of evidence in political TV spots. *Speaker & Gavel,* 47(1), 2.

Iyengar, S., & Simon, A. F. (2000). New perspectives and evidence on political communication and campaign effects. *Annual Review of Psychology,* 51(1), 149–169.

Iyengar, S., & Vavreck, L. (2012). Online panels and the future of political communication research. In *The Sage handbook of political communication* (pp. 225–240). Thousand Oaks, CA: Sage.

Johnston, A., & Kaid, L. L. (2002). Image ads and issue ads in US presidential advertising: Using videostyle to explore stylistic differences in televised political ads from 1952 to 2000. *Journal of Communication,* 52, 281–300. http://dx.doi.org/10.1111/j.1460-2466.2002.tb02545.x.

Kahn, K. F., & Geer, J. G. (1994). Creating impressions: An experimental investigation of political advertising on television. *Political Behavior,* 16(1), 93–116.

Kaid, L. L. (2004). Political advertising. In L. L. Kaid (Ed.), *Handbook of political communication research* (pp. 155–202). Mahwah, NJ: Lawrence Erlbaum.

Kaid, L. L., & Davidson, D. K. (1986). Elements of videostyle: Candidate presentation through television advertising. In L. L. Kaid, D. Nimmo, & K. R. Sanders (Ed.), *New perspectives on political advertising* (pp. 184–209). Carbondale, IL: Southern Illinois University Press.

Kaid, L. L., Postelnicu, M., Landreville, K., Yun, H. J., & LeGrange, A. G. (2007). The effects of political advertising on young voters. *American Behavioral Scientist,* 50(9), 1137–1151.

Kaid, L. L., & Tedesco, J. C. (1999). Tracking voter reactions to television advertising. In L. L. Kaid & D. G. Bystrom (Eds.), *The electronic election: Perspectives on the 1996 campaign communication* (pp. 233–246). Mahwah, NJ: Lawrence Erlbaum.

Kates, S. (1998). A qualitative exploration into voters' ethical perceptions of political advertising: Discourse, disinformation, and moral boundaries. *Journal of Business Ethics,* 17(16), 1871–1885.

Klofstad, C. A. (2015). Exposure to political discussion in college is associated with higher rates of political participation over time. *Political Communication,* 32(2), 292–309.

Lapowsky, I. (2015, November 4). Facebook now lets candidates target political fanatics. Retrieved from www.wired.com/2015/11/facebook-now-lets-candidates-target-election-2016-fanatics/.

Lee, C., & Benoit, W. L. (2004). A functional analysis of presidential television spots: A comparison of Korean and American ads. *Communication Quarterly,* 52(1), 68–79. http://dx.doi.org/10.1080/01463370409370179.

Meirick, P. (2002). Cognitive responses to negative and comparative political advertising. *Journal of Advertising*, 31(1), 49–62.

Parmelee, J. H., Perkins, S. C., & Sayre, J. J. (2007). "What about people our age?" Applying qualitative and quantitative methods to uncover how political ads alienate college students. *Journal of Mixed Methods Research*, 1(2), 183–199.

Phillips, J. M., Urbany, J. E., & Reynolds, T. J. (2008). Confirmation and the effects of valenced political advertising: A field experiment. *Journal of Consumer Research*, 34(6), 794–806.

Pinkleton, B. (1998). Effects of print comparative political advertising on political decision-making and participation. *Journal of Communication*, 48(4), 24–36. doi:10.1111/j.1460-2466.1998.tb02768.x.

Pinkleton, B. E., Um, N.-H., & Austin, E. W. (2002). An exploration of the effects of negative political advertising on political decision making. *Journal of Advertising*, 31(1), 13–25.

Prior, M. (2001). Weighted content analysis of political advertisements. *Political Communication*, 18(3), 335–345.

Prior, M. (2009). Improving media effects research through better measurement of news exposure. *The Journal of Politics*, 71(3), 893–908. doi:10.1017/s0022381609090781.

Prior, M. (2013). The challenge of measuring media exposure: Reply to Dilliplane, Goldman, and Mutz. *Political Communication*, 30(4), 620–634.

Reyes, G. M. (2006). The Swift Boat Veterans for Truth, the politics of realism, and the manipulation of Vietnam remembrance in the 2004 presidential election. *Rhetoric & Public Affairs*, 9(4), 571–600.

Richardson, G. W. (2000). Pulp politics: Popular culture and political advertising. *Rhetoric & Public Affairs*, 3(4), 603–626.

Roberts, C. (2013). A functional analysis comparison of web-only advertisements and traditional television advertisements from the 2004 and 2008 presidential campaigns. *Journalism & Mass Communication Quarterly*, 90, 23–38. doi:10.1177/1077699012468741.

Roddy, B. L., & Garramone, G. M. (1988). Appeals and strategies of negative political advertising. *Journal of Broadcasting & Electronic Media*, 32(4), 415–427. doi:10.1080/08838158809386713.

Schenck-Hamlin, W., Procter, D., & Rumsey, D. (2000). The influence of negative advertising frames on political cynicism and politician accountability. *Human Communication Research*, 26(1), 53–74. doi:10.1111/j.1468-2958.2000.tb00749.x.

Shah, D. V., Cho, J., Nah, S., Gotlieb, M. R., Hwang, H., Lee, N. J., … & McLeod, D. M. (2007). Campaign ads, online messaging, and participation: Extending the communication mediation model. *Journal of Communication*, 57(4), 676–703.

Shapiro, M. A., & Rieger, R. H. (1992). Comparing positive and negative political advertising on radio. *Journalism & Mass Communication Quarterly*, 69(1), 135–145. doi:10.1177/107769909206900111.

Sheckels, T. F. (2002). Narrative coherence and antecedent ethos in the rhetoric of attack advertising: A case study of the Glendening vs. Sauerbrey campaign. *Rhetoric & Public Affairs*, 5(3), 459–481.

Shen, F. (2004). Chronic accessibility and individual cognitions: Examining the effects of message frames in political advertisements. *Journal of Communication*, 54(1), 123–137.

Slater, M. D. (2016). Combining content analysis and assessment of exposure through self-report, spatial, or temporal variation in media effects research. *Communication Methods and Measures*, 10(2–3), 173–175.

Sparrow, N., & Turner, J. (2001). The permanent campaign: The integration of market research techniques in developing strategies in a more uncertain political climate. *European Journal of Marketing*, 35, 984–1002.

Strach, P., Zuber, K., Fowler, E. F., Ridout, T. N., & Searles, K. (2015). In a different voice? Explaining the use of men and women as voice-over announcers in political advertising. *Political Communication*, 32(2), 183–205. doi:10.1080/10584609.2014.914614.

Tak, J., Kaid, L. L., & Khang, H. (2007). The reflection of cultural parameters on videostyles of televised political spots in the US and Korea. *Asian Journal of Communication*, 17, 58–77. doi:10.1080/01292980601114570.

Valentino, N. A., Hutchings, V. L., & Williams, D. (2004). The impact of political advertising on knowledge, internet information seeking, and candidate preference. *Journal of Communication*, 54(2), 337–354. doi:10.1111/j.1460-2466.2004.tb02632.x.

Wen, W., Benoit, W. L., & Yu, T. (2004). A functional analysis of the 2000 Taiwanese and US presidential spots. *Asian Journal of Communication*, 14, 140–155. doi:10.1080/0129298042000256785.

4

GENDER AND POLITICAL ADVERTISING

Content and Effects

Dianne Bystrom

Because female political candidates are often framed in stereotypical terms by the media, political advertising – and the control it affords candidates over campaign messages about their images and issues – may be even more important for women running for elected office. Over time, researchers have found both differences and similarities in the ways in which female and male candidates use political advertising – primarily on television – in communicating with voters.

In addition to studies conducted on the content of television ads sponsored by female political candidates, another line of research has investigated the effects of this campaign medium on women voters. This chapter will summarize the research on the content of women candidates' political ads – as compared to their male opponents – as well studies investigating the gendered effects of television spots on voters. As very few studies (Carlson, 2001; Walter, 2013) have looked at gender differences in the televised campaign communications of female and male candidates and party leaders in other countries, this chapter will focus on the research to date on the political spots of women running for governor, Congress and president in the US. Through this examination of studies on the content and effects of political ads sponsored by female candidates and targeted toward women voters, I will suggest an agenda for future research on gender and political advertising.

The Content of Television Ads Sponsored by Women Candidates

As much research shows that political ads on television are effective in reaching and influencing voters, it is interesting to compare how female and male political candidates are presenting themselves – and defining their images and issues – through this campaign medium. Research on the content of female versus male political ads dates back to the 1964 election and has increased as more women ran for political office in the 1980s and, especially, the 1990s and 21st century. Over time, research has shown differences as well as similarities in how female and male candidates use television ads in their political campaigns – sometimes to confront and at other times to capitalize on gender stereotypes held by voters and the news media.

In the 1980s, female candidates' political ads were more likely to emphasize social issues, such as education and health care, whereas men were more likely to focus on economic issues such as taxes (Kahn, 1993; Trent & Sabourin, 1993). In highlighting their personal traits, women were more likely to emphasize compassion and men to stress their strength, although sometimes both sexes emphasized stereotypically masculine traits such as competence and leadership (Benze & Declercq, 1985; Kahn, 1993). In their nonverbal communication, men were more likely to dress in formal attire, whereas women preferred "feminized" business suits and office or professional settings (Johnston & White, 1994; Trent & Sabourin, 1993).

Shames (2003) examined the content of 526 television commercials of 95 male and female candidates in US House, Senate and governor races from 1964 to 1998 for their image and issue emphasis. She found that candidates of both sexes, and especially challengers, increasingly turned to femininity to showcase an outsider status. Candidates most likely to use a feminine outsider status over this timespan were Democrat female challengers, who Shames dubbed the "un-candidates."

As for issue emphasis, Shames found differences in the policies raised by women candidates before and after the 1992 election – which is commonly referred to the "Year of the Woman" due to the then-record numbers of women who ran for and were elected to the US Congress that year. Four key feminine issues – education, sex discrimination, health care and reproductive rights with a prochoice stance – increased in prominence beginning with the 1992 election. Three feminine issues – race discrimination, the environment and the care of children – and two masculine issues – defense/foreign policy and agriculture – decreased in prominence in women's political ads between 1992 and 1998. Overall, Shames (2003) found that the importance of masculine issues declined significantly as the focus on feminine issues rose through the 1990s, probably due in part to the end of the Cold War and the good economy in this time period.

As more women ran for political office in the US, beginning in 1992 and continuing through the 2014 election, most research has shown that female and male candidates are increasingly similar in their use of the verbal, nonverbal and production techniques – or videostyle – that make up the content of their television ads. In studies analyzing female and male political commercials in mixed-gender gubernatorial, congressional and presidential campaigns from 1990 through 2014, researchers have found that female and male candidates have becoming increasingly similar over time in their use of negative ads as well as in the issues discussed and, especially, in the image traits emphasized and appeal strategies used (Banwart & Winfrey, 2013; Bystrom, Banwart, Kaid, & Robertson, 2004; Bystrom & Brown, 2011; Fridkin & Kenney, 2014; Winfrey, 2015).

The similarities and differences that have emerged over the past 30 years are interesting from a gender perspective in terms of the tone of the ad (negative or positive), issues mentioned, image traits emphasized, and appeal strategies used as well as in their nonverbal content, including the candidate's dress and who is pictured in the ad.

Negative Versus Positive Tone

In their 2004 book, *Gender and candidate communication: VideoStyle, WebStyle, and NewsStyle*, Bystrom et al. found that female and male candidates running for governor and the US Senate between 1990 and 2002 were similar in the use of negative spots. Overall, these candidates employed attacks in about 45% of their total ads, primarily to attack their opponents on the issues. However, the ads of women candidates were significantly more likely to criticize their opponents' personal character and to call them names. The ads of male candidates were significantly more likely to attack their opponents' group affiliations/associations and background/qualifications.

In studying the 2008 election, Bystrom and Brown (2011) examined the television ads aired in female versus male general election races for governor and the US Senate as well as the primary race for the Democratic nomination for president between Barack Obama and Hillary Clinton. Contrary to earlier studies, they found that female candidates in 2008 were more likely than male candidates to use positive-focused ads. This was true not only for the overall sample of ads, but also for female gubernatorial candidates and Clinton. The fact that Clinton ran so many candidate-positive ads, perhaps contrary to perceptions, no doubt affected this result.

Consistent with previous research, female candidates running for state and federal office in 2008 were more likely than male candidates to criticize their opponents' personal characteristics and call them names, usually employing an anonymous announcer, whereas male candidates were significantly more likely to attack their opponents' group affiliations or associations and background or qualifications.

This consistent finding over time may indicate that female candidates have more latitude than male candidates to make personal attacks, because they enter the race with the stereotypical advantage of being considered kinder. Male candidates, in contrast, may feel more constrained by expectations that they treat women with some degree of chivalry by refraining from attacks on their personal characteristics. Instead, male candidates may lash out more often at their opponent's group affiliations as guilt by association may be a more acceptable and indirect way to question their character.

In their study of the 2012 election, Banwart and Winfrey (2013) contributed to our understanding of female versus male videostyle by studying the television commercials of mixed-gender races for the US House of Representatives. They found that male candidates were significantly more likely than female candidates to air "candidate-focused" – or positive – ads, whereas female candidates were significantly more like to run "opponent-focused" – or negative – spots. And, while both female and male candidates for the US House tended to end their 30-second spots on a positive note, men were significantly more likely to do so.

In the 2014 midterm elections, women and men running against each other for governor, the US Senate, and in the 15 most competitive races for the US House of Representatives were mostly similar in their use of negative television ads (Winfrey, 2015). Both sexes employed negative attacks in 56% (women) to 58% (men) of their ads, primarily to criticize their opponent on the issues. However, male candidates were significantly more likely to use the attack strategy of guilt by association in 28% of their attacks compared to women, who used this strategy in 16% of their attacks.

"Feminine" Versus "Masculine" Issue Discussion

In their 2004 book, Bystrom et al. found that female and male candidates running for governor and the US Senate had become increasingly similar in the issues they discussed in their television spots. However, they detected some differences in various election cycles. For example, the top issue in ads aired by female candidates running for office between 1990 and 2002 – and one that was discussed significantly more often by women than men – was the stereotypically feminine concern of education and schools. These female candidates discussed other issues more commonly associated with women – health care and youth violence – significantly more often than their male opponents. However, these female candidates also were significantly more likely than male candidates to discuss the economy in general, which is usually considered a masculine issue.

A study investigating the issues emphasized in the televisions ads – as well as websites and press releases – of 32 female and male candidates running for the US Senate in 2006 found that women were more likely to focus on communal issues in their spots whereas men were more likely to highlight competitive issues (Fridkin & Kenney, 2014). Women discussed communal issues – such as health care, the elderly, child care, education, and the environment – in 67% of their television ads compared to male candidates, who mentioned these topics in 46% of their spots. Men discussed competitive issues – such as defense, foreign policy, budget, energy and taxes – in 54% of their television ads, compared to female candidates, who mentioned these topics in 33% of their spots.

In their study of the 2008 mixed-gender gubernatorial and US Senate general election races and the Clinton versus Obama presidential primary campaigns, Bystrom and Brown (2011) found that male candidates were significantly more likely than female candidates to discuss ethics and declining morals and the price of gasoline. Women were most likely to discuss education, health care, social security and energy dependence, but not significantly more often than men (Bystrom & Brown, 2011).

In their study of mixed-gender races for the US House of Representatives in 2012, Banwart and Winfrey (2013) found that both female and male candidates mentioned stereotypically masculine issues in 62% of their ads. However, female candidates were more likely to discuss economic issues whereas male candidates were more likely to mention the federal budget. Female candidates were significantly more likely than male candidates to mention feminine issues in their television ads – 62% to 53% – with senior citizen concerns discussed the most by these women.

In the 2014 midterm elections, women and men running against each other for governor, the US Senate and in 15 US House races discussed mostly the same issues (Winfrey, 2015). Jobs/unemployment was the issue mentioned most frequently in the ads of women (31%) and men (23%). However, women were significantly more likely than men to discuss the economy in general, the cost of living and equal pay.

These results lend support to the observation by Bystrom et al. (2004) that the context of the election year may be more important than gender in determining what issues candidates emphasize in their political ads. Over time, the only consistent result is that female candidates do tend to discuss a variety of feminine issues – education, health care, pay equity and senior citizen concerns – more often than their male opponents.

"Feminine" Versus "Masculine" Image Traits

Even fewer differences are evident between female and male candidates in the images they emphasize. However, the traits they choose to emphasize both defy and underscore stereotypical expectations about the roles and behaviors of women and men in today's society. In their television ads, women candidates often portray themselves as successful, action-oriented, aggressive and tough leaders – commonly considered masculine attributes – but also have consistently emphasized their honesty, more commonly considered a feminine quality. In their ads, men often portray themselves as successful, action-oriented, aggressive and tough leaders with experience in politics – all masculine attributes.

For example, in their study of 32 female and male candidates running for the US Senate in 2006, Fridkin and Kenney (2014) found that both sexes were more likely to emphasize male agentic traits – such as experience, strength, accomplished, independent and ambitious – over such female communal traits as caring, moral, compassionate and honest. However, female candidates were much more likely than male candidates to mention agentic traits in their ads.

Among these traits, male candidates have been significantly more likely than women to discuss their experience in politics until the 2008 election, when female candidates were significantly more likely than men to emphasize this trait (Bystrom & Brown, 2011). Women overall, female Democrats, female executive office candidates and Clinton were all significantly more likely to emphasize their experience compared to men overall, male Republicans, female legislative candidates and Obama. Again, these results can be attributed to the number of Clinton ads in the sample of 2008 commercials studied (Bystrom & Brown, 2011).

Also in 2008, contrary to previous research, male candidates were significantly more likely than women to emphasize their honesty. Male candidates overall, male Republicans and Obama were more likely to emphasize honesty than female candidates overall, female Democrats and Clinton. The feminine trait of cooperation was emphasized by women US Senate candidates and Obama as compared to male US Senate candidates and Clinton. Similar to previous recent studies, female candidates were more likely to emphasize their toughness/strength in their campaign ads than males were in 2008 (Bystrom & Brown, 2011).

In the 2012 mixed-gender races for the US House of Representatives, both female and male candidates balanced masculine and feminine traits in their ads, with men mentioning feminine characteristics slightly more often (61% to 57%) than masculine ones and women discussing masculine images more often (51% to 49%) than feminine ones. As for feminine traits, male candidates were most likely to emphasize that they were sensitive and understanding whereas female candidates focused on their ability to cooperate with others. As for masculine traits, female candidates once again emphasized that they were aggressive fighters whereas male candidates focused on their competence (Banwart & Winfrey, 2013).

In the 2014 mixed-gender races for governor, the US Senate and 15 US House races, past performance and being "of the people" were the two most frequently discussed traits by both sexes. However, male candidates discussed the feminine trait of honesty/integrity more frequently than female candidates and women discussed the feminine trait of cooperation significantly more often than men did.

"Feminine" Versus "Masculine" Appeal Strategies

The appeal strategies used in female and male candidate ads are closely related to the traits they emphasize. Both female and male candidates have been equally as likely to use all of the elements of "feminine style," which is characterized by an inductive structure (moving from specific observations to broader generalizations), personal tone, addressing viewers as peers, use of personal experiences, identifying with the experiences of others, and inviting audience participation (Campbell, 1989).

Some differences in male versus female candidate appeals have been consistent over time. For example, male candidates have relied on statistics – a masculine strategy – significantly more often than female candidates, and female candidates have been significantly more likely to make gender an issue in their ads, an indication that at least some women are campaigning as female candidates and not political candidates who happen to be women.

In the 2008 sample of ads studied by Bystrom and Brown (2011), male candidates were more likely than female candidates to address viewers as peers, call for change and emphasize hope for the future. Male Democrats running for governor and the US Senate as well as presidential candidate Obama addressed viewers as peers in more than 70% of their ads, which probably affected the overall result. Similarly, men overall, male US Senate candidates, male Democrats and Obama were more likely than women overall, female US Senate candidates, female Republicans and Clinton to talk about change – perhaps, not surprising, as Obama centered his campaign theme on hope and change. And, male candidates were more likely than female candidates to make direct appeals to women voters in their 2008 ads (Bystrom & Brown, 2011).

In 2008, female Democrats were more likely than male Republicans to use the feminine style appeal strategy of personal tone in their ads, whereas male Republicans – consistent with previous research on male political candidates overall – used statistics, a masculine appeal strategy (Bystrom & Brown, 2011).

Nonverbal Content of Female and Male Candidate Television Ads

In the nonverbal content of their television ads, female candidates have been significantly more likely to dress in business, as opposed to casual, attire and to smile more often than male candidates. Both of these nonverbal characteristics reflect gender-based norms and stereotypical expectations faced by women in their everyday lives – to dress for success and smile to gain acceptance.

Consistent with years of previous research findings, female candidates in 2008 and 2012 were far more likely than their male counterparts to dress formally in their television commercials, whereas male candidates were much more likely to dress casually. Women overall, female Democrats, female executive office candidates and Clinton all dressed more formally than men overall, male Republicans, female legislative candidates and Obama in 2012. Men overall, male Senate candidates, and male

Democrats and Republicans dressed casually in their ads significantly more often than women overall, female Senate candidates, and female Republicans and Democrats.

Interestingly, Obama was more likely to dress formally, in about 84% of his ads, compared to men overall, at 53%. However, Clinton was dressed in formal attire in 100% of her television commercials in the study's sample. Clinton's formal dress no doubt affected the study's finding that women running for governor or president dressed formally in 97% of their ads compared to women running for the US Senate, who wore formal attire in 79% of their ads (Bystrom & Brown, 2011).

In 2012, female candidates for the US House of Representatives were significantly more likely to dress formally – in 63% of their television ads – whereas male candidates were significantly more likely to dress casually – in 78% of their spots (Banwart & Winfrey, 2013). In 2014, male candidates running for governor, the US Senate, and in 15 US House races more frequently appeared in casual attire (81.3%) whereas women balanced casual (57.4%) and formal (42.6%) attire (Winfrey, 2015) in their ads.

Also consistent with previous research, female candidates were more likely than men to smile in their ads in 2008. Women overall, female Democrats, female executive candidates and Clinton all smiled more often than men overall, male Republicans, female legislative candidates and Obama (Bystrom & Brown, 2011).

In addition to their dress and facial expressions, it is interesting to note who female and male candidate choose to picture in their television ads. Compared to male candidates, women are less likely to picture their families in their ads. In 2008, women candidates were significantly more likely than men to picture young children in their ads, but not their own children. Women overall, female Democrats, female executive candidates and Clinton all pictured young children more often than men overall, male Republicans, female legislative candidates and Obama (Bystrom & Brown, 2011).

In choosing to picture their families or not, both male and female candidates are confronting societal stereotypes. Women candidates may wish to show voters that they are more than wives and/or mothers and to dismiss any concerns voters may have about their abilities to serve in political office because of family obligations. Male candidates, in contrast, may wish to round out their images beyond politics by portraying themselves as loving husbands and/or fathers.

"Female" Versus "Male" Videostyle

In summary, research conducted over the past 30 years on the television ads of female and male political candidates running against each other for governor, the US Congress, and the Democratic nomination for president have shown that women and men are more similar than different in the tone of their messages, the issues mentioned, the image traits emphasized, the appeals used, and the nonverbal content included. Thus, it can be speculated that when women and men run against each other for political office, they are both drawn into a communication environment that favors a balance of feminine and masculine styles and strategies.

Still, the differences that have emerged over the years are interesting from a gender perspective. Although both female and male candidates often include about the same proportion of negative television ads in their appeals to voters, the most recent elections show that tone also may vary with the context of the election. For example, female candidates ran television ads with more positive messages than male candidates in 2008 – a finding largely influenced by Clinton's positive appeals – whereas male candidates aired more positive spots than female candidates in 2012. It is also interesting to note that the 2012 election marked a historical milestone in the number of women who ran for (184) and were elected to (89) the US Congress (Center for American Women and Politics, 2012).

The issues emphasized by female and male candidates in their television spots also tend to vary with the context of the election year. That is, both sexes are likely to discuss the issues most important to voters in any election year whether they are considered masculine or feminine. Still, it is interesting to note that female candidates emphasize such issues as education, health care and senior citizens issues – which voters believe women have some expertise – more often than male candidates.

The traits emphasized by female and male candidates also underscore how women and men running against each other for political office are drawn into a communication strategy that balances mostly masculine but also feminine characteristics. Surveys have shown that voters prefer their elected officials to exhibit such masculine characteristics as leadership, experience and toughness, but also want them to be honest, sincere and, in more recent years, willing to cooperate with others.

The fact that both female and male candidates employ a feminine rhetorical style in their television ads may indicate that such strategies work best in 30-second spots. Still, it is interesting that male candidates use more statistical evidence – a masculine strategy – and female candidates make gender an issue in their television ads.

Finally, the nonverbal content differences between the ads of female and male candidates seem very much tied to the role of women in society. That is, female candidates have continued over time to dress more formally, smile more often and avoid picturing their families in their television ads to communicate with voters that they are professional, seek their acceptance and should be considered in roles beyond being a wife and/or mother.

In addition to the content of political candidates' television ads, it is interesting to look at the effects these appeals have on potential voters. Next, recent research on the effects of television political ads on women voters is summarized to help assess whether the styles and strategies used by male and female candidates work or not.

The Effects of Television Political Ads on Women Voters

In addition to research analyzing the content of television ads sponsored by female and male candidates, studies have examined the effects of political commercials on voters, including women. Recent studies have focused on the effects of television ads of female and male political candidates on voter evaluations of their image traits and issue competencies, the effect of negative messages on women and men voters, and the impact of presidential candidate commercials targeted to women voters.

The Effects of Female Versus Male Candidate Ads on Voters

Results of studies that have examined viewer reactions to the television ads of female and male candidates appear to confirm what numerous content analyses show: women and men are best advised to balance stereotypically feminine and masculine images and issues in their campaigns, taking into consideration the context of the election year.

Early studies (Kaid, Myers, Pipps, & Hunter, 1984; Wadsworth, Patterson, Kaid, Cullers, Malcomb, & Lamirand, 1987) found that masculine strategies work best for women candidates in their political ads. However, more recent studies (Banwart, 2010; Banwart & Carlin, 2001) have found women were most effective when balancing stereotypical feminine and masculine traits.

In her 2010 study of the effects of television ads from two mixed-gender congressional races in 2008, Banwart investigated whether gendered trait stereotypes are still used by voters in evaluating female and male candidates. Confirming earlier studies, she found that female candidates were rated higher than the male candidates on a warmth/expressiveness (feminine trait) scale whereas male candidates were rated higher on an instrumental (masculine trait) scale. Moreover, the candidate's political affiliation did not influence evaluations of their traits by study participants.

As far as issue competency, male candidates were rated as more competent than females to handle military and economic issues. However, female candidates were not rated significantly more competent than male candidates to handle compassion issues. Evaluations of issue competency were influenced by the candidate's political party affiliation – the female Democrat was considered more competent to handle compassion issues than the female Republican, and the male Democrat was considered more competent to handle compassion issues than either the female or male Republican. Thus, Banwart (2010) concluded that while traditional trait stereotypes continue to influence the evaluation of female candidates, the generation of policy stereotypes is more complicated.

The Effects of Negative Advertising Messages on Female and Male Voters

Recent studies also suggest that the use of negative political advertising appeals may backfire with women voters. In their 2011 study focusing on negative campaign communication, Fridkin and Kenney found that men were more tolerant of negative commercial content than women. Moreover, according to a 2010 study by Brooks, men were more likely to be motivated to vote by a negative campaign message. She found that 88% of men compared to 77% of women in her sample of voters said they were likely to vote in highly negative campaigns. In political races with the least amounts of negative campaigning, women were slightly more likely than men to indicate their likelihood of voting.

Brooks also tested the effects of civil and uncivil negative messages on women and men. Uncivil messages were those characterized as divisive, inflammatory, or gratuitous. She found that men were disproportionately motivated by uncivil campaign messages. After viewing uncivil negative television ads, only 9% of men compared to 21% of women said they definitely would not vote for the candidate. However, women were slightly more likely than men to say they would vote after viewing ads with civil negative messages.

The Effects of Presidential Television Ads on Women Voters

Studies by Kaid and her colleagues have tested for the effects of presidential ads on voters, including female versus male voters, in several election cycles. For example, in an experimental design studying the effects of television ads sponsored by George W. Bush and John Kerry in 2004, her research team found no major differences in the responses of female and male participants (Kaid, Postelnicu, Landerville, Yun, & LeGrange, 2007). However, women were significantly more likely than men to rate both Bush and Kerry less qualified after viewing their ads. Also, women found Bush significantly more aggressive and Kerry less sophisticated after viewing their commercials.

Similarly, in their experimental study of the effects of television advertising in the 2008 presidential campaign on young voters, Kaid, Fernandes and Painter (2011) found no significant gender differences in the overall image evaluations of Obama or John McCain in either the pretest or posttest scores. However, after viewing the ads, female voters found Obama to be significantly more believable than males did. Females also found McCain to be less sincere than males did. They also found interesting gender differences in cognitive effects from exposure to televised political ads, as female participants perceived that they learned more about the candidates' issues and personal qualities from watching the ads than did male voters.

The 2012 presidential campaign provided an interesting look at how campaigns can target women voters in their television commercials. Whereas Mitt Romney made more traditional television ad buys, President Obama's campaign targeted women through daytime talk shows – who, at the time, represented three-fourths of the viewing audience during those timeslots – and on cable television networks such as the Food Channel, Lifetime and Hallmark (Fowler & Ridout, 2012).

Using an experimental research design, Winfrey, Banwart and Warner (2014) investigated whether presidential candidate ads targeted toward women voters were effective, or not, in 2012. Their study produced mixed results. Contrary to previous studies of the effects of presidential advertising on candidate favorability (Kaid et al., 2007, 2011), Winfrey et al. found that female voters were influenced by exposure to television ads, but male voters were not.

Following exposure to the presidential candidates' ads, women in the general message condition and the targeted message condition rated Obama more favorably, with approximately a 5% increase in both conditions. Although female participants rated Romney more favorably in the general message condition, they did not significantly change their favorability toward him after viewing the targeted advertisements. For male participants, changes in favorability for both Obama and Romney remained non-significant across the general message and targeted message conditions. Thus, Winfrey et al. concluded that Romney's targeted messaging strategy to frame the economy as a women's issue was less successful than Obama's strategy to focus on more traditional women's issues such as pay equity, birth control, and reproductive rights.

In addition to measuring the effects of television advertising on candidate favorability, Winfrey et al. tested participants' perception of each candidate's sincerity in standing up for women and women's issues. They found that participants considered Obama's sincerity to be higher than Romney's across all experimental conditions.

Final Observations and Directions for Future Research

Combining the research on the content of female versus male political candidate television advertising with the results of studies on the effects of commercials on voters, a few observations emerge. First, female candidates are best advised to balance feminine and masculine image traits in their television ads. Second, as far as issue emphasis, female candidates should balance feminine and masculine issues, depending on the context of the election, in their campaign commercials. That is, they should emphasize their competence on the issues that matter with voters in the election.

Third, female candidates should concentrate their negative messages toward the beginning and middle of their campaigns – and finish with positive messages – in their television ads. Fourth, presidential candidates can best target women voters through their television commercials on issues on which their political parties are perceived as more effective.

Finally, this examination of research on the gendered content and effects of televised political ads provides ideas for future research. Clearly, more research is needed that examines both the content and effects of the same set of television ads in an election year. In their 2014 book, *The changing face of representation: The gender of US Senators and constituent communications*, Fridkin and Kenney provide an example on how content analyses of the messages of female and male politicians – including their websites, press releases, and television ads – as well as their media coverage can be combined with the results of survey research to more thoroughly evaluate the role of gender in today's political environment. In their study, they evaluated the information presented by female and male US Senators at both the governing and campaigning stages as well as their media coverage and assessments by voters in 2006.

In addition to providing a research design that can be adapted in future studies of the contents and effects of the political ads of female and male political candidates, Fridkin and Kenney propose an original theory – strategic stereotype theory – to explain why representational communications may vary by the senator's gender. This theory can be further tested through future research on the content and effects of televised political ads, including those using an experimental design.

Also, more research is needed on the content and effects of candidate political ads that air on their websites and social media, such as YouTube, instead of television. According to an article in the September/October 2015 issue of *Mother Jones* magazine, the amount of money spent by political candidates on digital advertising is expected to nearly double in the 2016 election cycle compared with 2012 (Choma, 2015). Online spots cost a fraction of traditional television ads and, with new and improved technology, can cheaply and creatively bombard voters with political candidate messages. According to the article, the 2016 US presidential nominees will likely devote nearly 25% of their ad-buy budgets to digital media. "Considering that each side could spend more than $2 billion to get into the White House, that's potentially hundreds of millions of dollars allocated" to digital media ads, Choma noted.

According to the digital media consultants interviewed for this article, television ads will remain the dominant tool for US political campaigns. However, through online advertising outreach, campaigns can pinpoint and analyze who is clicking to view candidate ads. This allows campaigns and candidates to microtarget potential supporters with more precision than ever before (Choma, 2015).

Additional research also is needed to investigate whether – or not – the findings of research on the television advertising of political candidates in the US is replicated by studies on candidates running for office in other countries. In an exploratory study, Walter (2013) sought to build on existing research on political candidate television advertising in the US by using similar operationalizations of negative campaigning. Although election campaigns in Western Europe are still largely party-centered, as compared to US campaigns that focus much more on the candidate him/herself as a representative of the political party, she notes that many of the parliamentary democracies "are witnessing a process of increased presidentialization or personalization" (Walter, 2013, p. 158).

In her study of 377 party election broadcasts aired in Germany, the Netherlands and the United Kingdom between 1980 and 2006, Walter (2013) found that female party leaders were much more likely to use negative campaigning than men. However, she attributed her overall finding to British Prime Minister Margaret Thatcher, whose 1983 and 1987 campaigns were more negative than those under the leadership of male candidates. She suggests extending research to study the television campaigns of party leaders in other countries – such as the Scandinavian countries, which have more female party leaders – to delve further into the possible effects of political context on their communication strategies.

Researchers have learned a lot over the past 30 years about the content, especially, and effects of televised political commercials sponsored by female candidates and targeted toward women voters. But, we still have much more to learn as more women run for state and federal office and seek to create messages that resonate with potential voters.

References

Banwart, M.C. (2010). Gender and candidate communication: Effects of stereotypes in the 2008 election. *American Behavioral Scientist*, 54(3), 265–283. doi: 10.1177/0002764210381702.

Banwart, M. C., & Carlin, D. B. (2001, November). *The effects of negative political advertising on gendered image perception and voter intent: A longitudinal study.* Paper presented at the meeting of the National Communication Association, Atlanta, GA.

Banwart, M., & Winfrey, K. (2013, November). *Is it the message or the medium? Female and male candidate messages in 2012.* Paper presented at the annual meeting of the National Communication Association, Washington, DC.

Benze, J. G., & Declercq, E. R. (1985). Content of television political spot ads for female candidates. *Journalism Quarterly*, 62, 278–283, 288.

Brooks, D. J. (2010). A negativity gap? Voter gender, attack politics, and participation in American elections. *Politics & Gender*, 6(3), 319–341. doi: http://dx.doi.org/10.1017/S1743923X10000218.

Bystrom, D. G., Banwart, M. C., Kaid, L. L., & Robertson, T. (2004). *Gender and campaign communication: VideoStyle, WebStyle and NewsStyle.* New York, NY: Routledge.

Bystrom, D. G., & Brown, N. J. (2011). Videostyle 2008: A comparison of female vs. male political candidate television ads. In M. S. McKinney & M. C. Banwart (Eds.), *Communication in the 2008 US election: Digital natives elect a president* (pp. 211–240). New York, NY: Peter Lang.

Campbell, K. K. (1989). *Man cannot speak for her: A critical study of early feminist rhetoric* (Vol. 1). New York, NY: Greenwood.

Carlson, T. (2001). Gender and political advertising across cultures: A comparison of male and female political advertising in Finland and the US. *European Journal of Communication*, 16(2), 131–154. doi: 10.1177/0267323101016002001.

Center for American Women and Politics. (2012). *Record number of women will serve in Congress; New Hampshire elects women to all top posts.* Retrieved from www.cawp.rutgers.edu/sites/default/files/resources/pressrelease_11-07-12.pdf.

Choma, R. (2015, September/October). Get ready for a flood of online campaign ads that will target and track you. *Mother Jones.* Retrieved from www.motherjones.com/politics/2015/07/digital-political-election-ads-dark-money.

Fowler, E. F., & Ridout, T. N. (2012). Negative, angry, and ubiquitous: Political advertising in 2012. *The Forum,* 10(4), 51–61. doi: 10.1515/forum-2013-0004.

Fridkin, K. L., & Kenney, P. (2011). Variability in citizens' reactions to different types of negative campaigns. *American Journal of Political Science,* 55(2), 307–325. doi: 10:1111/j. 1540–5907.2010. 00494.x.

Fridkin, K. L., & Kenney, P. J. (2014). *The changing face of American representation: The gender of US Senators and constituent communications.* Ann Arbor, MI: University of Michigan Press.

Johnston, A., & White, A. B. (1994). Communication styles and female candidates: A study of political advertisements of men and women candidates for US Senate. *Political Research Quarterly,* 46, 481–501.

Kahn, K. F. (1993). Gender differences in campaign messages: The political advertisements of men and women candidates for US Senate. *Political Research Quarterly,* 46(3), 481–502.

Kaid, L. L., Fernandes, J., & Painter, D. (2011). Effects of political advertising in the 2008 presidential campaign. *American Behavioral Scientist,* 55(4), 437–436. doi: 10.1177/0002764211398071.

Kaid, L. L., Myers, S. L., Pipps, V., & Hunter, J. (1984). Sex role perceptions and television advertising: Comparing male and female candidates. *Women & Politics,* 4, 41–53.

Kaid, L. L., Postelnicu, M., Landerville, L., Yun, H. J., & LeGrange, A. G. (2007). The effects of political advertising on young voters. *American Behavioral Scientist,* 50(9), 1137–1151.

Shames, S. L. (2003). The "un-candidates": Gender and outsider signals in women's political advertising. *Women & Politics Journal,* 25(1/2), 115–147.

Trent, J., & Sabourin, T. (1993). Sex still counts: Women's use of televised advertising during the decade of the 80s. *Journal of Applied Communication Research,* 21(1), 21–40.

Wadsworth, A. J., Patterson, P., Kaid, L. L., Cullers, G., Malcomb, D., & Lamirand, L. (1987). "Masculine" vs. "feminine" strategies in political ads: Implications for female candidates. *Journal of Applied Communication Research,* 15, 77–94.

Walter, A. M. (2013). Women on the battleground: Does gender condition the use of negative campaigning? *Journal of Elections, Public Opinion and Parties,* 23(2), 154–176. doi: 10.1080/17457289.2013.769107.

Winfrey, K. L. (2015). *Gender and campaign messaging.* Paper presented at the annual meeting of the Iowa Association of Political Scientists, Des Moines, IA.

Winfrey, K. L., Banwart, M. C., & Warner, B. R. (2014). Communicating with voters 30 seconds at a time: Presidential campaign advertising 2012. In D. G. Bystrom, M. C. Banwart, & M. S. McKinney (Eds.), *alieNATION: The divide and conquer election of 2012* (pp. 48–65). New York, NY: Peter Lang.

5

NEGATIVE ADVERTISING

Todd L. Belt

Negative advertising is sometimes called attack advertising because the point of the advertisement is to diminish the political fortunes of the subject of the attack, providing an advantage to the attacker. Negative advertisements are distinguished from positive ads, also called promotional ads, that seek to advocate for a policy or the election of an individual. Contrast ads contain elements of both positive ads and negative ads, extolling the benefits or virtues of one candidate or idea while disparaging another candidate or idea. Because contrast ads contain an element of attack, they are also considered to be negative ads. These ads have become ubiquitous in US politics. In 1960, just over 10% of political ads in the presidential campaign were negative, but by 1988 the number had jumped to 80% (Jamieson, 1996). Since that time, negative advertisements have continued to comprise the majority of political ads seen in the US (West, 2014).

Negative advertisements come in different styles and formats, deal with different types of subject matter, are used in different contexts and may have differing effects. Negative advertising may take the form of still images and words (such as an ad in a newspaper or on a billboard), audio format (such as an ad heard on the radio) or an audiovisual format (such as an ad on television). Several techniques are used in crafting negative ads that are quite distinct from positive ads, including color, music, speed, narration and the associations made in the ad. Negative advertising is most commonly used in political campaigns, but is also used in non-campaign contexts in order to influence the politics surrounding an issue on the public agenda (or to raise an issue onto the public agenda). Finally, the influence of negative advertising has generated much scholarly interest and debate, with researchers finding evidence of a multitude of different effects that come to bear not only on a given election, but on the conduct of politics more generally.

Who Engages in Negative Advertising?

Political advertising is an extraordinarily lucrative industry. Political campaigns spend over half of their revenues on media. Consulting groups are contracted to create and to run focus group tests in order to gauge the ads' appeal to voters in different media markets. Finally, broadcasters accumulate ad revenue by selling air time. In the US, a broadcaster must charge the "lowest unit rate" – no more than they charge to their most preferred advertisers – to political advertisers for a designated period prior to an election. However, broadcasters do not have to guarantee to run an ad for the time period purchased, causing campaigns to pay higher rates in order to secure desired air times prior to an election (Alexander & Corrado, 1995). The result is a windfall of profits for advertisers – in 2016, campaigns in the US are expected to spend $4.4 billion on television advertising (Kurtzleben, 2015).

Changes in campaign finance laws in the US explain a great deal of the uptick in advertising spending. New regulations and court decisions have allowed the formation of "super-PACs" that are far less regulated than the political action committees (PACs) of the past and have less of an ongoing connection to traditional interests groups (Franz, 2012). These super-PACs have dramatically increased the amount of money that interest groups have spent on political campaigns, the overwhelming majority of which is on advertising (Dowling & Miller, 2014). In the 2008 presidential election, super-PACs spent $286 million compared to $1.1 billion in 2012 (Smith & Kimball, 2013). A study of the advertising done by super-PACs in the 2012 election found the tone of advertisements to be overwhelmingly negative (Smith & Powell, 2013).

Whether candidates approve of attacks against their rivals or not, interest groups provide a veil of plausible deniability and innocence for the candidate that benefits from the attack. This is because super-PACs and other independent expenditure groups are required to be uncoordinated with candidate campaigns. But beyond that, these groups are not required to face their victims, as candidates must do in debates where they might face a backlash for airing negative ads. Since these groups are often fleeting and not tied to candidates or traditional organizations, they may be much less responsible in assertions made in their advertisements.

While candidates cannot control whether interests groups "go negative" against their opponents, they can decide whether their own campaign will do so. In the US, a candidate's own campaign ads are easily identified by a quote heard at the end of their ad that states: "I'm [candidate's name] and I approve of this message." As mentioned above, going negative can often cause a backlash, and a candidate who does so will be criticized by his/her opponent for "mudslinging." Additionally, negative advertising that is perceived as extraordinarily harsh or unfair may backfire on a candidate (Jasperson & Fan, 2002; Merritt, 1984; Roese & Sande, 1993; Shapiro & Rieger, 1992; Sonner, 1998).

To a large degree, underdog candidates choose to mount negative campaigns. Frontrunners have no incentive to engage in attacks that might potentially backfire. Accordingly, candidates that are first to go negative are often behind in the polls, in fundraising, or in name recognition. Negative advertising puts the opponent on the defensive, and if left unanswered, these ads may be devastating (Sonner, 1998).

During the 1988 US presidential election campaign, Michael Dukakis found out the hard way that attack ads cannot go unanswered for long. Negative ads sponsored by George H. W. Bush and independent expenditure groups portrayed Dukakis as an ineffective liberal governor who was weak on defense and soft on crime. Dukakis failed to volley Bush's attacks until it was too late, providing an air of credibility to the attacks. In 1992, Bill Clinton established a campaign "war room" to respond to attacks instantaneously, so that assertions would not go unchallenged.

There are ways by which ads can have an augmented influence beyond the targeted media buy. Attack and comparative ads are more likely to generate "amplification" – free media coverage in the form of news attention to the ads (Ridout & Smith, 2008). This process results from broadcast news coverage of negative ads in order to police their validity, or to cover and comment on particularly harsh or controversial attacks (Jamieson, 1992; Kendall, 2000; Min, 2002, 2004; West, 2014). An example involves probably the most famous negative ad in history – Lyndon Johnson's 1964 "Daisy Girl" ad. In the ad, a young girl is counting as she plucks petals from a daisy, only to have her counting replaced by a countdown issued by a male voice. The camera then draws closer to focus on her pupil, revealing a nuclear explosion. An announcer then states: "Vote for President Johnson on November 3rd. The stakes are too high for you to stay home."[1] The terrifying ad was aired only once before it was pulled from circulation, but received tremendous media coverage and generated a great deal of public discussion (Leighley, 2004).

Style and Format

Negative advertisements are designed to provoke fear and sow doubt about candidates and their policies. As such, a number of different techniques may be employed to heighten anxiety produced by audio and visual content. For example, anti-smoking ads around the world have used frightening – and sometimes quite graphic – imagery of maladies associated with smoking. Many of these techniques are believed by those who work in advertising firms to strengthen the emotional impact of negative ads, making them more effective (Brader, 2006). Of course, styles and techniques that can be used in negative ads are mitigated by the medium in which they are transmitted.

Medium

Certainly, still images, such as newspaper ads, buttons and lawn signs, have been an important part of political campaigning for some time. The broadcast revolution of the early 20th century facilitated circulation of campaign messages on a grand scale. Political campaigns began buying time on the radio as early as 1924 (Diamond & Bates, 1992). The first candidate to forcefully embrace the medium was Dwight Eisenhower in 1952. These ads were designed to strengthen the general's credibility on issues other than war and foreign policy. In the ads, titled "Eisenhower Answers America," the Republican candidate answers questions from voters, occasionally attacking the Democratic Party.

Since the 1950s, political advertising on television has ballooned. While radio and newspapers are still used for political advertising, estimates for 2016 indicate that two-thirds of spending will be on televised ads, with another 10% spent on digital media (James, 2015). In other words, the trend is toward audiovisual advertising instead of visual-only (newspapers) or audio-only (radio) ads.

The medium of communication of political ads matters. Often, the adage that "a picture is worth a thousand words" holds in advertising – visual images increase information recall more than audio messages, and visuals often obstruct audio message recall (Garramone, 1983). Additionally, visuals are more memorable for negative ads than positive ads (Lang, 1991). Audiovisual ads permit an entire range of production techniques to be applied in order to enhance their effectiveness.

Color, Speed and Grain

Visual characteristics of negative advertisements can enhance their effectiveness. Candidates under attack are portrayed in black-and-white, whereas brighter colors are used for sponsors of ads (West, 2014). The use of gray imagery is used to appeal to fear (Brader, 2006). For example, a 1996 attack ad by Bill Clinton on Republican Nominee Bob Dole portrays the president in full color, but shifts to black-and-white for Dole, with red-colored text contrasting against Dole's image to underscore points of attack.[2] Moreover, the imagery of Dole is particularly grainy, whereas the imagery of Clinton is crisp, making Dole's appearance bleak. Finally, Dole's movements are slowed down, further imparting a haunting visage. The result is an ad that is much more effective than its narrative alone.

Color tones can also be used to exploit racial prejudice. During the 2008 presidential primaries, Hillary Clinton's campaign was accused of airing an attack ad that portrayed Barack Obama with darker skin tone than his appearance in the original source image (Aravosis, 2008). While questions have been raised as to whether the skin tone effect on Obama was intentional (Kolawole, 2008), the effect was to activate negative stereotypes about him (Messing, Jabon, & Plaut, 2016).

Audio and Music

Similar to how visuals can be used to augment the impact of negative advertising, so can music or other audio effects. Just as patriotic music can be used in positive ads, sound effects can be used to attack candidates, as well. For example, in a 2012 attack ad against Republican nominee Mitt Romney, an Obama/Biden ad showed Romney singing the song "America the Beautiful" as text recounted the number of jobs his firms had sent to Mexico and China while he maintained bank accounts in tax havens such as Bermuda and the Cayman Islands.[3] The use of the candidate's own voice singing a patriotic song while the ad disclosed unpatriotic business and financial practices made for a particularly powerful attack advertisement.

Frequently, negative ads feature eerie or disquieting music to increase the viewers' anxiety. In 1988, an attack ad by George H. W. Bush on Michael Dukakis criticized the Massachusetts governor's environmental record with respect to Boston Harbor. As the camera moves across the harbor, focusing on drains, sewage and floating debris, ominous music can be heard in the background creating a "horror film" like quality of eeriness and tension.[4]

Once Dukakis decided to respond to George H. W. Bush's attacks, he took aim at Bush's choice for vice president, Dan Quayle, using a different audio technique. In one ad, the president's chair in the oval office is empty, and a narrator states: "The most powerful man in the world is also mortal. We know this all too well in America. One in five American vice presidents has had to rise to the duties of commander-in-chief." In the background, a heartbeat can be heard, as a photo of Lyndon Johnson taking the presidential oath of office following John Kennedy's assassination, is shown. At the end of the ad, the narrator states, "after five months of reflection, George Bush made his personal choice J. Danforth Quayle. Hopefully we will never know how great a lapse of judgment that really was."[5] The beating heart in the ad implies human mortality, underscoring the importance of the office, and providing a chilling backdrop to the advertisement.

Narration

Negative advertising often features individuals speaking in their own voices, but even more frequently provides a "voiceover" in the form of a narrator speaking over images. The narrator's voice not only tells the story of the advertisement, but also provides context and suggests a specific interpretation of the images on the screen. Generally, authoritative male voices are used to underscore the seriousness of accusations in attack ads. However, female narrators are occasionally used in order to "soften any potential backlash" (West, 2014, p. 20) of particularly harsh criticism, or to appeal directly to female voters.

The intonation and audio quality of the narrator's voice-over can have a strong impact on the overall tone of an attack ad, particularly when used in conjunction with a candidate's own words. In 1992, the Bush/Quayle campaign aired an ad showing two candidates (with gray dots over their faces to hide them) with the narrator explaining their different statements on the same issue. Following the statements, the narrator revealed that both candidates were Bill Clinton.[6]

Similarly, in an attack ad on George H. W. Bush in 1992, the Clinton/Gore campaign ran an ad reminding the public of Vice President Bush's famous 1988 campaign promise: "Read my lips. No new taxes." The ad then showed President Bush signing a tax increase after assuming the presidency.[7] Using a candidate's own words against them can be particularly effective, especially when juxtaposed against other incongruous statements and actions.

Visual Imagery, Symbols and Association

While positive ads are filled with imagery to inspire enthusiasm for candidates – such as flags, balloons, and throngs of smiling people – negative ads make associations to both positive and negative imagery. These images are used to metaphorically link the targeted candidate to an undesirable action, position, or idea. Other times, images are chosen for their humorous content in order to ridicule the target candidate. The visuals used in advertising are extremely important because images are remembered for a longer period of time than are the spoken words used in ads (West, 2014, p. 17).

In 1996, the Clinton campaign used images of the unpopular Speaker of the House of Representatives Newt Gingrich in order to attack Republican presidential nominee Bob Dole. Ads repeatedly showed Dole and Gingrich together, and the printed text referred to the both of them as "Dole/Gingrich." Following the 9/11 terrorist attacks, several candidates used images of Osama bin Laden and the burning World Trade Center towers in order to attack their opponents' credentials in the War on Terror.

In a 1988 ad by the Bush/Quayle campaign attacking Michael Dukakis, a revolving door is shown with criminals filing in and out of a prison. The image was so memorable, that the ad is sometimes referred to as the "Revolving Door" ad. The ad criticizes Dukakis for a weekend furlough program for criminals.[8] In an attempt to correct the record on the subject, Dukakis aired an ad that insisted that he had ended the furlough program for first degree murderers. However, the very first image in Dukakis' ad is a television replaying the revolving doors from the original attack ad, thus reinforcing the initial attack against Dukakis and undermining the effectiveness of the "correction" ad.[9]

Often, imagery is chosen in order to validate claims made in attack ads. Clippings of newspaper headlines have been traditionally used to provide evidence of the target candidate's record and actions. Digging deeper into stories, an attack ad by the McCain/Palin ticket against Barack Obama in 2008 used newspaper mastheads with dated quotes from the same paper.[10]

One curious use of imagery took place during the 2000 US presidential election, when a Republican attack ad on Democratic nominee Al Gore criticized Gore's policy proposal for prescription drugs. In the ad, a photo of Gore is shown, replaced for one-thirtieth of a second by the word "rats" in large, all capitalized letters, followed immediately by the phrase "bureaucrats decide" (Berke, 2000).[11] Alex Costenellos, who was hired by the Republican National Committee to produce the ad, denied that he noticed the word in the ad and that any use of the word was "purely accidental" (Berke, 2000). While the use and impact of subliminal advertising may seem akin to a conspiracy theory, there is support for its effectiveness in negative political advertising. In an experimental study, researchers found that the subliminal use of the word "rats" increased viewers' negative ratings of an unknown politician (Weinberger & Westen, 2008).

Subject Matter

Very few topics seem to be off limits for negative advertising. Criticizing a candidate's record or policy proposals seems to be fair game. Attacks on a candidate's character may seem a bit nasty, but is understandable considering that leaders must possess a variety of traits in order to govern effectively. A candidate's personality seems to be an even less relevant topic of discussion for an attack advertisement, although an argument could be made that a certain temperament is desirable in elected officials. Particularly dirty attacks go after a candidate's friends or family (for whom the candidate should bear no responsibility), but these attacks are rare.

Policy, Issues and Ideas

Negative advertising frequently targets unpopular decisions or stances taken by a candidate. The point of these attacks is to portray a candidate as out of the mainstream, or worse, potentially dangerous. Tax increases, ever unpopular, are a common subject in negative ads. Similarly, support for policies that can be seen to threaten the safety of communities can provide a basis for attack. For example, a 2004 Bush/Cheney attack ad against John Kerry spoke of his opposition to "weapons vital to winning the war on terror."[12]

Controversial issues, especially those that are perceived to benefit one group over another, are often common topics for negative ads. In a controversial ad aired by US Senator Jesse Helms, his opponent, Harvey Gantt, was attacked for his support of affirmative action (without the term being used). The ad begins with the narrator stating, "You needed that job, and you were the best qualified, but they had to give it to a minority, because of a racial quota." Under the narration, a pair of Caucasian hands are seen crumbling a freshly opened letter in frustration. The narrator continues, "Is that really fair? Harvey Gantt says it is. Gantt supports Ted Kennedy's racial quota law that makes the color of your skin more important than your qualifications."[13] Not only did the attack ad criticize Gantt's stance on affirmative action, it associated him with Ted Kennedy (considered by many to be a very liberal senator).

Of course some ads can use issue positions in order to call into question a candidate's character and/or judgment. In 2004, another attack ad by the Bush/Cheney campaign showed Democratic nominee John Kerry windsurfing back and forth. When surfing in one direction, Kerry was reported to have voted a certain way on a policy issue. Kerry and his wind surfboard then immediately switch direction, and the narrator reports how Kerry had reversed his position on the same issue. Among other policy issues, the ad was aided by Kerry's comment that he had "voted for the Iraq War before he voted against it." At the end of the ad, the narrator concludes, "John Kerry – whichever way the wind blows," in order to criticize Kerry's lack of consistency as compared to George W. Bush's decisiveness.[14] This sort of issue-based "flip-flop" attack is used to undercut candidates by portraying them as political opportunists without the courage of their convictions, willing to tell people whatever they want to hear in order to get elected.

Character and Personality

A line of attack against a candidate's character that seems reasonable (if true) is to highlight issues of corruption. In 1972, an ad by Democratic candidate George McGovern used multiple newspaper headlines to point out issues of corruption – embezzlement, special deals and spying – by President Nixon and his aides.[15] Certainly, charges of corruption bring forth legitimate issues of a candidate's character and the personality traits of honesty, integrity, judgment and credibility.

In 2006, a more unseemly personal attack implying sexual promiscuity was leveled by the Republican National Committee against Democratic candidate Harold Ford, Jr. during the race for US Senate in Tennessee. Among other satirical attacks on his policy positions, a blonde woman with a high pitched voice chimes in, "I met Harold at the Playboy party." Later, a shifty-looking man with sunglasses says, "So he took money from porn movie producers. I mean, who hasn't?" At the very end of the ad, the same woman from earlier in the video reappears and implores, "Harold, call me!" and winks at the camera.[16] The ad targeting Ford, an African American, was widely decried for sparking racial fears (Toner, 2006).

Context

Negative advertising may take place in either a campaign context or a non-campaign context. In non-campaign contexts, the goal may be to shift opinion on an issue in order to impact a policy outcome, or merely to raise an issue onto the public or policy agenda. In a campaign context, the goal is clear – to win an election.

Non-campaign Advertising

Negative ads may be aired for a variety of non-electoral purposes. As noted earlier, they have been frequently employed in public health efforts. Many nations have taken to placing disturbing images of body parts on packages of cigarettes in order to discourage smoking. For example, Brazil requires cigarette labels that show images such as blood pouring out of a man's head (to indicate risk of stroke), and a fetus in an ashtray (to underscore premature birth from smoking). A meta-analysis of experimental studies found these graphic images to be more effective than text warnings alone (Noar et al., 2015).

In the US, the "Not Even Once" advertising campaign warns individuals about methamphetamine use. These ads focus on deterioration in physical appearance as well as potential life changes associated with the drug, such as violence, psychotic episodes, prostitution and even suicide.[17]

Finally, drunk driving has been the subject of negative ad campaigns around the world for many years. For example, an Australian ad recalling an anti-drunk driving advertising campaign, started in 1989, illustrated the dangers associated with drunk driving. The ad features individuals being arrested and landing in jail, injured drivers and passengers, and bicyclists and pedestrians (including children) killed by drunk drivers. The audio ends on a chilling note with sad music replaced by a woman screaming and wailing.[18]

Of course, more overtly political negative ads not associated with electoral politics abound. One famous case involved what came to be known as the "Harry and Louise" ads. These advertisements were aired between 1993 and 1994 in order to derail the health-care initiative proposed by President Bill Clinton. In the ads, a suburban middle-aged couple discusses changes to their health care. The ads focus on the prospect of the couples' loss of choice over doctors and health plans. A study of individuals' opinions about the health-care plan found that the "Harry and Louise" ads were effective in developing negativity among viewers to certain aspects of the plan (West, Heith, & Goodwin, 1996). More recently, non-electoral negative ads have addressed issues such as abortion, trade and aspects of foreign policy.

Campaign Advertising

Obviously, the point of political campaigns is to win elections, and negative advertising can help achieve this goal in three ways. The first way is to convince voters to select the preferred candidate, which is often done through positive promotional advertising that extols the virtues and experience of the candidate. However, contrast ads, which include attacks on the opposition as well as promotion, can be particularly helpful in distinguishing the merits of one candidate over another, clarifying the choice facing voters.

A second method in which advertising is used to pursue election is partisan reinforcement. It is important for a candidate not only to appeal to undecided voters, but to reinforce the commitment of voters within his/her own party predisposed to the candidate. Moreover, it is important for a candidate to mobilize voters – to imbue them with a sense of enthusiasm so that they actually go to the polls – and encourage others to do so as well. Negative advertising can help in these efforts.

The third way to use negative advertising is to dissuade individuals from showing up to vote for the opposing candidate. Since it is difficult to convince strong supporters of an opposing candidate to not show up, the target audience is often undecided voters. In two-party contests, candidates may use negative advertising when they perceive that independents are leaning in favor of their opponent (Ansolabehere & Iyengar, 1995). Thus, minimizing the independent vote could be beneficial. However, this assumes that negative ads are effective in lowering voter turnout. The scholarly research on this subject has shown mixed results and has sparked a great deal of controversy.

Effects of Negative Advertising

As noted at the beginning of this chapter, the 1988 US presidential election represented a high point for the percentage of negative advertisements aired on television. While there had been scholarly interest in the topic prior to the election, research into the various effects negative advertising erupted following it. In 1999 and again in 2007, Lau and his colleagues collected and performed a meta-analysis of the effects of numerous research studies on the effects of negative advertisements (Lau, Sigelman, Heldman, & Babbitt, 1999; Lau, Sigelman, & Rovner, 2007). Their studies demonstrate that research has focused on two general areas of effects: electoral effects – specific to an election – and systemic effects – related the broader practice of electoral politics and the health of a democracy.

Electoral Effects

Do negative ads help candidates win elections? The answer is complicated. Beyond influencing actual vote choice (or in some studies, intended vote choice), negative ads may impact a number of other variables that in turn may influence the outcome of an election. Additionally, negative ads stimulate emotional responses of viewers both toward the target candidate and the attacking candidate. These emotional responses may not only influence vote choice, but they may also stimulate voters' interest and information seeking behavior. Finally, negative ads can influence elections to the extent that they are memorable and increase voters' knowledge about the candidates and issues.

The most fundamental question is: If candidates decide to engage in negative advertising, does it help them win elections? Negative advertisements are designed to impact emotions toward candidates. Theoretically, negative ads should increase emotions such as anger, fear and worry while decreasing positive emotions such as hope and enthusiasm (causing "negative affect") about the target candidate. The negative ads should simultaneously reduce negative affect about the sponsoring candidate. On balance ("net affect") should work to the attacker's advantage.

It is well established in the scholarly literature that negative advertising increases negative affect toward the targets of the ad (Basil, Scooler, & Reeves, 1991; Crigler, Just, & Belt, 2006; Fridkin & Kenney, 2004, 2011; Houston & Doan, 1999; Jasperson & Fan, 2002; Kaid, 1997).[19] However, a majority of studies also find that negative affect is increased for the attacker, resulting in a backlash effect (Brader, 2005; Chang, 2003; Fridkin & Kenney, 2004; Hill, 1989; Hitchon & Chang, 1995; Houston & Doan, 1999; Jasperson & Fan, 2002; Kahn & Geer, 1994). The results show that attackers, on balance, do not harm their target any more than they harm themselves (Lau et al., 2007). It is not surprising, then, that in individual studies, some scholars have found negative advertising to be effective for the attacker (Roddy & Garramone, 1988; Shen & Wu, 2002), while others have not (Capella & Taylor, 1992; Lemert, Wanta, & Lee, 1999).

Several studies have shown that negative ads are more memorable than positive ads (Brader, 2005; Brians & Wattenberg, 1996; Chang, 2001; Merritt, 1984; Roberts, 1995; Shapiro & Rieger, 1992). Thus if these ads are better remembered than positive ones, they may actually produce an effect that is beneficial to electoral politics. In their meta-analysis in 2007, Lau and his colleagues showed the overall impact found by these studies to be neither particularly strong nor consistent.

There is more good news about negative ads – particularly those that stimulate fear – in that they provoke information seeking behavior and interest in the political campaign (Bartels, 2000; Brader, 2005; Lang, 1991; Newhagen & Reeves, 1991). Consequently, negative ads have been demonstrated to increase knowledge about candidates and policies (Craig, Kaine, & Gainous, 2005; Kahn & Kenney, 2004; Niven, 2006). The seemingly paradoxical conclusion is that bad candidate behavior is good for electoral democracy – at least in terms of educating voters.[20]

Systemic Effects

Some effects of negative ads may not pertain to a specific election at hand. As noted above, negative ads may be used to influence citizens' intent to turn out to vote which has spillover consequences for other elections, ballot initiatives and referenda. In addition to voter turnout, negative advertising may have a long-term effect on citizen's political efficacy and their trust in government, which are essential to the healthy functioning of a democracy.

Perhaps the most controversial topic in the study of negative advertising is whether these ads reduce viewers' likelihood of voting. Differing results seem to be due to differing methods used by researchers. In experimental studies, negative ads have been found to reduce the likelihood of voting (Ansolabehere & Iyengar, 1995; Ansolabehere, Iyengar, Simon, & Valentino, 1994; Crigler et al., 2006; Houston, Doan, & Roskos-Ewoldsen, 1999; Min, 2004). However, studies that use surveys and other aggregate data sources find that the prevalence of negative ads have no impact on voter turnout, or may actually increase turnout (Djupe & Peterson, 2002; Finkel & Geer, 1998; Freedman & Goldstein, 1999; Geer, 2006; Jackson & Sides, 2006; Wattenberg & Brians, 1999).

The results of scholarship evaluating the impact of negative political ads on other democratic values seem to be more consistent. Citizen's political efficacy – the degree to which they feel that their individual actions can have an influence on politics – declines as a result of the use of negative ads (Brader, 2005; Freedman & Goldstein, 1999; Pinkleton, Um, & Austin, 2002). Trust in government is also reduced by negative ads (Brader, 2005; Brooks & Geer, 2007; Leshner & Thorson, 2000; Pinkleton, Um, & Austin, 2002). So, when candidates use attack ads, it is not clear that it works to their advantage individually, but it is clear that it works to the disadvantage of the political system more generally.

Regulation of Negative Advertising

There are many reasons that nations may consider regulating negative advertising, beyond the fact that it is merely distasteful. The power of interest groups that fund negative ads is often asymmetrical, and in the US, their impact on elections is growing. As discussed earlier, interest groups and super-PACs have less of an incentive to act responsibly than candidates in how they use ads. In other words, there is a greater risk that groups not aligned with candidates will engage in misinforming the public. Research shows that the sponsor of an attack ad also matters in terms of its influence – ads sponsored by interest groups are more effective than those sponsored by candidates (Dowling & Wichowsky, 2015; Ridout, Franz & Fowler, 2014).

Even when negative ads are used by candidates, the truth is often stretched and words and actions are taken out of context. A case could be made that some negative advertising amounts to "false advertising." However, in the US, constitutional law protects political advertising as free speech – and political speech is afforded the highest degree of protection of any form of speech. Other nations have significant restrictions on campaign advertising.

On the positive side, there is valuable information in negative political advertising (Mattes & Redlawsk, 2014). Additionally, private sector news fact-checking seems to be helpful to voters, especially as they cut through misrepresentations made in negative ads (Fridkin, Kenney, & Wintersieck, 2015). Without negativity, we can't expect that candidates would willingly expose their own flaws to the electorate. Negative advertising, just like the adversarial system of justice in courtrooms, provides incentives for the promulgation of full information. Nations would be well advised to weigh the full costs and benefits of regulation.

Conclusion

Long ago, Walter Lippman (1922) observed that the press shines a spotlight on the workings of government for the public to see. Today, mass media convey information through broadcast news as well as increasingly popular online and digital formats. As E. E. Schattschneider (1960) noted, nothing attracts attention as much as a fight – especially in politics. Negative advertising supplies much desired material for broadcast media's search for large audiences by focusing on campaign strategy and the horserace among candidates (Patterson, 1994; West, 2014). In recent years, Internet technology has advanced, and platforms exist for citizens to be involved in the ad amplification process, further augmenting the impact of ads. Negative ads are sure to be with us in one form or another for some time to come.

Acknowledgments

The author thanks Tyler Hoffman for research and editing assistance.

Notes

1 Video archived at: www.livingroomcandidate.org/commercials/1964/peace-little-girl-daisy.
2 Video archived at: www.livingroomcandidate.org/commercials/1996/signed.
3 Video archived at: www.livingroomcandidate.org/commercials/2012/firms.
4 Video archived at: www.livingroomcandidate.org/commercials/1988/harbor.
5 Video archived at: www.livingroomcandidate.org/commercials/1988/oval-office.

6 Video archived at: www.livingroomcandidate.org/commercials/1992/gray-dot.
7 Video archived at: www.livingroomcandidate.org/commercials/1992/second.
8 Video archived at: www.livingroomcandidate.org/commercials/1988/revolving-door.
9 Video archived at: www.livingroomcandidate.org/commercials/1988/furlough-from-the-truth.
10 Video archived at: www.livingroomcandidate.org/commercials/2008/education.
11 Video archived at: www.livingroomcandidate.org/commercials/2000/priority-md-rnc.
12 Video archived at: www.livingroomcandidate.org/commercials/2004/weapons-florida.
13 Video archived at: www.youtube.com/watch?v=KiyewCdXMzk.
14 Video archived at: www.livingroomcandidate.org/commercials/2004/windsurfing.
15 Video archived at: www.livingroomcandidate.org/commercials/1972/newspapers#4046.
16 Video archived at: www.youtube.com/watch?v=kkiz1_d1GsA.
17 Videos available at: www.methproject.org/ads/tv/kevin.html.
18 Video archived at: www.youtube.com/watch?v=7l5Wa94ynss.
19 According to Lau et al., these findings occurred in roughly two-thirds of the studies they analyzed. They caution that the largest effects were found in studies with the smallest sample sizes (Lau et al., 2007, p. 1182).
20 Lau et al. warn in their meta-analysis that, taking the studies together, the impact of negative advertising on campaign knowledge is not particularly strong (2007, p. 1180).

References

Alexander, H. E., & Corrado, A. (1995). *Financing the 1992 election.* New York, NY: M. E. Sharp.

Ansolabehere, S., & Iyengar, S. (1995). *Going negative: How political advertisements shrink & polarize the electorate.* New York, NY: Free Press.

Ansolabehere, S., Iyengar, S., Simon, A., & Valentino, N. (1994). Does attack advertising demobilize the electorate? *The American Political Science Review,* 88(4), 829–838.

Aravosis, J. (2008, March 28). Obama skin tone darker in Clinton ad? HuffingtonPost.com. Retrieved from www.huffingtonpost.com/2008/03/04/obama-skin-tone-darker-in_n_89829.html.

Bartels, L. (2000). Campaign quality: Standards for evaluation, benchmarks for reform. In L. M. Bartels & L. Vavreck (Eds.), *Campaign reform: Insights and evidence* (pp. 1–61). Ann Arbor, MI: University of Michigan Press.

Basil, M., Scooler, C., & Reeves, B. (1991). Positive and negative political advertising: Effectiveness of ads and perceptions of candidates. In F. Biocca (Ed.), *Television and political advertising volume 1: Psychological processes* (pp. 245–262). New York, NY: Routledge.

Berke, R. L. (2000, September 12). The 2000 campaign: The ad campaign: Democrats see, and smell, rats in G.O.P. ad. *New York Times.* Retrieved from www.nytimes.com/2000/09/12/us/the-2000-campaign-the-ad-campaign-democrats-see-and-smell-rats-in-gop-ad.html?pagewanted=all.

Brader, T. (2005). Striking a responsive chord: How political ads motivate and persuade voters by appealing to emotions. *American Journal of Political Science,* 49(2), 388–405.

Brader, T. (2006). *Campaigning for hearts and minds: How emotional appeals in political ads work.* University of Chicago Press.

Brians, C. L., & Wattenberg, M. P. (1996). Campaign issue knowledge and salience: Comparing reception from TV commercials, TV news and newspapers. *American Journal of Political Science,* 40(1), 172–193.

Brooks, D. J., & Geer, J. G. (2007). Beyond negativity: The effects of incivility on the electorate. *American Journal of Political Science,* 51(1), 1–16

Capella, L., & Taylor, R. D. (1992). An analysis of the effectiveness of negative political campaigning. *Business and Public Affairs,* 18(Spring), 10–17.

Chang, C. (2001). The impacts of emotion elicited by print political advertising on candidate evaluation. *Media Psychology,* 3(2), 91–118.

Chang, C. (2003). Party bias in political-advertising processing: Results from an experiment involving the 1998 Taipei mayoral election. *Journal of Advertising,* 32(2), 55–67.

Craig, S. C., Kane, J. G., & Gainous, J. (2005). Issue-related learning in a gubernatorial campaign: A panel study. *Political Communication,* 22(4), 483–503.

Crigler, A. N., Just, M. R., & Belt, T. L. (2006). The three faces of negative campaigning: The democratic implications of attack ads, cynical news and fear arousing messages. In David P. Redlawsk (Ed.), *Feeling politics: Affect and emotion in political information processing* (pp. 135–163). New York, NY: Palgrave Macmillan.

Diamond, E., & Bates, S. (1992). *The spot: The rise of political advertising on television* (3rd ed.). Cambridge, MA: MIT Press.

Djupe, P. A., & Peterson, D. A. M. (2002). The impact of negative campaigning: Evidence from the 1998 senatorial primaries. *Political Research Quarterly,* 55(4), 845–860.

Dowling, C. D., & Miller, M. G. (2014). *Super PAC!: Money, elections, and voters after Citizens United*. New York, NY: Routledge.

Dowling, C. D., & Wichowsky, A. (2015). Attacks without consequence? Candidates, parties, groups, and the changing face of negative advertising. *American Journal of Political Science*, 59(1), 19–36.

Finkel, S. E., & Geer, J. G. (1998). A spot check: casting doubt on the demobilizing effect of attack advertising. *American Journal of Political Science*, 42(2), 573–595.

Franz, M. M. (2012). Interest groups in electoral politics: 2012 in context. *The Forum: A Journal of Applied Research in Contemporary Politics*, 10(4), 62–79.

Freedman, P., & Goldstein, K. (1999). Measuring media exposure and the effects of negative campaign ads. *American Journal of Political Science Association*, 43(4), 1189–1208.

Fridkin, K. L., & Kenney, P. J. (2004). Do negative messages work? The impact of negativity on citizens' evaluations of candidates. *American Politics Research*, 32(5), 570–605.

Fridkin, K. L., & Kenney, P. J. (2011). Variability in citizens' reactions to different types of negative campaigns. *American Journal of Political Science*, 55(2), 307–325.

Fridkin, K., Kenney, P. J., & Wintersieck, A. (2015). Liar, liar, pants on fire: How fact-checking influences citizens' reactions to negative advertising. *Political Communication*, 32(1), 127–151.

Geer, J. G. (2006). *In defense of negativity: Attack ads in presidential campaigns*. University of Chicago Press.

Hill, R. P. (1989). An exploration of voter responses to political advertisements. *Journal of Advertising*, 18(4), 14–22.

Hitchon, J. C., & Chang, C. (1995). Effects of gender schematic processing on the reception of political commercials for men and women candidates. *Communication Research*, 22(August), 430–458.

Houston, D. A., & Doan, K. (1999). Can you back that up? *Media Psychology*, 1(3), 191–206.

Houston, D. A., Doan, K., & Roskos-Ewoldsen, D. (1999). Negative political advertising and choice conflict. *Journal of Experimental Psychology: Applied*, 5(1), 3–16.

Garramone, G. M. (1983). Issue versus image orientation and effects of political advertising. *Communication Research*, 10(1), 59–76.

Jackson, R. A., & Sides, J. C. (2006). Revisiting the influence of campaign tone in senate elections. *Political Analysis*, 14(2), 206–218.

James, M. (2015). Political ad spending estimated at $6 billion in 2016. *Los Angeles Times*. Retrieved from www.latimes.com/entertainment/envelope/cotown/la-et-ct-political-ad-spending-6-billion-dollars-in-2016-20151117-story.html.

Jamieson, K. H. (1992). *Dirty politics: Deception, distraction, and democracy*. New York, NY: Oxford University Press.

Jamieson, K. H. (1996). *Packaging the presidency: A history and criticism of presidential campaign advertising* (3rd ed.). New York, NY: Oxford University Press.

Jasperson, A. E., & Fan, D. P. (2002). An aggregate examination of the backlash effect in political advertising: The case of the 1996 US senate race in Minnesota. *Journal of Advertising*, 31(1), 1–12.

Kahn, K. F., & Geer, J. G. (1994). Creating impressions: An experimental investigation of political advertising on television. *Political Behavior*, 16(1), 93–116.

Kahn, K. F., & Kenney, P. J. (2004). *No holds barred: Negativity in US senate campaigns*. Upper Saddle River, NJ: Pearson Prentice Hall.

Kaid, L. L. (1997). Effects of the television spots on images of Dole and Clinton. *The American Behavioral Scientist*, 40(8), 1085–1094.

Kendall, K. E. (2000). *Communication in the presidential primaries: Candidates in the media, 1912–2000*. Westport, CT: Praeger.

Kolawole, E. (2008). Did Clinton darken Obama's skin? FactCheck.org. Retrieved from www.factcheck.org/2008/03/did-clinton-darken-obamas-skin/.

Kurtzleben, D. (2015, August 19). 2016 campaigns will spend $4.4 billion on TV ads, but why? NPR.org. Retrieved from www.npr.org/sections/itsallpolitics/2015/08/19/432759311/2016-campaign-tv-ad-spending.

Lang, A. (1991). Emotion, formal features, and memory for televised political advertisements. In F. Biocca (Ed.), *Television and political advertising volume 1: Psychological processes* (pp. 221–243). New York, NY: Routledge.

Lau, R. R., Sigelman, L., Heldman, C., & Babbitt, P. (1999). The effects of negative political advertisements: A meta-analytic assessment. *The American Political Science Review*, 93(4), 851–875.

Lau, R. R., Sigelman, L., & Rovner, I. B. (2007). The effects of negative political campaigns: A meta-analytic reassessment. *The Journal of Politics*, 69(4), 1176–1209.

Leighley, J. (2004). *Mass media and politics: A social science perspective*. Boston: Houghton Mifflin.

Lemert, J. B., Wanta, W., & Lee, T. T. (1999). Party identification and negative advertising in a US senate election. *Journal of Communications*, 49(2), 123–134.

Leshner, G., & Thorson, E. (2000). Overreporting voting: Campaign media, public mood, and the vote. *Political Communication*, 17(3), 263–278.

Lippmann, W. (1922). *Public opinion*. New York, NY: Free Press.

Mattes, K., & Redlawsk, D. P. (2014). *The positive case for negative campaigning.* University of Chicago Press.

Merritt, S. (1984). Negative political advertising: Some empirical findings. *Journal of Advertising*, 13(3), 27–38.

Messing, S., Jabon, M., & Plaut, E. (2016). Bias in the flesh: Skin complexion and stereotype consistency in political campaigns. *Public Opinion Quarterly*, 80(1), 44–65.

Min, Y. (2002). Intertwining of campaign news and advertising: The content and electoral effects of newspaper ad watches. *Journalism and Mass Communication Quarterly*, 79(4), 927–944.

Min, Y. (2004). News coverage of negative political campaigns: An experiment of negative campaign effects on turnout and candidate preference. *The International Journal of Press/Politics*, 9(4), 95–111.

Newhagen, E. & Reeves, B. (1991). Emotion and memory responses for negative political advertising. In F. Biocca (Ed.), *Television and political advertising volume 1: Psychological processes* (pp. 197–220). New York, NY: Routledge.

Niven, D. (2006). A field experiment on the effects of negative campaign mail on voter turnout in a municipal election. *Political Research Quarterly*, 59(2), 203–210.

Noar, S. M., Hall, M. G., Francis, D. B., Ribisl, K. M., Pepper, J. K., & Brewer, N. T. (2015). Pictorial cigarette pack warnings: A meta-analysis of experimental studies. Tobacco Control. Published online. Retrieved from http://tobaccocontrol.bmj.com/content/early/2015/05/03/tobaccocontrol-2014–051978.full.pdf+html.

Patterson, T. E. (1994). *Out of order.* New York, NY: Vintage.

Pinkleton, B. E., Um, N., & Austin, E. W. (2002). An exploration of the effects of negative political advertising on political decision making. *Journal of Advertising*, 31(1), 13–25.

Ridout, T. N., Franz, M. M., & Fowler, E. F. (2014). Advances in the study of political advertising. *Journal of Political Marketing*, 13(3), 175–194.

Ridout, T. N., & Smith, G. R. (2008). Free advertising: How the media amplify campaign messages. *Political Research Quarterly*, 61(4), 598–608.

Roberts, M. S. (1995). Political advertising: Strategies for influence. In K. E. Kendall (Ed.), *Presidential campaign discourse: Strategic communication problems* (pp. 179–199). Albany, NY: SUNY Press.

Roddy, B. L., & Garramone, G. M. (1988). Appeals and strategies of negative political advertising. *Journal of Broadcasting & Electronic Media*, 32(4), 415–427.

Roese, N. J., & Sande, G. N. (1993). Backlash effects in attack politics. *Journal of Applied Social Psychology*, 23(8), 632–653.

Schattschneider, E. E. (1960). *The semisovereign people: A realist's view of democracy in America.* New York, NY: Holt, Rinehart and Winston.

Shapiro, M. A., & Rieger, R. H. (1992). Comparing positive and negative political advertising on radio. *Journalism & Mass Communication Quarterly*, 69(1), 135–145.

Shen, F., & Wu, H. D. (2002). Effects of soft-money issue advertisements on candidate evaluation and voting preference: An exploration. *Mass Communication & Society*, 5(4), 395–410.

Smith, J., & Kimball, D. (2013). Barking louder: Interest groups in the 2012 election. *The Forum: A Journal of Applied Research in Contemporary Politics*, 10(4), 80–90.

Smith, M. M., & Powell, L. (2013). *Dark money, super PACs, and the 2012 election.* Lanham, MD: Lexington Books.

Sonner, B. S. (1998). The effectiveness of negative political advertising: A case study. *Journal of Advertising Research*, 38(6), 37–43.

Toner, R. (2006, October 26). Ad seen as playing to racial fears. *New York Times.* Retrieved from www.nytimes.com/2006/10/26/us/politics/26tennessee.html?ref=politics&_r=0.

Wattenberg, M. P., & Brians, C. L. (1999). Negative campaign advertising: Demobilizer or mobilizer? *The American Political Science Review*, 93(4), 891–899.

Weinberger, J., & Westen, D. (2008). RATS, we should have used Clinton: Subliminal priming in political campaigns. *Political Psychology*, 29(5), 631–651.

West, D. M. (2014). *Air wars: Television advertising and social media in election campaigns, 1952–2012* (6th ed.). Los Angeles: Sage.

West, D. M., Heith, D., and Goodwin, C. (1996). Harry and Louise go to Washington: Political advertising and health care reform. *Journal of Health Politics, Policy and Law*, 21(1), 35–68.

6

THE EFFECTS OF POLITICAL ADVERTISING

Travis N. Ridout and Jenny L. Holland

Research in the field of political advertising has advanced considerably since one of us wrote a review on the topic over a decade ago (Goldstein & Ridout, 2004). Those who study ads are still interested in their persuasive power, but instead of asking "do ads matter?" the field has moved on to more interesting questions, such as "for how long do ads matter?" and "how does the content of the ad influence its effectiveness?" The question that scholars grappled with a decade ago, "do ads demobilize?" now has a much more nuanced answer: on average, no, but certain types of ads in certain circumstances may demobilize certain people. And scholars who study ad effects have situated the study of advertising into larger contexts, examining, for instance, the impact of advertising not just on individuals but on media coverage.

This is all good, though the conclusions that scholars draw about the effects of advertising lean heavily on research coming from the US. This is understandable given the sheer volume of ads aired in the US during election campaigns. Still, research on political advertising in other parts of the globe is growing. Much of that research speaks to the conditions under which parties engage in negative advertising (e.g., Sullivan, 2008; Walter, Van der Brug, & Van Praag, 2014), but some research is starting to examine advertising effects in places like Switzerland (Nai, 2013, 2015) and Brazil (Da Silveira & De Mello, 2011). It is difficult to know to what extent conclusions drawn about the effects of American television ads – which are short, sophisticated and shown over and over again – generalize to other countries with different institutional arrangements.

In this review, we examine current research on the effects of political advertising, focusing on how advertising can affect people's vote choices, evaluations of candidates, political knowledge and participation, and attitudes toward the political system. We also explore how long the effects of advertising endure and how advertising can influence the news media's agenda. We find that research on the effects of political advertising has advanced considerably over the past decade but that new questions remain to be addressed – and we argue that one important avenue for answering those questions will be making the study of advertising effects more cross-national.

Vote Choice

One of the indicators that campaign ads "work" is persuasion. Put simply, persuasion occurs when ads influence the choices of voters. Studies have shown that candidates who air more ads than their opponents typically enjoy a larger share of the vote, though this finding is not consistent across all electoral contexts. Shaw (1999) examined the effects of ads aired across US states in three different presidential elections and found that, in many cases, when a presidential candidate's ad volume increased in a state, that candidate's vote share also increased. The size of the effects, however, varied across races. Franz and Ridout (2010) focused on the relationship between market-level ad buys and county-level vote returns in the 2004 and 2008 US presidential races, finding that an ad advantage for a candidate in those years also led to a vote advantage for that candidate, though the effects were larger in 2008 than 2004, presumably because both candidates were less well-known in that year. They also found that the effects of ads on vote choice were even larger in non-battleground states than in battleground states, likely because battleground states are saturated with campaign activity above and beyond television advertising (e.g., candidate visits, door-to-door canvassing and direct mail), which may moderate the effects of ads themselves. Advertising, then, can influence the outcome of a presidential race, particularly in competitive states where a few thousand votes can make a difference in the Electoral College vote. In fact, Gordon and Hartmann (2013) found, using a statistical simulation, that if no political advertising had been aired in the 2000 presidential race, Al Gore would have beaten George W. Bush.

In addition to these aggregate-level studies, there has been work on the persuasive power of campaign advertising at the individual level. Much of it uses the method developed by Goldstein and Freedman (1999), who combine ad tracking data at the market level and survey responses to create a an individual-level measure of ad exposure.

This method has been applied across many types of races. At the presidential level, for instance, there were no significant effects of advertising on vote choice in 2000 (Ridout & Franz, 2011). But increased exposure to ads for John Kerry in 2004 significantly increased both his favorability and the likelihood of voting for him (Franz & Ridout, 2007). These studies also indicated that, generally speaking, increased exposure to a candidate's ads can lead to a decrease in evaluations of his opponent.

In the US Senate context, Goldstein and Freedman (2000) found that in the 1996 contests, as exposure to ads for incumbents and challengers increased, support for each type of candidate also increased. Ridout and Franz (2011), examining ad effects in US Senate races, found that the persuasiveness of advertising varies depending on electoral context. For example, ads had the most consistent effects in open-seat races, likely because both candidates were less well-known than an incumbent candidate. Additionally, challengers' ads were effective, particularly in competitive races against an incumbent.

One reason ad effects are not larger, it has been argued, is that resources are generally pretty evenly matched across candidates in high-profile campaigns, especially at the presidential level. But instances of imbalanced message flows may be increasing because advertisers are strategic in their ad placements, airing them on different channels and at different times in order to reach specific audiences. For instance, audiences for some programs in the US skew Democratic, independent or Republican (Ridout, Franz, Goldstein, & Feltus, 2012), and thus campaigns can direct their ads at shoring up base voters and trying to convince the most persuadable.

Candidate Evaluations

Related to the question of voter choice is whether ads have the power to move a candidate's favorability. This question is important because of the assumption that having a favorable view of a candidate is a precursor to voting for that candidate. Much of this research focuses on how the tone of the ad, whether positive, negative or contrast, influences candidate evaluations.

The intended effects hypothesis suggests that positive ads should increase favorability of the sponsoring candidate, while negative ads should decrease the favorability of the targeted candidate. The literature, however, is mixed on whether ads do indeed have these intended effects. For example, negative ads can decrease the favorability of the targeted candidate (Fridkin & Kenney, 2004; Lau, Sigelman, & Rovner, 2007), but may also result in a backlash against the sponsor (Fridkin & Kenney, 2004; Garramone, 1984; Kahn & Geer, 1994). But contrast ads may allow a candidate to escape the unwanted backlash effect (Pinkleton, 1997) because these critiques are seen as less severe. More recent research indicates that even when using negative ads, the spacing of those ads over a program may make a difference. Using an experimental design, Fernandes (2013) found that evaluations of the sponsor decreased under larger and more frequent airings of an attack, whereas only the target suffered when the attacks were not as concentrated. The message: It may be better to space out attack ads than to place them close together.

Although much research focuses on positive, negative or contrast ads, more recent research has pushed scholars to move beyond the traditional three-category typology. For example, civil and uncivil negative ads may have different effects (Fridkin & Kenney, 2008), and the specific emotional appeals in the ad may also matter. Brader (2006) found that appeals to enthusiasm activate existing loyalties (as can appeals to anger), while appeals to fear motivate viewers to reconsider their choices.

Others make a distinction between trait-based and issue-based ads. Kahn and Geer (1994) found that an unknown candidate is evaluated more favorably when using positive trait-based or issue-based ads (both had a similar effect). The least effective ad was a trait-based negative ad, as these are usually seen as unfair and below the belt, especially if they concern a candidate's family or religion (Mattes & Redlawsk, 2015).

Candidates, then, should be wary of attacking opponents on personal characteristics, but recent experimental research has shown that backlash against a candidate may be avoided if an outside group does the attacking (Brooks & Murov, 2012; Dowling & Wichowsky, 2015; Weber, Dunaway, & Johnson, 2012). The type of group sponsor also matters. Weber et al.'s (2012) experimental study showed that an ad sponsored by an unknown group, the hypothetical "Citizens for a Safer America," was more persuasive than an identical ad that was sponsored by a more well-known and ideologically identifiable group, the National Rifle Association.

Additional research has focused on whether the electoral context influences the effectiveness of advertising. Research shows, for instance, that incumbent politicians have less to gain with their use of campaign ads relative to challengers, and that challengers are less likely to experience a backlash for using negative ads (Fridkin & Kenney, 2004; Ridout & Franz, 2011), ostensibly because voters expect incumbents to run on their successes in office. By contrast, a challenger is expected to define herself and provide a rationale for why she should be elected over the incumbent. But Fridkin and Kenney (2011) found that in US Senate races, incumbents enjoy a credibility advantage when it comes to the content of their ads. And when incumbents address their opponents with messages relevant to the campaign – whether civil or uncivil – it can lower voters' evaluations of the challenger to a greater degree than when the challenger attacks an incumbent (Fridkin & Kenney, 2008).

The Role of Ad Content

The audiovisual techniques used in political ads help sell the message. Persuasive ads typically include a combination of images, music and other sounds that work together to evoke emotional reactions and reinforce the ad's message. As Brader (2006) explains, ads that appeal to emotions tend to be more persuasive than ads that do not contain such overt cues. A positive ad without any music, for example, is less persuasive than the same ad with an uplifting soundtrack playing in the background. Music can set the mood of an ad and signal to the viewer whether the message is uplifting or not. Ads that aim to generate enthusiasm or pride tend to include uplifting music that is pleasing to the ear, and may even include patriotic themes. On the other hand, ads that intend to evoke fear or anger may use music that is not pleasing to the ear and full of discordant sounds.

Visual imagery is also chosen carefully. Positive ads generally use bright colors and crisp images in contrast to negative ads that generally use dull colors such as black-and-white and grainy or unclear images (West, 2014). Bright, sunny images send a message of hope and optimism compared to dark and dull colors that might seem scary or unpleasant. Positive ads, with appeals to enthusiasm and pride, tend to include children, images of the American flag, children in school, people hard at work, and beautiful landscapes (Brader, 2006). Negative ads, with appeals to anger or fear, tend to include fewer people than positive ads, and they include unpleasant sights such as pollution, war or violence, desolate or abandoned locations, guns and violent crime (Brader, 2006). Ads that appeal to enthusiasm may shore up support among already existing supporters (Brader, 2006), though not all research supports this claim (e.g., Ridout & Franz, 2011).

In addition to visual images and music, the narration (or voice-over) can have an impact on the effectiveness of an ad. One study showed that the sex of the voice-over announcer interacts with type of issue such that women's voices are more effective when the issue is a feminine one (i.e., a women's issue) while a man's voice is more effective when the issue is a masculine one (Strach, Zuber, Fowler, Ridout, & Searles, 2015).

Clearly, those who study political advertising have made progress in the past decade in learning how the content of an advertisement influences its effectiveness; scholars have moved beyond ad tone to consider things like visual images, music, emotional appeals and narration. But all of these should be investigated more fully, and there are dozens of other content features that remain to be investigated.

Political Participation

Scholars have debated for decades whether political advertising encourages political participation, reduces it or has no effect. Most of this research has focused on voter turnout. The consensus view leans in the direction of no effect, at least on average, with the view that advertising stimulates turnout coming in second. That said, there remain certain circumstances under which – and certain individuals for whom – the impact of advertising may be negative.

There are theoretical reasons to believe that advertising could have both positive and negative impacts on turnout. In favor of advertising's having a positive impact on turnout, scholars point out that advertising can raise the stakes: it can make the citizens realize that there is a lot to be gained – or a lot put at risk – if a particular candidate or party wins (Djupe & Peterson, 2002; Franz, Freedman, Goldstein, & Ridout, 2007). Second, political advertising may reduce the costs of voting by informing citizens of where the candidates stand on various issues. Citizens who learn which candidate is closest to them from the political ads they watch do not need to spend time researching those candidates in order to make an informed decision.

Yet, there are also arguments in favor of the idea that exposure to political advertising reduces people's incentives to vote. These arguments focus, in particular, on negative political advertising. One argument is that the negativity and cynicism found in modern-day ad campaigns leads voters to decide they do not want to be involved in such a process (Ansolabehere & Iyengar, 1995). Moreover, the negativity makes people dislike specific things about the candidates such that they see less reason to vote for any of them. Why vote if neither candidate has anything positive to offer?

Of course, another option is that the net effect of exposure to political advertising may be essentially nil. Perhaps the impact of advertising is minimal, regardless of the individual citizen. Or perhaps some citizens are mobilized while others are demobilized. For instance, Krupnikov (2011) argues that negative political advertising can demobilize, but only after a person has decided for whom to vote. That is, seeing an ad that makes the candidate you support look bad may make you less enthusiastic about going out and voting for that candidate, but it will not lead you to vote for the other candidate.

There are really two debates about advertising and turnout: one about how advertising, taken as a whole, influences turnout and another about whether negative advertising affects turnout. Concerning the first debate, Krasno and Green (2008) and Franz, Freedman, Goldstein and Ridout (2008) argue about whether the effects of advertising on turnout are nil or positive. Much of the debate hinges on methodological questions, such as whether to examine all ads or just presidential ads, and what the appropriate unit of analysis is. Although the two sides ultimately disagree, they do agree that there are no negative effects of advertising on turnout.

The other debate concerns the impact of negative advertising, in particular, on voter turnout. The most definitive study on this question is Lau et al.'s (2007) meta-analysis, which takes into account 57 studies addressing the question. They conclude that there is no evidence that negative advertising demobilizes. "If anything, negative campaigning more frequently appears to have a slight mobilizing effect" (p. 1184).

The pace of research into the relationship between negativity and turnout picked up steam, especially after Ansolabehere and Iyengar (1995) provided strong experimental evidence that attack ads were causing people to stay home on Election Day – a finding that raised many normative concerns. Over the past decade, however, new research examining the question of ad tone and turnout has slowed down. In part, that is due to the emerging consensus that negativity is probably unrelated to turnout, and if it is related, its impact is positive. What is more, voter turnout in the 2004, 2008 and 2012 presidential races was considerably higher than in the 1980s and 1990s, which served to calm those concerned about the apparent decline in voter turnout in the US since the 1970s (McDonald & Popkin, 2001).

Still, some research on the relationship between negativity and turnout is being produced. One direction in which that research has turned is to the study of down-ballot races. For instance, negativity in state supreme court races appears to increase turnout, with races with more attack ads experiencing less ballot roll-off (Hall & Bonneau, 2012). Moreover, negativity in Swiss ballot proposition campaigns reduces turnout when the campaign is defending the status quo, but negativity increases turnout when policy change would take place as a result of the proposition's passage (Nai, 2013).

Research has also examined the impact of advertising on measures of participation in addition to turnout. One study found no relationship between exposure to advertising and attending a rally, circulating a petition or contacting a public official, nor was there any effect of advertising on the volume of political chatter, whether talking with family, friends or political opponents (Franz et al., 2007). And, in general, the relationship between exposure to advertising and feelings of internal efficacy (confidence in one's ability to participate in politics) and external efficacy (a belief in the responsiveness of the political system) is non-existent (Jackson, Mondak, & Huckfeldt, 2009).

Advertising may even influence people's willingness to give money to candidates. Urban and Niebler (2014) find that running ads in a particular zip code raises contributions from that zip code by, on average, $6,800. Collins (2012) similarly argues that advertising can increase donations, but that only occurs with positive ads when they use partisan cues. Negative ads can increase donations to the sponsor – and even donations to the candidate who is attacked.

Attitudes Toward the System

How does advertising influence peoples' perceptions of the political system? Certainly, it seems intuitive that exposure to advertising, especially negative advertising, might result in increased political cynicism and distrust, and this is what some early studies found (Ansolabehere & Iyengar, 1995; Cappella & Jamieson, 1997; Tedesco, 2002). But more recent research has tended to step back from that claim.

For instance, Jackson et al. (2009) find no relationship between people's exposure to negative advertising and their views about the legitimacy of the political system. This was true among partisans and nonpartisans, as well as those with high and low levels of political knowledge. Work by Pinkleton, Um and Austin (2002) backs these claims.

Other research finds that advertising can occasionally have a positive impact on people's feelings toward the political system. An analysis of survey and ad-tracking data from 2004 found that exposure to the total ad environment led to a decrease in negative feelings about the electoral process and a decrease in the belief that the electoral system needed change (Franz et al., 2007). Additionally, increases in advertising exposure led to modest increases in trust in government.

Still more research suggests that the impact of advertising is conditional. Schenck-Hamlin, Procter and Rumsey (2000) suggest that just those ads focused on candidate characteristics increased voters' cynicism while Dardis, Shen and Edwards (2008) found that issue-based ads led to higher cynicism.

Knowledge of Politics

Can political advertising increase people's knowledge of politics? At first blush, it is difficult to imagine that people could learn much from 30 seconds of flashy images, but the evidence tells a different story. In spite of being short, ads contain a considerable amount of policy content. Most ads aired in the 1992 US presidential campaign contained at least some policy content (Just et al., 1996, pp. 82–83). And 85% of House and Senate ads from the 2014 campaign made at least some mention of policy, and 60% were primarily focused on policy issues as opposed to candidates' personalities (Fowler, Franz, & Ridout, 2016). At the very least, then, advertising contains information for viewers to acquire.

Much research confirms that citizens can and do learn information from political advertising (Just, Crigler, & Wallach, 1990; Patterson & McClure, 1976). For instance, Freedman, Franz and Goldstein (2004) create a measure of survey respondents' likely exposure to advertising that aired in the media market in which they lived, finding that increased exposure to congressional ads is positively associated with people's claims to know the names of the House candidates in their districts and the accuracy of their reports. Furthermore, increased exposure to presidential advertising is positively associated with the respondents' ability to correctly place Gore to the left of Bush in 2000 on a series of issues scales. Ridout, Shah, Goldstein and Franz (2004) draw similar conclusions. Zhao and Chaffee (1995), however, are less optimistic about the ability of political advertising to inform. Although they find that increased attention to television advertising does improve political knowledge, its impact is generally less than the increase provided by exposure to television news. Lipsitz (2013) finds, in general, that greater exposure to political advertising clarifies candidates' issue positions, but when people were exposed to more Republican ads in 2000, they were less likely to correctly identify Al Gore's position on prescription drug coverage, suggesting that sometimes greater exposure to advertising can confuse voters.

Research in this field has also addressed not just whether advertising increases political knowledge but whether certain types of advertising do a better job of increasing knowledge. Many suggest that negative advertising may have a particularly strong impact on political learning because it generally contains more policy information than positive advertising (Franz et al., 2007; Geer, 2006) and because it is more attention-grabbing (Lau, 1985; Martin, 2004). Another study – this one focusing on young people – finds that increased exposure to negative advertising in the 2008 presidential campaign was positively correlated with human-interest candidate knowledge, such as which candidate was a community organizer, but exposure to negative advertising was not associated with policy-relevant candidate knowledge (Wang, Gabay, & Shah, 2012). Yet, Lau et al. (2007) conclude on the basis of a meta-analysis examining 15 different studies that negative campaigning (not always defined in terms of negative advertising) has a positive impact on campaign-related knowledge.

Another debate centers on whether learning from political advertising occurs more among the highly knowledgeable or those without much political knowledge. Although Freedman et al. (2004) argue that the least aware should benefit the most from political advertising given advertising's emotionally rich content and ease of understanding, the analysis of their data does not support this expectation. At least for their most direct measures of political knowledge, such as for respondents' ability to recall the name of House candidates, it is the most aware who learn the most. Work from Valentino, Hutchings and Williams (2004) confirms this finding. They argue that while all may benefit from learning information contained within the ads themselves, it is only the most politically sophisticated who are able to make inferences about candidate positions based on what they see in the ads. Their expectations are supported by an experiment, which finds both low and high-aware individuals learn candidate issue positions from watching Bush and Gore ads, but those with high awareness were better able to infer issue positions not directly mentioned in the ads viewed.

Duration of Ad Effects

Scholars have recently made strides in assessing how long the effects of advertising last. Answering this question is difficult, in part, because of the data requirements. One must assess citizens' attitudes – and their exposure to advertising – at multiple points in time, which requires either panel data or multiple cross sections. Much of the research looking into the duration of ad effects has focused on the direct, persuasive effects of advertising and has concluded that such effects are relatively ephemeral. For example, Gerber, Gimpel, Green and Shaw (2011) worked with a gubernatorial campaign in Texas in 2006, which allowed the research team to experimentally assign television and radio ads to different media markets. In brief, they find some substantial impacts of exposure to advertising on voter preferences, as measured through campaign tracking polls, but these effects decay rapidly, within two weeks.

Hill, Lo, Vavreck and Zaller (2013) matched up data from rolling cross-sectional surveys with data on ad buys in the respondents' media markets. They examined both the 2000 presidential race and several subnational races in 2006. Like Gerber's team, they find relatively short-lived ad effects, especially for the subnational races, but do suggest that for some voters, especially those engaging in online processing, that the persuasive effects of advertising may last for up to six weeks.

Bartels (2014) uses a survey experiment to try to better understand the mechanism behind the decline in ad effectiveness over time. One wave of the panel survey that he examines was fielded during the heart of the 2012 US presidential campaign. During this wave, respondents viewed an anti-Romney video aired by the Obama campaign. Respondents were re-interviewed 1–3 weeks later, after Election Day. Exposure to that single pro-Obama ad increased support for Obama immediately after watching that ad, and much of that increased support held up post-election among pre-existing Obama supporters and the undecided, but the increase in Obama support among those predisposed to vote for Romney disappeared. Bartels interprets this not as people forgetting the messages of the ad but as people counter-arguing the ad's message.

These studies should not be interpreted, however, to say that airing ads early in a race is pointless. Early ads can, as Hill et al. (2013) suggest, send a message to donors that the sponsor is a viable candidate, can deter weaker candidates from throwing their hat in the ring and may, as we explore in the next section, have a considerable influence on media coverage. Thus, while the direct persuasive effects of advertising may generally be short-lived, their indirect effects may be much longer.

Recent research has also looked beyond persuasion in attempting to assess the duration of ad effects. In fact, Gotlieb and colleagues (forthcoming) suggest that when it comes to outcomes like political trust, social trust and political talk, the effects of advertising may endure long after Election Day, may depend on ad exposure over several election cycles, and may even emerge after the campaign has ended. They find, for instance, that cumulative ad exposure from 2000 to 2004 has an influence on frequency of cross-cutting political talk, measured both right after the 2004 campaign and in 2005.

Effects of Advertising on Media Coverage

The effects of advertising are not confined to voters or citizens. Advertising also has an impact on journalists and their coverage. For example, the infamous "Willie Horton" ad from the 1988

US presidential campaign "suckered the press into covering crime, an issue on which the public prefers Republicans" (Iyengar, 2011).

Advertising as a topic of news coverage is not just an American phenomenon. Britain's Labour Party crafted a Party Election Broadcast in 1992 that is commonly referred to as "Jennifer's Ear," which describes the "story of a little girl who had to wait for an ear operation due to the Conservative's government neglect of the National Health Service" (Scammell & Langer, 2006, p. 74). The advertisement and subsequent controversy about Labour's exploiting a child for political purposes, made front-page headlines.

Media coverage of political advertising in the US has risen since the early 1980s. Geer (2009) shows that in the 1970s and early 1980s, the *New York Times* and *Washington Post* printed about 100 articles each election season that mentioned political advertising, but that rose to 200 in 1988 before rising to approximately 250 in 2004 and 2008. Media coverage of advertising also extends to local news outlets. About 30% of coverage of US Senate races in local newspapers – and 20% of coverage on local television stations – mentioned political advertising (Fowler & Ridout, 2009).

Media coverage is slanted toward negative advertising. Negative ads aired in US Senate races in 2004 received almost four times the newspaper mentions of positive ads (Ridout & Smith, 2008), though this unrepresentative focus on negativity may not extend to coverage in other countries (Ridout & Walter, 2015).

The disproportionate media attention to negative advertising, at least in the US, matters because it influences people's perceptions of the tone of the race: media coverage of political advertising, when framed strategically, leads people to perceive campaigns as more negative (Ridout & Fowler, 2010).

The Future of Advertising Effects Research

With rare exception, the research cited in this review uses data from the US to draw conclusions about the effects of advertising. How far, then, do these effects travel, especially given the relatively unique campaign environment in the US, one of extremely long campaign seasons and ubiquitous television advertising? One way forward is to tap theories of media and campaign effects to help develop (and test) hypotheses about how advertising should matter elsewhere. For instance, in those countries that enforce a balance in campaign communications across parties by imposing spending limits or only allowing for free air time, might we find less impact of advertising? Should we find more impact of advertising in countries with more sophisticated ad production? A more comparative approach to the study of ad effects will be one important avenue for future research.

Another promising path forward is more investigation into how the content features of political advertising condition its effectiveness. Answering this question may require more collaboration with colleagues in marketing and advertising disciplines who study non-political advertising. It might also be fostered by partnerships with commercial firms that do online testing of ads in real campaigns. Instead of altering one or two ad features experimentally as has been our practice, we may be able to code the features of dozens of real ads to see how those features relate to the effectiveness of the ad. Mattes and Redlawsk (2015) provide a small-scale example of how this might be done.

Third, it may be helpful for scholars to think beyond just the most obvious effects of political advertising, such as persuasion and turnout, to consider how advertising might have an impact on the larger political system. How does advertising influence media coverage, for instance, and thus election results? How might advertising set expectations about candidate and party issue agendas and thus establish criteria for how those candidates and parties perform while in office?

The good news, of course, is that what we know as scholars about the impacts of political advertising has grown considerably in the past decade, closing some debates but opening up new and interesting questions for us to explore.

References

Ansolabehere, S., & Iyengar, S. (1995). *Going negative: How political advertisements shrink & polarize the electorate*. New York, NY: The Free Press.

Bartels, L. M. (2014). Remembering to forget: A note on the duration of campaign advertising effects. *Political Communication*, 31(4), 532–544.

Brader, T. (2006). *Campaigning for hearts and minds*. University of Chicago Press.

Brooks, D. J., & Murov, M. (2012). Assessing accountability in a post-*Citizens United* era: The effects of attack ad sponsorship by unknown independent groups. *American Politics Research*, 40(3), 383–418.

Cappella, J. N., & Jamieson, K. H. (1997). *The spiral of cynicism, the press and the public good*. New York, NY: Oxford University Press.

Collins, K. (2012). *Who gives? Political messages, activist motivations, and campaign contribution behavior*. Working paper. Retrieved from www.princeton.edu/politics/about/file-repository/public/Job_Market_Paper-Collins.pdf.

Da Silveira, B. S., & De Mello, J. M. (2011). Campaign advertising and election outcomes: Quasi-natural experiment evidence from gubernatorial elections in Brazil. *The Review of Economic Studies*, 78(2), 590–612.

Dardis, F. E., Shen, F., & Edwards, H. H. (2008). Effects of negative political advertising on individuals' cynicism and self-efficacy: The impact of ad type and message exposures. *Mass Communication & Society*, 11(1), 24–42.

Djupe, P. A., & Peterson, D. A. (2002). The impact of negative campaigning: Evidence from the 1998 senatorial primaries. *Political Research Quarterly*, 55(4), 845–860.

Dowling, C. M., & Wichowsky, A. (2015). Attacks without consequence? Candidates, parties, groups, and the changing face of negative advertising. *American Journal of Political Science*, 59(1), 19–36.

Fernandes, J. (2013). Effects of negative political advertising and message repetition on candidate evaluation. *Mass Communication and Society*, 16(2), 268–291.

Fowler, E. F., Franz, M. M. & Ridout, T. N. (2016). *Political advertising in the United States*. Boulder, CO: Westview Press.

Fowler, E. F., & Ridout, T. N. (2009). Local television and newspaper coverage of political advertising. *Political Communication*, 26(2), 119–136.

Franz, M. M., Freedman, P. B., Goldstein, K. M., & Ridout, T. N. (2007). *Campaign advertising and American democracy*. Philadelphia: Temple University Press.

Franz, M. M., Freedman, P. B., Goldstein, K. M., & Ridout, T. N. (2008). Understanding the effect of political advertising on voter turnout: A response to Krasno and Green. *The Journal of Politics*, 70, 262–268

Franz, M. M., & Ridout, T. N. (2007). Does political advertising persuade? *Political Behavior*, 29(4), 465–491.

Franz, M. M., & Ridout, T. N. (2010). Political advertising and persuasion in the 2004 and 2008 presidential elections. *American Politics Research*, 38(2), 303–329.

Freedman, P., Franz, M., & Goldstein, K. (2004). Campaign advertising and democratic citizenship. *American Journal of Political Science*, 48(4), 723–741.

Fridkin, K. L., & Kenney, P. J. (2004). Do negative messages work? The impact of negativity on citizens' evaluations of candidates. *American Politics Research*, 32(5), 570–605.

Fridkin, K. L., & Kenney, P. J. (2008). The dimensions of negative messages. *American Politics Research*, 36(5), 694–723.

Fridkin, K. L., & Kenney, P. J. (2011). Variability in citizens' reactions to different types of negative campaigns. *American Journal of Political Science*, 55(2), 307–325.

Garramone, G. M. (1984). Voter responses to negative political ads. *Journalism & Mass Communication*, 61(2), 250–259.

Geer, J. G. (2006). *In defense of negativity: Attack ads in presidential campaigns*. University of Chicago Press.

Geer, J. G. (2009). *Fanning the flames: The news media's role in the rise of negativity in presidential campaigns*. Working paper, Vanderbilt University. Retrieved from www.vanderbilt.edu/csdi/research/files/CSDI-WP-03-2010.pdf.

Gerber, A. S., Gimpel, J. G., Green, D. P., & Shaw, D. R. (2011). How large and long-lasting are the persuasive effects of televised campaign ads? Results from a randomized field experiment. *American Political Science Review*, 105(1), 135–150.

Goldstein, K. M., & Freedman, P. B. (1999). Measuring media exposure and the effects of negative campaign ads. *American Journal of Political Science*, 43(4), 1189–1208.

Goldstein, K. M., & Freedman, P. B. (2000). New evidence for new arguments: Money and advertising in the 1996 senate elections. *The Journal of Politics*, 62(4), 1087–1108.

Goldstein, K., & Ridout, T. N. (2004). Measuring the effects of televised political advertising in the United States. *Annual Review of Political Science*, 7, 205–226.

Gordon, B. R., & Hartmann, W. R. (2013). Advertising effects in presidential elections. *Marketing Science*, 32(1), 19–35.

Gotlieb, M. R., Scholl, R. M., Ridout, T. N., Goldstein, K. M., & Shah, D.V. (forthcoming). Cumulative and long-term campaign advertising effects on trust and talk. *International Journal of Public Opinion Research.*

Hall, M. G., & Bonneau, C. W. (2012). Attack advertising, the white decision, and voter participation in State Supreme Court elections. *Political Research Quarterly*, doi: 1065912911433296.

Hill, S. J., Lo, J., Vavreck, L., & Zaller, J. (2013). How quickly we forget: The duration of persuasion effects from mass communication. *Political Communication*, 30, 521–547.

Iyengar, S. (2011, April). The media game: New moves, old strategies. *The Forum*, 9(1), 1–6.

Jackson, R. A., Mondak, J. J., & Huckfeldt, R. (2009). Examining the possible corrosive impact of negative advertising on citizens' attitudes toward politics. *Political Research Quarterly*, 62(1), 55–69.

Just, M., Crigler, A., Alger, D., Cook, T., Kern, M., & West, D. (1996). *Crosstalk: Citizens, candidates, and the media in a presidential campaign.* University of Chicago Press.

Just, M., Crigler, A., & Wallach, L. (1990). Thirty seconds or thirty minutes: What viewers learn from spot advertisements and candidate debates. *Journal of Communication*, 40(3), 120–133.

Kahn, K. F., & Geer, J. G. (1994). Creating impressions: An experimental investigation of political advertising on television. *Political Behavior*, 16(1), 93–116.

Krasno J. S., & Green, D. P. (2008). Do televised political ads increase voter turnout? Evidence from a natural experiment. *Journal of Politics*, 70(1), 245–261.

Krupnikov, Y. (2011). When does negativity demobilize? Tracing the conditional effect of negative campaigning on voter turnout. *American Journal of Political Science*, 55(4), 797–813.

Lau, R. (1985). Two explanations for negativity effects in political behavior. *American Journal of Political Science*, 29, 119–138.

Lau, R. R., Sigelman, L., & Rovner, I. B. (2007). The effects of negative political campaigns: A meta-analytic reassessment. *Journal of Politics*, 69(4), 1176–1209.

Lipsitz, K. (2013). Issue convergence is nothing more than issue convergence. *Political Research Quarterly*, 66(4), 843–855.

Martin, P. S. (2004). Inside the black box of negative campaign effects: Three reasons why negative campaigns mobilize. *Political Psychology*, 25, 545–562.

Mattes, K., & Redlawsk, D. P. (2015). *The positive case for negative campaigning.* Chicago: University of Chicago Press.

McDonald, M. P., & Popkin, S. L. (2001). The myth of the vanishing voter. *American Political Science Review*, 95(4), 963–974.

Nai, A. (2013). What really matters is which camp goes dirty: Differential effects of negative campaigning on turnout during Swiss federal ballots. *European Journal of Political Research*, 52(1), 44–70.

Nai, A. (2015). The maze and the mirror: Voting correctly in direct democracy. *Social Science Quarterly*, 96(2), 465–486.

Patterson, T. E., & McClure, R. D. (1976). *The unseeing eye.* New York, NY: Putnam.

Pinkleton, B. (1997). The effects of negative comparative political advertising on candidate evaluations and advertising evaluations: An exploration. *Journal of Advertising*, 26(1), 19–29.

Pinkleton, B. E., Um, N. H., & Austin, E. W. (2002). An exploration of the effects of negative political advertising on decision making. *Journal of Advertising*, 31(1), 13–25.

Ridout, T. N., & Fowler, E. F. (2010). Explaining perceptions of advertising tone. *Political Research Quarterly*, 65(1), 129–145.

Ridout, T. N., & Franz, M. M. (2011). *The persuasive power of campaign advertising.* Philadelphia: Temple University Press.

Ridout, T. N., Franz, M., Goldstein, K. M., & Feltus, W. J. (2012). Separation by television program: Understanding the targeting of political advertising in presidential elections. *Political Communication*, 29, 1–23.

Ridout, T. N., Shah, D.V., Goldstein, K. M., & Franz, M. M. (2004). Evaluating measures of campaign advertising exposure on political learning. *Political Behavior*, 26(3), 201–225.

Ridout, T. N., & Smith, G. R. (2008). Free advertising: How the media amplify campaign messages. *Political Research Quarterly*, 61(4), 598–608.

Ridout, T. N., & Walter, A. S. (2015). How the news media amplify negative messages. In A. Nai & A. S. Walter (Eds.), *New perspectives on negative campaigning: Why attack politics matters* (pp. 267–286). Colchester: ECPR Press.

Scammell, M., & Langer, A. I. (2006). Political advertising in the United Kingdom. In L. L. Kaid & C. Holtz-Bacha (Eds.), *The Sage handbook of political advertising* (pp. 65–82). Thousand Oaks, CA: Sage.

Schenck-Hamlin, W. J., Procter, D. E., & Rumsey, D. J. (2000). The influence of negative advertising frames on political cynicism and politician accountability. *Human Communication Research*, 26(1), 53–74.

Shaw, D. R. (1999). The effect of TV ads and candidate appearances on statewide presidential votes, 1988–96. *American Political Science Review*, 93(2), 345–361.

Strach, P., Zuber, K., Fowler, E. F., Ridout, T. N., & Searles, K. (2015). In a different voice? Explaining the use of men and women as voice-over announcers in political advertising. *Political Communication*, 32(2), 183–205.

Sullivan, J. (2008). Campaign advertising and democracy in Taiwan. *The China Quarterly*, 196, 900–911.

Tedesco, J. C. (2002). Televised political advertising effects: Evaluating responses during the 2000 Robb-Allen senatorial election. *Journal of Advertising*, 32(1), 37–48.

Urban, C., & Niebler, S. (2014). Dollars on the sidewalk: Should US presidential candidates advertise in uncontested states? *American Journal of Political Science*, 58(2), 322–336.

Valentino, N. A., Hutchings, V. L., & Williams, D. (2004). The impact of political advertising on knowledge, Internet information seeking, and candidate preference. *Journal of Communication*, 54(2), 337–354.

Walter, A. S., Van der Brug, W., & Van Praag, P. (2014). When the stakes are high: Party competition and negative campaigning. *Comparative Political Studies*, 47(4), 550–573.

Wang, M., Gabay, I., & Shah, D. V. (2012). The civic consequences of "going negative": Attack ads and adolescents' knowledge, consumption, and participation. *The ANNALS of the American Academy of Political and Social Science*, 644(1), 256–271.

Weber, C., Dunaway, J., & Johnson, T. (2012). It's all in the name: Source cue ambiguity and the persuasive appeal of campaign ads. *Political Behavior*, 34, 561–584.

West, D. M. (2014). *Air wars: Television advertising and social media in election campaigns 1952–2012* (6th ed.). Washington, DC: CQ Press.

Zhao, X., & Chaffee, S. H. (1995). Campaign advertisements versus television news as sources of political issue information. *Public Opinion Quarterly*, 59(1), 41–65.

PART II

Airtime With No Charge for Electoral Advertising

7

POLITICAL ADVERTISING IN ARGENTINA

Martín D'Alessandro

Introduction[1]

It is a well-known fact that television advertisements have been present in electoral campaigns since the candidate Dwight Eisenhower used them in the US election of 1952. From there, the use of political television ads has disseminated and intensified in almost all modern democracies. Increasingly, in various areas of the world there are political advertisements, candidates are selected in part for their attractive image projected on the screen, experts advise candidates on marketing strategies, voters' attitudes and electorate's feelings, and media professionals are hired to produce convincing campaign pieces. Mass media have become the principal outlet for campaigns (Mancini & Swanson, 1996). In effect, the appearance, growth and development of the advertisements is a good example of the transformation of the role of communication media – television in particular – in electoral campaigns, and of the growth of independent voters (Ansolabehere & Iyengar, 1995). Since television campaign advertisements often attract public attention on a grand scale, parties and candidates put a lot of attention in the production of ads; journalism makes reference to them in their campaign coverage, and voters use ads to inform themselves before deciding their vote. Still, the study of electoral campaigns has not become an attractive object of study in Argentina.

We begin reviewing the increasing importance of political campaigns and ads in Argentina, especially taking into account external variables – political system, political context, media system and campaign regulations – that determine the way in which the ads are produced and also the way in which they distribute information about electoral politics. Next, we summarize the Argentine literature on television spots, and then present an empirical analysis of Argentine campaign ads in terms of their thematic and communication content. Later we examine the impact that changes in law regulations have had on Argentinian campaign communication. In addition, we consider the uses of Internet and social media for the last presidential campaign in Argentina, before offering some conclusions.

Television Advertisements: Institutions, Context and Regulation in Argentina

After some disagreement in the academic literature about campaign advertising, it is widely accepted that election advertisements are political messages televised in a campaign that are persuasive, produced by the parties themselves, and not mediated by the media. The defining element of ads is not the purchase of television space itself but the fact that the ads are non-mediated channels of communication between the party or the candidate and the electorate (Holtz-Bacha & Kaid, 2006; Kaid, 2004; Sádaba Garraza, 2003). This direct and almost unique relationship between the candidate and the electorate is further intensified because television language achieves a personal and intimate approach (Just et al., 1996), and because the advertisements have the power to be present along the whole campaign – with the corresponding legal restrictions in each case – while other forms of communication – like acts, rallies or pseudo-events – are episodic.

Argentina is a presidential democracy. So, the presidency is by far the most important political office. The president is elected directly by a two-round system for a term of four years with the possibility of one consecutive reelection. The legislative branch is bicameral. The 257 deputies are elected from closed party lists through proportional representation. Deputies terms last four years, and half of this chamber is renewed alternatively every two years. The Senate – Argentina is a federal country, and its 24 provinces have their autonomous constitution and their own governor and legislature – has three members per province, directly elected using closed party lists for a term of six years, with a limited allocation formula so that the plurality party gets two seats, and the follower obtains the third seat for the province in the Senate. One third of this chamber renews every two years. Presidents have important legislative powers – they can initiate laws, veto Congress' decisions, and issue decrees – and have immense budget discretion which allows them to build political power beyond their party or coalition.

The Argentine political party system has two large traditional parties, the PJ (Partido Justicialista) and the UCR (Unión Cívica Radical). Between 1946 and 2015, with the exception of military governments, presidents have been *justicialistas* (Peronists, from the PJ party) or *radicales* (from the UCR). Nonetheless, the Argentine political party system has not always been characterized as a two-party system, but as an inchoate system of moderate pluralism – with predominance of the PJ – due to the absence of ideological linkages between parties and voters, and the presence of "third parties" (Mainwaring & Torcal, 2005). Although almost all third parties have been flash parties, they have constituted important parliamentary blocks and/or participated in coalitions with the PJ or the UCR. Rather unexpectedly, a new "third party", PRO (Propuesta Republicana) arose in 2003, consolidated itself as a stable party and won the presidency in coalition with the UCR in 2015.

Proselytizing styles are the result of institutional dynamics, such as presidentialism and the electoral system, but also of cultural provisions. The return of democracy in 1983 – when more than 90% of Argentine households had at least one television (Martínez Pandiani, 2004) – marked the birth of a new phase in Argentine politics. The new willingness to make decisions collectively and substantive changes in social structure, such as the transfer of many employees to the self-employed worker sector, produced new perceptions and expectations, the weakening of old loyalties and the consequent growth of the independent vote (Cheresky, 2003; Mora y Araujo, 1991). Gradually, and with the acceptance of democratic rule, a perception of a disenchantment has emerged (Echegaray & Raimondo, 1987) in which citizens have retreated into private life and politics has been depreciated. At the same time, citizens have largely developed a new cultural interpretation characterized by a critical attitude to the ways in which power is exercised and to the linkages between the representatives and the represented. In fact, there has been a steady decline in the traditional identification of the people with the PJ and the UCR, and a sustained increase of people who cannot identify themselves in partisan terms. In sum, dealignment and voter volatility have emerged.

Even so, since 1983 the Argentine parties have been strong mechanisms of campaigning and they are still important in mobilizing traditional advocacy resources. In fact, there is a widespread practice of using public spaces as arenas of street actions and meetings. On the other hand, democratic stability has renewed electoral practices, in which the important role of the media and the use of professional communication techniques gained a strategic place.[2]

In this new context, campaigns actually have more weight than in previous periods of democracy in Argentina. Indeed, Argentine campaigns have been modernized from 1983, mainly due to this weakening of party identities (Waisbord, 1996) and also to a process produced by market-oriented reforms in the 1990s: increasing commercialization of traditional media, intensified competition among them, and the rise of Internet media. In sum, a "new context of media institutions" has emerged (Swanson, 2013). Nowadays there are four private and one public nationwide television channels, 103 local channels, and more than 600 cable-operators firms. Public television is not an important or competitive player in the market.

It has been argued that the characteristics of advertisements depend on the degree of regulation of the campaign environment in a given country; basically, the possibility of buying television airtime for ads (Kaid & Holtz-Bacha, 1995). Up to 2009, regulation in Argentina was minimal and television advertising time was freely available for purchase.

The first regulation was passed in the National Electoral Code in 1972, but it has been modified over time. Before 2009, free television airtime for political parties on radio and television were insignificant for Argentine presidential campaigns. As a further step in the difficult path of institutionalization of Argentina's political parties, the Law 16652 of 1963 provided some benefits and franchises to campaigns, such as media spaces, postal rights and free telephone lines (Jackisch, 1990). This particular law was repealed, reinstated and repealed again – however, the rules established no limits to the quantity of airtime that parties could buy on television for electoral purposes during campaign periods. As a result, paid ads were the highest expenditures of parties since the restoration of democracy.

At the end of 2009, the Argentine Congress passed Law 26571 that contains modifications in a number of important regulations about parties and elections. Specifically in relation to television ads, the new law prohibited private contracting for airtime. Half of radio and television time is distributed equally among all parties, and the other half is allotted in proportion to the quantity of votes received in the previous legislative election. The law includes the provision that all parties have access to prime-time space. Another law establishes that for presidential elections at least 600 hours must be distributed on television during the 25 days before the election. Finally, a decree states that television channels must assign 10% of their time free to parties, distributed in four time zones in such a way that political publicity should not exceed 120 seconds in each commercial break. Television spaces are raffled by the government, but parties can decide which spot to broadcast in each raffled space. The spots can last from one to ten units of 12 seconds each.

Because they are free of charge, electoral television ads democratize electoral competition by providing equal resources to all parties; however, since the parties produce the spots themselves, the production differences make disparity remain in the quality of the emitted pieces.

The State of Research in Argentina

The study of television ads is a very important area in the investigation of election campaigns (Farrell, 1996). Studies on their effects have evolved and become more sophisticated, but there is still controversy about whether the effects are concentrated on people who observe campaigns carefully on the less committed partisans and more apathetic voters (Just et al., 1996; Patterson & McClure, 1976), or on the most committed and the most indifferent at the same time (Ansolabehere & Iyengar, 1995; Kaid, 1981). Besides, one of the main characteristics in the US television ads is their negative character. This type of advertising – about half of total advertising – is what generates a reaction from independent voters, even if their disillusionment with politics is reaffirmed (Ansolabehere, Iyengar, & Valentino, 1994). If the effect of positive ads is, according to these authors, to reaffirm the loyalties of each party, then negative ads discourage the vote of the independents and provoke electoral abstention (Ansolabehere & Iyengar, 1995; Ansolabehere et al., 1994).

In Argentina voting is mandatory for all adult citizens (except those older than 70), and for that reason it is more difficult to evaluate those effects. We know that the means of mass communication have high impact on voters during campaigns in Argentina (D'Adamo & García Beaudoux, 2009), but we have no studies about spots effects. It is widely assumed that many people have learned to derive inferences from appearances of physical movements and visual information about candidates, and it has been argued that this learning may be more accessible and useful for voters than verbal messages (Landi, 1992). Nonetheless, most of the authors agree that the greatest effect of television ads is the – yet not measured – extent to which they provide information about candidates and issues.

The US perspective of television advertisements concentrates on candidates' attributes, but the scope of television ads is much broader, and ads have important cognitive effects: they are much more substantial and serious than many other campaign coverage. In this vein, a study of television news reports during the 2003 Argentine presidential campaign found that 71% of mentions of candidates referred to "horse race" and only 7% to candidates' proposals, and also that the content of their platforms suffered reductionism and limited time (Bitonte, 2005).

There is no systematic research on television ads content for the Argentine case. The few pieces on the topic are very descriptive, usually from the perspective of advertising techniques, analyzing few ads or one single election. Borrini (2005) provides the pioneer systematic study of campaigns, including some spots in its analysis. Martínez Pandiani (2004) concentrates much more on "videopolitics" than on spots. D'Adamo, García Beaudoux and Slavinsky (2005) made an exhaustive theoretical and empirical study of the 2003 presidential election, as well as García Beaudoux and D'Adamo (2006), while Chejter, Oberti and Varela (2000) analyze qualitatively some spots of the 1999 presidential election. Donot (2011) develops explanations on two spots of the PJ candidate Cristina Fernández' 2007 presidential campaign, and Aruguete (2013) and Slavinsky (2013) discuss some spots of her 2011 presidential campaign. Finally, in a Latin American comparative perspective, Riorda and Farré (2012) and Riorda (2013) study the 2007 Argentine presidential campaign, concluding that spots contain less ideology than traditional discourses.

Television Advertisements of Argentine Political Parties: Content Analysis

This section presents a content analysis of campaign television ads for the seven Argentine presidential elections between 1983 and 2011. A total of 343 ads were analyzed, of which 210 are of the PJ and 133 are of the UCR.[3]

The average duration of the ads is about 43 seconds. This data has comparative relevance, as well as it allows to deduce the impact of institutional variables that regulate the media system. Although it is accepted that the duration of the television advertisements depends on the media system and the regulations (Semetko, 1996), we will cast some doubt on this point in the next section. The peak in the duration of the spots occurred in 2007, when the average duration of the spots was 114 seconds for the incumbent PJ and 20 seconds for the UCR.

What are the issues that parties and candidates have addressed in their television ads? Content analysts usually code issues into several variables (Aruguete, 2013; Canelas Rubim, 2003; Cho, 2008; Just et al., 1996; Kaid, 2002; Norris, Curtice, Sanders, Scammell, & Semetko, 1999). We follow the basic lines of MARPOR's (Manifesto Research on Political Representation) methodology, originally designed for content analysis of party platforms but versatile for other types of discourse genres. Figure 7.1 shows, first, that the predominant issue area in television spots is the economy. It is apparent that, in general, the emphasis on issues is quite similar between the parties.

The relative convergence of issues in the ads is also found in the party manifestos (D'Alessandro, 2013). This convergence does not necessarily mean an ideological vacuum in the Argentine political system. It should be understood, however, that there is a basic consensus among the political elite.

Communicational Analysis

Basically, television ads can be positive or negative, and may relate to issues or to candidate's images (Kaid & Johnston, 2001). We take the variable "predominant communication" from Just et al. (1996), which encodes all possible combinations along these two cleavages. Each spot was analyzed if it

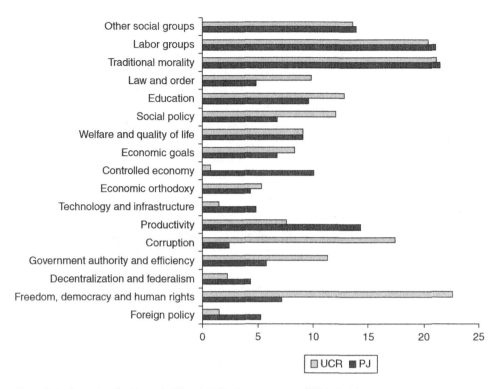

Figure 7.1   Issues in television ads, PJ and UCR, in percentages (1983–2011)

mentions: (a) candidate's character and achievements; (b) issues or candidate's issues; (c) the combination of both of them; and (d) some kind of attack (attack on opponent's character, attack on opponent's issues, attack on the combination of these two, attack on opponent's issues and promotion of the own, and attack on both opponent's character and issue and promotion of the own). Figure 7.2 shows the ads through these classic content analysis categories. Like the vast majority of countries in the world – with the notable exception of the US (Kaid, 1999; Kaid & Holtz-Bacha, 2006; Kaid & Johnston, 2001; Plasser & Plasser, 2002) – negative and/or image-centered messages do not have much weight in Argentina.

Do these communication outputs emerge as strategic alternatives according to parties' positions in the electoral competition, or are they linked to traditions and/or partisan decisions? As Figure 7.3 shows, although incumbents' ads attack slightly more, they also make more references about their own candidates and issues. Values and proportions are similar for the opposition.

One distinguishing characteristic of televised campaign messages is the ability to include emotional components. While there is not necessarily an inverse relationship between substantive information and the presence of emotional components, appealing to peoples' feelings does not increase the possibility of transmitting objective and substantive information. Television ads have been criticized for being superficial, by appealing to emotions, and therefore, not being compatible with "communicative rationality" and deliberation (Habermas, 2004 [1962]). According to this point of view, if an ad relies mainly on emotions, it probably tends to manipulate information. However, the audiovisual nature of television ads allows the transmission of messages using a number of resources that cannot be delivered exclusively on their discursive character.

Indeed, ads information is both visual and verbal, and there is no clear separation between issues and candidate's images (Holtz-Bacha, 2003; Kaid, 2002). In presidential systems, the image of candidates

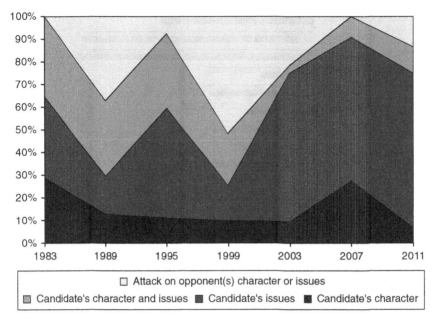

Figure 7.2 Type of predominant communication, PJ and UCR (1983–2011)

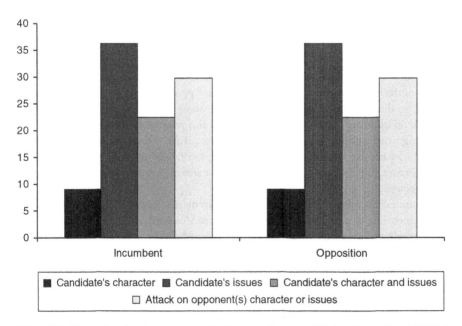

Figure 7.3 Type of predominant communication according to political position, PJ and UCR, in percentages (1983–2011)

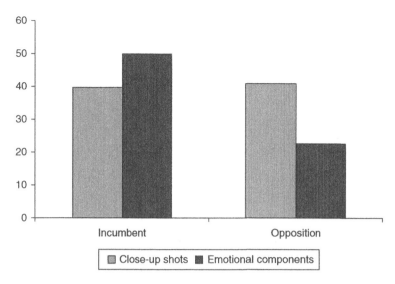

Figure 7.4 Close-up shots and emotional components according to political position, PJ and UCR, in percentages (2003–2011)

is an essential element in generating differences between presidential candidates. The negative or positive feelings that the images generate serve as cognitive shortcuts that voters use to decrease the cost of information collection (D'Adamo et al., 2005). For this reason, candidates try to use brief images with emotional symbols to synthesize far more abstract issues. In effect, the "videostyle" of a candidate combines verbal (substantive content), nonverbal (tone, movement, body, clothing, etc.) and production elements (scenes, angles, special effects, etc.) (Kaid, 2002, 2004). For the Argentine case, nonverbal images increase the attention given to verbal information: between 80 and 85% of what people retain of an election advertisement is visual (Aruguete, 2013; Sádaba Garraza, 2003). For that reason, the way in which visuals are staged in an advertisement is important, based on various esthetic and technical decisions.

Therefore, two other variables were designed to gather the kind of information that has been incorporated. First, according to the literature and to experts (Sádaba Garraza, 2003), pointing the camera at the candidate's face – if he/she is present in the ad – produces a non-rational "honesty effect." The indicator identifying "close-up shots" refers to whether the camera is (or not) on the candidate's face. Close-ups generate feelings of closeness and trust in the candidates whether or not there are references to their agenda issues. Second, "emotional components" refers to whether the ad effectively uses non-rational elements that appeal to voters' emotions. This is useful to estimate to what extent ads seek to generate emotions such as fear, anger, discontent, frustration, gratitude, hope, pride, etc. Figure 7.4 shows that the utilization of close-up shots is similar between government and opposition, while appealing to emotional components is never more than 50%, and much more used by incumbents than by challengers.

The Effects of the Rules

As mentioned above, electoral rules and norms that regulate campaign communication have an impact on the communication strategies of political parties and candidates (Mieres, 2013). The second section of this chapter referred to the prohibition of purchasing television ads that was adopted in Argentina in 2009. Has this produced any effect in the campaign strategies of parties? While it

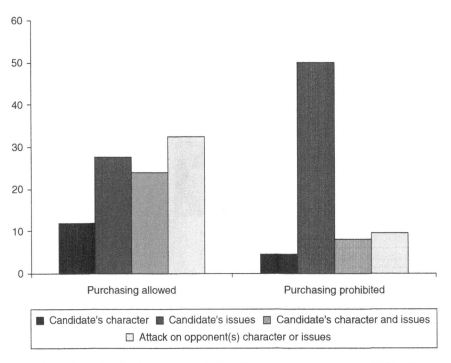

Figure 7.5 Type of predominant communication, PJ and UCR, in percentages (1983–2011)

would be too hasty to draw conclusions from such a recent change, an exploration of the topic could provide some partial insights.

A main argument of the empirically based comparative literature about advertisements (Holtz-Bacha & Kaid, 2006; Kaid & Holtz-Bacha, 2006; Tedesco, Jones, & Chanslor, 1999) states that the duration of the ads depends mainly on the available party funding, and that messages' information quality depends on the duration of the ads. In our case, after the prohibition of buying television space, the length of the ads has not been altered. Unexpectedly, however, the information contained in the ads does not indicate a quality reduction. On the contrary, a comparative glance suggests a more complex scenario. First, the campaign of 2011 under restrictive laws seems to have had more substance in terms of relevant political information for the public than the average presidential campaigns of the past: in 2011 there were fewer references to the candidates' character, fewer attacks on opponents, and more explanation on candidate's issues (see Figure 7.5). And second, in the 2011 campaign there was less use of the visual effect of close-up shots and less use of emotional resources that would reduce the probability of the implementation of rational public messages. It seems that a de-americanization of the ads has occurred unrelated to their length, but linked to the (de)regulation of the television space market.

Internet and Social Media

As recently argued, the Argentine environment is highly regulated for television. However, it is very poorly regulated with regard to Internet feeds. This is an additional reason why parties and candidates seek to use the Internet widely in periods close to Election Day, when television and radio advocacy is forbidden.

In Argentina, Facebook is the most popular social network. There are about 25 million Argentine registered users. For the 2015 presidential elections, the PJ candidate's Facebook site had almost 1.5 million likes, while Mauricio Macri's[4] Facebook site had more than 2.6 million likes. On Twitter, Argentina has almost 12 million accounts. About one million of them are politically active. Therefore, social media constitute a market of interest to politicians and candidates, who hire community managers and robots to spread information. Social media are dominated by institutional actors and by a hyperactive minority of users, whose messages circulate very fast and to a great extent (Calvo, 2015), and provide a great deal of information to traditional media (Parmelee, 2014). Although social networks have potential structural opportunities to transform democratic political communication (Tedesco, 2004) there is as much information concentration in the online world as in the traditional media (Boczkowski & Mitchelstein, 2013), and the issues that dominate public opinion are those of the traditional media more than the issues of the online social networks (Aruguete, 2015).

Although Twitter is more politically sensitive than Facebook (Calvo, 2015), during the last 10 days before the 2015 presidential election, there were only 2,453 tweets and re-tweets containing links or hashtags related to spots prepared for television broadcasting that originated in all parties' and candidates' Twitter accounts. Taking into account that Macri had more than 1.7 million followers and the PJ candidate, Daniel Scioli, had more than one million followers, tweets with links or hashtags related to spots are poorly re-tweeted. In other words, spots do not generate 2.0 interaction because they are evidently not the kind of information interesting to this community. On the contrary, on their YouTube channels, the former achieved more than seven million views of all his 43 ads, and the latter achieved more than five million views of all his 46 ads.

Conclusion

Television advertisements are key pieces of information that parties and candidates make to reach the citizenry during electoral campaigns. Despite the fact that audiovisual support makes it easy to appeal to emotions, television advertisements have cognitive effects: they offer useful information about parties, candidates and issues of each election. Furthermore, they can also stimulate the consumption of another type of political information and potentially generate greater discussion and deliberation. In fact, Argentine campaign ads between 1983 and 2011, despite their frequent appeal to emotional elements – and the utilization of audiovisual resources to generate the sensation of closeness with the electorate – offer important information about the priorities and agendas of presidential candidates. This compels the reconsideration of the general belief that the ads, and the personalization of campaigns, damage political content.

In terms of the specific issues contained in the ads, and their relative weight, there is a high degree of coincidence between the different parties in Argentine presidential elections. But that consensus does not mean that all parties agree about which issues to prioritize in each election. In other words, parties are not alienated but rather there is some consensus on public policy priorities. Overall, and despite the growing presence of US agencies and consultants, the ads do not contribute to negative campaigning, which these consultants often recommend.

In Argentina, election campaigns and particularly television ads have become more crucial as traditional identifications and certainties have waned. Democratic regime stability, political dealignment and disenchantment have made elections more and more decisive. In this context, electoral campaigns have professionalized, modernized and post-modernized organizationally and technologically. They have adopted new tools for marketing – such as the identification of different voter segments – and have increased the sophistication of their techniques through televised discourse, and gradually they have reorganized human resources and campaign methods.

Argentina shifted from a free market of television space to broadcast campaign spots to the complete prohibition of purchasing television spaces. It is still too difficult to make concrete statements about the impact of changes to Argentina's campaign regulation in terms of the quality of campaign messages. But unexpectedly, our data shows that the duration of spots, the references to the candidate's character and the attack strategy have not increased, but references to issues did.

Campaigns and advertisements are key factors of the functioning of democracy and representative government, so, further research is needed for the case of Argentina and also for other cases. Robust and empirically based theory can enlighten democratic knowledge and practice, strengthen democratic accountability, and benefit citizens around the world.

Notes

1   The author is grateful for research collaboration with Cecilia Rodríguez, Lara Goyburu and Paula Szewach.
2   Before 1983, the only precedent was the center-right winged party New Force, which carried out a professional campaign, including modern television spots in 1973.
3   The ads were gathered from private archives, consultants and the Internet. No "third party" ads have been included due to the extreme difficulty of finding them: some parties do not exist any more or are reduced to a minimal role, and key informants usually do not remember who made the ads or who kept a copy. Neither PJ nor UCR spots are in any partisan or public archive. The ads from UCR in 1989 include a few advertisements from minor parties that supported the UCR candidate, Eduardo Angeloz: Confederación Federalista Independiente, Partido Acción Transformadora and Partido Socialista Unificado. I also labeled as UCR the spots of the coalitions led by the UCR: Alianza para el Trabajo, la Justicia y la Educación in 1999, Concertación por Una Nación Avanzada in 2007 and Unión para el Desarrollo Social in 2011. While in the 1995 and 2011 presidential elections the coalitions Frepaso and Frente Amplio Progresista, respectively, came in second, they are still understood as "third parties."
4   Mauricio Macri belongs to the party PRO and won the presidency in 2015.

References

Ansolabehere, S., & Iyengar, S. (1995). *Going negative: How political advertisements shrink and polarize the electorate*. New York, NY: The Free Press.

Ansolabehere, S., Iyengar, S., & Valentino, N. (1994). Does attack advertising demobilize the electorate? *American Political Science Review*, 88, 829–838.

Aruguete, N. (2013). Argentina: Los valores en los spots de la campaña electoral de Crsitina Fernández (2011). In I. Crespo & J. Del Rey (Eds.), *Comunicación política & campañas electorales en América Latina* (pp. 269–283). Buenos Aires: Biblos.

Aruguete, N. (2015). *El poder de la agenda. Política, medios y público*. Buenos Aires: Biblos.

Bitonte, M. E. (2005). *Notas al pie. Monitoreo cualitativo de la campaña 2003*. Florida: Proyecto.

Boczkowski, P. J., & Mitchelstein, E. (2013). *The news gap: When the information preferences of the media and the public diverge*. Cambridge, MA: MIT Press.

Borrini, A. (2005). *Cómo se vende un candidato. Un siglo de camañas políticas en la Argentina*. Buenos Aires: La Crujía-KAS.

Calvo, E. (2015). *Anatomía política de Twitter en Argentina. Tuiteando #Nisman*. Buenos Aires: Capital intelectual.

Canelas Rubim, A. A. (2003). As imagens de Lula Presidente. In A. F. Neto & E. Verón (Eds.), *Lula Presidente: televisão e política na campanha eleitoral* (pp. 43–64). San Pablo: Hacker-Unisinos.

Chejter, S., Oberti, A., & Varela, G. (2000). Palabras de campaña. La campaña presidencial en Argentina. In *Silencios y susurros. Ciudadanía y género en las campañas presidenciales de Argentina, Chile y Uruguay*. Santiago de Chile: Programa Mujer y Democracia en el Mercosur.

Cheresky, I. (2003). En nombre del pueblo y de las convicciones: Posibilidades y límites del gobierno sustentado en la opinión pública. *POSTData*, 9, 83–123.

Cho, J. (2008). Political ads and citizen communication. *Communication Research*, 35, 423–451.

D'Adamo, O., & García Beaudoux, V. (2009). Medios y ciudadanos: Percepción pública del comportamiento de los medios de comuncación de masas durante la campaña paras las elecciones presidenciales de 2007 en Argentina. *POSTData*, 14, 65–95.

D'Adamo, O., García Beaudoux, V., & Slavinsky, G. (2005). *Comunicación política y campañas electorales. Estrategias en elecciones presidenciales*. Barcelona: Gedisa.

D'Alessandro, M. (2013). Las plataformas electorales en la Argentina moderna. *América Latina Hoy*, 65, 107–139.

Donot, M. (2011). Cristina Fernández de Kirchner, de "una reina" a la encarnación del pueblo de la Argentina. *Ensemble. Revista Electrónica de la Casa Argentina en París*, 12.

Echegaray, F., & Raimondo, E. (1987). *Desencanto político, transición y democracia*. Buenos Aires: CEAL.

Farrell, D. M. (1996). Campaign strategies and tactics. In L. LeDuc, R. G. Niemi, & P. Norris (Eds.), *Comparing democracies: Elections and voting in global perspective* (pp. 160–183). Thousand Oaks, CA: Sage.

García Beaudoux, V., & D'Adamo, O. (2006). Comunicación política y campañas electorales. Análisis de una herramienta comunicacional: el spot televisivo. *Polis*, 2, 81–111.

Habermas, J. (2004 [1962]). *Historia y crítica de la opinión pública*. Barcelona: Gustavo Gili.

Holtz-Bacha, C. (2003). Political advertising during election campaigns. In P. J. Maarek & G. Wolfsfeld (Eds.), *Political communication in a new era* (pp. 95–116). London: Routledge.

Holtz-Bacha, C., & Kaid, L. L. (2006). Political advertising in international comparison. In L. L. Kaid & C. Holtz-Bacha (Eds.), *The Sage handbook of political advertising* (pp. 3–13). Thousand Oaks, CA: Sage.

Jackisch, C. (1990). *Los partidos políticos en América Latina. Desarrollo, estructura y fundamentos programáticos. El caso argentino*. Buenos Aires: CIEDLA-KAS.

Just, M. R., Crigler, A., Alger, D., Cook, T., Kern, M., & West, D. (1996). *Crosstalk: Citizens, candidates and the media in a presidential campaign*. University of Chicago Press.

Kaid, L. L. (1981). Political advertising. In D. D. Nimmo & K. R. Sanders (Eds.), *Handbook of political communication* (pp. 249–271). Beverly Hills, CA: Sage.

Kaid, L. L. (Ed.). (1999). *Television and politics in evolving European democracies*. New York, NY: Nova.

Kaid, L. L. (2002). Videostyle and political advertising effects in the 2000 presidential campaign. In R. E. Denton Jr. (Ed.), *The 2000 presidential campaign: A communication perspective* (pp. 183–197). Westport, CT: Praeger.

Kaid, L. L. (2004). Political advertising. In L. L. Kaid (Ed.), *Political communication research* (pp. 155–202). New York, NY: Routledge.

Kaid, L. L., & Holtz-Bacha, C. (1995). A comparative perspective on political advertising: Media and political system characteristics. In L. L. Kaid & C. Holtz-Bacha (Eds.), *Political advertising in Western democracies: Parties and candidates on television* (pp. 8–18). Thousand Oaks, CA: Sage.

Kaid, L. L., & Holtz-Bacha, C. (2006). Television advertising and democratic systems around the world. In L. L. Kaid & C. Holtz-Bacha (Eds.), *The Sage handbook of political advertising* (pp. 445–457). Thousand Oaks, CA: Sage.

Kaid, L. L., & Johnston, A. (2001). *Videostyle in presidential campaigns: Style and content of televised political advertising*. Westport, CT: Praeger.

Landi, O. (1992). *Devórame otra vez. Qué hizo la televisión con la gente. Qué hace la gente con la televisión*. Buenos Aires: Planeta.

Mainwaring, S., & Torcal, M. (2005). La institucionalización de los sistemas de partidos y la teoría del sistema partidista después de la tercera ola democratizadora. *América Latina hoy*, 41, 141–173.

Mancini, P., & Swanson, D. L. (1996). Politics, media, and modern democracy: Introduction. In D. L. Swanson, & P. Mancini (Eds.), *Politics, media, and modern democracy* (pp. 1–26). Westport, CT: Praeger.

Martínez Pandiani, G. (2004). *Homo zapping. Política, mentiras y video*. Buenos Aires: Ugerman.

Mieres, P. (2013). Uruguay: Sistemas electorales y sus efectos sobre las estrategias de campaña. In I. Crespo & J. Del Rey (Eds.), *Comunicación política & campañas electorales en América Latina* (pp. 197–214). Buenos Aires: Biblos.

Mora y Araujo, M. (1991). El cuadro político y electoral argentino. In D. Nohlen & L. De Riz (Eds.), *Reforma institucional y cambio político* (pp. 207–235). Buenos Aires: CEDES-Legasa.

Norris, P., Curtice, J., Sanders, D., Scammell, M., & Semetko, H. A. (1999). *On message: Communicating the campaign*. London: Sage.

Parmelee, J. H. (2014). The agenda building functions of political tweets. *New Media & Society*, 16, 434–450.

Patterson, T., & McClure, R. (1976). *The unseeing eye: The myth of television power in national elections*. New York, NY: G. P. Putnam.

Plasser, F., & Plasser, G. (2002). *La campaña global. Los nuevos gurúes del marketing político en acción*. Buenos Aires: KAS-Temas.

Riorda, M. (2013). América Latina: ¡Ey, las ideologías existen! Campañas presidenciales y discursos ideológicos. In I. Crespo & J. Del Rey (Eds.), *Comunicación política & campañas electorales en América Latina* (pp. 25–54). Buenos Aires: Biblos.

Riorda, M., & Farré, M. (Eds.). (2012). *¡Ey, las ideologías existen! Comunicación política y campañas electorales en América Latina*. Buenos Aires: Biblos.

Sádaba Garraza, T. (2003). Los anuncios de los partidos en televisión. El caso de España. In S. Berrocal (Ed.), *Comunicación política en televisión y nuevos medios* (pp. 163–205). Barcelona: Ariel.

Semetko, H. A. (1996). The media. In L. LeDuc, R. G. Niemi, & P. Norris (Eds.), *Comparing democracies: Elections and voting in global perspective* (pp. 160–183). Thousand Oaks, CA: Sage.

Slavinsky, G. (2013). Argentina: Orquestación audiovisual en la campaña electoral de Cristina Fernández (2011). In I. Crespo & J. Del Rey (Eds.), *Comunicación política & campañas electorales en América Latina* (pp. 237–245). Buenos Aires: Biblos.

Swanson, D. L. (2013). Political news in the changing environment of political journalism. In P. J. Maarek & G. Wolfsfeld (Eds.), *Political communication in a new era: A cross-national perspective* (pp. 11–31). New York: Routledge.

Tedesco, J. C. (2004). Changing the channel: Use of the Internet for communicating about politics. In L. L. Kaid (Ed.), *Political communication research* (pp. 507–532). New York, NY: Routledge.

Tedesco, J., Jones, C. A., & Chanslor, M. (1999). Political television in evolving European democracies: Political, media, and legal system issues. In L. L. Kaid (Ed.), *Television and politics in evolving European democracies* (pp. 11–32). New York, NY: Nova Science Publishers, Inc.

Waisbord, S. (1996). Secular politics: The modernization of Argentina electioneering. In D. L. Swanson & P. Mancini (Eds.), *Politics, media, and modern democracy* (pp. 207–225). Westport, CT: Praeger.

8

PRIME TIME ELECTORAL PROPAGANDA

The Brazilian Model of Free Airtime

Alessandra Aldé and Felipe Borba

Our goal with this chapter is to introduce the reader to the particularities of the Brazilian model of electoral broadcast. To explain its features, we will begin by describing the legal provisions and the reintroduction of political advertising after the 1964–85 military dictatorship. Due to its historical and political relevance, the Brazilian Free Electoral Broadcast Airtime (FEBA) has been a central object of academic investigation, especially since the 1989 presidential election, primarily in the Communications Studies field and increasingly in Political Science. We will also broach the main characteristics of the Brazilian media system and pinpoint some relevant research results across time on the subject. Given the vast range of issues implied, our main object will be the presidential elections of the more recent period.

Brazilian Political and Electoral Systems: An Overview

Brazil, as all other Latin American countries, is a presidential republic. Presidents, as well as the other chief offices of the executive and deputies of the legislative branches, are elected by direct vote, which is compulsory for every citizen aged between 18 and 70 and optional for 16- and 17-year-olds, as well as for seniors above 70. Citizens may cast blank or null ballots in the electronic machine used since 1996, but unjustified absence is charged with a small fine and legal consequences such as not being able to apply for civil service employment and for passport issuance. Citizens may cast their vote for parties ("legendas") or for the parties' individual candidates, usually the preferred option.

Between October 2000 and October 2014, the year of the most recent general election in Brazil, the electorate expanded from a total of 109,826,263 voters to almost 143 million, which amounts to more than half the population, making Brazil one of the largest voting democracies in the world.

This electoral magnitude is combined with a pervasive media system that reaches almost every individual across the continental extent of the country. In spite of fast growth of the Internet, television is still the main communication medium, watched by 97% of the population, while 61% are habitual radio listeners and 47% routinely access the web. Print media such as newspapers and magazines are less popular, reaching 25% and 15% respectively. Television is also the preferred medium of 76.1% of the population, with radio preferred by 7.9%. More than two-thirds, 67%, of Brazilian women and 63% of men watch television daily, for an average of three hours and 30 minutes per day (Secretaria de Comunicação da Presidência, 2014). Brazilian voters, as much as ordinary citizens from other democracies, do not rank political issues among their main interests when seeking media outlets, but attend to them during the electoral period, sometimes called "the time of politics"

(Palmeira & Heredia, 1993). Thus, elections assume special relevance in everyday conversation, as do scandals and a few other extraordinary political subjects. Brazilian FEBA, the main focus of this chapter, contributes to the prominence of elections – especially for election to executive offices – due to its legal features as well as its discursive character, based mainly on audiovisual broadcast communication.

National-level elections, the "general elections" – for president, state governors and deputies, as well as federal representatives for the two chambers of Congress, Deputies and Senators – are held every four years, alternating in even years with municipal elections for mayors and city representatives (called "vereadores"), also for four-year mandates, except senators, who are elected by majority vote for eight-year mandates, contesting either one-third or two-thirds of the higher chamber seats in each election. All three levels of deputies (federal, state and municipal) are elected by a proportional open list system.[1]

Under the military dictatorship, following a coup in 1964, with severe setbacks for political and human rights, the regime held regular indirect elections for chief of state, which were all military until 1985. Elections were kept direct for federal and state representatives, as well as both branches of the municipal level, but parties were reduced to two, the pro-regime Arena and the moderately oppositional MDB, all other critical organizations being banned and persecuted. From 1966 to 1978, also governors and mayors of capitals and larger cities were chosen by the electoral college or appointed directly by the regime. By the beginning of the 1980s, responding to political and social pressure, the military initiated political redemocratization, gradually reinstating direct elections for all offices, allowing party formation in 1980 and direct election of governors and mayors in 1982. The years thereafter saw growing demands for political rights, probably best symbolized by the massive campaign for presidential direct vote, joined by all pro-democracy forces and various segments of civil society in 1984. Although not enough to achieve an amendment that would grant the right to voters, the movement further strengthened political opposition, contributing to the election of civilian Tancredo Neves (PMDB) in the 1985 indirect presidential election. Direct presidential elections were banned until 1989, when Fernando Collor de Mello, of PRN, won a tight contest against more than 20 candidates.

For the office of president, as well as for governors and mayors of larger cities, whenever a candidate does not reach the absolute majority of valid votes (50% + 1) in the first round, there is a second round between the two candidates with the highest vote totals. The last four Brazilian presidential elections were all decided on the second round, as was the 1989 election. The presidential term has a fixed duration of four years, and from 1998 to 2014 the president could be re-elected for a second consecutive term. However, legislation is currently under revision by the Congress and re-election may be banned for executive offices in coming elections. As is, executive incumbents of the three levels may still run for a third non-consecutive term.

According to Shugart and Carey's classification (1992), Brazilian presidents are considered among the most powerful in the world. They have total and partial veto power, the initiative in proposing laws (and the exclusive initiative of proposing budget and fiscal legislation). Presidents may issue binding decrees and may demand urgent action by the legislature. Presidents are both chiefs of state and of government. They nominate all of the cabinet of ministers, which is formed after negotiation with allied parties. They also appoint Supreme Court judges. Although the term of office has a fixed duration of four years, Brazilian legislation allows for its interruption through a process of impeachment by Congress, such as the one Dilma faced in 2016. This mechanism was used once, to oust the first president elected after the military regime, Fernando Collor de Mello, who resigned to avoid the process.

Brazil combines a majoritarian system for the executive branch with elections for state and federal legislative offices which are simultaneous and unbinding – a candidate may be elected president from a minority party or a party with no elected representatives. In the 2014 elections, 11 candidates ran for president, while the number of parties with representatives in the lower chamber rose from

22 to 28, a world record of party fragmentation. The party of the president elected (PT or Partido dos Trabalhadores, the Workers' Party) had only 70 deputies, or 13.6% of the total 513 House seats. The resulting coalition presidentialism implies heavy dependency on legislative alliances and support to ensure governability (Power, 2010).

In spite of the high degree of fragmentation in the Brazilian party system, in the recent democratic period presidential elections have been characterized by stability. Since 1994, the second election after the end of military regime, the PT and the PSDB (Brazilian Social-Democratic Party) have polarized the presidential vote. In 1994 and 1998, the PSDB elected Fernando Henrique Cardoso and re-elected him on first round in 1998. From 2002 until the present, however, the PT came out on top with the election of Luis Inácio Lula da Silva in 2002 and 2006, and Dilma Rousseff in 2010 and 2014. The difference between first and second place has fallen gradually since Lula's first election. PT's fourth consecutive presidency was won in the most disputed election in Brazilian history since redemocratization.

History and Regulation of Electoral Broadcasting

To understand the scope and relevance of Brazilian electoral advertising, it is useful to briefly describe Brazil's media system. According to the Federal Constitution of 1988,[2] Brazilian broadcasting is a public concession controlled by central government and is required to observe a "principle of complementarity of the private, public and state systems" (Art. 223). Nevertheless, this power has been traditionally used to grant concessions to political allies. Until today most radio and television companies are privately owned by politicians, their relatives or associates (Lima, 2006). Many federal deputies are involved in the corporate media business, which makes regulation a difficult matter. There are neither anti-monopolistic nor cross-ownership limitations, and with the exception of a few public channels with low audience numbers, all major media outlets are owned by private family corporations.

The main television channel, Rede Globo, flourished thanks to its support of the military dictatorship, as an important asset to the regime's plan of national integration. In fact, it was the military that financed the microfiber net which enabled national television to be broadcast all over the country. During the following decades, there were moments in which Globo's main newscast, Jornal Nacional, was watched by 70% of the country's population, and the company has always played an active political role, supporting preferred candidates and governments throughout the democratization and recent democratic period (Porto, 2006, 2012).

Given this biased journalistic landscape, party access to broadcasting has become crucial to citizen information and alternation of power. Political advertising is aired twice a year on radio and television during the FEBA (in Portuguese usually HGPE or Horário Gratuito de Propaganda Eleitoral). The model regulates the distribution of time slots to parties for free access to electronic media. Paid political advertising is forbidden in electronic media, but allowed in print. Although it is free for parties and mandatory for broadcasting companies, the government pays for it in the form of a fiscal waiver. Airtime is divided in two types: longer programs at fixed hours and shorter 30-second spots inserted during regular programming. In addition to electoral airtime in election years, parties are entitled to Free Party Broadcast Airtime, also mandatory for all open access channels and aired in both formats twice every year, except for electoral ones. Although these broadcasts are supposed to be used exclusively to disseminate party values and platforms, they end up serving as accessory electoral propaganda spaces for party leaders.[3]

The FEBA was instituted by Law n. 4737 in July 1965, as part of the Brazilian electoral code created by the military government. Since its creation, although keeping its central features, electoral airtime has undergone several changes relative to its length, distribution among parties and candidates and daily time allocated to the campaigns – the most recent law was approved in September 2015.

Brazilian elections are highly regulated, falling under both the Electoral Code and decisions by an assigned branch of the justice system, the Superior and Regional Electoral Courts (TSE and various TREs), staffed by professional judges. Campaign use of communication strategies is thus limited by specific national law, as well as the interpretation of appeals by Electoral Judges. Regulation also includes content and format specifications, on several occasions tailored to suit party interests.

During the earlier democratic intervals in Brazilian political history (1889–1930 and 1945–64) electoral advertising was also used, possible with limited role of electronic media such as radio and television. Even during the military dictatorship, some episodes exemplify the historical relevance of FEBA. In the 1974 elections for the legislature, the oppositional MDB (Brazilian Democratic Movement) organized a very successful campaign, winning the majority of the Federal Chamber. The government's reaction was to strictly regulate electoral broadcasting: In the following elections, parties were only authorized to air the candidate's still photograph and brief description, without filmed footage, jingles or editing. This legislation, known as the Falcão law on behalf of the minister who enacted it, was cleverly interpreted by the MDB in 1978 through an electoral program that stated the party's achievements and principles (instead of the individual candidates, as expected) while the slow succession of the candidates' pictures suggested they were all members of the opposition's great project. In the 1982 state elections, with parties already re-established, the opposition kept challenging the regime, winning governor mandates in important states such as Rio de Janeiro and São Paulo.

Only in 1985, in the elections for state capitals, was the FEBA allowed more freedom, with the use of filmed footage, music and other audiovisual resources. In that election, well designed campaigns by media professionals helped unknown politicians obtain success against well-established party machines or political oligarchies, such as in the election of Maria Luiza Fontenelle, a radical member of PT who was elected against all odds as mayor of Fortaleza thanks to a series of appealing programs.

In 1989, almost 30 years since the 1960 election of Jânio Quadros, Brazilians were again entitled to choose their president directly. Important constitutional modifications were introduced. For the first time, the president's election would be decided over two rounds and singular, that is, not bound to the Senate, governors and deputies elections, which had been the case in the previous year. Law n. 7.773/1989 established that electoral broadcasts would be aired for a total of 59 days, with 140 daily minutes, divided in two 70-minute slots, in early afternoon and in the evening. Distribution of airtime among parties followed the size of each party's parliamentary representation in Congress. Parties without congressional representation would be allowed 30 seconds daily. A total of 22 candidates took part in the presidential race, including several of the most prominent political leaders.

The 1994 presidential election occurred in a markedly different institutional and political context, where Electoral Law n. 8.713/1993 introduced significant changes. The president's election was bound to the vote for Senate, Chamber of Deputies, state governments and state assemblies, which deeply altered the politics of electoral alliances and coalitions, which were bound to consider simultaneously the various seats up for office. The new electoral legislation also introduced changes in campaign rules. The most controversial topic was the article that forbade candidates and parties to air outdoor filmed footage, computer graphics and other audiovisual resources in their FEBA programs – only studio-generated images could be produced and transmitted. The official argument was to limit manipulation, given the previous election of Collor, a well-trained media-savvy candidate who bypassed more traditional politicians and was unable to finish his term due to corruption charges. In fact, the governing coalition and its candidate, then Minister of Finance, Fernando Henrique Cardoso, also feared the strength of images from Lula's well-documented Caravan of Citizenship. Central to the PT's strategy for the 1994 election, it showed Lula traveling all over Brazil to "get to know" – and become known by – its people and problems. In more recent elections, the ban on outdoors filmed footage was limited to spots.

For the first time, the legislation also defined the schedule of broadcast and time distribution for different offices. Candidates for president were allowed 30 minutes in each slot, for governor 20 minutes, and for senator 10 minutes. Airtime for deputies was divided equally between federal and state levels. The overall time for each office was then divided among parties following Article 74, which states that, for presidential office, 10 minutes are distributed equally among all parties or coalitions running; the 20 remaining minutes were distributed according to each party or coalition's representation in the Chamber of Deputies. As for the Senate, the total ten minutes were divided equally, while for governors half the time was equally distributed and the other half according to parties or coalitions size in the Federal Chamber. Distribution of airtime for deputies (federal and state levels) followed the same rule as the presidential campaign (see Table 8.1).

The fact that FEBA distribution follows party size in the Federal Chamber has, as political byproduct, caused parties and politicians to behave strategically, seeking electoral coalition with already well established organizations and providing for much party changing after elections (which is legal in Brazil), ideology being considered depending on the party (Krause, Dantas, & Miguel, 2010). Particularly the PMDB, as the main congressional force, has also become an important electoral player, courted by both PT and PSDB, in spite of not having had its own presidential candidate since 1994. Electoral coalitions then turn into government power, with many ministries and secretaries being assigned to electoral allies.

Electoral Law 9.504/1997 introduced some significant changes to the 1998 general elections. The principal novelty was making it possible for the re-election of incumbents of the executive branch, altering a norm in effect since the beginning of the Republic in 1889. It also changed the length of campaigns to 45 days, with two 50-minute free airtime slots. Electoral broadcasting was no longer aired on Sundays, and federal candidates (president and deputies) were allocated three days per week, alternating with state candidates (governors, state deputies and senators).

The 1998 electoral law brought to the national level the use of short spots, which had already been used in previous municipal elections: radio and television outlets would reserve additional 30 daily minutes, divided equally among all offices. This meant access to six minutes' worth of spots each for president, governor, federal and state deputies and senators, again subdivided by the parties' size in Congress. Spots could be 15, 30 or 60 seconds long. Distribution of spots during regular broadcast programming is regulated as well (Borba, 2015a). Campaigns do not choose when and where to air their spots, but must follow the media map designed by the TSE, which defines, in advance and by random draw, the days and audience slots in which parties air their spots. The rules determine that spots be divided equally by the number of campaign days and, for each particular day, be distributed among different audience slots, granting all parties access to hours of lesser and greater visibility (see Table 8.2). Thus, for example, if a candidate is allocated 45 campaign spots, they must air one per day in alternate slots, refraining from concentrating their spots closer to Election Day or in hours with larger audiences. Candidates also do not control the programs and specific hours during which spots will be aired, a decision made by the radio or television companies. This leaves little room for targeting specific constituencies or social segments.

Finally, TSE rules over content aired both in the programs and spots, with direct bearing on the negativity of campaigns. FEBA follows the general principle of free content and there is no prior censorship, but it is prohibited to air messages that may "degrade or deride candidates or parties." Legislation provides two possible effects: TSE may order the withdrawal of the campaign piece and/or concede right of reply in equivalent airtime, taken from the offender's allowance, to answer offensive attacks.[4] Although the concession of right to reply is not frequent, its existence affects campaigns tactics: the cost of being punished by the justice system and losing television time to opponents makes candidates more cautious when using negative campaign spots. Another consequence is the growing judicialization of campaigns, with professional legal counselling to guide campaign appeals and avoid improper attacks.

Table 8.1 Regulation of presidential FEBA programs distribution

	1989	1994	1998–2014	2016
Electoral law number	7.773	8.713	9.504	9.504 (modified by Law 13.165)
Beginning and end of propaganda term	Between September 15 and November 12	60 days running until two days before election	45 days running until two days before election	35 days running until two days before election
Airing days	Daily	Sundays, Mondays, Wednesdays and Fridays	Tuesdays, Thursdays and Saturdays	Tuesdays, Thursdays and Saturdays
Number of programs	59 programs	34 programs	20 programs	15 programs
FEBA total time	140 daily minutes divided in two 70-minute slots	60 daily minutes divided in two 30-minute slots	50 daily minutes divided in two 25-minute slots	25 daily minutes divided in two 12.5-minute slots
First round distribution of airtime	30 seconds for parties with no deputies. For parties or coalitions with elected representatives: up to 20 (5 min) 21 to 60 (10 min) 61 to 120 (13 min) 121 to 200 (16 min) above 200 (22 min)	10 minutes equally divided among all parties and coalitions and 30 minutes divided proportionally to the number of representatives each party or coalition had when the law was published (September 30, 1993)	One-third equally divided among all parties and two-thirds divided proportionally to the number of representatives each party or coalition had on previous election day	One-tenth equally divided among all parties and nine-tenths divided proportionally to the number of representatives each party or coalition had on previous election day
Second round distribution of airtime	40 daily minutes equally divided between candidates since the day after the official proclamation of first round results until 48 hours before election	30 daily minutes equally divided between candidates during 20 days up to two days before election	40 daily minutes equally divided between candidates since 48 hours after the official proclamation of first round results until two days before election	40 daily minutes equally divided between candidates since 48 hours after the official proclamation of first round results until two days before election

Source: Authors on the basis of data from the Supreme Electoral Court (Tribunal Superior Eleitoral at www. tse.jus.br/).

In 2015, electoral legislation underwent new changes with the proposition of Law 13.165, applying to the 2016 municipal elections and thereafter. Radio and television campaigns were reduced from 45 to 35 days, with half the time per day: from two 25-minute slots to two 12.5-minute ones. Legislation has further concentrated FEBA access to major parties: the new formula allows 90% of total time distributed proportionally to the size of parties in Congress, and only 10% equally divided among all.

On the other hand, the total time for slots was increased from 30 to 70 minutes per day, to be divided in equal shares among the campaigns for president, governors, senators, federal and state

Table 8.2 Regulation of FEBA spots distribution

	1998–2014	2016
Electoral law	9.504	9.504 (modified by Law 13.165)
Beginning and end of FEBA	45 days running until two days before election	35 days running until two days before election
Broadcast days	Daily	Daily
Broadcast time	6 daily minutes	14 daily minutes
Audience slots	1: 8h to 12h 2: 12h to 18h 3: 18h to 21h 4: 21h to 24h	1: 5h to 11h 2: 11h to 18h 3: 18h to 24h
Duration of pieces	15, 30 or 60 seconds	30 or 60 seconds
Time division among candidates (first round)	One-third equally divided among all parties and coalitions and two-thirds divided proportionally to the number of representatives elected for previous term of office	One-tenth equally divided among all parties and coalitions and nine-tenths divided proportionally to the number of representatives elected for previous term of office
Time division between candidates (second round)	40 daily minutes, equally divided between the two candidates, beginning 48 hours after the proclamation of first round results and running until two days before the election	40 daily minutes, equally divided between the two candidates, beginning 48 hours after the proclamation of first round results and running until two days before the election

Source: Authors on the basis of data from the Supreme Electoral Court (www.tse.jus.br/).

representatives (14 minutes each) during the daily broadcasting period. FEBA spot distribution now has three audience slots: from 5 a.m. to 11 a.m., 11 a.m. to 6 p.m. and 6 p.m. to midnight. Campaigns may no longer subdivide 30-second spots into shorter ads. Live and outdoors footage is permitted again, as well as editing, computer graphs, animation and special effects.

Regulation of the Internet campaign is relatively new. Seen as a strategic medium to reach opinion leaders, it has had growing investment from parties and candidates, especially due to looser regulation, which has made negative propaganda easier than in traditional mass media, subject to strict legal monitoring. Since 2002, although the Internet was not yet widespread among most the electorate, it has been used to publicize attacks, slanders and satires, often aimed at journalistic media, who in turn gave them a visibility that could not be obtained solely online (Aldé & Borges, 2006).

Presently Internet electoral use is governed by Law 12.034, of 2009, incorporated into Law 9.504, still in force and basically unchanged. Internet advertising is permitted beginning August 15 of the electoral year and forbidden in the 48 hours before Election Day and the 24 hours thereafter, whenever a second round is to take place. Official electoral campaign materials may be exhibited on sites belonging to candidates, their parties or coalitions, through electronic addresses by Internet service providers established in Brazil that must be listed to the respective Electoral Court. Candidates, parties and coalitions may also campaign through blogs, social media, and instant or electronic free message services to registered addresses. In this latter case, voters must be able to unregister, the sender being obliged to comply within 48 hours. Finally, it is forbidden to publish electoral broadcast pieces or other electoral advertising on sites belonging to private or public companies, agencies or hosted by direct or indirect public administration offices.

As with FEBA, the law establishes the right of response also for Internet offenses, to be aired through the same outlet, in equivalent space, time, page, size and features as the piece judged offensive. Response must remain available online for at least twice the time during which the offensive message was available.

The Internet may be growing as an electoral communication platform, involving dedicated teams and social media strategists, but television still accounts for the main share of campaign expenditures, along with opinion polling. Although parties and candidates do not pay for air-time, major candidates' budgets include the cost of producing professional television programs that can be several minutes long, as well as the expensive fees charged by high-profile marketers, their crews and studios, in what has become a million-dollar business in Brazil. Values officially declared to the TSE for the 2014 elections reached, considering all candidates running for office (president, governors, senators, state and federal deputies), the total sum of R$5.1 billion (around US$2 billion at the time). Legal and illegal campaign financing, through slush funds (known as "caixa dois"), is at the core of most corruption scandals revealed in Brazil during the past decades, involving all major parties.

FEBA Language and Content Research

Brazilian FEBA follows a distinctive model, its distribution and language differing from the more commercial American model of political advertising, as well as from the ones where parties are granted specific spaces that have to be actively sought by citizens, such as in France or the UK, where they are limited to certain (usually public) channels. The system combines access which is free for parties and highly visible for citizens, since it occupies national prime-time broadcasting and is mandatory for all open radio and television channels simultaneously, while penetration of paid television channels and other alternative media outlets is still relatively small. According to Albuquerque (2005), it should be analyzed as electoral propaganda, due to the more political nature of the latter concept. Featuring lengthier programs, sometimes several minutes long, campaigns in Brazil resort to a variety of audiovisual formats and styles, in addition to high impact commercial advertising.

The specific rhetorical language of FEBA is influenced by television journalism as well as commercial advertising. In Brazil, the progressive professionalization of campaigns mobilized not only marketing admen, but also some television journalists and editors, who frequently take temporary leaves to pursue the challenges (and high pay) of electoral campaigns. Many of TV Globo's former news people opened up their own publicity agencies. Television news language and aesthetics are especially relevant to the longer programs, where larger parties were entitled up to 12 daily minutes of prime-time broadcast. Journalistic formats such as interviews, documentaries and anchor people contribute to the perceived credibility of programs, although other formats, such as fiction sketches and chat shows, were also used on occasion.

As we saw, the Brazilian model is party oriented: even executive campaigns are granted time according to their size in Congress. Studies show that parties have used this space to strengthen their image (Dias, 2013). Nevertheless, votes tend to be personalistic, and so do FEBA main communication strategies. Despite the variety of formats, personal features, past achievements and positions on issues are more relevant than party ideology and platform.

Brazilian academic research on political and electoral broadcasting has focused mainly on presidential elections, with specialization and publications increasing alongside the redemocratization process. A search through the Directory of Masters Dissertations and Doctoral Theses kept by Compolítica, the Brazilian Association of Researchers on Political Communication, counted more than 80 publications under the "Political marketing and advertising" category (Aldé, Chagas, & Santos, 2013).[5]

The 1989 election was a landmark for political communication studies, all main parties investing and experimenting with the new communication and persuasion possibilities. The election results, where newcomers Collor and Lula achieved the second round, leaving behind established politicians, contributed to the perception that FEBA had played a significant role. Albuquerque (1999) analyzed in detail three of the most innovative campaigns, stressing the creative use, by Lula's PT, of television formats that were parodies of popular Globo Network programs.

During the 1990s, FEBA reached a high degree of professionalization, with party leaders and platforms submitted to marketing strategies and opinion polls, all major campaigns relying on multiple daily focus groups to assess the efficiency of programs and spots. Campaign costs escalated accordingly.

The elections of 1994 and 1998 brought more conservative communication strategies. In both cases, the front runner was the incumbent Fernando Henrique Cardoso (PSDB), and the campaign was heavily based on the popular success of an economic stabilization plan, which for the first time in years managed to control inflation. FEBA programs and spots were used to strengthen the positive feeling toward the economy, supported by news coverage that stressed the role of Cardoso, as Finance Minister, in the government's economic success. PT's television campaign, on the other hand, was impaired by legal restrictions on content, which kept the party from using the main narrative it had been preparing, namely Lula's Caravan of Citizenship, based on outdoors film footage.

Shorter spots, introduced in the 1996 mayoral contests, emphasized strategies closer to the American model, with more high impact and visual appeals. Even in this format, Brazilian FEBA maintained a less aggressive approach, compared to international experiences (Figueiredo, Aldé, Jorge, & Dias, 2000). However, negative campaigning is more usual in spots (as well as radio and Internet) than in the lengthier programs, because it is easier to conceal the identity of attackers, avoiding possible negative side effects on voters. Negative campaigning is more intensive in second rounds, among candidates running behind in the polls and in re-election years (Borba, 2015b).

In 2002, another much analyzed campaign was seen as crucial in helping Lula finally to get elected president – directed by a high-profile adman, Duda Mendonça, the campaign set an emotional tone to programs and spots, addressing Lula's main obstacles to obtain the support of the majority of voters: his perceived radicalism as a union leader, and his lack of formal education skills, up to then an expected feature of Brazilian political leaders. Professedly aimed at softening Lula's image into a new "Lulinha paz e amor" (Little Lula peace and love), more palatable to the general voter, the campaign also benefited from the negative assessment of the Cardoso government. José Serra, the candidate supported by the incumbent President Cardoso, concentrated in presenting his personal qualifications as former Minister of Health, trying to avoid the burden of incumbency and to show his differences from Cardoso, but Lula's identification as "the change" made it difficult to campaign on similar grounds.

Lula's re-election, in 2006, although explained mainly by the success of government's social and economic results, managed to block the opposition's strategy of pointing at the corruption scandal known as the Mensalão. As is usual with incumbent candidacies, it followed a more journalistic approach, presenting the government's feats in more journalistic language, with data on achievements, news media reproductions and documentary style stories. It still relied on Lula's identification as "one of the people," contrasting with oppositional PSDB's more elitist discourse and candidate, São Paulo former governor Geraldo Alckmin. Since his first participation in presidential campaigns, Lula was able to establish his image as a popular leader, committed to a social agenda (Panke, 2015).

The Mensalão scandal involved several of PT's leaders who were accused and arrested for bribing parliament members to approve party proposals. As a result, the election of 2010 found the party short of natural candidates. Lula's choice was for Dilma Rousseff, a former cabinet member who, however, had never stood for election. The campaign strategy counted on Lula's success and persona to popularize Dilma, using her more technical profile to the advantage of the candidate, presented as a loyal follower of Lula's successful policies and not a "typical politician," negatively viewed by most of the electorate. The campaign did not stress the gender factor, in spite of stating that Dilma would be "the first woman president"; femininity had to be dosed with "masculine" authority to dodge gender prejudice, an important feature of Brazilian politics, where female representation is amongst the smallest worldwide.

The polarization of presidential contests, in this respect, favored PT both in this and the next election, in 2014, which relied heavily on the comparison argument and the underlying threat that the country could lose the conquests of the Lula years and "go back" to the previous negative scenario, attributed to the rival PSDB, then headed by the former Minas Gerais governor Aécio Neves. This strategy resonated mainly with the majority of the population that benefited from PT's policies. That support was sufficient to give the party a narrow victory, although it faced a mounting economic crisis and new corruption charges, this time linked to the country's state oil company, Petrobrás.[6]

Impact on Brazilian Voters of FEBA and Campaign Strategies

The different formats of electoral free broadcasting airtime – lengthier regular programs versus 30-second spots aired during normal programming – each have their advantages. Advocates of the traditional programs argue those longer propaganda programs are important as they allow candidates to develop their campaign arguments to a greater extent.

Other political analysts and consultants argue in favor of shorter spots and against longer programs, their impact being considered disproportionate in regard to the campaign budget share needed to produce them (Lavareda, 2009). Short spots are valued by campaign strategies focusing on agility and unpredictability. Inserted in the middle of regular broadcasting, electoral spots reach a broader audience, which has no time to divert its attention, contrary to what happens during longer programs, when voters may turn to paid television, the Internet or simply turn off the television. FEBA longer programs have overall fewer viewers than spots. Coimbra (2008), analyzing opinion polls on the media habits of Brazilian voters during 2002 and 2006 presidential elections, states that half the population had watched the programs "rarely" or "not at all."

Since the 1989 presidential election, several surveys were conducted to assess how voters relate to the FEBA. The picture offered by Coimbra on the level of exposure in 2002 and 2006 has not changed much since then, although longitudinal analysis is hampered by the different phrasing of the question over time and surveys being conducted by institutes with diverse methodologies.

Even so, evidence suggests that audience varies over the length of campaign and also between the two electoral turns. It also varies according to voters' profiles, being significantly greater among viewers who are interested in politics and support for the mandatory vote – and, to a lesser degree, among those with higher income and higher educational level.

The number of people who report having seen at least one of the electoral broadcasts grows over campaign time and is greater for second round programs. In the 2010 presidential election, Datafolha Institute carried out a series of surveys asking citizens about their exposure to FEBA. The question did not mention the intensity of exposure – if FEBA was viewed many or few times – but only if voters had or not watched at least one program. According to Figure 8.1, we note the percentage of voters who declare having seen it at least once starts low, rises and stabilizes at around half the electorate, then rises markedly in the passage from first to second round. In 2010, the first round was held on October 3, and the second round electoral airtime went from October 6 to 28; Election Day was on October 31.

Although relevant, the viewer percentage by itself is not a given measure of the success or failure of electoral broadcasts. It is important also to analyze whether electoral advertising has some kind of effect on voters. Most studies about electoral campaigns suggest that television broadcasts have an effect on voting. These studies used different methodological approaches, such as aggregate data analysis, experiments, surveys, focus groups and in-depth interviews (Borba & Figueiredo, 2014; Borba, Veiga, & Bozza, 2015; Figueiredo, 2007; Figueiredo & Aldé, 2010; Figueiredo & Coutinho,

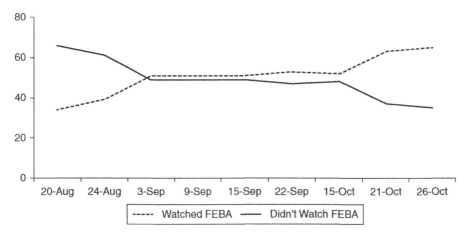

Figure 8.1 Electoral broadcast television programs viewing
Source: Datafolha Research Institute.

2003; Lourenço, 2009; Mundim, 2010, 2012; Pimentel, 2016; Veiga, 2001), finding evidence that significant shifts in voter preference during presidential campaigns can be attributed to the presence of advertising on radio and television.

Electoral advertising has also an impact on the level of citizens' knowledge about parties, candidates and their proposals, campaign issues and the level of trust. In 2010 and 2014, surveys by Datafolha provided evidence to back these findings. The opinion poll available on October 15, 2014, one week after the beginning of the second round, showed that watching FEBA allowed for significant change in the levels of knowledge about candidates. Both Dilma Rousseff and Aécio Neves became better known when voters claimed to have watched at least one FEBA program (see Table 8.3). For example, while 44% of the electorate stated they knew President Dilma Rousseff "very well," this rose to 51% among voters who had watched the programs, versus 36% among those who had not. The same thing happened when voters were asked about their knowledge of the Petrobrás corruption scandal. Among voters who had watched the FEBA, 38% considered themselves well informed, against only 18% among those who had not. Likewise, while 12% of FEBA viewers had no knowledge at all about the scandal, this percentage rose to 30% among non-viewers.

Another survey conducted by Datafolha during the second turn of the presidential election of 2010 adds additional evidence to the claim that electoral broadcasting changes voters' perceptions of candidates. Voters' opinions about the personal traits of Dilma Rousseff and José Serra and about their preparedness to deal with public policies varied according to the level of exposure to the FEBA. Rousseff's percentages rose in almost all the questions evaluated. Positive assessment of her capacity to maintain economic stability, for example, went from 46% among those who did not watch to 51% among viewers. The candidate's perceived authoritarianism, however, also rose among voters who had watched the broadcasts (see Table 8.4).

Conclusion

We pointed at FEBA's distinctive features and its central role in the Brazilian electoral system. In spite of the growing role of segmented and online media, electoral radio and television broadcasts still play a significant role in Brazilian elections. With the distrust of politics by ordinary citizens, party and electoral communication tends to be criticized as well, regarded by many as sheer manipulation, where the most expensive campaigns, by the least reliable politicians, contribute to the low opinion of political elites.

Table 8.3 FEBA and knowledge about candidates

	Level of knowledge	Watched (%)	Did not watch (%)	Total (%)
Dilma Rousseff	Very well	51	36	44
	A little	31	36	34
	Only heard about	17	26	21
Aécio Neves	Very well	26	16	21
	A little	36	33	35
	Only heard about	31	43	37
Corruption in Petrobrás	Well informed	38	18	29
	More or less informed	40	37	39
	Not well informed	10	15	12
	Did not know of	12	30	20

Source: Authors on the basis of data from the Datafolha Survey Institute, October 14 and 15, 2014.

Table 8.4 FEBA and perception of candidates' attributes

	Dilma Rousseff (PT)		José Serra (PSDB)	
	Watched (%)	Did not watch (%)	Watched (%)	Did not watch (%)
Will defend the wealthy	19	21	53	48
Will defend the poor	55	52	27	27
More likeable	42	41	42	39
More intelligent	34	30	47	47
More authoritarian	51	45	34	36
More prepared to be president	41	36	49	49
More prepared to fight unemployment	49	45	37	37
More prepared to fight violence	42	36	40	39
More prepared to care for health	34	31	56	55
More prepared to care for education	46	40	43	43
More prepared to maintain economic stability	51	46	38	37

Source: Authors on the basis of data from the Datafolha Survey Institute, October 14 and 15, 2010.

However, in the context of partisan news corporations and low access to alternative media, FEBA is an important means to balance the information available to voters. Given the political activism of mainstream media outlets, it has the democratic role of providing political actors with broadcast visibility.

We regard FEBA as a relevant feature of Brazilian democracy also with regard to access by parties, since it covers the entire political spectrum and even parties with no representation are granted some degree of exposure. Viewing FEBA is almost compulsory for voters in a democracy in which voting is mandatory, and contributes to the great visibility of elections in Brazil. The evidence is that FEBA is more important to executive majority candidates than to proportional ones, since voting behavior on this level is more influenced by other dynamics (family, closer social group, district logic, local campaign) than by mass communication. However, the role played by party in the distribution of broadcast time to candidates makes it a major political asset in party and congressional political life as well.

Further regulation of campaign financing and media spending may be helpful for the model, without hindering what we consider to be an important role played by mass media in Brazilian elections.

Notes

1   Adopting the D'Hondt method for distribution of seats among parties.
2   Article 21, regulated by ensuing laws.
3   For official information regarding political airtime distribution, as well as electoral results and data from the Electoral Justice System, see www.tse.jus.br/.
4   Right of reply is stated in Law 7.773 (1989), 8.713 (1994) and 9.504 (1998, 2002, 2006 and 2010).
5   Updated until 2013. http://compolítica.org/diretorio/index.php/diretorio/.
6   It is worth noting that the corruption schemes revealed and prosecuted under PT's government are not new to Brazilian politics, but have been framed by mainstream media as belonging almost exclusively to its administrations. If anything, the fact that they are being investigated and punished on such a scale is a novelty.

References

Albuquerque, A. (1999). *Aqui você vê a verdade na tevê: A propaganda política na televisão [Here you see the truth on TV: Political propaganda on television].* Niterói: MCII-UFF.

Albuquerque, A. (2005). Advertising ou propaganda? O audiovisual político brasileiro numa perspectiva comparativa [Advertising or propaganda? Brazilian political broadcast in a comparative perspective]. *Alceu – Revista de Comunicação, Cultura e Política,* 5, 215–227.

Aldé, A., & Borges, J. (2006). Internet, the press and Brazilian elections: Agenda-setting on real time. *Journal of Systemics, Cybernetics and Informatics,* 4, 61–66.

Aldé, A., Chagas, V., & Santos, J. G. B. (2013). Teses e dissertações defendidas no Brasil (1992–2012): Um mapa da pesquisa em comunicação e política [Theses and dissertations presented in Brazil: A map for political communication research]. *Revista Compolítica,* 3, 7–43.

Borba, F. (2015a). The strategy of electoral spots in Brazilian presidential campaign: The decision on when and where to broadcast an attack. In A. Nai & A. Walter (Eds.), *New perspectives on negative campaigning: Why attack politics matters* (pp. 183–200). Colchester: ECPR.

Borba, F. (2015b). Propaganda negativa nas eleições presidenciais brasileiras [Negative campaigning in Brazilian presidential elections]. *Opinião Pública,* 21, 268–295.

Borba, F., & Figueiredo, M. (2014). Quanto vale o voto da TV? [How much is worth the TV vote?]. *Insight Inteligência,* 64, 101–114.

Borba, F., Veiga, L., & Bozza, F. (2015). Propaganda negativa na eleição presidencial de 2014. Ou como tudo que é frágil se desmancha no ar [Negative advertising in 2014 presidential election: Or how everything fragile melts into air]. *Revista Estudos Políticos,* 6, 171–189.

Coimbra, M. (2008). Quem se importa com o horário eleitoral? [Who cares about electoral broadcasting?]. In R. Figueiredo (Ed.) *Marketing político em tempos modernos [Political marketing in modern times]* (pp. 87–110). Rio de Janeiro: Fundação Konrad Adenauer.

Dias, M. R. (2013). Nas brumas do HGPE: A imagem partidária nas campanhas presidenciais brasileiras (1989 a 2010) [In the mists of FEBA: Party image in Brazilian presidential campaigns (1989 to 2010)]. *Opinião Pública,* 19, 198–219.

Figueiredo, M. (2007). Intenção de voto e propaganda política: Efeitos da propaganda eleitoral [Vote intention and political advertising: Effects of electoral broadcasting]. *Logos: Comunicação & Universidade,* 14, 9–20.

Figueiredo, M., & Aldé, A. (2010). Intenção de voto e propaganda política: Efeitos e gramáticas da propaganda eleitoral [Vote intention and political propaganda: Effects and grammar of electoral propaganda]. In L. F. Miguel & F. Biroli (Eds.), *Mídia, representação e democracia [Media, representation and democracy]* (pp. 19–40). Brasília: Hucitec.

Figueiredo, M., Aldé, A., Jorge, V., & Dias, H. (2000). Estratégias de persuasão em eleições majoritárias: Uma proposta metodológica para o estudo da propaganda eleitoral [Persuasion strategies in majoritarian elections: A methodological approach to the study of electoral advertising]. In R. Figueiredo (Ed.), *Marketing político e persuasão eleitoral [Political marketing and electoral persuasion]* (pp. 147–203). Rio de Janeiro: Fundação Konrad Adenauer.

Figueiredo, R., & Coutinho, C. (2003). A eleição de 2002 [The election of 2002]. *Opinião Pública*, 9, 93–117.

Lavareda, A. (2009). *Emoções ocultas e estratégias eleitorais [Hidden emotions and electoral strategies]*. Rio de Janeiro: Editora Objetiva.

Lima, V. (2006). *Mídia: Crise política e poder no Brasil [Media: Political crisis and power in Brazil]*. São Paulo: Editora Fundação Perseu Abramo.

Lourenço, L. C. (2009). Propaganda negativa: Ataque versus votos nas eleições presidenciais de 2002 [Negative adverstising: Attacks versus votes in the presidential elections of 2002]. *Opinião Pública*, 15, 133–158.

Krause, S., Dantas, H., & Miguel, L.F. (Eds). (2010). *Coligações partidárias na nova democracia brasileira: Perfis e tendências [Party coalitions in Brazilian new democracy: Profiles and trends]*. Rio de Janeiro and São Paulo: Fundação Konrad Adenauer and Fundação Editora da UNESP.

Mundim, P. S. (2010). Um modelo para medir os efeitos da cobertura da imprensa no voto: Teste nas eleições de 2002 e 2006 [A model to measure the effects of media coverage on the vote: Test in the 2002 elections and 2006]. *Opinião Pública*, 16, 394–425.

Mundim, P. S. (2012). Imprensa e voto nas eleições presidenciais brasileiras de 2002 e 2006 [The press and the vote in the 2002 and 2006 Brazilian presidential campaigns]. *Revista de Sociologia e Política*, 20, 123–147.

Palmeira, M., & Heredia, B. (1993). Le temps de la politique [The time of politics]. *Études rurales*, 131/132, 73–88.

Panke, L. (2015). *Lula del sindicalismo a la reelección: un caso de comunicación, política y discurso social [Lula from unionism to re-election: A case of communication, politics and social discourse]*. Ciudad de México: UAM Unidad Cuajimalpa.

Pimentel, J.T. P. (2016). *Quem bate perde? Os efeitos afetivos dos spots eleitorais de TV no Brasil [Hitting means losing? The emotional effects of election TV spots in Brazil]*. Rio de Janeiro: Autografia Editora.

Porto, M. P. (2006). Political advertising and democracy in Brazil. In L. L. Kaid & C. Holtz-Bacha (Eds.), *Handbook of political advertising* (pp. 129–143). Newbury Park, CA: Sage.

Porto, M. P. (2012). *Media power and democratization in Brazil: TV Globo and the dilemmas of political accountability*. New York, NY: Routledge.

Power, T. J. (2010). Optimism, pessimism and coalitional presidentialism: Debating the institutional design of Brazilian democracy. *Bulletin of Latin American Research*, 29, 18–33.

Secretaria de Comunicação da Presidência. (2014). *Pesquisa brasileira de mídia 2014: Hábitos de consumo de mídia pela população brasileira [2014 Brazilian survey on media: Use habits of the Brazilian people]*. Brasília: Secom.

Shugart, M., & Carey, J. (1992). *Presidents and assemblies: Constitutional design and electoral dynamics*. Cambridge University Press.

Veiga, L. (2001). *Em busca de razões para o voto: O uso que o cidadão comum faz do horário eleitoral [In search of reasons for the vote: The use of Electoral Broadcast by ordinary citizens]*. Unpublished doctoral thesis. Rio de Janeiro: Instituto Universitário de Pesquisas do Rio de Janeiro.

9

POLITICAL ADVERTISING IN CHILE

State of Play in a Period of Changes

Alberto Pedro López-Hermida Russo

Tradition of the Post-dictatorship Political System

With 25 years of uninterrupted democracy, it does not seem premature to assert that Chile is already among the countries that have a solid political system, although it is currently undergoing the same crisis of confidence and citizen disaffection with politics that pervades all five continents (Altman & Luna, 2007; Contreras & Morales, 2014; Mardones, 2007; Rodriguez-Virgili, López-Escobar, & Tolsá, 2011).

On the return to democracy in 1989, one of the legacies of Augusto Pinochet's military government – as well as a far-from-healed wound resulting from human rights violations – was a Constitution, which, together with a package of laws, made it possible for the country to move steadily toward its democratic rebirth. This legal framework permitted the country to run like clockwork, with no threat of or temptation for authoritarian relapses, regardless of how unpopular the successive master clockmakers may have been.

Chile has a direct-election strong presidential system with a bicameral legislative branch of government, which, so far, has been elected by means of a binomial system (two-member constituencies). Among other things, this has prevented the atomization of political forces in the legislature, although the other side of the same coin has been that the binomial system has systematically excluded from any parliamentary representation the political forces that have been emerging while the country has been growing in political maturity. In addition, the climate of citizen disaffection has become more pervasive.

Since 1990, stability has been evident as far as the party political system is concerned, and its representatives have always come from a sufficiently strong political tradition for the government and legislature to be renewed without major disruption (Agüero, Tironi, Valenzuela, & Sunkel, 1998; Angell, 2002; Castillo, 2014; Garretón, 2000; Godoy, 1994; Oppenheim, 1999). Something similar can be observed in economic matters (Larraín & Assael, 1997) and in the mass media system (Arriagada & Navia, 2011; Bresnahan, 2003; Tironi & Sunkel, 1993).

After 17 years of dictatorship, the Palacio de La Moneda has housed several presidential incumbents: Patricio Aylwin Azocar (1990–4) and Eduardo Frei Ruiz-Tagle (1994–2000), both members of the Christian Democratic Party, a crucial actor in the transition to democracy; Ricardo Lagos Escobar (2000–6) and Michelle Bachelet Jeria (2006–10), both of them with socialist beginnings and a personal history of experience of the harshness of the dictatorship; Sebastián Piñera Echenique (2010–14), entrepreneur and leader of the center-right; and at the time of writing, Bachelet once again. Thus, in the Executive Branch, the political forces have managed to alternate in a mature and enlightened way, so much so that Chile was the first country in the region to elect a woman president, not only once but twice (Angell, 2005; Dussaillant, 2005; Fermandois & Soto, 2005; Navia, 2005).

The party political system, which is reflected in the forces represented both in the Chamber of Deputies and in the Senate, has also attained an uneventful alternation, mainly because the binomial electoral system has compelled the parties to aggregate around two large blocs, whose only substantial changes have been in name (Valenzuela, 1995).

On the one hand, the center-left – mostly grouped under the consecutive names of Concertación and Nueva Mayoría – has historically gathered together the Christian Democratic Party (DC, Spanish acronym), the Socialist Party (PS), the Party for Democracy (PPD) and the Social Democratic Radical Party (PRSD). Off and on, the center-left coalition has included lesser political denominations such as the Humanist Party (PH), the Ecologist Party (PE), the Christian Left (IC) or the Communist Party (PC). It was not until the 2013 elections that the PC became an official member of the electoral bloc. This permitted it to take part from the outset in the design of an ambitious political platform and, once the bloc was voted in, to be represented in the cabinet. However, by the parliamentary elections of 2009, the historic Concertación had already allocated the PC a limited electoral quota in some specific electoral districts. This made it possible for the PC to be represented in parliament, which had not happened since before the dictatorship.

On the other side of the political spectrum, the center-right – under the umbrella names of Democracia y Progreso, Unión por el Progreso and Alianza por Chile – has historically consisted of the Unión Demócrata Independiente (UDI) and Renovación Nacional (RN). This conglomerate of political forces has been occasionally joined or abandoned by splinter groups from RN or even the DC.

The stability and maturity of Chile's executive and legislative branches of government, also mirrored in the judiciary branch, combined with the solidity of its economic model – also largely inherited from the dictatorship – have given this country its particular standing in the region, particularly, in relation to others, which have been undergoing long periods of political uncertainty, economic volatility and social unrest (Barrenechea & Villagarcía, 2014; Bonvecchi & Giraudy, 2007; Deheza, 2007; Tanaka & Vera, 2007; Tironi & Agüero, 1999).

Winds of Change

Having said that, in the last few years and, particularly from 2012 to date, just as the country has been hit by strong earthquakes, the political stability described above has also experienced some quakes. Although there is no need to be alarmed, these changes, like any other, have generated uncertainty about the future (Castiglioni, 2014).

In addition to the outbreak of serious cases of corruption, which have disrupted the political class as well as entrepreneurs, a series of bills have been passed and others are being discussed or are about to be introduced to Congress. These changes will affect politics and elections and campaign advertising. This is certainly true for the amendments promised or already introduced to the Law on Transparency, Limit and Control of Electoral Spending (Law 19,884), which impinges directly on the way in which campaigns are run.

As early as 2012, voter registration ceased to be voluntary and became automatic, while voting, which had been compulsory, became voluntary (Law 20,568). This change generated uncertainty about the election campaigns and the reliability of election polling (Traugott, 2015a) not to mention, a considerable drop in citizen participation (Contreras & Morales, 2014; Contreras & Navia, 2013; Navia & del Pozo, 2012; Traugott, 2015b). For the first time there were a large number of political ads urging people to go to the polls and asking for their votes. The new voluntary nature of the act of voting resulted in messages about the relevance and importance of voting, which had not arisen in the previous system of mandatory voting.

Another change in voting procedure approved in 2014 (Law 20,748) is that for the first time in the presidential elections of 2017, Chileans residing in other countries will have the right to vote, which obviously adds a new dimension to the electorate. There is an ongoing discussion about whether the candidates will be allowed to advertise in foreign mass media to canvass votes beyond Chile's borders.

Lastly, in 2015 there was a substantive amendment (Law 20,840) to the electoral law in aspects such as the new distribution and creation of constituencies, the increase in number of deputies and senators and, in some cases, the requirement of gender quotas. The Law's main change was the replacement of the binomial electoral system with an inclusive proportional representation model using the D'Hondt coefficient. This new system promises increased representation of parties so far excluded and gives independent candidates the chance of a campaign that is not merely symbolic, as has been up to now. This structural change to the legacy of the military government will be put to the test for the first time in the 2017 elections (Pastor, 2004).

It is necessary to add that in 2015 the National Congress began discussing a Political Parties Bill that, among other things, addresses party creation. Another ongoing discussion in Chile is the reform of its Constitution. This is a problematic issue given the origin of the present Charter in the Pinochet era and the uncertainty that has pervaded the process of writing a new document.

Despite the fact that the regulations associated with election campaigns and, specifically, political advertising, appear to be already defined, it is undeniable that a change in the country's Constitution would have significant effects on the election system.

Regulation of Political Ads

Amid this scenario of changes, the law that, among other things, regulates campaign advertising has remained practically untouched since it was passed. Because of this, there is a certain degree of uncertainty about how the possible changes described above may affect it.

Obviously, political advertising had been regulated before, in the 1950s and early in the 1960s. Holding the Football World Cup in Chile generated the mass consumption of television sets and, by the same token, of television itself (García, 2013).

The Organic Constitutional Law on Elections and Vote-Counting (Law 18,700) was issued in 1988 and forms part of the legal framework which, together with the Constitution, is still part of the legacy of the military government.

Campaign advertising can only begin 30 days before Election Day and must end three days before. During this period, the law permits advertising through mass media. The written media and radio can sell political spots with no time restrictions, just as they sell commercial spots, but television is treated differently.

Article 31 of the Law stipulates that paid television channels are forbidden to air any electoral campaign spots and free television channels should allocate a daily free-of-charge 30-minute slot in their grid to advertise presidential or parliamentary elections. When both elections coincide – as is the case since 2005 and unless the law is changed, will continue to be the case – free television channels must allocate two free 20-minute segments to each election.

Candidates running for president of the Republic will each get an equal share of the 20 minutes. In the case of the parliamentary election, the 20 minutes will be distributed in proportion to the votes obtained in the latest election. Candidates belonging to non-parliamentary parties and independent candidates will get the same share of time as the party in Congress with the lowest vote share.

All this has led to some peculiar and always striking situations, such as candidates who end up having no more than one second of airtime. This has generated complaints and claims for changes in the regulations, but has also sharpened the wit of the campaign teams.

The National Television Council – an autonomous constitutional body whose Chairperson is elected by the president of the Republic and whose other ten members are elected by the Senate, subject to the president's consent – establishes the length and timing of the ads, receives the spots before they are aired and coordinates the television networks that ANATEL, the National Television Association, has formed for this purpose

Thus, although the law regulating campaign advertising on television remained intact despite the structural and normative changes in the country, it is highly likely that changes in the funding of political campaigns may affect the quality of the spots. Similarly, the new developments of voluntary voting and the voting of Chileans residing abroad may result in incorporation of new discourses in television spots.

As for campaign advertising on the Internet, it is still unregulated in Chile. In fact, there is a striking contrast between the legal push to use digital platforms to promote Open Government – which requires a detailed publication of electoral expenses on campaign websites – and the absolute silence of the law via-à-vis political advertising on the web.

Key Points in Research on Electoral Ads

At the outset of the transition to democracy in Chile at the end of the 1980s, research on political advertising at that time reached a common conclusion, namely, that television was the most widely used of all media, and also the medium through which Chileans got most of their information about the 1988 plebiscite and the 1989 elections. In fact, debates on television (56.5%) and television news (47.8%) and political spots (46.1%) were the Chileans' preferred sources of information on the days preceding the first democratic elections, well beyond radio and the written press (CEP, 1989).

However, despite the contribution of television to the plebiscite and the first democratic elections – which even inspired a successful movie on the plebiscite, (*No*, 2012) – television audiences for and the perception of the influence of electoral spots has been steadily decreasing. This decline is due to the political disaffection and to the eruption of digital media in audiovisual campaigns, which permit greater targeting accuracy (Arriagada & Schuster, 2008).

A large part of the research has focused on the analysis of the audience for campaign ads rather than on the analysis of their content (Alvarado, Medel, Vergara, & Uribe, 2007; López–Hermida, 2007). Television continues to be the leading format, receiving most of the media attention when a spot is first aired, regardless of the size of the audience. Even now, in the Web 2.0 era, this is the case, at least in Chile (Carvajal, 2007; Dussaillant, 2007).

At a very early stage after the return to democracy, there was a decline in the number of citizens watching free airtime ads, as well as a decline in the value that voters attributed to ads in deciding how to vote (Hirmas, 1989; Uribe, Hidalgo, Selman, & Albornoz, 2007). These are the spots that the media are forced by law to "give away" at the beginning of prime time and just before the nine o'clock news, even though research demonstrates that there is a very low correlation between the content of political ads and coverage of campaigns by television and other media (Porath, 2009; Scherman, 2012).

In addition, some research carried out in Chile has confirmed that the consumption of campaign messages – including political ads – almost exclusively consolidates opinions already formed rather than modifies citizen opinions (Arriagada, Navia, & Schuster, 2010a, 2010b).

Electoral Funding and Political Ads

Another line of research, which has aroused interest lately, is the funding of electoral campaigns in connection with the legal changes already in effect and those in the offing.

Thanks to new laws, funding of Chilean election campaigns has been increasing in amount and transparency in terms of campaign expenses (Agostini, 2012; Nogueira, 2015). However, the use of reserved funds is still pending. This is a particularly tricky issue, given the number of political funding scandals exposed in 2015. These transgressions have cut across the political class and prompted new proposals for reform (Ramírez, 2015).

However, candidates still have television airtime free of charge. There is no doubt that free air time provides campaigns with significant savings compared to the situation in other countries where airtime must be purchased (Espíndola, 2002). Therefore, any modification in general funding should have not have a major impact.

As for television spots, the legal modifications that may materialize will eventually only affect the technical quality and content of the spots. Should there be no changes in Law 18,700, there will be no particular incentive to carry out concrete research on the link between the source of the money and the content of the electoral spots.

Bachelet and the Feminization of Research

The fact that Michelle Bachelet should have gained prominence in 2004 and that shortly afterwards she was voted in as president of the Republic in 2006, made research on gender stereotypes turn to Chile. As she was the first woman to reach the most important political post in her country in South America, she has been the subject of research ever since she launched her campaign.

Although the participation of Chilean women in elections and as well as the presence of minorities in ads have always been the subject of research (Alles, 2014; Alvarado et al., 2007; Hinojosa & Franceschet, 2012; Mardones, 2012; Shair-Rosenfield & Hinojosa, 2014). It is obvious that having a woman in the presidential race has resulted in a range of research, some of them specifically focusing on the purely ideological aspect of what this implied (Morales, 2008; Stevenson, 2012; Valdés, 2010; Vera, 2009; Vitale, 2014).

Other researchers focused on the Bachelet campaign itself, exhaustively reproducing what had already been done in other countries that had undergone a similar development (Banwart, 2010; Khan, 1994; Van Zoonen & Holtz-Bacha, 2000). Some studies concluded that in her political ads Bachelet explicitly used her status as a woman to assume a verbal and visual discourse against which her three male competitors could do little (López-Hermida, 2007, 2011). Her framing as a middle-class single mother, successful in her career, was reproduced with some innocence – attributable to inexperience – by the media (Valenzuela & Correa, 2009).

Bachelet's campaign ads, both for the first round in December 2005 and for the run-off in January 2006 extensively displayed the candidate's personality traits and skills – stereotypically attributed to women – whereas her discourse made it clear that she, the country's imminent ruler, had the qualities and skills generally attributed to male candidates.

Similarly, while Bachelet displayed her talent in feminine roles – mother and homemaker – and, to a certain extent, exposed her private life, she also portrayed other roles, which, theoretically, might be considered masculine: those of dedicated worker and politician (López-Hermida & Cerda, 2012).

The themes in the political ads during the campaign were curious. Stereotypically, there are some topics that are attributed as masculine and others, as feminine. Thus, the campaign that led Bachelet to La Moneda the first time showed that the two main candidates, Bachelet and Piñera, were using up some valuable advertising time to prove that they could handle and come up with proposals that are generally attributable to the opposite sex (see Table 9.1).

After Bachelet was voted in for the second time in 2014, research on this gender is still quantitatively scant, probably because by then she was not the first woman president in the region. Other countries such as Argentina and Brazil have woman presidents and, thus, the novelty has worn off.

Having said that, the fact that the two main presidential candidates for election in 2014 were women has prompted some new research. These studies have shown that there was a strong masculine framing in the media coverage of the political ads and the campaign in general (Leiva & López-Hermida, 2014).

Table 9.1 Time allocated to different issues by Piñera and Bachelet 2005 and 2006

Candidate	First round		Second round	
	Piñera	Bachelet	Piñera	Bachelet
Women	17:39	07:28	02:48	00:00
Senior citizens	04:24	01:18	07:16	00:20
Education	02:53	03:14	06:32	00:06
Health	04:43	03:33	00:56	00:00
Family	03:42	00:00	00:36	02:25
Minorities	04:19	02:32	00:28	00:00
Security	03:02	09:30	00:48	03:20
International relations	00:00	00:00	00:00	03:06
Industry	05:37	09:24	00:00	00:00
Employment	04:21	08:09	00:48	06:12

Source: López-Hermida (2009).

In addition, some of these studies have concluded that compared to the second campaign, the content of the spots of Bachelet's first campaign are markedly more ideological, with minimal references to the candidate's gender. This has also been the case of a similar comparison of the spots of Cristina Fernández de Kirchner and Dilma Rousseff in their successive campaigns (López-Hermida, 2013a, 2014).

Personalization and Storytelling

In Chile, as elsewhere, personalization and storytelling have gained in importance as new research fields. One of the conclusions these studies have reached is that primary campaigns – including the use of television spots – have become mechanisms for strong personalization of candidates, rather than for the institutionalization of political parties or electoral coalitions (Cantillana, Contreras, & Morales, 2015, Portales, 2009).

Although not exclusively related to research on political ads, Sebastián Piñera's government prompted some interesting studies on personalization in the coverage of his campaign – including the electoral television spot – by the traditional mass media; Piñera's storytelling efforts in an adverse political environment (Funk, 2011) and, certainly, the cinematographic-campaign treatment of the rescue of the 33 miners trapped in a 720-meter deep pit in 2010 (López-Hermida, 2015), have become a source of inspiration for political campaigns, from 2014 on.

Obviously, the two presidential campaigns in which Michelle Bachelet took successful part generated studies on the personalization and storytelling approaches used when the candidate is a woman, particularly in terms of the public exposure of her biography and her family life (López-Hermida & Cerda, 2012). Also the quality of unified narrative of the package of spots that made up her electoral slot have been the object of interest of academic studies. Both in her primary campaign and later in the first and second rounds of the presidential election, instead of showing specific messages, Bachelet opted for a serialized narrative story consisting of short episodes presented on television or in digital platforms (López-Hermida, 2014).

Social Media: A Promising Growth

The emergence of digital media has hit the Chilean electoral campaigns in a major way. Digital growth has been exponential since the first attention-seeking websites of the 1999/2000 elections, in which the digital campaign of the right-wing candidate Joaquín Lavín was particularly striking.

For the presidential campaigns of 2009/10 all the candidates deployed digital strategies explicitly. Particularly striking was Sebastián Piñera's decision to highlight social networks. Between the first and second rounds, he launched an electoral "spot" specially tailored for the Internet, in which he resorted to humor and protocol-breaking innovations. This is not very usual in entrepreneurial circles, and marked an enormous difference from the personality of his opponent, the former president Eduardo Frei Ruiz-Tagle (González & Henríquez, 2012, 2013). In turn, the then independent candidate Marco Enríquez-Ominami attracted most of the attention for the Web 2.0 campaign with his antics and the fact that he demonstrated that he himself was in charge of managing his digital profile. Despite his age, MEO, as he is generally known, was the first native digital presidential candidate that Chile has ever had.

Michelle Bachelet's proclivity for a digital scenario has been somewhat erratic. During her first presidential campaign she came up with an appealing campaign attuned to the penetration of digital media in Chile. During the second, she made good use of audiovisual digital material, even producing some special episodes which were for exclusive use in the web and took an active part in social networks, albeit not directly but through a team. Because of this, it is curious that once in office, Bachelet should have relinquished her digital presence, a decision she reluctantly reversed at the end of 2015 in an attempt to reverse her declining popularity.

It is worth mentioning that in terms of social networks and digital media, Chile is quite a distinctive country. This inevitably has a bearing on the way in which politics and electoral campaigns have been and will be conducted. In the year 2010, an earthquake that measured 8.8 on the Richter scale, followed by a tsunami, hit the center-south regions of the country. One of the consequences of this catastrophe was that the number of social networks users, particularly Twitter, increased enormously since they used Twitter to search for friends and family (López-Hermida, 2013b). A few months after this, 33 miners were trapped in a 720-meter deep corridor in a mine in the north of Chile, and became the protagonists of a human, political and social story that lasted 69 days, was covered by the media all over the world and once again resulted in a boom of social network use (López-Hermida, 2015; Pujol, 2010). Finally, during all that year and the next, students took to the streets demanding structural reforms in educational policy. The social media were used once again the means of information and calls for coordinated demonstrations (Cabalin, 2014; Valenzuela, Arriagada, & Scherman, 2012, 2014).

Presumably, although in the last campaign and during the current Bachelet administration the use of the digital media has not been particularly striking, it will become more prominent in the future. This is particularly true if changes in the law will encourage a larger number of candidates to run for office, many of whom will be independent and with no financial resources.

Conclusions

Political advertising in Chile should attract particular attention. Since the publication of the *Handbook of political advertising* in 2006, which included an excellent chapter on Chile by Markus Moke (2006), Chilean scholarship has contributed many studies of the effect of a woman on the content and reception of televised campaign ads.

In fact not many countries can boast having had on two occasions a victorious woman candidate and, on one of these, a strong competition between two female candidates of opposite political ideologies. Only a few years ago, this scenario would have been a mere pipe dream.

In addition, the emergence of digital platforms combined with Chile's wide use of social networks supports the view that in the near future Chile will continue to be a rich field for research. The same can be said of the impact of electoral storytelling as a strategy to attract the attention of today's hyperconnected audience.

Besides these factors, social, political and economic change and, particularly, the changes in regulatory legislation will no doubt inspire future research in the field of campaign advertising.

The fact that voting is now voluntary will make it necessary for Chilean candidates explicitly to ask for votes. The right to vote for Chileans who reside in other countries will bring about the emergence of messages especially addressed to that particular audience on television or digital platforms. Changes in funding will probably affect content, including the technical quality of political spots. New political party political legislation and the end of the binomial election system will generate more competition between parties and more candidates. Unless increased competition is accompanied by changes in laws regulating campaign advertising on television, there will be very little time for the messages of numerous candidates, which will require wiser solutions and digital environments.

There is no denying that after a quarter of a century of stability, thought-provoking winds of change are blowing in Chile.

References

Agostini, C. (2012). Financiamiento de la política en Chile: Campaña electoral 2009–2010 [The funding of politics in Chile: Electoral campaign 2009–2010]. In F.J Díaz & L. Sierra (Eds.), *Democracia con partidos: Informe para la reforma de los partidos políticos en Chile [Party political democracy: Report on the reform of political parties in Chile]* (pp. 269–319). Santiago: CEP-Cieplan.

Agüero, F., Tironi, E., Valenzuela, E., & Sunkel, G. (1998). Votantes, partidos e información política: La frágil intermediación política en el Chile post-autoritario [Voters, political parties and information: The fragile political mediation in post-authoritarian Chile]. *Revista de Ciencia Política*, 19(2), 59–193.

Alles, S. (2014). Ideología partidaria, competencia electoral y elección de legisladoras en cinco democracias latinoamericanas: Argentina, Brasil, Chile, Perú y Uruguay, 1980–2013 [Party ideology, electoral competition and election of members of Congress in five Latin American democracies: Argentina, Brazil, Chile, Peru and Uruguay, 1980–2013]. *América Latina Hoy*, 66, 69–94. doi:10.14201/alh2014666994.

Altman, D., & Luna, J. P. (2007). Desafección cívica, polarización ideológica y calidad de la democracia: Una introducción al Anuario Político de América Latina [Civic disaffection, ideological polarization and democracy quality: An introduction to the Latin American Political Yearbook]. *Revista de Ciencia Política*, 27, 3–28. doi: 10.4067/S0718-090X2007000100001.

Alvarado, M.V., Medel, T., Vergara, S., & Uribe, R. (2007). *Marketing político en Chile: El caso de la franja presidencial en televisión [Political marketing in Chile: The case of the presidential election slot on TV]*. Unpublished master's thesis, Universidad de Chile, Santiago.

Angell, A. (2002). The Pinochet factor in Chilean politics. *Revista Bicentenario*, 1(1), 53–73.

Angell, A. (2005). La elección presidencial en 1989: La política de la transición a la democracia [The 1989 presidential election: The politics of democratic transition]. In A. San Francisco & A. Soto (Eds.), *Camino a La Moneda: Las elecciones presidenciales en la historia de Chile. 1920–2000 [On the road to La Moneda: Presidential elections through the course of Chilean history. 1920–2000]* (pp. 401–434). Santiago: Centro de Estudio Bicentenario.

Arriagada, A., & Navia, P. (2011). La televisión y la democracia en Chile, 1988–2008 [Television and democracy in Chile, 1988–2008]. In C. Rodríguez & C. Moreira (Eds.), *Comunicación política y democratización en Iberoamérica [Political communication and democratization in Latin America]* (pp. 169–194). México D.F.: UIM y CPES.

Arriagada, A., Navia, P., & Schuster, M. (2010a). ¿Consumo luego pienso, o pienso y luego consumo? Consumo de medios, predisposición política, recepción económica y aprobación presidencial en Chile [Media consumption, political predisposition, economic perception and presidential approval in Chile]. *Revista de Ciencia Política*, 30(3), 669–695. doi: 10.4067/S0718-090X2010000300005.

Arriagada, A., Navia, P., & Schuster, M. (2010b). ¿Creer para ver o ver para creer? Consumo de medios y aprobación presidencial en Chile [Believe to see or see to believe? Media consumption and presidential approval in Chile]. *Observatorio*, 4(1), 349–377. doi: 10.4067/S0718-090X2010000300005.

Arriagada, A., & Schuster, M. (2008). Consumo de medios y participación ciudadana de los jóvenes chilenos [Media consumption and participation of the Chilean young]. *Cuadernos de Información*, 22(1), 34–41. doi: 10.7764/cdi.22.87.

Banwart, M. (2010). Gender and candidate communication: Effects of stereotypes in the 2008 election. *American Behavioral Sciences*, 54(3), 265–283. doi: 10.1177/0002764210381702.

Barrenechea, R., & Villagarcía, P. (2014). Perú 2013: La paradoja de la estabilidad [Peru 2013: The paradox of stability]. *Revista de Ciencia Política*, 34(1), 267–292. doi: 10.4067/S0718-090X2014000100013.

Bonvecchi, A., & Giraudy, A. (2007) Argentina: Crecimiento económico y concentración del poder institucional [Argentina: Economic growth and institutional power concetration]. *Revista de Ciencia Política*, 27, 29–42. doi: 10.4067/S0718-090X2007000100002.

Bresnahan, R. (2003). The media and the neoliberal transition in Chile: Democratic promise unfulfilled. *Latin American Perspectives*, 30(6), 39–68.

Cabalin, C. (2014). Online and mobilized students: The use of Facebook in the Chilean student protests. *Comunicar*, 43(22), 25–33. doi:10.3916/C43-2014-02.

Cantillana, C., Contreras, G., & Morales, M. (2015). Elecciones primarias y personalización de la política: El caso de las elecciones locales en Chile 2012 [Primary elections and personalization of politics: The case of local elections in Chile 2012]. *Revista de Ciencia Política*, 35(2), 273–298. doi:10.4067/S0718-090X2015000200002.

Carvajal, J. (2007, March). Algunas reflexiones sobre la relación entre TV y política [Thoughts on the relationship between TV and politics]. In Secretaría de Comunicaciones, Ministerio Secretaría General de Gobierno de Chile, La función política de la TV: Tendencias, contenidos y desafíos en el Chile de hoy [The political role of TV: Trends, contents and challenges in Chile of today]. Retrieved from http://transparencia.msgg.gov.cl/encuestas/documentos2006/archivo_de_356.pdf.

Castiglioni, R. (2014). Chile: Elecciones, conflictos e incertidumbres [Chile: Election, conflicts, and uncertainty]. *Revista de Ciencia Política*, 34(1), 79–104. doi:10.4067/S0718-090X2014000100004.

Castillo, M. (2014). Clases medias y trabajadores frente a la política. Sobre el ascenso electoral de la derecha en Chile [Middle classes and workers against the policy: About the rise of right-wing politics in Chile]. *Universum*, 29(2), 65–82.

Centro de Estudios Públicos (CEP) (1989, December). Estudio social y de opinión pública [Public opinion and social study]. Retrieved from www.cepchile.cl/enc_main.html.

Contreras, G., & Morales, M. (2014). Jóvenes y participación electoral en Chile 1989–2013: Analizando el efecto del voto voluntario [Young people and electoral participation in Chile 1989–2013: Analyzing the effect of the voluntary vote]. *Revista Latinoamericana de Ciencias Sociales, Niñez y Juventud*, 12(2), 597–615. doi:10.11600/1692715x.1226100414.

Contreras, G., & Navia, P. (2013). Diferencias generacionales en la participación electoral en Chile, 1988–2010 [Generational differences in electoral participation in Chile, 1988–2010]. *Revista de Ciencias Políticas*, 33(2), 419–441. doi:10.4067/S0718-090X2013000200001.

Deheza, G. (2007). Bolivia 2006: Reforma estatal y construcción del poder [The reform of the state and the construction of power]. *Revista de Ciencia Política*, 27, 43–57. doi:10.4067/S0718-090X2007000100003.

Dussaillant, P. (2005). La elección presidencial de 1999–2000: El siglo terminó en empate [The 1999–2000 presidential election: The century ended in a tie]. In A. San Francisco & A. Soto (Eds.), *Camino a La Moneda: Las elecciones presidenciales en la historia de Chile. 1920–2000 [On the road to La Moneda: Presidential elections in Chilean history. 1920–2000]* (pp. 463–490). Santiago: Centro de Estudios Bicentenario.

Dussaillant, P. (2007). La televisión y el debate público [TV and public debate]. In Secretaría de Comunicaciones, Ministerio Secretaría General de Gobierno de Chile, La Función Política de la TV: Tendencias, contenidos y desafíos en el Chile de hoy [The political role of TV: Trends, contents and challenges in Chile of today] (pp. 55–66). Chile: SEGEGOB. Retrieved from http://transparencia.msgg.gov.cl/encuestas/documentos2006/archivo_de_356.pdf.

Espíndola, R. (2002). *The effect of professionalized campaigning on the political parties of the Southern Cone*. Paper presented at the 52nd Annual Conference of the Political Studies Association, Scotland.

Fermandois, J., & Soto, A. (2005). El plebiscito de 1988: Candidato único y competencia [The 1988 plebiscite: An only candidate and competition]. In A. A. San Francisco & A. Soto (Eds.), *Camino a La Moneda: Las elecciones presidenciales en la historia de Chile. 1920–2000 [On the road to La Moneda: Presidential elections through the course of Chilean history. 1920–2000]* (pp. 371–400). Santiago: Centro de Estudio Bicentenario.

Fernández, M. A., & Rubilar, F. (2011). En el nombre del género: El caso de Michelle Bachelet [In the name of gender: The case of Michelle Bachelet]. *Desigualdade & Diversidade*, 9, 135–156.

Funk, R. (2011). El relato político en el primer año del gobierno de Piñera [The political narrative in the first year of the Piñera's government]. *Revista de Ciencia Política*, 49(2), 151–159. doi:10.5354/0716-1077.2011.17318.

García, J. I. (2013). Las franjas electorales en la experiencia chilena [The party political broadcast in Chile]. *Revista de Derecho Electoral*, 16, 279–293.

Garretón, M. A. (2000) Chile's election: Change and continuity. *Journal of Democracy*, 11(2), 78–84. doi:10.1353/jod.2000.0037.

Godoy, O. (1994). Las elecciones de 1993 [The 1993 elections]. *Estudios Públicos*, 54, 301–337.

González, B., & Henríquez, G. (2012). Campañas digitales: ¿Branding o participación política? El rol de las redes sociales en la última campaña presidencial chilena [Digital campaigns: Branding or political participation? The role of social networks during the last Chilean presidential campaign]. *Más Poder Local*, 12, 32–39.

González, B., & Henríquez, G. (2013). Chile: la campaña digital 2009–2010 [Chile: The 2009–2010 digital campaign]. In I. Crespo & J. Del Rey (Eds.), *Comunicación política y campañas electorales en América Latina [Political communication and electoral campaigns in Latin America]* (pp. 288–298). Buenos Aires: Biblos.

Hinojosa, M., & Franceschet, S. (2012). Separate but not equal: The effects of municipal electoral reform on female representation in Chile. *Political Research Quarterly*, 65(4), 758–770. doi:10.1177/1065912911427449.

Hirmas, M.E. (1989). La franja: Entre la alegría y el miedo [The party political broadcast: Between joy and fear]. In D. Portales & G. Sunkel (Eds.), *La política en pantalla [On-screen politics]* (pp.107–158). Santiago: Ilet-Cesoc.

Khan, K. F. (1994). Does gender make a difference? An experimental examination of sex stereotypes and press pattern in statewide campaigns. *American Journal of Political Science*, 38(1), 162–195. doi: 10.2307/2111340.

Larraín, F., & Assael, P. (1997). El ciclo político económico en Chile en el último medio siglo [The Chilean political-economic cycle of the last half century]. *Estudios Públicos*, 68, 197–214.

Larraín, P. (Director) (2012). *No* [Motion picture]. Chile: Fábula. www.imdb.com/title/tt2059255/.

Leiva, R., & López-Hermida, A. P. (2014). *Female campaign, masculine press: The Chilean press coverage of the presidential runoff*. Paper presented at the VI WAPOR Latinoamerica Congress, Universidad Diego Portales, Chile.

López-Hermida, A. P. (2007). *El estereotipo de género en política: La imagen de la mujer candidata en las elecciones presidenciales chilenas 2005–06 y su continuidad en el primer año de gobierno de Michelle Bachelet [Gender stereotypes in politics: The image of the female candidate in the 2005–06 presidential elections in Chile and its continuance during Michelle Bachelet's first year in office]*. Unpublished doctoral dissertation. Universidad de Navarra, Pamplona.

López-Hermida, A. P. (2009). La imagen de la mujer en política: La campaña electoral televisiva de Michelle Bachelet [The political image of women: The Michelle Bachelet TV campaign]. *Cuadernos de Información*, 24, 7–18. doi: 10.7764/cdi.24.30.

López-Hermida, A. P. (2011). Mujer y política desde la triangulación metodológica [Women and policy from an ideological triangulation]. *Revista Chilena de Comunicación*, 2, 63–79.

López-Hermida, A. P. (2013a). El estereotipo de género como factor estratégico: Comunicación política sin corbata [Gender stereotypes as a strategic factor: Political communication with ties off]. In K. Sanders, G. Velasco, & A. P. López-Hermida et al. (Eds.), *Hacia una profesionalización de la comunicación política en México. Retos y desafíos para conformar gobiernos cercanos a la sociedad [T]* (pp. 57–113), México D.F.: Porrúa.

López-Hermida, A. P. (2013b). *Comunicación en tiempos de Twitter: Reflexiones, ilusiones, sugerencias y silencio* [Communication in the times of Twitter: Reflections, illusions, suggestions and silence]. In M. McCombs & Martín M. Algarra (Eds.), *Communication and social life: Studies in honor of Professor Esteban López-Escobar* (pp. 761–775). Pamplona: EUNSA.

López-Hermida, A. P. (2014). *El papel de la mujer en campañas políticas [The role of women in political campaigns]*. Paper presented at the VI International Seminar of Electoral Strategies, ITAM, México.

López-Hermida, A. P. (2015). *(Nuevas) Narrativas y esfera pública: Análisis cualitativo del rescate de 33 mineros en Chile [(New) Narratives and the public sphere: Qualitative analysis of the rescue of 33 miners in Chile]*. Atenea (manuscript accepted for publication).

López-Hermida, A. P., & Cerda, F. (2012). Women and politics: The privacy without Necktie. *Revista de Comunicación*, 11, 196–211.

Mardones, R. (2007). Chile: Todas íbamos a ser reinas [Chile: We were all going to be queens]. *Revista de Ciencia Política*, 27, 79–96. doi:10.4067/S0718-090X2007000100005.

Mardones, R. (2012). Un pacto entre hombres: De las mujeres en la política postdictadura de Chile [A pact between men: Women in post dictatorship politics in Chile]. *Revista electrónica de Psicología Política*, 29, 37–46. Retrieved from www.psicopol.unsl.edu.ar/2012-12-Art%EDculo3.pdf.

Moke, M. (2006). Political advertising in Chile. In L. L. Kaid & C. Holtz-Bacha (Eds.), *The Sage handbook of political advertising* (pp. 145–159). Thousand Oaks, CA: Sage.

Morales, M. (2008). La primera mujer presidenta de Chile: ¿Qué explicó el triunfo de Michelle Bachelet en las elecciones de 2005–2006? [The first female president of Chile: What explains Michelle Bachelet's triumph in the 2005–2006 election?]. *Latin American Research Review*, 43(1), 7–32. doi: 10.1353/lar.2008.0013.

National Library of Congress of Chile, Ley 18.700. (1988). Ley Orgánica Constitucional sobre votaciones y escrutinios [Law 18,700 (1988) Constitutional act on voting and ballots], Chile. Retrieved from http://bcn. cl/1m9ud.

National Library of Congress of Chile, Ley 19.884. (2003). Sobre transparencia límite y control del gasto electoral [Law 19,884 (2003) Transparency and campaign spending limits and control], Chile. Retrieved from http:// bcn.cl/1m3aj.

National Library of Congress of Chile, Ley 20.568. (2012). Regula la inscripción automática, modifica el servicio lectoral y moderniza sistema de votaciones [Law 20,568 (2012) Regulates automatic enrollment, makes changes in the electoral office and modernizes the voting system], Chile. Retrieved from http://bcn.cl/1m1j3.

National Library of Congress of Chile, Ley 20.748. (2014). Regula el ejercicio del sufragio los ciudadanos que se encuentran fuera del país [Law 20,748 (2014) Regulates the voting process of citizens abroad], Chile. Retrieved from http://bcn.cl/1maj9.

National Library of Congress of Chile, Ley 20.840. (2015). Sustituye el sistema electoral binominal por uno de carácter proporcional inclusivo y fortalece la representatividad el Congreso Nacional [Act 20,840 (2015) Replaces the binominal electoral system with a proportional and inclusive system and strengthens the representativeness of Congress], Chile. Retrieved from http://bcn.cl/1qoq6.

Navia, P. (2005). La elección presidencial de 1993: Una elección sin incertidumbre [The 1993 presidential election: An election devoid of uncertainty]. In A. San Francisco & A. Soto (Eds.), *Camino a La Moneda: Las elecciones presidenciales en la historia de Chile. 1920–2000 [On the road to La Moneda: Presidential elections through the course of Chilean history. 1920–2000]* (pp. 435–462). Santiago: Centro de Estudio Bicentenario.

Navia, P., & del Pozo, B. (2012). Los efectos de la voluntariedad del voto y de la inscripción automática en Chile [The effects of voluntary vote and automatic enrollment in Chile]. *Estudios Públicos, 127*, 161–191.

Nogueira, H. (2015). Democracia, representación política y financiamiento de partidos y campañas electorales en Chile [Democracy, political representation, political parties and electoral campaign funding in Chile]. *Teoría y Realidad Constitucional, 35*, 543–575.

Oppenheim, L. H. (1999). *Politics in Chile: Democracy, authoritarianism, and the search for development*. Boulder, CO: Westview Press.

Pastor, D. (2004). Origins of the Chilean binominal election system. *Revista de Ciencia Política, 24*(1), 38–57.

Porath, W. (2009, July). *La publicidad política en televisión y la agenda de los medios: Las elecciones presidenciales de Chile 2005 [Political advertising in TV and the media agenda: The 2005 Chilean presidential election]*. Paper presented at the XXI Mundial Congress of Political Science, IPSA, Santiago de Chile.

Portales, J. C. (2009). A test of personalization of politics in Chile's 2009 presidential election. *Cuadernos de Información, 25*, 69–82. doi: 10.7764/cdi.25.48.

Pujol, F. (2010). *El rescate de los 33 mineros: Una epopeya coral. Análisis del impacto mediático y de reputación [The rescue of 33 miners: An epic acomplishment. Analysis of the media and reputation repercussions]*. Media reputation intangibles. España, Universidad de Navarra. Retrieved from www.unav.es/econom/sport/files/resourcesmodule/@random4562ca6fb6e9a/1287698834_R_2_33_mineros_de_Chile.pdf.

Ramírez, J. (2015). Financiamiento de la política: Evaluación, experiencia comparada y propuestas [The funding of politics: Evaluation, comparative experience and proposals]. *Libertad y Desarrollo, 146*, 2–35. Retrieved from http://lyd.org/wp-content/uploads/2015/03/SIP-146-Financiamiento-de-la-Politica-Evaluacion-JRamirez-Enero2015.pdf.

Rodriguez-Virgili, J., López-Escobar, E., & Tolsá, A. (2011). La percepción pública de los politicos, los partidos y la política, y uso de medios de comunicación [Media use and public perception of politicians, politics and political parties]. *Comunicación y Sociedad, 24*(2), 7–39.

Scherman, A. (Ed.). (2012). *Jóvenes, participación y medios 2011 [The young, participation and media 2011]*. Chile: Universidad Diego Portales. Retrieved from www.udp.cl/funciones/descargaArchivos.asp?seccion=documentos&id=135.

Shair-Rosenfield, S., & Hinojosa, M. (2014). Does female incumbency reduce gender bias in elections? Evidence from Chile. *Political Research Quarterly, 67*(4), 837–850. doi: 10.1177/1065912914550044.

Stevenson, L. (2012). The Bachelet effect on gender-equity policies. *Latin American Perspectives, 39*(4), 129–144. doi: 10.1177/0094582X12441518.

Tanaka, M., & Vera, S. (2007). Perú: Entre los sobresaltos electorales y la agenda pendiente de la exclusión [Peru: Between electoral commotion and the pending exclusion agenda]. *Revista de Ciencia Política, 27*, 235–247. doi: 10.4067/S0718-090X2007000100014.

Tironi, E., & Agüero, F. (1999). ¿Sobrevivirá el nuevo paisaje político chileno? [Will the new political landscape in Chile survive?]. *Estudios Públicos, 74*, 151–168.

Tironi, E., & Sunkel, G. (1993). Modernización de las comunicaciones y democratización de la política. Los medios en la transición a la democracia en Chile [The modernization of communications and the democratization of politics: The media in the transition to democracy in Chile]. *Estudios Públicos, 52*, 215–246.

Traugott, M. (2015a). Problemas relacionados con las encuestas preelectorales desde una perspectiva comparada [Problems related to pre-election polls from a comparative perspective]. *Estudios Públicos, 138*, 7–46.

Traugott, M. (2015b). Métodos alternativos para la estimación de resultados electorales [Alternative methods for estimating election outcomes]. *Estudios Públicos, 137*, 7–42.

Uribe, R., Hidalgo, P., Selman, E., & Albornoz, E. (2007). Las audiencias de la franja presidencial chilena [The audiences of the Chilean presidential election spot]. *Cuadernos de Información, 21*(2), 12–19. doi: 10.7764/cdi.21.101.

Valdés, T. (2010). El Chile de Michelle Bachelet. ¿Género en el poder? [Michelle Bachelet's Chile: Gender in power?]. *Latin American Research Review, 45*, 248–273. doi: 10.1353/lar.2010.0036.

Valenzuela, J. S. (1995). Orígenes y transformaciones del sistema de partidos en Chile [Origins and transformations of the party system in Chile]. *Estudios Públicos, 58*, 5–78.

Valenzuela, S., Arriagada, A., & Scherman, A. (2012). The social media basis of youth protest behavior: The case of Chile. *Journal of Communication, 62*(2), 299–314. doi: 10.1111/j.1460-2466.2012.01635.x.

Valenzuela, S., Arriagada, A., & Scherman, A. (2014). Facebook, Twitter, and youth engagement: A quasi-experimental study of social media use and protest behavior using propensity score matching. *International Journal of Communication, 8*, 2046–2070.

Valenzuela, S., & Correa, T. (2009). Press coverage and public opinion on women candidates: The case of Chile's Michelle Bachelet. *The International Communication Gazette*, 71(3), 203–223. doi: 10.1177/1748048508100913.

Van Zoonen, L., & Holtz-Bacha, C. (2000). Personalisation in Dutch and German politics: The case of talk show. *Javnost –The Public*, 7(2), 45–56.

Vera, A. (2009). Una crítica feminista a la madre pública postdictatorial: Los discursos de género en la campsaña presidencial de Michelle Bachelet [A feminist critique of the postdictatorial matriarch: Gender discourse in Michelle Bachelet's presidential campaign]. *Nomadías*, 10, 111–129. doi: 10.5354/0719-0905.2009.15133.

Vitale, M. A. (2014). Èthos femenino en los discursos de asunción de las primeras mujeres presidentes de América del Sur: Michelle Bachelet, Cristina Fernández de Kirchner y Dilma Rousseff [Female ethos in the inaugural addresses of South America's first women presidents: Michelle Bachelet, Cristina Fernández de Kirchner and Dilma Rousseff]. *Anclajes*, 18(1), 61–82.

10

THE ROLE OF POLITICAL ADVERTISING IN THE CZECH REPUBLIC

Jan Jirák and Anna Shavit

Political campaigning belongs among those innovations in the public sphere which were introduced to Czech society after the socio-political changes which began in the fall of 1989. With the process of democratization, the former Czechoslovakia and the Czech Republic as its successor since 1993 accepted methods of contemporary political marketing and advertising. The first post-1989 parliamentary election (in 1990) was accompanied by a campaign and political parties and associations struggled for voters' attention, using meetings, mass media and outdoor advertising, including billboards, print, television and radio advertising, as well as direct marketing methods (for more see Jirák & Šoltys, 2006).

It was the first experience with an election campaign that involved tools widely used in other democratic countries for almost all voters (the number of people returning back from exile was marginal). However, attitudes toward political marketing were quite ambivalent. On one side, there was still a memory of political competition and party struggles from the interwar period (from establishing Czechoslovakia after World War I in 1918 until the Munich Treaty in September 1938 and following the annexation of Czechoslovak territory with German-speaking inhabitants by Nazi Germany) and of course of Communist Party propaganda in the period 1948–89. In both cases, more or less bitter experiences were recalled. The former exposed political campaigning as an unscrupulous, highly personalized fight; the latter brought the experience of ineffective, hypocritical self-promotion of one party and one political point of view. On the other side, the methods of political marketing introduced after 1989 were part of the "package for the West," in other words they were accepted and welcome as a part of the process of democratization (and "Westernization") of the country.

During the following more than 25 years, the modern methods of political marketing became a standard part of political communication and have been shaping the politics and policies of the country ever since. It is an inherent part of decision-making processes, election campaigning, as well as of forming new political bodies (parties, associations, movements) and introducing political projects, grassroots movements, protests, etc. Marketing itself is determined and shaped by the specific Czech socio-political context, including the dynamics of public sphere, public, political parties and media agendas, legal framework, economic situation, etc.

In this chapter, the socio-political context of contemporary political advertising and its legal framework as well as immanent development of political communication in the Czech Republic will be characterized and illustrated by case studies of two remarkable milestones in Czech political marketing: the process of establishing a new political subject and the experience of the first direct election of Czech president in 2013.

Brief Overview of the Socio-political Context

By its Constitution,[1] the Czech Republic is a parliamentary democracy with a two-chamber parliament (House of Representatives with 200 members elected every four years and Senate which consists of 81 members elected for six years; one-third of the senators are elected every two years), president (elected by members of parliament originally and in direct election by voters since 2013), government appointed by the president and the Constitutional Court. The country is a member of NATO and the European Union, signed the Schengen Treaty but has not entered the Eurozone yet.

The fundaments of the political system of the Czech Republic have been developing within the framework of former Czechoslovakia since 1989, when the political and economic structure of the Soviet Union and its Eastern satellites collapsed. The following developments took place with the declared and widely accepted aim to establish a market economy, adopt basic human rights and build up a state based on individual freedom, values of liberal democracy and integration into the "West." The process of privatization of state-run industry and agriculture took place, democratic institutions were newly re-established, and huge properties were returned to their former owners, from whom they had been taken during the postwar Soviet dominance between 1948 and 1989 (Večerník & Matějů, 1999). On January 1, 1993, Czechoslovakia peacefully split into two independent states – the Czech Republic and the Slovak Republic. Because the former Czechoslovakia had been a federation of two republics anyway, both new countries had most of their political institutions already organized at the time of the split, and citizens had already had their first experience with free democratic elections and with election campaigning as well (during the parliamentary elections of 1990 and 1992). The further development of both countries took quite a different route (Slovakia entered the Eurozone in 2009).

There are several types of elections in the Czech Republic: election to the House of Representatives (every four years), election to the Senate (every two years, but because of the graduated change in senators, only in a limited number of counties), regional and local (municipal) elections (every four years) and since 2013 direct election of the president. The election of members of the House of Representatives is understood as the most important event in the political life of the nation (for more information on the Czech political system see Malíř & Marek, 2005; Strmiska, 2001). Since 1993, the Czech Republic held elections to the House of Representatives (1996, extraordinary election in 1998, 2002, 2006, 2010 and 2013), the Senate (after establishing this chamber in 1996 every two years one-third of the senators is re-elected), regional and municipal elections, elections to European Parliament and in 2013 also the first election of the president (for details see Charvát & Just, 2014).

The main actors participating in the political struggle are traditional political parties and their candidates (who may or may not be party members), "independent" candidates (their real influence is marginal) and political "groupings" or "movements" (party-like formations with small or non-existing formal structure and membership). Groupings are quite important political actors in the Czech Republic since trust in traditional parties has been weakened by two decades of corruption, scandals and non-transparent cabinet policy. The voters have a tendency to interpret the groupings as an alternative to traditional parties.

Still, the leading actors on the Czech political stage are political parties and groupings in a close orbit around the political center between the traditional "left" and "right." There are currently seven political objects in the House of Representatives, and many marginal political bodies are not represented there.[2] The two strongest political parties are Česká strana sociálně demokratická (the Czech Social Democratic Party, ČSSD, which won the last election), a traditional social-democratic party with a strong pro-EU orientation and welfare state political program, and grouping ANO 2011,[3] which has quite an unclear orientation with a strong populist tone. The founder and leader of ANO is Andrej Babiš, an entrepreneur and media mogul (and currently the member of the cabinet and Minister of Finance of the Czech Republic). Other parties are Komunistická strana Čech a Moravy (the Communist Party of Bohemia and Moravia, KSČM) clearly a leftist party, with an electorate still identified with the pre-1989 regime; Křest'ansko-demokratická unie–Česká strana lidová (the Christian Democrats), a middle-sized but quite stable centrist party (it has been a member of all coalition governments since 1990); the Občanská demokratická strana (the Civic Democratic Party, ODS), which has a more conservative orientation, some nationalistic characteristics, and a very cold approach to the European Union; TOP 09, a neoliberal party with quite a strong populist undertone and strongly xenophobic, populist Úsvit (The Down – from The Down of Direct Democracy), a political grouping founded in 2013.

Financing for the political parties and their campaigns comes from a state budget (funding is granted according to the number of votes a party wins in the election, as long as it is more than 3% of the votes, and according to the number of seats for parties represented in parliament), from membership fees, and from sponsorship and money offered by donors.

The Media/Public Communication System in the Czech Republic

To understand the shape and role of political advertising in the contemporary Czech Republic, some knowledge about the Czech public communication system is necessary, including the foundations of the contemporary system rooted in the previous regime. The media in the former "socialistic" Czechoslovakia had a highly centralized structure with a clearly defined goal: to serve the communist power elite and to support its image and decisions. The whole system was very close to the description offered as a "Soviet model" in *Four theories of the press*[4] (Siebert, Peterson, & Schramm, 1963). In the print media sector, national dailies were published mainly by the political parties.[5] There was a rich variety of regional and local weeklies and specialized magazines published in all major cities by the local and regional authorities. One type of daily was missing: the sensational paper. All broadcasting in the former Czechoslovakia was run and controlled by the state and financed via the state budget. The alternative media, *samizdats*, were marginal and, in comparison with other countries (for instance, Poland), underdeveloped. On the other hand, foreign radio broadcasting in Czech language (the BBC, Voice of America and Radio Free Europe) was commonly available in the former Czechoslovakia despite the effort of the state to control and jam the signal.

After 1989, the whole public communication structure changed profoundly. The media system has been decentralized and started to operate independently of the state and in a completely new legal framework. "The new media are embedded in legal forms and social practices and are no longer a matter of hope, fear or speculation," concluded Sparks (1998, p. 174) in his observations of media transition in Central Europe.

Some national dailies changed into employee shareholding companies in the first step. The former daily of the Socialistic Union of Youth, *Mladá fronta* (Young Front; after 1989, *Mladá fronta dnes*, Young Front Today), is an excellent example. Finally, the shareholders sold their shares to owners based in other countries. The new owners were of different origin (French, Scandinavian, Swiss), and as such, they did not provoke any negative reaction from the general public. Only potential owners based in Germany were understood as a danger to the country. However, most of the Czech dailies moved into the hands of German owners during the 1990s. Only one national daily, *Právo*, has been owned by a Czech citizen. The situation started to change after 2006, nowadays, most of the daily press (and its Internet versions) is owned by Czech owners, almost exclusively big financial moguls with major ownership in other sectors besides media (for details see Mediaguru, 2014 – the only substantial later change in ownership is the withdrawal of German family publishing house Diekmann and its Verlagsgruppe Passau – replaced by Czech-Slovak corporation Penta in 2015). In some cases, the ownership represents a combination of media, economic and political power. For instance, the *Mladá fronta dnes* daily and its publishing house (which includes other daily, set of magazines and radio station), mentioned above, is nowadays owned by Andrej Babiš, the founder and head of ANO and minister of finance in current government.

Within the field of broadcasting media, the dual system (i.e., a system in which both public service and private commercial broadcasting operate side by side) was established both for radio and television (see for instance Jirák, 1997, p. 44). The state media established in the previous regime were transformed into public service media and formed *Český rozhlas* (Czech Radio) and *Česká televize* (Czech Television).[6] Both public service media are financed primarily by fees paid by households for the ownership of functioning receivers and by the sale of some limited broadcasting time to advertisers.

Private radio and television stations also appeared after 1989. Local and regional radio stations have come first, then nationwide private radio stations appeared, and then television channels. Private television stations appeared in 1993, with the first (regional) commercial television called *TV Premiéra* (transformed into *TV Prima* in 1998). The real victory of commercial television broadcasting came in 1994, when *TV Nova* started to broadcast. This mass audience entertainment television channel was the most successful media project of the 1990s, gaining the attention of about two-thirds of viewers at the beginning and with a long-term weekly share of over 40% for more than 10 years. In 2005, after some changes in *TV Prima*'s programming, *TV Nova*'s audience share started to drop. Nowadays, more channels are available even in terrestrial broadcasting (for instance *TV Barrandov* since 2009) and both public service and private broadcasters took the route toward fragmentation of the audience, establishing more and more thematic and niche channels (sports, news and children's channels of public service television, variety of sport, document, action movies, television series, etc. run by commercial broadcasters). Recently, the mobile phone network providers (first O2 and then T-mobile) have been developing their own "broadcast" services offering the whole package of television and radio channels including their own channel (where it is possible to download the programs and/or to watch them with a 30-hour delay).

Digitalization of communication media is quite advanced in the Czech Republic, both in terms of media production and media consumption. Digitalization progressed rapidly especially since 2010. Digital switch-over from terrestrial television broadcasting was completed in 2012 (terrestrial broadcasting is still the dominant way of delivering signal to the television sets), the number of users of new media platforms is increasing continuously as well as the consumption of media content of via "platform independent" applications. Consequently, the print media (especially dailies) suffered a significant fall in the circulation and news production has undergone a strong shift toward massive commercialization and tabloidization and weakening of journalistic production, caused by a huge increase of user-generated content (for more details on digitalization in the Czech Republic see Rybková & Řiháčková, 2013).

After 1989 the advertising market opened in the Czech Republic as a new field of economic activity and has been developing extremely quickly since then. With no regard for the frequent ups and downs of the Czech economy, the finances pumped into advertising have increased steadily – even during the digitalization when the economic model of financing media is under pressure, since the traditional "Northcliffian" model of mass media economics has not been moved from "old" to "new" media successfully. However, "the Czech media system is a market-driven media structure deeply rooted in the trends of economic globalization and commercialization. Unlike other countries, in the Czech Republic, the process of commercialization has not been slowed down by 'quality' media" (Jirák & Šoltys, 2006, p. 380). The political elite, experienced in using "media logic" and hiring communication and marketing agencies, use the media not only as tools for communication with voters but mainly as part of the communication mix aimed at persuasion and manipulation of the public.

Political Advertising as a Part of Czech Media Communication

Generally, political advertising (in election campaigns as well as in "normal" periods of political life of the country) is not regulated in print, outdoor or Internet media by any specific law and is widely present in all kinds of communication channels from dailies, magazines, on billboards and other outdoor advertising carriers and through means of direct marketing. The demand for fairness of political competition as a legal frame is reflected only by prohibiting the publication of any public opinion poll results three days before and during Election Day in any type of media. This rule is an obligatory part of the "election laws" passed before any election by the parliament. The same laws also set the rules of the election campaign, and doing that, they provide a framework for political advertising as well. The fundamental principle of the campaign supposed to be the equality of political parties (or movements) and coalitions. For instance, the city mayors are allowed to reserve public space for political posters 16 days before an election.

The only field of public media communication where political advertising is regulated is television and radio broadcasting. No "business messages" of political parties and movements, independent candidates for MPs, senators, president and members of regional or local bodies is allowed on radio or television according to the Broadcasting Law (Zákon 231/1991, 2001, in which the definition of "business message" can be found in section 2). The fact that the definition of political advertising is based on the concept of "business message" ("obchodní sdělení") is important: the general assumption behind the concept is that we can speak about political advertising only when a political body *pays* for broadcast time and fills it with its own self-promotion (for instance, a news reel from a party press conference or the appearance of a candidate in a public affairs television show is not part of political party self-promotion from this point of view). The definition in reality caused some conflicts in the last election to the House of Representatives in 2013: the chair of ANO 2011 Andrej Babiš, mentioned above, is also an owner of a huge chicken farm and appeared in an ad for the products of the farm.[7] He was immediately accused of placing a hidden political ad.

Political advertising in broadcast media is allowed only during election campaigns. For instance, according to the election law, all political parties, political movements (groupings, formations) and coalitions are allowed a total of 48 hours of free broadcast time, both on Czech public radio and Czech public television before the election to the House of Representatives. The broadcast time must be used during a period that starts 16 days before the election and ends 48 hours before voting begins. This free broadcast time must be divided equally among all political parties, political movements and coalitions registered for election. The time slots for each political party, movement and coalition are determined randomly. Political parties, movements and coalitions are responsible for the content of the message broadcast in their time slot. The election law is an exception from the Broadcasting Law, according to which forbids any political advertising in broadcast media.

Political Advertising and Political Communication

Political advertising has been established as a regular feature of political communication in the Czech Republic after 1989. In pro-Soviet regimes, with the dominant position of the Communist Party, it had no place (the existing propaganda was more or less formal ritual with very little persuasive impact). From a very modest and in a sense naive initial phase, political advertising became an integral part of complex, planned, professionalized communication strategies of political entities within the last two decades. However, political advertising itself is still predominantly a tool of election campaigning, it is quite clear that it is embedded within an ongoing image-building process which takes place during the whole election period.

Political bodies have adopted all available means of communication from the traditional ones (print, radio, television, outdoor advertising, direct marketing) and their web derivatives to direct face-to-face communication (political meetings) and its interactive quasi-equivalent on social networks Facebook and Twitter. Among all available communication channels, television broadcasting and social networks seem to be understood as the most important ones (but not necessarily as the best channels for advertising: according to Transparency International, for instance almost 50% of all financial resources invested in advertising before the 2013 election were allocated to outdoor advertising[8]). Social media are playing a crucial role in campaigning and they do represent a significant part of campaign budgets (Šíma & Králiková, 2013). The candidates try to present themselves not only in their legally allowed free airtime but also in political debates, via various "media events," on Facebook profiles, disseminating self-promoting "news" via Twitter and so on. Although most parties have broadcast promotional advertisements, more attention has been devoted to televised debates between the competing candidates and parties (Gregor, 2012). The number of viewers and range of popular coverage – which is truly "mass" – is a highly appreciated quality of political communication in Czech television broadcasting, monitored both by political parties and media. However, a mass audience was not actually in front of their television sets when campaign clips were broadcast, because public television (and public radio as well) traditionally scheduled them during late at night or early in the morning.

The political debates and self-presentation on the web (YouTube party television, television ads, Facebook videos, etc.) seem to be interpreted as more effective by political actors and their professional advisers. The complexity of communication and sound communication strategy is considered among professionals as the most appreciated aspect of pre-election political communication (Gregor & Matušková, 2014).

Because of the dynamics of the development of available communication means, some crucial changes in the political communication took place since 2006. Campaigns are becoming more professional, marketing driven, research based and data driven (Chytílek, Eibl, & Matušková, 2012; Matušková, 2010). The milestones in modern campaigns and political communication in the Czech Republic were the following events: parliamentary election of 2006, 2010 (hugely influenced by PSB Associates, a US based polling company) and direct presidential elections of 2013, and recently the parliamentary elections of 2013 which basically changed the electoral map of the country and brought new political actors into the game (see above).

The first direct popular vote for the president of the country was hugely influenced by strategically planned negative campaigning, extensive polling and message delivery. These changes have influenced the nature and role of political advertising deeply – especially the shift in importance of advertising via television and the Internet. Presidential campaigns and parliamentary elections in 2013 were largely influenced by usage of social media. Tactical messaging was echoed online, as the "non-advertising" political communication generated more media audience (Šíma & Králiková, 2013).

The presidential election 2013 was a two-round election. In the first round nine candidates ran for the presidency – two of them proceeded to the second (and final) round: candidates Karel Schwarzenberg and Miloš Zeman (who became the president). The campaign showed the importance of a simple and strong message and how important or damaging the televised debates can be. It was the very first campaign in the country clearly centered on candidates. It received strong support from all media and the media also played an important role by openly supporting some candidates (Gregor & Matušková, 2014). In general, television advertising was marginalized during the campaign, while social media and television debates became crucial (for the overview of the election see for details Charvát & Just, 2014). The outdoor ads were quite important but only in the first round: the billboards, which appeared before the election, blamed one of the strong candidates, former Prime Minister Jan Fišer, for his supposed political engagement with the pre-1989 regime.

Television ads were aired during the campaign and carried the messages the candidates want to deliver to the voters and general public. For example, Miloš Zeman offered an ad focusing on harmony and integrity. The 60-second spot represents a symbolic "pilgrimage" of the candidate from the countryside to the city full of people and to Prague Castle, the traditional residence of the president. In a voice-over, the reflections of Mr. Zeman can be heard with his main messages, "Lepší než proklínat tmu je zapálit alespoň jednu svíčku" [Better than blame the darkness, it is better to light at least one candle] (Zeman, 2013, 0:25) and "Každý prezident má pracovat pro budoucnost" [Any president should work on the future]" (0:53). For the last few seconds the candidate, sitting in an armchair with his daughter on his left, speaks directly to the audience: "a budoucnost: to jsou I naše děti" [and future: it is also our children] (0:56). The spot, produced by a successful feature movie director Filip Renč, is in clear, warm colors, with soft music in the background and provided a self-portrait of the candidate. The spot in a nutshell reminded voters that Zeman, a social democrat and important political actor in the post-1989 development, decided to leave his political career. He made a statement about being closer to nature and himself, which was symbolized by "hugging trees." The video shows the motive of tactile contact with a tree as a starting point of the spot (0:07). Gradually voters are reminded about his career and main goals as future president. The ad closes with a close-up of his 19-year-old daughter, Kateřina. She played an important role in the campaign in generating support among younger voters but also in improving Zeman's image. Her presence proved to be very successful.

Zeman's spot is clearly a professional piece of audiovisual work – especially when compared to the television ad of his rival, Karel Schwarzenberg. His spot is a set of stand-ups of people – mostly Czech celebrities – who express support for the candidate. At the end, Karel Schwarzenberg appears himself (Schwarzenberg, 2013, 0:57). His messages are presented in written form at the beginning of the spot: "Přemýšlejte, než zvolíte" [Think before you vote] (Schwarzenberg, 2013, 0:01) and at the end "Stojím o podporu slušných a čestných lidí" [I appreciate support of decent and honest people] (0:57). The messages do not seem to play a dominant role in Schwarzenberg's advertisement. The focus is more on intertextuality and emotional support:

(1) Some of the speakers carry the signs of Schwarzenberg's campaign (a female student, Veronika Vichnarová, has a T-shirt with the candidate shown as a punker, which was the "logo" of Schwarzenberg's campaign (0:05); the same picture is on the button of the next student, Karolína Chlupíková (0:08)). The television spot acts as a supplement to the campaign, which took place via social media and outdoor advertising.

(2) The appearance of the candidate himself at the end of the spot is a "reminiscence" of Vaclav Havel, the icon of the "Velvet Revolution" and the president of former Czechoslovakia after 1989. Karel Schwarzenberg, who served as Havel's chancellor in 1990–2, tried to take a position of his successor. In the spot he is wearing a plain sweater (Havel was well-known for his informal dress code) and offering just a shy smile (a shy performance was typical for Havel).

(3) The celebrities expressing support for Schwarzenberg (successful movie director, pop music singer, actor and writer, etc.) are building up a feeling of general support for the candidate.

These examples from the second round of the presidential campaign 2013 show the importance of social media over television broadcasting and over traditional media. Because they are broadcast in marginal time slots, the ads only serve as supportive messages showing a positive aesthetic image of the candidate such as Zeman, who was constantly shown in the news media in a negative way. Alternatively, spots may strengthen awareness of candidates who present themselves via other channels of communication (such as Schwarzenberg).

The presidential race was followed by parliamentary elections in 2013, which represent yet another interesting example of television advertising. The political grouping ANO 2011 was established in 2011 and remained rather unknown to the general public until the election of 2013. The party ended up second in the whole race with 18.65% (which represents 47 MPs out of 200 in the House of Deputies).[9] The success of ANO 2011 was partly caused by the unique political situation in the country – massive corruption and political scandals – which led to the complete discrediting of traditional center-right parties. ANO 2011 positioned itself as center-right liberal formation focused on creating jobs and better conditions for employers as well as reducing taxes. Its founder, Andrej

Babiš, is a billionaire and one of the biggest employers in the country operating in the food industry among others – he is predominantly associated with chicken products.

The ANO 2011 campaign started in August 2013 along with systematic PR strategy and visual communication. A variety of advertising tools were used – mainly billboards (to help to create brand awareness – 67% voters claimed they did not know ANO and Mr. Babiš). Meanwhile new web pages were launched and social media networks (such as Facebook, Twitter and YouTube). The campaign was prepared and managed with wide and sophisticated use of data, public polls and other marketing tools. It followed the rules defined by law – with the possible exception of a loophole in the fall of 2013, just in the time for the election. An advertisement on "Vodňanské kuře" [The Chicken from Vodňany – one of Mr. Babiš famous products] appeared among regular commercial advertisements with ice hockey player Jaromír Jágr (Vodňanská drůbež, 2013). At the end of the ad not only Jágr but Andrej Babiš himself appeared on the scene and they spoke to each other. The ad raised a debate about the legal and ethical aspect of the advertisement. Babiš argued that he can promote his products as an entrepreneur, but his opponent accused him of presenting himself outside the regulated time slots for presenting candidates (for details see for instance Nová, 2013).

Conclusion

The framework of political advertising in the Czech Republic has a level of planned, evaluated and dynamic strategic persuasive communication.

In election campaigns, political actors and their advisers trust non-advertised persuasion and thus campaigning is governed by the media logic of the contemporary mass media while traditional types of political advertising – especially television advertising – are undertaken more as a ritual. Guaranteed free airtime on public television has been shown to have particularly little impact, and the political parties and candidates engage in it for ritualistic reasons.

Election results (especially the success of Karel Schwarzenberg in the first round of presidential election among young voters) suggest that direct contact or contact via social media with voters is more effective than any communication through the mass media. The "mass communication" qualities of election campaigning will probably diminish in the future and another means of campaign communication will become dominant: the Internet, personal meetings and direct mail. Television advertising as a tool of persuasion may become a complementary type of communication.

There are some points of dispute in the current legal framework of political communication in the Czech Republic. First, there has been some discussion of the potential synergic effects of legally guaranteed broadcast time and the news coverage of election campaigns. Second, the question of hidden political advertising has been raised (especially in connection with the legal concept of a "business message"). Third, the danger of manipulative interventions in media content by media owners who support candidates, chair political bodies or are candidates themselves has been discussed.

Notes

1   The Preamble to the Constitution of the Czech Republic (Ústava České republiky), passed on December 16, 1992, claims that the Czech Republic is *svobodný a demokratický stát, založený na úctě k lidským právům a na zásadách občanské společnosti, jako součást rodiny evropských a světových demokracií* (a free and democratic state, founded on respect for human rights and principles of civic society as a part of the family of European and world democracies).
2   To enter the House of Representatives, a party has to gain at least 5% of the votes.
3   ČSSD is a traditional political body in Czech society (established in the 1880s, swallowed by the Communist Party after World War II, and re-established in 1989). ANO 2011 is a political grouping ("movement"), founded in 2012 by entrepreneur and media magnate Andrej Babiš. The analysts interpret the grouping as a center-right political formation.

4   However simplifying and biased the model is, it can be used as a good frame for the basic characteristics of the Czech media's situation before 1989.

5   Formally, there was a multi-party system in Czechoslovakia before 1989 and "democratic" elections took place regularly, but political parties (and other public organizations) were obliged to be members of an umbrella association called the *Národní fronta* (National Front), and as members of *NF*, all parties were supposed to support the policy of the leading Communist Party.

6   The whole concept of "public service" broadcasting was inspired by the German public service broadcasting model and the British BBC and has not been welcomed very warmly by the liberal-conservative segment of the Czech political elite.

7   In 2013, the anti-establishment movement ANO 2011 entered the parliament. The party was founded by billionaire Andrej Babiš. It also used a lot of local and foreign consultants.

8   For details see www.transparentnivolby.cz/snemovna2013/2013/10/16/monitoring-financovani-volebnich-kampani-ti-medii-protece-stranickymi-ucty-nejmene-134-mil-korun/.

9   Electoral results are based on data from the Czech statistical office online at http://volby.cz/pls/ps2013/ps2?xjazyk=CZ.

References

Charvát, J., & Just, P. (2014). *První přímá volba prezidenta v roce 2013 [The first direct election of the president in 2013]*. Praha, Czech Republic: Metropolitan University Press.

Chytílek, R., Eibl, O., & Matušková, A. (2012). *Teorie a metody politického marketingu [Theory and methods of political advertising]*. Brno, Czech Republic: Centrum pro studium demokracie.

Gregor, M. (2012). Politická reklama [Political advertising]. In R. Chytílek, O. Eibl, & A. Matušková, *Teorie a metody politického marketingu* [Theory and methods of political advertising] (pp. 178–194). Brno, Czech Republic: Centrum pro studium demokracie.

Gregor, M., & Matušková, A. (2014). The presidential election in the Czech Republic: A case study of Karel Schwarzenberg's campaign strategy. In J. Lees-Marshment (Ed.), *Political marketing: Principles and applications* (2nd ed., pp. 191–193). London: Routledge.

Jirák, J. (1997). The Czech Republic: Media accountability system – an unknown concept. In U. Sonnenberg (Ed.), *Organising media accountability: Experiences in Europe* (pp. 43–48). Maastricht, The Netherlands: European Journalism Centre. Retrieved from www.ejc.nl/pdf/pub/mas.pdf.

Jirák, J., & Šoltys, O. (2006). Political advertising in a "new" democracy: The Czech Republic. In L. L. Kaid & C. Holtz-Bacha (Eds.), *The Sage handbook of political advertising* (pp. 377–386). Thousand Oaks, CA: Sage.

Malíř, J., & Marek, P. (2005). *Politické strany. Vývoj politických stran a hnutí v českých zemích a Československu 1861–2004. II. díl: Období 1938–2004 [Political parties: The development of political parties and movements in Czech lands and Czechoslovakia, 1861–2004. Volume II: 1938–2004]*. Brno, Czech Republic: Doplněk.

Matušková, A. (2010). *Politický marketing a české politické strany [Political marketing and Czech political parties]*. Brno, Czech Republic: MPU.

Mediaguru. (2014). *Infografika: Vlastníci českých médií a jejich dosah na trhu [Infographics: The owners of Czech media and their position on the market]*. Retrieved from www.mediaguru.cz/2014/06/infografika-vlastnici-ceskych-medii-a-jejich-dosah-na-trhu/#.VyyKlCEleVl.

Nová, E. (2013). Porušuje Babišova reklama na vodňanské kuře s jágrem zákon? Radní to chtějí prověřit [Is Babiš's advertisement violating the law? Members of the Council want to check it out]. Hospodářské noviny 9.10.2013. Retrieved from http://domaci.ihned.cz/c1-60981160-porusuje-babisova-reklama-na-vodnanske-kure-s-jagrem-zakon-radni-to-chteji-proverit.

Rybková, E., & Řiháčková V. (2013). *Mapping digital media: Czech Republic. A report by the Open Society Foundations*. Retrieved from www.opensocietyfoundations.org/sites/default/files/mapping-digital-media-czech-20130820.pdf.

Schwarzenberg, K. (2013). *České prezidentské volby 2013 | Karel Schwarzenberg – TV spot*. Retrieved from www.youtube.com/watch?v=Y3u89V_SU_c.

Siebert, F., Peterson, T., & Schramm, W. (1963). *Four theories of the press*. Urbana: University of Illinois Press.

Šíma, P., & Králiková, M. (2013). *Volební kampaně 2013 [Election campaigns 2013]*. Brno, Czech Republic: Barrister & Principal/IPM.

Sparks, C. (1998). *Communism, capitalism and the mass media*. Thousand Oaks, CA: Sage.

Strmiska, M. (2001). *Challenges of consolidation and post-communist party systems*. Brno, Czech Republic: International Institute of Political Science.

Večerník, J., & Matějů, P. (Eds.). (1999). *Ten years of rebuilding capitalism: Czech society after 1989*. Praha, Czech Republic: Academia.

Vodňanská drůbež. (2013). *TV spot KŘÍDLO.* Retireved from www.youtube.com/watch?v=ymq426Dv7Bw.

Zákon 231/2001 Sb. o provozování rozhlasového a televizního vysílání [Law on radio and television broadcasting]. Retrieved from www.rrtv.cz/cz/static/cim-se-ridime/stavajici-pravni-predpisy/pdf/231–2001.pdf.

Zeman, M. (2013). *Miloš Zeman – TV spot od Filipa Renče, plná verze.* Retrieved from www.youtube.com/watch?v=rz1FgsSFGKo.

11

POLITICAL ADVERTISING IN FRANCE

The Story and Effects of a Slow Liberalization

Alexandre Borrell and Jamil Dakhlia

From the beginning, the history of French audiovisual political advertising has been marked by distrust and drastic regulation. In 1936, between the two rounds of the legislative elections, the Pathé Company decided to broadcast speeches of the main political parties' leaders in movie theaters, just after its newsreels. It caused such violent collective reactions that this kind of political advertising stopped immediately (Delporte, 2007, pp. 28–30). In December 1955, a few weeks before the general election, each of the parties that already had at least one MP was allowed a five-minute program, aired between 7:30 and 8:30 p.m. on what was the only public television channel, as well as two 10-minute and one five-minute programs on public radio. The day and hour of broadcast were determined by drawing lots, to ensure the equality between parties. This official campaign was the real starting point for the practice of providing candidates in national elections access to dedicated programs on television.

Though significant, the development of the television programs allotted to the candidates in French national elections since the 1950s did not result in the creation of a specific word for them. In the 1990s, French authors used the word "clip" – especially when they studied the new formal aspects of these programs. Since then, terms like "spots" or the more general "official campaign" – that also encompasses radio programs, official posters and party manifestos – are more frequently used, whereas "political videos" seems the most frequent to designate online programs. Incidentally, the foreign researchers who conduct transnational studies or a study focused on France, use various words in relation to the media concerned, their political content, and/or the specific circumstances of elections ("television/election/political broadcasts"), or even the commercial appearance of these programs, probably influenced by countries where spots are quite similar to other television commercials ("televised/electoral/political advertising/ads/commercials"). In this chapter, we will use the terms "spots," "political advertising" or "official campaign" ("*campagne officielle*" being the official formula used by the French regulation board), or even "programs," to underline the audiovisual rules and constraints.

A first literature review of political advertising studies was written by Kaid and Gagnère (2006). After a presentation of the French political and electoral system, we will specifically focus on spots and shed light on the recent development of research on online political videos.

Political and Electoral System

Political Institutions

France under the Fifth Republic (since 1958) is a semi-presidential system, with both a president and a prime minister. The presidency is the most powerful position in the French political system. The president's duties include appointment of the prime minister, the power to dismiss the National Assembly, chairing of the Council of Ministers, appointing the members of the State Court (*Conseil d'État*) and the Constitutional Court (*Conseil Constitutionnel*), chairing the Higher Council of the Judiciary (*Conseil de la Magistrature*), negotiating all foreign treaties, and the power to call referenda. However, all domestic decisions must be approved by the prime minister. The French president is also supreme commander of the military. The president determines policy with the aid of the Council of Ministers (*Conseil des ministres*).

The head of the government is the prime minister who is appointed by the president for an indefinite term. The prime minister recommends ministers to the president, sets out ministers' duties and responsibilities, and manages the daily affairs of government. When the president and the prime minister do not come from the same political party or wing of the political spectrum, as was the case in 1986, 1993 and 1997, they must practice a process of "*cohabitation*," which means that the prime minister and the president will have to coordinate their policies in spite of their opposite political orientations.

The French Parliament is made up of two houses. The lower and principal house, the National Assembly (*Assemblée nationale*) is elected via a two-round system. The prime minister is always from the political majority in the National Assembly, but the president chooses who from the winning party becomes prime minister (the president supposedly chooses whoever he wants, but the prime minister needs the approval of the National Assembly to govern). The Senate co-writes the laws with the National Assembly. The president of the Senate is the "second most important person of the State." If the president of the Republic dies or is incapacitated, the president of the Senate assumes his function until the president comes back to work or a new president is elected. Bills, proposed by the government, and Parliament Members' bills must be approved by both houses before becoming law. Nonetheless, a government can in rare instances use Article 49.3 of the French Constitution to override parliamentary opposition and pass a law without a parliamentary vote. Laws and decrees are promulgated when the official text is published in the Official Journal (*Journal Officiel*) of the French Republic.

The State Court advises the executive for all administrative cases. The Constitutional Court determines the constitutionality of new laws or decrees. It can strike down a bill before it passes into law, if it is deemed unconstitutional, or demand the withdrawal of decrees even after promulgation. This Court is made up of nine members, appointed (three each) by the president of the Republic, the president of the National Assembly, and the president of the Senate, plus all living former heads of state. While the Minister of Justice (*Garde des Sceaux*) has power over the judicial system and public prosecutors through the *Parquet*, the judiciary is strongly independent of the executive and legislative branches.

Local government units consist of almost 36,000 *communes*, headed by a municipal council and a mayor, grouped in 101 *départements*, each of them headed by a *Conseil Général* (general council) and its president, grouped in 13 *régions* (reduced from 22 in 2014–16), headed by a regional council and its president.

Electoral System

The presidential election attracts the most predictions and news coverage because of the prominent role and effective powers of the head of state. The election now takes place every five years, however prior to 2000 it was only every seven years. The goal of the reform of the presidential term was to synchronize the presidential and legislative elections, reducing the odds of a *"cohabitation."* The presidential election has two rounds. Usually, more than 10 candidates run for the office, and the top two are chosen for the second round.

The legislative elections are for seats in the National Assembly. Its 577 members are elected, as is the president, by universal suffrage in a two-round voting system. A candidate who gets more than 50% of the vote in the first round is elected. If no candidate gets 50%, there is a second round, one week later, between all those first-round candidates who receive more than 12.5% of the votes in that first round. The National Assembly votes laws and also investigates day-to-day government business. In cases of disagreement with the Senate, the National Assembly eventually prevails.

The 348 members of the Senate are elected, in each *département*, by a college of elected officials, such as members of the National Assembly, mayors, delegates from the municipal councils, etc. – about 145,000 electors all in all.

The European elections are held every five years. As in all other member states, and unlike other elections in France, seats are distributed according to proportional representation. French European deputies are usually less well known figures than the national deputies and they are sometimes suspected of participating in those elections because they were unable to be elected otherwise. This is one of the reasons why few French voters care about the European elections.

The main government parties are, on the left, the Socialist Party (*Parti socialiste*, PS), which has been in power since the 2012 presidential and legislative elections, and on the right, *Les Républicains* (former *Union pour un Mouvement populaire*).

History and Regulation of Political Advertising on Television

History

In the elections from 1956 to 1962, every party represented in the National Assembly was given airtime for both referendum campaigns and legislative elections. In 1962, despite the opposition of many political leaders and parties, French voters approved by a large majority Charles de Gaulle's proposal to elect the president of the Republic by direct popular vote. The 1965 presidential election was the first one by direct suffrage.

This time, each candidate was given two hours of airtime on the public radio and television, between 1:00 and 1:30 p.m. and 8:30 and 9:00 p.m., divided into statements, from 7 to 14 minutes, and interviews with supportive journalists, for about 30 minutes[1] (Vassalo, 2012). The political diversity of access on French television was a historical event, making it possible for voters to discover previously unknown candidates. In the past, television news had only given attention and airtime to members of the majority party. This official campaign gathered a large audience, at a time when about 46% of French families owned a television. In the beginning, de Gaulle refused to use that communication tool, presuming he was well-known enough to need to present himself on television. When public curiosity about the official campaign seemed more and more apparent, he finally agreed to appear twice in that kind of program before the first round (Cohen & Lévy, 2007). That official campaign was a "television event," extensively reported and commented on in newspapers: television was from then on considered as an "actor of democracy" in France (Cohen & Lévy, 2007, pp. 74, 81).

In 1969, the board of directors of the ORTF (*Office de radiodiffusion-télévision française*), the public television and radio, decided to promote pluralistic access to television and radio, dividing the airtime dedicated to political information and debates in three equal parts: one for the government, one for the majority and one for the parliamentary opposition. This is probably one of the reasons why the official campaign appears to be a less important element and event in the French presidential elections since then, and all the more so given that a televised debate has been ritually organized between the two candidates before the second round, since the 1974 presidential elections. The discussions about the adoption of modern techniques of communication and/or introducing paid political ads on television during the 1980s are reported in Dauncey (1999). It is important to keep in mind that political ads are forbidden during campaigns in newspapers since 1985, and on billboards since 1990.

Regulation of Broadcast and Production

Succeeding to the HACA (*Haute Autorité de la communication audiovisuelle*, 1982–1986) and the CNCL (*Commission nationale de la communication et des libertés*, 1986–1989), the CSA (*Conseil supérieur de l'audiovisuel*) monitors the implementation of television and radio regulations. It is aimed at ensuring plurality in the opinions expressed, and since 1989, at organizing the radio and television electoral campaigns.

During electoral periods, the CSA asks television channels and radio stations that follow the campaign on their programs to apply more precise rules and it checks their implementation regularly. In 2012, from January 1 to March 20 – the day of the publication of the list of candidates that are allowed to run for the presidential election – they had to give "fair" coverage and "fair" airtime to the potential candidates (and their party and supporters). Fairness takes into account their representativeness – based particularly on the results of the candidate or its party at the most recent elections and on electoral surveys – and their involvement in the campaign (CSA, 2011). During the second period, until April 9, they had to give fair coverage of all the candidates' campaigns and equal airtime to express themselves. Since the beginning of the official campaign, during the two weeks prior to the first and the second rounds, they had to give the same coverage and the same airtime to each of the 10 candidates' campaigns. The official campaign is the period when the candidate spots are broadcast on public television channels and radio stations; official posters can be put up on the dedicated boards near each polling station and all the electors receive by mail four pages of party manifestos and samples of ballot papers.

The organization of the official campaign is guided by a concern for equality. For audiovisual programming, the CSA ensures that production, scheduling and broadcasting conditions are equal. The candidates are provided technical equipment and a team for the shooting and editing of their spots.

The rules are similar for the official campaigns aired before the legislative elections, the European Parliament elections and referendum,[2] except for the length of spots: the airtime is divided between the parties represented in the *Assemblée nationale* depending on the number of their MPs; other parties that run at least 75 candidates for legislative elections or put forward lists in at least five of the eight European constituencies are allocated a shorter amount of airtime. The parties represented in the *Assemblée nationale* have to share three hours between them before the first round and one-and-a-half hours before the second round for the legislative elections in 2012, and a total of two hours for the European elections in 2014. The other parties may dispose of seven minutes before the first round of the legislative elections, five minutes before the second one, and share one hour for the European official campaign.

Like the newspapers, the Internet remains a free space where candidates and parties do not labor under such legal constraints of their political communication and are free to broadcast as many commercials and videos as they want, of any kind.

Regulation of Content

As far as their content is concerned, spots have other restrictions, as a legacy of the previous obligation to ensure equality between candidates: the candidates must appear and express themselves in each one of their spots; participants cannot use the national or the EU emblem, or pictures of official buildings (the *Elysée*, the *Assemblée nationale*, city halls, etc.); it is forbidden to use any expression meant to or having the effect of ridiculing other candidates or their representatives and each candidate is supposed to respect the related rights of all the people who appear in a recognizable way (right to privacy, rights of the image, CSA, 2012c).

As a consequence, negative ads are forbidden in France: although candidates regularly evoke – by naming them or not – their competitors, they are not allowed to use their image. However, a few exceptions were found in 2012, when some opponents were surreptitiously shown in some spots. Similarly, the rules were loosened and the presence of tri-color flags (in very large numbers in some meetings) was finally permitted, except when they appeared at the candidate's side.

Format

These constraints have a significant effect on the format of electoral spots, and supposedly on their success with viewers. In addition, the official campaign was aired at the same time in all public channels until 1981. Yet, the situation changed in the 1980s when the first private channels were created (Canal+ in 1984, La Cinq and M6 in 1986) and the older and most successful television channel TF1 was privatized in 1987. Given that private channels are not required to broadcast official campaign spots, they have faced tough competition by more entertaining fare since that time (Johnston & Gerstlé, 1995). That is why the length, the broadcast schedule and the visual content of campaign spots were liberalized afterwards.

Since the 1993 legislative elections, the length of campaign spots has been shortened (Drouot, 1995). Before the first round of presidential elections, the programs' length varied from 5–6 minutes to 18 minutes in 1981 and 1988, from one minute and 30 seconds to three minutes and 30 seconds in 2012 (see Table 11.1), and from two to five minutes before the second round.

Altogether, in 2012, each candidate of the first round of the presidential election was allocated 2:24 hours of airtime, divided between 18 spots broadcast on four public channels; the ten spots

Table 11.1 Airtime allocated to the official campaign on public channels before the first round of the French presidential elections

	Number and length of spots by candidate	Total length of the spots for each candidate	Total airtime (including broadcast on various public television channels)	Number of candidates	Total airtime allocated to the official campaign
1965	**7:** 1 x 8 min*, 4 x 14 min, 2 x 28 min	2 h	2 h	6	12 h
1981	**6:** 2 x 5 min*, 2 x 12 min, 2 x 18 min	1:10 h	3:30 h	10	38 h
1988	**6:** 2 x 5 min*, 4 x 15 min	1:10 h	3:30 h	9	31:30 h
1995	**12:** 2 x 1 min*, 4 x 2 min, 4 x 5 min, 2 x 15 min	1:15 h	2:30 h	9	22:30 h
2002	**9:** 1 x 1 min*, 4 x 1 min 45, 4 x 5 min	28 min	2:04 h	16	33:04 h
2007	**18:** 8 x 1 min, 6 x 2 min 30, 4 x 5 min 30	45 min	3 h	12	36 h
2012	**18:** 10 x 1 min 30, 8 x 3 min 30	43 min	2:24 h	10	24 h

* spots aired the first and/or the last day of the official campaign.

Source: The authors on the basis of data reported by CSA.

of the second round were also aired several times, representing a total of 3:10 hours of airtime for each candidate (Borrell, 2013b). The spots were broadcast at eight different times throughout the day, from 7:30 a.m. to 10 p.m., especially after the main television news programs. The aim was that all television viewers should have an opportunity to see some of the spots, even if they had not scheduled time for it – the audience ratings detailed below prove that it was partly successful. As in 1965, the official campaign was announced in the printed television programs or newspapers in 1988. But it was no longer the case for the 1995 campaign (Cong Huyen Nu, 1999), and Maarek and co-authors emphasize the lack of announcement of these programs on television and their erratic scheduling in the 2000s (Maarek, Pourtier-Tillinac, & Sebbah, 2012; Maarek & Sebbah, 2009, 2013).

Moreover, since the European election campaign of 1984 (Drouot, 1995), parties and candidates are allowed to insert videos pre-produced by themselves in increasing proportions. For the presidential official campaign of 2012, the candidates could produce their 18 spots with the human and material resources provided by the CSA, but were also allowed to produce 50% of the total duration of their spots by their own means, and 75% for the spots aired before the second round. These sequences represented about 22% of the total length of the 2007 official campaign and 27% in 2012, with a wide range of uses by the candidates, from 0.66% to 49% of their official campaign (CSA, 2012c).

Gerstlé (2012, p. 66) sees that significant transformation as a "compelling commercial tendency" ("*authentique dérive publicitaire*") with a bad influence on electoral debate and political life. For Ballet (2014), reducing the length of spots pushed the candidates to use much more emotional appeals. However, since spots received less and less public attention since the 1970s, the fragmentation of airtime allocated to the candidates may also be considered as a way to establish contact with many more voters. Seemingly, after some kind of an adaptation period to this new formal freedom during the 1990s, spots are again composed mainly of the candidates' speeches nowadays as they were before 1988.

Research on the Content, Reception and Effects of Ads

The evolution of research on French political ads follows the evolution of the official campaign itself. We have many pieces of information about the 1965 official campaign, depicted by many historians as a successful new era of political communication, but little is known about the spots broadcast in 1969, 1974 and 1981. Spots did not engage political communication studies again until 1988, when they became a more visually attractive object of research.

There is no standardization of French spots studies, nor a codebook that could be applied for each official campaign, but only infrequent references to former studies, even in the case of recurring studies conducted by the same team (Bras & Maarek, 2007; Maarek et al., 2012; Maarek & Sebbah, 2009, 2013). Using the same codebook to study 1988 and 2002 official campaigns and the effects of spots in 1988, 1995 and 2002, the studies by Kaid and her co-authors (Kaid & Gagnère, 2006) stand as an exception. Diachronic comparative studies are more frequently conducted through a specific approach of one dimension of the spots: emotions for Ballet (2006, 2012, 2014), pictures for Borrell (2006, 2013a, 2014). The comparison between French and US presidential elections in 1988 (Kaid, Gerstlé, & Sanders, 1991) later completed with the German general elections (Holtz–Bacha, Kaid, & Johnston, 1994) has not been repeated since then.

By making it possible to compare the political ads of many countries at the same time, the European elections are the main occasion where France has been included in synchronic comparative studies. The first occurrences of these studies were for direct elections in 1979 (Blumler, 1983), for the campaigns in 2004 (Maier & Tenscher, 2006), 2009 (Holtz-Bacha, Johansson, Leidenberger, Maarek, & Merkle, 2012) and 2014 (Holtz-Bacha, Novelli, & Rafter, in press). European elections offer an opportunity to apply similar methods and to underline some national trends.

Legislative elections, whose results are mainly seen as a consequence of the presidential election when they are organized a few weeks after it, have only been studied once (Dauncey, 1999). As for the 577 MPs that are elected in single-member districts, studying the communication of parties alone could be a very interesting subject of research, as is the case for the European Parliament campaigns.

The Predominance of Content Analysis

French spots are a unique object that allows a comparative study of various candidates' political communication and of the different French political cultures, both in synchrony and diachrony.

The general form of spots has led to different classifications from one study to another. Kaid and Johnston (2001) and then others studied the video-style of spots, taking the whole spot as the unit of analysis, assessing the verbal content, the nonverbal content (appearance, clothing, body movements, eye contact, presence of leaders, etc.) and the production techniques (length, video special effects, etc.). As European spots not only are generally longer than American spots, but deal with different issues and frequently are composed of several sequences, other researchers have studied each sequence of one spot, focusing on formal features, production techniques, content, personalization, style/argumentation and visualization (for a complete presentation, see Holtz-Bacha, 2000). As far as their results are concerned, we can distinguish between the studies that mainly focus on verbal content or visual content, and those that address both dimensions of the audiovisual message or more globally the political and communication strategy.

Discourses

A team of linguists have studied the first spot aired by the candidates for the presidential election of 1988, spots that were integrally transcribed in their book (Groupe Saint-Cloud, 1995). They analyzed particular elements of the discourses and arguments of each candidate – the use of pronouns, words such as "you," "me," "France," some elements of rhetoric, the gestures of candidates, etc. – in order to highlight the specific attributes of each of them. In the book that this team published about the 1995 presidential election, spots were studied much less, only with regard to the different uses of imperative tense by the candidates (Petitjean, 1999).

The commercials were a large part of the corpus studied by Ballet (2006, 2012, 2014), who aimed at bringing out the emotional patterns of discourse of the candidates during the presidential campaigns from 1981 to 2012, by focusing on their appeals of fear, hope, repulsion and sympathy in their announcement that they run for presidency, their printed manifesto sent to voters and their spots. She transcribed and studied the candidate spots of the seven main parties.[3] As a general result, she shows that the use of emotional patterns is much more important in the spots than in the candidates' announcement they run for presidency and printed manifesto. This use is quite stable from 1981 to 2002 and grows quickly in 2007 and 2012 campaigns, when she counted a tripled amount of emotional occurrences in the spots in comparison with the 1980s and the 1990s, one each eight seconds (Ballet, 2014, pp. 18, 37). The comparison also shows continuities and changes in the expression of specific political cultures. The parties that protest and do not govern more frequently use indignation than hope: the left-wing candidates emphasize indignation concerning economic and social matters, the green party expresses environmental fears and the far-right-wing party uses the fear of otherness and immigration, and the indignation about Europe. The mainstream candidates use less affective rhetoric, particularly when they are in power. Incumbents more frequently use hope, and challengers prefer to express their indignation toward the president or prime minister in charge. If the mainstream candidates tend to adopt the specific emotional patterns and matters of concern of their party, they mix them with specific emotions and topics related to their status in the majority or the opposition.

Applying a classical typology of political ads, papers showed that the spots of the 1988 presidential campaign relied on logical (as opposed to emotional) appeals and focused more on issue than on images (Holtz-Bacha et al., 1994; Johnston, 1991). In 2002, these logical and issue oriented trends were similar, but attacks and emotional appeals were more frequent in Le Pen and Chirac spots (Gagnère & Kaid, 2003). The French spots also seem to contain fewer attacks on the opponents than in other countries (Holtz-Bacha et al., 1994; Johnston & Gerstlé, 1995) – obviously a result of the legal constraint not to make a fool of other candidates nor show their images; as the candidates have to express themselves in each spot, they have to make these attacks personally (Johnston, 1991).

Pictures

Some other studies especially focus on the visual content of the official campaign, since political ads became visually much more varied in 1988. Renault (1995) studied the famous clip that appeared in many spots of Mitterrand in 1988, a 1:18 minute sequence composed of 800 pictures coming from 300 historical documents. He considers it as a brief "moderate republican, secular and glorious" history of France whose continuator would be Mitterrand (Renault, 1995, p. 26).

Gourévitch (1989) noted that clips were used in the spots of six of the nine candidates for the presidential election in 1988. He proposed to define the "clip" as a format influenced both by musical clips and television commercials: it inherited from musical clips the prominence of music over discourse on their soundtrack, a rapid pace due to editing and electronic effects, and shortness. Political clips were broadcast in a similar scheduling as television ads (hours of broadcast and succession of clips), and shared the same strategy: they focused on the product, i.e., in clips, the candidate himself. Gourévitch also proposes a typology of them ("jingle clips," "ideologic clips" and "allegoric clips") (1989, p. 28), but, in a statement written after the 1995 and 1997 elections, he notes that the use of clips has decreased, and that they are restricted to "introduction jingles" (1998, pp. 169–173). The fashion has changed and/or this audiovisual tool of communication is more controlled by the candidates.

Cong Huyen Nu (1999) studied the transformation of the visual strategy of Chirac and its homogenization. In 1988, spots had a new opportunity to present the candidates, their personality, relations with anonymous people or the heads of foreign states. That is what Maarek et al. call a "notoriety commercial" (2012, pp. 25, 36): although he has been mayor of Paris since 1977, and prime minister for the second time, and despite his being well-known, the personality of Jacques Chirac is still controversial, and he wanted to offer a more sympathetic image of himself. In 1995, the visual composition of his spots is much more elaborated, abstract and centered on his platform more than on his image.

Applying the video-style categories, Johnston (1991, p. 65) emphasized that the spots of Chirac and Mitterrand in 1988 were mostly "combinations" of "production technique" (75% of the spots), recorded live in formal indoors settings.

Other studies were conducted using a more cultural approach. Comparing the spots of the parties for the legislative elections in 1993 and those of the candidates to the presidential election in 1995, Dauncey (1999, section 52) showed that "the 'picturing' employed in French campaign spots may be more broadly 'political' than cultural, since parties and candidates competitively appeal to the traditions and values of republican society and to idealized geographical communities of indivisible rural and urban France, rather than a culture defined by race, ethnicity and multiculturalism." He also underlined some differences among political parties: "the imagery of broadcasts show how the Right tends to organize pictures of France dominated by a blend of 'traditional life' and France's modern prestige as an advanced industrial nation, whereas the Left emphasises the political and cultural values of Republican liberty, equality and fraternity" (Dauncey, 1999, section 1).

A later study focused on the specific use of pictures of the French scenery in the presidential campaigns in 1988, 1995 and 2002 (Borrell, 2006), analyzing whether they were used as a background of the candidate, as a reference to a specific issue (political, environmental, immigration, etc.) or as decorative postcards. These pictures are almost always made up of real footage and mainly show a green but urban background or rural landscapes. And the coast, when used as a setting, symbolizes the freedom of the candidate. More generally, the right-wing parties' spots keep on conveying a more traditional image of France, whereas the territory progressively disappears from the pictures used by the left-wing parties, which give more and more importance to anonymous portraits and endorsements. This aspect was studied in another comparative study that focused on the spots of the communists, socialists, right-wing and far-right-wing candidates in the presidential elections, from 1988 to 2007 (Borrell, 2014). The composition of the series of anonymous portraits, and of the panels of people that talk about their lives or ask questions of a candidate, shows that their main function is to represent French society, and/or one of the specific electorates that the candidate wants to address in order to persuade voters. As far as French people seen as Black or Arabic are concerned, a general evolution appears: their number slowly grows between 1988 and 2002, as political leaders become aware of the diversity of French people's skin color, and try to convey another image of the society and of their potential electors. Beyond the use of skin color as an additional means (with age, gender and profession) to depict the diversity of the French nation, some political trends appear. In the spots of the right-wing candidates, Black- and Arabic-looking French are frequently racialized as they only speak of immigration. In the left-wing spots this status is only used to denounce racism and racial discrimination, and Black- and Arabic-looking French people are frequently undifferentiated from other endorsements, since they have the same hopes and problems.

The conclusion from these results is that in France, presidential candidates' spots express, wittingly or unwittingly, their belonging to a political culture, linked to their party and, more generally, to the distinction between the left and the right. The differences go beyond the classical political strategy of addressing specific groups of voters, traditionally devoted to one's party.

Strategies

Strategies appear in visual and discursive content studies; they explain a large part of the content of the spots. The studies we discuss now take a more global approach to the spots. Two types of research are involved: one that applies a code sheet already used in other countries, and another that evaluates more generally the strategy of the candidate at an individual level, using their own methodology or sensibility.

In comparing the French and American presidential candidates in 1988, for instance, Johnston (1991) showed that an incumbent and a challenger style exist in both countries. Mitterrand was then president, with a cohabitation government headed by Chirac. He succeeded in presenting himself as an incumbent, the same way that US presidents do when they run for re-election.

The studies by Maarek and co-authors deal with the official campaigns of the European elections of 2004 (Bras & Maarek, 2007), 2009 (Maarek et al., 2012) and the presidential elections in 2007 (Maarek & Sebbah, 2009) and 2012 (Maarek & Sebbah, 2013). They focus on the specific strategy of the official campaign of the candidate or the party. As they are all studied separately, it is difficult to summarize their conclusions, which are specific for each party/candidate and election. In the European parliamentary elections, 21 parties produced spots in 2004 and 24 in 2009. The authors show that a majority of parties deal with national issues much more than European ones, oscillating between disqualification, denial and Euroskepticism, except the centrist and green parties. They also highlight the significant presence of some leaders although they are not candidates, specifically in 2009. The spots of the 2007 presidential campaign show two different strategies: the three candidates expected to receive the largest number of votes showed consistency and repetition of a few messages in their spots, while the other ones mainly produced many different "notoriety commercials" to promote their platform. There was a great contrast between the two candidates of the second round: the didactic spots of Sarkozy, based on his platform, and the much more emotional spots of Royal, focused on her personality and the main slogans of her campaign.

Despite useful remarks, this approach remains rather subjective and aims at determining if a campaign is more of a success or a failure – for instance, the official campaigns for the European elections are both considered to be "disappointing" (Bras & Maarek, 2007, p. 80; Maarek et al., 2012, p. 17).

Focusing on the pictures of the 2007 presidential spots, another researcher (Borrell, 2011) evaluates the audiovisual strategies of the candidates to promote their relations with voters, using the traditional face-to-face device, the contribution of anonymous citizens (talking about their experiences, asking the candidates questions or engaging in conversation with them), and interactions caught on camera, shaking hands in the streets or during rallies. Candidates use their own strategies. Considering that verbal interactions are deeper than visual interactions, it seems that, with exceptions, left-wing candidates engage in much more physical and verbal interactions with voters than the right-wing ones (Borrell, 2011).

Another study of the 2012 presidential campaign quantified the portion of airtime allocated to the speeches and the pictures of the candidates during their shortest spots (Borrell, 2013a, Table 1). It shows that candidates occupy most of the airtime, speaking all or virtually all of the time. The candidates not only conform to the obligation to appear in each spot, they choose to focus on three or four core elements of their platforms or develop a single issue in each spot.

That level of personalization could appear as a tautological effect of the presidential system – although several other leaders appeared in many presidential spots in 1988 and 1995. But the spots of the European elections suggest a specific national trend. For the first European elections in 1979, Suine stated that "the overall level of personalization was low everywhere except in France, where it was markedly higher than average" (1983, p. 235). A study of the 2009 European spots in four countries (Holtz-Bacha et al., 2012) showed that party representatives or candidates appeared in 61% of the sequences of the French spots (of which 86% were statements), and that French spots showed the smallest number of representatives, leading the authors to consider that French spots had "the highest amount of personalization" (Holtz-Bacha et al., 2012, p. 85).

The European comparison makes it possible to shed light on the specific qualities of French spots which are much more personalized than in other countries. That could be a result of the influence of the presidential election on all of political life and political communication, apart from the presidential campaign itself.

Reception

Political communication research in France has produced only a few studies about effects, although it was and remains a theoretical and heuristic matter of interest. Despite factual errors concerning political parties and media and interpretations about the effects of spots on voting choices, we do have the detailed review presented by Kaid and Gagnère (2006) about research on the effects of French official campaigns. No other research of this kind has been conducted since then. Kaid and Gagnère (2006) synthesized results from the presidential campaigns in 1988 (Kaid, 1991), 1995 (Cwalina, Falkowski, & Kaid, 2000; Kaid & Holtz-Bacha, 2000; Kaid, McKinnon, & Gagnère, 1996) and 2002 (Gagnère & Kaid, 2003; Kaid, Gagnère, Williams, & Trammel, 2003). They showed the modest effects of exposure to spots in the changing evaluation of the presidential candidates by young student voters, which only reinforced or weakened the relation between candidates and their supporters. It is possible that the emotional content of spots may be correlated with the evaluation of the presidential candidates, and there might be gendered differences in the effect of ads on the evaluation of these candidates.

A modest effects study was organized the day before the second-round election in 2012 (Borrell, 2013b). It mainly showed the ambivalence of television viewers: although a large portion of them found the spots boring, they appreciated the fictional and unusual spots of Philippe Poutou, the candidate of the New Anticapitalist Party, and evaluated negatively the other spots that departed from the usual format, especially those of Joly, as if television viewers had integrated a visual convention governing the effects of spots.

Relevance of Advertising as a Campaign Channel

According to a survey organized in 1975, 64% of the voters regarded television as the most useful and efficient way to "choose a candidate" (Kaid & Gagnère, 2006). More generally, in 2009, a representative survey reports that television is the first source of political information for 50% of the French, and the second for another 30% (Le Hay, Vedel, & Chanvril, 2011). But television's key role is still to verify information and depends on the type of program. According to a survey conducted in March 1988, people believe the best way to obtain campaign information is by programs in which politicians answer questions from several journalists (50%), debates between politicians (38%), political programs with a live audience (23%) and the official campaign spots (5%) (Gerstlé, 2002). It seems that the mediation of journalists is much more valued than the mere propaganda of the spots.

However, official campaign spots cannot be neglected as a way for candidates to directly address voters through television. The CSA asks the 13 main French television channels to measure precisely how long each political figure spoke during the previous month, in order to quantify the political balance and pluralism of television coverage of politicians, and to guarantee equity first, then equality during election campaigns. In 2002, during the last two weeks before the first round, public channels (France 2, France 3, France 5 and France Ô) and private channels (TF1, Canal +, M6, Direct 8), altogether allocated 24:39 hours of airtime to the candidates and their representatives, equally divided between them. That is only a few minutes more than the whole official campaign, which represented 24 hours of broadcast during the same two weeks (Borrell, 2013b). Spots whose content was completely controlled by candidates occupied the same airtime as the sound bites chosen by journalists to cover the campaign on full service channels; the private 24-hour news channels (LCI, i-Télé, BFM TV) allocated candidates 119:37 hours of airtime during the same two weeks. The quantitative comparison is less favorable to spots during the two weeks before the second round: they represented 6:20 hours, compared to 48:40 hours on full service channels (including the debate between the two finalists), and 142:17 hours on 24-hour news channels.

Audience ratings are not available to compare one presidential campaign to another. The television audience was low in 1988 – no more than five million viewers, decreasing day by day (Mariani, 1995) – and suffered from the existence of several private channels. Since then, the CSA mainly delivers general data. During the two weeks before each round of the presidential election, the official campaign program was seen by a total of 127 million viewers of 15 years of age and older in 1995, 108 million in 2002, 115 million in 2007 (CSA, 1995, 2002, 2007). In 2012, an average of 40% of French people watched a part of the official campaign of each of the 10 candidates; this average goes up to 51% for the candidates in the second round (CSA, 2012c). Because they were broadcast after the 8 p.m. newscast on the French public channel France 2 in 2012, the audience doubled for shortest spots compared to the 2002 and 2007 campaigns, when they were broadcast before the newscast. There were 3.7 million television viewers each evening during the two weeks before the first round according to Médiamétrie (Ménager, 2012), an audience size similar to the most successful broadcast scheduled in 1988, at 1:30 p.m. (Mariani, 1995).

In 2007, André Gunthert (EHESS) and Rémi Douine (Telecom Paris) created the "*Vidéomètre,*" a tool to measure the audience of online political videos on YouTube and Dailymotion. They found that the day before the first round, the spots were seen 360,000 times (Borrell, 2011). In 2012, we found 276 videos on YouTube and Dailymotion that were copies exactly the same as spots in the official campaign; altogether, they had 1.85 million viewers of at least part of the spot, between the beginning of the official campaign and the election day of the second round. With 48 videos online, Hollande's spots received 29.7% of the total views; the candidate of the little anti-capitalist party, Poutou, with 50 videos, received 18% of the online audience (Borrell, 2013b). Poutou's strategy – to produce varied and humorous spots – can be seen as a success as far as public attention is concerned. Moreover, these data show that audience interest was high at the very beginning of the official campaign, when online newspapers mentioned and showed the first broadcast spots, then quickly decreased from the second day of the campaign, and grew again only the day before the first-round election day. The results lead us to think that some people indeed use online spots for more information about the candidates and their platforms. More generally, the Internet offers free space to any candidate or party wishing to broadcast spots from the official campaign and other videos dealing with the election.

The Internet

In France, the use of the Internet for campaign advertising began to develop in 2005. Before the creation of YouTube and Dailymotion in February 2005, many ways of publishing videos online were already available but sharing videos was quite difficult, due to differences between the technological processes and the varied formats of each platform.

From a political point of view, 2005 is also a turning point because of the approaching 2007 French presidential election. According to Gunthert (2007), the ease of broadcast and access to video content constituted one of the historical contributions of this campaign; he keeps this novelty into proportion by pointing the modest daily viewing figures for a majority of these videos. In 2007, of the 12,000 videos identified through *Vidéomètre* as having political relevance, only 350 were seen more than 100 times and only 20 more than 1,000 times per day. Furthermore, the peaks of viewership are closely linked to mass media reporting, such as lemonde.fr's, which puts the role of political videos into perspective (Politique, Internet et vidéos avec le Vidéomètre, 2007).

Pourtier-Tillinac (2009, p. 2) sees three reasons for the French politicians' fad for online videos. The first and most obvious one, as far campaign advertising is concerned, is that the CSA doesn't take Internet videos into account when it measures the time allotted for speaking, unlike the politicians' appearances on radio or television. The second reason is a technical one. Such a system enables the low-cost publication of many kinds of contents. In the case of blogs or sites drawing on public platforms such as Dailymotion or YouTube, broadcasting is zero-cost. As for the set-up costs, they remain very low because politicians can use the Internet visual communication fashion of aligning a webcam or a mobile phone, with no apparent film direction. These two first elements provide an opportunity for "small" French parties. Outside of electoral periods, political audiovisual communication is regulated by a proportionality principle which makes the smallest political parties almost non-existent on television. Encouraged by the minimal cost of production and circulation on the web and freed from the CSA jurisdiction, the small parties can communicate as much as they wish on the Internet. A third reason is the freedom of political expression both on the form and the substance allowed by online videos. Politicians and their teams can control the whole interview process for example, but also the direction and the publication of each video. Pourtier-Tillinac highlights this very issue. She points out that if, at first, these broadcast modes allowed unchecked political expression, they were quickly followed, after Nicolas Sarkozy's first political podcast in 2006, by strictly monitored political communication (2009, p. 1).

Insisting that technological choices can impact the way politics is advertised, Pourtier-Tillinac identifies three types of French political videos from 2005 to 2009. The first category deals with the political sites or blogs using their own server to broadcast videos. The second one is all about WebTV. In this case, we should speak of semi-personal broadcasting since the distribution is aimed at collective use. The first French political WebTV dates back to the 2007 presidential campaign when Nicolas Sarkozy launched NS TV on January 14. The other parties soon imitated him. Beside party WebTV, the explosion of video channels dedicated to specific political leaders is particularly striking, confirming the personalization process of French politics (*Chaîne Alain Juppé*, *Web TV* of Luc Chatel, *Ma web TV* of Jean-Luc Mélenchon, *Eric Besson TV*, etc.). The third and last type of political Internet broadcasting is the use of a public video platform such as Dailymotion or YouTube. They have been chosen by a majority of political sites and blogs for financial reasons as we already mentioned, but also for the symbolical benefit of participating in a collective or generational movement, becoming a member, etc. (Babeau, 2014).

Gunthert (2007) builds his own typology of French political videos on pragmatic criteria. He distinguishes between activist videos – e.g., "*Le vrai Sarkozy*" (The real Sarkozy), "*Greenpeace livre du maïs OGM à Sarkozy*" (Greenpeace delivers GMO corn to Sarkozy) – satiric or parodic videos – e.g., "*Nicolas & Ségolène – Les Musclés*" inspired by a popular variety band – and editorialized events – e.g., "*Création d'émeutes à Gare du Nord*" (Riots created at the Gare du Nord Station), "*La bonne blague de Rachida Dati*" (Rachida Dati's Good Joke). Regarding satirical videos, he sheds light on an interesting case, which he names "*détournement d'intention*" (diversion of intention). He refers to the militant videos that become a subject of mockery in the eyes of the supporters of the opposite political side, because of their ridiculous or outrageous aspect. In November 2007 for example, the song "*Une rose, un projet, une femme*" (A Rose, a Project, a Woman) made many of Ségolène Royal's opponents laugh whereas it was meant for glorifying the Socialist candidate.

As for the social uses of French political videos, Gunthert (2007) judges by the variety of comments added to many videos that attention does not directly depend on partisan cleavages. A large audience is generally caused by popularity, but in this case, Gunthert prefers to speak of attractiveness. Priority is given to the contents, or more exactly what the contents are suggested to be by the titles, tags or any other pieces of information about it. Before accessing a video, the Internet user is generally referred by a news site, a militant network or a personal contact. Direct access to videos is a less usual scenario.

In any case, as Devars puts it, in line with Gunthert's study, the main motive for the watching French political videos is the search for further information, whether the user missed a program on television or whether he/she wishes to receive more complete, unmediated information, especially if it depicts politics from a different angle than the one taken by traditional media.

Nevertheless, Pourtier-Tillinac (2009, p. 4) defines French Internet political advertising as a kind of selective exposure, especially in the case of party or personal sites and blogs. Most of the time, politicians only address an audience that chooses to watch their videos. As shown by the annual electoral surveys of CEVIPOF, the profile of Internet users who visit political sites seems to be very specific. By focusing their audiovisual communication on the Internet, politicians and parties risk only addressing the most informed, and politicized part of the population and missing swing voters. This last point suggests that the role of the Internet political advertising is less about information and conviction than a propagandistic one, designed for promoting political leaders within their own camp (CEVIPOF, annually).

To conclude, as Devars (2015, p. 97) pointed out from his study of the videos released during Nicolas Sarkozy's five-year term (2007–12), political videos "lie at the intersection of new possibilities offered by computerized technologies, the various constraints of the digital devices that shape the ways these videos are made public and visible and of course the sociopolitical logic which gives worthiness to their circulation."[4]

Conclusion

A result of this review is that all authors do not utilize the existing literature on French political ads, and that there is a specific gap between French-speaking and English-speaking studies, which tend to ignore each another. That can be seen both as an effect of different research traditions and a consequence of the language barrier. But the few references to prior studies is also a distinctive feature and a shortcoming within French studies about political ads. Two academic reasons seem to be of particular significance: on the one hand, the dissemination of French research is in books more than in journals, and second, the weakness of the French political communication research community. That second reason might be explained in turn by the lack of an established journal specifically dedicated to this area of knowledge, and by the fact that political communication is not considered an academic area study and that researchers in France communicate within their disciplines. Relations between historians, political scientists, communication studies, discourse studies, etc. are rare, with only a few individuals bridging the gaps. Far from depending on the interest of each academic area, the connectivity of research should be one of the methodological goals of the studies about French political ads in the coming years.

We hope this first attempt of an exhaustive review of French- and English-speaking studies will help develop a better knowledge of the existing literature. Regular funding and strengthening of the political communication research community would be a great help.

Research about the reception and effects of ads could define another goal. Although they cannot be considered as representative, the comments on online videos posted on YouTube, Dailymotion, etc., could be a fruitful ground for research in order to understand on what criteria the reception of political spots is based.

Notes

1   A part of the official campaigns broadcast since 1965 to nowadays is available for free on the INA (*Institut national de l'audiovisuel*) website: www.ina.fr/recherche/search?search=campagne+officielle.
2   Parties of the *Outremer* territories benefit from a specific allocation system of airtime and broadcast designed for their specific political life and audiovisual media.
3   Complete transcription of the spots broadcast in 2002 are available in Ballet (2006, pp. 56–101).
4   "(Les vidéos politiques) s'inscrivent au carrefour des possibilités nouvelles offertes par les technologies informatisées, des contraintes plurielles des dispositifs numériques qui façonnent les modes de visibilité et de publicité des vidéos, et bien sûr des logiques sociopolitiques qui chargent de valeur leur mise en circulation."

References

Babeau, F. (2014). La participation politique des citoyens "ordinaires" sur l'Internet. La plateforme Youtube comme lieu d'observation. *Politiques de Communication, 2*(3), 125–150.

Ballet, M. (2006). *À cœur ouvert. Les ressorts émotionnels des discours de la campagne présidentielle officielle de 2002*. Master's thesis (dir. by N. Mayer). Paris: IEP Paris.

Ballet, M. (2012). *Peur, espoir, compassion, indignation. L'appel aux émotions dans les campagnes présidentielles (1981–2007)*. Paris: Dalloz.

Ballet, M. (2014). *Émotions et élections: Les campagnes présidentielles françaises (1981–2012)*. Paris: INA.

Blumler, J. G. (Ed.). (1983). *Communicating to voters: Television in the first European Parliament elections*. London: Sage.

Borrell, A. (2006). L'appropriation du territoire national par les candidats à l'élection présidentielle dans les campagnes télévisées officielles (1988–2002). In É. Ndiaye, C. Roméro, & E. Zayas (Eds.), *Territoires rêvés II. Du territoire rêvé au rêve de territoire* (pp. 188–208). Orléans: PU d'Orléans.

Borrell, A. (2011). Les citoyens ordinaires: Supporters, témoins, interlocuteurs? Les candidats mettent en scène leur proximité avec les Français dans les spots télévisés de la campagne officielle. In I. Veyrat-Masson (Ed.), *Médias et élections. La campagne présidentielle de 2007 et sa réception* (pp. 59–82). Paris: INA/L'Harmattan.

Borrell, A. (2013a). S'adresser aux électeurs face caméra dans la campagne officielle: figure imposée ou programme libre pour les candidats? *Nottingham French Studies, 52*(2), 227–239.

Borrell, A. (2013b, May). *Les stratégies de propagande dans les spots de la campagne officielle*. Paper presented at the Conference "Communication et médias dans la campagne présidentielle de 2012," Paris.

Borrell, A. (2014). "Un corps français traditionnel ?" Usages de la couleur de peau dans les spots des candidats à la présidentielle (1988–2007). In S. Denis, C. Sécail, & I. Veyrat-Masson (Eds.), *Sous les images, la politique… Presse, cinéma, télévision, nouveaux médias (XXe-XXIe siècles)* (pp. 195–210). Paris: CNRS Éditions.

Bras, A., & Maarek, P. J. (2007). Les spots audiovisuels électoraux français de 2004: un refus inconscient de l'Europe. In P. J. Maarek (Ed.), *Chronique d'un non annoncé: La communication politique et l'Europe (juin 2004-mai 2005)* (pp. 55–81). Paris: L'Harmattan.

CEVIPOF. (Annually). Les Chroniques électorales, www.cevipof.com/fr/les-publications/les-chroniques-electorales/.

Cohen, E., & Lévy, M.-F. (2007). Les élections présidentielles de décembre 1965 en France. In E. Cohen & M.-F. Lévy (Eds.), *La télévision des Trente Glorieuses* (pp. 69–87). Paris: CNRS Éditions.

Cong Huyen Nu, P. T. (1999). Les clips de J. Chirac: de l'homme ordinaire (1988) au symbole présidentiel (1995). In Groupe Saint-Cloud (Ed.), *L'image candidate à l'élection présidentielle de 1995: Analyse des discours dans les médias* (pp. 49–62). Paris: L'Harmattan.

Conseil supérieur de l'audiovisuel (CSA) (1995). *Les Documents du CSA: "Élection du président de la République, rapport sur la campagne électorale à la radio et à la télévision (20 septembre 1994–7 mai 1995)."* Paris: CSA.

Conseil supérieur de l'audiovisuel (CSA) (2002). *Élection présidentielle, rapport sur la campagne électorale à la radio et à la télévision.* Paris: CSA.

Conseil supérieur de l'audiovisuel (CSA) (2007). *Rapport sur la campagne présidentielle de 2007. Bilan et propositions.* Paris: CSA.

Conseil supérieur de l'audiovisuel (CSA) (2011). *Élection du Président de la République, 22 avril – 6 mai 2012. Présentation de la recommandation du Conseil.* Paris: CSA.

Conseil supérieur de l'audiovisuel (CSA) (2012a). Pluralism in broadcasting media. Retrieved from www.csa.fr/en/Media/Files/Pluralism-in-Broadcasting-Media.

Conseil supérieur de l'audiovisuel (CSA) (2012b). Abiding by the principle of political pluralism. Retrieved from www.csa.fr/en/Media/Files/Abiding-by-the-Principle-of-Political-Pluralism.

Conseil supérieur de l'audiovisuel (CSA) (2012c). *Rapport sur l'élection présidentielle de 2012: Bilan et propositions.* Paris: CSA.

Cwalina, W., Falkowski, A., & Kaid, L. L. (2000). Role of advertising in forming the image of politicians: Comparative analysis in Poland, France and Germany. *Media Psychology,* 2(2), 119–146.

Darlington, R. (2016). A short guide to the French political system. Retrieved from www.rogerdarlington.me.uk/Frenchpoliticalsystem.html.

Dauncey, H. (1999). French culture in party and presidential political spots of the early 1990s. *The Web Journal of French Media Studies,* 2(1). Retrieved from http://wjfms.ncl.ac.uk/daunceWJ.htm.

Delporte, C. (2007). *La France dans les yeux: Une histoire de la communication politique de 1930 à nos jours.* Paris: Flammarion.

Devars, T. (2015). Les vidéos politiques au prisme de la trivialité. *Communication & Langages,* 185, 89–106.

Drouot, G. (1995). La politique sur les ondes: Des premières émissions aux campagnes actuelles. In G. Drouot (Ed.), *Les campagnes électorales radio-télévisées* (pp. 15–43). Aix-Marseille: Presses universitaires d'Aix-Marseille/Economica.

Gagnère, N., & Kaid L. L. (2003, March). *Political broadcasting in the 2002 presidential election in France: Appeals and effects for young voters.* Paper presented at the European Communication Association Convention, Munich.

Gerstlé, J. (2002). Les campagnes présidentielles depuis 1965. In P. Bréchon (Ed.), *Les élections présidentielles en France: Quarante ans d'histoire politique* (pp. 73–107). Paris: La Documentation française.

Gerstlé, J. (2012). *La communication politique* (2nd ed.). Paris: Armand Colin.

Gourévitch, J.-P. (1989). Le clip politique. *Revue française de science politique,* 39(1), 21–33.

Gourévitch, J.-P. (1998). *L'image en politique. De Luther à Internet et de l'affiche au clip.* Paris: Hachette Littératures.

Groupe Saint-Cloud (Ed.). (1995). *Présidentielle. Regards sur les discours télévisés.* Paris: INA/Nathan.

Gunthert, A. (2007). Retrieved from www.arhv.lhivic.org/index.php/2007/04/10/365-petite-geographie-des-videos-de-.

Holtz-Bacha, C. (2000). *Wahlwerbung als politische Kultur: Parteienspots im Fernsehen 1957–1998 [Electoral advertising as political culture: Party spots on television 1957–1998].* Wiesbaden: Westdeutscher Verlag.

Holtz-Bacha, C., Johansson, B., Leidenberger, J., Maarek, P. J., & Merkle, S. (2012). Advertising for Europe: TV ads during 2009 European election campaign in four countries. *Nordicom Review,* 33(2), 77–92.

Holtz-Bacha, C., Kaid, L. L., & Johnston, A. (1994). Political television advertising in Western democracies: A comparison of campaign broadcasts in the US, Germany, and France. *Political Communication,* 11, 67–80.

Holtz-Bacha, C., Novelli, E., & Rafter, K. (Eds.). (in press). *Political advertising in the 2014 European Parliament elections.* Basingstoke: Palgrave.

Johnston, A. (1991). Political broadcast: An analysis of form, content, and style in presidential communication. In L. L. Kaid, J. Gerstlé, & K. R. Sanders (Eds.), *Mediated politics in two cultures: Presidential campaigning in the United States and France* (pp. 59–72). New York, NY: Praeger.

Johnston A., & Gerstlé J. (1995). The role of television broadcasts in promoting French presidential candidates. In L. L. Kaid & C. Holtz-Bacha (Eds.), *Political advertising in western democracies: Parties and candidates on television* (pp. 44–60). London: Sage.

Kaid, L. L. (1991). The effects of television broadcast on perceptions of presidential candidates in the United States and in France. In L. L. Kaid, J. Gerstlé, & K. R. Sanders (Eds.), *Mediated politics in two cultures: Presidential campaigning in the United States and France* (pp. 247–260). New York, NY: Praeger.

Kaid L. L., & Gagnère, N. (2006). Election broadcasts in France. In L. L. Kaid & C. Holtz-Bacha (Eds.), *The Sage handbook of political advertising* (pp. 83–96). Thousand Oaks, CA: Sage.

Kaid, L. L., Gagnère, N., Williams, A. P., & Trammel, K. D. (2003, May). *Political advertisement and the 2002 presidential election in France.* Paper presented at the International Communication Association Convention, San Diego.

Kaid, L. L., Gerstlé, J., & Sanders, K. R. (Eds.). (1991). *Mediated politics in two cultures: Presidential campaigning in the United States and France.* New York, NY: Praeger.

Kaid, L. L., & Holtz-Bacha, C. (2000). Gender reactions to TV political broadcasts: A multicountry comparison. *Harvard International Journal of Press/Politics,* 5(2), 17–29.

Kaid, L. L., & Johnston, A. (2001). *Videostyle in presidential campaigns: Style and content of televised political advertising*. Westport, CT: Praeger.

Kaid L. L., McKinnon, L. M., & Gagnère, N. (1996, May). *Male and female reactions to political broadcast in the 1995 French presidential election*. Paper presented at the International Communication Association Convention, Chicago.

Le Hay, V., Vedel, T., & Chanvril, F. (2011). Usages des médias et politique: Une écologie des pratiques informationnelles [Uses of the media and politics: An ecology of information practices]. *Réseaux*, 170(6), 45–73.

Maarek, P. J., Pourtier-Tillinac, H., & Sebbah, B. (2012). Les spots de la campagne officielle des élections européennes de 2009. In P. J. Maarek (Ed.), *La communication politique européenne sans l'Europe. Les élections au Parlement Européen de 2009* (pp. 17–44). Paris: L'Harmattan.

Maarek, P. J., & Sebbah, B. (2009). Les révélations des spots de la campagne audiovisuelle officielle. In P. J. Maarek (Ed.), *La Communication politique de la présidentielle de 2007. Participation ou représentation?* (pp. 121–136). Paris: L'Harmattan.

Maarek, P. J., & Sebbah, B. (2013). La campagne officielle à la télévision: Un bon révélateur des potentiels des candidats. In P. J. Maarek (Ed.), *Présidentielle 2012: Une communication politique bien singulière* (pp. 71–96). Paris: L'Harmattan.

Maier, M., & Tenscher, J. (Eds.). (2006). *Campaigning in Europe, campaigning for Europe: Political parties, campaigns, mass media and the European Parliament elections 2004*. Berlin: LIT.

Mariani, I. (1995). La perception de la campagne radiotélévisée et ses conséquences en France. In G. Drouot (Ed.), *Les campagnes électorales radio-télévisées* (pp. 229–243). Aix-Marseille: Presses universitaires d'Aix-Marseille/Economica.

Ménager, A. (2012). Présidentielle, la télévision au rendez-vous. *Médiamétrie – Actu 24/7*. Retrieved from www.audiencelemag.com/?article=43&cat=1.

Merkle, S. (2009). *Fernsehwahlwerbung in Frankreich – Die "spots télévisés" zur Präsidentschaftswahl 2007*. Nürnberg: Universität Erlangen-Nürnberg, Diploma thesis.

Ministère de l'Intérieur (French Ministry of the Interior). Retrieved from www.interieur.gouv.fr/Elections/Les-elections-en-France/Les-modalites-d-elections/Les-differentes-elections.

Petitjean, L. (1999). Des présidentiables à l'impératif. In Groupe Saint-Cloud (Ed.), *L'image candidate à l'élection présidentielle de 1995: Analyse des discours dans les médias* (pp. 171–182). Paris: L'Harmattan.

Politique, Internet et vidéos avec le Vidéomètre. (2007, June 13). *La Croix*. Retrieved from www.la-croix.com/Culture/Nouvelles-technologies/Politique-Internet-et-videos-avec-le-Videometre-_NG_-2007-06-13-523354.

Pourtier-Tillinac, H. (2009). Les podcasts politiques: Atout ou risque politique? In M. Burger, J. Jacquin, & R. Micheli (Eds.), *Actes du colloque "Le français parlé dans les médias": Les médias et le politique*. Lausanne: Université de Lausanne. Retrieved from www.unil.ch/clsl/home/menuinst/publications/actes-fpm-2009.html.

Renault, J.-J. (1995). Le clip, une inscription dans la légende. In Groupe Saint-Cloud (Ed.), *Présidentielle. Regards sur les discours télévisés* (pp. 20–26). Paris: INA/Nathan.

Siune, K. (1983). The campaigns on television: What was said and who said it. In J. G. Blumler (Ed.), *Communicating to voters: Television in the first European Parliament elections* (pp. 223–257). London: Sage.

Vassalo, A. (2012). Élection & télévision: La présidentielle 1965 (Acte 1 – Premier tour). Retrieved from https://audevassallo.wordpress.com/2012/04/01/election-television-la-campagne-presidentielle-de-1965-acte-1-premier-tour/.

12

DOES POLITICAL ADVERTISING STILL HAVE AN IMPACT ON THE OUTCOME OF ELECTION CAMPAIGNS?

Political Advertising in Hungary

Jolán Róka

Democracy was institutionalized in the Republic of Hungary between 1987 and 1989, as a result of which a multi-tier political system came into being and state power gained a totally new frame of parliamentary democracy. The media played a fundamental role from the very beginning of the democratization process. News coverage of the election campaigns both in print and electronic media became one of the crucial information sources about the events and candidates of the parliamentary, municipal and European parliamentary elections. Media influenced the citizens' ideological, political and aesthetic views, concepts and values using the marketing tools and verbal, nonverbal and visual means of persuasion. The tactics and strategies of ideological manipulation of citizens would surely have been less effective without their media presentation.

"The mediatization of politics," to put it in black and white, is the spread of a communication technique, by which the politicians try to force the media into an event – a following, passive role. Journalists – often despite their intentions – become the means of attempting to influence the voters' will. Mediatization does not fit the social expectation that the media should autonomously control the representatives of political power and should interpret the voters' expectations to the politicians. The media can meet these social demands only if the editors find a way for the media to play an active role in the political processes. They have to succeed in their attempts to influence representatives and also have to elaborate the methods for moving them (Bajomi-Lázár, 2005, p. 50).

Political and Electoral System

Political System

Hungarian political traditions are determined by more than a thousand years of Hungarian statehood. From the time of Saint Stephen (who reigned from 1000 until 1038), a constitutional concept of the state provided the framework for Hungarian political culture for a long time before the communist regime and after the democratic regime change in 1989–90. Before the democratic transition

Hungarian political evolution had been characterized by a weak democratic, but strong parliamentary tradition for more than a hundred years (Körösényi, Tóth, & Török, 2003, pp. 15–16).

In the Hungarian political system, the most prominent state and representative organ is its 386-member (between 1990 and 2010), 199-member (after 2011) parliament, the Hungarian National Assembly. Its legal status and functions are regulated by the Constitution. Members of the parliament are elected every four years in the course of a regular election campaign, and the winning party or coalition then has the legal right to nominate the prime minister, who formulates the program of the government. The head of the state is the president of the state, who is elected by the members of the parliament for five years (Gallai & Török, 2003, pp. 347–369).

Democracy became reality in the Republic of Hungary between 1987 and 1989, which led to the formation of a multi-tier system. Hungary is a "classic" parliamentary system (Sándor, Stumpf, & Vass, 2009, p. 34). The first democratically elected government in 1990 began abolishing the centrally planned economy in order to develop a new market-based economy.

Among the unusual characteristics of Hungarian parliamentary democracy mentioned by Körösényi (1999) are: (1) the parliamentary, institution-oriented concept of politics; (2) liberalism as the ruling political concept; (3) nationalism; (4) two versions of the emancipatory-normative concept of politics (institutionalist and anti-institutionalist); (5) a depoliticized concept of the public interest; (6) an antipolitical approach in Hungarian political thought; and (7) a consensus-oriented approach to politics (pp. 152–157). Körösényi considers political parties to be the main actors in Hungarian politics and the formation of public opinion. "By the early 1990s, three political camps had formed – the liberal, the national-conservative/Christian and the socialist. The parliamentary parties all belonged to one of these camps" (1999, p. 31). The socialist camp included the Hungarian Socialist Party (MSZP), the liberal camp the Alliance of Free Democrats and the Federation of Young Democrats (Fidesz), the national-conservative and Christian camp the Hungarian Democratic Forum (MDF), the Independent Smallholders' Party (FKgP) and the Christian Democratic People's Party (KDNP).

> During the second half of the 1990s, a change occured in this structure, with Fidesz moving from the liberal camp to the national-conservative camp. The extra-parliamentary parties and the parties formed by the defections from the larger parties were also, for the most part, associated with one of these camps. Each camp was tied together not only by common political and ideological orientation, but also by the very similar socio-cultural composition of their core political élites and electoral bases, and by the shared political attitudes and world-views.
>
> (Körösényi, 1999, p. 32)

The four most important political parties that determined the formation of the Hungarian political system, were the Federation of Young Democrats – Hungarian Civic Party (Fidesz-MPP), Hungarian Socialist Party (MSZP), Alliance of Free Democrats (SZDSZ), Hungarian Democratic Forum (MDF). The organizational structure of the parties showed a lot of similarities in their financing as well. Their finance bases drew on three sources: membership fees, donations and state subsidy.

The political landscape gradually went through radical changes in the subsequent parliamentary (1990, 1994, 1998, 2002, 2006, 2010, 2014) and European parliamentary (2004, 2009, 2014) elections. At present the main political actors are FIDESZ (Fidesz – Hungarian Civic Union, conservative), MSZP (Hungarian Socialist Party, social democratic), Jobbik (Movement for a Better Hungary, nationalist) and LMP (Politics can be Different, ecologist).

"The previous parliamentary elections took place on 11 April 2010 and resulted in a victory for the Fidesz-Hungarian Civic Union (Fidesz-Magyar Polgári Szövetség, Fidesz) and the Christian-Democratic People's Party (Kereszténydemokrata Néppárt, KDNP), which won a two-thirds majority in parliament" (Hungary, 2014, p. 4). The latest parliamentary elections were held on April 6, 2014.

The official results were announced on 23 April. The ruling Fidesz-KDNP gained roughly the same percentage of seats in parliament and thus retained its constitutional majority. Notably, this result was achieved with 45 per cent of national list vote, as opposed to 53 per cent in 2010. Some portion of this can be attributed to changes in the electoral system. The results also showed that 70 per cent of constituency candidates received fewer votes than required on their signature sheets.

(Hungary, 2014, p. 24)

Electoral System

Parliamentary elections between 1990 and 2010 were based on Act No. 34 of 1989 on the Election of Members of Parliament (1994), enacted by parliament on October 20, 1989 and also on Act C of 1997 on Electoral Procedure. Act No. 34 contained the regulations concerning suffrage, the electoral system (members of parliament, nomination, determination of election results) and electoral procedures (electoral campaign, polling, electoral bodies, polling wards, registration of voters, publicity of electoral procedures, legal remedies, by-elections, final provisions).

Act C of 1997 on Electoral Procedure declared that according to the Constitution of the Republic of Hungary, suffrage was equal, voting was direct and secret, the process of elections was democratic. "The aim of this act is that voters, candidates and nominating organisations as well as election bodies may exercise their election related rights on the ground of uniform, clearly arranged and simple rules of procedure, as laid down by law" (Act C of 1997 on Electoral Procedure).

This Act was applied to the election of the members of parliament, the election of the members of the European Parliament, the election of the representatives and mayors of local governments, and the election of minority municipalities. The election must be called at least 72 days before the polling day. Some of the basic principles applied in the electoral procedure were: to safeguard the fairness of elections; to ensure voluntary participation in the nomination, election campaign, and voting; and also the equality of candidates. These requirements and all the other regulations were enforced and monitored by the National Election Office Hungary.

Act C of 1997 in chapter 6 contained the regulations of the campaign period. It lasted from the call for the election to midnight of the day before voting when a period of campaign silence was required. During that period, it was prohibited to engage in any election campaigning (including organizing transportation to the polling station for the voters by the candidate or the nominating organization; supplying food and drink; distributing party's or candidate's symbols, posters). It was also prohibited to publish the results of opinion polls eight days prior to the elections, until the termination of elections.

Nominating organizations and candidates could produce posters without permission, and they might place them without limitation in certain parts of the public domain, but they could not cover the posters of other candidates or parties. Posters had to be removed 30 days after polling day. Radio and television program providers might broadcast political advertisements under equal conditions for candidates and parties if they did not attach explanation or opinion. The same regulation referred to national, local periodicals and news agencies.

National public service providers shall publish the political advertisements of nominating organisations putting forward national lists; regional public service program providers shall publish the political advertisements of nomination organisations putting forward regional lists in their region of reception; local public service providers shall publish the political advertisements of candidates announcing themselves in single mandate constituencies in their region of reception from the 18th day preceding the elections, the latest until the 3rd day before the elections, at least once, free of charge.

(Act C of 1997 on Electoral Procedure)

The new electoral law (Act CCIII of 2011 on the Elections of Members of Parliament) was passed by the governing parliamentary majority coalition of Fidesz – Hungarian Civic Union and KDNP (Christian Democratic People's Party). There are several main modifications to the previous election law:

- the number of members of National Assembly was reduced from 386 to 199 (106 MPs are elected in single-member constituencies, 93 from national lists instead of the former 210);
- the number of individual electoral districts were also reduced from 176 to 106;
- single-member constituencies cannot cross county boundaries or the boundaries of Budapest (capital city);
- 1990–2010: two rounds of voting on a regional list, on single-member constituencies, and the national list; 2011–: one round of voting on single-member constituencies and national list;
- nomination in a single-member constituency used to be subject to minimum 750 signatures of eligible voters, after 2011 the number of recommendations was reduced to 500;
- outside Hungary: 1990–2010: Hungarian citizens with legal residence in Hungary could vote at Hungarian embassies, consulates; 2011–: Hungarian non-resident citizens can also vote by mail;
- 1990–2010: no minority lists; 2011–: a national minority receiving 0.27 of national vote receives a seat in the National Assembly. Those who vote for minority lists, cannot vote on general lists (www.valasztas.hu). The law permitted "voters to register prior to elections to vote for single candidates from each of Hungary's 13 Nationality Councils (Gypsy, German, Slovak, Ukrainian, Ruthene, Romanian, Serb, Croatian, Slovene, Polish, Bulgarian, Greek and Armenian) instead of parties on the national party lists."

(The Orange Files, 2015)

Parliament passed more laws between 2010 and 2014 than any other cycle since Hungary's democratic transition and about 50 percent more than between 2006 and 2010.

But the opposition claims some of the new election rule Fidesz passed have given the party an unfair advantage. The opposition accuses the government of gerrymandering newly redrawn districts, which accompany a reduction of members of parliament from 386 to 199.

The government also passed a winner-take-all, simple plurality voting system which favors the largest party: in this case, Fidesz. Government spokesman … says the advantage of this system is that it can 'produce a healthy majority for forming a government which is a fundamental condition for political stability.'

(Jovanovski, 2014, p. 2)

History of Political Ads

The growing importance of communication technologies in the political process can be seen by examining election campaigns that took place in different political and media systems and at different times. This part summarizes the main conclusions of the analyses carried out on the 1990, 1994, 1998, 2002, 2006, 2010 and 2014 party election campaigns plus the 2004, 2009, 2014 European parliamentary elections in Hungary.

The intentional application of marketing techniques in political campaigns is a relatively new phenomenon in Western democracies. More than 15 years have passed since the first marketing-based election campaign in the US. Bill Clinton was the first American president whose successes and victory in 1992 and in 1996 were partly due to the introduction of a new type of campaign management and partly to the personality and physical endowments of the presidential candidate, who was apt and talented at using nontraditional campaign methods (Newman, 1999). This new type of American campaign management had a profound impact on Eastern and Central European political campaign conventions, and as a result they changed radically in the middle of the 1990s. In the Republic of Hungary, the marketing approach to parliamentary election campaigns has been applied since 1998. The switch to the marketing approach meant that politics became business, where success depends mainly on professional communication skills and unique public relations strategies. The final goal of this approach is to project the most positive image of the political candidate and the party and to sell them with the biggest possible "profit." The profit in this case is the voters' support and the winning of the elections.

What are the most widely used tools and channels for gaining citizens' attention in political campaigns? Since the advent of audiovisual media, television has played the most prominent role in political communication, and one of the major components of any candidates' campaign is good televised usage, including televised advertisements and the broadcast of the candidates' debate. Among the new technological advances, the Internet has a crucial potential for influence. In Hungary, multimedia on the Internet became part of the political battle in 1998 (Róka, 2006, pp. 347–348). Since 2002, new possibilities provided by the latest advances in telecommunication technology arose, and short message service (SMS) messages transmitted through mobile phones were added to the mix. Web 2.0 applications (Facebook, Twitter) were however of little importance in the 2010 and 2014 campaigns. The political parties used billboards and television spots to reach out to voters.

Relevance of Advertising as Campaign Channels

There are lots of different definitions of the term advertising. According to Vivian: "Advertising is vital in a consumer economy. Without it people would have a hard time even knowing what products and services are available. Advertising, in fact, is essential to a prosperous society. Advertising also is the financial basis of contemporary mass media" (Vivian, 2013, p. 289). Ads can be placed in print (newspapers, magazines, billboards, flyers, etc.) and electronic media (radio, television, online). There are different types of advertisements: commercial, political, nonprofit, local, global, glocal, just to mention some. In political election campaigns political advertisements play a significant role in campaign coverage, in political agenda-setting and agenda-building.

In election periods, political advertisements can be broadcast according to the laws about the election of members of parliament, the local and regional candidates, and the mayors. In any other period, political advertisements can only be communicated in connection with a decreed plebiscite. The law prohibits political advertisements in any programs broadcast to foreign countries. Although another person or institution is sponsoring the political advertisement, this does not decrease either the responsibility or the freedom of the broadcaster, and neither the sponsor nor the broadcaster may change the content or placement of the program because of the ad, just the timing. The broadcaster is not responsible for the content of the political advertisement. A political advertisement must be visually and acoustically separated from other pieces of the program, with special announcement about its character before and after the broadcast.

Parliamentary elections between 1990 and 2010 were based on Act No. 34 of 1989 on the Election of Members of Parliament (1994), enacted by Parliament on October 20, 1989 and also on Act C of 1997 on Electoral Procedure.

Parliamentary elections have been based on the new media law (Act CLXXXV of 2010 on Media Services and Mass Communication), which was passed by the Hungarian Parliament in December 2010, since 2011. The changes are described below ("Regulation of Political Advertising on Television and the Internet").

The Role of the Internet for Campaign Advertising

Among the new technological advances, the Internet has the potential to become very influential. In Hungary the Internet became a part of the political campaign in 1998, provided by the latest advances in telecommunication technology, such as: prerecorded messages through cable and SMS messages transmitted through mobile phones in 2002 and 2006. The Internet plays a growing role in spreading election information, in collecting donations, and also in mobilizing voters. However, the parliamentary parties' home pages do not reveal how they intend to mobilize potential "Internet" voters. Thus in the 2006 parliamentary election campaign the parties did not consider it important to let the citizens know about their plans and party programs well before the election day – the Hungarian Democratic Forum was an exception. The most informative and well designed home page was prepared by the Alliance of Free Democrats. It included podcasts, interactive interviews, RSS, a blog, and introduced the party's candidates for parliament. Blogs as an election campaign tool were also used by the prime minister. Interactive communication possibilities were characteristic only of the home pages of the governing parties and just for the registered users. Both the Hungarian Socialist Party and the Federation of Young Democrats used their home pages for recruiting volunteers, and they also had separate home pages for negative campaigning (www.hullamvadasz.hu/index.php3?tanulmany=879&fotip=6).

Internet penetration has been gradually growing in Hungary since 1990. The proportion of users was 52% in 2009, 57% in 2013 and 74% in 2014, according to a survey by Gemius. The Internet has become an influential mass medium. Citizens get most of their current information from online channels. As a result, they were no longer passive decoders of media messages and became active participants who set the public, political, mass media agenda.

There are some further advantages of social media: "the social web can be a cost-effective medium for targeted advertising. Whereas expensive television and print ads might blanket a wide swath of voters with uncertain viewership and impact, social media engagement costs pennies on the dollar, and can deliver highly targeted and measurable results if executed properly" (Silverman, 2010).

In the political campaigns of 2010 and 2014 the media landscape was fragmented. The "mass" political parties (Fidesz – KDNP and MSZP) used traditional political advertising options (mostly billboards and video spots), while the "smaller" parties (Jobbik = Movement for a Better Hungary, LMP = Politics can be Different) made use of Web 2.0 applications (social media, more precisely Facebook, Twitter, YouTube, blogs, etc.). The advantages of Web 2.0 applications are lower costs and the ability to reach a huge number of eligible voters. The Movement for a Better Hungary could recruit viewers for its YouTube channel through Twitter, while the Politics can be Different party managed to involve the citizens into its campaign through its blogs (Szabó, Mihályffy, & Kiss, 2011, p. 194).

Regulation of Political Advertising on Television and the Internet

As mentioned before, parliamentary elections between 1990 and 2010 were based on Act No. 34 of 1989 on the Election of Members of Parliament (1994). Article 11 in chapter 4 ("Electoral Campaign") of the act briefly defined the media presentation of the campaign:

(1) Until the day preceding election at the latest, the Hungarian Telegraph Agency, Hungarian Radio, and Hungarian Television must carry on an equal bases the electoral messages of parties putting forward candidates. Each party with a candidate must be given at least one electoral program free of charge. That same duty should devolve upon the local studios in their respective area of broadcast with regard to the electoral programs of candidates. Other advertisements that went towards making a party or any

of its candidates more popular could only be broadcast with a clear message declaring such publicity as "Paid Electoral Advertising."

(2) During the 30 days preceding the election, Hungarian Radio and Hungarian Television must cover the parties presenting national lists on an equal basis in their news of electoral events and, in their electoral reports, in proportion to the candidates nominated.

(3) On the last day of the electoral campaigns, Hungarian Radio and Hungarian Television must broadcast the electoral summary reports prepared by parties presenting national lists, under equal program conditions for all parties, for equal lengths of time and without comments.

(Act No. 34, 1994, p. 25)

The key concepts in the act were equality and proportionality in media presentation of the parties and the candidates. These principles guided the application of the regulatory system to campaigning (see Róka, 2006).

The new media law (Act CLXXXV of 2010 on Media Services and Mass Communication) was passed by the Hungarian Parliament in December 2010. This law granted the power to monitor the functioning of the Hungarian mass media system to the Media Authority and Media Council. In the introductory summary the new act states:

The Parliament, with a view to promote community and individual interests and social integrity, to ensure proper operation of the democratic order and to strengthen national and cultural identity, with due respect to the Fundamental Law, the constitutional principles, and the norms of international law and of the European Union, by taking into consideration the circumstances created by the developments in technology, by preserving freedom of expression, speech and the press, and considering the key importance of media services in cultural, social and economic terms, and the importance of ensuring competition on the media market.

(Act CLXXXV of 2010 on Media Services and Mass Communication; médiatörvény.hu)

Article 32 on Political Advertisements, Public Service Announcements, Public Service Advertisements summarizes some aspects of the new regulations concerning political advertisements:

(1) The person or entity ordering the publication of political advertisements, public service announcements, public service advertisements, and the person or entity with an interest in the publication thereof shall not exert editorial influence over the media service, except for the time of publication.

(2) The political advertisement, public service announcement and public service advertisement shall be immediately recognizable in nature and distinguishable from other media content. The method of distinguishing from other media contents in linear media services

(a) shall take place in the form of optical and acoustic notice in the case of audiovisual media services;

(b) shall take place in the form of acoustic notice in the case of radio media service.

(3) During the election campaign periods, political advertisements may only be published in accordance with the provisions of the Act on Electoral Procedures. Outside of election campaign periods, political advertisements may only be published in connection with referendums already ordered. The media service provider shall not be responsible for the content of the political advertisement. If the request for publication of the political advertisement is in compliance with the provisions of the Act on Electoral

Procedures, and in such case the media service provider shall be obliged to publish the advertisement without further consideration.

(4) Upon the publication of political advertisements, public service announcements and public service advertisements, the person or entity ordering the publication shall be identified unequivocally.

(médiatörvény.hu, pp. 12–13)

The new Media Act clearly distinguishes political advertisements from public service announcements and public service advertisements. Point 55 of Article 203 of the Media Act says "a political advertisement shall mean any program transmitted for or without consideration, promoting or advocating support for a party, political movement, or the Government, or promoting the name, objectives, activities, slogan, or emblem of such entities, which appears and is transmitted in a manner similar to that of advertisements" (Koltay, 2012, p. 240).

Political advertisements can be published during the election campaign according to the regulations set by Article 32 of Media Act on Electoral Procedure. The election date must be determined 60 days before voting. Political parties and different organizations are provided approximately two months to conveying their political messages. Besides the audiovisual messages the parties may produce posters. The posters can be placed "with the consent of rights holders" on buildings and fences 50 meters from major roads, or 100 meters from a highway. In Budapest posters were restricted to locations, according to environmental regulations. Posters could be placed in a manner not to cover other posters.

The national media service providers could publish political ads on equal terms for nominating parties and candidates during the election campaign. Commercial broadcasters also had to provide equal conditions for the nominating parties and candidates. The National Electoral Committee must examine the balance of coverage during the election period. On the day of the election campaign silence has to be kept until the closing of ballot-boxes. One more important regulation is that the results of public opinion polls can not be published eight days before the elections. "In Hungary, the financing of campaign costs is also provided for by the law … from the central budget in proportion to the number of their candidates. Such support, which may only be used to cover material type costs (travel, rents, etc.) must be accounted for … independent candidates and nominating organisations may spend a maximum of one million forints per candidate for the purposes of election. The above campaign financing amount must be accounted for, and the State Audit Office exercises control over such accounts as well (Act on Electoral Procedure, Articles 91–92)" (Koltay, 2012, p. 245).

Consequently, Article 32 provides some general regulations concerning political advertising. In the parliamentary elections of 2014 the campaign period lasted for 50 days. There was a limit to the campaign period, and also a limit for budgetary support to political parties, electoral and individual candidates. All parties on the national list received equal time on public television: 600 minutes were divided equally among the parties. Parties with national lists could run advertisements on commercial television if the given channel provided equal time for free. It wasn't provided by any of the channels. Even advertising on billboards was strictly regulated.

Hungarian lawmakers have established a set of comprehensive new media laws that critics say are inconsistent with democratic free-press principles and European practices and norms. Hungarian officials say the legislation conforms to EU standards and its elements are drawn from existing regulations in other European and EU-member states.

(Hungarian Media Laws in Europe, 2012, p. viii)

Research on the Content, Reception and Effects of Ads

An analysis of the symbolic content of campaign messages has been carried out since 1990 (Kapitány & Kapitány, 2014). At the beginning it focused only on the campaign video spots. In subsequent election campaigns the length, the amount and the importance of the spots gradually decreased, and the most important transmitters of the campaign messages became the flyers, posters, webpages (Internet), mobile phones (SMS), social media (Facebook, Twitter, blogs), YouTube.

The key values in the election campaigns barely changed during this time: family, safety, peace, human relationships, honesty. In 1990 the parties emphasized eight values: Hungarian, nation, freedom, Europe, democracy, democratic, home, Christianity. In 1994 the values changed except for Hungarian, then came enterpreneur, enterprise, enterpreneurship, support of enterpreneurship, the formation of a modern civilized society, nation, cooperation, democracy, safety, stability and development of the economy. In 1998 the individual values instead of ideological values became the leading values: family, honesty, together, welfare, safety, future, nation, lie (a negative value), Europe, continuity, stability, competition, Hungarian, freedom, democracy, civilian, oppression (negative value), robbery (negative value). In 2002: family, children, youth, welfare, development, support, help, reliability, education, Hungarian, home, nation. In 2006: tax reduction, Hungarian, job, employment versus unemployment, welfare, subsistence, joining forces, common action.

In 2010, due to the economic and value crisis, new symbolic meanings set the public agenda. The leading values in the campaign were crime, safety, social order, job, and also old-age pension, taxes, costs of services, importance of family, decreasing the difference between city and county life, future. There was a general tendency of losing credit in politics, emphasizing the importance of a peaceful, collaborative political style. New meanings were included in some parties's programs: determining the role of state, the negative influence of some EU initiatives, globalization, multinational companies, and more effective defense of national interests, the necessity of economic opening toward the East, improvement of the health-care system and a healthy environment.

In 2014 most of the parties emphasized the importance of welfare, healthy environment, public safety, job, employment, European (Kapitány & Kapitány, 2014). Kapitány and Kapitány also analyzed who were the people in the ads, the location and environment, music and sound effects, visual elements, lights, colors, montage, style, slogans, negative campaign messages, and mediatization.

The actors. In the 1990s the main characters of the campaign messages were the intellectuals, however this gradually changed and intellectuals were replaced by businessmen, economists, lawyers and professional politicians. The middle class became the determining social layer in the political messages. At the same time the campaigns represented the professionalization of politics. As for the genders, men still were the dominant actors in the political arena, while women were present in the traditional female roles both at the individual and professional levels. Almost all the parties however made use of the attractiveness of women, choosing pretty women for the role of spokespersons. Children were shown in symbolic roles, like the symbols of innocence, future, family harmony, though for 2014 children became supporting actors in the campaign, implying that politics is not for children. Minority groups played an insignificant role in the campaigns, though in 2014 in the campaign spots of the liberal coalition some ethnic groups were represented, saying "This is my homeland." The appearance of the actors also matched the characteristic features of the middle class with financially sound circumstances. The facial expressions also changed a lot from the 1990s until 2014: from smiling faces through half-smiles to serious expressions. In 2014 the faces showed healthy, white teeth (the symbol of youth), but the negative campaign messages of the Socialist Party used sorrowful, suffering faces demonstrating the critical economic and political situation of the country.

Environment. The most typical locations in the video spots and on the posters are the building of parliament, the Castle in Buda, the Heroes' Square (which are political locations and symbols), then the Hungarian land (the emblem of agriculture). Since the 1990s the role of the countryside, agriculture and villages has been declining, a message used primarily by conservative parties. In the election campaign of 2014, one can see the symbols of agriculture: tractors and agricultural land only in the video spots of the LMP (Politics can be Different). For other parties the most typical locations are nice landscapes and family homes. The liberal coalition prefers the public spaces of cities, especially of Budapest, the governing party coalition (Fidesz – KDNP) shows the interior of the National Assembly, the LMP (ecologist) uses pictures from different countries of the world, saying we live in a global village. Symbolic objects also may appear in the campaign messages: computer, laptop, cell phones, these are the symbols of modernity. The national symbols still have important roles: national flag, map of Hungary, as well as religious symbols. There are also new elements: bicycle, wind power plants, solar, green vegetables, fruits (LMP).

Music, sound effects. In the 1990s the parties experimented with different musical trends (Hungarian classical music, folk music, etc.), but nowadays pop music has become the most widely used style in accordance with the target group of voters: the young eligible voters. The Jobbik (Movement for a Better Hungary, nationalist party) and LMP (Politics can be Different) prefer dynamic music. In negative campaign spots by the liberal coalition, dramatic, threatening sound effects can be heard, while the spots of Fidesz – KDNP apply quiet, discreet background music.

Visual elements, colors. Lighting as an important visual element was first used by Alliance of Social Democrats (SZDSZ) in 1994, then in 1998 Fidesz and MSZP also included it in their spots. Darkness is the visual element of negative spots (MDF [Hungarian Democratic Forum], 1994), as well as the distortion of faces or the application of montage for juxtapositioning, e.g. a clown with a former prime minister (campaign of 2014).

Verbal style. The most striking change in verbal style during the last 25 years is a gradual transition from pathos to standard language. The elements of pathos remained to a certain extent in the messages of Fidesz – KDNP, but they are mixed up with humor, and standard Hungarian. If politicians want to be effective, their messages have to be repeated. Humor is used in different forms: self-humor by LMP ("Green is not just a color") refers to their ideology, being ecologist. The liberal coalition used the slogan "Together," the opposition's reaction is "They together ruined the country," or for the slogan of Fidesz – KDNP "We live better than four years ago" the answer is "They already live better than four years ago."

Slogans. There are two types of slogans, some are the parts of the parties' negative campaigns, some intend to strengthen the party image. Let's see some examples:

- "They already live better. And you? The mafia government of Simicska – Orbán" (MSZP).
- "We live worse than four years ago (Vote for MSZP) 109% increase of heart pills" (MSZP).
- "They ruined the country together. It was enough. We don't forget" (Fidesz – KDNP).
- "They would withdraw again the family tax. They don't deserve more chances" (Fidesz – KDNP).
- "Get on your feet Hungarian! Win the Better! It will succeed with you" (Jobbik).
- "Patient, clear power. Everyone knows: the future is green" (LMP).

The slogans serve propaganda purposes. They also identify the parties more or less clearly. In Hungary the different parties used most of their slogans as feedback to each other, very often in a negative way. This tendency has been typical in the parties' political battles since 2002.

Mediatization. As political campaigns move toward mediatization, they tranform messages into show-business. Visual design plays a significant role in campaign messages. The impact of campaign spots (such as posters) decreases, as there are fewer spots, but the quality of the spots improves. Since 2002 campaigns have become more and more interactive due to digital media. There are several new forms for reaching voters: SMS, blogs, YouTube, Facebook, Twitter, etc. In 2014 the period of campaign silence was cancelled, making SMS one of the most powerful means of political mobilization (Kapitány & Kapitány, 2014).

In 2014 the election campaign period was much shorter than previously (almost half of the previous campaign period), lasting from February 15 until April 4 at 12:00 p.m.), until one day before Election Day (April 6). The audiovisual campaign began on March 15. The new election law (Act CLXXXV of 2010 on Media Services and Mass Communication) contained some innovations: in the campaign period political advertisements can be broadcast free. The new law differentiated political announcements and political advertisements. Paid political announcements can be published in print media, on the Internet or presented in cinemas in order to popularize an organization or candidate. The goal of political advertisements is similar, but they can be broadcast on television or radio free of charge. As a consequence, the parties hardly had any media presence on commercial channels; rather they used billboards and flyers for campaign purposes. According to the new law, however, all print materials had to publish the name and location of the publisher and the name of the person responsible for the ad. While the audiovisual political advertisements had to be registered in advance, billboards could be published without limitation and did not have to be registered until the end of the campaign period.

In 2014, 19 political parties and 13 national councils participated in the campaign. Of these, 18 of the 19 parties and 8 of the 13 national councils prepared televised spots. Compared with 2010, there was a significant decrease in the number of advertisements, the participating television channels and the length of the advertisements. In 2010 10 registered television channels (ATV, COOL, F+, M1, M2, RTL Klub, Sport Klub, Story4, TV2, Hálózat TV) broadcast 1,366 political ads for 660 minutes. In 2014 just two public television channels (Duna TV, M1) showed 515 advertisements for 303 minutes (2014-es országgyűlési…, 2014). The parties could have used 470 minutes and the councils 130 minutes for advertising purposes, but none of them did.

The parties averaged one or two spots. The governing coalition (Fidesz – KDNP) showed four spots in 2010, but just two (24 times) in 2014. The Socialist Party (MSZP) also used two spots (11 times), the Jobbik (Movement for a Better Hungary) also two spots (but for a remarkable 54 times), and LMP (Politics can be Different) used one spot (34 times). The governing coalition broadcast its political ads only in evening prime time period (2014-es országgyűlési…, 2014).

> The change in the media's role and presence in this election cycle was demonstrable compared to previous election years when the media flurry around parliamentary campaigns would reach a fevered pitch. There were no televised debates after Fidesz dismissed invitations by opposition candidates. Restrictions on political advertising meant candidates were given no airtime on commercial TV, and just a few minutes of airtime on public TV during the course of campaign.
>
> OSCE delegates also noted a dominance of pro-government campaign coverage in the broadcast media. The organisation's monitoring of TV coverage since mid-March showed that three out of five monitored TV stations displayed a "significant bias towards Fidesz by covering nearly all of its campaign in a positive tone while more than half the coverage of the opposition alliance was in a negative tone" … The result was an eerily muted, heavily regulated campaign cycle – and an uneven political contest that analysts and the opposition have labelled as "free but not fair."
>
> (Brouillette, 2014, pp. 3–5)

The OSCE delegate observers also gave a detailed analysis of the election campaigning of 2014 and of the media environment. They noted that four political forces "dominated" the campaign: the alliance of Fidesz – KDNP; the opposition alliance of the Hungarian Socialist Party (MSZP), Together – Party for a New Era (Együtt – A Korszakváltók Pártja), Dialogue for Hungary (Párbeszéd Magyarországért, PM), Democratic Coalition (Demokratikus Koalíció, DK), Hungarian Liberal Party (Magyar Liberális Párt, MLP); the Movement for a Better Hungary (Jobbik Magyarországért Mozgalom); the Politics can be Different party (Lehet Más a Politika, LMP); non-governmental organizations (NGOs), e.g. the Fidesz-affiliated Civil Unity Forum (Civil Összefogás Fórum, CÖF). "Overall, the focus of the campaign was individual cases of alleged corruption at the expense of a discussion of party programmes" (Hungary, 2014, p. 12). The observers also emphasized that there was no campaign silence period, just one restriction: campaigning was banned within 150 meters of polling stations (Hungary, 2014, p. 12). Most of the parties used billboards, political advertisements in print media, leaflets and social media. Most of the billboards were rented by Fidesz, the opposition parties had insignificant access to billboards, and especially to broadcast media. "This contributed to an uneven playing field" (Hungary, 2014, p. 13).

The governing party started a campaign in March 2013 (until Election Day) using the slogan "Hungary is performing better." The cost of the campaign was EUR 4.5 million. Then the rights of the slogan were sold to Fidesz for EUR 640, and it used the slogan throughout the election campaign (Hungary, 2014, p. 13).

The media environment went through a radical change due to the new media law. The new guidelines underline that the public media (MTVA) should ensure a balanced representation of the polititical parties and candidates. Commercial television stations could air only unpaid political advertising. As a result of that regulation, there were no political advertisements on commercial channels.

The OSCE delegates also made a statement saying that the media coverage of the campaign was unbalanced, which meant that the campaign of the governing party was covered in positive tone, while the campaign and the representatives of the opposition alliance in negative. "The market-leading RTR Klub covered Fidesz in both positive and negative tone 45 per cent of the time monitored. The opposition alliance received 42 per cent positive and 33 per cent negative tone. However, the amount of campaign coverage on RTL was limited. Other contesting parties, including LMP and Jobbik, received considerably less coverage" (Hungary, 2014, p. 18).

Concluding the most characteristic feautures and trends of the Hungarian election campaign of 2014 one can say: the average number of political advertising (for all parties) was restricted for a few minutes on public television, the political candidates were given no airtime on commercial television channels, there was no silence period, and no political debates as in earlier parliamentary elections. The remaining advertising possibilities included billboards, leaflets, print political ads and social media. The billboards were mostly rented by the governing coalition, and the other marketing tools reached a limited segment of the eligible voters. The election campaign of 2014 – according to OSCE delegates – was uneven, unfair and ineffective.

References

2014-es országgyűlési választási kampány televíziós megjelenítésének elemzése. [Analysis of the televised presentation of the parliamentary election campaign of 2014]. Nemzeti Média- és Hírközlési Hatóság (NMHH). June 6, 2014. Retrieved on October 14, 2015 from www.mediatorveny.hu.

Act C of 1997 on Electoral Procedure. Retrieved January 1, 2007, from the National Election Office Hungary website: www.election.hu/parval2006/en/02/2_0.html.

Act CCIII of 2011 on the Elections of Members of Parliament. Retrieved October 7, 2015 from the National Election Office website: www.valasztas.hu.

Act CLXXXV of 2010 on Media Services and Mass Communication. Retrieved October 6, 2015 from médiatörvény.hu.

Act No. 34 of 1989 on the Election of Members of Parliament. (1994, January). Magyar Közlöny, (7). Retrieved January 1, 2007, from the National Election Office Hungary website: www.election.hu/parval2006/en/02/2_0.html.

Bajomi-Lázár, P. (2005). A politika mediatizálódása és a média politizálódása [The mediatization of politics and the politization of media]. *Médiakutató*, 6(1), 39–51.

Brouillette, A. (2014). Hungary elections: How the media failed the people. Retrieved on October 16, 2015 from www.aljazeera.com/indepth/opinion/2014.

Gallai, S., & Török, G. (2003). *Politika és politikatudomány [Politics and political science]*. Budapest: Aula Kiadó.

Hungarian Media Laws in Europe. (2012). *An assessment of the consistency of Hungary's media laws with European practices and norms*. Budapest: Center for Media and Communication Studies (CMCS).

Hungary. Parliamentary Elections, April 6, 2014. OSCE/ODIHR Limited Election Observation Mission, Final Report. Warsaw, 11 July 2014, OSCE (Office for Democratic Institutions and Human Rights).

Jovanovski, V. (2014). Hungary heads to the polls. Is it a "free but unfair" election? Retrieved on September 14, 2014 from www.csmonitor.com/WorldEurope/2014/0406/Hungary-heads-to-the-polls.

Kapitány, Á., & Kapitány, G. (2014). Értékválasztás 2014. A 2014-es választási kampány vizuális üzeneteinek szimbolikus és értékvonatkozásai. [Choice of values 2014: Symbolic and value aspects of the visual messages of the election campaign of 2014]. *Budapest, Studies in Political Science*, 3, 1–55.

Koltay, A. (Ed.). (2012). *Hungarian media law*. Budapest: CompLex.

Körösényi, A. (1999). *Government and politics in Hungary*. Budapest: Central European University Press, Osiris.

Körösényi, A., Tóth, Cs., & Török, G. (2003). *A magyar politikai rendszer [Hungarian political system]*. Budapest: Osiris Kiadó.

Newman, I. B. (Ed.). (1999). *Handbook of political marketing*. Thousand Oaks, CA: Sage.

The Orange Files. Notes on the end of liberal democracy in Hungary. Retrieved on September 28, 2015 from http://theorangefiles.hu/national-assembly-election-system.

Róka, J. (2006). Political advertising in Hungarian electoral communications. In L.L. Kaid & C. Holtz-Bacha (Eds.), *The Sage handbook of political advertising* (pp. 343–358). Thousand Oaks, CA: Sage.

Sándor, P., Stumpf, A., & Vass, L. (Eds.). (2009). *The Hungarian political system*. Budapest: Hungarian Center for Democracy Studies Foundation.

Silverman, M. (2010). How political campaign are using social media for real results. Retrieved on October 20, 2015 from http://mashable.com/20100609/political-campaigns-social-media.

Szabó, G., Mihályffy, Zs., & Kiss, B. (Eds.). (2011). *Kritikus kampány. A 2010-es országgyűlési választási kampány elemzése [Critical campaign: The analysis of the parliamentary election campaign of 2010]*. Budapest: L'Harmattan.

Vivian, J. (2013). *The media of mass communication*. Boston, MA: Pearson.

13

POLITICAL ADVERTISING IN ITALY

Edoardo Novelli

The history of Italian political spots has been marked by distinctive features of the country's political, institutional, historical and legislative structure that distinguish it from developments elsewhere. Like the periodization of modern political communication (Blumler & Kavanagh, 1999) – which in Italy's case seems to have developed mostly in the second age, marked by the presence of television (Novelli, 2006) – the history of Italian political ads also seems to have taken a distinctive course. The initial explosion of spots in the 1980s, characterized by euphoria matched by equally deep-seated suspicion between politicians and political parties, led to a phase when repeated attempts were made to introduce strict regulations that actually aimed to curtail political advertising. The result was a production of ads variable in quantity and quality down the years.

Moreover, ads have been considered to have a short shelf life, to be produced during election campaigns but not deemed worth keeping either by the political parties or by archives, foundations or research institutes. Nevertheless, political spots constitute an important audiovisual-heritage resource for the history not only of political communication but also of Italian culture and society, a resource that has risked being lost forever.[1]

Perhaps that also explains why studies of political spots in Italy have emerged in fits and starts, with great interest at the beginning and during particular phases (Mancini & Mazzoleni, 1994; Mazzoleni & Boneschi, 1980; Morcellini, 1995; Novelli, 1995, 2012) and indifference at others.

Because of these two factors, almost 40 years after political spots were introduced in Italy in 1979, there are but few analyses of their history, their characteristics and their effects on political communication (Novelli, 2012; Pezzini, 2001).

During this period, some of the structural aspects of the political audiovisual texts – those concerning packaging, discursive strategies and, not least, distribution channels and costs – have changed, diverging from what is defined as a political spot in professional and academic circles (Jamieson, 1992). Political spots have been accompanied in the second half of the 1990s by ads that are not based on the model of commercial advertisements but are usually longer, transmitted not only via television but also via the Internet. That change was also effected by strict control of election-campaign publicity (journalistic and infotainment programs, free electoral spaces, and debates) and spots during election campaigns. Examples are the film clips broadcast without charge during the party-political broadcast slots provided by public television channels or uploaded to political parties' and candidates' websites. From the early 2000s, the development of the Internet, together with the ban on spots on national television during election campaigns, has accentuated the Internet's importance in the dissemination of political ads. Finally, in recent years, Web 2.0 has resulted in spots created using the prevailing approaches and languages of social media.

We can identify four stages in the use of political ads in Italy, each characterized by different contents, regulations and modes of dissemination. In essence, spots and ads have been important forms of expression in which political parties and candidates have experimented with new languages and communication strategies in close relation to some of the main trends that have affected Italian politics.

The Origins of Political Spots in Italy

Political parties have used television for election-campaign publicity in Italy since 1960, when the Tribuna Elettorale program was introduced on the Rai, the monopoly public-service network. The broadcast gave Italian viewers the chance to see and listen to their political leaders, ministers and head of government for the first time. Structured around press conferences and appeals, it gave the parliamentary parties equal airtime, free of charge, and was subject to strict government control (Novelli, 1995). Tribuna Elettorale and Tribuna Politica, its companion program, used various formulas over the years (discussions, debates, interviews, etc.), but until private television channels arrived in Italy in the mid 1970s, parties could not buy television advertising space for their political messages.

The first political spots in Italy were shown during the campaign for the 1979 general and European elections.[2] This was a major change in the national political culture and customs. It happened spontaneously without any regulation or control, which is how the situation would remain until the mid 1990s.

The 1979 election campaign therefore marked the political world's "first assault on private television channels" (Mazzoleni & Boneschi, 1980, p. 409). The expenditure amounted to around one-and-a-half billion lire, and it triggered in Italy "that transformation of election campaigns that was already at an advanced stage elsewhere" (Mazzoleni & Boneschi, 1980, pp. 409–410). This still incipient phase continued with the campaign for the 1980 administrative elections, in which the candidates spent an estimated four billion lire, mostly on broadcasting spots on local television stations, with no coordination by the national parties. That electoral campaign marked an intensified use of spots, spectacularization of political messages driven by the increasing contamination between the traditional forms of appeals and television entertainment, and the personalization of electoral propaganda (Mazzoleni & Boneschi, 1980).

The explosion of local private television stations in the second half of the 1970s gave political communication and electoral appeals a new instrument and language for which the Italian parties seemed at least partly prepared. The four spots produced by the "*Comitato per il No*" for the campaign for the 1974 referendum on repealing the divorce law – intended, notably, for cinema and not television yet[3] – already contained many of the features that would characterize political spots in the future. Besides their brevity and their commercial nature, also worthy of note are their use of a comic-ironic register, a markedly seductive tone, the lack of any party-political reference, symbol or presence, and the use of extremely popular celebrity spokespeople from the worlds of cinema, such as actors Gigi Proietti and Nino Manfredi, and of entertainment, with singer Gianni Morandi.

The 1983 general election campaign saw the systematic use of spots by all the main parties, caused by the sudden political crisis. The widespread use of spots, combined with talk shows and debates about the election campaign on commercial television, made the 1983 elections the first "Italian tele-elections" (Grossi, Mancini, & Mazzoleni, 1983). The spots in this campaign showed that the parties had different ideas about the nature and potential of political advertising. The Italian Socialist Party (PSI), given the stature of its leader, Bettino Craxi, opted to personalize things.[4] The Italian Communist Party (PCI) was reluctant to personalize its communication despite the popularity of its leader, Berlinguer, and instead produced spots – of very cinematographic style – on specific topics.[5] The Christian Democratic Party (DC), which had been in power since 1946, was the party that most adopted the style and language of advertising. It produced the "*Decidi Dc*" (Choose DC) series of spots with strong emotional content that depicted critical or dangerous situations, all resolved by the DC's "providential" intervention.[6] The Social-Democratic Party (PSDI) relied on the endearing cartoon Gigi the Cat.[7] Words, images, emotions and humor were the different languages chosen by the main parties.

From the 1983 election campaign onwards, political spots were an important resource for the Italian parties, which they systematically used to speak new languages, pursue new strategies, and evoke emotions and feelings. In the form of the spots, political communication dealt with two distinct communicative domains, each with its own rules and features: television, with its rapidly evolving forms of delivery and consumption; and advertising, with its language, rhetoric and aims. Political discourse during ad breaks on television now had to function not as another political text – as in parliamentary proceedings, a political rally or an election debate – but as a text designed to entertain and amuse in order to sell a product. The political spots thus had to communicate not with citizens or voters but with the consumers of advertisements.

The Legislation Governing Political Spots in Italy

In 1993, Law no. 81 provided a very belated regulatory framework for the use of paid party spots for local elections, banning them from public, private national, and private local television stations for the 30 days before the vote. In the same year, Law 515 extended those rules to cover parliamentary election campaigns. That law was not very effective, however, partly because it did not appoint any institutes or bodies to monitor the television adverts, impose penalties and, above all, force spots immediately off air. Thus, the 1994 parliamentary elections saw considerable use of television spots throughout the campaign, especially by Forza Italia. This disrespect for the rules, along with the imbalance in the use of the spots between Forza Italia – which could count on free airtime on the networks owned by the party's founder, Silvio Berlusconi – and the other political groupings, prompted Romano Prodi's center-left government to pass a decree-law.

The decree-law of March 20, 1995 introduced an important distinction between election-campaign publicity (journalistic programs and debates) and election advertising (spots). Election campaign publicity was permitted – nay, encouraged – but election advertising was allowed only in the 15 days before the start of the campaign and was banned in the month prior to the elections.

Constitutional Court ruling no. 161 of May 10, 1995 relaxed those rigid rules, enabling paid spots to be broadcast during the election campaigns for referenda, which are different from parliamentary elections.

Under Law no. 28 of February 22, 2000, known as *par condicio*, in election season, the public and private national television and radio broadcasters could air only free party-political broadcasts offered equally to all parties. These messages were of 1–3 minutes' duration and had to be broadcast in dedicated slots separate from commercial ads and without interrupting other programs. The public service network was obliged to broadcast them; the national private television channels could decide for themselves; and the local television stations that agreed to air free messages could also do so for a charge of 50% of their regular advertising rates. No party or candidate could transmit more than two messages on the same channel on the same day. Those rules applied to all elections including referenda. Outside election campaigns, Rai had to air promotional messages if requested by the parties, whereas private national television and radio broadcasters could choose whether to do so; broadcasts were always free. These slots had the same duration as in the election season, although only two a day were permitted. Private local broadcasters could be paid for their airtime, albeit for less than their standard rates. Compliance with the rules was overseen by the telecommunications authority and by a parliamentary committee.

Law 3013 of 2003 put private local television channels on a different footing. It encouraged them to adopt a self-regulatory code for election campaigns to ensure pluralism and equal access. The self-regulatory code was approved by the local television and radio broadcasters and subsequently endorsed by the Ministry of Telecommunications Order dated April 8, 2004. Under the code, during election campaigns, local television stations could air party-political broadcasts free of charge or for payment (spots) at equal tariffs for all parties, on a first-come-first-served basis and with a 70% discount off commercial rates.

Essentially, the parties' use of television and spots was regulated in Italy after the phenomenon had already become widespread. A plethora of laws, decrees and other measures, all complex to enact, emerged from the early 1990s in an attempt to control a situation aggravated by the anomaly of a party leader who owned three national television networks. The result for political advertising was that, in preventing the parties from using them freely and in preventing the television broadcasters from making money with them, their effectiveness was diluted and, consequently, their use was drastically limited. Thus, political spots gradually evolved from a type of communication conceived and made for television to become an Internet phenomenon, with all that implies for its construction, language and nature.

Personalization

The personalization of Italian political communication, with a shift in focus from the party to the leader, is a major consequence of the spread of spots. Party leaders appeared in less than half of the early ads, but a trend was already apparent (Table 13.1). Indeed, the leader featured in the vast majority of the political spots produced between 1995 and 2004, the years when Italian politics became markedly personalized, and then in around half of the ads in recent years, which have been characterized by the Internet's emergence as a campaign tool and by a transformation in the spots' formal and expressive characteristics. However, besides the fluctuating trend, although already significant in itself, the phenomenon's most characteristic aspect is the quality and nature of the personalization engendered by political spots.

During the 1983 general-election campaign, the PSI and PRI centered their strategies on their party secretaries (leaders). This personalization, however, was still built on the strictly political themes of competence and quality. Putting the party leaders in the television spotlight did not yet focus on their image, let alone the nature of their performances.[8]

Table 13.1 Presence of national leader in spots produced for general-election campaigns by the different political parties during the First Italian Republic

	1983	1987	1990	1992
PCI			X	
DC				
PSI	X	X	X	X
PRI	X	X	X	X
PSDI		X		X
PR		X		
PLI			X	
MSI				X
Verdi			X	
Lega				X
Pensionati				X
Si Referendum				X

During the 1987 general election, the number of parties that used their leaders in at least one campaign spot increased to four. The PSI and the PRI continued with their personalization strategy and were joined by the PSDI and the PR. This represented a rise in both quantity and quality. The spots in which Craxi was interviewed by television journalist Giovanni Minoli were more elaborate in their direction and attention to image and detail than the "talking-head" spots of 1983. The composition of the shots, where Craxi is positioned looking down at Minoli, is a telling detail indicative of this closer attention.[9] The themes were still strongly political – unemployment, inflation, development, the environment – but the Craxi who turned to the camera at the end of the spot, smiled and invited viewers to wear the Socialist carnation, was a different leader from those in the election spots of four years earlier – a leader acting out a script, not just delivering a speech.[10]

The party leaders' presence in party-political spots continued to increase. In 1990, the PCI adopted this approach, too.[11] By then, the party that by tradition and culture had been the most critical of the ongoing modernization and personalization of political communication was going through a phase of internal turmoil that would soon see it dissolve and change name. The PCI decided to focus its strategy on its leader, Achille Occhetto. Among the large political parties, the DC was the only one that did not personalize its political spots, more because it had no face that could represent the party as a whole, an undisputed leader able to reconcile the party's various factions. In the 1992 general election – the last of the First Republic – using the party leaders in the spots was one of the most frequently used strategies, albeit often to the detriment of creativity and originality. Exceptions were the PSI spots featuring Craxi, in which images (usually the poor relation) were given equal footing with words. These spots' visual imagery acted independently from speech: through the use of slow-motion sequences, warm and vibrant colors, and musical accompaniment, it conveyed a new image of the PSI secretary.[12] This signaled that in Italy, too, the personalization of political communication was merging with construction of the leader's image – as already theorized and practiced in other countries (Séguéla, 1982).

Another aspect to consider is the further personalization of politics effected by spots produced not by the parties at national level but locally at the individual candidates' behest. The makers of these personal spots had no interest in keeping them for posterity, so they were difficult to retrieve, and the archive only has a few of them. Nonetheless, they show how political communication at local level was focused even more closely on the candidates' image and characteristics.[13]

In the early 1990s, the Tangentopoli political-corruption scandal and the "clean hands" investigation led by some judges prompted the collapse of the First Republic. With the disappearance of many of the political parties that had constituted the Italian political system since 1945, and with the advent of Forza Italia in 1994, the personalization of politics took a striking step forward. Berlusconi, founder of the "personal party *par excellence*" (Calise, 2000) centered his political manifesto, and consequently his communication, on a direct relationship with voters based on personal and pre-political components (Novelli, 2004). Berlusconi took center stage in almost all of the 47 spots stored in the Archive produced at national level by Forza Italia between 1994 and 2005. This is not just a purely quantitative statistic, for with Berlusconi, the personalization process had two distinct features. The first was a marked anti-political trait reflecting an attitude that was widespread in Italy at that time (Campus, 2006; Mastropaolo, 2000), fueled by the contrast between the myth of the man of action and success, on one hand, and "political hacks" on the other.[14] The second was that Berlusconi's leadership was popularized by going beyond the traditional confines of politics to show aspects of his private and personal life, partly through an intimate tone and informal linguistic registers. The trend is perfectly exemplified by Berlusconi's "Merry Christmas and Happy New Year" ads for Christmas 1999, where he comes across as a much-loved friend and neighbor, rather than a party leader, in a bright Christmassy background without any direct references to politics.[15] Hence, in Italy too, the individualization of politics gave way to its privatization, as a more accentuated form of personalization (Van Aelst, Sheafer, & Stanyer, 2012).

The spots produced by the parties in those years therefore contributed strongly to the personalization of politics and the humanization of the party leaders. Those two tendencies, although particularly apparent in Berlusconi's spots, also extended to other protagonists on the Italian political stage and were evident in different political cultures, too.[16]

The introduction of directly elected presidents of regional and provincial administrations, mirroring that of mayors of 1993, extended personalization from national to local level. The candidate has taken center stage and become the main content of a communication that is less about political and ideological themes but more about the candidates personally, their character and biography. These aspects are conveyed and enhanced through the pace of the editing, video effects, music and jingles.[17]

Thanks to the Internet, and social media in particular, recent years have seen the emergence of unofficial musical political spots devoted to the political leader. These are parodies of well-known songs or original compositions, produced by supporters and activists. These spots testify to the spread of a bottom-up form of personalization that elevates the leader to a figure endowed with extraordinary powers (almost an incarnation of divine providence) while annulling any formal and linguistic distance from the leader by calling them by name and using the informal form of address (*tu*).

Long live Italy, the Italy that has chosen to still believe in this dream.
Mister President, we are with you, thank goodness for Silvio.
> (*Meno male che Silvio c'è*, 2006, song for Silvio Berlusconi, Popolo delle Libertà
> candidate for prime minister)[18]

Walter, I trust you, I say Walter, a modern country with Walter,
You can reward talent with Walter and increase wages. Go for it, Walter.
> (*I'm PD*, 2006, song for Walter Veltroni, Partito Democratico candidate
> for prime minister)[19]

You, the son of our land, you who have chosen those who have chosen you,
You, the dream that protects against dark clouds; you, our safety net for today and tomorrow.
> (*Roberto tu sei uno di noi*, 2010, song for Roberto Formigoni,
> PDL candidate as president of the Lombardy region)[20]

Those are three examples of the personalization and popularization of politics from the bottom up, through one of the main vehicles of popular culture: music.

The Genres of Political Spots

One aspect of political spots is the tendency to construct and narrate stories by drawing on the entertainment genres offered by the media and the culture industry. In fact:

> the narrative and audiovisual conventions of popular forms of culture and entertainment are extremely attractive to political communicators because they embrace meanings and understandings already shared by ordinary citizens. These conventional understandings are the linchpins of what culture and film critics call genre … In visual media, genres are characterized by several reinforcing stimuli, where the music, sound effects, rhythms, and tones of narration exist in synergistic combination.
>
> (Richardson, 2008, pp. 11–12)

Spots, as a blend of cinema, advertising, television, music clips and art, constitute a privileged instrument for politics to appropriate the registers, models, languages and formats of other communicative registers.

A caveat is required when discussing the genres of political spots. Although a large body of research has considered these genres, each study seems to use categories of its own, largely deriving from its specific scientific approach and aims, so the same document may be classed differently (Richardson, 2008). Moreover, genre seems to be based on different factors: formal aspects, content or tone. Consequently, given the instability of the political genres – unlike the well-established literary, cinematic or televisual genres – this chapter uses the classifications predominant in the international, especially American (Devlin, 1986), scientific literature to analyze the history and characteristics of Italian political ads.

The most common genre of Italian political spots is the "talking head–declaration–appeal," characterized by two traditional elements of political communication: a speaker and a speech, to which background images are added sometimes. This approach, albeit of somewhat thin narrative construction, has been used consistently over time. Another very popular genre is "program–achievements," intended to present the candidates' political platforms or to emphasize their accomplishments.

Regarding the two most common genres, then, Italian parties have predominantly used political spots to disseminate content about their political function, using fairly traditional forms and methods.

To continue with the run–down of the most used genres, next come the "documentary" – which consists in the reconstruction of a situation, event or period through archive footage – and the "common folk," defined by the presence of ordinary people (sometimes played by actors) representing the supporters of a party or candidate. The "documentary" spot reached its peak in the 1990s, when it was used to reaffirm the identities and histories of political parties going through the profound crisis and upheaval in the Italian political scene.[21] The "common folk" genre has grown constantly over time, reflecting, on one hand, a progressive erosion of authoritativeness in political discourse, and on the other, an attempt by politics to come closer to the electorate.[22]

Ever since the advent of political spots in the US, one of the most characteristic and frequently used genres has been the "negative ad" (West, 2010). The large-scale use in the US of political ads to make direct personal attacks on opponents has prompted some commentators to use the expression "mud-slinging war" to emphasize how the tone and aims of public discussion have degenerated (Diamond & Bates, 1988). Some go so far as to blame this genre for falling turnouts (Ansolabehere & Iyengar, 1995). This highly critical view contrasts with the opinion of those in favor of renewed emotionalism in political communication, who claim that a certain kind of negative political advertising can increase citizens' interest and involvement in the public debate – or at least who tend to downplay its harmful consequences (Brader, 2006; Lau, Sigelman, Heldman, & Babbitt, 1999).

The Italian political scene and, consequently, its communication have experienced a high degree of conflict ever since the first republican electoral campaigns of the 1940s and 1950s, when direct attacks on political adversaries – with insults and even threats – were commonplace (Novelli, 2008). Not surprisingly, therefore, opponents are portrayed with a negative tone in many electoral spots. While this is the overall pattern, however, a change can be seen over time in both the tone and the content of *negative* political advertising. The political spots of the early years mostly made their attacks based on political arguments against political institutions, political parties and the government.[23]

More recent years have seen an increase in *negative* political ads, together with a change in their tone and targets – they have become more aggressive and explicit, with direct personal attacks increasingly against politicians, rather than a party or institution. This tactic is used especially (and this is another innovation) in regional and municipal election campaigns, by candidates from both left[24] and right.[25] Therefore, the more politics has become personalized and has made public the private lives of its protagonists (Meyrowitz, 1985), the more the *negative* genre has spread and taken root, and the more politicians, in Italy too, have become targets of direct attacks.

This tendency is closely linked with the spread of social media and the free online circulation of political ads. The great freedom of expression provided by the Internet, unfettered by any effective form of control or censorship, along with the need to attract attention in order to stand out from the vast mass of material online, seems to have exacerbated the use of a *negative* tone in political debate. Although especially marked in spots made by individual sympathizers or for local candidates' campaigns, such a tone is also apparent in some produced by the national parties.[26]

The "feel-good" genre seeks "to shape reception of the ad's message by eliciting positive emotions such as hope, enthusiasm and perhaps even pride" (Brader, 2006, p. 5). Visually, "feel-good" ads typically feature positive situations, warm images, happy people and uplifting choral music; as regards content, their hallmark is the absence of political points and issues.

In Italy, notwithstanding some earlier instances, this genre began with a famous spot produced in 1987 for the DC[27] by the Italian branch of the advertising agency RSCG – which had worked in France with Jacques Séguéla on François Mitterand's presidential campaigns. This spot is special because it takes the same language, visual register and narrative structure of a very famous Italian advertising campaign for Mulino Bianco biscuits made by RSCG for Barilla[28] and uses it for a political message. When the DC left the political stage in 1994, it was Berlusconi's nascent party that used this genre, in an entirely musical spot, to depict a serene and happy Italy, using a sequence of advertising locations, cultural stereotypes and postcard landscapes.[29] In the years that followed, this genre was seldom employed: perhaps it was unsuited to a climate of conflict in which, as mentioned, aggressive tones and negative registers prevailed; perhaps it was too closely identified with the style of Forza Italy – which, after its initial *feel-good* spot, abandoned the genre for the *talking-head/declaration* and *negative* ads. With some modifications, but still centered on serenity and happiness conveyed by emotional and sensory devices, *feel-good* has reappeared in some of the latest election campaigns.[30]

In the history of Italian political advertising, *feel-good* has been relatively little used. Nevertheless, it is precisely this genre that has marked salient moments in electoral-communication history while demonstrating the tendency for political discourse to transform into narrative built on emotional elements, popular interpretive frameworks, and strong visual stereotypes derived from other languages.

Irony, humor and sarcasm are seldom deployed as persuasive devices in Italian political spots. Very few parties used these communication registers in the early years.[31] The great unfettered expressive freedom characterizing the ads of the first period moved in other directions, then, and toward other genres. Irony and humor were also infrequent in the spots produced in the years that followed, which, as we have seen, witnessed a further deterioration in the tone and language of political debate. While political satire extended its scope, acquiring a greater role in Italian public life (Novelli, 2012), and while a process of hybridization between politics and entertainment on television continued, humor and irony had no place in political spots.

In recent years, however, the comic/satirical genre has spread, in parallel with a more general cross-fertilization between highbrow and lowbrow languages, and the increasing importance of satire in political discourse (Day, 2011; Gray, Jones, & Thompson, 2009). Once again, this change is largely driven by the Web and its close relationship with political satire (Cepernich, 2012), as seen both in viral amateur ads[32] and in the official campaign spots for parties and candidates.[33]

This tendency to accentuate the amusing component of political communication also concerns ads that explicitly draw on the most popular television entertainment formats and genres: reality shows[34] or sitcoms. In particular, the spots by the Ministero per gli Affari Sociali in 2001 used actor Lino Banfi in the guise of Nonno Libero, the popular central character in a well-known Italian sitcom, and it was set in a very similar location to the television series.[35] The Partito Democratico advertising campaign, *La famiglia Spera* – comprising five episodes with events in the life of a typical Italian family, produced with a deliberately televisual style and visual language – can be considered the first electoral sitcom in the history of Italian political communication.[36] Although these are minor cases within the overall advertising output, they are indicative of the progressive cross-fertilization between the language of politics and forms of television entertainment (Mazzoleni & Sfardini, 2009; Van Zoonen, 2005).

Diametrically opposed to the strategy of amusement is that of fear. This too was a minority genre, but it has recently grown and evolved. The few political spots in the early years that played on feelings of vulnerability and worry dealt with themes like terrorism, the menace of totalitarianism, or the threat of nuclear war.[37] Nevertheless, these messages were intended not to cause alarm but to exorcise it. Since the early 2000s, though, political spots in greater numbers have raised fears and worries, especially about security, crime and immigration issues. What distinguishes these ads from the earlier ones is that they no longer merely characterize and discuss topics to do with fear; rather, they are deliberately designed to inspire it. Accordingly, they use quick-fire editing, sound effects, cutaway shots, a narrative style, and music: in short, techniques clearly inspired by horror films and television crime thrillers.[38]

Amusement/comedy and fear/horror are two contrasting genres of political communication based on entertainment formats, and which in the Italian political tradition correspond to two opposite political sides. In fact, while humor/comedy is almost exclusively used by the leftist parties, the fear/horror genre is deployed by the center-right ones, which base their message on an emotive mix of tension and fear. This sharp divide demonstrates that cultural and ideological differences may persist within the more general popularization of politics and its merger with entertainment languages and formats.

Conclusions

In general, the overall output of Italian political spots can be divided into four distinct phases according to content, formal aspects, and legislative and production factors.

1. *1983–94.* During this initial phase, marked by great enthusiasm for the new tool and major concerns about its possible effects, political advertising developed rapidly and entirely without regulation. By the political-communication standards of the time, some of the most original, interesting, creative and innovative spots were produced in those years. They sprang from an encounter with advertising language and from a strong emphasis on the visual dimension over the verbal one. The spots actively reinforced some of the ongoing transformations in political communication at the time, especially personalization, with the involvement of party leaders, and the use of seductive registers and styles. But those political spots did not revolutionize political communication. Most of them belonged to the traditional talking-head/appeal genre; some, though, showed a clear endeavor to communicate through emotional, sensory and spectacular techniques, rather than through verbal logic, and a quest to present politics in a new light.

2. *1995–2004.* This was a phase of regulatory measures and restrictions that subjected political advertising to numerous limitations and stunted its potential. Indeed, it seemed to lose some of its creativity and effectiveness. Nevertheless, political spots continued to play an important role in the personalization of politics, which in those years was a key feature of the Italian political landscape. As the *negative* genre became more common, it contributed to a harshening of the tone of political discussion. It adopted the successful registers of other media and gave voice to ordinary people in an attempt to narrow the gap between political system and citizens that had widened during the 1990s.

3. *2005–11.* The legislative restrictions on the use of political spots remained, but the Internet, used increasingly often during election campaigns (Bentivegna, 2006; Vaccari, 2006), initiated a new phase in the use of political ads. Indeed, their timings, languages

and tones differed substantially from the paid-for political spots on television. In fact, videos produced for the Web were not subject to the rigid constraints imposed by the merger of advertising and television approaches. Because these ads were made to fill websites that were often short on content, they tended to expand, sometimes from the traditional 15 or 30 seconds to even two or three minutes. This radical change affected their pace and language, often reducing their impact. Moreover, while the spots on television were aimed at a mixed audience, the websites of the parties and candidates were mainly visited by supporters and sympathizers. Finally, because these ads had restricted, even if mixed, circulation (on websites and local television stations), and because they were made in large numbers (since they could be placed online without charge), the budgets for producing them were slashed. Hence, their quality and professionalism deteriorated, although some of these shortcomings were offset by greater originality and spontaneity.

4. *2012–15*. The spread of Web 2.0 and social media changed not only the processes of distributing and disseminating spots but also their logic, structure and language. The ease with which ads could be produced and uploaded, in fact, enabled more political players to make and distribute them. Indeed, in Italy, as in other countries (Richardson, 2008, p. 25), the phenomenon has recently spread of viral ads produced by ordinary citizens, sympathizers or creative groups. Their action from the bottom up – marked by creativity, originality and a strong, humorous tone – has proved highly popular and able to influence the information and election-campaign agenda (Cepernich, 2012). Their spontaneity and originality has various roots: the use of satire and irony; the adoption of the culture industry's styles and formats derived from cinema, television and popular music; the use of easy, low-brow and direct language; and narrative with strong emotional, amusing and sensational content. All these features, although most striking in the viral ads uploaded by activists or individuals, are also apparent in the spots produced by the parties.

Spots have been a means of linguistic and expressive experimentation, in close relation to certain traits of modern Italian political communication and the country's political scene:

- Personalization: the elevation of the leader as the main protagonist who makes a direct communicative pact with the voters, built on interweaving personal, biographical and physical features with popular-culture formats (Boni, 2002; Debray, 1977; Hart, 1999; Schwartzenberg, 1977); thus, the party is backgrounded and loses importance (Calise, 2000; Cavalli, 1992, 1998; Pasquino, 1983).
- Impoverishment of the language and content of politics. This is the consequence, on one hand, of the preference for increasingly rapid, elementary and universal rhetorical and discursive approaches (Cedroni & Dell'Era, 2002), and on the other, of high and low registers that are borrowed from the entertainment industry and that can engage an audience with little interest in the public debate (Baum & Jamison, 2006; Jones, 2005).
- Spectacularization: the adoption of linguistic registers and narrative styles centered on strongly emotional, entertaining and sensational components (Brader, 2006) drawn directly from commercial advertising and brief texts – like trailers, video games and music video clips – in which the visual dimension predominates over speech (Kaid & Holtz-Bacha, 2006; Saba, 2006).
- Transformation of political communication into stories – tales centered on commonplace genres and well-tested interpretive frames (Brants & Voltmer, 2011; Jamieson, 1992; Parry-Giles & Parry-Giles, 2002) shared with and taken jointly from television, the news media system, and the entertainment industry (Mazzoleni & Schulz, 1999; Postman, 1985; Riegert, 2007; Van Zoonen, 2005).

Notes

1 The *Archivio degli Spot Politici* (archive of political spots – ASP) was created only in 2012, thanks to a research project funded by the Italian Ministry of Education and Università degli Studi Roma Tre. The ASP is available online at www.archivispotpolitici.it and is the main Italian archive for this type of material. The ads and spots mentioned in this article can be viewed via their ASP URL stated in the notes.

2 On the Italian parties' use of cinema and audiovisual media for appeals and electoral purposes before the 1970s, through original films, short sketches and animated cartoons, see Novelli (2006).

3 The article's notes include ASP links for all cited spots. www.archivispotpolitici.it/dettaglio.spot. php?idspot=258; www.archivispotpolitici.it/dettaglio.spot.php?idspot=259; www.archivispotpolitici.it/dettaglio.spot.php?idspot=257.

4 www.archivispotpolitici.it/dettaglio.spot.php?idspot=75.

5 www.archivispotpolitici.it/dettaglio.spot.php?idspot=80; www.archivispotpolitici.it/dettaglio.spot. php?idspot=98; www.archivispotpolitici.it/dettaglio.spot.php?idspot=96; www.archivispotpolitici.it/dettaglio.spot.php?idspot=492.

6 www.archivispotpolitici.it/dettaglio.spot.php?idspot=78; www.archivispotpolitici.it/dettaglio.spot. php?idspot=81; www.archivispotpolitici.it/dettaglio.spot.php?idspot=85; www.archivispotpolitici.it/dettaglio.spot.php?idspot=88.

7 www.archivispotpolitici.it/dettaglio.spot.php?idspot=76; www.archivispotpolitici.it/dettaglio.spot. php?idspot=82; www.archivispotpolitici.it/dettaglio.spot.php?idspot=83; www.archivispotpolitici.it/dettaglio.spot.php?idspot=87.

8 www.archivispotpolitici.it/dettaglio.spot.php?idspot=77.

9 www.archivispotpolitici.it/dettaglio.spot.php?idspot=104; www.archivispotpolitici.it/dettaglio.spot. php?idspot=114.

10 www.archivispotpolitici.it/dettaglio.spot.php?idspot=121.

11 www.archivispotpolitici.it/dettaglio.spot.php?idspot=53.

12 www.archivispotpolitici.it/dettaglio.spot.php?idspot=226; www.archivispotpolitici.it/dettaglio.spot. php?idspot=231; www.archivispotpolitici.it/dettaglio.spot.php?idspot=235.

13 www.archivispotpolitici.it/dettaglio.spot.php?idspot=221; www.archivispotpolitici.it/dettaglio.spot. php?idspot=41.

14 www.archivispotpolitici.it/dettaglio.spot.php?idspot=166; www.archivispotpolitici.it/dettaglio.spot. php?idspot=165.

15 www.archivispotpolitici.it/dettaglio.spot.php?idspot=167.

16 www.archivispotpolitici.it/dettaglio.spot.php?idspot=193; www.archivispotpolitici.it/dettaglio.spot. php?idspot=467.

17 www.archivispotpolitici.it/dettaglio.spot.php?idspot=213.

18 www.archivispotpolitici.it/dettaglio.spot.php?idspot=439.

19 www.archivispotpolitici.it/dettaglio.spot.php?idspot=438.

20 www.archivispotpolitici.it/dettaglio.spot.php?idspot=331.

21 www.archivispotpolitici.it/dettaglio.spot.php?idspot=46; www.archivispotpolitici.it/dettaglio.spot. php?idspot=40.

22 www.archivispotpolitici.it/dettaglio.spot.php?idspot=79; www.archivispotpolitici.it/dettaglio.spot. php?idspot=454; www.archivispotpolitici.it/dettaglio.spot.php?idspot=485.

23 www.archivispotpolitici.it/dettaglio.spot.php?idspot=103; www.archivispotpolitici.it/dettaglio.spot. php?idspot=125; www.archivispotpolitici.it/dettaglio.spot.php?idspot=227; www.archivispotpolitici.it/dettaglio.spot.php?idspot=296.

24 www.archivispotpolitici.it/dettaglio.spot.php?idspot=266; www.archivispotpolitici.it/dettaglio.spot. php?idspot=348; www.archivispotpolitici.it/dettaglio.spot.php?idspot=435.

25 www.archivispotpolitici.it/dettaglio.spot.php?idspot=330; www.archivispotpolitici.it/dettaglio.spot. php?idspot=343.

26 www.archivispotpolitici.it/dettaglio.spot.php?idspot=444; www.archivispotpolitici.it/dettaglio.spot. php?idspot=384.

27 www.archivispotpolitici.it/dettaglio.spot.php?idspot=109.

28 Another curiosity of these ads is that they represent the first use of the expression "Forza Italia," which Berlusconi would employ just a few years later as the name of his new party.

29 www.archivispotpolitici.it/dettaglio.spot.php?idspot=328.

30 www.archivispotpolitici.it/dettaglio.spot.php?idspot=283; www.archivispotpolitici.it/dettaglio.spot. php?idspot=142.

31 www.archivispotpolitici.it/dettaglio.spot.php?idspot=76; www.archivispotpolitici.it/dettaglio.spot.
php?idspot=263; www.archivispotpolitici.it/dettaglio.spot.php?idspot=54.
32 www.archivispotpolitici.it/dettaglio.spot.php?idspot=437.
33 www.archivispotpolitici.it/dettaglio.spot.php?idspot=441; www.archivispotpolitici.it/dettaglio.spot.
php?idspot=350; www.archivispotpolitici.it/dettaglio.spot.php?idspot=491.
34 www.archivispotpolitici.it/dettaglio.spot.php?idspot=285.
35 www.archivispotpolitici.it/dettaglio.spot.php?idspot=397.
36 www.archivispotpolitici.it/dettaglio.spot.php?idspot=136. These five episodes have been broadcast in cinemas and distributed via the Internet.
37 www.archivispotpolitici.it/dettaglio.spot.php?idspot=111; www.archivispotpolitici.it/dettaglio.spot.
php?idspot=207; www.archivispotpolitici.it/dettaglio.spot.php?idspot=58.
38 www.archivispotpolitici.it/dettaglio.spot.php?idspot=281; www.archivispotpolitici.it/dettaglio.spot.
php?idspot=270; www.archivispotpolitici.it/dettaglio.spot.php?idspot=367.

References

Ansolabehere, S., & Iyengar, S. (1995). *Going negative*. New York, NY: Free Press.

Baum, M. A., & Jamison, A. S. (2006). The Oprah effect: How soft news helps inattentive citizens vote consistently. *The Journal of Politics*, 68(4), 946–959.

Bentivegna, S. (2006). *Campagne elettorali in Rete*. Roma-Bari: Laterza.

Blumler, J. G., & Kavanagh, D. (1999). The third age of political communication: Influences and features. *Political Communication*, 16, 209–230.

Boni, F. (2002). *Il Corpo mediale del leader*. Roma: Meltemi.

Brader, T. (2006). *Campaigning for hearts and mind: How emotional appeals in political ads work*. Chicago: University of Chicago Press.

Brants, K. and Voltmer, K. (Eds.). (2011). *Political communication in postmodern democracy*. New York, NY: Palgrave Macmillan.

Calise, M. (2000). *Il partito personale*. Roma-Bari: Laterza.

Campus, D. (2006). *L'antipolitica al governo: De Gaulle, Reagan, Berlusconi*. Bologna: Il Mulino.

Cavalli, L. (1992). *Governo del leader e regime dei partiti*. Bologna: Il Mulino.

Cavalli, L. (1998). Considerations on charisma and the cult of charismatic leadership. *Modern Italy*, 3(2), 159–171.

Cedroni, L., & Dell'Era, T. (2002). *Il linguaggio politico*. Roma: Carocci.

Cepernich, C. (2012). La satira politica al tempo di internet. *Comunicazione Politica*, 13(1), 73–88.

Day, A. (2011). *Satire and dissent: Interventions in contemporary political debate*. Bloomington: Indiana University Press.

Debray, R. (1977). *L'etat seducteur*. Paris: Gallimard.

Devlin, P. L. (1986). An analysis of presidential television commercials 1952–1984. In L. L. Kaid, D. Nimmo, & K. R. Sanders (Eds.), *New perspectives on political advertising* (pp. 21–54). Carbondale: Southern Illinois University Press.

Diamond, E., & Bates, S. (1988). *The spot: The rise of political advertising on television*. Cambridge, MA: MIT Press.

Gray, J., Jones, J. P., & Thompson, E. (2009). *Satire TV: Politics and comedy in the post-network era*. New York, NY: New York University Press.

Grossi, G., Mancini, P., & Mazzoleni, G. (1983). *Giugno 1983. Campagna elettorale. Vol. I-II*. Roma: Rai-Radiotelevisione Italiana.

Hart, R. (1999). *Seducing America: How television charms the modern voter*. New York, NY: Oxford University Press.

Jamieson, K. H. (1992). *Dirty politics: Deception, distraction and democracy*. New York, NY: Oxford University Press.

Jones, J. P. (2005). *Entertaining politics: New political television and civic culture*. Lanham, MD: Rowman & Littlefield.

Kaid, L. L., & Holtz-Bacha, C. (Eds.). (2006). *The Sage handbook of political advertising*. Thousand Oaks, CA: Sage.

Lau, R. R., Sigelman, L., Heldman, C., & Babbitt, P. (1999). The effects of negative political advertising: A meta-analytic assessment. *American Political Science Review*, 93, 851–875.

Mancini, P., & Mazzoleni, G. (Eds.). (1994). *I media scendono in campo. Le elezioni politiche in tv*. Roma: Rai Eri.

Mastropaolo, A. (2000). *Antipolitica: All'origine della crisi italiana*. Napoli: L'Ancora del Mediterraneo.

Mazzoleni, G., & Boneschi, M. (1980). Televisioni private ed elezioni. *Problemi dell'Informazione*, 5(3), 397–431.

Mazzoleni, G., & Schulz, W. (1999). Mediatization of politics: A challenge for democracy? *Political Communication*, 16(3), 247–261.

Mazzoleni, G., & Sfardini, A. (2009). *La politica pop*. Bologna: Il Mulino.

Meyrowitz, J. (1985). *No sense of place: The impact of electronic media on social behavior*. New York, NY: Oxford University Press.

Morcellini, M. (Ed.). (1995). *Elezioni di tv*. Genova: Costa e Nolan.

Novelli, E. (1995). *Dalla tv di partito al partito della tv*. Firenze: La Nuova Italia.

Novelli, E. (2004). Forza Italia: Origini, trionfo e declino del partito televisivo. *Comunicazione Politica (Special issue: Il Grande Comunicatore)*, 5(1), 143–154.

Novelli, E. (2006). *La turbopolitica. Sessant'anni di comunicazione politica e di scena pubblica in Italia 1945–2005*. Milano: Bur Rizzoli.

Novelli, E. (2008). *Le elezioni del quarantotto. Storia, strategie e immagini della prima campagna elettorale repubblicana*. Roma: Donzelli.

Novelli, E. (2012). Satira, politica e televisione in Italia. *Comunicazione Politica*, 13(1), 57–72.

Parry-Giles, S., & Parry-Giles, T. (2002). *Constructing Clinton: Hyperreality and presidential image making in postmodern politics*. New York, NY: Peter Lang.

Pasquino, G. (1983). Mass media, partito di massa e trasformazione della politica. *Il Mulino*, 33, 559–579.

Pezzini, I. (2001) *Lo spot elettorale*. Roma: Meltemi.

Postman, N. (1985). *Amusing ourselves to death: Public discourse in the age of show business*. New York, NY: Penguin.

Richardson, G. W. (2008). *Pulp politics: How political advertising tells the stories of American politics*. Lanham, MD: Rowman & Littlefield.

Riegert, K. (Ed.). (2007). *Politicotainment: Television's take on the real*. New York, NY: Peter Lang.

Saba, C. G. (2006). *Lo sguardo che insegue*. Milano: Lupetti.

Séguéla, S. (1982). *Hollywood lav plus blanc*. Paris: Flammarion.

Schwartzenberg, R. G. (1977). *L'état spectacle*. Paris: Flammarion.

Vaccari, C. (2006). La campagna 2006 su internet: Pubblico, siti, agenda. *Comunicazione Politica*, 7(2), 329–341.

Van Aelst, P., Sheafer, T., & Stanyer, J. (2012). The personalization of mediated political communication: A review of concepts, operationalizations and key findings. *Journalism*, 13(2), 203–220.

Van Zoonen, L. (2005). *Entertaining the citizen: When politics and popular culture converge*. Lanham, MD: Rowman & Littlefield.

West, D. M. (2010). *Air wars: Television advertising in election campaigns*. Washington, DC: CQ Press.

14

A STRING OF PHENOMENA

A Meta-ethnographic Synthesis of Qualitative Studies and Reviews of the Advertising Campaign of the 13th General Election in Malaysia

Aida Mokhtar

Introduction

The 13th general election in 2013 (GE13) was the most recent general election in Malaysia. It was a display of stiff competition as the main opposition coalition at the time, Pakatan Rakyat (PR), was a strong competitor for Barisan Nasional (BN), the ruling coalition. BN learned its lesson from the 12th general election campaign in 2008 (GE12) and came up with a large scale campaign and active participation on social media in GE13. The former prime minister of Malaysia who led the GE12 campaign, Abdullah Badawi, mentioned it was "a serious misjudgment" when BN depended on government-controlled newspapers and television as the opposition attracted young voters with mobile phone text messages and blogs for the elections ("Malaysian leader admits ignoring Internet was a mistake," 2008). PR performed better in the election compared to the ruling coalition in GE12, increasing their seats from 19 to 82 in a parliament of 222 members. That election denied BN a two-thirds majority in parliament.

GE13 was regarded as the first social media[1] election by the new leader of BN at the time, Najib Tun Razak, because politicians from the two main coalitions used social media to engage with voters online (Lim, 2013; Sani, 2014). Gomez (2013) dispels this notion due to what he claims as BN's poor election performance and describes the election as BN losing the social media election. BN used both traditional and social media in the GE13 campaign (Bakar, Yusoff, & Hussin, 2014). Whichever view one takes, it is clear that the Internet has transformed the political communication style of Malaysian elections from the use of traditional mass media to a symbiosis of both traditional mass media for predominantly one-way communication and online media for interactive communication with voters.

Of great interest to this chapter are previous qualitative studies and reviews of the GE13 campaign in terms of advertising. A meta-ethnographic synthesis of qualitative research studies and reviews of the political campaigns for the 13th general election in Malaysia has generated themes and identified keywords for comparison and contrast. These studies provide an insight into the GE13 campaign in relation to advertising. Before examining advertising in GE13, it is important first to understand the Malaysian populace and the country's aspirations, which determine the significant aspects of the election campaign in GE13 and in previous elections.

Background

Malaysia, situated in Southeast Asia, is a melting pot of diverse cultures. Its population is about 31 million people (Department of Statistics Malaysia, 2016). The main ethnic groups in Malaysia are the Malays, Chinese and Indians who are racially and culturally distinct from one another. In 2010,

Bumiputeras (Malays and indigenous ethnic groups) made up 67.4% of the population, Chinese 24.6%, Indians 7.3% and others 0.7% (Department of Statistics Malaysia, 2010).

The Alliance Party, the former name for BN, was formed in 1953 and, by 1954, it comprised the United Malays National Organisation (UMNO), Malaysian Chinese Association (MCA) and Malaysian Indian Congress (MIC). The Alliance Party successfully represented the three major ethnic groups of Malaya and won the first election in 1955 (Ooi, 2009). The mounting polarization between the Malays and Chinese was reflected in the general election result in 1969, which was a major disappointment for the Alliance Party. In that election, the party lost the two-thirds majority in parliament as well as majorities in the Penang and Kelantan states (Kua, 2011). The success of the opposition parties in this election (Gerakan and DAP) encouraged their supporters to stage a celebration on the nights of May 11 and 12, 1969, which was followed by a racial riot between the Malays and Chinese on May 13 and 14, 1969. The riot led to 137 deaths and more than 300 injured (Kua, 2011). On May 13, another rally, this time by UMNO supporters, countered the victory rally by the opposition that had jeered at the Malays and forecast the triumph of the Chinese. Violence again ensued, marking the profound distrust between the ethnic groups in Malaysia (Andaya & Andaya, 2001).

Against this background, the challenge has been trying to bring Malaysians together so as to successfully pursue a national goal – developed nation status by the year 2020. This goal was inspired by former prime minister, Dr. Mahathir Mohamad, through his Vision 2020 policy.

> Malaysia should not be developed only in the economic sense. It must be a nation that is fully developed along all the dimensions: economically, politically, socially, spiritually, psychologically and culturally. We must be fully developed in terms of national unity and social-cohesion, in terms of our economy, in terms of social justice, political stability, system of government, quality of life, social and spiritual values, national pride and confidence.
>
> (Mohamad, 1991, p. 1)

Dr. Mahathir's vision takes a multidimensional perspective on Malaysian development. His aspiration gives direction to the country while serving as a challenge for future Malaysian prime ministers as they endeavor to steer a country with an extremely fragile social fabric to development. Any form of disunity amongst Malaysians would be detrimental to national development because it could result in the nation not being able meet these goals. Malaysia faces several challenges as it pursues development. The first of these is in building an integrated Malaysian nation that senses a shared destiny and is made up of a single Malaysian national identity or "Bangsa Malaysia" (Mohamad, 1991).

In forging a strong national identity, "the official position is that the national (Malaysian) culture has to be based on Malay culture because it is the culture of the indigenous people who comprise a sizeable portion of the population" (Yong, 2004, p. 7). It is a great challenge to respect the differences of the main ethnicities, while acknowledging the Malay ethnic group as the dominant group based on its size and position as the earlier inhabitants of Malaysia. The Malays of the Malay peninsula have been around for centuries and the Chinese and Indians are largely descendants of migrants who entered Malaya[2] in the mid-19th century for employment when the country's economy was managed by British colonial rule (Andaya & Andaya, 2001).

Despite the challenges, the pursuit of the Vision 2020 goal and even plans for post-2020 were outlined by the government led by Prime Minister Najib as evident in the most recent Eleventh Malaysia Plan (2016–20):

> The Eleventh Plan is based on the theme "anchoring growth on people" and has six strategic thrusts and six game changers that will transform ideas into reality, and address in concert the goals set out in Vision 2020 so as to catapult Malaysia towards the end state of being an advanced economy and inclusive nation.
>
> (Government of Malaysia, 2015a, p. 18)

An endeavor to integrate all ethnic groups in Malaysia is manifested in the concept of "1Malaysia" that was officially introduced by Prime Minister Najib on September 16, 2010. It promotes the idea of integrating diverse cultures and inclusiveness as key to Malaysian development. It endeavors to ease the burden on Malaysians through the offer of 1Malaysia initiatives (Government of Malaysia, 2015b). 1Malaysia promotes eight values that are relevant to all ethnic groups in the nation supporting inclusiveness: the culture of excellence, perseverance, humility, acceptance, loyalty, meritocracy, integrity and education. The 1Malaysia concept was also associated with enhancing the life of Malaysians who are financially challenged. Some key government initiatives are: Back to School initiatives, 1Malaysia People's Aid, 1Malaysia clinic, and, the 1Malaysia book voucher. The repeated mention of 1Malaysia in the names of the initiatives reinforces in people's minds the ideal of a united Malaysia. 1Malaysia was an important element of the GE13 advertising campaign by the governing party, BN.

Politics and the Media in Malaysia

Malaysia is a constitutional monarchy with a political system that follows the Westminster model. The incumbent coalition is BN, which was established in 1973. BN is made up of parties that, like the former Alliance Party, represent the three main ethnic groups of Malaysia: UMNO, MCA and MIC[3] (Barisan Nasional, 2015). The opposition party in GE13 was PR, comprising Parti Keadilan Rakyat (PKR; People's Justice Party), Democratic Action Party (DAP) and Pan-Malaysian Islamic Party (PAS). The PR coalition is relatively new in comparison to BN as it was formed in 2008. The general election campaign in 2013 by BN was led by Najib Tun Razak and PR, by the former deputy prime minister, Anwar Ibrahim. After the disintegration of the Pakatan Rakyat alliance in early 2015, it was announced on September 22, 2015 that Pakatan Harapan was the newly formed alliance by PR comprising PKR, DAP and Parti Amanah Negara (PAN) (Goh, 2015). PAN is a splinter party of PAS.

There have been five Malaysian prime ministers[4] before Najib who is the current and sixth prime minister. All prime ministers were from UMNO under the Alliance Party and then from UMNO under BN. The dominance of BN as the ruling coalition for over 50 years has resulted in its political hegemony, which is reflected in the mass media (Muhamad, 2015). The developing opposition coalition has little access to the media. Control of the mass media is evident by governmental regulations that control media content and access to production (George, 2005). With BN in control of the mass media, it is no surprise that advertising messages in the mass media for GE13 predominantly originated from the governing coalition.

The BN mass media hegemony reflects Malaysia's practice of an authoritarian principle of the press (print and broadcast), based on direct or indirect control of the state or sovereign; truth is controlled by those in authority and they decide what should be published (Hachten & Scotton, 2002). According to Siebert (1963), the authoritarian concept proposes that the state is the highest form of group organization, surpassing the value of the individual. It further reiterates that the individual is dependent on the state in developing the attributes of a civilized man. Authoritarianism is one of the four theories of the press alongside libertarianism, social responsibility and Soviet communism (Siebert, Peterson, & Schramm, 1963).

In the Soviet press concept, the mass media were controlled by the government and the party in the absence of private media. The controlled press was monopolized by one party and informed the public with "positive" news that supported the party's goals without being customer-centric (Hachten & Scotton, 2002). The libertarian theory of the press is illustrated by the media system of democratic countries with the functions of informing and entertaining the public, free from the controls and domination of the government as it seeks truth (Siebert, 1963). The social responsibility theory of the press in the 20th century emphasizes the idea that the role of the press is in "servicing the political system, in enlightening the public, in safeguarding the liberties of the individual; but it represents the opinion that the press has been deficient in performing those tasks" (Peterson, 1963, p. 74).

The General Election 13 Campaign in Malaysia

GE13 or "the mother of all elections" was important for both parties. It was an opportunity for PR to wrestle more seats from the incumbent BN coalition after their GE12 conquest, which was marked by a 12% swing in popular votes to their side. For Najib, as head of the BN, GE13 was the opportunity to earn a new mandate from voters after taking over the prime minister's post from Abdullah Badawi in 2009 (Mustafa, 2014). Najib was competing against Anwar Ibrahim, the opposition leader, who was perceived as morally corrupt by the Malaysian mainstream media since his imprisonment for sodomy from 1998 to 2004.

Young voters made up a large percentage of the total number of voters and this made social media an important platform for the general election campaign.

> According to the statistics from the Suruhanjaya Pilihan Raya (SPR or Elections Commission [EC]),[5] young voters consist of up to 40% or 5.6 million voters … Voters between the ages of 21 and 45 years old were made up of more than 8 million voters. EC explains that there are over 85% of the country's 13.3 million eligible voters who went to the polls on 5 May 2013.
>
> (Sani, 2014, p. 136)

Political campaigning commenced on the day of nominating candidates on April 20, 2013, and ended on polling day on May 5, 2013. The election campaign by BN was described as having "grandeur-style political campaign exercises" but was said to have commenced many years before GE13 through the 1Malaysia transformational program (Bakar et al., 2014). BN's budget for the GE13 campaign was controlled by Najib, who centralized political communication management, akin to a war-room strategy dependent on consultants, quite unlike previous elections when the individual parties of the coalition promoted themselves (Welsh, 2013).

It was reported that BN incorporated both political advertising and social media together in their GE13 campaign (Bakar et al., 2014). There were about four advertising companies appointed by BN to work on an integrated GE13 campaign on television, radio, print media and direct mail (Mohamed, 2013). The banners, commercials, political songs and advertisements placed on traditional media were also put on the Internet (Bakar et al., 2014) reinforcing the same message on different platforms. BN advertisements swarmed national mass media outlets and websites during the GE13 campaign (Welsh, 2013). A study that examined political advertisements in selected mainstream newspapers from nomination day to polling day found that "*The Star, Utusan Malaysia* (UM) and *New Straits Times* (NST) carried 245 political advertisements. The Star carried 39.2 per cent of the total advertisements; NST 31.9 per cent and UM 29 per cent" (Mustafa, 2014, p. 84).

Despite aggressive political campaigning on both sides of the GE13 fence, the opposition did not win GE13 and BN is again in power in parliament albeit without a two-thirds majority.

> Throughout Peninsular Malaysia, BN was marginally ahead of PR in terms of parliamentary seats, marginally ahead in terms of state legislative assembly seats, but substantially ahead in terms of the control of state governments. Of course, BN had won power according to a "first-past-the-post" system, not a system of proportional representation (that had never been adopted by Malaysia).
>
> (Khoo, 2013, p. 21)

It appears that social media influenced the outcome for the opposition. The use of social media helped the opposition party to win popular votes in 2008 and 2013 against BN (Muhamad, 2015). BN had to come up with a better campaign in GE13 compared to previous elections.

Political Advertising

There are various definitions of political advertising, which highlight its key objective of persuading voters to decide on political candidates and parties for power and office. "Political advertising promotes candidates for office" (Thorson & Rodgers, 2012, p. 5). It is found in political systems where political power is competed for in elections by political parties and candidates who promote themselves through paid advertisements, predominantly through mass media, to voters (Holtz-Bacha & Kaid, 2006).

Political advertisements aim to move voters from being aware of politicians and political parties to voting for them. Political advertisements have the potential of affecting voters' political interests, knowledge, candidate assessments and ultimately their voting behavior (Moorman & Neijens, 2012). Advertising must balance strategic advertising information along with drama (Moriarty, Mitchell, & Wells, 2015). Finding the right balance between the two goals results in effective political communication – the target audience obtains information supported by evidence by inferring from the drama "staged" by characters in advertisements.

Research Methods

Reviewing previous qualitative research studies and reviews on political advertising for GE13 is the main focus of the study. It adapts Noblit and Hare's (1988) meta-ethnography synthesis approach of reviewing qualitative research studies which extends beyond a literature review by synthesizing interpretative studies. The qualitative research studies and reviews were chosen because of their interpretative orientation and depth in the examination of concepts. The interpretative paradigm, under which the meta-ethnographic synthesis approach falls, emphasizes a concern for comprehending the world in its current state through the lens of the participant rather than through the observer (Burrell & Morgan, 1979). The most attractive aspect of this research study is the absence of predetermined items which would influence the analysis.

Findings and Discussion

After examining previous studies of political advertising in the 13th general election in Malaysia, seven qualitative research studies and GE13 campaign reviews that were relevant to the intellectual interest of this study were found (Bakar et al., 2014; Gomez, 2013; Leong, 2014; Mohamed, 2013; Muhamad, 2015; Mustafa, 2014; Sani, 2014). The studies contained similar and different metaphors, key words and phrases, including: the importance of targeting for effective advertisement; BN advertised on both traditional and online media in GE13; political advertisements on social media encourages better engagement with voters; politicians can no longer hide in ivory towers; political advertisements exist in the public and state spheres; political advertising and diversity of views on traditional media in GE13; the social media transformation of mass media; the imagined society as a target of political advertisements; moving from negative to positive appeals in election advertisements; and political advertising regulation in Malaysia.

Targeting Important for Effective Advertisements in GE13

Targeting entails designing specific communication strategies to meet the needs and wants of audience members and positioning the product by identifying a specific location for it relative to its competitors so as to match the interests of the target audience (Moriarty et al., 2015). Targeting was practiced by BN and the Malaysian government through their promotion of the 1Malaysia concept. The Malaysian government had promoted 1Malaysia in the years after its launch in 2010 and before

GE13. The "1Malaysia" slogan by the government was reported to be used by BN in its GE13 campaign as evident through the print advertisements of selected Malaysian newspapers that used the theme "1Malaysia" with the tagline "People First" (Mustafa, 2014). The slogan and tagline were regarded as demonstrating the customer-oriented and inclusive side of BN by focusing on people's needs and by including diverse ethnicities through 1Malaysia. The repeated 1Malaysia logo in the advertisements seems to be an attempt to reinforce the united Malaysian identity and was the solution to the first strategic central challenge encountered by the government of uniting diverse Malaysians for the developed nation status, raised earlier by Dr. Mahathir in his Vision 2020 policy (Mohamad, 1991).

However, the discrepancy between the ideological messages and the dismal realities of the high costs of living, ethnic discrimination, corruption and religious extremism affecting people on the ground had marred the advertising effectiveness of BN (Mustafa, 2014) and freed up votes from BN (Gomez, 2013). An effort to close the gap between advertising messages and reality would make the BN advertisements more effective as this would underline the targeting effort in the way that meets people's needs for solutions to the problems they encounter. To succeed, the advertisements would have had to be relevant and resonate with the audience (Moriarty et al., 2015). The writers define relevant advertisements as those that contain ideas that mean something to the audience and resonant advertisements are those that ring true for the audience. All political parties have to profoundly understand their target audience members to make their advertisements relevant and resonate with the audience.

A study of first-time voters in Malaysia, from 21 to 23 years old and of different ethnicities, found that more apt advertising elements should have been included in GE13 campaign advertisements as without relevance and resonance, the advertisements were less effective (Mohamed, 2013). The study involved three focus groups of 15 participants comprising 12 Malays, one Chinese, one Indian and one participant categorized as "Other" from urban, semi-urban and rural areas. It is important to observe that in this study there were many more Malay respondents than other ethnicities and it did not represent the real proportions of the ethnic groups in the country. More BN advertisements than PR advertisements were also examined when there should have been an equal number for a fairer examination.

The participants in the focus groups expressed strong preferences and dislikes of the form and content of 21 print advertisements by political parties (14 by BN and 7 by PR) showcased during the GE13 campaign. There were commonalities in terms of their preferences for political advertisements that were relevant by mentioning the youth agenda in a simple manner, for soft-sell[6] political advertisements, for advertisements with graphics, simple copy, colorful visuals, and neutral topics and dislike of advertisements that attacked opposition parties or promoted candidate characteristics. Soft-sell advertising messages provided young voters with the freedom to make judgments rather than hard-sell advertisements that imposed messages.

Despite the commonalities, there were some preferences that were dissimilar across the groups, perhaps due to the different settings and educational levels of the respondents. The study found that the rural group were generally distrustful of political advertisements and politics but simultaneously commented that BN advertisements were attractive because of their creativity and individuality and PR advertisements had attractive design, an engaging factor and promoted profound thinking (Mohamed, 2013). The semi-urban group had people with strong emotional and physiological attachments to being ruled by BN for 57 years and, hence, preferred BN advertisements that promoted "peace, stability, progress, pride and developments." The urban group saw advertisements that contained percentages, figures and sources rather than "slanderous words" as trustworthy and reflecting the credibility of the party.

The study found that young voters are discerning "customers" due to their access to a variety of information on traditional and alternative media, do not favor advertisements that attacked competitors and felt that online and offline advertisements should have coherent messages as young people favored looking at the larger campaign. The soft-sell approach was used by BN in their GE12 campaign and was successful in leading the coalition to a landslide victory (Netto, 2007).

Other than the young voters being important targets in GE13 by BN and PR, the Chinese voters were also targeted by BN. In the campaign running up to GE13, BN strategists particularly targeted Chinese voters with television commercials and posters with Prime Minister Najib wearing traditional Chinese clothes (Foley, 2013). Najib played drums in the advertisement depicting his dedication to the Chinese community (Kaur, 2013).

BN Political Advertisements on Traditional and Online Media in GE13

In the previous few Malaysian general elections, the public has witnessed changes in political campaigns with advertisements on television, in newspapers, on websites and the aggressive use of social media in GE13 (Yaakop, Padlee, Set, & Salleh, 2014). For BN, political advertisements placed on traditional media were also placed on the Internet for GE13 (Bakar et al., 2014). This combination reinforced advertising messages.

Political advertisements combined with better engagement on social media could have improved the election result for BN. There was increased BN participation on social media during GE13 compared to GE12 but the coalition's election results were dismal despite their win. BN managed to win GE13 albeit with a simple majority of seats but lost the popular vote to the opposition (Bakar et al., 2014). Some recommendations were provided by the writers in terms of the need for better coherence, focus and engagement of political communication campaigns in future elections. "Finally, in the Prime Minister's Department gathering on 3 June 2013, Najib admitted that the failure of the BN government to handle negative perceptions on social media had cost them greater success in the election" (Sani, 2014, p. 142). Social media should have been aligned with mainstream media and focused on significant key election issues for BN's election campaign to be more effective (Gomez, 2013). That mass media advertisements should have been coupled with more intense activity[7] on social media became evident in light of the opposition group's greater engagement with voters through online media, which led to their success in GE13 (Muhamad, 2015; Sani, 2014).

> On the polling day of 5 May 2013, although there has been an increase of "Likes" on Najib's official Facebook page to 1,720,255, the engagement level was very low at 12%. Opposition leader Anwar's official Facebook page had an increase as well at nearly half of Najib's at 826,586 "Likes", but had an extremely high engagement rate of 75%.
>
> (Sani, 2014, p. 137)

The main lessons BN drew from the election was that more needs to be done to combat negative perceptions on social media. The mass media has its strengths and should play its role complementarily to social media to encourage voters in Malaysia to vote for BN. The Malaysian rural voters, who are less educated, conservative and pro-government, tend to use traditional media where BN is prominent (Sani, 2014). Social media should therefore be emphasized for urban voters. In 2011, household use of the Internet in rural areas was only 17.8% while in urban areas it was 82.2% (Malaysian Communications and Multimedia Commission, Q2 2013).

Political Advertisements on Social Media Encourages Better Engagement with Voters: No More Hiding in Ivory Towers for Politicians

People in "ivory towers" are cut off from the real world when they fail to engage with people and understand them better. When politicians make decisions, they may be unrealistic because they do not quite understand what is happening or what is expected in the real world. The media landscape has changed for politicians as it moves them from the ivory tower to being "on the ground" engaging with voters. "Politicians cannot hide behind ivory towers (office doors) any more as people expect them to be available to answer queries and address issues" (Leong, 2014, p. 34). The previous practice of one-way communication by politicians through traditional mass media has been transformed into a combined formula of both one-way and interactive communication online. With the emergence of Web 2.0, two-way communication occurs between political parties and consumers compared to Web 1.0 that uses the "We talk, you listen" approach (Thill & Bovee, 2015). Political advertisements put on social media for the reinforcement of messages in GE13 would encourage better engagement due to the media's interactive orientation. It would be best for the advertisements to be viral so as to allow them better reach.

Political Advertisements in the Public and State Spheres

The Malaysian political space for political advertising in GE13 was divided into two spheres: the public sphere and the state sphere (Bakar et al., 2014). "The public sphere itself appears as a specific domain – the public domain versus the private. Sometimes the public sphere appears simply as that sector of public opinion that happens to be opposed to the authorities" (Habermas, 1991, p. 2). It was mentioned that PR had limited presence on traditional media compared to the easy access for BN politicians and socio-political bloggers (Leong, 2014). Traditional media reflected BN's political hegemony by focusing on government views (Leong, 2014).

There are three means of mass media control in Malaysia: legal provisions, state ownership and ruling-party shareholding (Bakar et al., 2014). Mass media influence on the previous election is apparent in Malaysia as the writers contend that the controls, justified by the government as important for stable race relations, were responsible for the major BN victory in the 1990 general election. Most traditional media organizations in Malaysia are owned by political parties in the BN coalition or by people who are affiliated with BN (Mustafa, 2014). The Malaysian mass media are also regulated by laws that have been described as obstacles to media freedom (Bakar et al., 2014).

The most well-known laws for newspapers in Malaysia are the Printing Presses and Publications Act (PPPA) 1984, Official Secrets Act 1972 and Sedition Act 1948 (Muhamad, 2015). The PPPA requires the annual issuing of licenses by the Malaysian Home Affairs Ministry for organizations producing newspapers and magazines and the applications for operating television and radio station licenses require approval from the Ministry of Communications and Multimedia Malaysia. The ownership and affiliations of the government with media organizations are apparent: Radio Televisyen Malaysia (RTM) is a government-owned broadcasting agency; Media Prima Berhad, a media corporation that owns television stations (TV3, NTV7, TV9 and 8TV) and Astro, the key provider of satellite television in Malaysia, are affiliated to the ruling political party.

The mass media controls in Malaysia have made mainstream media a BN mouthpiece (Muhamad, 2015). The traditional media – television, radio and print – have provided a sphere for the state rather than for the public (Bakar et al., 2014). This explains why most political advertisements for GE13 in mainstream newspapers were by BN. PR and their allies faced significant challenges in trying to enter the state sphere for GE13 as their political advertising copy was scrutinized for content offensive to BN (Mustafa, 2014).

The political space for alternative views has grown nevertheless and allows for more diverse political advertisements and opportunities for discerning voters. The independent online media that provide viewpoints different from traditional mainstream newspapers are *The Malay Mail Online*, *The Malaysian Insider*, *Free Malaysia Today* and *The Ant Daily* (Mustafa, 2014). The opposition's need for more political space to communicate with voters has resulted in their use of new media (synonymous to social media by the writer) (Leong, 2014). Bakar et al. (2014) mention that mass media controls have led the opposition and all non-state actors (opposition parties, civil societies and individuals) to resort to social media for communication. The potential for the engagement and self-expression of alternative views compared to traditional media has made social media attractive for political parties and voters (Muhamad, 2015). In 2013, BN was involved in social media, however, the opposition social media campaign, though active, was obscured by BN's mainstream media presence, paid advertising and direct marketing spurred by greater financial resources (Gomez, 2013).

The question of whether there is a public sphere in Malaysia has been raised. It seems that freedom of the press and an open public sphere are essentially absent in Malaysia, in light of the government's controls on the mass media and restrictions on alternative media (Sani, 2014). Some people think there is a public sphere in spite of the state control of new media and BN's active participation in social media during GE13, since all parties could still express themselves openly on social media (Leong, 2014). The possibility of expressing alternative views by the opposition on social media was demonstrated during GE13. Social media helped to level the playing field. GE13 demonstrated the relevance of equalization theory, which argues that the Internet offers a convenient and inexpensive way for opposition political marketing. On the Internet, the opposition is able to engage with the electorate on equal footing with the ruling party (Muhamad, 2015). Equalization theory stands in opposition to normalization theory, i.e. that the political hegemony of political space by one party is maintained even on the Internet.

It is likely that traditional and digital media will co-exist and reinforce one another but not replace one another in Malaysia (Nor, Gapor, Bakar, & Harun, 2011; Salman, Ibrahim, Abdullah, Mustaffa, & Mahbob, 2011). This co-existence was evident in GE13 with the use of political advertisements on traditional media and social media in a fiercely fought campaign aimed at 13.3 million voters (Sani, 2014). Each form of media has its strengths and can be used to target audiences who access them most.

Political Advertising and Diverse Views on Traditional Media in GE13: Social Media Transformation of Mass Media

Social media has begun to transform traditional media in Malaysia. Social media's influence on traditional media has made radio, television and the press somewhat more accommodating and amenable to alternative views (Leong, 2014). Leong further mentions that in GE13, selected private traditional media gave a more balanced coverage of GE13 with *Sinar Harian* accepting a DAP advertisement, the radio station Business FM (BFM) and cable television *Astro Awani* giving space to views from the opposition.

Since the 2008 general election (GE12), social media has encouraged some positive treatment of opposition politicians by several publications in Malaysia, specifically by English-language newspapers sold in the urban parts of the west coast states. Such treatment would have been "unthinkable" prior to the emergence of social media (Brown, 2008, p. 744).

A Target of Political Advertisements: The Imagined Society

The public sphere or social media is occupied by an imagined community (Bakar et al., 2014). The nation is an imagined political community and imagined as limited and sovereign, with members who may not know one another but can imagine their communion (Anderson, 2006). There is a "silo effect" found when people restrict themselves to views they agree with (Leong, 2014). This silo effect causes the supporters of PR and BN to be more committed to their parties through social media (Sani, 2014). People are unified by their common interests through social media where political advertisers market to a united target audience.

BN Political Campaign with a Single Icon: Najib Tun Razak

Although young voters preferred political advertisements that touched on national growth and development, issues, racial stability, and the manifesto and finally candidates' characteristics (Mohamed,

2013), the single leadership icon of Najib was found in the BN political campaign for GE13 (Gomez, 2013; Mohamed, 2013). The GE13 campaign by BN was focused on Najib alone, akin to a US presidential campaign, with a huge amount spent on advertising (Welsh, 2013). The prominence of Najib in the campaign was a convincing form of singular branding in contrast to PR that had online and offline advertising posters encompassing its three leaders with separate social media platforms to promote the different PR parties individually (Gomez, 2013). It appears that the parties in the BN coalition were well-integrated under one leader compared to the PR coalition, which promoted separate leaders in a way that depicted the lack of unification. That the BN coalition has matured more significantly than PR is demonstrated by its agreement to be led by a single leader. The BN maturity is not surprising in light of its earlier establishment in 1973 compared to PR which was founded in 2008.

In contrast, another study mentioned that Najib Razak did not overtly employ his personality in BN's political advertisements as Abdullah did in GE11; instead, the 1Malaysia concept was reiterated (Mustafa, 2014). In the GE11 campaign, images of Abdullah dominated television, radio, billboards and newspapers, with a television advertisement portraying him as a caring and moderate leader. In the campaign, BN depended on Abdullah's popularity (Lau, 2004). Perhaps Abdullah was more intensely featured than Najib in the election campaign as a result of the contrasting views. According to an advertising agency director, BN television commercials for the GE11 campaign adopted Abdullah's approach to politics by focusing on the matters Malaysians usually talked about in terms of what they do, their beliefs and life that goes beyond politics (Netto, 2007).

Political Advertisers: Two in One

It was difficult to distinguish between the state and BN as separate advertisers in print media during GE13 as Malaysian government's achievements were promoted as BN's achievements in managing the country.

> There is no distinct differentiation between a party campaign and a state function in the advertisements and pullouts. For instance, the Federal Land Development Authority (FELDA) had a pullout supplement on what it claimed to be its achievements in improving the livelihood of the smallholders. The supplement page subtly communicated the achievements of the BN-led government over the years.
>
> (Mustafa, 2014, p. 85)

Other achievements were found in the supplement by the Ministry of Higher Education and its initiative of transforming Malaysia into a leading global education hub, a positive advertisement for Malaysia's economy endorsed by the International Monetary Fund, the World Bank and the Asian Development Bank, and a two-page supplement that hailed the achievements of the government agency, the Rubber Industry Smallholders Development Authority (RISDA) (Mustafa, 2014). The use of RTM as the government's and BN's mouthpiece for the general election speaks of this dual function of the state-owned television (Ingram, 1999). It conveyed the achievements of BN as the government of Malaysia.

From Negative to Positive Appeals in Election Advertisements

The negative appeals used in the 10th Malaysian general election in 1999 (GE10), were replaced with positive appeals in the 2004 11th general election (GE11). The feel-good appeal was used with BN branding and was featured in GE11 advertisements (Netto, 2007). BN launched the manifesto and slogan "Excellence, Glory, Distinction" for the GE11 campaign (Tsin, 2008). The slogan was used in exchange for threats and negative campaigning in GE10 (Lau, 2004). It appears that BN was later associating itself with positive attributes as the slogan exuded the towering and positive positioning of the coalition, thus distinguishing it from its political rivals.

The campaign approach by BN for GE10 was heavily criticized by DAP leader, Lim Kit Siang, as part of an election that was the "dirtiest" in the history of the nation (Lim, 1999). He accused BN of using dirty tactics in the GE10 campaign that was getting dirtier and dirtier as the days passed, by using advertisements with "fear and scare" tactics on radio, television and newspapers. He claimed that BN's ads were generated by the "dirty tactics" department to malign and defame opposition leaders with fictitious and biased media coverage of the opposition. The feel-good factor approach in GE11 seemed as though it was answering Lim's criticism of the previous election.

Political Advertising Regulations in Malaysia

Web 2.0 provides a democratic ecosystem in Malaysia but therein lies a paradoxical scenario since the government both participates in and controls social media (Bakar et al., 2014). The writers mention governmental control of social media in an unfavorable tone, calling it an act of "de-democratising" that is challenging to carry out due to the characteristics of social media, which are: interactive, consumer-centred and "almost-anarchic." The Internet is under the Malaysian government's watchful eye, but during GE13, the "cyberwar" between political parties saw more prominence of the production and manipulation of information rather than restriction on information (Tapsell, 2014). Nevertheless, the government took action against users of social media during the GE13 campaign when the police detained a pro-PR blogger Yusuf Al Siddique (also known as Milo Suam) under the Official Secrets Act (Sani, 2014).

There are no specific laws for political television, online and print advertisements in Malaysia but there are codes that guide them. Political advertisements on television, radio, online services (of online advertisements) and audiotext hosting services or premium rate services in Malaysia are guided by the Malaysian Communications and Multimedia Content Code issued by the Malaysian Communications and Multimedia Commission (MCMC). The code reflects its commitment in providing a guide for self-regulation of service providers in the Malaysian communications and multimedia industry in conformity with the Communications and Multimedia Act of 1998 (Act 588) (The Communications and Multimedia Content Forum of Malaysia, 2004). The Film Guidelines by the Film Censorship Board of Malaysia are used by the Malaysian government to screen films and television advertising content. They are used in accordance with the Film Censorship Act 2002 (Act 620) and other laws, regulations, policies and international conventions (Film Censorship Control and Enforcement, 2011). The guidelines also do not mention specific guidelines for political television advertisements in Malaysia.

Election and political advertisements in print media are guided by the Malaysian Code of Advertising Practice issued by the Advertising Standards Authority of Malaysia (ASA) which mentions that there should not be advertisements that offend the political sensibilities of any community (Advertising Standards Authority Malaysia, 2014). It appears that political advertisements online, on television and in print media are treated like goods and services advertisements.

Nevertheless, in July 1999 before GE10 in November 1999, the former Information Minister, Khalil Yaacob, mentioned that the opposition would be denied access to RTM which was state-run because of the country's developing status and ethnic sensitivities, but Yaacob was allowed to speak to private television stations about access (Ingram, 1999). This situation illustrates the association of the government with BN that has turned RTM into a political space.

There has been criticism with regard to the television news in Malaysia. Opposition leader Lim Kit Siang, referring to a 90-second video, called it a commercial dressed up in different clothing (Lim, 2002). He regarded the footage as political and against the opposition parties PAS and Parti Keadilan Nasional, during the Indera Kayangan by-election campaign in 2002. He recommended that there be a clear labeling of the footage as a political commercial instead of disguising it as prime-time news and the need for the opposition to be given airtime for their commercials so as to identify the footage as "legitimate, justified and valuable."

Conclusion

Political advertising has to be carried out adeptly by political parties for their messages to be convincing enough to garner votes. The previous literature on the GE13 campaign has identified several themes, such as: targeting is important for effective advertisements in GE13; the need to coordinate political advertisements on traditional and online media in GE13; political advertisements on social media encourages better engagement with voters; no more hiding in ivory towers for politicians; distinguishing political advertisements in the public and state spheres; political advertising and accommodating diverse views on traditional media in GE13; social media transformation of mass media; the imagined society as a target for political advertisements; political advertisers: two in one; from negative to positive appeals of election advertisements; and political advertising regulations in Malaysia.

In GE13, competition between BN and PR was stiff and required both coalitions to campaign intensely to the electorate (Mohamed, 2013). Some political advertisements have been placed on traditional and social media, and reach different target audiences, with the urban audience preferring the Internet and the rural audience preferring traditional media. Political parties cannot rest on their laurels as they have to promote themselves more effectively and one way is to understand the target audience well and to meet their need for advertising elements that are value laden.

The formula for success in political communication in Malaysian election campaigns would be the effective amalgamation of advertising on social media and traditional media that addresses the prospective policies of BN and the opposition, which they would implement in government. The changing media landscape has made young voters discerning as they have access to a variety of information from different parties before deciding on which candidate and political party to vote for in an election.

Notes

1   Social media includes blogs, news portal, Facebook, Twitter and YouTube (Sani, 2014).
2   Malaya consists of the parts of current Malaysia without Sabah, Sarawak and Singapore. Malaysia became independent in 1957. The Federation of Malaya consisted of nine states (Selangor, Perak, Negeri Sembilan, Pahang, Johor, Kedah, Kelantan, Perlis and Terengganu) and two Straits Settlements of Penang and Malacca.
3   Other parties in BN are: Parti Pesaka Bumiputera Bersatu (PBB), Sarawak United People's Party (SUPP), Parti Gerakan Rakyat Malaysia (GERAKAN), Peoples Progressive Party (PPP), Liberal Democratic Party (LDP), Parti Bersatu Rakyat Sabah (PBRS), United Pasokmomogun Kadazandusun Murut Organisation (UPKO), Parti Bersatu Sabah (PBS), Sarawak Progressive Democratic Party (SPDP) and Parti Rakyat Sarawak (PRS) (McGrath, 2013).
4   Former prime ministers of Malaysia were: Tunku Abdul Rahman Putra Al-Haj, Abdul Razak Hussein, Hussein Onn bin Dato' Onn, Dr. Mahathir Mohamad and Abdullah Ahmad Badawi.
5   Suruhanjaya Pilihan Raya or SPR is the Malay name for the Election Commission of Malaysia.
6   A soft-sell approach is "an emotional message that uses mood, ambiguity, and suspense to create a response based on feelings and attitudes" (Moriarty et al., 2015, p. 635).
7   According to Yu, the Meltwater marketing and communications manager for Asia Pacific, engagement is the number of people conversing about the webpage, divided by the number of people who like the webpage (Asohan, 2013).

References

Advertising Standards Authority Malaysia. (2014). *Malaysian code of advertising practice*. Petaling Jaya, Malaysia: Advertising Standards Authority Malaysia.

Andaya, B.W., & Andaya, L.Y. (2001). *A history of Malaysia* (2nd ed.). Basingstoke, UK: Palgrave.

Anderson, B. (2006). *Imagined communities: Reflections on the origin and spread of nationalism*. London: Verso Books.

Asohan, A. (2013). GE13: A "social media election" after all. Retrieved from www.digitalnewsasia.com/contactus.

Bakar, B. A. M., Yusoff, M. A., & Hussin, Z. H. (2014). The paradox of social media: The de-democratization of Malaysia. *International Review of Basic and Applied Sciences, 2*(7), 104–112.

Barisan Nasional. (2015). Barisan Nasional: Parti Komponen. Retrieved from www.barisannasional.org.my/parti-komponen.

Brown, G. K. (2008). Federal and state elections in Malaysia, March 2008. *Electoral Studies, 27*(4), 740–773.

Burrell, G., & Morgan, G. (1979). *Sociological paradigms and organisational analysis.* London: Heinemann Educational Books.

The Communications and Multimedia Content Forum of Malaysia. (2004). *The Malaysian communications & multimedia content code (Version 6).* Petaling Jaya, Malaysia: The Communications and Multimedia Content Forum of Malaysia.

Department of Statistics Malaysia. (2010). *Population and housing census of Malaysia: Population distribution and basic demographic characteristics.* Putrajaya, Malaysia: Department of Statistics Malaysia.

Department of Statistics Malaysia. (2016, July 18). Department of Statistics Malaysia Official Portal: Population Clock. Retrieved from www.statistics.gov.my/index.php?r=home/index&menu_id=b2ROaWpITmQ5NnAvMHVmRjRkZzlBQT09.

Film Censorship Control and Enforcement. (2011). *Guidelines on film censorship.* Putrajaya, Malaysia: Ministry of Home Affairs of Malaysia.

Foley, S. (2013, May 13). Malaysians vote: The Middle East watches. Retrieved from www.mei.edu/content/malaysians-vote-%E2%80%94-middle-east-watches.

George, C. (2005). The Internet's political impact and the penetration/participation paradox in Malaysia and Singapore. *Media, Culture & Society, 27*(6), 903–920.

Goh, M. (2015). Malaysia's opposition band together under new Pakatan Harapan alliance. *Channel NewsAsia.* Retrieved from www.channelnewsasia.com/news/asiapacific/malaysia-s-opposition/2143004.html.

Gomez, J. (2013). Malaysia's 13th general election: Social media and its political impact. In Direk Jayanama Research Center (Ed.), *TU-ASEAN political outlook* (pp. 57–72). Bangkok, Thailand: Direk Jayanama Research Center, Thammasat University.

Government of Malaysia. (2015a). *Eleventh Malaysia plan 2016–2020: Anchoring growth on people.* Putrajaya, Malaysia: Prime Minister's Department, Malaysia. Retrieved from http://rmk11.epu.gov.my/book/eng/Elevent-Malaysia-Plan/index.html.

Government of Malaysia. (2015b). The story of 1Malaysia. Retrieved from www.1malaysia.com.my/en/the-story-of-1malaysia#.

Gramsci, A. (1995). Hegemony. In J. Rivkin & M. Ryan (Eds.), *Literary theory: An anthology* (2nd ed., p. 673). Malden, MA: Blackwell.

Habermas, J. (1991). *The structural transformation of the public sphere: An inquiry into a category of bourgeois society.* Cambridge, MA: MIT Press.

Hachten, W. A., & Scotton, J. F. (2002). *The world news prism: Global media in an era of terrorism.* Ames, IA: Blackwell.

Holtz-Bacha, C., & Kaid, L. L. (2006). Political advertising in international comparison. In C. Holtz-Bacha & L. L. Kaid (Eds.), *The Sage handbook of political advertising* (pp. 3–14). Thousand Oaks, CA: Sage.

Ingram, S. (1999, November 16). Malaysia's much-maligned media. *BBC News.* Retrieved from http://news.bbc.co.uk/2/hi/asia-pacific/522848.stm.

Kaur, S. (2013, February 10). PM: Malaysians should respect all cultures in the country. *The Star Online.* Retrieved from www.thestar.com.my/news/nation/2013/02/10/pm-malaysians-should-respect-all-cultures-in-the-country/.

Khoo, B. T. (2013). *The 13th General Election (GE13) in peninsular Malaysia: An analysis of issues, outcomes and implications.* Retrieved from Chiba, Japan: www.ide.go.jp/English/Publish/Download/Report/2013/2013_malaysia.html.

Kua, K. S. (2011). *May 13: Declassified documents on the Malaysian riots of 1969.* Petaling Jaya, Malaysia: Suaram Kommunikasi.

Lau, L. (2004, March 20). Malaysia: BN's Pak Lah ads tug at heartstrings. *The Straits Times.* Retrieved from http://web.international.ucla.edu/institute/article/9174.

Leong, P. (2014). Political communication in Malaysia. In M. M. Skoric, P. Parycek, & M. Sachs (Eds.), *Conference for E-Democracy and Open Government (CeDEM Asia 2014)* (pp. 29–42). Hong Kong, China: Donau-Universität Krems.

Lim, K. S. (1999, November 27). Call on the police to investigate the funding of the Barisan Nasional election campaign as to how it could spend RM50 million in eight days just for its "fear and scare" political advertising on radio, television and newspapers and RM500 million for the whole campaign [Web blog post]. Retrieved from www.limkitsiang.com/archive/1999/Nov99/sg2122.htm.

Lim, K. S. (2002, January 11). Rais should ask Gani to study the prosecution of RTM and Barisan Nasional for the offence of publishing "false news" for the nightly 90-second political propaganda footage camouflaged as prime-time news [Web blog post]. Retrieved from www.limkitsiang.com/archive/2002/jan02/lks1401.htm.

Lim, Y. (2013). PM: GE13 will be Malaysia's 1st "social media election." *The Star Online*. Retrieved from www.thestar.com.my/news/nation/2013/02/27/pm-ge13-will-be-malaysias-1st-social-media-election/.

Malaysian Communications and Multimedia Commission. (Q2 2013). *Communications & multimedia pocketbook of statistics*. Retrieved from Putrajaya, Malaysia: www.skmm.gov.my/skmmgovmy/media/General/pdf/SKMM_Q2_Eng.pdf.

"Malaysian leader admits ignoring Internet was a mistake." (2008, December 28). *New York Times*. Retrieved from www.nytimes.com/2008/03/25/world/asia/25iht-malay.1.11396684.html?_r=0.

McGrath, C. (2013, May 9). Barisan Nasional wins fiercely contested election. *ABC News*. Retrieved from www.abc.net.au/news/2013-04-08/an-malaysia-votes/4615310.

Mohamad, M. (1991). *Malaysia: The way forward*. Kuala Lumpur, Malaysia. Retrieved from www.epu.jpm.my/.

Mohamed, N. S. P. (2013). Championing political campaigning towards first-time voters. *Jurnal Komunikasi; Malaysian Journal of Communication, 29*(2), 79–86.

Moorman, M., & Neijens, P. (2012). Political advertising. In S. Rodgers & E. Thorson (Eds.), *Advertising theory* (pp. 297–309). New York, NY: Routledge.

Moriarty, S., Mitchell, N., & Wells, W. (2015). *Advertising & IMC: Principles and practice*. Boston, MA: Pearson.

Muhamad, R. (2015). Online opposition and elections in Malaysia. *Asian Social Science, 11*(10), 281–291.

Mustafa, A. K. (2014). Election advertising in the mainstream print media politics for sale during Malaysia's 2013 General Election. *Asia Pacific Media Educator, 24*(1), 77–94.

Netto, A. (2007, July 29). Watch out for the BN ad agencies' election media blitz [Web blog post]. Retrieved from http://anilnetto.com/malaysian-politics/malaysian-elections/a-strange-phone-call-a-prelude-to-the-elections/.

Noblit, G. W., & Hare, R. D. (1988). *Meta-ethnography: Synthesizing qualitative studies*. Newbury Park, CA: Sage.

Nor, W. A. W. M., Gapor, S. A., Bakar, M. Z. A., & Harun, Z. (2011). Patterns of Internet and traditional media use for political information and political participation in Malaysia. *International Journal of Cyber Society and Education, 4*(1), 31–38.

Ooi, K. G. (2009). *The A to Z of Malaysia*. Lanham, UK: Scarecrow Press.

Peterson, T. (1963). The social responsibility theory of the press. In F. S. Siebert, T. Peterson, & W. Schramm (Eds.), *Four theories of the press: The authoritarian, libertarian, social responsibility and Soviet communist concepts of what the press should be and do* (pp. 73–104). Urbana: University of Illinois Press.

Salman, A., Ibrahim, F., Abdullah, M.Y. H., Mustaffa, N., & Mahbob, M. H. (2011). The impact of new media on traditional mainstream mass media. *The Innovation Journal: The Public Sector, 16*(3), 1–11.

Sani, M. A. M. (2014). The social media election in Malaysia: The 13th General Election in 2013. *Kajian Malaysia, 32*(2), 123–147.

Siebert, F. S. (1963). The authoritarian theory of the press. In F. S. Siebert, T. Peterson, & W. Schramm (Eds.), *Four theories of the press: The authoritarian, libertarian, social responsibility and Soviet communist concepts of what the press should be and do* (pp. 9–38). Urbana: University of Illinois Press.

Siebert, F. S., Peterson, T., & Schramm, W. L. (1963). *Four theories of the press: The authoritarian, libertarian, social responsibility and Soviet communist concepts of what the press should be and do*. Urbana: University of Illinois Press.

Tapsell, R. (2014). Negotiating media balance in Malaysia's 2013 General Election. *Journal of Current Southeast Asian Affairs, 32*(2), 39–60.

Thill, J.V., & Bovee, C. L. (2015). *Excellence in business communication*. Boston: Pearson.

Thorson, E., & Rodgers, S. (2012). What does "Theories of Advertising" mean? In S. Rodgers & E. Thorson (Eds.), *Advertising theory* (pp. 3–17). New York, NY: Routledge.

Tsin, S. L. (2008). Report card II: Excellence, glory, distinction. *Malaysikini*. Retrieved from www.malaysiakini.com/news/78779.

Welsh, B. (2013). Malaysia's elections: A step backwards. *Journal of Democracy, 24*(4), 136–150.

Yaakop, A.Y., Padlee, S. F., Set, K., & Salleh, M. (2014). Political advertising and media: Insights from a multicultural society. *Mediterranean Journal of Social Sciences, 5*(7), 510–518.

Yong, H. H. (2004). *5 Men & ideas: Building national identity*. Subang Jaya, Malaysia: Pelanduk Publications.

15

THE LOUSY AVALANCHE

Political Advertising in Mexico

Julio Juárez-Gámiz and Marco Arellano-Toledo

Regulation Framework of Electoral Advertising in Mexico

A review of the most outstanding literature on democratic transitions experienced in Latin American countries reveals that Mexico's case is still atypical (Alcantara, 2004; Méndez, 2006; O'Donell, Schmitter, & Whitehead, 1994). A lengthy period of electoral reformism, which was controlled and permitted by the authoritarian regime itself, granted an idiosyncratic level of stability to the change process. Nevertheless, as a result the process was slow and convoluted.

The 2006 presidential election put the electoral system to the test, particularly one of its weakest aspects until that point: media access for candidates and political parties. One of the main discussions after that heated process in 2006 focused on negative advertising campaigns and spots broadcast on the electronic media, especially on television and radio.

In terms of political communication, at least six problems were identified at the time. First, the way in which candidates and parties gained access to the electronic media and used that airtime; second, the influence and immediate effect that negative spots could have on electoral preferences and on the election itself; third, the existence of a legal vacuum that did not allow parties or candidates to appeal during the electoral process if they were targeted by negative spots broadcast by their political adversaries; fourth, the participation and interference of private interests taking out spots in favor of, or against, a given party or candidate; fifth, the economic and political empowerment acquired by radio and television concession holders with the model of buying and selling airtime for campaign spots, which allowed them to set differentiated rates for advertising slots depending on the political affiliation of the network or concession holder, in addition to the massive income that they obtained from the commercial sale of that airtime throughout the electoral process (Arellano & Guerrero, 2012);[1] sixth, the potential interference of federal and local executive branches, promoting their government's image and achievements during the electoral process by means of government communication campaigns.

The close result of that election evidenced the need for the electoral system to increase the effectiveness of its regulation of access to the media during electoral periods. While the state granted political parties access to free airtime under the previous model, by means of the IFE (Federal Electoral Institute), they were also allowed to hire commercial airtime in the electronic media for their political campaigns, and the cost that this entailed accounted for most of the campaign expenditure of all parties. In that context, and based on the political plurality resulting from the 2006 election, which proved to be the most hotly contested in Mexican history, the issue of media access for political parties was addressed. There was a lot at stake, namely the model of political electoral communication that the political parties would define for themselves, by means of their legislators, in contexts of political competition.

After a period of heated debate and agreements among all of the country's political parties, the 2007–8 electoral reforms were approved (Official Gazette, 2007, p. 13-11). These reforms enshrined a new model of state-controlled political communication, which sought to address the problems detected in the 2006 electoral process (Juárez, 2009; Langston, 2009; Torres, 2011). These were the main changes and new regulations:

1. Access to state media for all political parties and candidates, overseen by the electoral authorities.
2. A ban on buying airtime for political spots on radio and television, both for political parties and candidates, and for all private individuals and companies (Esteinou, 2009; Serra, 2009).
3. Restrictions on any political advertising and promotion campaigns on electronic media by the federal government, local governments and any other public institutions throughout the electoral process. The only exceptions allowed were information campaigns by the electoral authorities, campaigns on education and health services, and essential civil protection messages in cases of emergency (García, 2009; Vargas, 2009).
4. In order to put an end to negative electoral advertising, wording was written into the Constitution to establish that the political or electoral campaigns of political parties and candidates should "abstain from any expressions denigrating institutions and political parties, or slandering individuals."[2]
5. A series of punitive measures were established, including a special sanctioning procedure designed for swift judicial action, which aimed to prevent irreparable damage in advertising campaigns among political adversaries. For example, this meant that preventive measures could be ordered to take an ad off the air, if it was considered in any way slanderous (Alanís, 2011; Olmeda & Sánchez, 2013).

This new model took away from the market the role of regulating the advertising activities of candidates and political parties, imposing a much more forceful ban on access to electoral advertising by private individuals and companies, as well as restricting government access to the media throughout electoral processes. These reforms sparked a heated debate between legislators and the owners of television networks, who protested that not only was the state banning them from selling advertising airtime to candidates and parties, but was also demanding that all television and radio concession holders broadcast 48 minutes of political electoral advertising per day, from 6 a.m. to 12 a.m. The networks claimed at the time that this glut of electoral spots would hurt their ratings and thereby harm the entire television sector.

In 2009 these new reforms faced their first electoral test. In accordance with the provisions of the reforms, the IFE had an obligation to guarantee access to millions of campaign advertising slots (the number of productions depend on the communication strategies of each political party – indeed, the less spots are produced the more repetition each spot will get) on more than 2,000 broadcasting concession holders throughout the country. To that end, the IFE created an Integral System for the Administration of State Airtime (SIATE), which was placed in charge of guaranteeing the implementation of this new electoral ad model. In addition, during several sessions of the IFE's own Radio and Television Commission, operating rules were designed to regulate the provisions established in the reforms. These rules established that the 48 mandatory minutes of airtime on all television channels and radio stations were to be divided into three time zones: from 6 a.m. to 12 p.m., from 12 p.m. to 6 p.m., and from 6 p.m. to 12 a.m.[3] Although 70% of the airtime granted to the parties would be allocated in a proportional manner to their results in the preceding elections, the remaining 30% of the airtime would be divided equally among all of the registered parties. Furthermore, the law contemplated a differentiated use of those 48 minutes at the beginning of the electoral process, the pre-campaign, and the campaign itself, granting 41 minutes to the parties (split into 30-second spots) and 7 minutes to the electoral authorities over the three months of campaigns, while the ratio would be inverted during the pre-campaign period and the beginning of the process. These 48 minutes per day, throughout an electoral process lasting 190 days (including 90 days of campaign), multiplied by more than 2,200 radio and television broadcasting concession holders, casts a result of an estimated 44 million spots broadcast throughout the country during that election (IFE, 2012).

This wealth of advertising time granted to political parties generated a far-reaching public debate on the matter. Radio and television concession holders were seen as the most affected by these new provisions, not only because they had less airtime to sell throughout the electoral process due to the obligation to broadcast 48 minutes of electoral spots, but also because they had lost the lucrative revenues that they used to obtain from selling airtime to political parties, as well as having seen their political influence on the electoral process diminished. Nevertheless, the reforms also had other critics. A number of observers like Jara (2011) argued that the new model was excessive, and that in an attempt to guarantee free access to the media for all parties, it had generated a glut of campaign spots that would saturate the television airwaves and fatigue the electorate, driving people away from the vote rather than encouraging them to get to know the proposals of candidates and political parties.

Initial Appraisal of the Television Advertising Model in Mexico

A triad formed by politics, parties and media became firmly entrenched in a young Mexican democracy. A national survey on political culture and citizen practices conducted by the Mexican government in 2012 found that 76% of the population used television as their main source of information about politics (Jara, 2011). Based on that finding, and bearing in mind that the electoral reforms affected two different sources of information, namely advertising and news, which are the two main mechanisms whereby citizens can become acquainted with the political proposals of parties and candidates, the importance of analyzing the socio-political consequences detonated by these variables in the Mexican electoral process becomes evident.

Furthermore, the implications of a political communication model such as the one implemented in Mexico place the various actors in very different perspectives. For example, from the perspective of the legislators who designed the reforms, the objective is for the state to guarantee access to the media, thereby ensuring a fair distribution of airtime, allowing a regulated use of the media, saving resources, and above all granting parties and candidates a powerful, regulated channel for their electoral disputes.

On the other hand, from the perspective of voters, they become saturated by overexposure throughout the electoral process. Mexican voters are targeted by an avalanche of campaign spots which fail to convince them to vote for a given candidate or party, nor do they offer clear, convincing information on the political offer in question, but they merely generate confusion and, in many cases, rejection (Jara & Garnica, 2013).

From the perspective of political parties and candidates, the political communication model grants them access to free airtime on radio and television. This access is managed through the electoral authority, meaning that they only need to produce content and send it on. With little effort they obtain a large reward. Nevertheless, given that all parties are entitled to an excessive amount of airtime for their spots, that arena of the electoral struggle has become devalued (Juárez & Brambila, 2013). Since there is no exclusivity in terms of airtime or prime viewing time, nor is there any chance of directing differentiated spots with specific content for specific audiences, the media arena has lost interest and is no longer as helpful to differentiate among political parties and candidates.

Finally, from the perspective of media owners who now have a constitutional obligation to incorporate 48 minutes of political advertising per day in their programming, for the entire duration of the pre-campaigns and election campaigns, this is viewed as an imposition and a punishment. In fact, political influence of Mexican broadcasters has been well documented in the past. A terrestrial television market dominated by two broadcasters (i.e., Televisa and TvAzteca) has led to a 60% concentration of the television audience nationwide. This has been used as a roadblock for non-official competitors in elections.

Following the 2007–8 reform broadcasters lost the lucrative business of selling airtime to candidates and political parties. They also lost the price-fixing power attached to their political agenda. Furthermore, the Mexican media ecosystem has been altered, there is less airtime available for advertisers to buy, yet ad breaks are longer and viewers increasingly resort to channel surfing. As an effective measure, some broadcasters agree to program the mandatory electoral adverts at exactly the same time, which in turn affects viewers who only find the same bloc of campaign spots as they switch from one channel to another.

To conclude this section, it is important to mention that the new communication model showed a significant shortcoming in its regulation of electoral advertising in the electronic media. Although the legal framework was designed in 2007–8, when Internet penetration in Mexico was still uneven, legislators failed to pay enough attention to what was already happening internationally. During the early months of the Democratic Party primaries in the US, candidate Barack Obama and his team were already embracing the multiplying power of advertising on digital platforms, seeking to connect with a new, largely younger body of voters, who no longer consumed information solely through traditional media.

In the case of Mexico, this debate was postponed and there was no clear, convincing proposal regarding the position of the Mexican state on the regulation of electoral campaigning in the digital arena. A lack of long-term political strategy and projection by legislators, added to a dearth of experience and use of new technologies at the time, made it almost impossible to define legislation on this front, which ultimately proved to be a major shortcoming in the 2012 presidential election.

Television Advertising in Campaigns: Effects of Harmful Saturation

As a result of the above, the presidential election held in 2012 can be considered the single mass communication event with the greatest reach among Mexico's citizens during the country's young democracy. Nevertheless, it was not necessarily the most highly valued among those citizens to whom it was directed, nor was it the most effective at persuading voters. The media ecosystem, especially on television and radio, was characterized by the ubiquitous presence of candidates on all channels and radio stations, at all times, repeating the same messages over and over again. At certain moments, the election campaign reached the extreme that the same ad by the same party or coalition was broadcast twice in a single bloc of commercials.

According to data in a report from Delphos 2012 (Jara & Garnica, 2013), the advertising messages presented by each of the four presidential candidates reached more than 98% of the group of the Mexican television-watching audience that was 18 or older at the time. Each of those citizens watched up to 753 campaign spots during the 2012 electoral process in Mexico. In order to place in perspective how disproportionate this figure is, consider that an effective benchmark for conventional advertising among brands paying to broadcast commercials on television is to ensure that their target audience watches an advertising message three to five times during its time on air on different channels. This number allows audience members who watched the ad to clearly remember the product or service to which they were exposed. A frequency[4] of 753, which is substantially higher than the three to five times proposed as a standard metric of media research, could be indicative of a squandered advertising effort, as well as producing the adverse effect of transforming the desired persuasion into fatigue with the brand in question.

On the 10 television channels included in the report by Delphos 2012, all of the candidates to the presidency of the Republic obtained 30-second spots. The number of spots broadcast is overwhelming. For example, thanks to the generosity of electoral reforms, the Partido Acción Nacional's (PAN) candidate Josefina Vazquez Mota broadcast a total 17,891 spots; the Partido Revolucionario Institucional's (PRI) candidate Enrique Peña Nieto[5] had broadcast 29,146 spots by the end of his campaign. Meanwhile, the Partido de la Revolución Democrática's (PRD) candidate Andres Manuel Lopez Obrador was entitled to broadcast 17,395 spots, and the New Alliance Party's candidate Gabriel Quadri de la Torre broadcast 5,845 campaign spots. If we calculate the value of frequency of exposure, 95 out of every 100 citizens watching television saw at least 65 spots for the New Alliance Party, 182 for the Progressive Movement,[6] 196 spots for the National Action Party and 316 for the Commitment for Mexico Alliance.[7]

In order to place these numbers in context and to ascertain the protective nature of the political communication model created with the 2007–8 reforms, if we compare the figures described above with the number of presidential campaign spots broadcast in the years 2000 and 2006, when political parties and candidates bought airtime on television freely in accordance with their needs and means, we find that in 2012 there were seven times more campaign spots than in the presidential election of the year 2000.[8] Nevertheless, the number of different versions of those spots produced was lower. This is significant, because it reveals that when political parties have such generous access to airtime granted by the state for advertising campaigns, they tend to reduce their content and produce a less varied yet more forceful communication strategy. Less creativity in the execution of spots but greater access to airtime to broadcast them necessarily leads to increased saturation and lower advertising diversity offered to the electorate.

In the 2012 elections, all of the political parties reached practically all of the voting-age population. Nevertheless, the number of spots broadcast exceeded by more than 3,000% the number of commercials broadcast by conventional commercials on television. If we compare the five commercial products with the greatest reach among their target of people aged 18 and older, during the same period when the presidential campaigns were held, we find that none of those five brands broadcast more than 1,000 spots, and yet they still managed to reach levels of 85% penetration and a frequency curve of 23 repetitions. This result reveals important effectiveness criteria for commercial brands as compared to political parties, given that they achieved practically the same reach among spectators with far fewer spots than those allocated to political parties (Arellano & Jara, 2013).

In both cases connection was achieved with over 80% of the target population, but commercial advertising used a much smaller rate of insertions than political advertising to achieve this goal. The key to this is media strategy, effective knowledge of the target to be achieved, and understanding of viewers' habits. Unlike the practices of traditional advertising, the electoral authority and the political parties that designed the reforms opted for saturation of communication with a strategy that sought to reach the entire population by broadcasting two to three minutes of electoral spots per hour.

Furthermore, the large number of spots to which presidential candidates were entitled in 2012 appears to have generated a certain lack of interest among their campaign teams to communicate better messages. While the 2012 electoral spots were viewed and identified extensively, they also had four times as many negative associations than spots for consumer brands, which revealed the public's rejection of political advertising as a product category. Research on the subject indicates little difference across poor reception for all political parties, suggesting that party ID was not a significant explanatory variable for this rejection (Martínez, Cárdenas, & Barrueta, 2013).

Meanwhile, in 24% of all cases the candidates' spots were followed by the phrase "I am tired of seeing it." This figure is six times higher than what we see for an average commercial advertising campaign.[9] In other indicators of approval, advertising of consumer brands usually registers a 40% enjoyment rate, while political spots barely reach 6%. In terms of relevance, spots for parties and politicians barely reached 6% support, compared with an average 32% for product spots.

Electoral Advertising's Impact on Mexican Voters

Since the arrival of the current glut of electoral spots, campaigns in Mexico have recently taken on new forms. They have transitioned from classic campaign models and have become commercial phenomena promising a product (the candidate) and services (public policies). This format necessarily entails simplification, as 30 seconds is certainly not long enough to convey a project for the country, a government plan or a political ideology.

The presidential races are the elections most affected by this situation, which calls for an analysis of the way in which candidates and campaign teams determine the path to follow to win an election, and decide how to use the media and ad campaigns to achieve their goal. Speaking of television spots broadcast by political parties in the last presidential election in Mexico is synonymous with saturation. A relentless repetition of contents may have been the campaign's greatest communication problem.

Analysis of Television Advertising in the 2012 Presidential Campaign

In order to conduct an accurate analysis of the content of advertising campaigns in the 2012 presidential election, we organized these campaigns along thematic lines. Segmenting spots in accordance with these themes will enable us to understand the efforts made by the different candidates to articulate their campaign message. In advertising terms, these thematic lines are subcampaigns highlighting different attributes and benefits of the same product, in this case the presidential candidate or their political party. These themes are a series of advertising messages that share the same idea and topic, but which refer structurally to the candidate. Campaign themes are usually devised with the intention of using them for a very specific time period, and they are often reactive to factors and tensions generated by political competition and circumstances in the electoral campaign.

All four presidential candidates segmented their campaigns into various different thematic lines. Analyzing the commercials generated by the various campaigns and broadcast on 10 television channels in Mexico City, the greatest contrast could be seen between Enrique Peña Nieto and Andres Manuel Lopez Obrador. The former presented a wide variety of thematic lines (in other words, micro advertising campaigns within his global campaign). Some of these themes were clearly planned intelligently since before the campaign began, while others were developed in response to situations that arose during the campaign. Meanwhile, candidate Lopez Obrador only broadcast spots with three different thematic lines, which reveals less interest in responding to the circumstances and developments that occurred throughout the campaign's 90-day duration. By the end of the campaign period he broadcast several spots referring to the context of the election, but that was not the norm. On the other hand, Josefina Vazquez Mota clearly developed the thematic lines of her advertising campaign in response to developments, setting aside what we assume must have been her original campaign plan. These themes focused on criticizing her adversaries, but did not include ads that would justify a vote for her. Vazquez Mota's spots focused on describing her as "different" or "the best," without offering any proposals that could justify this differentiation.

As stated above, the number of different versions of campaign spots used by each of the presidential candidates is a clear sign of their interest in conveying their messages to the electorate. In this case, the PRI candidate Enrique Peña Nieto broadcast the largest number of different versions, with 81. Josefina Vazquez Mota was in second place with 52 versions of her spots; candidate Quadri came in third place, with 21 different versions, and Andres Manuel Lopez Obrador was last with 18 versions. Based on the above, each of the candidates followed a clear media strategy. In the first case, Peña's campaign firmly intended to reach the electorate in a variety of different ways, seeking to issue a message and to reach the segments of the electorate with differentiated strategies. We see the greatest contrast with candidate Lopez Obrador, who only broadcast 18 different versions and whose media strategy was short-sighted, lacking advertising acumen.

From an advertising perspective, the candidates made decisions in accordance with the initial contexts of their own campaigns. In Peña's case, the logical course of action was to maintain the lead that all of the polls appeared to grant him before the electoral process began, so the main aim of his campaign was to avoid controversy and to keep the candidate in first place. Thus, his campaign began with a neutral tone and with visits to several states throughout the Republic, in order to convey the idea that he had broad knowledge of the country and of its different needs and requirements.

As for Lopez Obrador, his priority was to reduce the negative points that he had accumulated since he led a sit-in on Mexico's City's central Reforma Avenue, to protest at the 2006 election results. Lopez Obrador's advertising campaign began with an offer of reconciliation addressed to anyone who had been affected in 2006 by the Reforma sit-in, and he offered to bring peace and calm to Mexico, in view of the terrible wave of violence affecting the country. He later broadcast a number of spots criticizing PAN and PRI governments, while highlighting his own role as mayor of Mexico City. He sought to establish a difference between those with experience in government, such as himself, and those who lacked any such experience.

In Vazquez Mota's case, the basic goal of her advertising efforts was to shake off the shadow of a government belonging to her own party, led by then President Felipe Calderon, as well as to maintain the media momentum that she had achieved thanks to a PAN primary election victory. Nevertheless, her strategy was never successful. As the campaign progressed its collapse became increasingly evident, until she was eventually left in third place. Her advertising campaign began inauspiciously in terms of production and communication. She tried to talk about her origins and her achievements in several different public offices. When this message did not resonate or generate an improvement of her poll ratings, she resorted to negative campaigning in order to bolster her recognition and support. Nevertheless, her campaign wandered without a clear direction, first attacking Peña, later presenting some proposals, and finally attacking Lopez.

As already stated, the large number of campaign spots available to the candidates in this race allowed them to appear in the media during the early stages of the campaign without having to offer any proposals of great impact. The candidates focused on maintaining their presence while avoiding any conflicts and controversy until it was absolutely necessary, with the exception of Vazquez Mota and the PAN, which began negative campaigning in the early stages with a series of attacks, first on Peña and later on Lopez Obrador.

Finally, negative campaigning is another element to be analyzed from the 2012 electoral process. According to the Delphos 2012 report, a total number of 12,106 negative campaign spots were broadcast. During the second part of the campaign, these spots reveal the urgency of the candidates to differentiate themselves from their opponents, by highlighting the flaws of their adversaries. This is not an ideal model of political campaigning, but it is a practice that is very difficult to avoid, especially once attacks become constant and widespread, creating the need to defend each campaign from rival attacks. In this case, even candidate Peña Nieto, who had claimed at the beginning of the campaign that he would not resort to this tactic, ended up attacking Lopez Obrador through his party when the left-wing candidate came close to taking over as frontrunner in the polls.

The 2012 electoral process can be viewed from several different angles. The first fact to be acknowledged is that the campaign reinforced recognition of the candidates. Whether they were known or unknown before the campaigns, they became firmly implanted in the minds of voters at least throughout the 90 days of campaigning. On the other hand, the election campaigns gave voters useful information to define their votes. Strictly speaking, the campaign was not a determining factor to win the election. It served to reinforce a series of previously acquired notions about the candidates, whether good or bad. It helped to confirm votes that had already been largely decided.

In other words, the campaigns were designed in such a manner as to ensure that no one would win or lose too much. The advertising campaigns launched in 2012 were not forward-looking, but moved sideways. They sought to create the impression that something was happening, when the real struggle occurred elsewhere. Despite appearances to the contrary, the real battlegrounds were not in the media, but in the territorial structures of political parties, in the governor's seats controlled by each party, and in the resources that they were able to distribute to obtain votes.

Thus, if the election campaigns were tedious and uninspiring, it was largely because of a lack of conditions and incentives to take any risks. The candidates were so exposed to public scrutiny through extensive multimedia coverage that any ad straying from the script would be tantamount to political suicide.

Ultimately, all the communication and advertising deployed by parties and candidates has a specific objective: persuading those who watch and hear those spots to vote for the person or party issuing the message in question. Nevertheless, according to an analysis by Millward Brown (Martínez et al., 2013), based on its Dynamic Tracking[10] method, electoral spots in 2012 were widely seen and identified.

If we accept the principle that the most effective and persuasive advertising campaigns are those that are most enjoyed by viewers, according to the Millward Brown report mentioned above, that variable was exceedingly low in the electoral spots broadcast during the 2012 election. For example, the enjoyment ratio of commercial advertising stands at an average of 40%, whereas the political advertising broadcast in 2012 barely reached a level of 6% (Martínez et al., 2013). Thus, if one of the defining features of electoral communication in 2012 was saturation, the other was fatigue among citizens.

Approaches and Perspectives for a New Model of Political Advertising

Throughout this text it has been questioned the way in which radio and television airtime has been used as a result of the reforms. By no means does this entail that this work advocates for a return to an old model of buying and selling campaign spots in electoral processes. It is acknowledged here that there is a need for the state to administer airtime, rather than following unilateral market considerations dictated by a web of businesses and media interests.

Here are some conclusions that could be used as a starting point for a more structured discussion on re-founding Mexico's current political communication model.

First, the evidence suggests that the greater the saturation during a lengthy period of exposure, the more citizens reject campaigns. This should lead to considering the possibility of shorter campaigns with less saturation in terms of radio and television presence. We believe that in essence, the current model favoring the use of state airtime by political parties should continue. Nevertheless, it would be desirable to reduce the current 48 minutes per day granted to political parties during electoral periods to a lower number. Let us remember that the state already has access to 30 minutes per day of official airtime on all media in non-electoral periods, which may represent an optimum balance point between saturation and fair access in electoral processes.

Second, another aspect of election campaigns in Mexico worth considering is the question of whether it is advisable to maintain the current model of spots on electronic media as the core mechanism of communication between candidates and citizens. This model was developed with the adoption of standards of paid advertising on radio and television media, both in Mexico and in other countries, since the 1950s. Under that model, whoever had the most money could afford to buy more 30-second spots, just like any other brand wishing to advertise. Nevertheless, conditions of access have changed, and now a minimum amount of airtime is guaranteed in Mexico to equally broadcast the messages of all candidates. Under these circumstances, it is relevant to ask how that airtime could be used most effectively, rather than by flooding it with countless repetitions of 30-second spots. Perhaps a "hybrid" solution would be the best option, combining some short spots with lengthier blocs, in which the candidates could outline their ideas, either alone or in contrast with others. This method has been tested and used in countries such as Great Britain, Chile and Israel, and their results could be useful for understanding a possible deploy in Mexico.

Third, election campaigns around the world occur in a media environment in which political-electoral events compete on equal footing with numerous other offers of commercial and entertainment content, and there is a temptation to try to attract the attention of audiences and engage with them to shape their attitudes toward candidates, issues and political parties. Nevertheless, this represents a challenge that calls for a broad understanding of communication, which extends beyond regulatory and electoral aspects. Election campaigns and politics in general represent one element within a broader experience of media and entertainment consumption available to citizens. The Mexican media landscape is changing rapidly, with terrestrial television losing its once predominant place as the primary channel for gathering political information. From an academic perspective it is desirable to encourage political parties to go beyond the beaten track of free-to-air television.

Fourth, as mentioned, electoral reformism was responsible for a long-awaited transition to democracy in Mexico. Nevertheless, we believe that hyper-regulation has started to obstruct the strategic flow of election campaigns in terms of political advertising. Furthermore, this excessive regulation generates an impoverishment of the political development of citizens, preventing them from deciding for themselves whether or not a campaign is negative, and whether the campaign in question slanders or vilifies an adversary. Current regulations affecting this stage of political communication and others within a campaign should be subject to review (Juárez, 2014).

Fifth, one of the main shortcomings of Mexico's political advertising model is the limited or non-existence of criticism of campaigns on media news coverage. Simply stated, campaign spots do not set the agenda, nor are they able to change the course of a conversation between candidates. This work reviews some of the reasons for this: premature campaigning, a high volume of repetition, few different versions, etc. Let us add another important element, which is that under the current system campaign spots lose their original purpose of conveying the candidate's proposals to citizens, while the media narrative focuses instead on which campaigns are fined or otherwise sanctioned by the electoral authorities, in response to protests from rival camps.

This appears to be an endless loop in which the main topic becomes whether or not the electoral authorities should ban any campaign ad considered offensive by another candidate, while ignoring any content and message in the ad. This triangulation leads to a well-documented erosion of the institutions.

Sixth, in a growing digital arena, the political communication model should take advantage of this new reality and not make the same mistake of attempting to over-regulate. It is essential to learn from the regulatory model on traditional media in order not to make the same mistakes with new media. It has been observed how the positive aspects of social media (their interactive and horizontal nature) have been offset by more negative aspects (anonymity and lack of credibility).

Seventh, 90 days is too long for a presidential campaign. Media coverage of the process across a wide range of platforms increases gradually as election day approaches, and it should be considered whether shorter campaigns are a possible measure to reduce the current saturation. The times when 90 or 120 days were required in order to give candidates enough time to take their message throughout the country are long gone. Nowadays, given the possibility of accessing multi-platform content, we must ask ourselves how much such a lengthy campaign really contributes to the process, especially considering that media coverage of issues increasingly occurs in real time.

In view of all of the above, it is inevitable to ask what characteristics an effective political advertising model should have, both from a normative perspective (offering citizens information to enrich democratic deliberation) and from a strategic perspective (positioning interpretative frameworks aligned with an electoral objective). Based on our findings and previous research on this topic, we list three key elements that must be reformulated within a new political communication model.

One, reducing the number of times people are exposed to a message. Today all evidence suggests this proliferation, the origin of the lousy avalanche in this chapter's title, produces the opposite desired effect. Citizens are overwhelmed by political advertising given the *quantitative logic* behind the distribution model implemented by the state.

Two, favoring more agile programming of spots. The current model establishes a period of up to five days before an ad can be incorporated into the official grid presented by the INE to radio and television concession holders. Under current technological conditions, it is unthinkable that an ad cannot be produced and broadcast faster than that, especially considering the need to encourage dialogue among spots, in which issues can be proposed and responded to within a matter of hours. The current model generates a delay in the exchange of points of view on the television format. If spots appear on social media and news websites before they are officially broadcast, and if the response of parties or candidates only occurs five days later, the informative and persuasive relevance of those spots is greatly diminished. In other words, spots become yesterday's news, while social media and electronic media are today's debate.

Finally, maximizing platforms without sacrificing expectations. In view of the digital convergence of platforms, which is conducive to disseminating audiovisual content, one would expect an end to the current method of broadcasting these messages exclusively on radio or television. It is necessary and logical to take full advantage of these new platforms to spread the message of political parties. Nevertheless, as stated in the first point, the factor that determines the impact of a message, beyond the ease with which citizens can see it, is the value of its content in the eyes of the electorate, as well as its capacity to affect the agenda of the media.

It is clear that political advertising is here to stay. The suggestions seek to align a key element in modern-day campaigning with an increasingly fragmented audience. This work underlines the amount of time parties already have to air their messages precisely because according to the Mexican law this time is a public good. Nevertheless, adjusting the amount and scheduling of televised political advertising will be meaningless if political parties are not willing to engage the public in their communication strategies. A commitment from all Mexican political parties is required in order to transform the current model into a more engaging one.

Notes

1 The total investment in campaign spots during the 2006 election has been estimated at 2.24 billion pesos (based on gross rates published by the media).
2 Article 41 of the Political Constitution of the United Mexican States valid on May 7, 2008. Official Gazette 07-05-2008.
3 Agreement of the General Council of the Federal Electoral Institute, reforming the Regulations on Electoral Access to Radio and Television, published in the Official Gazette on 30-06-2011.
4 Audience variable indicating the number of advertising impacts to which a television viewer was exposed during an advertising campaign. This number designates the number of spots viewed out of the total advertising campaign.
5 By the time the election concluded, this candidate won a majority with 38.21% of the votes cast.
6 This coalition included all of the political parties in Mexico identified ideologically with the left wing, namely the PRD, the Partido del Trabajo and the Convergence Party.
7 Political coalition formed by the Institutional Revolutionary Party (PRI) and the Mexican Green Ecologist Party (PVEM).
8 Source: Delphos 2012 study, the base of comparison are 10 open television channels: five national channels (2, 5, 7, 9 and 13) and five more that are broadcast in the metropolitan district of Mexico City (4, 11, 22, 28 and 40).
9 This regulation refers to the historic average developed by Millward Brown over several years of evaluating the effectiveness of advertising among the Mexican consumer population.
10 This study was conducted among a sample of people above the age of 18 with regular access to the Internet. "the interviews were conducted daily … throughout a 10 month period, from the beginning of the electoral process until shortly after the vote." In other words, this is a non-representative sample of the entire universe of voters, which is nonetheless representative of those with Internet access. The findings of this report are well worth reading.

References

Alanís, M. C. (2011). Retos en la distribución de competencias respecto de las infracciones a los Artículos 41 y 134 constitucionales. *Revista Justicia Electoral*, 1(7), 15–40.

Alcántara, M. (2004). Partidos políticos en América Latina: Precisiones conceptuales, estado actual y retos futuros. *Estudios Políticos*, 124, 55–94.

Arellano, M., & Guerrero, M. (2012). *Campañas negativas en 2006 ¿Cómo afectaron el voto?* Mexico: Universidad Iberoamericana.

Arellano, M. & Jara, J. R. (2013). Estrategias de spoteo en el contexto de una nueva reforma. In J. R. Jara & A. Garnica (Eds.), *Audiencias saturadas comunicación fallida. El impacto de los spots y las noticias en la campaña presidencial 2012* (pp. 21–140). Mexico: Grupo Delphi.

Esteinou, J. (2009). El boicot a la Reforma Electoral y la crisis de gobernabilidad nacional. *El Cotidiano*, 155, 19–29.

García, C. (2009). Reforma electoral y televisión. Los formatos de los mensajes políticos despues de la reforma electoral. *El Cotidiano*, 155, 5–11.

IFE. (2012). Informe general sobre la administración de los tiempos del Estado en radio y televisión en materia electoral durante el Proceso Electoral Federal 2011–2012. Consulted on March 3, 2015. Retrieved from www.ine.mx/documentos/proceso_2011-2012/documentos/Actividad_093.pdf.

Jara, J. R. (2011). Spotización electoral: Las cifras del 2009. *Este Pais*, 243, 20–24.

Jara, J. R. & Garnica, A. (Eds.). (2013). *Audiencias saturadas, comunicación fallida. El impacto de los spots y las noticias en la campaña presidencial 2012*. Mexico: Delphi.

Juárez, J. (2009). *La televisión encantada. Publicidad política en México*. Mexico: CEIICH-UNAM.

Juárez, J. (2014). Medios, equidad y libertad de expresión en la justicia electoral mexicana. In C. Báez & L. Ríos (Eds.), *Los derechos políticos en el siglo XXI, un debate judicial* (pp. 176–194). Mexico: Tirant lo Blanch.

Juárez, J., & Brambila, J. A. (2013). La publicidad política televisiva en el proceso electoral federal 2012 en México. *Revista Mexicana de Derecho Electoral, Especial sobre Observación Electoral 2012*, 4, 303–319.

Langston, J. (2009). Las reformas al Cofipe, 2007. *Política y gobierno*, 16(2), 245–272.

Martínez, M., Cárdenas, I., & Barrueta, R. (2013). Recepción e impacto de los spots y la mercadotecnia electoral en los votantes. In J. R. Jara & A. Garnica (Eds.), *Audiencias saturadas comunicación fallida. El impacto de los spots y las noticias en la campaña presidencial 2012* (pp. 193–247). Mexico: Grupo Delphi.

Méndez, I. (2006). *Transición a la democracia en México. Competencia partidista y reformas electorales. 1977–2003*. Mexico: FLACSO-Fontamara.

O'Donnell, G., Schmitter, P., & Whitehead, L. (Eds.). (1994). *Transiciones desde un gobierno autoritario*. Barcelona: Paidós.

Official Gazette. (2007). Consulted on April 20, 2015. Retrieved from www.dof.gob.mx/nota_detalle.php?codigo=5005999&fecha=13/11/2007.

Olmeda, M. P., & Sánchez, A. (2013). El procedimiento especial sancionador en el sistema electoral mexicano. *Revista de Ciencias Jurídicas*, 130, 43–74.

Serra, G. (2009). Una lectura critica de la reforma electoral en México a raiz de la elección de 2006. *Política y gobierno*, 16(2), 411–427.

Torres, E. (2011). Una nueva legislación para la democracia mexicana: La reforma electoral 2007–2008 y los medios de comunicación. *Estudios políticos*, 24, 107–129.

Vargas, P. (2009). México: Reforma electoral de 2007 y su impacto en las elecciones locales. *Revista Justicia Electoral*, 7, 117–149.

16

POLITICAL ADVERTISING IN TURKEY

Baki Can

Turkish people have been familiar with elections and voting throughout their history. Turks have been familiar with elections and voting both during the period they lived in their own homeland, Central Asia, and during the time they have lived in Land of Anatolia, where they intermingled with the natives about 1,000 years ago. Elections, impressing voters and voting were significant in Turkish political life. Especially after they adopted Islam, Turks promoted voting and elections. After the death of the prophet Muhammed, the process of electing the four great caliphs was held up as an example of the peaceful passing power. Although from time to time Turks abandoned that process, the principle of elections and voting were maintained and highly valued in Turkish attitudes and ideals.

Political and Electoral System

Turkey transitioned to a multi-party system beginning with the 1946 elections. Having survived sporadic periods of military and antidemocratic intervention, the system has been in effect to date, and the historical trajectory of the system is often considered to be that of an overall progress (Tuncer, 2002).

Currently, three kinds of election co-exist in Turkey; parliamentary, presidential and local elections. Beginning with the advent of the multi-party system, parliamentary elections have been considered to be the most fundamental and significant among those, since legislation takes place principally in the parliament. The president and the ministers chosen from members of the parliament govern the country (Kalender, 2014). Since local elections determine the local governors responsible for providing local, mostly municipal services, they are considered secondary in importance as far as the long-term political administration and political orientation of the country is concerned. A presidential election has only been held once to date, in August 2015, and is likely to rise in importance if the efforts to extend the authority of the president (currently led by the ruling party) come to realization.

During parliamentary elections, a total of 550 members of parliament are elected on a city basis, with the number of members of parliament from each city determined by the proportion of its population to that of the entire country. Additionally, a city is divided into two electoral districts if the quota of members of parliament for the city ranks between 19 and 35, and into three if it ranks equal to, or above, 36. Accordingly, Ankara and Izmir are split into two electoral districts, and Istanbul into three. This leaves Turkey, spanning 81 cities, with an electoral district count of 85.

Turkey utilizes proportional representation, with the addition of an election threshold per party. Apart from this countrywide 10% vote rate threshold on a party basis, there are no additional thresholds on the city or election-district level. The countrywide threshold has been in effect since the legislation was passed in 1983. Following the general elections, the president of the Republic tasks the leader of the party with the greatest number of members of parliament with forming a government. The party leader, in turn, needs to secure the support of at least 276 members of parliament – the majority number necessary to win the parliament's vote of confidence – to form the government. If the total number of members of parliament from the largest party is less than that, the party leader seeks the support of additional parties, by either pursuing a coalition government with those parties or asking for their external, provisional support.

The Historical Background and the Precedents of the Election

The election in November 2002, and the four general elections preceding it, were snap elections, as were most of the yet earlier ones. In contrast, elections after 2002 – June 2015 included – have been held according to schedule. Three main reasons behind the prevalence of snap elections in Turkey appear to be conflicts within the coalition government, opposition parties' discontent and disinclination to wait until the scheduled election time, and the ruling party's fear of losing majority support. The reasons for the snap election of 2015 present an exception to this generalization, for the Justice and Development Party (the AK Party), which had been the ruling party throughout the period between the 2002 and November 2015, was in favor of elections being held as scheduled for 2015. However, following the election in June 2015, no party turned out to be able to attain the support of the majority in the parliament in the allotted time (45 days), and the efforts to form coalitions failed. Thus, the president of the Republic, utilizing his constitutional rights, asked for a new election to be held, and which was subsequently scheduled for November 2015. After the expiration of the 45-day period following the June 2015 election, an electoral government, in the form of a temporary cabinet of ministers, was established that was exempt from the requirement of attaining the parliament's vote of confidence, for the first time in the history of the country. The temporary government stayed in power until the AK Party, attaining the requisite number of members of parliament in the November 2015 election, formed a one-party government in November 2015.

The election of June 2015 transformed into a bipolar political clash, with the AK Party aiming to extend its one-party government for another four years, and opposition parties hoping to prevent the AK Party from getting enough votes to form a one-party government, thus effectively forcing the party to seek coalition governments. The AK Party had been in power since 2002, steadily increasing its votes with every election.

To better understand the dynamics of the June 2015 and November 2015 elections, and the atmosphere of electoral advertising they exhibited, it is necessary to briefly revisit the election of December 1995. For, as we will argue, the results of the December 1995 election, and the process begun by the military intervention in February 1997, despite its gradually declining effect on collective voting behavior, had an impact on the November 2015 election campaign, the content of the advertisements for the campaign, and consequentially the result of the election.

Following the election on December 1995, the parties ranking second and third formed a coalition, since a single-party government did not turn out to be possible. The resulting coalition proved unstable and dissipated short of four months, giving way to a new coalition among the Welfare Party (Refah Partisi, RP), ranked first, and the True Path Party (Doğru Yol Partisi, DYP) in June 1996. The RP and coalition leader, and ministers from RP, were all decidedly and conspicuously pious, and the effects of their beliefs was observable in their political actions. Faced with the prospect of an unusually religious government, parties outside the coalition, the president of the Republic, generals, media corporations and various NGOs joined forces in an effort to oppose the government. The National Security Council (Milli Güvenlik Kurulu, MGK) held a meeting led by the president of the Republic, as per the constitution, and forced the government to resign. Subsequent governments chose to avoid conflicts with the MGK. One of the Welfare Party-based, prominent political actors in the process was Recep Tayyip Erdoğan, then the mayor of Istanbul, who was soon to be the leader of the emerging AK Party, and subsequently the prime minister, and finally the president. None of the parties forming the coalition subsequent to the February 1997 intervention ended up getting enough votes in the November 2002 election to pass the threshold for senate-presence. Most notably, the Democratic Left Party (Demokratik Sol Parti, DSP), the party of the incumbent president Bülent Ecevit, despite having the biggest presence in the senate prior to the 2002 election, ended up winning only 1.22% of the votes in the 2002 election.

The AK Party and the CHP were the only parties to pass the threshold of having members of parliament in parliament following the November 2002 elections. The AK Party, which was founded merely 14.5 months prior to the 2002 elections, formed the government exclusively after the 2002 election, and after the two subsequent elections in 2007 and 2011. In the June 2015 election, despite ranking first in vote rate for the fourth time in a row, it failed to get enough votes to form another government exclusively, and in the absence of a viable coalition, a new election was scheduled for November 2015.

The elections of 2015 provided opposition parties with opportunities to re-establish themselves in the senate, with the founding leader now serving as the president of the Republic, and being replaced by the inexperienced Ahmet Davutoğlu (previously the Minister of Foreign Affairs, following years as an academician). Having been elected as the leader of the AK Party merely nine months before, his political rhetoric throughout the June 2015 campaign was that of an academician or diplomat. Despite having a reputable academic background and intellectual approach, his powers of political persuasion were limited. His political rhetoric during the November 2015 election campaign was better geared toward the audience, the Turkish voters liable to support him in the approaching election. Despite all efforts, the opposition parties failed to turn the June 7 elections into an opportunity.

Turkey witnessed a total of four elections between March 2014 and November 2015. The first one was the local authority general elections held in March 2014, the second one was the election of the president of the Republic (held for the first time) in August 2014, the third was a general election in June 2015, and the fourth, in November 2015, was another general election intended to replace the June election, and transcend the political cul-de-sac following fruitless coalition-building efforts. The rapidity of elections can be regarded as auspicious for a country that has been subjected to many antidemocratic interventions – military and otherwise – in its short history, considering the centrality of elections to a culture of democracy and democratic political institutions.

Prior to the June elections, political parties other than the AK Party coincided on a common strategy, that of weakening the AK Party. The latter, having risen to power shortly after its inception, and steadily increasing its vote rate with each election, had stood a good chance of forming yet another one-party government; and all the opposition parties, a considerable portion of mass media outlets, television channels – especially those with headquarters abroad – and certain NGOs gave spirited support to this strategy.

The campaigns prior to the November 2015 general election were relatively subdued, with meetings, political discussions on television and party ads being kept to a minimum, since the messages intended for the voters had been conveyed four months and three weeks earlier before the preceding June election. Nevertheless, television and electronic media ads and social media messages were utilized by parties to influence the public to vote in their favor.

Information Technology

The use of information technology has been gaining momentum in Turkey, paralleling the global trends, as the data gathered by the Turkish Statistical Institute (Türkiye İstatistik Kurumu, TÜİK) reveals. This data approximates the percentage of domestic households with access to the Internet at 69.5% by April 2015. The same data indicates that the percentage of domestic households with at least one cell phone or smartphone is 96.8% (TÜİK, 2015).

A report from TNS market research company rates the use of smartphones in Turkey at 13% in 2012, 34% in 2013, and up to 55.5% in 2015. The corresponding data from the the the Turkish Statistical Institute closely approximates this at a smartphone usage rate of 53.8%, with a 63% male and 37% female distribution (www.cepfix.com, 2015).

Among the smartphone users, 31% are between the ages of 18 and 25, 38% between 26 and 30, and only 10% are below 18. Since only the last group among these is not eligible to vote, we can observe that the percentage of Turkish smartphone users who are not allowed to vote is only 10%. Furthermore, the ages of 18 to 25 are when a person's political inclinations and voting behavior become recognizable for the first time, only to stabilize and become more predictable in the subsequent period (26 to 30).

The Turkish public has of late been following advances in information technology ardently, especially in the realm of electronic media. This could be observed in the political campaigns preceding the November election. As Table 16.1 reveals, electronic media was employed extensively by the parties for this process.

The political parties seem to have preferred electronic media over alternatives at this juncture owing to the speed and ease of reaching out to the younger population, getting immediate feedback, and revising their messages on the go in light of received feedback. The most heavily used websites were Facebook and Twitter.

Campaign ads for the November election were viewed by a total of 6,345,000 people, which amounts to 13.45% of the votes cast subsequently. The ad most clicked on among them was by the CHP, promising the rescission of credit card debts. The most clicked ad for the AKP was the ad concerning the minimum wage, which received 672,605 total clicks. Overall, the AK Party received 3,799,035 ad clicks, CHP 2,556,661, MHP 56,844 and HDP 21,483.

The Legal Regulation of Political Ads

Four distinct sets of laws regulate the broadcast of campaign advertising in Turkey: the parliamentary election law (Milletvekili Seçimi Kanunu), the law on basic principles and ledgers (Seçimlerin Temel Hükümleri ve Seçmen Kütükleri Hakkında Kanun, part of the Political Parties Act), the law on the establishment and broadcasting of radio and television corporations (Seçmen Kütükleri Hakkında Kanun, Radyo, Televizyon Kuruluş ve Yayın Hizmetleri Hakkında Kanun) and the law on the regulation of electronic commerce (Elektronik Ticaret Kanunu). These laws set limits on both the formal properties and the broadcast schedule. As a judicial institution, the Supreme Electoral Council of Turkey (Yüksek Seçim Kurulu or YSK) regulates the broadcast of electoral ads on television and electronic media, in addition to other activities related to the election process (Yüksek Seçim Kurulu, 2015). Under the regulation of these laws and statutes, any party and candidate is allowed political ads through the electioneering period. To ensure the election's compliance with democratic ideals, media channels are expected to practice objectivity, integrity and reliability in the allocation of screen time to the parties and the candidates, as enforced by the Supreme Electoral Council. The parties are free to work with media outlets of their choosing, and either the party or the ad agency it works with is allowed to be in charge of the allocation of ads to preferred media outlets.

Before the emergence of private radio and television channels in Turkey in the early 1990s, broadcast of campaign speeches was limited to slots on the radio and television branches of the state-owned Turkish Radio and Television Corporation (TRT). As the service was provided to eligible candidates free of charge, these efforts cannot be subsumed under advertising. Once the private radio and television channels emerged, however, ads on the radio and television quickly became routine and a prominent part of campaigning. In subsequent years, the global adoption of the Internet and smartphones in electioneering transformed the Turkish campaign scene. The use of electronic media, computers and smartphones, in particular, was particularly prevalent during the March 2014 local elections, August 2014 presidential election, and the June and November 2015 general elections.

Campaign ads are regulated by the aforementioned four statutes. As can be discerned by their respective names, each statute pertains to another aspect of campaign advertising. In addition, the Regulation of Electronic Commerce Law (No. 6563) evaluates and regulates campaign advertising as it pertains to commercial communications (Resmi Gazete, 2014).

As expected, campaign ads are all paid. Nearly all campaign ads in Turkey are commissioned by the party headquarters to a varying group of agencies. Accordingly, the production and broadcast costs of ads are paid by the parties. The money the parties spend on campaigns is provided by four sources of income: membership fees, donations, fees paid to apply for parliamentary candidacy, and financial support from the treasury, proportional to the number of members of parliament a party has in the senate.

Scope

This study focuses on the campaign ads broadcast on television and electronic media ahead of the November 2015 general elections. Since the November elections took place under particular, unprecedented conditions, a summary of the conditions and the political atmosphere surrounding the elections follows.

A total of 16 parties took part in the November elections. Since the majority of these parties had no hopes of an election victory, they did without paid campaign ads and other electioneering activities, settling for the limited screen time allotted gratis to every party for pre-election speeches on the state-owned Turkish Radio and Television Corporation (Türkiye Radyo Televizyon Kurumu – TRT, 2007).

While a few parties which ended up failing to get members of parliament in the parliament took part in electioneering, this study focuses only on the parties which eventually achieved seats in the parliament, and of those, only on the television and electronic media ads. Subsequently, 10 ads (financed by a variety of parties) considered by the author and the coders to be lacking in quality and craftsmanship were kept out of consideration. Of the remaining 100 ads that made it into this evaluation, 69 were for the AK Party, 14 for the CHP, 13 for the MHP and 4 were for the HDP.

The Content of Ads

What follows is a breakdown of the content of television and electronic media ads through the November campaign, with a bird's-eye view of recurring themes, without concentrating on the details. For this purpose, it was necessary to classify the content. Accordingly, two coders were employed, one a master's student and one a Ph.D. candidate, both in the public relations department. The two coded independently, and their results converged by 91% subsequently. The distribution of ads based on the party, length and the medium is presented in Table 16.1.

Three patterns are readily observable in the table: first, more than two-thirds of the ads are commissioned by the AK Party. Second, most ads were broadcast simultaneously on television and electronic media. Third, the majority of ads are short, with 76% below 30 seconds, two ads between two and three minutes, and two ads above three minutes.

Overall, only seven ads are in black-and-white, and six are partly in color and partly in black-and-white. Color is effective for persuasive messages (Parsa & Parsa, 2014). All of these 13 ads were commissioned by the opposition parties. The sequences in black-and-white were used to criticize the AK Party government.

Of all the AK Party ads, 35 are composed solely of on-screen text read by a voice-over. Eleven feature moving images with sound. Ads featuring people usually have crowds representing the populace, as observed in 25 ads by the AK Party, seven by the CHP, three by the MHP and two by the HDP. These ads were interpreted by the coders as an attempt to underline the voters' support of the party in question.

Table 16.1 Ad distribution by party, length and the medium throughout the November 2015 campaign

		0–30 sec.	30 sec.–1 min.	1–2 min.	2–3 min.	3> min.	Total
AK Party	TV + Int	41	4	1	1	–	47
	Internet	20	1	–	–	1	22
	Total	61	5	1	1	1	69
CHP	TV + Int	5	5	–	–	–	10
	Int	3	1	–	–	–	4
	Total	8	6	–	–	–	14
MHP	TV + Int	6	5	–	–	–	11
	Internet	–	–	1	–	1	2
	Total	6	5	1	–	1	13
HDP	TV + Int	–	1	–	–	–	1
	Internet	1	–	1	1	–	3
	Total	1	1	1	1	–	4
Total		76	17	3	2	2	100

Sixty-three out of 69 ads by the AK Party refer to future projects; nine out of the CHP's 14 refer to both the past and the future, and two exclusively to future projects; whereas six out of the 13 MHP ads refer to both the future and the past, and two exclusively to the past; and two out of four ads by the HDP refer to both the past and the future.

All ads by the AK Party focus on the party itself, concentrating more on future plans than past achievements. Since the opposition is never referred to in the AK Party ads, there is no criticism of other parties. Ads by the remaining three parties focus both on the party in question, and a rival party, which is in all instances the AK Party. Eight of these ads belong to the CHP, nine to the MHP, and one to the HDP.

None of the ads by these four parties feature any tables, graphs or animation. Images within the ads most commonly depict the adoration the parties' supporters feel for the corresponding party president, and the sense of belonging they feel toward the party itself, with the very occasional shot of enthusiastic crowds during grand party meetings. Two ads each by the AK Party, the CHP and the MHP and one by the HDP feature footage from past party meetings.

The vast majority of ads are devoid of music, as observed in 65 out of the 69 AK Party ads. The presence of music on the soundtracks for the CHP ads is hard to characterize, as the background noise falls somewhere in between music and an indiscernible background hum. Three of the MHP ads, and all of the HDP's, feature music. Considering the centrality of music in the transmission of political messages in Turkish history (Can, 2015), it is surprising to note the limited utilization of music throughout the November campaign.

Lastly, our coders were asked to rate how consistent and how convincing the ads were for each of the parties, and their 95% correspondence rate fell below 87%. Accordingly, the answers are presented in broad strokes: most of the AK Party ads were considered average, except a few that were deemed outstanding, those of the CHP were often found outstanding with a few average efforts, and for both the MHP and the HDP ads, roughly half of the efforts were considered to be average, and the other half dissatisfactory.

Conclusion and Evaluation

STAR 1, the first ever private television channel in Turkey, and founded extralegally, began the process of campaign ad transmission on television with the – extralegal – broadcast of the ANAP's ads during campaigns for the 1991 elections (Can, 1999). As the 1990s progressed, campaign ads saw an increase in popularity, paralleling legislative regulations to create the grounds for lawful campaign broadcasting. As the number of channels, including national, regional and international ones, increased, and they gained access to close to 100% of the households, the value of campaign ads on television boomed in response (Can, 2006).

In the 2000s, paralleling the popularization of (greatly advanced) electronic-media devices, political ads permeated electronic media. A perfect substitute for earlier mass media outlets, electronic media increased the value of political advertising once again, in the wake of the earlier impact of television. This increase in value can be observed in the availability of devices, the accessibility of electronic media ads, and predictions about the number of views per ad. The total view count of 6,435,000 is notable, considering the total number of Turkish voters at 56,965,100.

In the determination of individuals' political stance and voting behavior in Turkey, the interaction with the immediate family, relatives and one's social sphere is more decisive than individual decision-making. Considering this, it is safe to assume that the aforementioned ads influenced a wider range of the population than the total number of clicks would indicate. The prevalence of political content shared on Facebook and WhatsApp these days is a case in point.

So far, we have gauged the influence of campaign ads on the results of the election based on the availability and accessibility of ads for the voters, and the number of clicks the ads attracted. However, the situation of the country prior to the election, and the relevance of the parties' political messages to the situation also figure in the results of the election. Two aspects of the pre-election political atmosphere of Turkey at the time are relevant and worth mentioning. First, the ongoing situation of political uncertainty was a cause of anxiety for every member of the society excepting civil servants, and this uncertainty benefited the AK Party, by far the likeliest candidate for a one-party government. Second, the 2015 interim election government, founded by the AK Party president and composed for the most part of the AK Party members, steadfastly responded to the escalating terror attacks, signaling that another one-party government by the AK Party would be capable of responding to the terror-related problems efficiently.

Another process that may have influenced the results of the election concerns the Gülen movement. Members of the movement, some of whom were prosecuted with charges ranging from murder to corruption and espionage, responded by utilizing the channels of mass communication they own to propagate negative messages concerning the AK Party at the time. These attempts by the media outlets associated with the Gülen movement are believed to have contributed to the consequent AK Party victory, instantiating the positive overall impact of a negative message propagated by a source with a negative public image.

This study focused on the Turkish electoral system, campaign ads, and the television and electronic media ads commissioned by the parties that subsequently achieved seats in the parliament. All of the ads were broadcast on both national and regional television channels. Sixty-six of them were broadcast on television and the Internet simultaneously, and 24 exclusively on the Internet. Seventy-six of the ads are shorter than 30 seconds, and 17 are between 30 seconds and a minute. Sixty-nine out of 100 ads were commissioned by the AK Party.

We see a convergence of themes in the ads of all parties except for the HDP. While the AK Party, the CHP and the MHP underlined the sanctity of the unity and the indivisibility of the country, and the promise of a peaceful Turkey untethered by violent civil conflict, the HDP notably decided on the "inadına HDP" slogan, which translates approximately as "the HDP, in spite of it all." Another message by the HDP, "We are going to lift the embargo against Armenia," was not well-received by the public. Identity politics underline ethnic difference at the expense of unitary tendencies. Paralleling analogous instances in the political history of Bulgaria and Kyrgyzstan (Can, 2014), the practice of anti-unitary identity politics, based on foregrounding ethnic difference, proved unfruitful for the proponents, in this case causing the vote rates of Turkish parties in question to decline and get further away from the 10% threshold.

All but 13 of the ads are in color. The remaining 13, utilizing black-and-white, belong without exception to the parties other than the AK Party. These ads all have the inclusion of a negative message in common, with the criticism being directed toward the AK Party in all cases. Most of the ads appeal to rational, logical thinking, with the AK Party ads making up the majority of the category. Notably, none of the ads employed any tables, graphs or animations. The relative scarcity of the use of music can also be observed in the ads of all the parties.

While few of the ads prepared for the November 2015 election qualify as outstandingly well made in terms of technique and content, they still proved effective in propagating the parties' political messages to the population, especially to the relatively apolitical younger generation avidly using electronic means of communication.

References

Can, B. (1999). Television and electoral success in Turkey. In L. L. Kaid (Ed.), *Television and politics in evolving European democracies* (pp. 171–185). New York: Nova.

Can, B. (2006). *Persuading voters and political advertising in Turkey.* In L. L. Kaid and C. Holtz-Bacha (Eds.), *The Sage handbook of political advertising* (pp. 387–397). Thousand Oaks, CA: Sage Publications.

Can, B. (2014). Türk gazetelerinde 2011 Kırgızistan cumhurbaşkanlığı seçimleri [The coverage of 2011 Kyrgyzstan presidential elections in Turkish newspapers]. In M. Bulut (Ed.), *Medeniyetler güzergahı ipek yolu* (pp. 333–242). Istanbul: Sabahattin Zaim Universitesi Yayınevi.

Can, B. (2015). Political advertising and its music on television and electronic media in Turkey. *ADAM Academy Journal of Social Sciences*, 5, 71–88.

Kalender, A. (2014). *Siyasal iletişim seçmenler ve ikna stratejileri [Political communication: Voters and persuasion strategies].* Konya: Tablet Kitabevi Yayınları.

Parsa, S. V., & Parsa A. T. (2014). *Göstergebilim çözümlemeleri [Semiological analysis].* İzmir: Ege Üniversitesi Basımevi.

Resmi Gazete. (2014). Elektronik Ticaretin Düzenlenmesi Hakkında Kanun. Retrieved from http://www.resmigazete.gov.tr/eskiler/2014/1120141105-1htm.

Tuncer, E. (2002*). Osmanlı'dan günümüze seçimler [The evolution of elections, Ottoman State to contemporary Turkey].* Ankara: Tesav Yayınları.

Türkiye İstatistik Kurumu (TÜİK). (2015). Hanehalkı Bilişim Teknolojileri Kullanım Araştırması, 201. Retrieved from http://www.tuik.gov.tr/PreHaberBultenleri.do?id=18660.

Türkiye Radyo televizyon üst kurulu. (2007). *Kadınların televizyon izleme eğilimleri [The disposition of female spectators].* Retrieved from www.rtuk.org.tr/Icerik/DownloadReport/13.

Türkiye'de rakamlarla akıllı telefon kullanımı [Smartphone usage numbers in Turkey]. (2015). *Cepfix Blog.* Retrieved from www.cepfix.com/blog/turkiyede-rakamlarla-akilli-telefon-kullanimi.

Yüksek seçim kurulu [The supreme electoral council of Turkey], sect. 1571. (2015). Retrieved from www.ysk.gov.tr/cs/groups/public/documents/document/ndq0/mde0/~edisp/yskpwcn1_4444014600.pdf.

17

POLITICAL ADVERTISING IN SPAIN (1977–2015)

From Education to Indirect Effects

Teresa Sádaba and Matias Jove

The role of advertising in electoral campaigns in Spain has evolved a great deal since the advent of democracy in the country. The progressive Americanization of European political communication and the emergence of the Internet as a basic communication channel have shaped a very different political scene to the one that existed during the first elections in the 1970s.

In spite of these developments in electoral campaigning, both the Spanish political system and electoral legislation continue to determine political communication to a large extent during election periods. The multi-party system, parliamentary government, the proportional representation electoral system, shorter campaign periods and the existence of public media are just some of the conditioning factors that restrict the so-called Americanization of campaigns (Dader, 1999), although, as Swanson and Mancini have pointed out: "Even prohibitions of political advertising on television and limits on campaign expenditure have not been sufficient to forestall the modernization of political communication" (Swanson & Mancini, 1996, p. 274).

In addition to all of this, we must also take into account certain changes that have been made to the very foundations of the political system over the last decade that could alter the status quo of political campaigning as we have known it up until now.

On the one hand, the political arena has changed substantially due to the emergence of new political forces, parties that have arisen from public discontent. In this respect, the national elections of 2015 promise a very different picture in terms of parliamentary representation. On the other hand, recent changes in party financing and in the financing of public television have changed the roles of the players that form part of the electoral process.

For all these reasons, in order to understand the role of televised electoral advertising in Spanish political campaigns, it is essential to carry out an analysis that takes these developments into account, whilst also encompassing legal, historical and communicational factors (including the emergence of the Internet).

Due to space limitations, we shall focus specifically on state or national elections, with some occasional comments regarding European, regional or local elections. It is important to bear in mind that, since the end of the Franco regime and the advent of democracy in 1977, elections have been held in Spain at different levels:[1] state (12 general elections), regional (33 elections), local (10 elections) and European (7 elections) (see Table 17.1).

Furthermore, due to the fragmentation of political representation in Spanish parliamentary life, our analysis shall focus largely on the main political parties, although reference shall be made to other smaller parties at certain times.

Table 17.1 General, regional, local and European elections held in Spain since 1977

	General	Regional	Local	European
1977	Adolfo Suárez (UCD) 166 (34.44%)			
1978				
1979	Adolfo Suárez (UCD) 168 (34.84%)		★	
1980		★ (Catalonia and Basque Country)		
1981		★ (Galicia)		
1982	Felipe González (PSOE) 202 (48.11%)	★ (Andalusia)		
1983		★ (13)[a]	★	
1984		★ (Basque Country)		
1985		★ (Galicia)		
1986	Felipe González (PSOE) 184 (44.06%)	★ (Andalusia and Basque Country)		
1987		★ (13)	★	★
1988		★ (Catalonia)		
1989	Felipe González (PSOE) 175 (39.6%)	★ (Galicia)		★
1990		★ (Andalusia and Basque Country)		
1991		★ (13)	★	
1992		★ (Catalonia)		
1993	Felipe González (PSOE) 159 (38.78%)	★ (Galicia)		
1994		★ (Andalusia and Basque Country)		★
1995		★ (13 + Catalonia)	★	
1996	José M. Aznar (PP) 156 (38.79%)	★ (Andalusia)		
1997		★ (Galicia)		
1998		★ (Basque Country)		
1999		★ (13 + Catalonia)	★	★
2000	José M. Aznar (PP) 183 (44.52%)	★ (Andalusia)		
2001		★ (Galicia and Basque Country)		
2002				
2003		★ (13 + Catalonia)	★	
2004	J.L. Rodríguez Zapatero (PSOE) 164 (42.59%)	★ (Andalusia)		★
2005		★ (Basque Country and Galicia)		Referendum CT
2006		★ (Catalonia)		
2007		★ (13)	★	
2008	J.L. Rodríguez Zapatero (PSOE) 169 (43.87%)	★ (Andalusia)		
2009		★ (Basque Country and Galicia)		★
2010		★ (Catalonia)		
2011	Mariano Rajoy (PP) 186 (44.6%)	★ (13)	★	
2012		★ (Basque Country, Galicia, Andalusia, Asturias and Catalonia)		
2013				
2014				★
2015	Mariano Rajoy (PP) 123 (28.07%)	★ (Andalusia and Catalonia)	★	
2016	Mariano Rajoy (PP) 137 (33%)			

Note:

a Meaning the 13 regional governments whose elections take place at the same time as local elections.

Source: By the authors. Based on Spanish Home Office data.

The Spanish Political and Electoral System

According to the Constitution, members of the State Parliament are elected every four years following the D'Hondt system and they possess the power to elect the prime minister of Spain (Aja, 1999). Due to this system, fragmentation is one of the main characteristics of the Spanish political arena. This is because the electoral system promotes two main national political parties (currently the Popular Party, PP, and the Socialist Party, PSOE), but also a number of other smaller political parties (including the regional or nationalist parties). However, these small parties have historically played an important role in the country's political history, because at certain times they have been key to achieving an absolute majority. Since the European elections of 2014, as well as the local and Catalan elections of 2015, two alternative political parties have emerged quite strongly due to the current climate of discontent and the economic and political crisis of recent years: Ciudadanos and Podemos.[2]

From the point of view of the media system, unlike the press and the radio, television in Spain was initially set up as a state monopoly, originally financed by both advertising and state subsidies.[3] The only national television station which broadcast in Spain between the mid-1950s and the early 1980s was Televisión Española (TVE), the public channel whose programs have been controlled entirely by successive governments, both during the dictatorship and under democracy (Palacio, 2001). The year 1998 marked the entry of various private television channels onto the market, which were to compete with the public channel in terms of audience figures and advertising up until 2009, when a new regulation modified the financing of TVE. Law 8/2009 regarding the Financing of the Spanish Radio and Television Corporation (RTVE), dated August 28, completely removed all advertising on all of its channels, which meant that RTVE emerged for the first time as a true state-run television corporation, one that no longer had to compete for advertising revenue and that was obliged to treat viewers as both citizens and consumers (López Gil & Valderrama, 2011).

With regard to the financing of election campaigns, there has also been a number of changes in recent years. The Political Parties Financing Act (LO 3/1987) was overhauled by Law 8/2007, dated July 4, and then modified by Law 5/2012, dated October 22.

Campaigns are mainly financed with public money. The Spanish model is largely based on public subsidies granted to the political parties and supervised by the Court of Auditors (TC). The main principle is that the state should subsidize the national and local campaigns. Private donations are limited to 100,000 euros in the case of individuals and associations, and to 150,000 euros in the case of foundations. Meanwhile, financing that derives from the dues paid by party members, from the contributions made by elected representatives, etc., represents only around one-fifth of the total revenue generated (Pérez Francesch, 2009).

Another aspect we should mention is that the parties in Spain traditionally financed their campaigns with bank loans. This gave rise to debt write-offs, which were used to cover up donations and possible preferential treatment. The reform of 2012 forbade "all credit bodies from writing off any party's debts equivalent to amounts higher than one hundred thousand euros a year" (Coello de Portugal, 2012, p. 340).

Regulation of Political Advertising

The legal framework for campaigns takes into account the current context of fragmentation in the realm of politics, a strong public television corporation and public funding for electoral campaigns. Furthermore, legislation pays special attention to electoral advertising on television in light of its importance regarding the dissemination of party messages.

The first attempt to regulate campaign ads on television was enshrined in Royal Decree-Law 20/1977 on Electoral Rules, dated March 18. Article 40 provided that "associations, federations, coalitions and groups will have the right to spots on State-owned television and radio and in the State-owned press free of charge." In 1977, although television was a state monopoly at the time, various private radio channels and press publications did exist, and this Decree made no mention of the possibility of contracting advertising space in these media (Herrero & Connolly-Ahern, 2004).

In 1985, Law 5/1985 on the General Electoral System, dated June 19,[4] commonly known as LOREG, established the key framework for electoral campaigns and the use of the media during electoral periods. This law, which was partially amended in 1994,[5] established the duration of the campaign, the financing model based on a maximum for expenses, the use of political advertising in the mass media and certain basic principles regarding election coverage.[6] Since then, there have not been any substantial legislative changes regarding electoral communication and there is a complete legal void regarding the role that the Internet plays in electoral campaigns.

Whereas the 1985 law established that electoral campaigns would last at least 15 days and no more than 21, the 1994 law limited electoral campaigns in Spain to 15 days. The day before voting is a reflection day and electoral activities are forbidden, which means that it is only during the previous 15 days that parties can organize electoral activities to ask citizens for their vote. However, before this regulated period, political parties exercise all kind of strategies of political communication.

Regarding the role of the media, the LOREG is based on two fundamental and constitutional principles: no discrimination and access to the mass media.

By *no discrimination* the law understands the right to equality on the part of all the political parties, in terms of advertising rates, spots, etc. *Access* refers to the political parties' capacity to use the public media, because the parties are, according to Article Six of the Spanish Constitution, an expression "of political pluralism, contribute to the formation and manifestation of the popular will and constitute a key instrument for political participation." This principle is reaffirmed in Article Twenty of the Constitution, which states that "the law shall regulate the organization and parliamentary control of the means of social communication owned by the State or any public entity and shall guarantee access to those means on the part of significant social and political groups, respecting the pluralism of society." These principles apply both to advertising and reporting time for political parties during campaigns.

The legal framework regarding political advertising and propaganda in the media is complex (see Table 17.2). We shall focus here specifically on advertising on television, which constitutes a special case in Spain.

Table 17.2 Spain: main principles of political advertising

	Printed press	Commercial radio	Public radio	Public television	Commercial television
Purchase of space	Freely purchased	Freely purchased	Free	Free	Banned
Limitations	Only limited in relation to total campaign expenses	Only limited in relation to total campaign expenses	According to the proportion of the vote	According to the proportion of the vote	
Content restrictions			Not specifically restricted regarding content	Not specifically restricted regarding content	

Because of the role of the public media and the restricted funding system for political parties, the law guarantees that all political parties, regardless of their importance, shall have some exposure in the media. Therefore, public television stations are required by law to provide free broadcast time to political parties. During electoral campaigns, parties, federations, coalitions and groups running in the elections have a right to free advertising space on public television and radio stations. The distribution of time for these free slots follows a series of complex rules, but the main principle is that it should correspond to the number of votes each party achieved in the previous election of the same kind.

An interesting point is that the free slots for political advertising are not considered to be commercial advertising and, therefore, legal restrictions for commercials (such as subliminal messages, comparative content, etc.) do not apply to electoral advertising. Consequently, there are no restrictions on negative advertising.

The distribution of free electoral advertising time is carried out in accordance with the following scale (LOREG, Article 64): (1) 10 minutes for the parties, federations and coalitions that did not participate or did not obtain representation in the previous equivalent election; (2) 15 minutes for the parties, federations and coalitions that, having obtained representation in the previous equivalent election, did not achieve 5% of the total number of valid votes in the national territory or in smaller constituencies or in the European Parliament elections; (3) 30 minutes for those parties, federations and coalitions that obtained representation in the previous equivalent elections, having achieved between 5% and 20% of the total number of votes; and (4) 45 minutes for those parties, federations and coalitions that attained representation in the previous equivalent elections with at least 20% of the total number of votes. However, this right to free electoral advertising time does not apply unless the parties present candidates in at least 75% of the electoral districts covered by the specific media body in question. Furthermore, specific rules apply for local elections. Nevertheless, even those political parties, associations and coalitions that do not present candidates in a sufficient number of districts can enjoy 15 minutes of broadcast time in the public national media if they achieved 20% of the total number of votes in the previous election.

Article 65 establishes that the Central Electoral Board (JEC) shall make decisions regarding the length and timing of broadcast of electoral advertising spots, based on the proposals made by a Commission set up by the Board itself. This Commission is made up of a representative of each party represented in the Lower Chamber of Spain's Parliament, the Congreso de los Diputados (Article 67).

As an example, in the 2004 general election, PP and PSOE were granted 45 minutes each, being authorized to broadcast 22 ads of two minutes' duration, as well as an additional spot of three minutes' duration. Izquierda Unida was granted 30 minutes, distributed in a similar fashion, while the three regional parties, CiU, PNV and CC, each enjoyed 15 minutes in the geographical area where the parties presented candidates. The same amount of broadcasting time was given to these parties on public radio.

Up until the elections of 2008, these free advertising spots were broadcast after the daily news programs on Channels 1 and 2 on Spanish state-owned television, RTVE. In 2008, the Central Electoral Board accepted RTVE's proposal to distribute the total amount of free time corresponding to each political party into 30-second spots throughout the entire program schedule, instead of in concentrated electoral blocks. In this respect, an electoral block lasting ten minutes under the old system became 20 30-second spots under the new formula. Furthermore, in order to enhance the impact on viewers, the majority of these spots were broadcast within programs themselves rather than between different commercial spots (Rodríguez & Sádaba, 2010).

In conclusion, legislation explicitly restricts television advertising in terms of exposure on television channels, but not in relation to contents. Proof of this is provided by the banning of political broadcasting on commercial television channels with the 1988 law.[7] In contrast, parties are free to broadcast political ads on commercial radio and to print them in the press.

We can take for granted that the large political parties have more exposure time and are more visible and that this inequality established by law prevents the small parties from presenting their proposals in a more effective manner (Sádaba, 2003). Furthermore, due to the fact that the bigger parties have more money, they can produce better spots in terms of quality. Nevertheless, the benefits of the present regulation are clear, because it guarantees free electoral advertising time, both on radio and television, for all the parties. This means that they can compete even if their budgets are low (López-Escobar, Sádaba, & Zugasti, 2008).

Finally, the law, as it was drafted in 1985, reflected the broadcasting situation at the time, which meant it did not encompass commercial television or new technologies. With the emergence of private television channels, a debate arose regarding the law's limitations (Herrero & Connolly-Ahern, 2004; Sádaba, 2003). Today we find ourselves in the midst of the YouTube video and video-blog era and the validity of this law has been called even further into question.

The History of Ads

The development of ads in Spain is directly linked to three variables. First is the logical development of democracy, in a country that staged its first elections in 1975 and has continued to the point of political saturation in the first decade of the 21st century. Second is the advances that have occurred throughout this period in terms of professionalizing political communication and the incorporation of new audiovisual techniques. These developments have led to a significant change regarding the format of advertising spots, which have become increasingly similar to commercial spots. And third, a combination of the two previous factors can be witnessed in the increasing sophistication of members of the public, who are more enlightened in the ways of democratic life and television culture itself: "The political rhetoric that we see today – in the midst of the Information Society – is directed at an audience that is educated in the audiovisual medium and, therefore, accustomed to the mass consumption of messages of this kind" (Peña-Jiménez, 2011, p. 75).

During the earliest elections, ads were used for the purposes of electoral education, featuring a simple and monotonous enumeration of the different proposals, summarized for a television format, based on the candidates' talking heads. However, little by little they have become more agile, featuring the use of illustrative videos, which have become veritable advertising or camouflaged spots. These broadcasts can only be distinguished from Americanized electoral advertising by the fact that they were inserted into short general party presentation blocks. They also differ in that the party does not have to pay for their broadcast, although this does reduce the number of spots.

These spots have evolved from 10- or 20-minute slots:

> mainly featuring a discourse-based approach and usually a medium close-up view of the candidate talking into the camera and explaining the political program or proposal, to a series of more carefully planned spots based on a duration that ranges from 30 seconds on intermediate campaign days to three or four minutes on the opening and closing days of the campaign. The way the spots are made has also been perfected, based on more daring formats that endow the image with greater rhythm and make more intelligent use of audio-visual resources in order to achieve a product that is striking at the very least.
>
> (Herrero & Connolly-Ahern, 2004, p. 166)

This development has changed the very concept of the traditional spot: "Political television campaign messages that are eminently persuasive and are created by the parties themselves without being leveraged by the media" (Sádaba, 2003, p. 166). With the emergence of the Internet, the traditional spots that are broadcast on television now co-exist alongside others that are not shown on television and, furthermore, that are not always created by the party itself, but by like-minded platforms. In some cases, sympathizers create videos that generate more hits than those created by the parties themselves (Jove, 2009). However, they continue to present certain characteristic features – they seek out a wide-ranging public and, therefore, bring together the main ideas that make up the message; they focus on the electoral programs that the parties present to the public. The intention is obvious: unlike other campaign messages, these ads do not attempt to conceal the reasons why they have been made. Their aim is explicitly persuasive. Although these messages may have an informative element, their tone and content seek to sway the voter.

In order to review the history of political advertising spots in Spain, we can distinguish between three distinct periods: the beginning of political campaigns; the period of maturity; and the changes that have occurred since the emergence of the Internet.

The Origins of Electoral Advertising in Spain: 1977–93

The general elections of 1977 and the advent of democracy as of 1978 presented a series of new communicational challenges to all of the political forces in Spain. In the face of this new communicational environment between politicians and members of the public, the response mainly consisted of imitating the models that already existed in Europe – Germany, mainly – and, in particular, the US (Muñoz-Alonso & Rospir, 1995).

The first electoral spots in Spain had a clearly pedagogic dimension. They were aimed at inexpert voters who did not know how the democratic system worked. The political parties endeavored in their spots to explain their position and their program. They even presented candidates who were often quite unknown to the general public. This political education was, therefore, carried out explicitly and voters were informed about how they should place their vote in the urn. They were also left with a very clear idea of the parties' ideals, their place in the political spectrum and the origin of their leaders. The majority of the parties opted for the "talking heads" model in order to present these proposals and candidates.

In this brief review of the early electoral advertising initiatives that took place in Spain, we might highlight the campaign waged by the PSOE in 1982, which became known for its slogan, "Por el cambio" ("For Change"). The spot in this campaign was also striking because it abandoned the traditional format in order to show a succession of images in which a series of doors and windows opened and a new political horizon finally emerged, together with a new leader in the form of the candidate, Felipe González.

We might also point out that, from the very beginning of these campaigns, it was relatively easy to distinguish between the more professional campaigns and spots associated with the parties that had greater resources and the financial capacity to tackle a professional campaign and the minority parties that, either due to lack of resources or due to ideological reasons, resorted to a more "home-made" and less professional approach. It is also important to bear in mind that at this stage of development, televised commercial advertising and programs at the time were very much in line with the poor quality of electoral advertising.

Whatever the case may be, the spots in these early campaigns were generally characterized by a strong verbal communication dimension as opposed to a visual approach, while also being quite long (between 10 and 15 minutes' duration). During the 1980s, the format evolved and, by the end of the decade and during the early 1990s – for example, in the general elections of 1989 and 1993 – we come across formats that use the technique of video-clips.

Negative Advertising and Commercial Formats: 1996–2004

By the 1990s, Spain had left the Transition years behind; it was a member of the European Union and NATO and the idea of an alternative option in government had become a real possibility.

Certain trends were consolidated. On the one hand, the duration of the spots decreased, now lasting approximately two and a half minutes. On the other, video-clip techniques made a timid debut, with interchanging images and accompanying up-beat music, a technique that had already been anticipated in the controversial Socialist video of 1989.[8]

In the 1996 campaign all of the parties used audiovisual techniques, which modernized their spots. The contents also changed. There was a decline in specific proposals and an increasing emphasis on general values such as trust, truth, dialogue, peace, regeneration, integrity and efficiency. These messages lost their specific appeal in search of a wide-ranging audience. These values had appeared in all campaigns since 1977, but rather than any specific references, these values were alluded to in a general and increasingly symbolic manner.

The 1996 campaign introduced negative advertising to Spain for the first time, a format that would gain ground in successive elections. It was PSOE, under the slogan *España en positivo* ("Positive Spain"), which created a purely negative spot in Spain for the first time. Over a period of two-and-a-half minutes, this spot contrasted the "positive Spain" of PSOE with the "negative Spain" of the right (the PP was not mentioned at any point), in what has become known as the "Doberman video."

This video took full advantage of the formal and technical possibilities of audiovisual media. "Negative Spain" was presented in black-and-white, which created daunting shadows and endowed the images with a sense of anxiety and tension. This feeling was enhanced by the use of sound, in this case a deafening siren, and the employment of original camera perspectives and movements: fused or superimposed images, high-angle and low-angle shots, close-up shots, distorted images, photo-negative images and slow-motion images. A morphing technique was used to make a PP candidate turn into a Doberman, effectively associating the party with the Civil War period. In contrast, "positive Spain" employed opposing techniques: striking colors full of life, cheerful and catchy music (rhythmic guitars and drums), a rapid succession of images, a predominant use of wide shots, and the occasional complementary use of extremely close-up shots of smiling people or attractive looks.

When the video was broadcast, there was also much talk of subliminal messages, which is to say messages that influence the public without their being aware of it. Negative advertising had been used in Spanish electoral campaigns since the beginning, but never in such a direct and aggressive manner. In 1996, PSOE produced an advertising campaign that directly attacked its adversary, a campaign that was negative, aggressive and explicit.[9] The impact of this campaign went far beyond television and evoked comment both by the media and members of the public.[10] This spot created a considerable amount of controversy and was considered to be potentially illegal, something which, as we have seen, is not encompassed by Spanish electoral law, given that the spots are not conceived as being advertising, but simply as free slots.[11]

The PP prepared four videos using cinematic techniques in 35-millimeter film, featuring a series of spots that employed camera techniques such as traveling shots, high-angle and low-angle shots, colorful images and fade-outs. Throughout a duration of two and a half minutes, the slogan "the new majority" was repeated nine times. The positive tone was also reinforced by key-words such as "optimism," "progress," "hope" and "solutions."

Izquierda Unida (IU) commissioned Dexiderius, a production company belonging to a group of young sympathizers with the party, to create four different videos. These followed the trend of segmenting different sections of the audience, based on a clear social message: military service, unemployment, pensioners and solidarity.

The electoral campaign in the year 2000 demonstrated the progress the parties had made in terms of audiovisual technique, achieving some meaningful effects in the case of PSOE and PP and some rather chaotic results in the case of IU. Audiovisual techniques were used to go beyond the rational realm, enabling the parties to play around with emotions and arguments in order to present their proposals. The video-clip format became the norm, with the static talking head almost disappearing completely. The candidates' appearances were also shortened. The PSOE candidate did not speak to the camera at any point, which may have even reduced the impact of the spot.

In these elections, the modernization of the spots presented by the Partido Popular was the most obvious development. In the year 2000 campaign the party openly adopted the formats and techniques of commercial advertising. Certain spots completely removed the candidate's talking head and all speeches at political rallies, presenting the entire verbal message by means of a voice-over.

The Socialist Party once again resorted to a negative advertising campaign, although not based on the fear format of 1996, but by turning to comparative advertising. The promises made by the Aznar government were compared with reality, with the incumbent prime minister being accused of lying and manipulation. A new alternative was presented to the electorate in the person of the PSOE candidate. The spots maintained the same structure: the first part devoted to attacking the other party, and the second, shorter section, devoted to presenting the Socialist candidate.

Another of the videos produced by PSOE in the year 2000 had a quick moving appeal, based on a video-clip montage. A series of docu-drama images played around with a large number of symbols, although the guiding thread of the video was the idea of time ("The right-wing government is running out of time") represented by a series of ticking clocks. The party's position was also reflected in the verbal language employed, which reminded voters of the reasons for voting for the Socialists. Repetition of the verbal structure, the ticking clock and the sound of drums marked the driving rhythm of a series of images. The ideas raised did not correspond to any particular program, but constituted an appeal to support the basic principles of the Left, the principles of progress.

Izquierda Unida's campaign, "Somos necesari@s" ("We Are Necessary") maintained the party's more sectorial and programmatic approach, although, on this occasion, the party introduced its new candidate, Francisco Frutos. The spots created by IU were very different from those it had produced up until that time. They were both original and ingenious. Both the argument and the combination and superimposition of techniques, images and formats constituted a series of spots that were extremely new, but too Baroque, which may have caused a certain degree of bewilderment amongst viewers. At the end of the video, a scene in a cinema was included where the main leaders of Izquierda Unida were shown watching the ad. At the end, Frutos declared: "This is going to wake up the abstaining voters for sure. Nobody will be indifferent."

The elections of March 14, 2004 were conditioned by the terrible terrorist attacks of March 11. On the day of the massacre, the parties suspended the electoral campaign.

Previously, the Partido Popular had presented a spot lasting barely two minutes in which it showed "ordinary people" and presented a clear party line, based on the promise of effective management. It sought electoral support based on the guarantee provided by the party's management capabilities during eight years of government.

PSOE once again opted for a negative advertising spot, directly attacking the PP government, although the presentation and arguments were less radical than in the two previous campaigns. Featuring a cinema format, a spot was created that revolved around a ballot-box. The video fused various sequences, each of which was based on a similar pattern: someone, in different circumstances, wrote a specific complaint against the government and placed it in the ballot-box in the form of a vote. In this sense, a young person wrote "No to war!", a fast-food deliveryman wrote "No to the 10-day contract!" and a pensioner wrote "Elderly, not stupid!" After this initial minute of denunciation, in which the spot encouraged voters not to support PP, the video contrasted this with Zapatero and concluded with a close-up sequence shot, "Until When?" This shot magnified the value of the candidate over the party or the program.

This period, which concluded with the tragic events of 2004, witnessed a very significant change in the way advertising spots were used by the political parties, ranging from the advent of negative advertising (which, from then on, was here to stay) to the modernization of formats and the involvement of commercial advertising professionals. The developments witnessed by this communication tool would open up the possibility of its adaptation to campaign changes founded on the strategic use of the Internet.

Electoral Advertising on the Web: 2008–15

The campaign of 2008 went down in history as the first occasion on which the parties strategically considered how to use the Internet in their national campaigns (Peytibi, Rodríguez, & Gutiérrez-Rubí, 2008). Specific videos were created to be disseminated via the Web (López García, 2008), a trend that was to be consolidated in subsequent campaigns. In this manner, YouTube became an electoral campaign channel in Spain (Carceller, 2013).

For example, in the European elections of 2009, the parties made especially strong use of Internet videos (Table 17.3). The number of hits obtained, however, did not correspond proportionally to the electoral importance of each party (Sádaba et al., 2012). In fact, the videos of a more minority-based party such as UPyD, very much an outsider in the intense Web campaign, had a more significant impact than those of larger parties.[12]

Likewise, in the general elections of 2008, taking advantage of the participative nature of the Web, various parties launched a video competition amongst their members (such as PP with its www.tupropuestaen30segundos.com). The advertising spot, which could previously be defined as a message produced and broadcast by the party, now also became the property of sympathizers and detractors, who used the Web to present their visual proposals. In this respect, we can observe how non-official channels have sometimes come to achieve greater levels of success than the institutional channels (Jove, 2011).[13]

In 2008, the first consequence of the emergence of spots on the Internet was a general increase in their number. Gómez and Capdevila counted 15 corresponding to PP, 12 corresponding to PSOE and 11 for IU (Gómez & Capdevila, 2013). The spots also became shorter and the language used was simpler.

The argument adopted by PSOE continued to be that of a confrontation of two worlds, one positive and the other negative, a formula already established in its campaign formats. In this case, the world of participation was set against the world of abstention, which was attributed to PP. And in terms of the leading players in its spots, the Socialist Party continued to turn more to the voice on the street than to the voice of its own candidates.

In 2008, PP created a negative spot format for the first time that was critical of the Socialist government. Featuring a strong dose of irony, the video presented a reality that was diametrically opposed to that presented by PSOE. One ad that had a certain impact was entitled "Castillo de naipes" ("House of Cards"), in which a deck of cards collapsed, whilst another featured a woman who had been deceived in love, which served as a metaphor for the electorate's disenchantment under Zapatero. The PP's use of metaphors as of this time was to become a recurring feature of its spots.

In the case of IU, in addition to other spots, the party presented a series of videos on the candidate's web page entitled *Las cosas que importan* ("Things That Matter"). These consisted of a number

Table 17.3 European elections 2009: Internet videos impact

Party	Percentage of votes	Number of hits
PP	42.23%	5,771
PSOE	38.51%	126,000
IU	3.73%	20,833
UPyD	2.87%	65,959

of cartoon stories featuring a super-hero known as Gaspi (a reference to the party leader, Gaspar Llamazares) who was placed in different threatening situations which Gaspi tackled in the typical manner portrayed in comics. This was an entirely relaxed and open campaign, far removed from the constraints of traditional spots and even the ads created by the party. This campaign also reflected, in some respects, the infotainment element that has emerged in recent years and which has led to new ways of communicating about political matters (Brants & Neijens, 1998).

Nevertheless, in 2008 the smallest parties with the lowest budgets continued to resort to the talking head formula (Peña & García, 2011).

The elections of 2011 presented few new developments from the point of view of electoral advertising (the PSOE campaign was more person-based, the PP campaign more party-based), although they focused more strongly on the most significant new feature of the moment, which consisted of the use of Twitter (García, García, & Varona, 2012; Zamora & Zurutuza, 2014). A spot broadcast by PSOE on YouTube that went viral had an impact almost a month before the campaign in which the issue of education and class difference was introduced. It generated comments in the media and both positive and negative criticisms on the Web. Furthermore, YouTube itself created a "cyber-journalist" platform for the campaign, which brought together information and videos, as well as questions aimed at the candidates (García, García, & Varona, 2012).

Today, the visual dimension predominates over the verbal dimension and brevity is favored at the expense of thorough exposition. Pace is essential and the narration is dependent on (or adapted to) the available images. Furthermore, this format corresponds to a more emotional and connotative style, focusing on generic ideas or values, as opposed to the previously rational and referential approach.

With the emergence of Internet these trends have been accentuated. It is important to achieve a spectacular appeal in order to stand out amongst the millions of messages that compete with one another on the Web, while combining this appeal with a certain agility and rapidity, so that the message can possibly go viral and achieve mass dissemination. The parties have ceased to exercise a monopoly over the spots. In this respect, specific campaigns revolving around political interests and carried out by private individuals have begun to play a significant role. These campaigns very often generate more hits than those of the parties themselves. The costs of the productions have also been substantially reduced and the spot format, which was destined to play the starring role in the campaign, has acquired a series of completely different characteristics within the new communicational environment (Rodríguez & Sádaba, 2010).

The 2015 campaign has incorporated a series of new players and television has been key for these candidates. Spots have created again some degree of discussion; some of them just created for YouTube and some others broadcast on television. This time, spots from PP employing a medical metaphor of the country's recovery, and another one about the "hipsters" voting PP, have been very notorious in the social media. One more institutional spot entitled "In which country do you want to get up in four years?", conceived for television, has been the most re-tweeted spot of the campaign. Also, the PSOE has created many videos both for television and the Internet with some success. New political parties such as Podemos and Ciudadanos, usually very active in social media, have not reached the same number of likes and re-tweets for their spots. Maybe this is because traditional spots talking about programs and candidates (such as the Ciudadanos spot about a letter from the candidate) live together with commercial, viral and humor spots (the ones created by the Youth branch of both PSOE and PP).

Reception and Effects of Advertising

Although research into the question of political communication and campaigning in Spain stretches back a number of decades, the specific and specialized study of spots began at the last decade of the 20th century (Sádaba, 2003). This recent interest is reflected in various contributions, especially with regard to the content of these spots, their rhetoric and their capacity to concentrate the parties' messages (Capdevila, 2004; García-Beaudoux & D'Adamo, 2007; Herrero & Connolly-Ahern, 2004). Various studies have also focused on the types of spots used and, specifically, the question of negative advertising (Feliu García, Feliu Albaladejo, & Martín Llaguno, 2002; Peña-Jiménez, 2011).

Following the directions pursued by certain international studies, research has also analyzed whether the spots in question focused on the theme of the campaign or on the candidate (Kaid & Holtz-Bacha, 1995; Sánchez-Aranda et al., 1997).

Within this context, only a few studies have focused on the impact that electoral advertising may have on voters, perhaps because the audiences are not large (Sádaba, 2003) or because the effects of these campaigns in Spain are limited (Fernández Mellizo-Soto, 2001; Martínez i Coma, 2005). Studies also show that negative advertising tends to be recalled better than positive advertising (Peña-Jiménez, 2011), although no empirical analyses have been carried out based on the spots broadcast in Spain.

Following our analysis of the development of Spanish campaign spots in this study, we can state that electoral advertising in Spain, which was perhaps initially created in order to have a direct impact on the voter (featuring the pedagogical content that can be observed in the early years), went on to have a more agenda-creating role vis-à-vis the campaign in the 1990s. Its impact must, therefore, be measured in this sense. That is to say, these spots began to be commented upon by the media and generated content that, subsequently, exercised an impact on the audience. Therefore, there is an indirect effect as it has been demonstrated in the US campaigns (Roberts & McCombs, 1994). This was especially so in the case of negative spots. A good example is provided by the PSOE spot of 1996, which occupied newspaper front-page headlines and generated an intense debate regarding the question of subliminal messages, negative advertising and the limits of political communication. However, an impact can also be achieved when spots are not necessarily negative; for example, when they become viral, such as the spot broadcast by PP in the 2015 campaign featuring hipsters. This kind of spot demonstrates the capacity of this approach for agenda-setting.

Notes

1   Regional elections are held at the same time as local elections, except in the Basque Country, Catalonia, Galicia and Andalusia. The heads of these regional governments are able to dissolve the regional parliament themselves and so follow their own election timetables.

2   Although these were very different types of election, these parties emerged due to a general disaffection regarding the traditional parties and seem destined to play an important role in national politics. See López García (2014).

3   In 1980, a law established the Spanish public television statute, which presented a considerable degree of continuity with the past.

4   Parliamentary Law 5/1985 on the General Electoral System, dated June 19.

5   Parliamentary Law 13/1994 for the Reduction of Electoral Campaign Expenditure and Institutional Advertising in the State-Owned Media, dated March 30.

6   In addition to the LOREG, two other laws were passed that relate to electoral advertising on television. Law 2/1988 Regarding the Regulation of Electoral Advertising on Private Television Channels, dated May 3, establishes in its sole article that "electoral advertising spots shall not be contracted on private television channels under concession." For its part, Law 14/1995 Regarding Electoral Advertising on Local Television Channels Via Terrestrial Waves, dated December 22, establishes that: "electoral advertising spots shall not be contracted on local television channels via terrestrial waves." The law accepts the possibility, solely in the case of municipal elections, that free spots may be granted on channels managed by Local Councils, based on criteria similar to those established in the LOREG, and also on cable.

7   Law 2/1988 on Electoral Advertising on Commercial Television, dated May 3.

8   The Socialist Party ad for these elections was an interesting and not uncontroversial case. By means of a quick succession of shots, the spot showed the most significant moments of the Socialist government's time in office. These images included various famous people who had been successful in their careers, such as Arancha Sánchez Vicario, Montserrat Caballé, Salvador Dalí, Juan Echanove and the pop group, Mecano, as well as scenes from the Olympics and Expo 92. Controversy arose because the individuals who appeared in the video had not been consulted by PSOE so that they could authorise the association of their image with

the party's merits. Some even explicitly supported other parties. PSOE was forced to remove these figures and create another version of the video with those who either agreed to appear or were not bothered about appearing in the ad.

9 Another spot created by PSOE attacked the PP candidate directly. This spot generated a direct and negative contrast, setting the political prestige of Felipe González against the ridiculous image of José María Aznar repeating the words "Váyase, Señor González" ("Just go, Mr. González"), a phrase familiar to all Spaniards and taken from a famous speech that Aznar had delivered in parliament.

10 For instance, the front page of *El Mundo* was devoted to explain this spot. See *El Mundo* February 18, 1996. But also, *El País*, February 19 and 23, 1996.

11 Something else all together was what happened during the same campaign with the electoral videos of Herri Batasuna (HB), where HB ceded its free slot to talk about the option of the terrorist group, ETA, for the Basque Country. In this case, the party was accused of the crime of collaborating with a terrorist group and the spot was removed from the electoral campaign.

12 Whilst the PP's videos, which had a more institutional message, achieved few hits (the party's most popular video generated just 5,771 hits), PSOE's videos, which had a more ideological message, reached a larger Internet audience (the most popular generated 126,000 hits).

13 In spite of the impact that all of the PP's initiatives had in the media, the number of hits generated by the platform, Yo Rompo, at least tripled those launched by the PP. Some of the videos created by Yo Rompo achieved 300,000 hits, compared to an average of 25,000 for the PP's videos. Yo Rompo and other initiatives of this kind show that a large part of the mobilization of the Spanish Right, which would contribute 10,169,973 votes to PP, had taken place via the Internet (Jove, 2009).

References

Aja, E. (1999). *El Estado autonómico. Federalismo y hechos diferenciales.* Madrid: Alianza.

Brants, K., & Neijens, P. (1998). The infotainment of politics. *Political Communication*, 15(2), 149–164.

Capdevila, A. (2004). *El discurso persuasivo. La estructura retórica de los spots electorales en televisión.* Barcelona: Aldea Global.

Carceller, C. J. (2013). La videopolítica en campaña: Evolución del spot electoral en España entre 2004 y 2011. *Vivat Academia*, 124, 1–20.

Coello de Portugal, J. M. (2012). La "Ley Orgánica 5/2012, de 22 de octubre", una buena reforma en una buena dirección del régimen de financiación de los partidos políticos. *Foro, Nueva Época*, 15(2), 337–344.

Dader, J. L. (1999). Entre la retórica mediática y la cultura autóctona: La comunicación política electoral española como encrucijada de la 'americanización' y el pluralismo democrático tradicional. *Cuadernos de información y comunicación*, 4, 63–87.

Feliu García, E., Feliu Albaladejo, Á., & Martín Llaguno, M. (2002). La publicidad negativa en las campañas electorales: Un análisis y algunas reflexiones. Universidad Pontificia de Salamanca. Servicio de Publicaciones.

Fernández Mellizo-Soto, M. (2001). ¿Para qué sirven las campañas electorales?: Los efectos de la campaña electoral española de 1993. *Reis: Revista Española de Investigaciones Sociológicas*, 93, 61–87.

García, A., García, I., & Varona, D. (2012). Incidencia de las redes sociales vs cibermedios, en las elecciones en España, 2011. *Enl@ce Revista Venezolana de Información, Tecnología y Conocimiento*, 9(2), 11–29.

García-Beaudoux, V., & D'Adamo, O. (2007). El anuncio político televisivo como herramienta de comunicación electoral. Análisis de caso: Los anuncios de la campaña para las elecciones legislativas de marzo de 2004 en España. *Revista de Psicología Social*, 22(1), 45–61.

Gómez, L., & Capdevila, A. (2013). Variaciones estratégicas en los spots electorales de televisión y de Internet en campaña electoral. *Zer-Revista de Estudios de Comunicación*, 17(33), 67–86.

Herrero, J. C., & Connolly-Ahern, C. (2004). Origen y evolución de la propaganda política en la España democrática (1975–1996): Análisis de las técnicas y mensajes en las elecciones generales de 2000. *Doxa*, 2, 151–172.

Jove, M. (2009). Influentials: Lecciones para el PP de la campaña de Obama. *La Ilustración Liberal: Revista Española y Americana*, 39, 17–24.

Jove, M. (2011). *Influentials: Localizando líderes de opinión en el "El confidencial."* Pamplona: Eunate.

Kaid, L. L., & Holtz-Bacha, C. (1995). *Political advertising in Western democracies: Parties and candidates on television.* Thousand Oaks, CA: Sage.

López García, G. (2008). *La eclosión del vídeo como mecanismo de comunicación política en Internet.* Paper presented at the I Congreso de la Asociación Española de Investigación de la Comunicación, Universidad de Santiago de Compostela.

López García, G. (2014, September). *Estrategias de movilización política de los partidos para un público desmotivado: Internet y las Elecciones Europeas de 2014.* Paper presented at the III Congreso Internacional en Comunicación Política y Estrategias de Campaña, ALICE, Universidad de Santiago de Compostela.

López Gil, N. L., & Valderrama, M. (2011). La nueva televisión pública española: Ley de Financiación, flujo de las audiencias y análisis de las promociones de canal tras la supresión de publicidad. *Revista Comunicación*, 9(1), 205–221.

López-Escobar, E., Sádaba, T., & Zugasti, R. (2008). Election coverage in Spain: From Franco's death to the Atocha massacre. In J. Strömbäck & L. L. Kaid (Eds.), *The handbook of election news coverage around the world* (pp.175–191). New York, NY: Routledge.

Martínez i Coma, F. (2005). ¿Cuáles fueron los efectos de la campaña electoral española del 2000? *Reis. Revista Española de Investigaciones Sociológicas*, 112(1), 231–257.

Muñoz-Alonso, A., & Rospir, I. (1995). *Comunicación política.* Madrid: Editorial Universitas.

Palacio, M. (2001). *Historia de la televisión en España.* Barcelona: Gedisa.

Peña, P., & García, A. (2011). Tipología del spot electoral: Una aproximación a partir de la campaña de 2008. *Pensar la Publicidad. Revista Internacional de Investigaciones Publicitarias*, 4(2), 51–70.

Peña-Jiménez, P. (2011). El spot electoral negativo. *Revista Latina de Comunicación Social*, 66, 399–425.

Pérez Francesch, J. L. (2009). La financiación de los partidos políticos en España. Consideraciones a partir de los informes del Tribunal de Cuentas y de la nueva Ley Orgánica 8/2007, de 4 de julio. *Papers, Revista de Sociología*, 92, 249–271.

Peytibi, X., Rodríguez, J. A., & Gutiérrez-Rubí, A. (2008). L'experiència de les eleccions generals 2008. *IDP: Revista d'Internet, Dret i Política*, 7.

Roberts, M., & McCombs, M. (1994). Agenda setting and political advertising: Origins of the news agenda. *Political Communication*, 11(3), 249–262.

Rodríguez-Virgili, J., & Sádaba, T. (2010). Publicidad electoral: La evolución de los spots electorales en España (1977–2004). In M. Montero (Ed.), *La edad de oro de la comunicación comercial, desde 1960 hasta 2000: Historia de la publicidad y de las relaciones públicas en España.* (Vol. 2, pp. 133–160). Sevilla: Zamora, Comunicación Social.

Sádaba, T. (2003). Los anuncios de los partidos en televisión. El caso de España (1993–2000). In S. Berrocal (Ed.), *Comunicación política en televisión y nuevos medios* (pp. 163–206). Barcelona: Ariel.

Sádaba, T., Rodríguez-Virgili, J., & Jove, M. (2012). Dans un pays en crise, une élection aux multiples préoccupations sous-jacentes. In P. J. Maarek (Ed.), *La communication politique européenne sans l'Europe: Les élections au Parlement Européen de 2009* (pp. 141–159) Paris: L'Harmattan.

Sánchez-Aranda, J. J., Canel, M. J., & Llamas, J. P. (1997). *Framing effects of negative political advertising.* Paper at the WAPOR Regional Conference, Universidad de Navarra.

Swanson, D. L., & Mancini, P. (1996). *Politics, media, and modern democracy: An international study of innovations in electoral campaigning and their consequences.* New York, NY: Praeger.

Zamora, R., & Zurutuza, C. (2014). Campaigning on Twitter: Towards the "personal style" campaign to activate the political engagement during the 2011 Spanish general elections. *Comunciación y Sociedad*, XXVII(1), 83–106.

18

THE LONGEST RUNNING SERIES ON TELEVISION

Party Political Broadcasting in Britain

Simon Cross and Dominic Wring

Introduction

Political advertising in Britain comes in various guises. In a pioneering survey of campaigning activities during the 19th century Ostrogorski used the term to refer to the literature candidates disseminated during election time (Ostrogorski, 1902). The advent of mass democracy and changes in media and communication after World War I led to a shift away from politicians relying on this kind of printed material and their increasing embrace of other forms of publicity including the ubiquitous and surprisingly enduring medium of the poster. The rise of mass circulation newspapers led to parties purchasing space in the best-selling titles to disseminate key messages to the growing audiences of readers. But it was the introduction of radio that led to politicians being granted airtime that enabled them to communicate with potential supporters in a more intimate way that mimicked the personal address of a public meeting. This format, known as the Party Election Broadcast (PEB), has become a familiar feature of British politics. And like the election poster, the medium has proved to be an enduring feature of successive campaigns.

British broadcasting has long been subjected to rules that enforce impartiality laws including during election times. This regulatory approach also means there has been a long-standing ban on paid radio and television advertising of the kind seen in other democracies. PEBs therefore function as the British equivalent of the American political spot. They still exist because, despite inquiries and reviews, they offer politicians the rare (and free) opportunity to directly communicate with the millions who watch PEBs and who would otherwise not choose to see them online. Moreover, the fragmentation of the party system from the duopoly that dominated the 20th century to the more diverse competitive environment of recent times has meant ever more politicians with a vested interest in protecting their entitlement to publicly subsidized airtime. This chapter explores the origins and development of a now 90-year-old tradition and considers some of the continuities as well as changes to these outputs.

Political and Electoral System

In his pioneering analysis of the British "political market," Andrew Gamble identified three components: "the existence of a mass electorate; competition between two or more parties for the votes of this electorate; and a set of rules governing this competition" (Gamble, 1974, p. 6). While the 1832 Great Reform Act and successive laws in 1867 and 1883–4 paved the way for the development of both the modern party and electoral systems, it was the 1918 Representation of the People Act that marked the emergence of the country as a democratic state. Overnight this legislation more than trebled the electorate, enfranchising the overwhelming majority of men and also some women for the first time. Further reforms followed with the reduction of the voting age to every citizen over the age of 21 in 1928 and 18 in 1969. General election turnouts have ordinarily exceeded 70% although in 2001 this dropped below 60% for the first time before recovering to 66.1% in the most recent poll of 2015. The voting system is a majoritarian one whereby electors support a single candidate in their local constituency: the winner is the politician who receives more votes than any rival. Currently there are 650 Members of Parliament returned in this way and historically most British governments have been formed by a single party achieving anything between 36% (2005) to 55% (1935) of the poll (Butler & Butler, 2010). The postwar norm to form an administration has required between 40–45% of the vote.

Labour and the Conservatives have been the primary beneficiaries of the Westminster parliament's majoritarian, "first past the post" electoral system. However, these parties' once seemingly hegemonic position has been increasingly challenged with the rise of various rivals such as the Liberal Democrats (and the merger of its "parents," the Liberals and Social Democrats, in the late 1980s), the Scottish Nationalists (SNP), the Greens and the UK Independence Party (UKIP). Combined the Conservative and Labour share of electoral support has declined to just over two-thirds of the total poll although the majoritarian system still ensures them disproportionately favorable representation in the House of Commons. The 2010 general election resulted in no single party winning an overall majority for the first time since 1974 and the formation of the first coalition government since World War II. The Liberal Democrats subsequently became junior partners in a Conservative-led administration.

The 2015 general election was won by the Conservatives with only 36.9% of votes but a slim majority of 50.9% or 331 of the seats. By contrast the millions of votes now routinely won by the various challengers have not given them significantly more MPs with one exception. The outlier here was the Scottish Nationalists, unique among the aforementioned challenger parties due to its support being, by definition, so geographically concentrated that when it reached 50% of the ballots cast north of the border it resulted in them winning all but three of the country's seats in 2015 and increasing their representation from 6 to 56 MPs. This remarkable result followed the 2014 referendum on independence that ended with 45% of Scots voting to leave the Union (Mitchell, 2015). Although this meant the continuation of the UK the result nonetheless provided the impetus behind the Nationalists' surge in the polls and with it a massive increase in people joining the party. The SNP's expansion is in contrast to most other parties in Europe where the overall trend has seen organizations experiencing significant declines in membership (Van Biezen, Mair, & Poguntke, 2012). That said, other British based parties have experienced growth, albeit for different reasons: UKIP and the Greens have developed because of dissatisfaction with mainstream politics on the right and left respectively. Since 2015, there has also been a surge of members joining Labour to participate in the election of a radical new leader, Jeremy Corbyn; his victory provided the catalyst for a further upsurge in those affiliating.

Origins and Developments

The earliest political advertising in Britain took the form of individuals promoting their candidatures by buying space in an increasingly popular print media. This practice has continued, to varying degrees, in subsequent campaigns and most especially in the latter part of the 20th century when newspaper circulations were highest (Butler, 1995). Allied to this political parties also took to commissioning outdoor advertisements in the form of posters that enabled messages to be disseminated simultaneously throughout the country. Even with the rise of digital media, this practice continues offline in a bid to target the still sizeable number of citizens who are not regular consumers of traditional news or social media. Following the introduction of near universal suffrage the interwar period was characterized by the interlinked development of mass democracy, media and communication.

Somewhat presciently the pioneering political scientist Graham Wallas foresaw the growing importance of the emotive "image" in what would be increasingly impersonal campaigns designed to cultivate larger numbers of voters than any candidate could realistically expect to meet individually during an election. Wallas observed "advertising and party politics are becoming more and more closely assimilated in method" and would likely supplement traditional methods such as canvassing and meetings (Wallas, 1910, p. 87).

The growing interest in using image-based appeals was part of the rationale behind politicians' earliest experimentations with using film for persuasive purposes, particularly to cultivate the less informed and involved citizen who might nonetheless participate by voting. Consequently, the first sustained attempts to use cinema came in the guise of the Conservative Film Association, which deployed mobile vans to disseminate short moving image animated and live action features to audiences in impromptu screenings up and down the country during the 1929 general election. This novel approach was overshadowed, however, by what amounted to the introduction of broadcast political advertising into British politics earlier that decade (Hollins, 1981). The development of radio during the 1920s, in the guise of the British Broadcasting Company (BBC) set up in 1922 provided an obvious opportunity to enhance and enrich the mass democratic process. BBC founder John Reith voiced a concern that the new medium might evolve into an American-style, overly commercial system in his 1924 book *Broadcast over Britain* (Reith, 1924). Rather Reith's belief in "public service" meant he saw radio as a key (if not the) forum for the dissemination of quality information to a citizenry now consisting of a sizeable mass electorate. The BBC's pioneer also believed that the new system should be scrupulously independent of party and government interference.

Following the return of the first Labour-led government PEBs were introduced for the 1924 campaign. Initially these consisted of radio speeches featuring the three main leaders explaining their policies (Antcliffe, 1984). Following the restructuring of the BBC and its re-launch as the Corporation rather than the Company in 1927 the number of PEBs increased. Two years later the general election featured several more PEBs, thereby establishing an enduring system guaranteeing the main electoral contenders access to the airwaves and hence the rapidly expanding audience. Although British television started broadcasting in 1936 it was not until well after World War II that the medium attracted a mass viewership. The first televised PEBs were broadcast in 1951 to be followed two years later by the introduction of advertising in non-campaign periods in the guise of so-called party political broadcasts (PPBs). The opening broadcast featured an elderly Liberal politician, Herbert Samuel, reading from a script adhering to a classic talking head format.

In the first televised PEB Samuel inadvertently gave the signal that he was finishing mid-sentence which led to him being prematurely cut-off during his live appearance. The rival parties' presentations were somewhat better. The Conservatives featured one of the earliest television personalities, Leslie Mitchell, posing questions to Foreign Secretary Anthony Eden. Eden, who would become prime minister four years later, was regarded as a more accomplished television performer than his leader, Winston Churchill, who felt uncomfortable appearing on the medium (Cockerell, 1989). Clips of Mitchell's questioning have often been mistakenly used as examples of the so-called deference demonstrated by early media interviewers toward politicians. Labour also deployed its own double act in an attempt to stimulate viewer interest. The party recognized relatively few voters had ready access to television. The subsequent broadcast had former journalist turned MP Christopher Mayhew introducing his colleague and celebrated lawyer, Hartley Shawcross, who made an explicit pitch to a viewing public of relatively affluent voters in which he tried to promote Labour as a party for those from wealthy as well as less privileged backgrounds.

Television rapidly developed during the 1950s in terms of the sophistication of its programming as well as its popularity with the general public (Seymour-Ure, 1974). By the end of the decade over 70% of households had their own television set on which they could view the BBC as well as its new commercial rival, Independent Television (ITV), launched in 1955. ITV transformed the coverage of

British politics so that its opening general election of 1959 came to be widely regarded as the "first TV campaign." That year saw television ownership rising to 11 million sets; in 1946 it had been a fraction of this at just 15,000. ITV adopted a more questioning approach to politics and politicians between and during elections. Television duly became the most popular medium for entertainment but also for providing many voters with information that they came to value as more objective than their other major source, the highly partisan press (Blumler & McQuail, 1968). The success of commercial television did not herald the end of PEBs and ITV, like its BBC rivals, were subject to laws that required them to offer impartial coverage of politics and to also allocate airtime to politicians free of charge. This state subsidy in kind remains to the present time. Following the growth of television broadcasting there were further innovations in PEB production and presentation. Influential BBC current affairs editor Grace Wyndham Goldie liaised with the major parties to help them finesse their broadcasts and many other senior Corporation figures such as future Director General Alisdair Milne were seconded to help politicians make these films as appealing and effective as possible (Negrine, 2011).

Alisdair Milne had been a producer on the popular BBC program *Tonight* which pioneered a more human interest, less solely hard news style of journalism that eventually came to dominate current affairs broadcasting to mass audiences. He and other colleagues working on the series were seconded to help Labour during the 1959 general election and helped create a highly innovative series, "Britain Belongs to You," presented by Tony Benn (Rose, 1967). The by now Labour MP Benn had previously worked for the BBC in North America and had got to know the Democrats' presidential candidate Adlai Stevenson and witnessed the impact of television on the 1952 US election. Significantly, the then head of Conservative broadcasting John Profumo also made the trip to experience Ike Eisenhower's strategists' use of advertising spots to successfully promote a not particularly telegenic candidate (Tunstall, 1964, p. 168). Benn proved a more effective television communicator than his friend Stevenson and was keen on ensuring his "Britain Belongs" series retained audiences through use of sounds. Music was seen as a means of preventing mass viewer desertion when the PEB began with the formal requirement to be prefaced "There Now Follows ...." Maintaining voter interest was a challenge given the ensuing slots each typically lasted 20 minutes. Labour, like rival parties, took to segmenting their broadcasts to include shorter items featuring leaders, candidates, experts (with or without graphics) and members of the public. The Conservatives deployed a former international athlete and ex-journalist Christopher Chataway to front their rival series of PEBs, one of which pointedly criticized what it alleged to be the artificial headquarters Benn and his colleagues had suggested existed in their films. It was an early example of how politicians were able to use their allotted time to undermine their rivals' reputations or rebut claims.

An estimated 15 million viewers saw PEBs on either BBC or ITV in the prime-time 9 p.m. slot during the 1960s. When the third channel, BBC2, was launched in 1964, it too joined in simultaneous transmissions of the broadcasts during the general election held that year. Critics bemoaned this amounted to the forced feeding of politics to mass audiences for the now established and highly popular medium (Black, 2010). Politicians appeared reluctant to end the arrangement and it was only later in the 1970s that broadcasters began to vary their scheduling of PEBs. Since then the practice has been for what were the five terrestrial channels and the satellite Sky News service to air the films before or after one of their main evening news bulletins (Rosenbaum, 1997). In terms of content the "talking head" soon became and remained a familiar PEB technique, particularly when involving the party leader addressing the nation. Harold Wilson was anointed the "first television prime minister" on account of his ability to use the medium in a more effective way than his predecessors and rivals (Seymour-Ure, 1974). But greater experimentation with various formats also followed courtesy of parties working with professional film-makers such as Stanley Baker, who advised Wilson, or Conservative-supporting director Bryan Forbes.

Fusing Politics with Advertising

Professional film-makers were increasingly conscious of changes in popular culture and the subsequent PEBs they produced drew on contemporary television genres such as talk and game shows, drama, documentary and even comedy. The experimentation was designed to appeal to the (by definition) more elusive audience of so-called "floating voters" who are prone to changing their allegiance and who also tend to be less politically engaged than their more firmly partisan peers. Representatives of the typical target audiences began to appear in PEBs aimed at them. For instance in one of the first to be made under the supervision of a commercial advertising agency, a 1964 Conservative film featured an actor playing a woman vacuuming her home and evidently annoyed that her husband had forgotten their wedding anniversary. But later it is revealed he has remembered and bought her a motor car apparently made affordable by the then Tory government's increase in an individual's tax allowances. The wife subsequently questions her husband's hitherto allegiance to the opposition Labour Party.

The fusion of politics and advertising was not new and had been pioneered decades before when, during the 1920s, the Conservatives had hired the services of the then leading agency SH Benson, soon to be famous for their iconic campaign "Guinness is Good for You." But the 1970s witnessed advertisers taking more responsibility for helping their political clients devise suitable copy. Edward Heath, elected Conservative leader in 1965, lost his first campaign in 1966 but succeeded four years later aided by a strategy devised by Barry Day. Recognizing the patrician, remote figure of Heath was not as telegenic as his principal rival, Prime Minister Wilson, Day focused on promoting the party to potential supporters from groups not traditionally associated with voting Tory (Day, 1982). These included married women from less socio-economically advantaged households and out of this an archetypal representative of this segment called "Sylvia" was identified. The eponymous character appeared in a short biopic with a child talking about her personal philosophy and decision to reject her husband's support for Labour in favor of voting Conservative as the best option for herself and family. Forty years later, during the 2010 general election, David Cameron adopted and used a very similar approach in a campaign PEB that narrated the story of Julie, a mother of two who could have been Sylvia's daughter (Harmer & Wring, 2013).

It was the broadcast advertising developed up to and during the Conservatives' successful 1979 general election campaign that is widely seen as offering a paradigm shift linked to the central strategic role of the Saatchi & Saatchi agency. The firm's formidable creative team devised memorable copy including the poster "Labour Isn't Working" (Scammell, 1995). The agency took responsibility for all aspects of the party's promotion, including PEBs that looked noticeably more like conventional adverts than political films. Characteristically few words were featured, either in written or spoken form, in Saatchi copy that focused on narrating Britain's decline and how the Conservatives could and would turn things around if elected. Significantly the party voluntarily halved its allotted time from the then standard 10 minutes to five in the belief that less was more. The shorter the film the more it resembled the kind of conventional television advertising that was thought likely to have some impact. Memorable copy included clips of actors playing voters defending their aspirational behavior in a courtroom to an unseen authority figure representing the incumbent Labour government. Another had athletes running backwards as a metaphor for the Conservative belief that the country was going in the wrong direction. A particularly memorable scene focused on the intercutting footage of striking workers with an increasingly fraught voice-over restating the newspaper headline "Crisis? What Crisis?" to remind viewers of the incumbent Labour government's alleged complacency and inability to acknowledge the scale of the UK's economic problems. These kinds of brief film extracts resembled the American-style 30- or 60-second spot advertising, particularly in the way they deployed emotive imagery in their attempts to engage with voters (Rees, 1992).

Neil Kinnock was not the first Labour leader to work with professional advertisers but the strategic reforms he oversaw during the 1980s ceded more control and authority to marketers than had previously been the case (Wring, 2005). Consequently, members of the so-called Shadow Communications Agency, a network of communications specialists, were recruited to work for the party on a voluntary basis. These professional advisers included a group hired to produce PEBs that, like Saatchi for the Conservatives, began to routinely feature actors playing voters talking about their aspirations and how these might be realized under a future Labour government (Gould, 1998). Here the emphasis was on countering the narrative that the party was somehow overly ideological in its use of language and thereby out of touch with "ordinary people." The nature of PEBs changed with the outputs becoming increasingly slick and professional in nature. Another significant influence on them from the 1980s onwards was that of American campaign consultants who began coming to the UK to advise British politicians. Ronald Reagan's pollster Dick Wirthlin started working with the Conservatives, Democrat strategist Rick Ridder began his long association with the Liberal Democrats, and President Kennedy's former adviser Joe Napolitan was hired by Labour.

Joe Napolitan had been the consultant who helped invigorate Hubert Humphrey's 1968 campaign partly through making a stirring biopic, "What Manner of Man," that focused on the private side of the public figure. The same technique was memorably adopted by Labour in the 1987 general election with the production of a PEB that became popularly known as "Kinnock: The Movie" (Wring, 2005). The film, directed by *Chariots of Fire* director Hugh Hudson, departed from British conventions by devoting itself to profiling the leader and was emblazoned with his name and not that of the party. This increasingly presidential approach was underlined when John Schlesinger, who made the classic film *Midnight Cowboy*, shot a feature on Prime Minister John Major called "The Journey" in which Thatcher's successor was chauffeured around parts of South London and talked about his humble background growing up there. This trend in personalized political advertising, long a feature of American elections, was confirmed in 1997 when another director Molly Dineen, a specialist documentary maker, followed and filmed hours of "fly on the wall" style footage of Tony Blair before editing selected highlights together. The effect was to create the impression of a youthful, dynamic leader who was also a dedicated family man. Subsequent political leaders, notably David Cameron, have emulated this approach in campaign communications including their PEBs.

Marginal Effect?

Like its commercial counterpart, political advertising is widely believed to be of limited value in terms of being able to persuade audiences and change behavior. This is because recipients of such messages tend to be aware that the information being presented has been created by the originating source for the obvious purposes of influencing them. By definition what is being communicated is partial and therefore questioned. But this has not stopped strategists in the US and elsewhere from continuing to invest vast finances in the medium. The most obvious rationale is because to not do so would cede a potentially invaluable advantage to the opposition should they continue to advertise. This alone does not explain the ongoing popularity of this kind of campaigning. Rather strategists still devote considerable time and money to crafting television spots to be aired on mainstream television as a means of reaching so-called "low involvement" citizens who, although largely uninterested in politics, are habitual media consumers who tend to vote. Within this group "floaters," that is those most likely to switch allegiance between elections, are vigorously targeted with adverts shown alongside conventional commercials in between programs selected because of their widespread or niche popularity among certain demographic groups. In the British context, with the ban on politicians purchasing airtime, televised appeals take for the form of PEBs. This necessarily limits their efficacy because audiences, particularly those consisting of low (or lower) involvement voters, are easily able to avoid seeing the broadcasts. This is because the minutes-long slots are required to be prefaced with a formal introduction; albeit this is now shorter than the original "There Now Follows a PEB from …," a prompt that a strategist working on the first "TV election" of 1959 recognized was a major turn-off for many viewers.

As has already been noted, the major broadcasters are still obliged to provide politicians with free airtime including during elections. Some prominent figures in the media industry such as Peter Bazalgette resent this continuing practice, not least because they think it outdated for schedulers to be compelled to accommodate such "dull and boring" fare given the advent of phenomena like YouTube (Settle, 2009; see also Scammell & Langer, 2006). Although some strategists might agree with Bazalgette they nonetheless persist with PEBs because they constitute a public subsidy in kind. Further to this, parties increasingly use the slots to air extracts of material available on their online platforms including YouTube channels. During the postwar era the (by a long way) third placed Liberals traditionally benefitted from the increased exposure during election time on television and PEBs were a part of this extended coverage (Blumler & McQuail, 1968). More recently, beneficiaries of this kind have been those parties that have gained support at the expense of their larger counterparts. Leaders of the SNP, UKIP and Greens have, in particular, appreciated the opportunity to reach and directly address potential supporters unmediated by any editorial interference from journalists. And even though PEBs may be of potentially limited value in campaign terms compared to news coverage and other forms of media exposure, the broadcasts have provided millions of prospective voters with information direct from the party source (Norris, Curtice, Sanders, Scammell, & Semetko, 1999).

Since 1979, there was a marked decline in the focus on issues in part because of the various experimentations with the PEB format (Gunter, Kostas, & Campbell, 2006). This in part reflects the way by then truncated broadcasts were regularly a quarter or less the time of their more policy dense equivalents during the 1950s. But regardless of differing styles of approach, many of which have been incorporated in attempts to capture the public imagination, the question remains as to whether the present format can survive as a viable method of political communication. The challenge for contemporary politicians and their strategists was to identify and cultivate voters in a rapidly changing media landscape where audiences were beginning to increasingly fragment. For roughly 40 years from the 1950s a few terrestrial channels counted for most viewers' television experience (Scammell, 1990); but the rise of satellite, cable and online services has meant audiences can obviously more easily avoid political content, including PEBs.

Audience desertion from news and current affairs has led to parties distributing VHS tapes and then DVDs in the 100 or so so-called "swing seats" that are prone to changing allegiance and that historically have decided the national electoral outcome. Labour, for instance, used this approach to strongly promote Blair's leadership credentials in his first victory of 1997 before switching to provide voters with individualized films about their by now incumbent MP in the subsequent triumphs of 2001 and 2005 (Electoral Commission, 2005). The PEB has nonetheless outlasted the brief fashion for distributing DVDs although the films themselves have been further reduced and in the most recent general elections of 2010 and 2015 most of the parties used two- to four-minute opportunities to promote themselves. Several of these broadcasts were reproduced on the party's own websites as well as YouTube and other channels where further information about the personalities and issues featured in them could be explored. PEBs, not to mention British broadcasting, have come a long way from their Reithian origins. But the free-to-air slots remain if only because they provide a low-cost opportunity for politicians. Such promotions can and do feature in the wider online viral campaigns.

Regulatory Issues

In Britain, as has been noted, there is a long-standing regulatory tradition whereby broadcasting is subject to laws ensuring "due impartiality" when television and radio journalists are covering politics. The BBC's oversight body was originally the Board of Governors, later re-launched as the Trust in 2007. Commercial and other broadcasters are regulated by Ofcom, the UK organization covering most media and communication formed in 2003. The latter body replaced various others previously responsible for monitoring outputs including political reporting and PEBs. These regulators' work has been made more complex by recent developments involving the fragmentation of support for what were once the dominant Labour and Conservative politicians and the rise of several more formidable electoral alternatives. Once routinely labeled "minor" these parties now command and retain not insignificant backing: in some cases, their rapid rise to prominence has tasked the regulators with having to make some controversial decisions. Ofcom's decision to grant what it labels "major party status" to the once fringe United Kingdom Independence Party (UKIP) in advance of the 2015 general election provoked debate. Despite polling only 3% in the previous national campaign of 2010 the party had nonetheless picked up enough support to place them first in the 2014 European elections. This provided the UKIP leadership with momentum going into the 2015 general election and enabled them to gain PEB airtime comparable to their political rivals for the first time. Other parties also qualified, albeit more on account of the numbers of candidates they were standing rather than their previous levels of electoral support.

Prior to World War II there were few PEBs. Moreover, the new monopoly BBC service was often criticized by politicians from across the partisan spectrum who argued their party was poorly served by the existing system either because of its limitations or alleged bias. During the 1930s one leading Labour figure, Herbert Morrison, even suggested his colleagues should explore the possibility of purchasing airtime on the increasingly popular Radio Luxembourg, a station broadcasting in to the UK from continental Europe and therefore free from domestic legal restriction (Wring, 2005). This did not happen but the increasing popularity of radio continued to exercise debate among politicians and led to the formation of the Committee on Party Political Broadcasts in 1947. It was convened by the main parties and traditionally involved the senior figure of the Chief Whip from the Labour, Liberal and Conservative parties together with representatives from the BBC who were later joined by colleagues from the newly formed ITV. The Committee was not a proactive body because there was general agreement for continuing with the arrangements established when PEBs were first introduced in 1924, specifically that there should be fair access to the airwaves for the main electoral protagonists. The formula that has been adopted to allocate airtime does, however, differentiate between larger and smaller parties by acknowledging the number of seats being contested together with votes won (Negrine, 1989, p. 170). More recently programmers have also had to take account of polling trends due to the fluctuating levels of support for certain alternatives, most notably UKIP. The range of politicians gaining the right to at least one broadcast increased during the 1970s onwards with the notable fall in the combined Conservative/Labour vote. In recent decades, what were once "minor" parties have come to greater prominence in campaigns. UKIP's success in receiving an eighth of the vote in the 2015 general election together with the SNP winning an unprecedented 56 out of the 59 MPs elected north of the border in the same poll has considerably strengthened their case for more PEB airtime in future campaigns.

There have been periodic reviews of the PEB system, most notably under the supervision of the UK Electoral Commission. These have considered the case for ending the provision of free airtime to parties but also confirmed the long-standing ban on paid political advertising on radio and television. This reflects the public service ethos of British broadcasting as well as the consensus among politicians, particularly those not in or aspiring to government, that PEBs provide an additional platform that would otherwise be prohibitively expensive to purchase at commercial rates. Broadcasts represent the continuing commitment to offer a protected space for political actors to communicate in a more complex and crowded media environment (Rozenberg, 2013). Threats to the continuation of the present arrangements come from those advocating a significant liberalization of regulations including the dilution of the laws requiring radio and television news outputs to be impartial. Should this happen it would likely be as part of a wider series of changes potentially involving the privatization of some BBC divisions. Paid political advertisements might logically follow because the existing ban on them could be challenged as a restriction on the freedom of expression.

A further threat to the ban on paid political advertising has emerged from changes in the UK legal system. In 2013, the European Court of Human Rights in Strasbourg was called on to adjudicate in a case brought by an animal rights group seeking the right to buy airtime in order to broadcast on commercial television. The campaigners' advert was controversial, featuring a young girl acting as a caged primate. The Court's adjudication was, however, concerned with the legal context rather than the specific content and upheld the UK's existing ban on American-style paid spots of the kind this particular ad, should it have been aired, would have represented. Critically the ruling accepted the campaign involved a "political" organization, a category of group specifically mentioned in the existing UK Communications Act of 2003. But perhaps most intriguingly the adjudication came about after deliberations and the closest of votes with nine to eight in favor. Should this (or a future) verdict have resulted in a different outcome the Electoral Reform Society warned the result would have led to an "arms race" of campaign spending primarily driven by the most wealthy interest groups (BBC, 2013).

The UK's current regulator, Ofcom, has primary responsibility for the media having emerged during the period and debates that produced the 2003 Act. The body is required by parliament to oversee the maintenance and enforcement of the official Broadcasting Code covering commercial radio and television and, in particular, what were once formally designated the "terrestrial" channels – ITV, Channel 4 and Five – as well as leading satellite outlets such as Sky News (Ofcom, 2015). Currently separate regulatory arrangements cover the BBC in the guise of its own Trust but these are set to change with Ofcom taking over the role. In theory, the two regulators could have acted independently of one another in matters pertaining to PEBs over the last decade or more. However, in practice they have worked closely together in the Broadcasters Liaison Group that includes representatives from the Electoral Commission as well as services operating in each nation of the UK. The Group helps coordinate its members' activities in this regard and ensured a coherent and consistent approach has been taken in allocating airtime to parties. This has meant the committee interpreting the various regulations governing the different broadcasters and taking account of the BBC guidelines as well Ofcom's Party Political and Referendum Broadcasts (PPRB) rules. The Group consequently devised a common set of guidelines for the allocation, length and frequency of PEBs and identified the channels required to transmit them.

Ofcom has an important responsibility for adjudicating whether a given electoral rival has "major" status and, by definition, whether others can be regarded as more minor parties although the latter description is not formally used. This has significance in terms of the amount of news coverage broadcasters are required to offer the different organizations. UK law requires providers comply with rules requiring radio and television journalism to exercise due impartiality as explained in Ofcom's Broadcasting Code and the BBC guidelines. The directives are also important in terms of PEB allocations. According to the PPRB, major parties should be offered at least two slots on the so-called Channel 3, the UK's main commercial service, which in practice means ITV1 in England and Wales, and Scottish TV and Ulster TV for the other nations. The same applied to Channel 4 and Five as well as the major non-BBC radio stations, Absolute, Talksport and Classic FM. During the 2015 general election the two largest parties, Labour and Conservative, received five PEBs each in England. Their main opponents, the Liberal Democrats and UKIP, were granted four and three respectively with the Greens qualifying for two. England aside, major party status is enjoyed in the other nations by a wider range of contenders including the Scottish Nationalists, Plaid Cymru (the Party of Wales) and various Northern Irish rivals. There are separate recommendations for smaller parties which, if they qualify, have received a single PEB because they have been able to field candidates to stand in at least a sixth of the seats being contested (BBC, 2015). This principle applies to each of the UK nations and so when the Cannabis is Safer than Alcohol party was able to stand four parliamentary candidates in Northern Ireland, the smallest country, it afforded this new fringe group the right to a PEB to be aired in the province's 18 constituencies.

Although increasingly produced by marketing experts, PEBs are not subject to the Advertising Standards' Authority's Code governing the content of television and radio commercials. PEBs are of course advertisements in the conventional sense that they are wholly controlled by their sponsors, the rival political parties, but are not technically paid for spots because the airtime continues to be granted free of charge. However, the growing fluidity in British electoral politics has meant an ever changing range of organizations qualifying for a broadcast and with this some occasional controversy regarding their content. Whereas mainstream parties tend to avoid producing material that might alienate viewers some of their smaller rivals relish provoking a reaction. In the 1997 general election broadcasters refused to show the anti-abortion ProLife Alliance's PEB because of the graphic medical content (Cull, 1997). Censorship has also been applied to parts rather than the whole of a film. For instance, in the 2014 European campaign, a PEB of the far right British National Party (BNP) was shown but subjected to the obscuring of certain scenes that were deemed racially offensive toward Muslims. The BNP subtitled their film to make clear they had been forced to make the alterations and encouraged the public to view the original version online.

The BNP's publicizing of the online version of its 2014 PEB demonstrated the potential of "viral" campaigns whereby the televised edition could be used to encourage voters to access related, more extensive material on the web. There are as yet no regulations governing online election campaign content or spending, although in practice mainstream politicians tend to carefully monitor their own digital outputs to ensure this kind of advertising does not bring them in to disrepute. In practice, parties have increasingly begun to invest in social media or video-sharing websites to disseminate the kind of American-style spots currently banned on television and radio (Wring & Ward, 2015). During the 2015 general election, for instance, the Conservatives spent hundreds of thousands of pounds on video clips (some as little as 16 seconds long) to try and reach millions on Facebook. One commentator described it as "unmediated media" where "party spin trumps press spin" (Greenslade, 2015). The point was underlined by a BBC report showing that, in the year leading up to polling day, the Conservatives spent £100,000 per month on Facebook advertising including paying for email collection to target potential voters. Furthermore, an estimated average of £3,000 online was spent on targeting within key individual constituencies (Hawkins, 2015). By comparison Labour's social media advertising spend was approximately a tenth of this amount.

Conclusion

The UK system of political advertising in the guise of the PEB has proved to be surprisingly enduring. Since first appearing on radio during the 1924 general election and on television in the 1951 campaign the format has developed and been subject to several innovations. Most obviously, the content has moved away from the traditional single talking head approach that was long associated with the PEB. But it would be an over-simplification to suggest the formats, particularly on television, were ever so one-dimensional. Rather two of the three earliest broadcasts featured double acts and both included at least one presenter with the experience to exploit a still young medium. Although quaint by modern standards these innovations nonetheless point to greater sophistication on the part of those involved than is sometimes appreciated, especially compared to the professional marketers who later on increasingly took responsibility for producing the films and used the opportunity to promote themselves as well as their political clients.

It remains to be seen how long the current arrangements for PEBs will endure. Should, as seems likely, the BBC continue to experience reductions in its budget as well as greater competition from commercial rivals both domestically and internationally, this will likely contribute to further fragmentation in audiences for what were once mainstream services. Given this scenario, the wisdom of maintaining the present arrangements whereby politicians are afforded state subsidies in kind will be challenged by broadcasters. Programmers are likely to question the maintenance of what they will see as a costly (to them, at least) anachronism that increasingly fails to engage the voting public beyond the older, more politically engaged citizens who take an active interest in news and current affairs broadcasting. Certain strategists, particularly on the right, might also argue for the further liberalization of broadcasting involving an end to the ban on paid election advertising or, as they will likely argue, "freedom of expression." The result will almost inevitably lead to the introduction of the kind of shorter campaign spot seen elsewhere. It is debatable, however, whether these commercials will ever reach the mass audiences once experienced by the longer form PEBs that have been in existence for almost a century.

References

Antcliffe, J. (1984). The politics of the airwave. *History Today*, March, pp. 4–10.

BBC. (2013, April 22). Electoral court upholds UK political advert ban. Retrieved from www.bbc.co.uk/news/uk-politics-22238582 [accessed November 25, 2015].

BBC. (2015). Party Election Broadcasts in 2015 – final allocation criteria: General Election and local elections. Retrieved from www.bbc.co.uk/bbctrust/our_work/editorial_standards/peb_allocation [accessed November 25, 2015].

Black, L. (2010). *Redefining British politics: Culture, consumerism and participation, 1954–70*. Basingstoke: Palgrave Macmillan.

Blumler, J., & McQuail, D. (1968). *Television in politics: Its uses and influence*. London: Faber & Faber.

Butler, D. (1995). *British general elections since 1945* (2nd ed.). Oxford: Blackwell.

Butler, D., & Butler, G. (2010). *British political facts* (10th ed.). Basingstoke: Palgrave Macmillan.

Cockerell, M. (1989). *Live from Number 10: The inside story of prime ministers and television*. London: Faber & Faber.

Cull, N. (1997). Censored! The Pro-Life Alliance. *Historical Journal of Film, Radio and Television*, 4, 515–522.

Day, B. (1982). The politics of communication, or the communication of politics. In R. Worcester & M. Harrop (Eds.), *Political communications: The general election of 1979*. London: George Allen and Unwin.

Electoral Commission (2005). *Election 2005: Engaging the public in Great Britain: An analysis of campaigns and media coverage*. London: Electoral Commission.

Gamble, A. (1974). *The Conservative nation*. London: Routledge Kegan and Paul.

Gould, P. (1998). *The unfinished revolution*. London: Little Brown.

Greenslade, R. (2015, April 12). General election uncertainty sets news cycle spinning. *The Guardian*. Retrieved from www.theguardian.com/media/2015/apr/12/general-election-press-tv-facebook-twitter [accessed November 25, 2015].

Gunter, B., Kostas, S., & Campbell, V. (2006). The changing nature of party election broadcasts: The growing influence of political marketing. Discussion papers in mass communication, Department of Media and Communication, University of Leicester. Retrieved from https://lra.le.ac.uk/bitstream/2381/845/1/mc06-1.pdf [accessed November 25, 2015].

Harmer, E., & Wring, D. (2013). Julie and the cybermums: Marketing and women voters in the UK 2010 general election. *Journal of Political Marketing*, 12(2–3), 262–273.

Hawkins, R. (2015, February 5). Tories' £100,000 a month Facebook bill. *BBC News*. Retrieved from www.bbc.co.uk/news/uk-politics-31141547 [accessed November 25, 2015].

Hollins, T. (1981). The presentation of politics: The place of party publicity, broadcasting and film in British politics. Unpublished Ph.D., University of Leeds.

Mitchell, J. (2015). Sea change in Scotland. *Parliamentary Affairs*, 68(supplement 1), 88–100.

Negrine, R. (1989). *Politics and the mass media in Britain* (2nd ed.). London: Routledge.

Negrine, R. (2011). British party election broadcasts in the 1950s: What was the American influence? *Media History*, 17(4), 389–403.

Norris, P., Curtice, J., Sanders, D., Scammell, M., & Semetko, H. (1999). *On message: Communicating the campaign*. London: Sage.

Ofcom. (2015). Ofcom broadcasting code guidance. London: Ofcom. Retrieved from http://stakeholders.ofcom.org.uk/broadcasting/guidance/programme-guidance/bguidance/ [accessed November 25, 2015].

Ostrogorski, M. J. (1902). *Democracy and the organization of political parties*. New York, NY: Macmillan.

Rees, L. (1992). *Selling politics*. London: BBC Books.

Reith, J. C. W. (1924). *Broadcast over Britain*. London: Hodder & Stoughton.

Rose, R. (1967). *Influencing voters: A study of campaign rationality*. London: Faber & Faber.

Rosenbaum, M. (1997). *From soapbox to soundbite: Party political campaigning in Britain since 1945*. Basingstoke: Macmillan.

Rozenberg, J. (2013). Government will be mightily relieved at decision to uphold political ads ban. Retrieved from www.theguardian.com/law/2013/apr/22/government-relieved-decision-political-ad [accessed November 25, 2015].

Scammell, M. (1990). Political advertising and the broadcasting revolution. *Political Quarterly*, 61(2), 200–213.

Scammell, M. (1995). *Designer politics: How elections are won.* Basingstoke: Macmillan.

Scammell, M., & Langer, A. (2006). Political advertising: Why is it so boring? *Media, Culture and Society*, 28(5), 763–784.

Settle, M. (2009, May 6). Are election broadcasts a turn off? *BBC News.* Retrieved from http://news.bbc.co.uk/1/hi/uk_politics/8036645.stm [accessed November 25, 2015].

Seymour-Ure, C. (1974). *The political impact of the mass media.* London: Constable.

Tunstall, J. (1964). *The advertising man in London advertising agencies.* London: Chapman & Hall.

Van Biezen, I., Mair, P., & Poguntke, T. (2012). Going, going, … gone? The decline of party membership in contemporary Europe. *European Journal of Political Research*, 51, 24–56.

Wallas, G. (1910). *Human nature in politics* (2nd ed.). London: Constable.

Wring, D. (2005). *The politics of marketing the Labour party.* Basingstoke: Macmillan Palgrave.

Wring, D., & Ward, S. (2015). Exit velocity: The media election. *Parliamentary Affairs*, 68, 224–240.

PART III

Purchase of Airtime for Electoral Advertising

19

BULGARIA

Election Advertising in Mediatized Politics

Lilia Raycheva

Introduction

The Republic of Bulgaria is located in Southeast Europe and borders on five other countries: Romania to the north (mostly along the Danube), Serbia and the Republic of Macedonia to the west, and Greece and Turkey to the south. The Black Sea defines the extent of the country to the east. The resident population is 7,202,798, grouped into about 3,000,000 households, on a territory of 110,910 km². It consists of Bulgarians (84%), Turks (9%), Roma (5%), and others (2%). The large majority of the population (84%) professes the Eastern Orthodox faith, while 12% are Muslims. The official language is Bulgarian and the official alphabet is Cyrillic. The present urban inhabitants amount to 70.6% of the Bulgarian population, and the rural ones to 29.4% (National Statistical Institute, 2015b).

The period of transformation to democracy and market economy, which started in 1989, has posed significant social challenges to the people of Bulgaria. The transition was slowed down by delayed legislation, aggressive political behavior and underdeveloped markets. All this caused rapid impoverishment, a high rate of unemployment and a loss of established social benefits such as free health care and free education. Thus the country lost the momentum generated by the rapid pace of democratic reforms and entered the 21st century under a Currency Board. Among the major political achievements during that transformation period of more than 25 years were the stabilization of pluralistic political life in the country, joining of NATO in 2004, and accession to the EU in 2007 (Raycheva, 2009). Despite these achievements, the pace of development was not satisfactory. In many parameters, Bulgaria ranks at the bottom of the list of the 28 member countries of the European Union. In 2014 GDP per capita was €5,800 – less than half the EU-28 average (Eurostat, 2015).

According to the World Bank, Bulgaria is an industrialized upper-middle-income country. The Gross Domestic Product (GDP) amounted to €42 billion in 2014. The average monthly salary was settled at 882 Leva (€451). The national currency – Lev (BGN) – is pegged to the euro at a fixed rate of 1.95583 Leva for 1 euro. However, the Lev is considered to be among the strongest and most stable currencies in Eastern Europe (World Bank, 2015).

Since the beginning of 2008, the Bulgarian income tax is a flat rate of 10%, being one of the lowest income rates in the world and the lowest income rate in the European Union. As of January 2007, the corporate income tax has also been kept at the flat rate of 10%, which makes it one of the lowest in Europe.

Data from the National Statistical Institute shows that the number of employed persons in 2014 was 2,166,199. The number of unemployed amounted to 300,900 and the unemployment rate in 2015 was 10.1% (National Statistical Institute, 2015a).

The Country Report on Bulgaria for 2015 by the European Commission states that the country is experiencing excessive macroeconomic imbalances, which require decisive policy action and specific monitoring. The Commission has made five country-specific recommendations to Bulgaria to help it improve its economic performance. These recommendations are in the areas of: fiscal consolidation, taxation and health; the financial sector; the labor market and wage-setting; education; and insolvency (European Commission, 2015).

The Political System

During a period of a little more than 20 years, Bulgarian citizens voted 26 times (on average, once yearly). Starting with the vote for the Grand National Assembly (in 1990), there were six presidential elections (in 1992, 1996, 2001, 2006, 2011 and 2016), eight parliamentary elections (in 1991, 1994, 1997, 2001, 2005, 2009, 2013 and 2014), seven local elections (in 1991, 1995, 1999, 2003, 2007, 2011 and 2015), three European parliamentary elections (in 2007, 2009 and 2014), three referenda and the appointment of 15 governments.

In normative terms, political life in Bulgaria is based mainly on the Constitution, the Election Code and the Political Parties Act. After the country's accession to the European Union, election rules have been harmonized with the European Community law – *acquis communautaire*.

The new Constitution was adopted by the Grand National Assembly on July 12, 1991. Under its terms, Bulgaria is a republic with a parliamentary system of government. Elections and national and local referenda are based on universal, equal and direct elections by secret ballot. Article 11 stipulates that: (1) Political life shall be based on the principle of political pluralism; (2) No single political party or ideology may be proclaimed or asserted as being that of the state ... (4) Political parties may not be founded on ethnic, racial, or religious grounds, nor shall it be permitted to found a party which seeks to assume state power by violent means. And further on: Citizens who are age 18 or older, with the exception of those who are legally incapacitated or serving prison sentences, have the right to elect state and local authorities and to participate in public referenda (Article 42 (1), National Assembly…, 1991).

After the accession of the country to the European Union in 2007, this Article of the Constitution was supplemented in the Election Code with the rules about the right to elect members to the European Parliament as well as with the rules about the right of the EU citizens to participate in local elections in Bulgaria.

The Election Code defines the organization and the procedures for holding elections for president and vice president of the Republic; members of the national parliament; members of the European Parliament from Bulgaria; municipal councillors, mayors and city councils. Article 4 provides that the right to be elected national representative shall be vested in any Bulgarian citizen over the age of 21 years by the polling day, who does not hold another citizenship, is not under indictment and is not in prison. As a member country of the European Union, the Bulgarian Election Code provides further requirements for the right to be elected member of the European Parliament for the Republic of Bulgaria, as well as for the right to be elected municipal Councillor and mayor, based on the length of residence of the candidate in the Republic of Bulgaria or in another member country of the European Union (National Assembly…, 2011).

Bulgaria has a multi-party political system. The Political Parties Act regulates the establishment, registration, organization, activity and dissolution of political parties. According to Article 15, every political party shall be registered in the Public Register of Political Parties with the Sofia City Court. Although, according to this Article, publicity of the Register shall be ensured by the website of the

Court in compliance with the Law on Protection of Personal Data, so far information about the political parties is not available on the website of the Court.

The Act provides also that the activities of political parties shall be financed from their own income and from a state subsidy. They have no right to incorporate or participate in commercial companies and cooperatives. The state subsidy is granted annually in four equal instalments to fund proportionally the political parties or coalitions that have registered at the Central Election Commission, have participated in the previous parliamentary elections, and have elected MPs. State subsidy is also granted annually to parties that are not represented in the National Assembly, but have received at least 1% of all valid votes in the previous parliamentary elections. Financial control over the activities of political parties and the management of property made available to them is exercised by the National Audit Office. Political parties are subject to administrative and penal provisions (National Assembly..., 2005).

According to Article 6 of the Political Parties Act, political parties conduct their public events, make public addresses and draw up their documents in the Bulgarian language. This is a very important requirement, especially during election campaigns. Article 133(2) of the Election Code reconfirms this provision in the canvassing procedure, requiring that election campaigns shall be conducted in the Bulgarian language. This legal requirement is most often violated by the political party Movement for Rights and Freedoms, which canvasses in Turkish – the mother tongue of most of its supporters.

Article 92 of the Bulgarian Constitution provides that the president is head of state. He embodies the unity of the nation and represents the Republic of Bulgaria in international relations. In his work, the president is assisted by a vice president (National Assembly..., 1991). The president is elected directly by the people for a term of five years. The president and vice president may be re-elected to their positions only once. Every Bulgarian citizen by birth, who is 40 years of age, who is eligible to be a member of parliament, and has resided in the country for the past five years, is eligible to run for president. The last requirement was used to block any possible attempts on the part of Tsar Simeon II, the Bulgarian monarch in exile who lived in Madrid, Spain, to run for head of state in 2001. The presidency is an autonomous institution within the system of state authorities. The president's powers are set out in the Constitution. The head of state does not belong to any of the three branches of authority – legislative, executive and judicial – but interacts with each of them (President..., 2015). The president of the Republic schedules elections for National Assembly, for members of the European Parliament and for local administrative bodies, as well as for national referenda decided upon by the National Assembly.

The Grand National Assembly is a specialized legislative institution in Bulgaria. In comparison with the National Assembly it has exclusive rights to decide a certain range of issues. Article 158 of the Constitution provides that a Grand National Assembly may be convened for matters of special jurisdiction, such as: adoption of a new Constitution; amendment of certain articles of the Constitution, e.g., those related with the basic civil rights; changes in the territory (gain or loss) of the Republic, etc. According to the latest Constitution, adopted in 1991, it consists of 400 deputies (200 members being elected by proportional representation and the other 200 by majority vote) (National Assembly..., 1991). The Grand National Assembly can also serve as an ordinary National Assembly, taking care of regular legislative activities, in urgent cases only. After it has concluded its work on the matter for which it was elected, the Grand National Assembly is dissolved *ex lege* and the president of the Republic appoints elections for an ordinary National Assembly (National Assembly..., 1990).

The National Assembly is the unicameral parliament of the country, which deals with the legislation and exercises the parliamentary control over the government. It consists of 240 members elected for a four-year term mainly by proportional representation in multi-seat constituencies with a 4% total vote threshold. The National Assembly is responsible for the enactment of laws, approval of the budget, scheduling of presidential elections, selection and dismissal of the prime minister and other ministers, declaration of war, concluding of peace and deployment of troops outside Bulgaria, and the ratification of international treaties and agreements. Article 86 of the Constitution provides that the

National Assembly passes laws, resolutions, declarations and appeals. The laws and resolutions passed by the parliament are binding for all state authorities, organizations and citizens.

The parliament also has a constitutive function, connected to its power to approve the structure of the Council of Ministers as proposed by the prime minister as well as appointments to high government positions. In case it is not possible to form a government, the newly elected National Assembly is dissolved by the president. The same happens when the current government ends its mandate ahead of schedule. In both cases, the president appoints a caretaker government and schedules new elections.

Members of the European Parliament (MEPs) are elected for five-year terms by direct universal suffrage and proportional representation. Currently, Bulgaria has 17 MEPs out of the total of 751. The Commissioner at the 28-member European Commission is nominated by the National Government.

According to Article 19 of the Administration Act, the bodies of executive power are central and territorial. The central executive bodies are: Council of Ministers; prime minister; deputy prime ministers; and the other ministers. The regional bodies of executive power are: the governors, the mayors of districts and the deputy mayors (National Assembly…, 1998).

Dynamics of the Media System

The Bulgarian Constitution guarantees freedom of expression to all citizens. Article 40(1) specifically defends freedom of the mass media, providing that the press and the other mass information media shall be free and shall not be subjected to censorship (National Assembly…, 1991). Of all institutions in the country, the mass media specifically contributed to the transformation to democracy and to a market-based economy in a rapid and profound way. The transition period has provided journalists with a strong hold on public opinion. Thus, the mass media system often operated as a Fourth Estate, influencing social attitudes, political opinions and decisions about national priorities (Raycheva, 2006, p. 361).

Although external media pluralism has been established in the country, the existence of many media providers is not a sufficient guarantee for the normal functioning of the market or for independent regulation or for the provision of widely varied and quality content. Research on the Bulgarian media environment by the European Commission, Transparency International, Balkan Media Barometer, IREX, Freedom House and Reporters without Borders abundantly criticizes the political dependency of the Bulgarian media. Unclear ownership and funding, attempts to exercise political and corporative influence, the inefficiency of the regulatory and self-regulatory mechanisms, and the deficit of professional standards compromise the concept of media pluralism (Raycheva, 2013b, pp. 151–152).

Political and media pluralism in Bulgaria still experiences systematic difficulties. Civil society – still in the making – fails to create a stable public basis for professional journalism. According to the World Press Freedom Index 2016, Bulgaria has dropped down to 113th place (out of 180 countries), which proves that freedom of speech and independent journalism is still vulnerable for most of the media outlets (Reporters without Borders, 2016). Although many non-government organizations disbursed funds from European and transatlantic institutions their activities proved erratic, limited and ineffective.

Data provided by the National Statistical Institute vividly show the trends in media development since 1989. In terms of print media, 301 newspapers (17 dailies) with annual circulation of 895,265,000 were published in 1989, as compared to 436 newspapers (70 dailies) with annual circulation of 370,789,000 20 years later, in 2008, after the country's accession to the European Union. The corresponding figures for magazines and bulletins were 827, with annual circulation of 57,849,000 in 1989 versus 775 with annual circulation of 14,708,000 in 2008. There has been a significant trend for preserving and even increasing diversification of supply, while considerably reducing circulation. Currently due to the economic crisis, the number of the print media has been reduced: 307

newspapers (54 dailies) with annual circulation of 324,310,000 and 668 magazines and bulletins with annual circulation of 27,831,000 are now available (National Statistical Institute, 2014).

In contrast to the turbulent transformation of print media, changes in the electronic media were slower, incomplete and lacking in general consistency. They started and were carried out in an atmosphere of deregulation – the Radio and Television Act, as well as the Telecommunications Act was not adopted until 1998. Both have been amended frequently. Bulgaria joined the Television without Frontiers Directive (1989) and subsequently ratified the European Union's Convention on Transfrontier Television (1997). Current media legislation has been closely aligned with EU regulations. The two national institutions that regulate the electronic media – the Council for Electronic Media (CEM) and the Communications Regulation Commission (CRC) – jointly issue radio and television licenses and register cable and satellite broadcasters. CEM (formerly the National Council for Radio and Television) is the regulatory body that monitors compliance with the Radio and Television Act, including such issues as advertising, sponsorship, product placement, copyright and protection of minors (Council for Electronic Media, 2012). The Council also considers complaints by citizens and organizations. It also appoints the management bodies of public service broadcasters. CRC (formerly the State Commission of Telecommunications) enforces the Telecommunications Act and manages the radio frequencies spectrum.

In the course of 25 years, a highly saturated radio and television landscape has been gradually established. Radio broadcasting has displayed an enormous increase. In 1988, prior to the political transition, some 46,810 hours of programming were aired. In 1989 the number had increased to 48,498 hours; in 1993 the introduction of private radio bounced the total number of on-air hours up to 161,278. By 2008, 20 years after the changes, the public was enjoying 797,683 hours of programming, more than 16 times the number of hours broadcast in 1988. Program supply has been strongly diversified. Dynamics of the structure and format of the programs is notable: news programs have drastically increased: from 19,090 hours in 1988 to 26,154 hours in 1989, 72,358 hours in 1994 and 92,070 hours in 2008 (National Statistical Institute, 2009b).

As compared to the other media, changes in television came much more slowly. Some major reasons for that included: a state monopoly over national telecasting; political pressures resulting in frequent replacements of television executives (in the course of 25 years, a succession of 15 General Directors headed the public National Television and only three of them have completed their term of office without suspension); the lack of research and development concepts and strategies; inefficient management; economic constraints, obsolete equipment, etc.

Television program dynamics were accompanied by several important trends. Television broadcasting has significantly increased. In 1988, prior to the transition, 5,886 hours of television programming were aired. A dramatic growth of 500 hours of telecasts was registered during the critical year of 1989. By 1994, when private television was officially introduced, audiences enjoyed 7,178 hours of television programming, while in 2008 the number of hours reached 747,036 – an increase of more than 120 times (National Statistical Institute, 2009a). The diversified program supply made for greater audience selectivity. Digitalization, mobile- and web-casting are the current technological challenges facing Bulgarian television broadcasters.

Although the advertising market is still not very big, the radio and television environment is oversaturated. Lack of clarity about the media ownership obscures how dependent the electronic media can be on political and business interests and their impact on media policies. A weak market, which fails to maintain the numerous licensed radio and television stations, has left an opening for companies with capital of doubtful origin. At the present moment, the legal, technological, regulatory and social framework is rather contradictory and often serves corporative interests.

In 2014, 337 radio stations and 187 television channels were present in the CEM public register, operating on national, regional and local level terrestrially, via cable or satellite. Radio and television broadcasting on the Internet is developing intensively (Council for Electronic Media, 2014). Privately owned radio- and television stations undoubtedly challenge the monopoly of state-owned public television. However, public service broadcasters still enjoy the greatest audience credibility: BNT is approved by 72.5% of the population and BNR by 58.6%, as compared to other institutions such as the police – 42.3%, the army – 41.9%, parliament – 23.4%, and the courts – 17.0% (National Center…, 2012).

The increasing popularity of the Internet during the last two decades has definitely impacted the media system. The online media business model, however, is still problematic. The combination of content sales, subscription fees and advertising revenues cannot generate sufficient income to assure the kind of trustworthy content variety for attracting larger audiences. Furthermore, the practices of Internet trolling, the publication of contradictory announcements in online discussion fora, aimed basically at provoking users, have become a top communication issue, particularly during election campaigns. Searching for their identity in the changing social and market environment, online and traditional media are more eagerly serving advertisers rather than audiences. Because of its quicker reaction to breaking news, online-only media has slowly but steadily taken over niches in the breaking news, competing successfully with traditional media. In addition, some citizen-generated content has entered the World Wide Web. Furthermore, almost every political leader has a presence in the online media, including web logs, social networks, sites of political parties and online television. These media are used intensively as channels of political populism in election campaigns (Raycheva, 2013a).

Besides the rapid pace of development of the online media and taking the public debate online, television is still the most trusted medium in Bulgarian society: 64% against 45% for the radio, 42% for the Internet and 35% for the press (European Parliament, 2014).

Mediatization of Politics and Politicization of Media

Dynamics of pre-election campaigns during the period of democratization since 1989 has been developing alongside demonopolization, liberalization and transformation of the media system. Deregulation of the radio and television broadcasting sector dragged on, giving way to the development of two mutually interdependent processes – politicization of media and mediatization of politics.

In spite of the fact that Bulgaria has taken considerable steps toward democratization, the political system faces an immense challenge owing to its unclear identity, both at conceptual and at representative level. The long years of one-party dominance were replaced by an ever-growing host of new political parties, unions and organizations, which constantly split, regrouped and entered into coalitions, especially on the eve of upcoming elections. The breakdown of the bipolar model (socialists versus democrats) with the aid of some newly formed structures of leadership, has failed to bring sustainability to the political system, which is weighed down by difficult economic and social tasks. Gradually, the situation of social disintegration and shortage of social synergy has become a good environment for the revival of populism, primarily by non-systemic political parties. The model of democracy established in the country delegated the difficult tasks of transition mainly to the political elite, thus eliminating the broad participation of the people in the process. Although superficially heterogeneous, the political as well as the media environment (especially during campaigns) are still not fully aware of the parameters of pluralism, or of independence (Raycheva, 2013b).

On the other hand, politicians fail to carry out the necessary reforms that would meet the European commitment of the country and the expectations of the people. Even the unique Bulgarian ethnic model, formed after long years of effort on the part of all ethnic groups and not by the contemporary parties and politicians, has been put to abusive purposes. The ever deeper gap between rulers and society has proved a grave obstacle for the trust and entrepreneurship of citizens. The absence of distinct program platforms encourages inter-party migration and erodes the foundations of political pluralism and decreasing election participation: from 90.79% in the first round of elections for the Grand National Assembly in 1990, to 28.6% in the first elections for European Parliament in Bulgaria in 2007, and further down to 20.22% for the First National Referendum in 2013 (Central Election Commission, 2015). Slowly but steadily, Bulgarian electors have refused to yield to the instruments of political, survey and media propaganda, have rejected joining the process of social imitation, and have acquired a position of active passiveness. As a result, the efforts of state regulation fail to effectively overcome self-regulation that can be traced back to the dawn of democratic changes achieved at the National Round Table, back in 1990. A telling example is the Code of Conduct for Election Campaigns, which forbids the offering, demanding, giving out, or promising any monetary amounts, or any other advantage for the elector's signature in support of, or for nomination of a candidate, or for voting in favor of any political party, movement or an independent candidate (National Round Table, 1990). The observance of this self-regulatory norm has proved unattainable for participants in the country's elections and thus, years later, it had to be legally decreed that the purchase and sale of votes is a criminal offense. However, this mantra, repeated as a must after every piece of political advertising, has failed to rid the country of the problem.

The process of transformation of legislation, its optimization, consolidation and harmonization with the EU *acquis communautaire* still suffers lapses in the formulation of clear definitions, decrees and effective documents for the organization and television coverage of the election campaigns. Thus, in the Election of the Grand National Assembly Act (1990), only one article explained candidate access to the BNT – the public service broadcaster. In 1994, its regional radio and television centers were also allowed to take part in political campaigning. In 1997, commercial television broadcasters joined in election advertising. Regulation of the election campaigns was described in detail in 24 articles of the Election Code of 2011, as well as in its revision of 2014. Nevertheless, legislation and regulatory practices of the various election campaigns have not been structured with sufficient precision and often the Central Election Commission had to specify their conduct. Political forces that have parliamentary representation are still in a more favorable position with respect to media access than those that are outside the national or the European Parliament. The opinion of the growing number of non-voters is neglected.

Financial sanctions for unregulated violation of the legal norms during elections are strangely low and ineffective for achieving free, fair and democratic elections as well as fair media coverage of the process of the national campaign. Attempts at coordinated self-regulation between the parties, pollsters, PR agencies, media, non-government sector and the academic community have proved fragile and unstable. It appears that the legislative framework will have to be revised and the regulatory application will have to be improved for effective functioning of the political system.

Forms of Television Political Advertising

Since the turn of the century, all elections (parliamentary, presidential, local and for MEPs) have been conducted under the conditions of a competitive media system strategically used for political campaigning. Both campaigns and election returns, however, manifested grave professional problems in the domain of public opinion surveys and media that have failed to meet the requirement for unbiased information and predictability of election results. The paradox is that parliament (2001, 2005 and 2013) and president (2001) were elected contrary to public opinion forecasts. A steady tendency toward low voter turnout has occurred in all elections.

For more than a quarter of a century, political, economic and social upheavals notably impacted the development of the mass media system in Bulgaria producing rapid and flexible reactions to social processes. The significance of media was manifested in several critical situations during the years, including: the television attack against President Petar Mladenov in 1990 that compelled him to resign; the resignation of the BSP government headed by Andrey Loukanov in 1990; the mass media war launched by the UDF government of Filip Dimitrov, which led to its toppling in 1992; the exit of the government of Lyuben Berov (under the Movement for Rights and Freedom mandate) in 1994; the withdrawal of the BSP government of Zhan Videnov in 1996; the siege of the House of the National Assembly in the situation of a governmental crisis in 1997, which led to radical power shift; the forced restructuring of the UDF government of Ivan Kostov in 1999, based on corruption allegations; the attacks that brought about ministerial replacements in the Simeion Saxe Coburg-Gotha government in 2005 and in the three-party coalition (Coalition for Bulgaria, Movement for Rights and Freedoms and National Movement Simeon II) government of Sergei Stanishev; the constant corrective to the government of Boyko Borisov (Citizens for European Development of Bulgaria), and the wide coverage of social protests which led to an earlier resignation of this government in 2013; the coverage of pressure of the continuous social protests against the government of Plamen Oresharski (Coalition for Bulgaria), which also led to its earlier resignation in 2014.

Article 128 of the new Election Code provides that the campaigns for all types of elections shall be open 30 days before election day. A special chapter (with six sections and 34 articles) is dedicated to election canvassing procedures. Canvassing and publication of public opinion polls in connection is forbidden during a period commencing 24 hours in advance of polling day and on polling day. Each item of campaign material (print, audio- or audio-visual) has to contain a statement that vote buying and selling is a criminal offense. Surveys on election day are supposed to include brief information about their author and are supposed to be conducted outside the voting areas, the results being announced after 7:00 p.m. on election day.

According to the Election Code, the campaign in the press is not subject to such strict regulations as those for the electronic media, and especially for television. Since 2011 media service providers have been obliged to offer identical terms and rates to all parties, coalitions of parties and nomination committees registered to participate in the elections. These terms for prepaid services have to be published on the Internet site of the providers not later than 40 days in advance of election day. The process is closely monitored by the Bulgarian National Audit Office and the Central Election Commission. The Election Code imposes strict regulations on the financing and accountability of election campaigns.

The parties, the coalitions of parties and the nomination committees that have registered candidates may finance the election campaigns with their own financial resources, financial resources of the members of the nomination committees and of the candidates as well as contributions by individuals.

The purpose of political advertising is to promote and enforce political parties, personalities and ideas to the public. Usually it focuses on creating the image of the candidate, supporting the motto of the campaign or promoting the political products. It follows the practices of commercial advertising: induction, maintenance (affirmation) and reminder. In can also be construed on rational or irrational levels; with emotional or subliminal impact; with positive or negative calls. Over the years, a number of appeals to people to vote or refrain (especially in referenda) were included in the campaigns.

In Bulgaria the term "political advertising" is not subject to explicit legal regulation. The Election Code establishes the legal regime on election campaigning, which is a private case of political campaigning (National Assembly…, 2011). The Radio and Television Act only considers commercial ads (Council for Electronic Media, 2012). However, the concept of political advertising is widely used in public discourse. On the eve of the European Parliament elections in 2009 the Council for Electronic Media (CEM) adopted a Standpoint, which distinguishes political advertising from commercial ones. It announced that it will distinguish political advertising from other forms of election campaigning. The regulator sets the cumulative parameters of political advertising: a clear indication separating political ads from other program content; warning for the criminalization of buying and selling votes; direct election political advertising message, including negative ones and appeals for refraining from voting; ballot number/name of the candidates (Council for Electronic Media, 2009).

The Electoral Code differentiates three types of political campaigning: opening and closing campaign addresses, spots, and news briefs. Article 140 prohibits the use of elements of commercials in political advertising as well as participation of candidates and representatives of political parties, coalitions of parties and initiative committees in commercial ads, broadcast by the public service broadcasters – the Bulgarian National Television and the Bulgarian National Radio.

Public Service Broadcasters

Even tighter terms are imposed on the public service broadcasters (PSBs) – the Bulgarian National Television and the Bulgarian National Radio. They allocate time slots for campaigning and are restricted to the use of specific format of spots, news briefs and debates as well as other formats agreed to in advance. The PSBs are also obliged to respect the principles of equality and objectivity in covering the campaign appearances of the candidates. A special agreement signed between the representatives of the participants and the Directors General of the PSBs no later than 31 days in advance of the polling day specifies the production crews, the formats of appearance and the topics of the debates. The Central Election Commission determines the order of presentation of the candidates by publicly drawn lot for each format separately. Any political insinuation in commercial advertising to the benefit or to the detriment of any contestant in the elections is prohibited. The campaign broadcasts on the PSBs and their regional centers are prepaid before airing by the contestants according to a rate schedule determined by the Council of Ministers not later than 40 days in advance of polling day.

Opening and Closing Campaign Addresses

An important format for televised election campaigns are the presidential addresses of the candidates. Over the years, this form of political advertising has undergone a metamorphosis in its duration as well as in its presence within the different types of elections (Raycheva, 2006). Since 2011 only the campaigns for elections of president and vice president of the Republic are framed in the PSBs with these addresses. Their length for the first round is not supposed to exceed three minutes for each pair. In the second round, the candidates have the right to broadcast unpaid addresses not longer than ten minutes in the PSB program on the last day of the election campaign between the two rounds of voting. The order of the addresses is determined by lot according to a procedure established by the Central Election Commission.

Spots

Political advertising aims to present the priorities of a party and convince the electors to vote for it. Over the years it has filled in the paradoxical niche opened due to the fact that the electorate did not vote for specific political platforms, because they were not clearly articulated. Content analysis of election publicity spots shows that there is a strong similarity between the messages of the various political forces on several levels: pre-election slogans, general political messages, positive review of the work done by them.

Focused political ads on important social issues such as unemployment, social security, health, education, security, foreign policy, etc. are not a common phenomenon. During the European parliamentary elections campaigns national issues most often replace the issues of the European Community. Nationalist parties are those that present specific populist messages. Several stable trends can be traced down: the negative advertising, the number of broadcast commercials, the invested funds in political advertising and forecasts of pollsters do not affect the election results.

In all election campaigns the one-minute spots by the parties, coalitions of parties and nomination committees frame the PSBs. The assignment of time slots for the spots is determined by an agreement between the Directors General of the PSBs and authorized representatives of the participants.

The spots have been the most popular forms for political campaigning since the very beginning of democratic elections in the country in 1990. A public drawing of lots, televised live, determined the order of the broadcasting of video ads in the 1994 parliamentary election campaign. Until television coverage was allowed in the commercial sector at the turn of the century the terms of broadcasting the spots followed a similar pattern. The gratuitous enthusiasm of the earlier elections was replaced by appearances of famous pop-singers and football players in support of the respective political formations.

In addition to the opening and closing spots, the candidates have the right to provide to the PSBs other spots for the purpose of making them popular and soliciting voter support. The length of these spots, the time slot and the number of broadcasts is also determined by agreement at identical terms and identical rates.

News Briefs

Since the 1997 parliamentary election campaign another form has been added to political advertising on the PSBs: news briefs. They report the marches, meetings, concerts and other events organized by the participants in the elections and have an informative rather than an appealing character. The news briefs are conditioned on equal presentation of the parties, the coalitions of parties and the nomination committees, especially of those which lack sufficient creative and financial capacity to produce spots.

With the introduction of the Election Code of 2011, news briefs of no more than one minute in length, which cover the campaign appearances of the candidates, are broadcast daily. They are grouped into several blocks: for the parties and coalitions of parties represented in parliament; for the parties and coalitions of parties that have members in the European Parliament but are not represented in parliament; and for the non-parliamentary parties and coalitions of parties and the nomination committees which have registered candidates, respecting the principle of non-discrimination. Similar to the other forms of political advertising, the time slots for the broadcast of the news briefs are assigned by the above mentioned agreement.

Debates

Obviously, the most important form of political advertising on television for the campaigns of all elections is the debates on some of the country's important political, social and economic issues.

The Election Code of 2011 provides that the PSBs shall allot air time to the parties, the coalitions of parties and the nomination committees which have registered candidates for not fewer than three debates on topics coordinated in advance and of a length aggregating not less than 180 minutes. The debates may alternatively take place with the simultaneous participation of candidates and representatives of all parties, coalitions of parties and nomination committees. The time is distributed evenly among the participants.

As for the conduct of a second round in elections of president and vice president of the Republic, in the period between the two rounds of voting, by mutual agreement the candidates may hold an unpaid debate not exceeding 60 minutes within the appointed time on the PSB – the Bulgarian National Television and the Bulgarian National Radio. The presidential debate of Zhelyo Zhelev (UDF) and Velko Valkanov (BSP) in 1992 was the first debate aired live on television.

The program services of the regional radio and television centers of the PSBs (five for BNT and 10 for BNR) allot air time for a total of not less than 60 minutes for debates among the representatives of the parties, the coalitions of parties and the nomination committees that have registered candidates.

Commercial Broadcasters

The broad invasion of commercial media in political campaigning since the beginning of the new millennium has liberalized the rules for organizing campaigns, which previously has been assigned only to PSBs. The Election Code of 2011 provides that commercial broadcasters may also allot time for political advertising during the election campaign of the parties, the coalitions of parties and the nomination committees which have registered candidates on identical terms and at identical prepaid rates. Similar to the requirements for the PSBs these terms are supposed to be made public on the Internet site of the respective broadcaster not later than 40 days in advance of polling day. The terms, procedure and rate schedules should be provided to the monitoring authorities not later than 10 days before the start of the campaign transmissions.

The inclusion of the commercial media in the election campaigns allowed for more varied presentation by the participants. Many candidates preferred to meet the public on mainstream commercial media with their higher ratings.

Taking advantage of the liberalization of the rules for political advertising, some media managed to get involved in the political life of the country through their popular journalists. The case of the television program "Attack" broadcast by the cable television station SKAT is a telling example of how the television program built the basis of a new political formation of the same name, which had won the fourth (out of seven) position in the 40th National Assembly in 2005. Following the initiative of its leader – former television anchorman Volen Siderov – this political party has founded its own media pool, "Alpha" (television station, newspaper and news site). There was a similar case with the anchorman Nikolay Barekov who founded in 2014 the party "Bulgaria without Censorship" with the support of TV 7 of which he was executive director. Currently he is an MEP. Other famous journalists were elected MPs because of their active presence in the media.

Developing dynamically, commercial broadcasters also created a variety of forms used for political campaigning in reality shows and entertainment programs. Television appearances by politicians are quoted in other television programs, and then multiplied in the social networks.

Conclusion

In contemporary Bulgarian society, the media have become a main source of information about politics and a transmitter of political communication techniques. While developing under conditions of new technologies and new business models, they face a great challenge in retaining their social purpose. This task becomes ever more difficult to accomplish not only owing to the multi-channel character of communication, but also because of the growing selectivity of a fragmented audience, which has become active users, as both consumers and producers of information.

Thus the media, and especially television, involuntarily or on purpose have imposed on society a personalized matrix on the coverage of world events. The media increasingly sink into their own reality, removed from its genuine parameters. An interpenetration of the media, capital and politics – dangerous for democracy – has emerged, which leads to auto-censorship and distorts the functions of free journalism. Although the media system has drastically changed in a very short period, deregulation has lagged behind, commercialization and neglect of professional standards have distorted the normal functioning of the market and developed two interlinked processes: politicization of the media and mediatization of politics.

The country still lacks a stable foundation on which to test the maturity and professionalism of the media as a source information for voter decision-making in a representative democracy. The media environment has experienced a lack of self-regulation. The market mechanism is stronger than the norms of social responsibility and professional standards.

The robust factors that push the media away from democratic values and bring them into the orbit of obscure political and corporative interests are:

- vague legal framework of media legislation;
- formal application of the European Directive on Audiovisual Media Services;
- lack of adequate definition and regulation of political advertising;

- unregulated product placement of political subjects and of political markers for audio-visual identification;
- imprecise financial and program rules for the election campaigns which favor the commercial media outlets;
- unreliability of opinion surveys and conscious self-regulation inertness on the part of providers of media services;
- inadequate reactions of the non-government sector;
- de-professionalization of journalists and creative deficit in the audiovisual domain.

Analysis of political advertising in election campaigns in Bulgaria during the period of transition prompts the following inferences:

- although political pluralism has been established in the country after four decades of one-party rule, smaller political formations have a limited presence in political advertising, mainly due to financial and organizational reasons;
- competition among the mass media, including the Internet, is fully in progress. Public service broadcasters have to follow more restrictions concerning political campaigning than the commercial ones;
- although challenged by the Internet, television is still the most important medium for political advertising;
- political advertising is the most popular form for political campaigning in media in comparison to addresses, news briefs and debates;
- slowly but steadily creativity in the production of political ads plays a significant role in major forms of political marketing;
- the negative advertising, the number of broadcast commercials, the invested funds in political advertising and forecasts of pollsters do not affect the election results;
- a lack of perspective in advertising strategies is felt by almost all political groups.

Professional inadequacy and bias of some political scientists, pollsters and media professionals are often on display during campaigns. As a result, although considerable progress has been made in the audiovisual quality of political advertising products, the media system still fails to fulfill its major purpose in campaigns, namely, to inform society impartially and on equal footing about the participants and their platforms in political contests.

References

Central Election Commission. (2015). Archives. Retrieved from https://portal.cik.bg/.

Council for Electronic Media. (2009). Standpoint. Retrieved from www.cem.bg.

Council for Electronic Media. (2012). Radio and Television Act. Retrieved from www.cem.bg.

Council for Electronic Media. (2014). Public Register. Retrieved from www.cem.bg.

Council of Europe. (1985). European charter of local self-government. Retrieved from http://conventions.coe.int/Treaty/EN/Treaties/Html/122.htm.

European Commission. Directorate-General for Economic and Financial Affairs. (2015). Macroeconomic imbalances. Country report – Bulgaria 2015. Retrieved from http://ec.europa.eu/economy_finance/publications/occasional_paper/2015/pdf/ocp213_en.pdf.

European Parliament. (2014). Standard Eurobarometer 80: Media use in the European Union. Report. Retrieved from http://ec.europa.eu/public_opinion/archives/eb/eb80/eb80_media_en.pdf.

Eurostat. (2015). National accounts and GDP. Retrieved from http://ec.europa.eu/eurostat/statistics-explained/index.php/File:GDP_at_current_market_prices,_2003%E2%80%9304_and_2012%E2%80%9314_YB15.png.

National Assembly of the Republic of Bulgaria. (1990). Election of the Grand National Assembly Act. Spravochnik normativni aktove [Legislation Guide]. Retrieved from http://lex.bg/laws/ldoc/2132293633.

National Assembly of the Republic of Bulgaria. (1991). Constitution. Retrieved from www.parliament.bg/bg/const.

National Assembly of the Republic of Bulgaria. (1998). Administration Act. Retrieved from www.lex.bg/en/laws/ldoc/2134443520.

National Assembly of the Republic of Bulgaria. (2005). Political Parties Act. Retrieved from www.lex.bg/en/laws/ldoc/2135501352.

National Assembly of the Republic of Bulgaria. (2011). Election Code of Bulgaria. Retrieved from www.parliament.am/library/Electoral%20law/bulgaria.pdf.

National Center for Public Opinion Research. (2012). Socio-political preferences. Retrieved from www.parliament.bg/pub/NCIOM/Bul-02-2012_press.pdf.

National Round Table. (1990). Code of Conduct for Election Campaign. Retrieved from www.omda.bg/public/bulg/k_masa/dokumenti_round_table/ethical_code_campaign.htm.

National Statistical Institute. (2009a). Television programs in kind. Retrieved from www.nsi.bg/ORPDOCS/Culture_6.2.xls.

National Statistical Institute. (2009b). Radio programs in kind. Retrieved from www.nsi.bg/ORPDOCS/Culture_5.2.xls.

National Statistical Institute. (2014). Publishing activity: Books, newspapers and magazines. Retrieved from www.nsi.bg/en/content/4551/publishing-activity-books-newspapers-and-magazines.

National Statistical Institute. (2015a). Labor market. Retrieved from www.nsi.bg/en/content/6316/labour-market.

National Statistical Institute. (2015b). Population by districts, municipalities, place of residence and sex as of 31.12.2014. Retrieved from www.nsi.bg/en/content/6704/population-districts-municipalities-place-residence-and-sex.

President of the Republic of Bulgaria. (2015). Constitutional provisions. Retrieved from www.president.bg/cat72/konstitucionni-pravomoshtia/&lang=en.

Raycheva, L. (2006). Fifteen years of televised political advertising in Bulgaria. In L. L. Kaid & C. Holtz-Bacha (Eds.), *The Sage handbook of political advertising* (pp. 359–375). Thousand Oaks, CA: Sage.

Raycheva, L. (2009). Mass media developments in Bulgaria. In A. Czepek, M. Hellwig, & E. Novak (Eds.), *Press freedom and pluralism in Europe: Concepts and conditions* (pp. 165–176). Bristol, UK: Intellect.

Raycheva, L. (2013a). The TV political advertising between politicization of media and mediatization of politics (1990–2013). Retrieved from www.newmedia21.eu/izsledvaniq/televizionnata-predizborna-reklama-mezhdu-politizatsiyata-na-mediite-i-mediatizatsiyata-na-politikata-1990–2013/.

Raycheva, L. (2013b). *The television phenomenon*. Sofia, Bulgaria: Tip-Top Press.

Reporters without Borders. (2016). 2016 World press freedom index. Retrieved from https://rsf.org/en/ranking.

World Bank. (2015). Data. Bulgaria. Retrieved from http://data.worldbank.org/country/bulgaria.

20

AUDIOVISUAL POLITICAL ADVERTISING IN FINLAND

Tom Moring

Introduction: A Nordic Frontrunner in Deregulation

In the context of the political and media system in the Scandinavian region, Finland has an exceptional history of audiovisual electoral broadcasts and spots produced for television by parties, candidates or non-affiliated groups. While broadly situated within the "Democratic-Corporatist Model" that according to Hallin and Mancini (2004) developed in Northern and Central Europe, and often compared to its Scandinavian neighbors (Pfetsch, 2014, p. 29), Finland is a special case. The country was earlier than its Scandinavian neighbors in introducing paid advertising on television and allowing commercial political spots on television. Finland also has an election system that is more personalized than the party-list election systems in Sweden, Denmark or Norway. Thus, Finland stands out as an interesting test-case for how the introduction of political advertising on television and Internet and the growing campaign activities in social media affect the political system. Interestingly, 25 years of political advertising on television and 10 years of growing activities on the Internet would indicate that the answer is: not much.

The State of Research

Audiovisual political advertising in Finland has attracted research from its beginning. Election campaigns have been covered in close connection to national election studies (Borg & Moring, 2005; Moring & Mykkänen, 2009, 2012; Pesonen & Moring, 1993). Some separate studies have been published on entertainmentalization of political television (Rappe, 2004) and the style, content and gender issues related to campaign material on television and the Internet (Carlson, 2000, 2001; Moring, 2008; Moring & Himmelstein, 1996; Mykkänen, 2005). The mediatization of the Finnish political system has been portrayed in a series of texts (Ampuja, Koivisto, & Väliverronen, 2014; Moring, 2006a; Moring & Mykkänen, 2012; Reunanen, Kunelius, & Noppari, 2010) and the effects of new interactive formats on Internet have been analyzed (Carlson & Strandberg, 2005; Mykkänen & Moring 2012; Strandberg, 2013, 2014). The professionalization of political campaigns has been studied in internationally comparative research (Moring, Mykkänen, Nord, & Grusell, 2011; Tenscher, Mykkänen, & Moring, 2012).

Together, these studies show a shift from what Carlson (2000) has called a modern mode of political communication toward a postmodern mode. In the latter, the individual candidate stands out more in the campaign, and traditional – also quite regulated – formats of campaigning have exploded into a multitude of new performance platforms for political parties and candidates (Moring et al., 2011; Moring & Himmelstein, 1996). Notwithstanding the high costs, campaign managers keep investing in paid television advertising, quite aware of its limited effect on turning voters' minds. Television campaigns are seen as complementary to other modes of campaign, reinforcing images in order to convince voters of the party message (Mykkänen, 2005). The orientation toward masculine issue traits have remained dominant in spite of new media formats (Moring, 2008) and possibilities to gender-profile candidates in television and Internet spots (Carlson, 2001). However, some formatted talk shows have been introduced where female candidates have expanded the repertoire to also include softer issues (Moring, 2008).

Large numbers of voters have found new ways of informing themselves through "candidate selectors," an originally Finnish gadget allowing voters in a list voting system with personalised voting to compare their views with the views of single candidates that have been assembled through pre-election campaign questionnaires. While comparisons between views of voters and parties have been developed elsewhere, the particular personalized feature that is characteristic for the Finnish selectors is less feasible in countries with elections based on party-lists where votes are cast for the list as a whole (for more details on the Finnish electoral system, see below).[1] In recent Finnish elections a multitude of such selectors have been offered by media and some political organizations. However, the versions offered by the public service broadcaster (Yle), the biggest commercial broadcaster (MTV3) and the biggest Finnish newspaper (*Helsingin Sanomat*) have remained most popular (Mykkänen & Moring, 2012). In some political segments young voters have turned toward new media on the Internet (Strandberg, 2014), but traditional forms of campaigning have remained important and even (e.g., door-to-door visits) in some cases returned in the last two parliamentary elections (Blomberg, 2015; Politiikan kulmapöytä: Kop, 2012).

In spite of the explosion in party and candidate activities on social media, the effect on voters of the increasing use of social media remains marginal (Carlson & Strandberg, 2005; Moring, 2006a; Strandberg, 2013). Effects have been found mainly among those young voters who are already interested in off-line politics (Strandberg, 2014), thus any activation effect of political campaigning on the Internet has not been realized. In spite of the non-regulatory regime in Finland, the level of professionalization has remained relatively low (Tenscher et al., 2012), and populist right-wing movements have gained popularity that has turned into electoral success in spite of their comparatively minute investments in new campaign methods or slot campaigns on television (Moring et al., 2011). As will be shown in subsequent sections of this chapter, the much discussed process of mediatization of campaigns (Asp & Esaiasson, 1996; Mazzoleni & Schulz, 1999) has so far had more effects on the political elites and their perceptions than on the behavior of voters in Finland (Ampuja et al., 2014; Moring, 2006a; Reunanen et al., 2010).

In light of the research referred to in this section, the empirical findings to be presented later in this chapter will mainly focus on a series of comparative election survey studies since 1995, the first parliamentary election where ads were used. These surveys have focused on the exposure to different media, the (self-reported) sources of information that support the voting decision, the choice of candidate versus choice of party as a basis for decision, and the timing of the voting decision – all key parameters of mediatization and all part of the context in which political campaigning on television and the Internet can be analyzed. But before going into this analysis, the Finnish political system, the media system and the history of audiovisual campaigning will be briefly described.

The Political and Electoral System

Finland is a parliamentary democracy with a multi-party political system and a president as the head of state. The Finnish election system deviates from the election systems in many other European states particularly due to the individualized character of the voting system.

The president is elected by a direct vote, in two rounds, as in France. Even though the new constitution adopted in 2000 (and adjusted in 2012) significantly reduced the powers of the president in favor of the government and parliament, presidential elections have continued to attract more voters to the polls than other types of elections.

The parliamentary elections are a combination of voting for party lists and individual candidates. The country is divided into 13 electoral districts. Votes are cast in direct proportional elections, where voters vote for individual candidates. The proportional calculation system in Finland is based on a formula named after the Belgian mathematician Victor d'Hondt. The ranking order of elected candidates in a party is determined by the number of personal votes given to the candidates. The candidates are given a comparative index according to their personal votes (Election Act, 1998, para. 89). The 200 seats are shared by eight parties.[2] The Finnish party system has been quite stable – the three biggest parties (the Social Democratic Party, the Centre Party and the National Coalition Party) together regularly shared about two-thirds of the seats from 1983 to 2007 – but in the election of 2011 a populist party (the True Finns, later the Finns Party) broke into the top tier that now consists of four parties.

In local elections, each of Finland's more than 300 towns and municipalities form a separate district, according to the same voting rules as apply to parliamentary elections. The rules apply also to EU elections, where the entire country forms one district.

The History of Ads

From the beginning, television in Finland developed on two pillars. Unlike their Scandinavian neighbors, Iceland and Finland were the only states that developed a television system in the 1950s, financed in part by advertising. As a small and sparsely populated country, Finland required a broader financial base to invest in a television network (Salokangas, 1996, pp. 134–135).

The Broadcasting System

The Finnish Broadcasting Company (Yleisradio, hereafter Yle) was the dominant actor at the start, based on the organization it developed in the early years of the radio. In Finland, as in many other European nations, radio broadcasting was a monopoly of the state-owned public service companies.

Yle established two television channels. A commercial television company (Mainostelevisio, hereafter MTV3), however, was allowed to broadcast on the same license. In the beginning the commercial channel broadcast in slots on Yle's two channels, but in the late 1980s commercial television started to grow. MTV3 got its own license to broadcast and its own television network in 1993, and one year later the biggest newspaper publisher in Finland, Sanoma Oy, got a license for what came to be a fourth channel (hereafter Nelonen).

With the growth of cable television, and particularly since the digitalization of television in the early years of the new millennium, the number of television outlets has grown considerably. However, the four main channels still have a dominant role in the Finnish television landscape (Table 20.1), with Yle in a leading position. The three main channels carry news and current affairs programs, and also broadcast election programs. These three channels all have a daily share of almost 55% of prime-time viewing, and each one reaches more than 70% of the audience.

Whilst the details vary from election to election, all channels have election debates. In addition, Yle has party leader interviews with all parties that have seats in parliament, and party leaders also appear in current affairs programs and talk shows on all channels. Also, before the parliamentary elections in 2015, all in all 1,823 candidates were presented in short interviews displayed on the Internet and linked to the *candidate selector* (see above). The interviews were conducted by journalists of Yle. Information provided by the broadcaster shows that there was little correlation between viewing rates for the interviews and electoral success. Many marginal candidates with non-conformist views

Table 20.1 Share and weekly reach of the main Finnish television channels (including side channels in brackets), 2014

Channel	Share, prime time (%, 18–23)	Weekly reach (%)
Yle TV1	22.4 (39.8)	73 (85)
MTV3	22.1 (32.2)	79 (85)
Nelonen	10.1 (17.2)	72 (79)
Three main channels (total)	54.6	

Note: 4–99 years old. Total weekly reach of all channels: 92%; average weekly viewing time: 20 hours, 31 minutes.

Source: Data from Finnpanel, electronic Finnish television people meter (online document, www.finnpanel.fi/en/tulokset/tv/vuosi/share/2014/4plus.html#, last accessed January 10, 2016).

attracted attention although their success in the election was minor (Sipola, 2015). While young people watch less television than older people, and tend to prefer commercial channels with fewer election programs, our surveys (to be discussed in subsequent sections of this chapter) show that election coverage in television news and current affairs, and also political debates on television, continue to play a major role among all segments of voters.

The Arrival of Commercial Political Spots

Finland was also early in allowing paid television advertising. In a decision of the license holder of broadcasting, state-owned Yle, restrictions on political advertising by parties were lifted in 1990. The neighboring Scandinavian countries maintained restrictions well into the new millennium. Whilst these restrictions were in individual cases circumvented, they by and large kept paid political spots outside the main television outlets (Moring, 1995, 2006b). Soon the purchase of television time was extended to candidates and to electoral alliances that were not registered parties. In combination with a personalized voting system, this created a potentially ideal playing field for Finnish parties that wanted to reach the electorate through television without the interference of journalists. Political television advertising soon became one of the most costly aspects of the parties' election campaigns. In the parliamentary elections of 2003, 43% of total campaign budgets were used for political advertising on television. Newspaper advertising still dominates the campaigns of single candidates, but by 2003 one in six candidates also purchased television-time in the form of slots (Borg & Moring, 2005).

In the early 1990s, deregulation of political television programs before elections changed profoundly, and not only in regard to paid political advertising. The television networks played down earlier rules of electoral quarantine which prevented candidates from television exposure except on news programs and allowed candidates to perform on entertainment programs in different roles. Also the formal interview programs with party leaders, and the party leader debates, became a freer discussion where an equal share of speaking time was given less prominence; a development often referred to as more "journalistic" (Moring & Himmelstein, 1996).

However, as research has shown (Moring, 2006a; Moring & Mykkänen, 2012, to be discussed in subsequent sections of this chapter), the effect of paid political advertising has not achieved a position in the (self-reported) perceptions of the voters that would correspond to its position in the organization of campaigns. Quite the contrary, in several cases the main effect of commercially driven television campaigns has been devastating to the campaign of single parties, as the political ads have backfired and shifted campaigns from offensive to defensive.

The Arrival of the Internet

In the most recent elections, broadly speaking since the beginning of this millennium, the Internet has played an increasing role in the campaigns of parties and candidates. Finland is among the countries that introduced Internet technology early and with widespread access to the web. In regard to this new approach to campaigning, however, the hype has been overrated. According to available research, traditional media outlets have kept their position as the main sources for voting decisions. The most prominent exception is the emergence of candidate selectors on the Internet, maintained by the same main media companies that direct newspaper and television outlets (Mykkänen & Moring, 2012).

In the recent most development, in the election in 2015, the public service broadcaster Yle presented each candidate in a four-minute video-interview available on the Internet. As noted above, though these interviews had considerable audiences in some cases, there is no evidence of an immediate effect on candidates' success; the most viewed video attracted 280,000 hits. This young candidate from Northern Finland, however, got less than 500 votes.[3] Some parties and particularly young candidates, however, believe strongly in the growing importance of the Internet and an active presence on social media. In the 2015 election, the Social Democratic Party invested €100,000 in supporting its presence on Facebook and Twitter. The party came out as a loser in the elections. In contrast, the Centre Party, which was the largest party and a winner in the election, used only "a couple of thousand (Euros) on Facebook and Twitter" (Mäntymaa, 2015).

The Relevance of Advertising as Campaign Channel

According to available research, the self-reported impact of paid political advertising and campaigning on the Internet has remained relatively minor. The impact of various media has been charted systematically since the parliamentary election in 1995 in a series of panel surveys by TNS Gallup, Finland.[4] This research has also covered other types of elections in Finland (presidential, local and EU elections). The time series presented in the tables will, to maintain comparability, be based on the six parliamentary elections since 1995, whilst additional observations from other types of elections will be inserted in the text (Tables 20.2 and 20.3). The focus on elections for parliament is also supported by the fact that parties prioritize these elections in their use of campaign resources.

The self-reported media effects in the election campaigns are presented here in two tables, to demonstrate the obvious difference between age groups. The generation that has grown up with the Internet (18–34 years old) also includes many voters who enter the electorate as new voters, and voters who have not yet established their voting behavior. Before discussing separate observations that can be found in the tables, some general observations will be presented.

First, the generation shift is clearly visible in the difference between the way that the two age groups lean on different types of media, particularly in regard to the shrinking importance of the press and the increasing importance of all categories of the Internet among young voters. Also, young people's reliance on relatives and friends stands out.

Second, the general consistency in media behavior over the 20 years covered by this research catches the eye. The time period covers a crucial era of media-politics development, that according to modernization theory (see Carlson, 2000, discussed above) and mediatization theory (Asp & Esaiasson, 1996; Mazzoleni & Schulz, 1999) should have profoundly changed the relation between the two. It should be noted that Finland was early in broadband penetration and remains comparatively advanced even in 2015 due to almost total mobile penetration of the population.[5] But in terms of how voters rely on media, in Finland traditional behavior prevails to a remarkable extent.

Table 20.2 Media impact in the parliamentary elections 1995–2015. Voters aged 18–34 years

	1995	1999	2003	2007	2011	2015
TV news, current affairs	22	25	23	21	18	26
TV election programs	17	20	15	18	26	21
TV ads	7	11	6	5	3	10
TV entertainment	★	6	3	4	3	5
Newspaper articles	25	30	24	23	17	13
Newspaper ads	11	26	19	8	7	9
Candidate selectors	★	9	31	36	35	50
Parties Internet sites	★	★	20	16	19	19
Candidate Internet sites	★	★	21	33	31	26
Social media	★	★	★	★	7	12
Campaign meetings	3	5	4	4	3	4
Friends, relatives	15	16	17	15	18	15

Note: "To what extent do you consider that the following source informed you in support of your decision how to vote?" Much or very much influence (on a four-point scale) 18–34 years old (%).
Source: The project 'Changes in Finnish TV Election Campaigns 1991-' and TNS Gallup, Finland.

Table 20.3 Media impact in the parliamentary elections 1995–2015. Voters aged 35 years and older

	1995	1999	2003	2007	2011	2015
TV news, current affairs	18	23	20	24	32	33
TV election programs	17	21	17	21	28	30
TV ads	7	10	5	7	6	9
TV entertainment	★	5	2	5	4	5
Newspaper articles	18	33	26	24	28	26
Newspaper ads	9	19	12	11	12	14
Candidate selectors	★	4	9	12	13	22
Parties Internet sites	★	★	5	6	6	7
Candidate Internet sites	★	★	6	6	10	11
Social media	★	★	★	★	2	5
Campaign meetings	6	7	6	7	6	7
Friends, relatives	8	10	9	8	9	7

Note: "To what extent do you consider that the following source informed you in support of your decision how to vote?" Much or very much influence (on a four-point scale) +35 years old (%).
Source: The project 'Changes in Finnish TV Election Campaigns 1991-' and TNS Gallup, Finland.

The older generations (35 years and older) clearly have a media behavior that is established before the digital revolution in the media world. This is visible in many parameters, the most obvious being a stronger and stable reliance on newspapers and an only slowly growing use of sources available on the Internet. A greater stability in voting behavior in the older age groups is indicated by less reliance on sources such as family and friends.

In reading these tables, a word of warning is required. Self-reported influence is not unproblematic, particularly because of the different status of various types of media. Therefore, the changes over time are more significant than the absolute levels of influence of any single medium at any single point in time. By and large, however, our findings show a remarkable stability compared to the societal and media changes that have occurred during this time. Paid political advertising on television remains relatively unimportant, as do entertainment programs with politicians or political content. Social media have become established, but at a relatively low level. Traditional sources, such as current affairs programs and election debates on television remain important in all age groups, and newspapers have maintained their importance among voters over 35 years of age.

The most remarkable exceptions to this stability are the emergence of the aforementioned Internet gadget, the candidate selector, that has established a strong position among both young and old voters, the decreasing interest of young voters in newspaper articles and newspaper ads, and the emerging interest among young voters in the Internet sites, particularly of single candidates. In subsequent sections, we will come back to the questions raised by this general picture in more detail.

The Role of Election Programs and Party Leader Debates in Election Campaigns

Traditional television has maintained its position in Finnish election campaigns. This holds true not only in the parliamentary elections (as is clearly seen in Tables 20.2 and 20.3), but also, and even more so, in presidential elections. In the three elections that we have surveyed approximately 30–40% of respondents report, irrespective or age,[6] that they were informed by the traditional television debates between presidential candidates. Thus, a fair conclusion is that traditional election programs on broadcast media have maintained their role in the campaign, as has visibility in news and current affairs programs.

An interesting newcomer in the election campaigns, since the de-regulation of election-time television, is the talk show. Such shows, offering platforms for candidates from different parties, have become part of the election campaign, both on public service and commercial television channels, particularly in the most personalized presidential elections. As has been indicated (although with a small number of cases) by Moring (2008), different types of programs offer quite distinctive platforms for candidates. The more traditional male voice is better served by the formal debate, whereas more intimate talk shows offer platforms that are better tuned for softer issues. It would be too straightforward a conclusion to say that these differences translate directly into a gender advantage, although this is also indicated by the study mentioned. However, candidates operate in a multidimensional space and may play out their different agendas skillfully on different arenas irrespective of sex – such as in the presidential election in 2012 where a homosexual male candidate from the Green Party quite successfully competed with the frontrunner in the campaign, a male candidate from the conservative National Coalition Party.

However, pure entertainment programs of different sorts are not highly valued by the viewers as sources for decision-making. Furthermore, their position has remained low throughout and in both age groups during the time period studied. One exception should be mentioned: in the second round of the presidential campaign in 2000, the two front-runners together with their spouses met in a quiz program. In a panel study (Moring, 1997) it was found that this one program left a small but distinct mark in the behavior of voters who saw the program, in favor of the candidate who won the election.

The Role of Paid Political Spots in Election Campaigns

Paid political advertising on television in Finland is not specifically regulated in legislation. Since 1991, when the then license holder Yle lifted the prohibition on political advertising, only general rules and restrictions concerning media and freedom of expression pertain to political ads. While the lengths of spots are not regulated, the format of political spots that was established in the first elections in the 1990s (Moring & Himmelstein, 1996) has, with some single exceptions, prevailed: spots are normally five to not more than 30 seconds long, sometimes with a brief repeat in the same time slot. The most notable exception was a telethon by the Centre Party candidate in the presidential election in 1994.

In 1991, the biggest commercial broadcaster MTV3 bound itself to certain internal rules of conduct (Moring, 1995, p. 168). In their first version, slots would be sold only to registered parties, spots could include comparative and critical elements but not negative assessments of single candidates, and political advertising could not contain other advertisement messages, such as names of sponsors or financers, logos or products. In connection with election programs (debates, etc.), only image advertising for parties or organizations could be inserted, not advertising for single candidates. No party or organization has been allowed to buy exclusive rights to appear in connection with an election program.

However, the first rule was not applied in presidential election campaigns, where slots were sold to larger campaign organizations that were formed, often by several parties, or as independent support groups, to support particular candidates (Moring, 2006b, pp. 190–191). The first rule was also removed when MTV got its own license to broadcast in 1993 and continued broadcasting on its own channel under the name MTV3. Since then civic movements that are not parties (e.g., trade unions) have been allowed to air political advertising in election campaigns. Also single candidates have been allowed to place ads in connection to election programs (Särkelä, 2015, Account Group Manager MTV). The other rules still stand as a self-regulatory mechanism for MTV3.

This internal rule system of the biggest commercial broadcaster has had decisive impact on political advertising both on television and on the Internet in Finland. As MTV until today has been the biggest actor in the television advertising market, parties and candidates have adapted their spot production to fit the company rules. When resources for producing spots are scarce, they then tend to go with the same concept throughout the audiovisual media. Thus, these rules have in practice restricted personal attack advertising on television in Finnish election campaigns.

A further particularity that merits mention is that legislation does not consider paid political advertising on television in Finland as being on par with commercial advertising in terms of rules regarding maximal advertisement time per time unit. As political advertising in this respect is considered to be public information, the advertising quota included in the EU Audio-visual Media Services Directive and reflected in Finnish media legislation does not apply. Thus, broadcasting of political spots can exceed the 12 minutes per hour limit that applies to prime-time broadcasting in Finland (Laakso, 2011, Sales Director MTV3).

Since 1995 most parties have used a significant share of their campaign budgets for political advertising on television. As noted above, the share in 2003 was more than 40%. In 2007, it was 37% for the five parties that aired paid political ads on television (the Green Party did not invest in such ads for the party in that election). In recent elections, however, parties' investment in television advertising has decreased, partly due to an increasing investment in campaigning on the Internet. The decrease started already in the 2011 election (Moring & Mykkänen, interviews with party campaign leaders 2011, unpublished), and according to the figures reported by parties to the Ministry of Justice after the parliamentary election in 2015, only 15% of the total campaign costs of the parties was allocated to television broadcasting, whereas the printed press and print works took 23% and Internet-related activities took 7%.[7] Whilst the tendency is clear, it should be noted that the figures compared here are based on the allocation of resources by the central parties; party districts and single candidates have their own campaigns that may deviate in allocation of resources.

Certain parties – in several parliamentary elections the Greens, in some elections the Finns Party, the Swedish People's Party, and the Centre Party – have refrained from paid television campaigns at the party level. Single candidates may, however, have aired some television ads. In 2011, all parties aired television spots. In 2015, the Greens, the Left Alliance and the Swedish People's Party refrained from television advertising at the party level.

It was mentioned before – and becomes evident in the low ratings in self-reported voting behavior as presented in Tables 20.2 and 20.3 – that political advertising has not been a road to success in elections in Finland. Self-reported behavior is not necessarily a safe measure, particularly when respondents react to questions relating to (possibly) less esteemed stimulus such as advertising. The well-known *third person effect* (Davison, 1983) has shown that people tend to estimate media influence on themselves as lesser than on "ordinary people." However, the conclusion here is that it is safe to say that television advertising in Finnish parliamentary elections has not increased its influence over the years. This conclusion is based first of all on the consistent low rating of television advertising in our data in all the parliamentary elections that we have covered, compared with other indications of dramatically growing influence (particularly the influence of the candidate selectors). It is further supported by the voters' response to explicit questions in our interview surveys, which consistently show that the majority of voters consider the general influence of political television advertising to be low on the success of the party that they support. Only between 10% and 18% consider the effects of political television advertising to be positive. There are single examples of campaigns that have lifted the party image, usually through a charismatic party leader. Such were the campaigns of the Left Alliance in the elections of 1999 and 2003. In these campaigns, a charismatic female party leader featured in the ads. In the 2003 election, 21% of the voters for this party thought the spot campaign was to the benefit of the party, and there were no negative reactions. In the same election in 2003, another party leader featured in the ads; the chairman of the National Coalition Party did not receive the same appreciation, only 8% of the voters of the party considered the campaign to be beneficial, whereas 16% thought it actually harmed the support for the party. Thus, for this party the campaign clearly backfired. Other parties had a slightly positive balance, but with rather low scores. Other examples of campaigns that backfired are the Centre Party campaign in 1996, portraying Finland as a threatened Wild West and using the image of John Wayne as savior; and the campaign of the biggest trade union organization, SAK, in 2007, in which a caricature of a capitalist was displayed mocking workers. These examples of negative campaigning on a general, not personal, level, clearly backfired among all but the youngest voters. The ratio among voters for the Social Democratic Party in 2007 was 6% positive to 30% negative (Moring & Mykkänen, 2009, pp. 43–46). In the 2011 election campaign the same party scored better. Against a general 16% rate of positive assessment of the influence of the television ad campaign for their chosen party among all voters, 27% of the Social Democratic Party voters thought that the television ad campaign affected the party positively, whereas only 1% thought it failed. In this election the Center Party suffered, only 6% of its voters thought that the television ad campaign had a positive effect, against 10% negative (in the 2015 election study this question was not asked).

The examples above, and particularly the failure of the trade union's spots in 2007, led to what has been called a "meta-campaign." Although the ads of the union were never actually aired as paid ads on television, their presentation to the press led to strong reactions. News programs aired the ads and they went viral. Consequentially, the union withdrew the ads and presented another spot on the theme "you may vote for whoever, as long as you turn up to vote." This ad clearly raised less interest than the failed attack ads (Moring & Mykkänen, 2009).

Surveys show, however, that television advertising attracts attention. Between 50% and 80% of the television viewers report that they have noticed the spot campaigns of the largest parties, while the campaigns of smaller parties are noticed by 20–50% of the voters. Audiovisual advertising on television may also – together with Internet campaigning – increase its importance in the future, as the slight increase in self-reported influence of spots and certain forms of Internet campaigns in the 2015 election would indicate (Tables 20.2 and 20.3).

The Role of the Internet in Election Campaigns

There are no particular regulations regarding audiovisual campaigning on the Internet in Finland. In recent years, all parties have invested much of their personal resources and also increasingly financial resources to support their visibility on the web (see figures above, also Mäntymaa, 2015). Whilst the prominence of the Internet has been increasing in the strategy of most campaign managers in recent elections, our data show little measurable effect of this activity on actual voting behavior. In light of self-reported influence on voting decisions, the aforementioned candidate selectors maintained by the biggest media companies are the most influential newcomers on the web.

It could be argued that the relatively late attention by the parties to the potential of the Internet in Finland compared to its Scandinavian neighbors (Moring, 2006b, pp. 189–190, 203) could be explained by the existence of television advertising in Finland whereas this type of advertising was not allowed in Denmark, Norway and Sweden. Thus, the audiovisual material in these countries early on was produced for the web, whereas in Finland it was produced for television.

The most spectacular political campaign on the Internet so far was during the presidential elections in 2012, where the candidate of the Greens, leaning on young, predominantly urban, support succeeded making it to the second round of the election. His supporters were among the most active Internet users in the population, and they used all types of platforms and formats including blogs and social media in the campaign. However, these Internet-savvy supporters were obviously already convinced supporters of the candidate, as our data show little influence of Internet activities on the voting behavior among voters in general, even among those who voted for this exceptional candidate.

Thus – and consistent with findings presented by Strandberg (2013, 2014) on behavior in parliamentary elections – the campaigns on the Internet appear to have had relatively limited effect also under these quite special conditions where two candidates compete and one represents the most Internet-savvy segment of the voters. In the first round of the election, traditional media clearly dominated as a source for the voting decision (Table 20.4). Most voters were informed through election programs on television, television news and current affairs and by the press. In spite of the active Internet campaign, few voters mentioned this as the source of information supporting their choice; even the voters for the Green candidate Pekka Haavisto (who got 37.4% of the votes in the second round) did not – according to their own witness as portrayed in our data – lean much on Internet sources. Only among young voters under 25 years of age a clearly greater preference for these sources

Table 20.4 The elections for president, 2012

	Round 1 All voters	Round 2 All voters	Voters for the Green's candidate in round 2	Voters 18–25 years old in round 2
TV news, current affairs	27	28	30	22
TV election programs	34	33	35	28
TV ads	6	4	5	11
TV entertainment	4	4	4	9
Newspaper articles	21	19	20	20
Newspaper ads	5	3	4	8
Candidate selectors	13	8	11	22
Parties Internet sites	★	★	★	★
Candidate Internet sites	4	4	5	11
Social media	4	4	6	8
Campaign meetings	4	4	4	10
Friends, relatives	12	8	10	23

Note: "To what extent do you consider that the following source informed you in support of your decision how to vote?" Much or very much influence (on a four-point scale) 18–34 years old (%). (Number of cases in the survey in round 1 = 1,011; in round 2 = 890)
Source: The project 'Changes in Finnish TV Election Campaigns 1991–' and TNS Gallup, Finland.

could be found. This, again, may point to potential changes in future elections. However, traditional broadcast television still dominated as a source of information also in the youngest age group.

Conclusions

The quite liberal media regulatory regime in Finland, allowing for paid commercial advertising and campaigning on the Internet without legal restrictions, has to date brought rather minor changes to the political system. The biggest differences are seen in the party and candidate campaign budgets and organization of the campaigns.

The contents of the mainly quite short paid political spots in election campaigns have been modified by policy decisions of the biggest commercial broadcaster that has restricted personal attack ads. Parties have also been careful in their campaigns, as the few cases of negative campaigning on a more general base have backfired. The rather tame campaign culture following from these self-restrictions may have contributed to the modest impact of paid political advertising on television.

The most important campaign media are still the candidate debates and current affairs broadcasts on television. The newspapers have lost ground among young voters, the youngest of whom have, to some extent, turned to web-based campaign media – although also these young voters still take much of their information from traditional media. One remarkable exception is the emergence of candidate selectors that allow voters to compare their views with the views of candidates. The selectors have grown in importance and have reached a stable popularity not only among young, but also among middle-aged voters.

In comparison with some other countries in Northern Europe that share many of the same traits, the level of professionalization of election campaigns is still relatively low in Finland. Furthermore, in the surge of the populist movements in Europe, the (populist) party that is weakest in terms of professionalization has in recent parliamentary elections had remarkable success, which is yet another indication of the limited effects of audiovisual political campaigning. This, indeed, is not a prediction of the future which may eventually see dramatic changes in the campaign culture as the media landscape is re-molded due to the rapid digitalization of the entire media sector.

Notes

1   The first version of this kind of a selector was presented by CNN in the 1996 US presidential elections. The same year the idea was further developed by Yle in Finland for the coming EU elections. Similar gadgets exist in many countries under different names, "Stem Wijser" in the Netherlands; "Wij kiezen partij foor u" in Belgium; "Wahl-O-Mat" in Germany; "Politarena" and "Smartvote" in Switzerland and "Test din stemme" in Norway, just to mention some examples. The particular version in Finland – with its personalized voting system – allows the voter to compare views with single candidates, a feature that is less feasible in countries with elections based on party-lists.

2   The eight parties are (number of seats in the 2015 election in brackets) Centre Party (49); Finns Party (38); The National Coalition Party (37); The Social Democratic Party (34); The Greens (15); Left Alliance (12); Swedish People's Party (10); Christian Democrats (5). For an overview of the Finnish political system, see Moring et al. (2011).

3   Online document, available at http://yle.fi/uutiset/eduskuntavaalit_2015/ (last accessed January 9, 2016), also Sipola (2015).

4   The surveys have been carried out on a web-based electronic representative panel in cooperation between the author and TNS Gallup, Finland. The number of respondents of voting age (at least 18 years old) was 1,445 in 1995; 1,511 in 2003; 1,171 in 2007; 1,253 in 2011 and 1,046 in 2015.

5   In 2003, Finland was the fifth in the number of broadband connections per capita in the EU after Denmark, Belgium, the Netherlands and Sweden (Tuomi, 2004, p. 1). According to the report "Implementation of the EU regulatory framework for electronic communications" (2015, p. 5) for the EU Commission, in 2014–15 Finland was moderately placed in fixed broadband access (60% of households). Finns were, however, best

connected in the EU through mobile broadband penetration (140% residential and business subscriptions as percentage of population).

6   Our surveys cover the presidential elections in 1994, 2006 and 2012.

7   Figures according to the financial reports of the parties to the Ministry of Justice, available at www.vaalira-hoitus.fi/fi/index/puoluetukiilmoituksia/ilmoituslistaus/tilinpaatostiedot.html (last accessed June 30, 2016).

References

Ampuja, M., Koivisto, J., & Väliverronen, E. (2014). Strong and weak forms of mediatization theory – a critical review. *Nordicom Review*, 35, 111–123.

Asp, K., & Esaiasson, P. (1996). The modernization of Swedish campaigns: Individualization, professionalization, and medialization. In D. L. Swanson & P. Mancini (Eds.), *Politics, media, and modern democracy: An international study of innovations in electoral campaigning and their consequences* (pp. 73–90). Westport, CT: Praeger.

Blomberg, A.-L. (2015, February 7). Vaalien alla oveesi saattaa koputtaa demari – "Keskustelut ovat laadukkaampia". *Demokraatti*. Retrieved from https://demokraatti.fi/vaalien-alla-oveesi-saattaa-koputtaa-demari-keskustelut-ovat-laadukkaampia/ (last accessed January 18, 2017).

Borg, S., & Moring, T. (2005). Vaalikampanja. In H. Paloheimo (Ed.), *Vaalit ja demokratia Suomessa* (pp. 47–72). Helsinki: WSOY.

Carlson, T. (2000). *Partier och kandidater på väljarmarknaden: Studier i finländsk politisk reklam*. Åbo: Åbo Akademi University.

Carlson, T. (2001). Gender and political advertising across cultures: A comparison of male and female political advertising in Finland and the US. *European Journal of Communication*, 16(2), 131–154.

Carlson, T., & Strandberg, K. (2005). The 2004 European parliament election on the web: Finnish actor strategies and voter responses. *Information Polity*, 10, 189–204.

Davison, W. P. (1983). Third person effect in communication. *Public Opinion Quarterly*, 47(1), 1–15.

Election Act 714/1998, unofficial translation. Ministry of Justice, Finland. Retrieved from www.finlex.fi/fi/laki/kaannokset/1998/en19980714.pdf (last accessed January 9, 2015).

Hallin, D. C., & Mancini, P. (2004). *Comparing media systems: Three models of media and politics*. Cambridge: Cambridge University Press.

Implementation of the EU regulatory framework for electronic communications. (2015). Commission Staff Working Document, Brussels, 19.6.2015, *SWD(2015) 126 final*. Retrieved from https://ec.europa.eu/digital-agenda/en/connectivity (last accessed January 12, 2015).

Laakso, M. (2011, August 8). Personal communication.

Mäntymaa, E. (2015). *Näin puolueet ostavat somenäkyvyyttä – SDP satsaa jopa sata tonnia*. Retrieved from http://yle.fi/uutiset/nain_puolueet_ostavat_somenakyvyytta__sdp_satsaa_jopa_sata_tonnia/7908833 (last accessed January 9, 2015).

Mazzoleni, G., & Schulz, W. (1999). "Mediatization" of politics: A challenge for democracy? *Political Communication*, 16(3), 247–261.

Moring, T. (1995). The North European exception: Political advertising on TV in Finland. In L. L. Kaid & C. Holtz-Bacha (Eds.), *Political advertising in western democracies* (pp. 161–185). Thousand Oaks, CA: Sage.

Moring, T. (1997). "Amerikaniseras" politiken? Medieförändring, väljarmobilitet och nya former för val i samverkan. In S. Lindberg & Y. Molin (Eds.), *Festskrift till Sten Berglund* (pp. 77–114). Vasa: Pro Facultate Nr 2.

Moring, T. (2006a). Between medialization and tradition: Campaigning in Finland in a longitudinal perspective. In M. Maier & J. Tenscher (Eds.), *Campaigning in Europe – campaigning for Europe: Political parties, campaigns, mass media and the European parliament elections 2004* (pp. 81–100). Berlin: LIT.

Moring, T. (2006b). Political advertising on television in the Nordic and Baltic states. In L. L. Kaid & C. Holtz-Bacha (Eds.), *The Sage handbook of political advertising* (pp. 181–209). Thousand Oaks, CA: Sage.

Moring, T. (2008). Television and gender in Finnish presidential elections. In C. Holtz-Bacha (Ed.) *Frauen, Politik und Medien* (pp. 208–234). Wiesbaden: VS Verlag für Sozialwissenschaften.

Moring, T., & Himmelstein, H. (1996). The new-image politics in Finnish electoral television. In D. L. Paletz (Ed.), *Political communication research: Approaches, studies, assessments. Volume II.* (pp. 117–143). Norwood: Ablex.

Moring, T., & Mykkänen, J. (2009). Vaalikampanja. In S. Borg & H. Paloheimo (Eds.), *Vaalit yleisödemokratiassa. Eduskuntavaalitutkimus 2007* (pp. 28–59). Tampere: Tampere University Press.

Moring, T., & Mykkänen, J. (2012). Vaalikampanjat ja viestinnällistyminen. In S. Borg (Ed.), *Muutosvaalit 2011/ Förändringsval 2011* (pp. 62–78). Oikeusministeriö, Selvityksiä ja ohjeita/Utredningar och anvisningar.

Moring, T., Mykkänen, J., Nord, L., & Grusell, M. (2011). Campaign professionalization and political structures: A comparative study of election campaigning in Finland and Sweden in the 2009 EP elections. In M. Maier, J. Strömbäck, & L. L. Kaid (Eds.), *Political communication in European parliamentary elections* (pp. 45–59). Farnham: Ashgate.

Mykkänen, J. (2005). Strategia, relevanssi ja merkitys: Televisiomainonnan kontekstuaalisuudesta vuoden 2004 eurovaalikampanjoissa. *Politiikka*, 47(4), 282–303.

Mykkänen, J., & Moring, T. (2012). Aktivoivaa tietoa? Vaalikoneet suomalaisessa julkisuudessa. In K. Karppinen & J. Matikainen (Eds.), *Julkisuus ja demokratia. Professori Hannu Niemisen juhlakirja* (pp. 161–180). Tampere: Vastapaino.

Pesonen, P., & Moring, T. (1993). Vaalikampanjan puitteet, rytmi ja yleisö. In P. Pesonen, R. Sänkiaho, & S. Borg (Eds.), *Vaalikansan äänivalta* (pp. 255–274). Helsinki: WSOY.

Pfetsch, B. (2014). The idea of political communication cultures and its empirical correlates. In B. Pfetsch (Ed.), *Political communication cultures in Europe: Attitudes of political actors and journalists in nine countries* (pp. 13–30). London: Palgrave Macmillan.

Politiikan kulmapöytä: Kop (2012, October 1). Politiikan kulmapöytä: Kop kop kop, avaa oves. *Helsingin Sanomat*.

Rappe, A. (2004). *Valbevakning i förändring. 1990-talets riksdagsval i finsk television*. Åbo: Åbo Akademis förlag.

Reunanen, E., Kunelius, R., & Noppari, E. (2010). Mediatization in context: Consensus culture, media and decision making in the 21st century, the case of Finland. *Communications*, 35(3), 287–307.

Salokangas, R. (1996). The Finnish Broadcasting Company and the changing Finnish society, 1949–1966. In R. Endén (Ed.), *Yleisradio 1926–1996: A history of broadcasting in Finland* (pp. 107–228). Helsinki: Oy Yleisradio Oy.

Särkelä, S. (2015, December 28). Personal interview.

Sipola, T. (2015, April 17). Valtavirrasta poikkeavat poliitikot kiinnostavat Ylen vaaligalleriassa. *Yle news*. Retrieved from http://yle.fi/uutiset/3-7936161 (last accessed January 18, 2017).

Strandberg, K. (2013). A social media revolution or just a case of history repeating itself? The use of social media in the 2011 Finnish parliamentary elections. *New Media & Society*, 15(8), 1329–1347.

Strandberg, K. (2014). Mapping the on-line campaign audience: An analysis of the on-line "participatory class" in the 2011 Finnish parliamentary campaign. *Journal of Information Technology & Politics*, 11(3), 276–290.

Tenscher, J., Mykkänen, J., & Moring, T. (2012). Modes of professional campaigning: A four-country comparison in the European parliamentary elections, 2009. *The International Journal of Press/Politics*, 17(2), 145–168.

Tuomi, I. (2004, March). *Broadband in Finland*. Report for the BREAD consortium. IPTS Working Paper.

21

MEDIA, POLITICAL ADVERTISING AND ELECTION CAMPAIGNING IN RUSSIA

Sergei A. Samoilenko and Elina Erzikova

Political advertising in Russia is a multilayered topic. It is highly contextualized and deeply ingrained in post-Soviet history. Russia's political culture is inevitably tied to the institutional background, the state of the media, the values of the previous (Soviet) system, and vision for the future of the society and its public discourse. In this chapter the discussion of Russian political advertising is linked to the important issues of "power, television, and electoral choice" (Oates, 2006a, p. 309), and addressed from the perspective of political institutions, mass media and civic engagement.

In transitional polities the persistence of long-existing institutional structures is widespread and influential. This political and administrative heritage impacts institutional decision-making in all post-Soviet transitional states including Russia (Porfiriev & Svedin, 2002). Naturally, the knowledge, collective memory, and previous administrative and management practices formed under the Soviet system are still in use and frequently applied to address modern realities. Political actors attached to a particular system are typically resistant to any change and run into value conflicts with the changing society.

Often, new national identities in post-Soviet countries are built upon the historical meanings of power and power relations, such as submission to the state, hierarchical administrative management, and paternalistic expectations of welfare (Korostelina, 2013). Porfiriev and Simons (2012) use the word *vlast* ("power") to define general authority within a hierarchical system implying that "political power guides and determines personal relations between various individuals in all spheres of Russian life" (p. 3). People located within the social system of norms and symbols of power accept this power as legitimate even if they have a disadvantaged position within this system (Bourdieu, 1991).

This chapter will first address the historical implications for the current conditions of the Russian mass media and its failure to meet public expectations for objectivity and accountability in the 1990s. This will explain how interdependence with the state turned the Russian media into an even more powerful propaganda machine than it used to be during the Soviet time. The following section will define the notion of political advertising and outline a legal framework related to election campaigning. Next, the chapter will provide an overview of the use of political advertising during Russian parliamentary and presidential campaigns from 1993 to 2014. The new strategies and tactics of national political advertising will be subsequently introduced. Finally, the chapter will address the state and the future of Russian public sphere in relation to the current state-imposed propaganda doctrine. Conclusions and lessons learned will be included.

The State of Mass Media

Historically, the media have served as an intermediary between the government and the public. As an important source of vital information, the media is assumed to demonstrate higher accountability and help the public make informed choices. It is expected to remain nonpartisan in the analysis of social issues and political decisions and serve as a conduit for citizen voices and alternative views to inform the authorities and the public (McQuail, 1993).

In the Soviet Union, the media were merely seen by the government as a means for political propaganda that served the needs of the state ideology. During the political reforms by Mikhail Gorbachev in the late 1980s, the press became the mouthpiece for the ideas of *perestroika* and *glasnost* (public transparency) helping the government to uncover the crimes of the communist past and to support a new political vision. Despite the policy for increased openness in government institutions, the media was still largely dependent on information from official sources.

There was a brief time period (1988–96) known as the "golden years" of journalism, when the media became less dependent on political power and was considered by 65% of Russians as the "Fourth Estate" in September 1993 (Fedorov, 2007, p. 38). However, the late Yeltsin period (1996–9) was marked by a steady decrease in trust toward all democratic institutions including the media. In the early 1990s the media struggled for survival without regular state sponsorship. In order to stay afloat, most print media had gradually to reduce the amount of "hard" news and substantially increase entertainment content. Finally, media outlets started to sell out to the oligarchs who happily embraced the media as a powerful tool in political competition. As expected, the level of objectivity declined according to the expectations and political interests of their new owners (Gatov, 2015). In the 1990s, oligarchs became increasingly influential in politics and played a significant role in Yeltsin's re-election. In fact, the 1996 presidential elections ended the period of independent journalism by introducing a new era of the televised political spectacle. The oligarchs bankrolled Boris Yeltsin's election campaign, and media owners guaranteed favorable media coverage of the president, helping him to win his second term. As a result of the 1996 presidential elections, the new cast of "spin doctors" was born.

During Putin's two presidential terms (2000–8) Russia saw economic growth with GDP increasing 6.9% annually (Trading Economics, 2016) and an emerging middle class. Ironically, it was the urban middle class that showed discontent about the course proposed by the state. One of the key reasons for dissatisfaction was that the government disregarded the growing need in the society for open public dialogue, political activism and civic engagement.

Medvedev's presidency (2008–12) was associated with a tremendous increase in the use of online media and news consumption in Russia. The Russian Internet community (Runet) became a public space for discussing and debating cases of state corruption and abuse of power, as well as a tool for civic activism and digital mobilizations during natural disasters, such as the 2010 Russian wildfires and the 2012 Krymsk floods.

Since the beginning of the new millennium, rapid digitization in Russia created a number of new platforms for news distribution and facilitated the production of user-generated content (UGC). The percentage of active bloggers and social media users in Russia became consistently higher than in the US and many other countries. In 2009, Russia had the world's most engaged social networking audience and four years later was named the country with the largest online audience (61.3 million) in Europe (Comscore, 2013). In 2014, the MGI Connectedness Index ranked Russia first on the list of the most connected emerging markets (McKinsey Global Institute, 2014).

During Medvedev's presidency the authorities were forced to use a more open and proactive communication strategy and more rigorous accountability measures. Russian politicians started actively promoting their own online presence by having government officials blog and use Twitter and by investing in eGov platforms, including online access to public data. For example, then President and now Prime Minister of Russia, Dmitry Medvedev was nicknamed a "blogger-in-chief" due to the frequency of his online activity. Since Putin's return to the presidency in May 2012, the rise of user-generated content on the Russian Internet, however, clashed with a series of legal measures imposing more control and administrative pressure on Internet media.

Legislation on Electoral Campaigning in Russia

Russia does not have a clear legal definition of *political advertising*. The 1995 Decree No. 18/149-II of the Central Election Commission of the Russian Federation defines "political advertising" as "the dissemination of information (announcements, calls, video and audio clips, etc.) in the mass media by participants in the electoral process concerning electoral associations, electoral blocs, and candidates by using tools and techniques that distinguish advertisements from other types and genres of information (a prevalence of the emotional impact over semantics, showiness, brevity, stress on the dominant advantages of the advertised object), and recognized by federal legislation and mass media practice as signs of advertising for the purpose of shaping public opinion in favor of electoral associations, electoral blocs, candidates for deputies" (ConsultantPlus, n.d.).

Current Russian legislation regulates the form of political advertising such as election campaigning. This legislation on election campaigning is broad and primarily relates to disseminating information about political forces and candidates to influence voting behavior or encourage citizens to follow a proposed action during a short election cycle. It follows the general rules governing freedom of speech, freedom of information, and general requirements for the electoral processes. A number of relevant regulations are provided in the following documents such as: Federal Law No. 67-FZ of June 12, 2002 "On Basic Guarantees of Election Rights and Citizen Rights to Participate in the Referendum of the Russian Federation"; Federal Law No. 5-FZ of June 28, 2004 "On Referendum of the Russian Federation"; Federal Law No. 114-FZ of July 25, 2002 "On Counteraction against Extremist Activity"; Federal Law No. 19-FZ of January 10, 2003 "On Election of the President of the Russian Federation"; Federal Law No. 20-FZ of February 22, 2014 "On Elections of the Deputies of the State Duma of Federal Assembly of the Russian Federation", and others (here and further as found in GARANT System).

Federal Law No. 67-FZ "On Basic Guarantees…" defines election campaigning (known in Russian as "pre-election agitation") as "the activities carried out during the election campaign which are intended to encourage or encouraging voters to vote for a candidate, candidates, list of candidates, or against it (them)" (Part 1, Article 2). This law lists election campaigning formats and methods (Part 7, Article 48) and outlines requirements for the content, distribution dates and placement order of campaign materials. The same legislation along with Law No. 5-FKZ "On Referendum…" requires the providers of political advertising to provide election candidates with equal opportunities for placing campaign materials.

According to Federal Law No. 20-FZ "On Elections of Deputies…," free airtime is reserved for discussions, round tables and other campaigning events and for the placement of election advertising materials. The campaigning period starts from the date of nominating a list of candidates by a political party and ends at midnight before Election Day. Election advertising on the radio and television and in print is only allowed 28 days before Election Day. Political campaigning on the day preceding Election Day is prohibited.

A number of articles of the Code of Administrative Law Offenses provides sanctions for violating rules about electoral or referendum campaigning and the production and distribution of anonymous campaign materials. The laws on extremism including Federal Law No. 114-FZ of July 25, 2002 "On Counteraction against Extremist Activity" and Federal Law No. 398-FZ of December 29, 2013, "On Modification of the Federal Law 'On Information, Information Technologies…'" ("The Lugovoi Law") prohibit candidates from using the Internet for extremist speech or promotion of extremist activities. The Criminal Code of the Russian Federation envisages liability both for libel and slander, i.e. for distribution of deliberately false information, defaming the dignity and honor of another person or undermining the person's reputation. According to Federal Law No. 2124-1 of December 27, 1991 "On Mass Media," a citizen has a right to request that an editor's office refute distributed information which is untrue and which defames his/her business reputation. The same law bans the use of subliminal information techniques or messages harmful to people's health (Baranova, 2007).

The lack of clear definition of political advertising in Russia presents many issues related to the implementation of campaigning procedures. For example, the current legislation does not define the difference between political news and political advertising on television or the extent of the daily coverage of political events. Ironically, Federal Law No.38-FZ of March 13, 2006 "On Advertising…" only regulates commercial advertising and would not apply to political advertising or election and referendum campaigning. Clearly, this law would not insulate viewers against the negative forms of political campaigning such as negative advertisements.

The State of Political Parties in Russia

Russia is routinely criticized for a tightly controlled political process with little room for opposition parties. In 2001, there were 190 political organizations officially registered in Russia (Nezavisimy Institut Vyborov, 2007). However, the number of parties very quickly decreased due to Putin's tight grip on the political system to the advantage of the governing United Russia Party. In his analysis of the marginal role of Russian parties in the State Duma elections, Kynev (2011) argues that the cast system in Russian politics divides the political landscape into "systemic," which are officially sanctioned (e.g., United Russia, Liberal Democratic Party of Russia (LDRP), the Communist Party of the Russian Federation (CPRF), Yabloko), and "non-systemic" parties which operate outside of the official political establishment and are normally not represented in the parliament. The pro-Kremlin United Russia is the only party in Russia holding primary elections.

The 2016 State Duma elections reverted to the former electoral process used between 1993 and 2003 according to which half of the 450 seats are elected by proportional representation from parties with a 5% electoral threshold, and the other half from single-seat electoral districts. In Russia, registered candidates and political parties that nominate candidates receive free airtime for campaign advertising on state-funded television, radio, and in print media. Candidates and political parties are eligible for one hour of campaign advertisements from every state-funded media outlet. State-funded newspapers are required to allocate 5% of the total weekly space for advertisements. Half of the space is split between candidates and the other half is split between political parties. Parties that receive less than 3% of the vote lose access to free mass media for the next campaign (International Foundation for Electoral Systems, 2012). There is no particular spending limit on paid advertising if parties do not spend more than their overall campaign-funding limit. Media organizations must charge all partisan candidates the same rate. Parliamentary elections are heavily slanted toward candidates affiliated with systemic parties, as they receive more free advertising than independent candidates. Smaller parties (e.g., the People's Freedom Party) are often rejected for official registration.

Since Putin's return to the presidency in May 2012, a number of restrictive laws have been enacted to further regulate the Russian public sphere and restrict the social activism of Russian citizens and nonprofit organizations, especially actions that could be construed as a "political activity." The Russian "foreign agent" law (Federal Law No. 121-FZ of July 20, 2012 "On Entering Amendments to Individual Legislative Acts…") requires non-profit organizations that receive foreign donations and engage in "political activity" to register as foreign agents. The foreign agent label imposes additional registration barriers for an NGO in Russia, such as extensive audits and restrictions on foreign personnel. Because in Russia "foreign agent" can be interpreted as "spy" or "traitor" (this negative connotation has been in use since Stalin's time), this law is seen as a way to discredit and marginalize independent advocacy groups. In 2013 the GOLOS Association, Russia's only independent organization monitoring referendums and elections, incurred a significant fine for failing to register under the law and then still listed as a foreign agent (Sud otklonil zhalobu "Golosa"…, 2013).

An important innovation in the Russian political elections was introduced in 2014 when Russia's Central Electoral Commission announced that it would draw up the map of the 225 single-member districts in the Russian Federation (Karpyuk, 2014). This *gerrymandering* technique, also known as "cracking," spreads voters of the non-systemic opposition among many districts to deny them a sufficiently large voting bloc in any particular district and minimize a number of unwanted voices in parliament. The "petal-shaped" mapping splits the voters in an urban area among several districts so that the majority of voters are suburban and more loyal to the authorities on the presumption that the two groups would vote differently.

Non-systemic politicians would also be less likely to get a seat from single-seat electoral districts at the pre-election stage because of this gerrymandering technique. Opposition groups will not be able to take full advantage of urban electoral campaigning such as lower costs, uninterrupted Wi-Fi connection, the convenience of organizing meetings with urban voters, or the full benefits of street campaigning (cubes, traffic, metro, etc.), among others.

Russian gubernatorial elections have been held since 1991 with the exception of a break from 2005 to 2011. In 2009 President Putin introduced the system of presidential appointment of governors, meaning that the president indirectly controls the appointment of members of the Federation Council. In 2012 President Medvedev signed a federal law to bring back gubernatorial elections. Although Russian law forbids the central government to be directly involved in political advertising during parliamentary campaigns, key government ministers have dominated political advertising and campaigning in every Duma election since 1993. The return to direct election of governors did not make the election process more competitive. The same political figures continue to be reelected on a regular basis. Their campaign managers often get the desired results without having to resort to any fraud or manipulation techniques. These elections are poorly attended and have a low turnout. This type of "referendum elections" normally leaves the opposition very little chance to win regional elections as the authorities have learned how to eliminate unwanted candidates at the early stage of election registration. This allows the officials to avoid unnecessary public scandals and additional media attention during an election period.

After Putin returned to power in 2012, he amended the legislation on gubernatorial elections by allowing the regions to choose appointments of the candidates recommended by political parties and nominated by the Russian president or by regional parliaments. The official reason for this amendment was the concern that in national republics, such as Chechnya, Dagestan, Ingushetia, representatives of national minorities would never have a chance to become governors through direct elections.

Political Advertising during Parliamentary and Presidential Elections

Under the terms of the 1993 Russian constitution, political parties and the mass media play important roles in elections to the new parliament. In 1993, individuals could choose to run with or without party affiliation in elections for both chambers. The 20-minute segments of free advertising were dominated by talking heads. Most major parties were not successful at making recognizable policy statements, apart from the xenophobic messages by Vladimir Zhirinovsky, the eccentric leader of the Liberal Democrats. Thanks to their charismatic leader, his party swept into power with 235 of the party-list vote (Oates, 2006a).

In 1995, the electoral commission provided guidelines for competing in the parliamentary elections. The guidelines outlined in Decree No. 18/149-P also delineated rules for debates and roundtable discussions even though almost all candidates and parties declined to participate in discussions during the 1995 campaign. Most candidates favored press conferences and rallies in which they could stick to limited and noncontroversial topics. Over time, the democratic features of political advertising, such as relatively equal access and representation, have faded (Oates, 2006a), and parties have been given shorter spots on television. The increasing involvement in the Duma elections by the central government has become more noticeable. In 1995, a study by the Institute for Media revealed "a strong bias towards the pro-government party 'Our Home is Russia' on five television networks" (Oates, 2006b, p. 100).

In the mid-1990s, political advertising gradually became less oriented toward the West and more hawkish (Oates, 1998). *Black PR* was introduced as one of the most potent smear campaign tools by political marketing specialists. Unlike negative advertising used in Western politics, black PR has been mostly known for using *kompromat* or compromising materials about politicians and other public figures (White & McAllister, 2006). Such materials were used for various purposes including negative publicity, blackmailing, or for ensuring loyalty. The wave of kompromat was generated not only by the demands of the media owners, but also by the journalists themselves. Credible falsehoods, transcripts of taped telephone conversations, and pseudo-events were thrown to the press in the guise of "the real news." This questionable practice flourished as journalists were not obliged under the law to reveal their sources except when ordered to do so by a court (Zassoursky, 2004). Russian news showed compromising materials in a biased or incomplete way not only to sling mud or report negative news about an individual or an organization, but also to obfuscate and confuse the viewer (Oates, 2006b, p. 116). Clearly, such detrimental practices contributed to a very low level of proved dialogue during election campaigns.

In 1995, Boris Yeltsin saw his lowest presidential approval rating of 5% (VCIOM, 1995), a result of failed economic reforms, the Chechen war, and multiple corruption scandals. At that time there was a decline in public trust in political and social institutions which "reflected the disillusionment with the role of government itself" (Clark, Goss, & Kosova, 2003, p. 10). The Communist Party (CPRF) leader Gennady Zyuganov, however, saw increased public approval by early 1996. CPRF, the only party with a coherent ideology and a significant popular support, has been consistently attacked and denigrated by the mass media. According to Oates (2006a), the 1996 Russian presidential campaign was the only one in which paid and free airtime were important tools for the incumbent leader. During the 1996 elections Yeltsin was given extensive coverage and was framed as an effective country leader. The coverage ignored the serious health problems of the president as well as corruption problems in his administration. Clearly, Yeltsin's improvement in the polls occurred mainly as a result of the application of new election marketing and "spin" techniques (Oates, 2006a).

The 1999 Duma campaign marked the battle between two "parties of power," with government ministers fronting a party called "Unity," supporting new Prime Minister Vladimir Putin, and some regional leaders launching the Fatherland-All Russia party. The early election campaign saw an initial surge in popularity of the latter party, led by the Moscow mayor Yuri Luzhkov and the former Prime Minister Yevgeny Primakov. Fatherland-All Russia leaders tried to capitalize upon the perceived incapacity of President Boris Yeltsin and the weakness of his administration. Enikolopov, Petrova, and Zhuravskaya (2011) argue for an impact of the alternative (non-state) media on voting behavior during the 1999 parliamentary elections. Their findings show that "the probability of voting for opposition parties increased for individuals who watched independent TV even controlling for voting intentions measured one month before elections" (p. 3282).

Political competition involved a new wave of intense mudslinging and character assassination practices (Sigelman & Shiraev, 2002). The late 1990s were known as the epoch of "television killers," especially Sergei Dorenko, who earned his reputation for scandalous accusations against Luzhkov and Primakov, two major opponents of Vladimir Putin, on prime-time news shows. Political advertising during this campaign became more personality-centered, leaving little room for discussion about policies and the problems facing Russia.

During the 2000 campaign, Putin's strategy was to avoid campaigning altogether. A new prime minister became popular among Russians for his resolute actions against Chechen separatists, making the younger, energetic politician a better alternative than seasoned KGB veteran Primakov. Putin did not use his free airtime or purchase advertising, but the Channel 1 news channel promoted him relentlessly during the campaign as an effective and authoritative leader. He was shown traveling around Russia and promising increased salaries, better pensions, and funding for various regional projects (Oates, 2006a). A study of voting behavior in the 2000 presidential elections found support for Putin and Channel 1 viewership to be closely related (White, Oates, & McAllister, 2005). According to Oates (2006a), Putin remained above the campaign fray and impervious to assaults from other candidates. As a result, they wound up attacking one another or discussing relatively trivial issues. For example, kompromat during the 2000 presidential elections against Grigory Yavlinsky, the leader of "Yabloko," included speculations about whether he had plastic surgery or if the West funded his campaign (Oates, 2006a).

By the 2003–4 elections cycle, political advertising had more emphasis on techniques favoring style over substance. The pro-government party Unified Russia dominated the Duma elections under the slogan "Together with the President." Only a handful of the parties in the 2003 Duma race used a significant amount of paid advertising. Three types of parties dominated the race: the parties in power, the Liberal Democrats and a selection of well-financed, but generally unpopular parties that had little aside from a paid television presence. In 2003, some experts (Efimov, 2003) saw the election campaign as less active due to many reasons, including the change in the law on pre-election campaigning. Although amendments to federal laws, such as Federal Law No. 2124-1 "On Mass Media," were made to address alleged concerns about the purity of the electoral process, in fact, they introduced rigid censorship. For example, the new legislation allowed suspending the activities of a mass media outlet for violating electoral rules during the election campaign, such as engaging in any communication that could be construed as political agitation. This could be literally applied to any activity, including expressing opinion or providing any analytical information about the possible consequences of elections, promoting appeals to vote for or against a candidate, or dissemination of information about the activities of a candidate unrelated to his professional activities (Memorial, 2003).

During the 2004 presidential elections the format of free broadcasts changed, and viewers could see a range of parties within the block, each with a shorter segment, instead of seeing each party for 20 minutes, as in 1993 (Oates, 2006a). But as there was no realistic opponent to Putin in the 2004 presidential elections, editorial coverage, free airtime and paid political advertising became largely irrelevant. Putin again did not use his free airtime or buy any advertising. This became unnecessary, as state-run news channels covered a wide range of Putin's most routine meetings, often in great detail.

The non-competitive conditions of the 2007 parliamentary elections and the implicit electoral victory of United Russia were largely criticized by election monitoring groups (Westall, 2008). Administrative resources were used extensively to promote United Russia. The opposition was largely excluded from the mainstream media, not all candidates had equal airtime, and the activities of some election monitoring groups were restricted. The surveys (VCIOM, 2007) demonstrated that the audience perceived politicians' statements as boring and political advertising mostly dull and annoying. The surveys also showed that important topical issues were not discussed and the election results were known to the audience in advance. During the 2007 election, Putin was deliberately ambiguous about his future plans. His leadership as the head of United Russia and the promise to become prime minister in many ways assured a positive result of the key party.

In 2011–12, Russia saw the biggest protests in Moscow since the 1990s. The protests were sparked by claims of alleged ballot-rigging in parliamentary elections and flawed results. Mass protests on the streets of Moscow, and in other cities, forced the Kremlin to confront the public outburst reflecting a lingering conflict between the state and the society that had been smoldering for years. Although the 2011 legislative elections were considered by the opposition to be rigged in favor of the ruling party, nationwide exit polls were very close to the final results. This suggests that there were no mass falsifications despite some isolated cases of fraud (Migranyan, 2011). United Russia, which was heavily criticized during the Duma elections, received less than 50% of the vote and lost its constitutional majority. During his campaign, Putin tried to distance himself from the pro-government party which faced decreasing public support. The representatives of United Russia declined an opportunity to participate in the televised debate or respond to critics. After 2011, however, their tactics changed as they began to pressure non-systemic opposition more actively. The popularity of political talk shows significantly increased during the 2011 election cycle. Some skeptics, however, explained that large audiences watched political debates as they were usually scheduled between the episodes of popular television sitcoms (Borodina, 2011).

The presidential elections in 2012 were characterized by increased civic activity that forced the state to make some electoral concessions and loosen its grip on the public sphere. After the mass protests following the parliamentary elections, the state sought to reduce the protest sentiment by promising changes in the political system. At the same time, there was little public debate with opposition leaders in the media. Television channels mainly ignored opposition parties. In early 2012, limits were put in place for Russia's talk shows and political programs were temporarily suspended on the major channels to prevent "the risk of false interpretations" during the election campaign (Luxmoore, 2015). The emotional tone of the print press was predominantly negative toward opposition leaders, who were often accused of working for foreign governments or of treason. The pressure from the government was exerted on the independent media, civil society organizations and opposition representatives. On December 9, 2011, a Russian independent television channel "Dozhd" was asked to provide copies of its coverage of the protests to determine if it had abided by Russian media laws. There were cases of government officials actively campaigning for Putin and imposing administrative pressure on their employees (Kynev, Vakhshtain, Buzin, & Lyubarev, 2012). President Putin's third term started with the enactment of laws in June 2012, which set strict boundaries on protests and imposed heavy penalties and fines for those taking part in unsanctioned protests.

In contrast to 2008, the focus of political campaigning in 2012 shifted from outdoor advertising and billboards to overwhelming mass media support of Putin. The intensity of Putin's media campaign and the disparity in the coverage of the other candidates are primarily explained by Putin's service as acting prime minister. Under the pretext of covering his "routine work activities," there was a massive information campaign to support him. Putin's heavy media exposure blurred the lines between political advertising and regular news coverage. Putin's campaign managers used the popular Internet sites, such as Yandex, Mail.ru and Odnoklassniki.ru, for posting pre-election polls that would be linked to Putin's election site, www.putin2012.ru.

It has become customary for Russian elections to have a significant imbalance in the media coverage between presidential candidates. For example, Mikhail Prokhorov, the self-nominated candidate, received less free airtime than the candidates nominated by political parties. An analysis of federal and regional media during the official campaign demonstrates a huge disparity in media coverage: 134,033 references for Putin and 24,476 references for the runner-up Mikhail Prokhorov (Kynev et al., 2012). This disparity was evident at both the federal and regional levels.

Kynev, Lyubarev and Maksimov (2015) argued that pre-election campaigning became even more pronounced during the regional and local elections in 2014. Campaigns usually started several months prior to the official kick-off time. Publications featuring the "right" candidate in regional or district newspapers were primarily financed from regional or city budgets and delivered free of charge to residents' mailboxes. Often, such intensive promotion in print media was unnecessary because of the widespread practice of "hidden advertising" disguised by regional television channels as the coverage of political candidates and their daily work. Formally, this practice might not seem like a pre-election campaign, but it has a significant impact on the voter's perceptions and, thus, can be regarded as inappropriate use of administrative resources. At the same time, the regional media would often deny free and paid airtime or print space to other candidates or offer them the graveyard slots on television.

It has also become a common practice for many candidates to avoid negative associations with the "party of power." They downplayed any party affiliation by declining to use the party's logo and other visual elements during the campaign. Other cloaking techniques used by pro-government parties involved the use of protest rhetoric and slogans calling for change, which are mostly typical for opposition parties. Traditional black PR techniques during the regional elections in 2014 included old-style compromising materials about the alleged criminal connections or past conviction of candidates, as well as information about their wealth, property and income.

The introduction of national primaries in May 2016 and allowing individual representatives from single-member districts to participate in parliamentary elections in September 2016 brought back higher demand for political consultants and election campaign managers. These recent reforms can be seen as the Kremlin's direct response to the public dissatisfaction about electoral rigging in previous years and consequent protests in 2011–12. The process of national primaries helps United Russia to reinvigorate the party system as it brings out not only party members but anybody with the right to vote. The primaries help the party of power spot promising candidates by attracting new politicians and making them debate and compete for the final place in the ballot, as well as screen out all flawed candidates during the registration phase. At the same time, critics point out that primaries allow United Russia to start their campaign early in the year before other parties (Why Russian primaries are little more…, 2016). Primaries are an excellent news topic that brings additional free media coverage and helps familiarize the electorate with new politicians ahead of the fall parliamentary elections.

Political Activism and Election Campaigning in the 2010s

In recent years, the Internet and mobile technologies have significantly altered traditional approaches to political advertising and election campaigning in Russia. Political organizations and parties actively embrace grassroots tactics and online applications for public outreach and citizen engagement. Grassroots campaigns refer to planned activity organized by the people from the ground up to mobilize public support and bring pressure on legislators and government officials. This form of political persuasion can be a highly effective way to alert legislators and elected officials about public concerns and spur them to action (Samoilenko, 2014). For example, the Society of Blue Buckets emerged in Russia in 2010 as a response to the arbitrary use of emergency rotating blue flashers by government officials. Inspired by blue toy buckets' strong resemblance to emergency blue rotating lights, members of this protest movement attached buckets to their vehicles' roofs during automotive flash mobs. On the other hand, cases of *astroturfing*, pseudo-grassroots campaigns, are also common in Russian politics. This kind of artificial grassroots action imitates public advocacy efforts started by individuals and often withholds information about the source's financial connections. For example, astroturfing was used during the 2012 presidential elections, as evidenced when a few pro-Putin rally participants complained that they were not paid as promised (Vinokurova, 2012).

Smartphones and mobile applications provided new approaches for public outreach. The Active Citizen mobile app for user participation in online referendums was launched in May 2014. Every week the Moscow mayor and the Moscow government introduced new vital issues for public consideration. Moscow residents can directly influence the decisions of the authorities by voting on the design for new metro stations, the dates for school holidays, or the areas where new parks will be created. Users are granted points for active participation in city referendums. After earning 1,000 points, they receive the "Active Citizen" status and can redeem their points for free parking or other city services.

In December 2011, Russia saw the largest protests against the ballot-rigging of legislative election results. The protests were organized by the leaders of non-systemic opposition and drew over 100,000 people to the street in 39 Russian cities. The opposition used two crowdsourcing platforms: "Karta

Narusheniy" [Map of Violations] for monitoring election violations and "Beliy Krug" [White Circle] for protest coordination in Moscow (Asmolov, 2015). "Karta Narusheniy" contained over 13,000 reports and was seen by many as a credible source of information about election fraud.

One of the protest leaders was Alexey Navalny, lawyer, politician and online activist, who gained prominence in Russia as a critic of government corruption. Navalny also became famous for his innovative crowdsourcing and crowdfunding projects. His anti-corruption platform RosPil is a perfect example of both civic activism and individual political branding. Ironically, RosPil takes advantage of the existing procurement regulation that requires all government requests for tender, government contracts and winning bids to be posted online. The idea is that all kinds of financial violations, budget schemes and unfair state competitions will be exposed by citizens and then investigated by the independent RosPil team. If a submitted report appears to be particularly suspicious, it will be flagged and reviewed by legal experts for modest compensation, funded by donations made to the site. In case of evidence of corruption, the lawyers will file a lawsuit and submit a complaint to the relevant government agency. As of January 2016, the RosPil website states that frauds totaling 59 billion rubles have been detected and prevented.

The difference in approaches to campaigning and political advertising between systemic and non-systemic candidates is best illustrated by the analysis of the 2013 Moscow mayoral election (Lipman, 2013; Suleimanov, 2013). Navalny, the candidate from the People's Freedom Party (or PARNAS), used a variety of advertising tactics. First, he refused to participate in mayoral debates, both televised and on the radio, during early-morning hours. Instead, he invested a significant amount of time and effort to meet face-to-face with residents of Moscow districts. About 15,000 volunteers canvassed for Navalny all over the city, distributing newspapers, printing leaflets, making banners, and producing and distributing T-shirts. Volunteers set up numerous "Navalny cubes," small, square tents with the politician's image and campaign goals printed on the walls. Campaigners actively used social media, especially public pages on "Vkontakte," sending up to 20 messages a day to random users who indicated Moscow as their place of residence in their profile. Navalny's campaign also used targeted Internet advertising via Google AdSense. This campaign drew on private fundraising and raised about a hundred million rubles (roughly three million dollars).

Sobyanin, acting mayor, used a different "silent campaign" approach, letting "Moscow speak for him" (Bodrunova, 2014). The media channels extensively covered the reconstruction of Moscow begun by the mayor. Testimonials by various supporters lauded the mayor's good deeds. The site, My Friend Agrees, featured domestic pets, snakes and goats supporting Sergei Sobyanin in one way or another. The use of video ads was another aspect of the pro-Sobyanin campaign. Another website, "Anybody but Sobyanin," featured "anti-Sobyanin" videos in which stereotypical characters, a Caucasian man, a traffic cop and a parking attendant, cursed Sobyanin for improving the city and depriving them of their ill-gotten gains. There were both pseudo-critical and complimentary videos about Sobyanin distributed across social networks. At the same time, several videos smearing Navalny were posted on YouTube.

Digital transparency, increased Internet literacy and real-time public engagement have changed Russian political communication in the 2010s. The real power of social media has been exercised through multiple campaigns aiming at building a critical mass of the informed public to address social and political concerns. Social media helps election campaigners to cut down on overheads and operating costs and reduces the need for both paid and volunteer staff. "Social media and especially blogs play an extremely important role in setting political agendas and forming collective opinions in the modern Russian hybrid media system, providing an alternative to government information channels and elite-controlled media" (Johansson, 2014).

Political advertising and election campaigning in the 2010s were largely influenced by new technological solutions and the mobile Internet. Bodrunova (2013) points out "a new ('anti-mediacratic') form of fusion of media and political activities" (p. 16) in Russia. Blogging political activists, such as Alexey Navalny, blur the lines between mainstream political practices (e.g., creating a political party, joining a coordination committee, and campaigning); grassroots activism, critical and opinion journalism, and media production (p. 16). The approach of these bloggers should be seen as a form of online anti-corruption activism and an effective means of political advertising in the context of the Russian political system.

Shaping the Russian Public Sphere

The concept of public sphere or *Öffentlichkeit* elaborated by Habermas (1962) involves the idea of the rational and critical discussion of public affairs. Public sphere as a practice has come under a lot of pressure lately. However, Golding and Murdock (2000) state that "the idea of public sphere is worth retaining, provided that we add that it needs to be open enough that all groups in society can recognize themselves and their aspirations as being fairly represented" (p. 77).

There is an ideal notion of the public sphere in terms of its potential and opportunity to enrich and develop society, especially the health of the democracy. Castells (2003) argues that there is a co-development between the society and the Internet, which has a profound effect upon citizens' daily lives. Thus, although power rests in the hands of the state, there are means available to challenge that power base through projecting competing sets of values and norms. Social media provides one possible avenue, linking and uniting individuals that could be otherwise separated by the constraints of time and space.

Introduced by President Putin in 2000, the Doctrine of Information Security signaled the intent to establish legal control over the flow of information with complete censorship of certain topics (Richter, 2002). Putin explained the need to create a "single information space" by filtering out disinformation as a way to build a better society. The media was relegated to maintaining public calm and providing a limited capacity for discussion of "minor" problems in society (Simons, 2005).

Federal and local governments apply pressure on media outlets in different ways. Various law enforcement agencies can be used to control the media. In addition, investors with close ties to the president's administration acquire shares of online media companies and turn them into state supporters. For example, financial control of VKontakte – Russia's largest social network and Europe's second most popular – was secured by investors loyal to the state in April 2014. In May 2016, three top editors of the independent news organization RBC, known for its in-depth investigative reports, had been dismissed. This became another illustration of a long-term trend in the Russian news media. Before then, two other Russian media outlets, Forbes and Vedomosti, got new owners in late 2015 in connection with a new federal law limiting foreign capital (Meduza, 2016).

A set of Internet laws in Russia allows the government to block, shut down or add a website to the blacklist without acquiring a court order. The official blacklists of banned websites and pages include sites that (1) are deemed extremist; (2) contain child pornography or promote suicide and drugs; (3) violate copyright laws in the online environment; and (4) call for non-sanctioned protests. There is also an unofficial fifth blacklist aimed not at sites but at hosting companies based abroad, who have proven to be uncooperative with Russian authorities. The applied measures primarily intend to instigate self-censorship of professional reporting and individual expression. By drafting broad and opaque bill proposals, legislators reserve the right to block entire portals or services and have the restrictions constantly expanded (Soldatov, 2014b).

Lately, the Russian government has enacted additional Internet restrictions. The notorious "bloggers law" (Federal Law No. 97-FZ of May 5, 2014) states that Internet bloggers who attract more than 3,000 daily visitors must register with Roskomnadzor as mass media. Popular bloggers are now obligated to store their electronic communications with Internet users for six months and submit this information to the authorized state bodies upon request. Roskomnadzor assigns the blogger status according to its own statistics. This law, however, does not protect bloggers from any manipulation of online statistics by fake accounts or spam bots.

These activities support President Putin's vision for nationalizing the online space of the country. At a media forum in 2014, the Russian president referred to the Internet as "a brainchild of the CIA" (Soldatov, 2014a) and called for protecting Russia's information in a field dominated by US companies. President Putin reproached the Russian search engine giant Yandex for falling under Western control. The two most popular search engines in Russia, Yandex and Google, share 62% and 27.6% of the market, respectively. A new national search engine, Sputnik, will have a competitive edge over other search engines in Russia as it will be required as the default service at state companies and government agencies. According to experts, the new search engine fits the Russian government's strategic perspective as it would reduce the influence of Yandex and Google on the search market (Bodner, 2014).

Since 2012 the Russian government has heavily invested in traditional propaganda strategies in an attempt to manipulate the public and replace an open public sphere and pluralism of voices with spiritual bonding and group-think. During the Ukraine political crisis in March 2014, the Kremlin continued toughening up its censorship policy over independent media and suppressing inconvenient narratives with saturated state-controlled propaganda. In 2014–15 more than a dozen political talk shows aired regularly on Russia's main channels, showing the popularity of television as a news source among Russians. The time Russians spend watching television rose in 2014 for the first time in over five years, with 72% tuning in to federal channels daily. News and analytical programs received a 9% boost in popularity – by far the largest across all categories (Luxmoore, 2015).

There are new sophisticated strategies employed by Russian political technologists. Recent research has revealed the work of infamous pro-Kremlin Internet trolls who are paid to flood Western news websites and forums and social networks with rumors and disinformation criticizing the opposition and praising the Russian government (Chen, 2015; Garmazhapova, 2013). The propaganda efforts seem to have had an impact on public opinion. A study by Nisbet (2015) shows that 49% of Russians think the Internet should be censored and 42% think foreign countries are using the Internet against Russia.

Furthermore, the Russian state is currently rewriting the country's doctrine of information security. The new doctrine is intended to be a protection mechanism against "special services" and Western countries' "controlled NGOs" that actively use information and communication technologies "to undermine the sovereignty and territorial integrity" and "destabilize the political and social situation" in other countries (Chernenko, Novy, & Safronov, 2015).

Conclusion

The media possess substantial power for political persuasion in countries characterized by weak democratic institutions (Oates, 2006a). Media effects in Russia are large due to the combination of such factors as an unstable party system, weak partisan attachments, unclear policy positions, and the lack of competitiveness in the media market. When other political institutions are weak, the role of television becomes even more critical and open to manipulation. State television is still among the most trusted institutions in the country. It remains central to the political education and orientation of Russians (Luxmoore, 2015; Simons & Samoilenko, in press).

The 2012 poll showed that Russians get information about elections primarily from informational and analytical television programs (66%) and televised debates between candidates (62%). Importantly, 36% of respondents said they get information about election campaigns from advertising on television, radio, print media and the Internet (36%) (VCIOM, 2012). At the same time, the majority of Russians do not remember the content of political trailers (VCIOM, 2007). The news, however, is quite carefully watched and relatively well received. The lack of trust or interest in advertising has made political advertising less relevant to electoral success, while access to the news has become more important in election campaigns (Oates, 2006b). Not surprisingly, news about the pro-government parties and candidates dominate the newscast on state-run television during every election campaign (Kynev et al., 2015).

The traditional boundaries between news and political advertising have eroded in Russia. Hidden advertising, black PR and biased news reporting were common in Russian election campaigns in 1993–2014. The majority of Russians believed that parties and candidates resorted to unfair methods of campaigning by taking advantage of administrative resources, using bribery and fraud (Shamseeva, 2003).

Political parties often spring up or show activity just before elections and inundate the media with populist messages to get elected. Russian Duma elections became an exercise of populism (promotion of demagogic figures, a preference for catchy slogans over real policy alternatives, nationalism and xenophobia) rather than a competition for preferred policy and leadership. As a result, both paid and free political advertising have done little to contribute to the growth of real political choices in Russia. Political advertising, which is sponsored by the elites, targets the base needs and desires of mass voters in order to preserve the status quo of the political system.

In recent years, a new practice of political communication has emerged, a hybrid form of online activism and political advertising (e.g., crowdsourcing). However, since 2012, the Russian Internet has become restricted by a number of laws and regulations. The law's vague language allows for multiple interpretations and thus allows the implementation of sanctions against "unfriendly" online media. The threat has a chilling effect on independent media, bloggers and opposition. The statement, "The internet is virtually the only platform where criticism of the government is tolerated" (Pankin, Fedotov, Richter, Alekseeva, & Osipova, 2011, p. 7) is quite outdated now. The participatory nature of the Internet or the ability to read and re-disseminate information online (Singer, 2013) has been severely undermined in Russia.

An old practice of suppressing traditional media reinforced by an attempt to regulate the Internet as a public space has a negative effect on the development of political advertising in Russia. As a relatively new field, development of political advertising would be possible in the environment with free competition and the exchange of ideas and public interest. However, in an environment with predetermined election results, citizens' political apathy and the threat of legal sanctions against online media, there are very few forces that would drive the development of the field. Future research should look at a possible resilience effect, or field development despite the political adversity. However, restrictions on street protests and heavy regulation imposed on online activities give Russian society a very limited choice of channels for self-expression and communicating their opinions and concerns to the government. The absence of an accurate monitoring system of public discontent and tightened steam valve on public communication makes it very hard to predict the next bifurcation point of political change in Russia.

References

Asmolov, G. (2015). Vertical crowdsourcing in Russia: Balancing governance of crowds and state–citizen partnership in emergency situations. *Policy & Internet*, 7(3), 292–318.

Baranova, M. V. (2007). Tekhiko-yuridicheskie problemy dinamiki struktury soderzhaniya bazovogo zakona "O reklame" [Technical and legal issues concerning the content structure dynamics of the basic law "On Advertising"]. *Yuridicheskaya Techika [Juridical Technique]*, 1, 92–98.

Bodner, M. (2014, May 22). Russia presents new state-owned search engine called Sputnik. *The Moscow Times*. Retrieved from www.themoscowtimes.com/business/article/russia-presents-new-state-owned-search-engine-called-sputnik/500727.html.

Bodrunova, S. (2013). Fragmentation and polarization of the public sphere in the 2000s: Evidence from Italy and Russia. *Global Media Journal. German Edition*, 3(1), Retrieved from www.db-thueringen.de/servlets/DerivateServlet/Derivate-27654/GMJ5_Bodrunova_final.pdf.

Bodrunova, S. (2014). "Humble and hard-working?" Sergey Sobyanin and Alexey Navalny as Moscow mayoral candidates of 2013. In J. Lees-Marshment (Ed.), *Political marketing: Principles and applications* (pp. 197–200). New York, NY: Routledge.

Borodina, A. (2011, December 7). Efir vybora [On the air by choice]. Retrieved from www.kommersant.ru/doc/1831949.

Bourdieu, P. (1991). *Language and symbolic power*. Cambridge, MA: Harvard University Press.

Castells, M. (2003). *The internet galaxy: Reflections on the internet, business, and society*. New York, NY: Oxford University Press.

Chen, A. (2015, June 2). The agency. *New York Times*. Retrieved from www.nytimes.com/2015/06/07/magazine/the-agency.html.

Chernenko, E., Novy, V., & Safronov, I. (2015, October 9). Zadachi gosudarstvennoy kibervazhnosti [The matters of national cyberimportance]. *Kommersant*. Retrieved from www.kommersant.ru/doc/2829842.

Clark, T. D., Goss, E., & Kosova, L. (2003). *Changing attitudes toward economic reform during the Yeltsin era*. Westport, CT: Greenwood.

Comscore. (2013). 2013 Europe digital future in focus. Retrieved from www.comscore.com/Insights/Presentations_and_Whitepapers/2013/2013_Europe_Digital_Future_in_Focus.

ConsultantPlus. (n.d). Decree N 18/149-P of 20.09.1995. Retrieved from www.consultant.ru/document/cons_doc_LAW_7857/a7e38703b688de5eebb7f6276d23d33622d5b383/.

Efimov, A. (2003, October 30). Kakoy zhe vybor bez piara? [What choice would it be without PR?] Retrieved from http://bd.fom.ru/report/map/d034325.

Enikolopov, R., Petrova, M., & Zhuravskaya, E. (2011). Media and political persuasion: Evidence from Russia. *American Economic Review*, 101(7), 3253–3285.

European Forum for Democracy and Solidarity. (2011, April 14). ECHR rebukes Russia's political party law. Retrieved from www.europeanforum.net/news/1132/echr_rebukes_russia_s_political_party_law.

European Institute for the Media. (2000). Monitoring the media coverage of the March presidential elections in Russia. Final Report. Düsseldorf, Germany.

Fedorov, F. (2007). *Ot Yel'tsina do Putina: Tri epokhi v istoricheskom soznanii rossiyan*. Moscow: VCIOM.

Garant. [n.d.]. GARANT System Documents. Retrieved from http://base.garant.ru/.

Garmazhapova, A. (2013, September 7). Gde zhivut trilli. I kto ikh kormit [Where trolls live. And who feeds them]. *Novaya Gazeta*. Retrieved from www.novayagazeta.ru/politics/59889.html.

Gatov, V. (2015, February). Putin, Maria Ivanovna from Ivanovo and Ukrainians on the telly. The Henry Jackson Society. Retrieved from http://henryjacksonsociety.org/wp-content/uploads/2015/03/Putin-Ivanovna-and-Ukrainians-on-the-Telly.pdf.

Golding, P., & Murdock, G. (2000). Culture, communications and political economy. In J. Curran & M. Gurevitch (Eds.), *Mass media and society* (pp. 70–92). London: Edward Arnold.

Habermas, J. (1962). *Strukturwandel der Öffentlichkeit. Untersuchungen zu einer Kategorie der bürgerlichen Gesellschaft [The structural transformation of the public sphere: An inquiry into a category of bourgeois society]*. Berlin: Neuwied.

International Foundation for Electoral Systems. (2012). Elections in Russia: The March 4 presidential election. Retrieved from www.ifes.org/faqs/elections-russia-march-4-presidential-election.

Johansson, E. (2014). Blogging in Russia: The blog platform LiveJournal as a professional tool of Russian journalists. *Baltic Worlds*, 7(2–3), 27–36.

Karpyuk, I. (2014, December 4). CIK prigotovilsya narezat [Central Election Commission is prepared to "cut" the districts]. Retrieved from http://polit.ru/article/2014/12/04/okrug/.

Korostelina, K. V. (2013). Identity and power in Ukraine. *Journal of Eurasian Studies*, 4(1), 34–46. DOI: 10.1016/j.euras.2012.10.002.

Kynev, A. (2011, November 14). State Duma elections 2011 and the marginal role of Russian parties. Part 2. EU Institute for Security Studies. Retrieved from www.iss.europa.eu/publications/detail/article/state-duma-elections-2011-and-the-marginal-role-of-russian-parties-part-2/.

Kynev, A., Lyubarev, A., & Maksimov, A. (2015). *Regionalnye i mestnye vybory 2014 goda v Rossii v usloviyah novyh ogranicheniy konkurencii [Regional and local elections in 2014 in Russia under new restrictions on competition]*. Moscow: Fond "Liberalnaya Missiya."

Kynev, A. V., Vakhshtain, V. S., Buzin, A. Y., & Lyubarev, A. E. (2012). *Vybory Prezidenta Rossii 4 marta 2012 goda [Russian presedential election of March 4, 2012]*. Moscow: Golos.

Lipman, M. (2013, September 6). Alexey Navalny's miraculous, doomed campaign. *The New Yorker*. Retrieved from www.newyorker.com/news/news-desk/alexey-navalnys-miraculous-doomed-campaign.

Luxmoore, M. (2015, December 28). Putin's no-spin zone. *Foreign Policy*. Retrieved from https://foreignpolicy.com/2015/12/28/putins-no-spin-zone-russian-political-talk-shows-television/.

McKinsey Global Institute. (2014). Global flows in a digital age: How trade, finance, people, and data connect the world economy. Retrieved from www.mckinsey.com/insights/globalization/global_flows_in_a_digital_age.

McQuail, D. (1993). *Media performance: Mass communication and the public interest*. London: Sage.

Meduza. (2016, May 18). 12 newsrooms in 5 years: How the Russian authorities decimated a news industry. Retrieved from https://meduza.io/en/feature/2016/05/18/12-newsrooms-in-5-years.

Memorial. (2003, July 29). O rabote Gosudarstvennoy Dumy v iyune 2003 goda (4–21 iyunya) [On proceedings of the State Duma in June 4–21, 2003]. Retrieved from www.memo.ru/hr/gosduma/61/14.htm.

Migranyan, M. (2011, December 9). What the recent Russian elections really mean. *The National Interest.* Retrieved from http://nationalinterest.org/commentary/what-the-recent-russian-elections-really-mean-6235.

Nezavisimy Institut Vyborov. (2007, February). Razvitie partijnoy sistemy v 2001–2005 godah [The development of political system in 2001–2005]. Retrieved from www.vibory.ru/Regs/b-2-part-2.htm#1.

Nisbet, E. (2015). Benchmarking public demand: Russia's appetite for Internet control. Center for Global Communication Studies. Annenberg School for Communication, University of Pennsylvania. Retrieved from www.global.asc.upenn.edu/publications/benchmarking-public-demand-russias-appetite-for-Internet-control/.

Oates, S. (1998). Party platforms: Towards a definition of the Russian political spectrum. *Journal of Communist Studies and Transition Politics*, 14(1–2), 76–97.

Oates, S. (2006a). A spiral of post-Soviet cynicism: The first decade of political advertising in Russia. In L. L. Kaid & C. Holtz-Bacha (Eds.), *The Sage handbook of political advertising* (pp. 309–324). Thousand Oaks, CA: Sage.

Oates, S. (2006b). *Television, democracy and elections in Russia.* London: Routledge.

Pankin, A., Fedotov, A., Richter, A., Alekseeva, A., & Osipova, D. (2011). *Mapping digital media: Russia.* Washington, DC: Open Society Foundation. Retrieved from www.opensocietyfoundations.org/sites/default/files/mapping-digital-media-russia-20130610.pdf.

Porfiriev, B., & Simons, G. (2012). *Crises in Russia: Contemporary management policy and practice from a historical perspective.* Farnham: Ashgate.

Porfiriev, B., & Svedin, L. (2002). *Crisis Management in Russia: Overcoming institutional rigidity and resource constraints.* Stockholm: Swedish National Defence College.

Richter, A. (2002). Media regulation foundation laid for free speech. In K. Nordenstreng, E. Vartanova, & J. Zassoursky (Eds.), *Russian media challenge* (pp. 115–154). Helsinki: Kikimora.

Samoilenko, S. (2014). Campaigns, grassroots. In K. Harvey (Ed.), *Encyclopedia of social media and politics* (pp. 190–194). Thousand Oaks, CA: Sage.

Shamseeva, E. (2003, October 30). Lizo i iznanka rossiyskogo agitpropa. [The face and underside of the Russian agitprop]. Retrieved from http://bd.fom.ru/report/cat/est_el/d034324.

Sigelman, L., & Shiraev, E. (2002). The rational attacker in Russia? Negative campaigning in Russian presidential elections. *The Journal of Politics*, 64, 45–62.

Simons, G. (2005, July). *Russian crisis management communications and media management under Putin.* Paper presented at the annual scientific meeting of the international society of political psychology, Lund, Sweden.

Simons, G., & Samoilenko, S. A. (in press). The effects of social media in the context of public sphere insularity in Russia. In F. Roumate & A. La Rosa (Eds.), *Civil society and democracy in the age of social media.* Marrakech: Institut International de la Recherche Scientifique.

Singer, J. B. (2013). User-generated visibility: Secondary gatekeeping in a shared media space. *New Media & Society*, 16(1), 55–73. doi: 10.1177/1461444813477833.

Soldatov, A. (2014a, June 18). In front of Putin, internet titans lose their nerve. *The Moscow Times.* Retrieved from www.themoscowtimes.com/opinion/article/in-front-of-putin-internet-titans-lose-their-nerve/502172.html.

Soldatov, A. (2014b, June 20). Voices from the frontlines of censorship. *Index on Censorship.* Retrieved from www.indexoncensorship.org/2014/06/voices-frontlines-censorship-andrei-soldatov/.

Sud otklonil zhalobu "Golosa" na vkljuchenie v spisok inostrannyh agentov [Russian court dismisses Golos' appeal in "foreign agent" case]. (2013, June 14). *Lenta.* Retrieved from https://lenta.ru/news/2013/06/14/golos/.

Suleimanov, S. (2013, August 28). Vo vseh utjugah strany Kak kandidaty v mjery Moskvy pokorjajut internet [Now in all national "irons": How the candidates for mayor of Moscow try to conquer the Internet]. Retrieved from https://lenta.ru/articles/2013/08/28/webelections/.

Trading Economics. (2016). Russia GDP: Annual growth rate 1996–2016. Retrieved from www.tradingeconomics.com/russia/gdp-growth-annual.

VCIOM (1995). Esli by v blizhayshee voskresenye sostoyalis prezidentskie vybory, za kogo by vy otdali svoy golos? [If the presidential elections were held next Sunday, who would you vote for?]. Retrieved from http://wciom.ru/zh/print_q.php?s_id=492&q_id=36352&date=10.12.1995.

VCIOM (2007, November 25). Chto v jetoj predvybornoj kampanii Vam bol'she vsego ne ponravilos'? [What didn't you like most about this pre-election campaigning?]. Survey. Retrieved from http://wciom.ru/zh/print_q.php?s_id=378&q_id=30605&date=25.11.2007.

VCIOM (2012, February 29). Izbiratelnaya kampaniya: Kak sledit za nei obshestvo? [The election campaign: How is the society paying attention]. Retrieved from http://wciom.ru/index.php?id=236&uid=112561

Vinokurova, E. (2012, February 7). Obshestvo obmanutyh mitinguyushih [The society of duped protesters]. Retrieved from www.gazeta.ru/politics/elections2011/2012/02/07_a_3992233.shtml.

Westall, S. (2008, February 27). No opposition or debate in Russia election. Retrieved from www.reuters.com/article/us-russia–election-rights-idUSL2689994320080227.

White, S., & McAllister, I. (2006). Politics and the media in post-Communist Russia. In K. Voltmer (Ed.), *Mass media and political communication in new democracies* (pp. 225–226). London: Routledge.

White, S., Oates, S., & McAllister, I. (2005). Media effects and Russian elections, 1999–2000. *British Journal of Political Science*, 35, 191–208.

Why Russian primaries are little more than a PR stunt political parties in Russia. (2016, May 23). *The Moscow Times*. Retrieved from www.themoscowtimes.com/news/article/why-russian-primaries-are-little-more-than-a-pr-stunt/570052.html.

Zassoursky, I. (2004). *Media and power in Post-Soviet Russia*. Armonk, NY: M. E. Sharpe.

22

SWEDEN

Ten Years with Television Advertising

Bengt Johansson

When political communication is addressed in Sweden, both scholars and party representatives point out that journalist-controlled media is seen as the most important channel in election campaigning (Grusell & Nord, 2015; Johansson & Grusell, 2013; Peterson, Djerf-Pierre, Holmberg, Strömbäck, & Weibull, 2006; Strömbäck, 2016). Even if this is true, political advertising has played a significant role in Swedish election campaigns for more than 100 years and has, during the last decade, become more and more important, not at least due to the advent of televised political advertising and the growing importance of the Internet (Grusell & Nord, 2015; Johansson & Grusell, 2013; Strömbäck, 2016).

Political advertising has a long history in Swedish election campaigns. Posters and newspaper ads have been a recurrent phenomenon since the breakthrough of the modern Swedish democracy at the beginning of the 20th century and are still significant features of the election campaigns (Esaiasson, 1991; Håkansson, Johansson, & Vigsø, 2017; Johansson & Odén, 2014). Over time, these have been complemented with other sorts of advertising. Political propaganda movies were shown in cinemas between 1928 and 1962. During this period, the Swedish political parties produced approximately 150 propaganda films, which were very popular in cinemas and were also used to attract people to join political meetings (Johansson & Odén, 2014). Showing political propaganda in cinemas became popular again during the 1980s and 1990s. In Sweden, as in many parts of the world, commercial ads are shown before the movie starts, and political parties produce political advertising spots and purchase slots in between commercials (Johansson & Grusell, 2013).

When the radio market was de-regulated in 1990, political parties began to produce and air political messages on commercial radio. But the most important change occurred when the legislation regarding political advertisements on television changed in 2005. Since then political parties can use television for political propaganda and this has changed the Swedish campaign culture in many ways (Grusell & Nord, 2010; Holtz-Bacha & Johansson, 2014; Holtz-Bacha, Johansson, Leidenberger, Maarek, & Merkle, 2012; Johansson & Grusell, 2013). But the Internet has also become an important channel for political campaigning. Political parties have, in the last decade, put a lot of effort into developing their websites, but they also purchase ads on different sites – both online media outlets and social media sites such as YouTube (Johansson & Odén, 2014; Karlsson, Clerwall, & Buskqvist, 2013). In addition to these channels, direct mail, leaflets and flyers have been used in the party propaganda repertoire for as long as political parties have been campaigning for public offices in Sweden.

So even if political advertising is still seen as less important compared to traditional news and debates/interviews in broadcast media, the Swedish political communicative landscape is more varied than ever. Political parties have more opportunities to reach voters, and various forms of political advertising have become more important in forming opinions. When the political parties are asked to evaluate the importance of different channels, they still mention news and debates in traditional media first, and the most effective party-controlled channels are believed to be door-to-door canvassing and meeting directly with voters (Grusell & Nord, 2015; Johansson & Grusell, 2013; Strömbäck, 2016; Strömbäck, Grandien, & Falasca, 2013). Nevertheless, political advertising – and especially television – has come to play a more important role, and the steeply increasing costs for political advertising in Swedish election campaigns are an indication of its growing importance.

Sweden: Media and the Political System

In terms of media and politics, Sweden belongs to what Hallin and Mancini (2004) call the Democratic Corporatist model. The role of state-intervention is strong at a structural level with press subsidies and public service broadcasting, and in terms of political communication, the focus has been on the role of the daily press and public service broadcast media – both radio and television (Nord, 2008; Peterson et al., 2006; Strömbäck, 2016).

There is a long tradition of mass-circulation press and an especially strong market for reading local daily newspapers with high circulation. In terms of political parallelism, the press used to be owned by political parties, but these ties have weakened over time and journalistic professionalization has developed standards of impartiality in news reporting and political independency of ownership (Nord, 2008; Peterson et al., 2006; Wiik, 2010). The widespread local press market is accompanied by a relatively strong and relatively autonomous public service broadcast tradition. Even if commercial broadcast media have gained significant market share during the past decades, public service media are still important players in the national media system (Djerf-Pierre & Weibull, 2008; Nord, 2008). During the past decade the traditional press has been under pressure because circulation and advertising revenues have fallen quite dramatically due to the digitalization of media use and the advertising market (Ohlsson, 2015).

In the course of development over time, Sweden, as well as other Nordic media systems, can today be characterized as a hybrid of the Democratic Corporatist and the Liberal Media models. The newspaper market is still relatively strong and the position for public service makes it special even in times of globalization and modernization. However, state intervention has become much less important and political parallelism appears to be overplayed (Nord, 2008).

Regarding the political system, Sweden is a parliamentary democracy, with a multi-party system and a proportional electoral system. Similar to the other Nordic countries – Denmark, Finland and Norway – Sweden has a well-developed social welfare state, comparatively high taxes, and a large public sector (Nord, 2008). Sweden joined the EU in 1994, but due to the referendum in 2003, it is not part of the Eurozone. The Social Democratic Party had a leading role after World War II, as in many other West-European countries. Sweden was led by Social Democratic governments between 1936 and 1976. After this period of Social Democratic dominance, the government has been shifting between coalition or minority Social Democratic governments or governments led by conservative/center parties.

The general support for the party system is relatively strong; the established parties with representation in the parliament still attract the great majority of votes in general. But during the last decade there has been – as in the rest of Europe – a rapid growth of right-wing xenophobic/populist parties. There is no indication of a decline in people's interest in politics, but party identification is decreasing and voters are more volatile. Up until the mid 1980s, five parliamentary parties dominated Swedish politics. The political blocs were relatively well-defined, and although the number of voters who switched party loyalties between elections was rising, the changes generally involved parties within the same bloc. Since then, the party system has become fragmented, and new parties have been established – both on the national and local levels (Peterson et al., 2006). In the contemporary

Swedish political landscape, voters decide which party to vote for during the late stages of the election campaign and they switch parties more easily than in the past. This suggests that Swedish election campaigns have become increasingly important and there more is at stake, and the parties stand to win (or lose) more (Strömbäck, 2016).

Unlike most other countries, national, regional and local elections are held on the same day, which, in essence, means fewer elections in which campaign strategies can be developed and practices can be improved (Nord, 2006). Even where it is possible to vote for a certain candidate, the parties have control over the nomination process and election campaigns are more focused on the struggle between parties than candidates (Hallin & Mancini, 2004).

Regulation of Political Advertising

Rather few regulations surround election campaigning in Sweden. The main principle is journalistic autonomy of election coverage in press, radio and television. The press is free to organize the journalistic coverage of the campaign as they please, even if journalistic norms of impartiality lead to balanced campaign news coverage (Asp & Bjerling, 2014; Ekström, Eriksson, Johansson, & Wikström, 2013). There is a strong professional norm of separating news and views and political opinions are restricted to the editorial page (Wiik, 2010). The only relevant legislation the press has to consider is the Freedom of Press Act, which covers general topics such as libel and threats to, or discrimination of, minorities. The Radio and Television Act regulates public service and commercial channels with terrestrial broadcasting. This Act specifies a balanced coverage of issues, if impartiality and accuracy is a part of the broadcasting license concession (e.g., public service) (Peterson et al., 2006).

Print political advertising has to follow the general principles of permissible expression according to Swedish law (the Fundamental Law of Freedom of Expression). Sweden has, for instance, laws against threatening or expressing contempt for groups with allusion to race, color, national or ethnic origin, religious faith or sexual orientation. Election posters, print ads and other printed political propaganda are – according to the same law – subject to libel and defamation rules. For posters there are also national regulations related to traffic security, where poster size and minimum distance from the roads is specified. Other regulations are local, which include placement and time frame. Election posters are allowed five weeks before Election Day, and they are supposed to be removed no later than one week after (Håkansson, Johansson, & Vigsø, 2014, 2017).

As mentioned above, broadcast media also have to take the Radio and TV Act into consideration. However, political advertising is not regulated for radio or television in this legislation if it is not a part of the license concessions. This de-regulated situation is quite new; Sweden had a long history of prohibiting political advertising in broadcast media (Grusell & Nord, 2010; Johansson & Grusell, 2013; Moring, 2006). The first weakening of this position came with the de-regulation of the radio market in the early 1990s. When commercial broadcast radio was established, a number of limitations on commercials were included in the legislation. Ads promoting alcohol, tobacco, infant formulas and some medicines were not allowed, but no restrictions about political advertising were incorporated.

Political advertisement on television was prohibited for a long time in the Swedish terrestrial television broadcast system. In the public service monopoly era, no advertisements were allowed – commercial or political. When satellite and cable television entered the Swedish media market in the 1980s, the system was put under pressure and in 1991 the first commercial terrestrial channel began broadcasting (TV4). But even if television advertising became an accepted part of the media system, political advertising was still not permitted, since the license agreement stipulated political advertising was prohibited for TV4 as well as for public service broadcasters (Grusell & Nord, 2010).

The situation in Sweden was quite extraordinary in that political parties had no opportunity to use television on their own terms during election campaigns. In many other countries, with or without political advertising on television, free airtime is made available in broadcast media (see

Holtz-Bacha, 2014), but the Swedish tradition was to let journalists control television as a campaign channel (Esaiasson & Håkansson, 2000; Grusell & Nord, 2010; Moring, 2006).

The political majority in the Swedish parliament has historically seen political advertising on television as a negative aspect of political communication. Fears were expressed that it would defame the quality of public sphere by offering emotional, personal and negative appeals lacking substance (Johansson & Grusell, 2013). All parties in the parliament supported the critical stance on political advertising in broadcast media – in public, as well as in private, media (Gustafsson, 2005; Nord, 2008).

But the prerequisites for using television during election campaigns changed when the television system converted from an analogue to a digital terrestrial broadcast system. Before the end of the analogue television broadcast system in 2007, many households had access to a large number of digitally distributed television channels via digital boxes, cable and satellite. These channels were not regulated under the existing Radio and TV Act that stipulated political impartiality. Therefore, these domestic "niche" channels could include political advertising. Some of these were predominantly carrying entertainment-oriented content, while others produced current affairs programs, documentaries, and international news. Consequently, political advertising in Swedish terrestrial television could appear for the first time during the 2006 elections. When the analogue system was shut down, the same rules were valid for commercial TV4 since no restriction concerning political advertising was included in the new license concession. During the European Parliament election (EUP) in 2009 and the general election in 2010, the breakthrough of televised political advertising in Sweden occurred, and most parties have used the opportunity to produce political television spots during election campaigns, although some parties have declined because of the high cost (Grusell & Nord, 2015). As a consequence, TV4 has almost a monopoly of offering political television advertising to political parties. Their internal rules are a strong predictor of when and how political advertising is broadcast, since TV4 is the one of the television channels reaching the greatest number of television viewers with 38% of the audience in 2014 (Mediebarometern 2014, 2014).

There are no specific legal restrictions on televised political advertising, except for a paragraph in the Radio and TV Act stipulating the content must not challenge the basic ideas of democratic government and principles of human equality and individual freedom and dignity. In line with this de-regulated system, there are no legal restrictions concerning the content, balance between parties, how much airtime can be purchased or when political ads are allowed to be aired (Holtz-Bacha, 2014; Johansson & Grusell, 2013). The only example where the restrictions of content have been challenged took place during the 2010 general elections. The Sweden Democrats purchased airtime on TV4 and produced a highly controversial spot telling voters that they had to choose between immigration and pensions. The message was visually represented by an old woman with a walking frame slowly approaching a desk where an immigration officer and a pension officer are sitting. Suddenly an alarm is heard and group of burqa-dressed women with baby strollers run past her to get to the counter before her. Two emergency brake handles are seen and the old woman and the group of women reach for the handles. The voice-over says: "On September 19th you have the choice between immigration or pensions, vote for the Sweden Democrats." The last picture shows an insert with the name of the party, the slogan "security and tradition" and a blue anemone, which is the party symbol.

TV4 refused to show the spot, claiming it was violating what was stipulated in the Radio and TV Act and also discriminated against minorities. The broadcaster demanded that the film be edited before being aired. However, the spot was available on the Internet and became probably the most viewed political advertising during the election campaign.

Television Advertising: Coping With a New Campaign Channel

As indicated earlier, Sweden has moved from a situation in which televised political ads were strictly prohibited, toward a political communication culture where televised political ads have become an integrated part. Due to the impact of television, the exposure to political advertising is widespread. In the national election campaigns of 2014, 85% claimed they had seen political ads on television (Berg & Oscarsson, 2015). But there is still to some extent an ideological cleavage among political parties regarding their views of political advertising on television. The left-wing parties (Social Democrats, Green Party and Left Party) have been more skeptical than parties on the right side of the ideological scale. The first parties to use spots in the digital niche channels were the Moderate Party (Conservative) and the Liberal Party. The same pattern was followed when it was possible to air spots during the EUP election in 2009. The red-green parties chose not to purchase airtime for television advertising, even though they produced films published on their websites (Holtz-Bacha et al., 2012). During the 2010 general election campaign all of the parties in the Swedish parliament decided to incorporate television advertising in their campaign toolboxes, but parties such as the Greens and the Left Party still had their doubts about television advertising, both in terms of the risk of rising campaign costs and the fear of negative campaigning. Parties supporting the new campaign channel claimed the fears were exaggerated. It was considered self-evident that political parties should have an opportunity to use television as a campaign channel on their own terms (Grusell & Nord, 2015; Johansson & Grusell, 2013). Even if voices have been heard sometimes criticizing political advertising on television, there are no suggestions for strengthening the regulations from the political parties. Televised political advertising became domesticated quite fast, which was a little surprising due to the historically critical views on the subject. This has to be understood in the development of the Internet and social media networks. Before the Internet, television (and cinema) was the only channel where voters could hear politicians speak and act. The situation changed radically when the parties started to use the Internet in the election campaigns. Even if the new possibility of using television in campaigning was an important change in 2005, it was maybe not such a big transformation as one might expect. This is because many voters watch the campaign spots on social media sites, online news sites and the websites of the political parties instead of via television. Due to the change of the media environment television has lost its monopoly of reaching voters with political messages using moving images. One could argue that this lack of debate and interest in legal restrictions mirrors a change in Swedish campaign culture, where television lost its central position to the Internet.

In the EUP and the general election of 2014, both the Green Party and the Left Party decided not to purchase televised advertising. The argument was now more related to economy than ideology. These parties judged that the price was too high in relation to the presumed effect and claimed they needed their campaign funds for other activities. Even if parties sometimes decline to purchase airtime for spots, they produce short spots for their websites or YouTube channels. One obvious example was when the Green Party, in the election campaign of 2009, chose not to purchase airtime for television advertising; instead they produced a series of long films which was published on the Green Party website. Another example occurred during the 2014 campaign, when the Sweden Democrats declared they were releasing a new spot, which could be previewed on the Internet. The spot circulated in social media and was also posted on online news websites. However, the Sweden Democrats never purchased airtime on television since they received so much viral attention.

All parties agree that the price of airtime for political advertising has risen quite dramatically since the first opportunity on TV4 during the 2009 EUP (Grusell & Nord, 2015). When analyzing campaign costs for political advertising since 2006 (Table 22.1), it is obvious that television advertising has led to increased costs. The total cost for political advertising during general election campaigns has risen from approximately €28 million to €37 million since 2006. This escalation of campaign costs is exclusively explained by the introduction of television advertising. Even if advertising costs of other channels like radio, Internet, outdoor signs and direct mail also increased, this growth is cancelled out by substantially weakened advertising in different types of press (and cinema).

Looking at the shares of campaign costs, television advertising has gone from being non-existent in the 2006 general election, to constituting 23% of the 2014 advertising budgets. Radio and Internet

Table 22.1 Political advertising in Sweden 2006–14 (euros (in thousands)/percent of advertising costs)

	EUP 2005	EUP 2009	EUP 2014	GE 2006	GE 2010	GE 2014
Television	0	2,300	2,800	0	6,310	8,750
Press	1,880	3,770	3,500	16,920	16,920	14,280
Radio	20	150	165	910	970	1,380
Internet	0	0	0	0	580	810
Cinema	0	10	10	240	150	90
Outdoor signs	180	1,830	2,000	6,780	7,910	8,900
Direct mail	110	470	750	3,010	2,660	3,050
Total	2,190	8,530	9,320	27,860	36,080	37,300
	EUP 2005	EUP 2009	EUP 2014	GE 2006	GE 2010	GE 2014
Television	0	27	30	0	17	23
Press	86	44	38	61	49	38
Radio	1	2	2	3	3	4
Internet	0	0	0	0	2	2
Cinema	0	0	1	1	0	0
Outdoor signs	8	21	21	24	22	24
Direct mail	5	6	8	11	7	8
Total	100	100	100	100	100	100

Note: EUP = European Parliament election, GE = general election. All political parties running for seats at local/regional/national or EU Parliament level during the analyzed period are included in the sample.

Source: TNS SIFO.

receive higher shares over time, while press and direct mail get lower shares. The segment for outdoor advertising is approximately the same.

Political parties spend more money on advertising during the EUP campaigns over time, but the costs are significantly lower compared with the general election. During the 2009 and 2014 elections the costs for political advertising were approximately 25% of the spending for the general elections in 2010 and 2014. But the same trend can be seen as for general elections; more money is spent on television advertising and its share of the total campaign costs increased over time.

Looking at the content and style of political television advertising there are some striking similarities. The length is almost always 30 seconds. When spoken words are used it is voice-over to emphasize and explain what is shown in the spot. Almost all spots use the technique of fast clips and music. The narrative is also similar in that they start with fast clips, with the explanation following at the end, through inserts or by text combined with voice-over. Like the pack-shot at the end of commercials, all parties show their name or party symbol at the end of the spot to remind voters who is responsible for the spot (Holtz-Bacha & Johansson, 2014; Johansson & Grusell, 2013).

Swedish political parties also favor the use of humor in televised political advertising. There are no jokes or slapstick used in the spots, but it is quite striking how parties use an amusing twist or irony when communicating politics. This has, of course, to do with a general tendency to use humor in commercial advertising in Sweden. The impact from commercial advertising is apparent and it is sometimes hard to tell the difference between political ads and commercial ads, if you miss the pack-shot at the end. The fear of more apparent negative campaigning due to the breakthrough of political advertising on television seems to be exaggerated. Even if some ads contain negative appeals, direct attacks are rare. Instead, the parties criticize policy consequences of the opposing parties by direct or indirect comparison to highlight their own policy or ideology. The focus on the party's own policy or ideology is also something TV4 included in its code of conduct for televised political advertising (Holtz-Bacha & Johansson, 2014; Johansson & Grusell, 2013).

Perceptions and Effects

Swedish election campaigns are, to a large extent, mediated. Most voters experience the campaigns indirectly and are exposed to them predominantly through the mass media. This emphasis on indirect political communication is also prevalent in other ways. Compared to many other Western democracies, only small minorities of Swedish voters are actively engaged in and have personal contact with the parties. Figures from the last general elections show that Swedes tend to follow politics from the sidelines, rather than actively engage in party politics or election campaigning (Strömbäck, 2016). Supporting a candidate by attending a meeting is rare (6%) and most voters are not contacted by candidates in their homes (10%) or their workplaces (4%). It is also rather uncommon to persuade someone else how they should vote (19%) or to convince other people (16%) (Berg & Oscarsson, 2015).

Mediated political communication is more widespread. When people are asked where they receive their information about politics and elections they emphasize news in television and the daily press as the most important channels (Strömbäck, 2016). But the breakthrough of television advertising has changed the picture since a vast majority claim they watched political advertising on television during the last general election campaign. Internet channels also seem to change the political communication culture, when 20% claim they searched for information on political party websites and 27% answered that they received political communication through social media platforms (Berg & Oscarsson, 2015).

A political communication channel often neglected in research is flyers and brochures. As Table 22.1 showed, direct mail containing campaign propaganda is a large budget item during the campaign, and it is also an effective way to reach voters. In an overview of where Swedish voters had contact with the 2014 election campaign, 56% answer they had read brochures/flyers from political parties (Berg & Oscarsson, 2015).

When citizens judge how they view different forms of political advertising during the 2010 election campaign (Table 22.2), there are a number of interesting results. One thing is citizens' different views on political advertising depending on the channel/platform used. Considering the balance (positive versus negative views), the results indicate a general negative opinion toward political advertising. Only two of eight forms of political advertising have a majority of respondents positively evaluating the channel (Press + 9 and Posters + 18). Political advertising on television, radio, Internet, direct mail or at cinemas is evaluated rather critically.

Table 22.2 The Swedish opinion on political advertising (percent)

	Television	Press	Radio	Internet	Cinema	Billboards	Posters	Direct mail
Very good	5	8	2	4	4	7	16	7
Fairly good	30	46	24	29	20	38	43	33
Not very good	28	28	41	38	39	33	23	33
Not good at all	36	17	33	29	37	22	18	28
Sum	100	100	100	100	100	100	100	100
N	994	991	948	955	915	981	1001	992
Balance	–30	9	–48	–35	–51	–10	18	–21

Note: The question asked was: "What do you think about political party advertising?"

Source: Novus Group International.

These results are not surprising since they reflect what previous research has shown about opinions on advertising in general. People are more positive toward advertising in the press compared with spots on television, radio and the Internet. On the whole it seems that people dislike being disturbed in their media use. If they want commercials, they want to choose to be exposed to them. It is considered annoying to be interrupted while watching television, listening to the radio or clicking on a clip on YouTube (Grusell, 2008; Reuters Institute, 2015). What might be a little puzzling is the different evaluation of billboards and posters, in which billboards are seen more negatively. Maybe this reflects an anti-professionalization perspective, where posters are viewed as a more grassroots channel compared to the expensive, purchased space on commercial billboards.

But the question is, of course, to what extent political advertising has any effect on citizens' perceptions and, in the end, their voting decisions. There is a long tradition of studying media effects during election campaigns in Sweden (Asp, 1986; Dimitrova, Shehata, Strömbäck, & Nord, 2014; Shehata & Strömbäck, 2013). However, effects of political advertising are under-researched. But the only studies conducted are on perceptions and effects of television advertising, even though television advertising is a rather new phenomenon in the Swedish political culture compared with other forms of political advertising.

One study on people's perception of political advertising was conducted right after the first attempts to introduce political advertising on television in 2006. The results indicated that Swedish opinions followed the general critique against televised political advertising. Political ads on television were not considered to be any guide to which party to vote for, the view of party positions was seen as too simplified, and the appeals were too emotional (Grusell & Nord, 2010). A number of studies have used data from the Citizen panel at the University of Gothenburg (the E-panel) to investigate perceptions and effects of political advertising (www.lore.gu.se). Analyses were conducted on how people evaluate spots they were exposed to during the 2009 EUP campaign. Results showed that party affiliation strongly affected voters' evaluation of the spots. The decision to vote for a specific party goes hand-in-hand with regarding this party's spot as more professional, more entertaining, as communicating the message effectively and arousing strong feelings, as presenting a positive image of the party and being able to convince other people to vote for the party producing the spot (Holtz-Bacha & Johansson, 2014). During the same campaign, an attempt was made to study if exposure to television spots had an effect on voting intention. Using panel data, the results showed a strong correlation between exposure and voting intention. However, when controlling for initial voting intention the results rejected a causal link between exposure and voting intention. Voters with intention to vote tended to be more willing to seek information about the election and therefore exposed themselves to a larger extent to television spots (or remembered they had seen the spots) (Dahlberg, 2010).

An Emerging Research Field?

This chapter has presented the development and the contemporary state of political advertising in Sweden, with a focus on the introduction of television advertising in the Swedish campaign culture. The field of political advertising has, to a large extent, been neglected by Swedish political communication scholars. Campaign research has mainly focused on news media content and its effects on the electorate. There has been a growing interest among Swedish scholars during the last decade to analyze political campaign strategies and the channels controlled by the political parties (i.e., the Internet) (Grusell & Nord, 2015; Johansson & Grusell, 2013; Karlsson et al., 2013). Along with the breakthrough of television advertising, this development has increased interest in analyzing political advertising in Swedish election campaign research (Grusell & Nord, 2010; Holtz-Bacha & Johansson, 2014). Important historical overviews of political advertising (print ads and posters) have also been written (Håkansson et al., 2014, 2017; Johansson & Odén, 2014).

However, there are still gaps to be filled, in terms of strategies, content and effects. The political process behind the changed policy of political advertising on television is still rather unknown. Was it an oversight in the process of adapting the legislation to the digital terrestrial television broadcast system, or was a political agenda behind the decision? Other questions waiting for answers include the process of producing political advertising. Researchers have so far produced limited knowledge on how political propaganda – and especially television advertising – is produced. To understand strategies and content of political advertising, we need to learn more about the tug-of-war between the political parties and advertising agencies. Another important area is the effects of televised political advertising. Previous research has mainly focused on the effects of the news media, even if there are some attempts made to analyze the effects of political advertising on television (Dahlberg, 2010; Holtz-Bacha & Johansson, 2014). But the general story on the effects of political advertising on television in a Swedish context is still waiting to be written.

References

Asp, K. (1986). *Mäktiga massmedier. Studier i politisk opinionsbildning.* Stockholm: Akademilitteratur.

Asp, K., & Bjerling, J. (2014). *Mediekrati. Mediernas makt i svenska val.* Stockholm: Ekerlids.

Berg, L., & Oscarsson, H. (2015). *Supervalåret 2014.* Stockholm: SCB.

Dahlberg, S. (2010). Premiär för personval. In H. Oscarsson & S. Holmberg (Eds.), *Väljarbeteende i europaval* (pp. 191–203). Gothenburg: Department of Political Science.

Dimitrova, D.V., Shehata, A., Strömbäck, J., & Nord, L. (2014). The effects of digital media on political knowledge and participation in election campaigns: Evidence from panel data. *Communication Research,* 41(1), 95–118.

Djerf-Pierre, M., & Weibull, L. (2008). From public educator to interpreting ombudsman: Regimes of political journalism in Swedish public service broadcasting 1925–2005. In J. Strömbäck, T. Aalberg, & M. Ørsten (Eds.), *Political communication in the Nordic countries* (pp. 195–214). Nordicom.

Ekström, M., Eriksson, G., Johansson, B., & Wikström, P. (2013). Biased interrogations? A multi-methodological approach on bias in election campaign interviews. *Journalism Studies,* 14(3), 1–17.

Esaiasson, P. (1991). 120 years of Swedish election campaigns: A story of the rise and decline of political parties and the emergence of the mass media as power brokers. *Scandinavian Political Studies,* 14(3), 261–278.

Esaiasson, P., & Håkansson, N. (2000). *Besked ikväll!* Stockholm: Stiftelsen Etermedierna i Sverige.

Grusell, M. (2008). *Reklam – en objuden gäst? Allmänhetens uppfattningar om reklam i morgonpress och tv.* Gothenburg: University of Gothenburg.

Grusell, M., & Nord. L. (2010). More cold case than hot spot: A study of public opinion on political advertising in Swedish television. *Nordicom Review,* 31(2), 95–111.

Grusell, M., & Nord, L. (2015). *Vinnande kampanjer, förlorade val. Partiernas politiska kommunikation i valrörelsen 2014.* Sundsvall: Mittuniversitetet.

Gustafsson, K.-E. (2005). *Reklamens makt över medierna.* Stockholm: SNS förlag

Håkansson, N., Johansson, B., & Vigsø, O. (2014). *Politik i det offentliga rummet. Svenska valaffischer 1911–2010.* Stockholm: Carlssons.

Håkansson, N., Johansson, B., & Vigsø, O. (2017). From propaganda to image building: Four phases of Swedish election poster history. In C. Holtz-Bacha & B. Johansson (Eds.), *Political communication in the public space: Election posters around the globe.* Heidelberg: Springer.

Hallin, D. C., & Mancini, P. (2004). *Comparing media systems: Three models of media and politics.* Cambridge: Cambridge University Press.

Holtz-Bacha, C. (2014). Political advertising in an international comparison. In H. Cheng (Ed.), *The handbook of international advertising research* (pp. 554–574). Malden, MA: Wiley Blackwell.

Holtz-Bacha, C., & Johansson, B. (2014). Through the party lens: How citizens evaluate TV electoral spots. *Journal of Political Marketing,* 13(4), 291–306.

Holtz-Bacha, C., Johansson, B., Leidenberger, J., Maarek, P. J., & Merkle, S. (2012). Advertising for Europe TV ads during the 2009 European election campaign in four countries. *Nordicom Review,* 33(2), 77–92.

Johansson, B., & Grusell, M. (2013). "Och nu blir det reklamfilm": Politisk reklam i svenska valrörelser. In J. Strömbäck & L. Nord (Eds.), *Kampen om opinionen: Politisk kommunikation under svenska valrörelser* (pp. 64–88). Stockholm: SNS Förlag.

Johansson, B., & Odén, T. (2014). *Politiska annonser. Partiernas valreklam i dagspressen under 100 år.* University of Gothenburg: Nordicom.

Karlsson, M., Clerwall, C., & Buskqvist, U. (2013). Political public relations on the net: A relationship management perspective. *Public Relations Journal,* 7(4), 1–23.

Mediebarometern 2014. (2014). Gothenburg: Nordicom.

Moring, T. (2006). Political advertising on television in the Nordic and Baltic states. In L. L. Kaid & C. Holtz-Bacha (Eds.), *The Sage handbook of political advertising* (pp. 181–210). Thousand Oaks, CA: Sage.

Nord, L. W. (2006). Still the middle way: A study of political communication practices in Swedish election campaigns. *The Harvard International Journal of Press/Politics*, 11(1), 64–76.

Nord, L. (2008). Comparing media systems: North between west and east? *Central European Journal of Communication*, 1(1), 95–110.

Ohlsson, J. (Ed.). (2015). *The Nordic media market 2015*. University of Gothenburg: Nordicom.

Peterson, O., Djerf-Pierre, M., Holmberg, S., Strömbäck, J., & Weibull, L. (2006). *Media and elections in Sweden*. Stockholm: SNS förlag.

Reuters Institute (2015). *Reuters Institute digital news report 2015*. Oxford: Reuters Institute for the Study of Journalism.

Shehata, A., & Strömbäck, J. (2013). Not (yet) a new era of minimal effects: A study of agenda setting at the aggregate and individual levels. *International Journal of Press/Politics*, 18(2), 234–255.

Strömbäck, J. (2016). Swedish election campaigns. In J. Pierre (Ed.), *The Oxford handbook of Swedish politics* (pp. 275–293). Oxford: Oxford University Press.

Strömbäck, J., Grandien, C., & Falasca, K. (2013). Do campaign strategies and tactics matter? Exploring party elite perceptions of what matters when explaining election outcomes. *Journal of Public Affairs*, 13(1), 41–52.

Wiik, J. (2010). *Journalism in transition: The professional identity of Swedish journalists*. Gothenburg: University of Gothenburg.

23

THE WILD, WILD WEST

Political Advertising in the United States

Marion R. Just and Ann Crigler

Political advertising is constructed by candidates, parties and groups and reconstructed by members of the public in the particular political, social, historical, economic and legal context of the system. This dynamic context consists of many different actors: candidates, opponents, political parties, consultants, interest groups, donors and journalists. Political advertising is no longer confined to broadcast media, but is increasingly resident on the Internet and spread through social media. This new form of delivery means a greater role for individual agency, especially in evaluating political ads and disseminating them across their social networks.

Political advertising in the US is unusually complex because of the large numbers of government elective offices and referenda, the nominating process, the length of the campaign, the lack of overlap between media markets and constituencies, and the private funding of campaigns. This chapter examines the context, content and effects of political advertising through the lens of social constructionism.

The Context of Political Advertising: Politics, History and Media System

Political Context

Voting is not required in the US and most elections are single-member, first-past-the-post races. The electoral system is dominated by two major parties with additional minor party candidates competing at the state and federal levels. Local level elections for mayor, city council or selectmen are often non-partisan. The US has a federal system of government and candidates at all levels of government – local, state and national – rely more or less on political advertising to inform voters. Each level contains dozens of contests. For example, local elections might include campaigns for mayor, other city officials, county supervisors, sheriffs, school boards and ballot measures. State elections include federal offices for US Congress, governors and executive level offices, state legislatures, and even judges and propositions. National elections for the president and vice-president are actually conducted within states through complex nominating processes and popular votes are represented in the Electoral College based on state representation in the Congress. Campaigns are lengthy and almost permanent in the US (Boyd, 1981). Long ballots and frequent elections lead many voters to rely on party label and political advertising in making electoral choices.

There is little electoral respite either for voters or candidates. Presidential campaigns begin only a few months after the previous midterm elections. The result is that presidential campaigns effectively last for two years. Members of the House of Representatives never stop campaigning and fundraising, because their terms are so short that they have no break. In fact, members of Congress must engage in fund-raising every week of their two-year terms (Currinder, 2009). Even Senators, who have six-year terms must begin their campaigns at least two years in advance. One reason for the increasing length of campaigns is the system of party nominations.

The parties control the nominating process using primary elections or caucuses of party members. The requirements for party "membership" vary among the states, but the bar is set very low. People do not carry cards of membership or pay dues and, in many states, membership amounts to nothing more than showing up for the caucus or primary. Given the fact that primaries and caucuses do not take place at a regular time, turnout tends to be low. The result is that only voters who are especially committed to the party participate. In general, the nominating electorate is highly ideological. In recent years, this means that voters tend to the ideological extremes of each party, but especially so for the Republican Party. Even party incumbents cannot be assured of re-nomination in the face of an extreme electorate. The system of almost constant elections and little-known candidates puts a heavy burden on voters. The result is low voter turnout for all elections. Turnout is greatest in presidential election years, when it is about half of all those who are age eligible – about 70% of those registered[1] to vote (DeSilver, 2015). In non-presidential years, turnout drops to about 35% – 36.5% in 2014 (Del Real, 2014). In primary elections during non-presidential elections, turnout can drop to the teens.[2] In presidential election states that rely on caucuses to nominate candidates, the electorate ranges from about 1% to 7.5% of the voter eligible population (2012 figures from United States Election Project, 2012). When voters do go to the polls, many have made up their minds in the last two weeks of the campaign. The late-deciders are typically not very attentive to politics and not strongly aligned with one party or the other. In a close election the proportion of unengaged, late-deciders can determine the outcome. For these voters, political advertising may be the main source of information.

History of Political Ads in the US

The presidential election of 1952 marks the beginning of televised political advertising in the US (West, 2014). The Republican Party engaged Madison Avenue advertising executive Rosser Reeves to create television ads for their candidate, Dwight Eisenhower, the World War II hero. From the beginning, political ads used television film technology to deceive audiences. For example, in the Eisenhower Answers America campaign the producers just filmed the General alone reciting answers and later lined up a series of diverse Americans to ask the questions. What appeared to be give-and-take was staged for the camera (The Living Room Candidate, 1952).

Eisenhower's opponent, Governor Adlai Stevenson, also aired television ads but would not appear on camera. One of Stevenson's ads featured a woman singing: "I'd rather have a man with a hole in his shoe than a man with a hole in everything he says." Stevenson also used cartoons to illustrate the policy differences between himself and Eisenhower. Advertising was Stevenson's secondary strategy, however. He preferred recorded half-hour speeches that were broadcast twice a week during the month before the election. Stevenson said about advertising: "I think the American people will be shocked by such contempt for their intelligence. This isn't Ivory Soap vs. Palmolive" (The Living Room Candidate, 1952). How wrong he was. Stevenson was the last presidential candidate *not* to appear in a television ad. In fact it is now required that candidates' pictures, if not the candidates themselves, appear in their ads.

In the following presidential election, with the same candidates, Eisenhower used a man on the street endorsement. An ordinary man standing under a lamppost says how reassuring it is to see the lights on in the White House where President Eisenhower is seemingly working. The man, who is walking a dog, says "a neighbor of mine lives there." This ad makes a bridge between the president and ordinary people. The man under the lamppost ad lasted 4.33 minutes. This ad was followed up with a series of 20-second ads featuring individuals drawn from different walks of life including a housewife, taxi driver, union member, college girl, and an African American woman. Clearly by 1956 many of the essential elements of ads (such as: visual images, sound, targeted appeals, biographical stories, issue spots, attacks against the opponent, and endorsements) were established, but with varying length.

Color television penetrated most US households in the mid 1960s. In 1964, candidates still relied on mostly black-and-white ads. The iconic "Daisy Ad" about the threat of nuclear war used extreme close-up, a mushroom cloud and white on black text to convey the message that the opponent would launch a nuclear war. Even now black-and-white is used to make an ad stand out from other ads, as Bill Clinton did with his policy messages in 1992, or to convey fear, as in the Revolving Prison Door ad by George H. W. Bush the same year (Kaid & Johnson, 2001; Kern, 1989; West, 2014).

The famous advertising guru, Tony Schwartz, introduced music and sound effects, including a laugh track, which were featured in the negative ad "Laughter?" which made fun of Richard Nixon's running mate in 1968. Length continues to vary on television, but most ads have settled at 30 seconds because of costs. In 1992, the independent candidate, Ross Perot, bought 30-minute ads with simple text rolling on the screen. The businessman found he could buy a whole television slot cheaper than some 30-second spots.

American political advertising was the model for television spots around the world. The techniques were exported by American political consultants who strategized with candidates in different political settings with more or less electoral success. Between 1997 and 2010, one consultant, Tad Devine, worked with major party candidates in Colombia, Ireland, Israel, Peru, Bolivia, Honduras and the Ukraine (Harvard Institute of Politics, 2015). Some critics have characterized the ad campaign, with its personalization of the political leader, as the "Americanization" of elections. Characterizing the leader as someone people can relate to or "a guy you can have a beer with" (which was the Reagan strategy in 1984) is central to many campaigns. In the US, candidates often appear with their families to demonstrate that they can relate to the lifestyle and problems of ordinary people. Candidates often picture themselves in casual settings with constituents. Male candidates tend to focus their visuals on themselves, while female candidates prefer more pictures of themselves with constituents (Just & Crigler, 2016).

Candidates use political advertising to promote themselves in the nominating process as well as the general election. The amount and placement of advertising varies according to the structure of the nominating process and the competitiveness of the constituency. So, for example, in presidential primaries, competitive states (i.e., without an overwhelming majority leaning to one party, such as Colorado, Florida, Iowa, New Hampshire) are inundated with political advertising while single party dominated states (e.g., California, New York, Texas, Wyoming) may be largely bypassed (Blumenthal & Edwards-Levy, 2014; *Washington Post*, 2012).

Media Delivery System

More than any other mode, Americans (45%) use television to get news about politics. Television users generally prefer local television to network news. The Internet is the second most used news platform at 37%. About 12% of Americans rely on radio, and print is a distant fourth at 6% (Pew Research Center, 2014). Liberals and conservatives trust very different news sources. While liberals depend on a variety of outlets – CNN, NPR, MSNBC, and to a lesser extent, the *New York Times* – conservatives mostly rely on Fox News (47%). Millenials (born in 1981 to 1996) and GenXers (born between 1965 and 1980) generally rely on social media, predominantly Facebook (Anderson & Caumont, 2014).

Traditional sources of news have been problematic for political news consumption. Media markets (newspapers and television) do not coincide with electoral constituencies for most of the population. As a result, political news does not cover most candidates (Just, Crigler, Alger, Cook, Kern, & West, 1996). The incongruence of candidates' districts and media markets also makes it difficult and expensive for candidates to advertise on these media, because they must pay to reach non-constituents along with potential voters. In large urban areas, there are too many constituencies for adequate or even any news coverage. For example, the New York City media market covers three states (New York, Connecticut and New Jersey) with all of their varied elections. Even in a large media market that does not cross state lines, such as Los Angeles or San Antonio, the limits of broadcast news make it impossible to cover all of the races that are contested (Fowler, Franz, & Ridout, 2016).

Candidates for the presidency and state-wide offices rely on television advertising, which is extremely expensive even at the lower electoral rate. To maximize the value of dollars spent, television advertising for president is concentrated in key competitive states (divided partisanship) with a large number of Electoral College votes. In the presidential nominating process, states with early contests receive the lion's share of the ads. Candidates place ads with cable and local stations, which reap huge profits in election years (Kang & Gold, 2014; Potter, Matsa, & Mitchell, 2015). During election years, television stations including cable are required to give federal candidates the lowest going rate for ads for 45 days before a primary election and 60 days before a general or special election (FCC, n.d.a). Television advertising for the nominating and general presidential campaign, however, begins earlier than the year of the election, and therefore, does not fall under the limitation on prices.[3]

Broadcast television advertising is expected to exceed $6 billion and capture more than half of all advertising expenditures in 2016. Cable and radio are projected to amount to over $1 billion each with 10% and 8.8% respectively. To mitigate the problems of the astronomical expense of broadcast advertising and the mismatch of media markets, candidates are increasingly turning to other media including online advertising and free media. Shifting to electronic media makes sense in the light of increasing audience reliance on the Internet. Online advertising spending is increasing faster than other media (see Figure 23.1) and is projected to total almost $1 billion in 2015, overtaking telemarketing and newspapers (Borrell Associates, 2015; West, 2014).

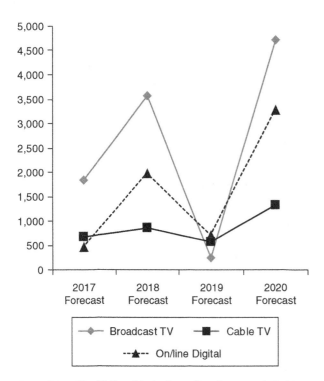

Figure 23.1 Total US political ad spending forecasts, 2017–20, in US$ millions
Source: Borrell Associates.

The rapid rise of social media and micro-targeting of audiences call for a whole new class of professionals (Kreiss & Welch, 2015). The costs of Internet advertising include managers of ad placement and targeting. Mobile is emerging as a significant platform for all advertising, including political campaigns. The recent development of ad blocking applications is an evolving threat, however, to online advertising.

In recent history, candidates in the primary and general election phases of the campaign have tried to augment advertising by appearing on talk shows and late night comedy. In the 2016 season, Donald Trump spent very little money on advertising during the pre-primary phase of the campaign, because he had so much free media. Journalists found Trump speeches, with their outrageous attacks on immigrants, highly newsworthy. He dominated the airwaves without advertising (Patterson, 2016).

Regulation of Political Advertising on Television and the Internet

The US is on the libertarian end of the spectrum of free speech and political speech is especially protected even in the face of discriminatory language and false information. While the Supreme Court does not protect obscenity, fighting words or words that are a "clear and present danger," hate speech, however, and symbolic speech (such as flag burning) have long been protected even in advertising. For example, the Supreme Court rejected a law that made it a crime for a politician to lie about his military service during a campaign (Lieffring, 2013). The "Fairness Doctrine," which required balanced political presentations on radio and television, was allowed based on the scarcity of channels (*Red Lion* v. *FCC*, 1969). With the advent of cable and digital media, the Court decided that principle was no longer needed. The Equal Time Doctrine, which provided for the right of reply, does not apply to news presentations including candidate debates, or syndicated entertainment programs such as talk shows. Television stations are not permitted to edit or refuse candidate ads, but they can refuse "third party" ads. Those ads are not eligible for the lower rate charged to candidates (Burgett, 2014).

Following the Watergate scandal, in which large donations were secretly extorted from political donors providing the Nixon campaign with a slush fund for illegal activities, Congress passed a law creating the Federal Election Commission (FEC). The job of the FEC was to oversee the donations and expenditures to political campaigns. While donations to political campaigns are regulated by campaign law, the provision of the law limiting expenditures was declared unconstitutional. In *Buckley* v. *Valeo*, the Supreme Court held that anyone (including a candidate) can spend an unlimited amount. The Court's decision rejected the concept that any one or several voices could drown out the speech of opponents. Other nations have held that voices in campaigns should be equalized to provide a level playing field for political ideas.

The US Supreme Court has taken the position that advertising is political speech and corporations are protected as persons under the Constitution's First Amendment. Although some justices avowed belief in the concept of disclosure, rulings such as *Citizens United* allowed donors to remain anonymous (Dowling & Wichowsky, 2013). Some argue that this decision has increased the diversity of voices in the discourse, especially in sponsoring political advertising (Creamer, 2012). Most observers agree, however, that the wealthiest donors including corporations and billionaires control a large percentage of advertising expenditures (see, for example, Confessore, Cohen, & Yourish, 2015). For example, several Republican candidates in the 2016 nominating contest had one or more billionaire backers. For example, Governor Chris Christie of New Jersey relied on Steve Cohen, an investor from his state. The most billionaire funding for Republicans comes from David and Charles Koch. The leading contributor on the Democratic side is George Soros who has backed Hillary Clinton (Vogel & Arnsdorf, 2016).

The advertising regulation that is familiar to most voters is aimed at negative ads. The rule requires all ads to show a "clear image" of the candidate along with a statement that the candidate "approves" the message. The same measure increased the required on-screen font size identifying who sponsored the ad so that viewers could actually read the text. Non-candidates' ads do not have an "approval" statement, but must include sponsorship information and the statement that it was not authorized by the candidate's campaign committee.

"Outside" or "independent" expenditures, including advertising, share one key element. They are not permitted to coordinate their advertising "materially" with the candidate or the party they support (Code of Federal Regulations, 2003). They are merely expressing their views about the campaign. The lack of coordination has become somewhat fictional. Often the head of the "outside" group has previously worked in the candidate's campaign or party and is privy to the general strategy. In addition, the candidate or the party may announce where and when they are *not* going to advertise, providing the super-PAC (the rubric for outside groups) with the information they need to fill in the gap. Another tactic is to announce on the candidate's website what their advertising strategy will be, allowing the outside group to choose from a readily available list of opportunities. This is coordination hiding in plain sight.

Outside groups have vastly increased their role in US political campaigns. Most of the devices used by third-party groups are named for specific exemptions from reporting in the US tax codes. The first prominent device was the "527" which represented groups that are permitted to express their views on issues. They were prohibited from endorsing a candidate during the last few months of the campaign. Another is the 501c4, which refers to groups that promote public welfare. The third, which is perhaps the most surprising, is the 501c3, which encompasses all charitable organizations, such as the Red Cross. What is surprising is the range of outside groups that consider themselves charitable. For example, the "Kentucky Opportunity Coalition" aired 10,000 ads in the first nine months of the 2014 Senate race on behalf of Mitch McConnell, the Republican majority leader (Confessore, 2014). In the presidential election of 2012, the overwhelming majority (85.2%) of ads by outside political groups was negative (Fowler & Ridout, 2013, p. 59, 2014).

Stating the name of the outside group sponsoring an ad usually provides voters with no useful information. Groups are named purposely not to reveal their ideological or political agenda. For example, Americans for Responsible Solutions is a gun control group, the Patriot Majority is a "charitable organization" (falling under 501c4 of the tax code) and is run by an aide to the former Democratic Senate leader, Harry Reid, while Crossroads GPS is the name of a conservative organization founded by Karl Rove, a Republican operative. After the Supreme Court's ruling in *Citizens United* v. *FEC* (followed two months later by appellate court's decision in *SpeechNow* v. *FEC*), super-PACs emerged as the main vehicle for unlimited and anonymous donations. The only restriction on them is that they may not "coordinate" with the official campaign. Super-PACs may accept donations from corporations (including international corporations) or labor unions, both of which had expressly been prohibited in prior campaign regulations.

Donations to the official campaign are limited by law, but another way around the provisions, especially in presidential campaigns, is for the candidate to establish an "exploratory committee" to "test the waters" to see if the candidacy is viable. The exploratory committee is in effect the candidate's committee up until the candidate declares that he or she is actually running for office. The exploratory committee may persist and receive donations until that point, often collecting a huge war chest. The amount collected then goes into the coffers of a super-PAC. Jeb Bush, the brother of President George W. Bush, amassed millions in funds for his "Right to Rise" PAC before the 2016 election. Unfortunately, he was not able to mobilize most of those funds as he was soundly defeated in the primary campaigns (Frum, 2016).

Oversight of Political Advertising

The FEC, charged with overseeing national elections, has been stymied by congressional refusal to fill vacancies in order to prevent the seating of the opposing party's nominees. Journalists, scholars and regulators have worked to reveal hidden funding sources (OpenSecrets.org, FEC.gov) and to correct misinformation (FactChecker.org, Politifact.org). One of the problems with disclosure is that deadlines for providing information about donations do not necessarily coincide with the optimal moment to inform voters. Until 2015, the reporting dates for federal elections were quarterly or monthly, with the last filing due after Election Day. Donations in the crucial period just prior to voting were essentially hidden from voters. In 2015, the filing dates were modified to make disclosure more timely, however, there are different rules for different kinds of political groups and offices, candidate versus "issue" advertising, and expenditures by groups that are or are not officially coordinated with the campaign. The rules are so complicated and confusing that candidates must hire specialists to keep the campaigns in compliance and some campaigns break the rules and worry about the penalties afterwards (Estrich, 2003; Fowler & Ridout, 2014). Moreover, because of the incomplete data available at any given time, reporting on political donations is daunting. Virtually every campaign amends its reporting after the election and almost all campaign committees pay fines for non-compliance disputes.

The Content, Reception and Effects of Ads

The primary goal of political advertising is to help candidates win elections. Advertising may influence voters cognitively, affectively and behaviorally. Appeals in ads may combine cognition and affect by offering information to the advantage of the sponsor and the disadvantage of the opponent. Even though attentive citizens receive more ads than less attentive citizens, advertising is a crucial avenue for disseminating information to the least interested, low information voters (Franz & Ridout, 2010). The language, symbols, music and color in positive or comparison ads forge emotional ties between potential voters and the sponsoring candidate. Effective ads aim to provide information and motivate supporters to register, donate, volunteer and vote or to demobilize the opponent's supporters. Emotions are key to the success of political ads (Brader, 2006; Crigler, Just, & Belt, 2006; Kaid & Johnson, 2001; Kern, 1989). Advertising manipulates emotions, especially enthusiasm for the sponsor and fear, anger or disgust with the opponent. Emotions can be elicited by visuals, text and/or music. A classic example of an ad in which visuals carry the burden of conveying positive emotions is President Ronald Reagan's 1984 campaign ad "Morning in America." The ad used images and political symbols to convey warm associations. Visuals included children raising the American flag (pride), a bride hugging her grandmother (family love), a milkman delivering milk to a neighborhood with white picket fences (American dream homes), even a sunset on the water. The text invited the audience to appreciate how much better things were under President Reagan than his Democratic predecessor, Jimmy Carter.

Many of the emotions addressed in ads are negative – fear and anger. The music is threatening as in the soundtracks of horror movies and the colors are dark, often black and grey. The visuals convey fear. An often mentioned negative ad in the 1988 presidential campaign was the "Revolving Door Ad." The spot was created by Roger Ailes, consultant to Fox News, and showed a revolving gate in front of a prison. The words on the screen conflicted with the spoken word, a technique which is intended to confuse the audience. The race of the men in the revolving gate was unclear. So many viewers thought the men were African American that Ailes insisted on showing the ad to journalists in slow motion. He claimed he was not responsible for the inferences the audiences drew from the ad based on their prejudices. No doubt the prejudices were exacerbated by the concurrently running "independent ad" about Willie Horton, an African American murderer and rapist, who was one of the handful of criminals who was accidentally released. The presidential candidate, George H. W. Bush, originally claimed the revolving door ad was not racist, and allowed it to run for two weeks before taking it down under journalistic pressure. Note that these negative ads and the positive "Morning in America" ad did not show the candidate, but were meant to associate emotions and ideas with the target or sponsor respectively.

Negative Advertising

There is a scholarly controversy about how to define and measure negativity. Some researchers view negativity in terms of a bimodal positive and negative valence. Others distinguish among discrete emotions such as fear, disgust and anger, which are identified with different behavioral consequences. In appraisal theory, for example, anger is action oriented while fear can be demobilizing. According to affective intelligence theory a circumplex of emotions is generated through specific neurological pathways. Anxiety about a stimulus is associated with a search for information, rather than relying on habitual thinking patterns (Marcus, Neuman, & MacKuen, 2015).

Some researchers define negativity based on the proportionality of the content of the ad. Some refer to ads as negative only if the whole ad attacks the opponent and does not make any positive comparison to the sponsor. If the attack compares the candidates on some dimension, those researchers consider the ad comparative – a combination of positive and negative. Some of these ads employ negative text, visuals and music in the attack portion. In contrast, the last part of the ad is often in full color with swelling music and an upbeat message. This "Wizard of Oz" effect provides a solution to the problem and leaves the viewer with a positive impression. The public credits candidates who use comparative ads with using less negativity than candidates that only attack (Jamieson et al., 2000; Kaid & Johnson, 2001; Kern, 1989). Some researchers distinguish negative ads from "mudslinging," which in some way transgresses advertising norms (Kahn & Kenney, 1999).

Some researchers distinguish attacks on personal qualities of the opponents or their relevant background in contrast to attacks on the opponent's issue positions, which they view as fair game. Many political scientists see issue oriented negative ads as informative (Geer, 2006). Issue oriented negative ads convey more information than "warm and fuzzy" ads that show what a nice looking family the candidate has or feature the endorsement of the candidate's mother. A frequent aspect of negative ads is to associate the lesser known candidate with a notable and reviled figure in the opposing party. An ad for Republic Senator Jesse Helms attacked affirmative action ("White Hands Ad," www.youtube/watch?v=KlyewCdMzk). The Helms ad pictured Democratic Senator Ted Kennedy and claimed he sponsored a "quota" bill favoring African Americans. Helms was facing an African American opponent, Harvey Gantt. The ad was misleading (about quotas) and played on racial cues, threatening that the opponent would favor blacks over whites.

These associative ads were especially common in Senate races during the Obama presidency, where Republican candidates did their best to tie the opposing Democrats to President Obama and his administration's policies, particularly the Affordable Health Care Act (Crigler & Hua, 2015). One of the goals of negative ads is to sow enough doubt about the candidate that supporters will be reluctant to go to the polls. In a focus group about the Helms Gantt race, participants picked up the implication in an attack ad that Harvey Gantt was a homosexual. The ad did not claim that he was, but noted that he had received a campaign contribution from a group supporting homosexual rights. Several participants reported they were not likely to go out to vote for Gantt after viewing that ad (Kern & Just, 1995). Decreasing turnout for the opponent is much easier to accomplish with advertising than actually persuading voters to support the sponsor.

In the heat of the campaign, eager staff may support "going negative" or even skirting the rules to produce a victory for their candidate (Estrich, 2003). A significant scholarly concern is that if both candidates produce negative ads, overall electoral participation decreases. Scholars on both sides of the negativity debate have produced evidence of turnout effects (Ansolabehere & Iyengar, 1995; Franz, Freedman, Goldstein, & Ridout, 2008; Geer, 2006; Krasno & Green, 2008).

One of the factors arguing against airing negative ads is the fear of "backlash," i.e. decreasing support for the sponsor of the attacks (Garramone, 1984). One way to avoid backlash is to couch the attack in humor. The candidate is disparaged in a humorous negative ad, but the sponsor is not tarred with mud. An early Roger Ailes attack ad is credited with turning around the campaign of current Senate Majority Leader, Mitch McConnell, whose personality was not inspiring support. The ad featured a man with a blood hound searching for the opponent who has been absent so often from the Senate. An ad against Barack Obama in 2008 argued that he had an inflated ego and sarcastically argued that "a light (from heaven) will come down" on Obama. While employing negative ads does not generally harm candidates, being perceived as the *most* negative can be detrimental. Candidates who are trailing are most likely to attack (Just & Crigler, 2016; Theilmann & Wilhite, 1998). Candidates who are persistently behind, are tempted to go negative all the time, as was the case for presidential candidate John McCain who ran against Barack Obama during the financial crisis in 2008 (Crigler, Just, & Belt, 2006). Studies of gender and negativity suggest that women get less backlash when they go negative (Fridkin, Kenney, & Woodall, 2009; Gordon, Shafie, & Crigler, 2003).

The cycle of attack and response to negative ads generally ends just before Election Day, when candidates make their final appeal for support. Occasionally, however, candidates launch last-minute attacks that cannot be answered by their opponents because television stations have run out of commercial time to sell to the target. Even though American elections are characterized by a long campaign, it is well documented that some voters do not make up their minds until the last two weeks and even the last three days of the campaign (Pew Research Center, 2004; Rahn, Krosnick, & Breuning, 1994). Since these voters typically have only a modest interest in the campaign, ads can be especially persuasive for this group. During presidential elections, the airwaves in "swing states" (i.e., those with roughly equal numbers of supporters of both major parties) are flooded with political ads. Citizens complain that they find it difficult to watch television because of the bombardment of political messages. The result is "advertising overload." Given the rapid decay of advertising influence (Gerber, Gimpel, Green, & Shaw, 2011), however, those last few days of the campaign may play a crucial role for both positive and negative ads.

While some observers thought women should not use attacks because negativity would contrast with their strength as caring human beings, the evidence shows women candidates air negative ads at a rate similar to men. Women, however, appear to benefit more from attack ads (Gordon et al., 2003). Women's ads have differed from men's ads primarily in terms of the issues addressed. For example, women candidates are less likely to promote war and more likely than men to discuss "women's issues," i.e., issues about family, healthcare, the elderly, as well as wage fairness and reproductive issues (Herrnson, Lay, & Stokes, 2003; Kahn, 1993; Schaffner, 2005), but these distinctions appear to be declining along with other gendered differences in campaigns (Just & Crigler, 2016).

Journalists have played a role in attempting to defang negative ads and to counter deception. When television news began covering ads, they gave free media time to the most outrageous ads, which made for compelling viewing. Sometimes the ads that were shown in the news had little life outside the newsroom. Candidates would make a small or geographically limited "ad buy" in the hope that news programs would run the ads for them at no cost. To counter that effect, news media developed the "ad watch" – an attempt to evaluate the claims made in political spots. Ad watches ran in newspapers, such as the *New York Times* and on television. One researcher developed a "grammar" for ad watches to reduce the impact of ads that were being critiqued. Techniques to counter the message included putting the ads in a box to one side of the screen, accompanied by assessments of their validity. Some ads were stamped FALSE in red text. A focus group study of the ad watch techniques, however, found that if the audience was interested in the ad, they leaned forward to better engage with the ad content, even though the disclaimers were on screen as well (Just et al., 1996, p. 132). Formal ad watches began to fade as journalists simply reported on the ad campaign as it progressed. Scholars continue to study how journalists can report ad events of the campaign without costless spreading of the candidate's message (Richardson, 2012).

While scholars and journalists may try to contain ad effects, political consultants are busy trying to enhance them. The Holy Grail for political consultants is to put ads only before those viewers who are likely to be persuaded by the messages. When television was the primary means of influencing voters, advertising was targeted by selecting television programming that attracts specific groups of people and placing ads in the commercial breaks of those programs. If an ad message were targeted to women, for example, the ad was placed on a program known to have many women viewers (Ridout, Feltus, Franz, & Goldstein, 2012). Targeting ads by program can be easy on cable stations that appeal to specific audience interests or a specific geographic area, as opposed to over the air broadcasting (Ridout, Franz, & Fowler, 2014). An ad targeting men might appear on a sports channel, while an ad targeting women might appear on a shopping channel.

With the increased availability of big data, targeting has become more refined. Parties and campaigns collect and employ information about individuals' buying habits, social media use, political donations and activities, as well as demographic data to micro-target their persuasive and motivational messages. The narrowest advertising targeting may take place on social media and the Internet, where ads can be placed on highly specific social networking sites and websites.

The Role of the Internet for Campaign Advertising

Since the Internet is a motivated medium, the audience for advertising tends to be supporters. Research shows that both positive and negative ads are posted and viewed online and that viewers remember Internet ads as they do television ads (Ridout, Fowler, & Branstetter, 2012). It is not clear exactly how negative ads will translate to the Internet. One study suggests that even humor will not deflect boomerang effects on negative ads online (Baumgartner, 2013). On candidates' websites or on their YouTube channels, supporters may click on negative ads attacking the opponent. As targeting increases, a more precise audience can be expected to include those who can be persuaded (Crigler, Just, Hume, Mills, & Hevron, 2011). It is well-known that Google algorithms increase the likelihood that individuals could be exposed to political ads consonant with their views, i.e., "accidental" viewing of ads on television can be replicated on the Internet. The difference is that the individual must still choose to be exposed to the ad by clicking on it. Some ads play on YouTube whether or not the viewer wants to see them. These "pre-roll" ads of 15 to 20 seconds appear before the video selected by the viewer. The viewer may "skip" some ads, but others cannot be skipped. YouTube charges more money for stubborn ads. One model of Internet ad effects suggests that a combination of anxiety level and web skills predict the efficacy of online ads (Thorson & Rodgers, 2000).

The significance of disposition of the audience brings us back to the theory of the active audience and the constructionist model of communication. This review of political advertising in the US shows how the contextual factors of the speech guarantees in the Constitution and the Supreme Court's interpretation have led to the explosion of advertising by outside groups as well as candidates and the parties. The changing media system has given new agency to individuals whose knowledge, attitudes and attachments have always accounted for the effects of political advertising.

Notes

1   Another burden on voters is the requirement to register with the local government so that they are eligible to participate in elections. In most jurisdictions voters must register two months before the actual election. The need to register is a particular burden for people who are less informed about the electoral process, usually those who are less interested or educated.

2   Even when citizens show up for elections they are confronted by the long ballot (i.e., the huge number of contested offices plus a list of referenda questions that can be greater than 200 in some states). Not only are some of the candidates entirely unknown to voters, but the function of the political offices on the ballot are also unknown. For example, citizens in the state of Massachusetts are expected to vote for a little known body, "the Governor's Council," as well as County Commissioners, and animal control officers. Citizens in California also vote for County Supervisors who are extremely powerful and the ballot can run to 40 pages because of the number of referendum questions. While most elections take place during "even" years, in some states, such as Virginia, incumbents do not want to compete for voter attention with federal elections. These states schedule their elections in odd numbered years. Presidential primary elections and caucuses begin at

the very beginning of January and end in late June, but primaries for state-wide offices may take place in the spring prior to the November elections, or as late as September.

3   In 2012, local stations were required to upload to the Internet their records for ad buys, including the names of executives or board members of the groups purchasing the ad (Federal Communication Commission, n.d.a; Waldman, 2011).

References

Anderson, M., & Caumont, A. (2014, September 24). How social media is reshaping news. Pew Research Center Fact Tank. Retrieved from www.pewresearch.org/fact-tank/2014/09/24/how-social-media-is-reshaping-news.

Ansolabehere, S., & Iyengar, S. (1995). *Going negative: How political advertisements shrink and polarize the electorate.* New York, NY: Free Press.

Baumgartner, J. C. (2013). Internet political ads in 2012: Can humor mitigate unintended effects of negative campaigning? *Social Science Computer Review*, 31(5), 601–613. doi:10.1177/0894439313490399.

Blumenthal, M., & Edwards-Levy, A. (2014, May 28). HUFFPOLLSTER: A state-by-state guide to party registration. Retrieved from www.huffingtonpost.com/2014/05/27/state-party-registration_n_53999770html.

Borrell Associates. (2015, August). 2015 to 2016 political advertising outlook. Retrieved from www.borrellassociates.com/industry-papers/papers/2015-to-2016-political-advertising-outlook-august-15-detail.

Boyd, R. (1981). Decline of US voter turnout: Structural explanation. *American Politics Research*, 9(2), 133–159.

Brader, T. (2006). *Campaigning for hearts and minds.* Chicago: University of Chicago Press.

Burgett, J. (2014, April 2). Political advertising 101: A refresher course for very busy people. *Advertising Issues, Broadcast Regulation, Political Broadcasting.* Retrieved from www.wileyonmedia.com/2014/04/political-advertising-101-a-refresher-course-for-very-busy-people/.

Confessore, N. (2014, October 10). Secret money fueling a flood of political ads. *New York Times.* Retrieved from www.nytimes.com/2014/10/11/us/politics/ads-paid-for-by-secret-money-flood-the-midterm-elections.html?_r=0.

Confessore, N., Cohen, S., & Yourish, K. (2015, October 10). Buying power. Retrieved from www.nytimes.com/interactive/2015/10/11/us/politics/2016-presidential-election-super-pac-donors.html?smid=tw-nytpolitics&smtyp=cur&_r=1b.

Creamer, M. (2012). Super PACs as scourge of political advertising battles? Not necessarily; they certainly merit scrutiny, but in the case of the GOP primary battle, these well-funded organizations have made the race more democratic. *Advertising Age*, 83(11), 2.

Crigler, A., & Hua, W. (2015, June 26–27). *Social media populism? A comparison of Tea-Party and MoveOn in 2014 Senate campaigns.* Paper presented at Conference on New Populism's Communication. CNRS, Paris, France.

Crigler, A., Just, M., & Belt, T. (2006). Voter responses to negative political ads. *Journalism and Mass Communication Quarterly*, 61(2), 250–259.

Crigler, A., Just, M., Hume, L., Mills, J., & Hevron, P. (2011). YouTube and TV advertising campaigns: Obama vs. McCain in 2008. In R. L. Fox & J. M. Ramos (Eds.), *i-Politics: Campaigns, elections, and governing in the new media era* (pp. 103–124). Cambridge: Cambridge University Press.

Currinder, M. (2009). *Money in the house: Campaign funds and congressional party politics.* Boulder, CO: Westview Press.

Del Real, J. (2014, November 20). Voter turnout in 2014 was the lowest since WWII. *Washington Post.* Retrieved from www.washingtonpost.com.

DeSilver, D. (2015). US voter turnout trails most developed countries. Pew Research. Retrieved from www.pewresearch.org/fact-tank/2015/05/06/u-s-voter-turnout-trails-most-developed-countries/.

Dowling, C. M., & Miller, M. G. (2014). *Super PAC! Money, elections, and voters after Citizens United.* London: Taylor & Francis.

Dowling, C. M., & Wichowsky, A. (2013). Does it matter who's behind the curtain? Anonymity in political advertising and the effects of campaign finance disclosure. *American Politics Research*, 41(6), 965–996.

Estrich, S. (2003). A tale of two worlds. In A. N. Crigler, M. R. Just, & E. McCaffrey (Eds.), *Rethinking the vote: The politics and prospects of American election reform.* New York, NY: Oxford University Press.

Federal Communication Commission. (n.d.a). FCC-12-44, Modernizing broadcast television public file availability. Retrieved from www.fcc.gov/document/modernizing-broadcast-television-public-file-availability.

Federal Communication Commission. (n.d.b). Statutes and rules on candidate appearances & advertising. Retrieved from www.fcc.gov/media/policy/statutes-and-rules-candidate-appearances-advertising.

Fowler, E. F., Franz, M. M., & Ridout, T. N. (2016). *Political advertising in the United States.* Boulder, CO: Westview Press.

Fowler, E. F., & Ridout, T. N. (2013). Negative, angry and ubiquitous: Political advertising in 2012. *The Forum*, 10(4), 51–61.

Fowler, E. F., & Ridout, T. N. (2014). Political advertising in 2014: The year of the outside group. *The Forum*, 12(4), 663–684. doi:10.1515/for-2014–5030.

Franz, M. M., Freedman, P., Goldstein, K., & Ridout, T. (2008). Understanding the effect of political advertising on voter turnout: A response to Krasno and Green. *Journal of Politics*, 70(1), 262–268.

Franz, M. M., & Ridout, T. N. (2010). Political advertising and persuasion in the 2004 and 2008 presidential elections. *American Politics Research*, 38(2), 303–329.

Fridkin, K., Kenney, P., & Woodall, G. (2009). Bad for men, better for women: The impact of stereotypes during negative campaigns. *Political Behavior*, 31(1), 53–77.

Frum, D. (2016, February 24). The twilight of the SuperPac. *The Atlantic*. Retrieved from www.theatlantic.com/politics/archive/2016/02/super-pacs-2016/470697.

Garramone, G. (1984). Voter responses to negative political ads. *Journalism and Mass Communication Quarterly*, 61(2), 250–259.

Geer, J. (2006). *In defense of negativity*. Chicago: University of Chicago Press.

Gerber, A. S., Gimpel, J. G., Green, D. P., & Shaw, D. R. (2011). How large and long-lasting are the persuasive effects of televised campaign ads? Results from a randomized field experiment. *American Political Science Review*, 105(1), 135–150.

Goldstein, K., Schweidel, D. A., & Wittenwyler, M. (2012). Lessons learned: Political advertising and political law. *Minnesota Law Review*, 96(5), 1732–1754.

Gordon, A., Shafie, D., & Crigler, A. (2003). Is negative advertising effective for female candidates? An experiment in voters' uses of gender stereotypes. *Harvard International Journal of Press/Politics*, 8(3), 35–53.

Harvard Institute of Politics. (2015). An American abroad: An inside look at how American consultants run high-level political campaigns around the world: An IOP Study Group. Led by Tad Devine. Retrieved from www.iop.harvard.edu/american-abroad.

Herrnson, P. S., Lay, J. C., & Stokes, A. K. (2003). Women running as women: Candidate gender, campaign issues, and voter-targeting strategies. *Journal of Politics*, 65, 244–255. doi: 10.1111/1468–2508.t01-1-00013.

Jamieson, K. H., Waldman, P., & Sherr, S. (2000). Eliminate the negative? Categories of analysis for political advertisements. In J. A. Thurber, C. J. Nelson, & D. A. Dulio (Eds.), *Crowded airwaves: Campaign advertising in elections* (pp. 44–64). Washington, DC: Brookings Institution Press.

Just, M., & Crigler, A. (2016). Candidate use of Twitter and the intersection of gender, party, and position in the race: A comparison of competitive male/female senate races in 2012 and 2014. In R. Davis, C. Holtz-Bacha, & M. Just (Eds.), *Twitter in elections around the world: Campaigning in 140 characters or less*. New York, NY: Routledge.

Just, M., Crigler, A., Alger, D., Cook, T., Kern, M., & West, D. (1996). *Crosstalk: Citizens, candidates, and the media in a presidential campaign*. Chicago: University of Chicago Press.

Kahn, K. F. (1993). Gender differences in campaign messages: The political advertisements of men and women candidates for US senate. *Political Research Quarterly*, 46(3), 481–502.

Kahn, K. F., & Kenney, P. (1999). Do negative campaigns mobilize or suppress turnout? Clarifying the relationship between negativity and participation. *The American Political Science Review*, 93(4), 877–889.

Kaid, L. L., & Johnson, A. (2001). *Videostyle in presidential campaigns: Style and content of televised political advertising*. Westport, CT: Praeger.

Kang, C., & Gold, M. (2014, October 31). With political ads expected to hit a record, news stations can hardly keep up. *Washington Post*. Retrieved from www.washingtonpost.com/business/technology/with-political-ads-expected-to-hit-a-record-news-stations-can-hardly-keep-up/2014/10/31/84a9e4b4-5ebc-11e4-9f3a-7e28799e0549_story.html.

Kern, M. (1989). *Thirty-second politics: Political advertising in the eighties*. New York, NY: Praeger.

Kern, M., & Just, M. (1995). The focus group method, political advertising, campaign news, and the construction of candidate images. *Political Communication*, 12(2), 127–145. doi: 10.1080/10584609.1995.9963061.

Krasno, J. S., & Green, D. P. (2008). Do televised political ads increase voter turnout? Evidence from a natural experiment. *Journal of Politics*, 70(1), 245–261.

Kreiss, D., & Welch, C. (2015). Strategic communication in a networked age. In V. Farrar-Myers & J. Vaughn (Eds.), *Controlling the message: New media in American political campaigns* (pp. 13–31). New York, NY: New York University Press.

Lieffring, S. (2013). First amendment and the right to lie: Regulating knowingly false campaign speech after United States v. Alvarez note. *Minnesota Law Review*, 97, 1048–1078.

The Living Room Candidate. (1952). Retrieved from www.livingroomcandidate.org/commercials/1952.

Marcus, G. E., Neuman, W. R., & MacKuen, M. B. (2015, November). Measuring emotional response: Comparing alternative approaches to measurement. *Political Science Research and Methods*, 1–22. doi:10.1017/psrm.2015.65.

Patterson, T. (2016). Pre-primary news coverage of the 2016 presidential race: Trump's rise, Sanders' emergence, Clinton's struggle. Shorenstein Center Report. Retrieved from http://shorensteincenter.org/pre-primary-news-coverage-2016-trump-clinton-sanders/.

Pew Research Center. (2004, October 27). Swing voters slow to decide, still cross-pressured, follow-up interviews find. Retrieved from www.people-press.org/2004/10/27/swing-voters-slow-to-decide-still-cross-pressured/.

Pew Research Center. (2014). American trends panel wave 1 topline March 19–April 29, 2014. Retrieved from www.journalism.org/files/2015/05/Millennials-and-News-TOPLINE.pdf.

Potter, D., Matsa, K., & Mitchell, A. (2015). Pew Research Center, state of the media 2015, local tv by the numbers. Retrieved from www.stateofthemedia.org/2013/local-tv-audience-declines-as-revenue-bounces-back/local-tv-by-the-numbers/.

Rahn, W. M., Krosnick, J. A., & Breuning, M. (1994). Rationalization and derivation processes in survey studies of political candidate evaluation. *American Journal of Political Science*, 38(3), 582–600. doi 10.2307/2111598.

Richardson, G. W. (2012). Ad watch 3.0: Developing audiovisual and narrative techniques for engaging the audiovisual content of political advertising. *Poroi*, 8(1). doi:10.13008/2151–2957.1089.

Ridout, T., Feltus, W., Franz, M., & Goldstein, K. (2012). Separation by television program: Understanding the targeting of political advertising in presidential elections. *Political Communication*, 29(1), 1–23. doi: 10.1080/10584609.2011.619509.

Ridout, T., Fowler, E., & Branstetter, J. (2012, March 8). *Political advertising in the 21st century: The influence of the YouTube ad*. Paper presented at the Western Political Science Association, Portland, OR.

Ridout, T., Franz, M., & Fowler, E. F. (2014). Advances in the study of political advertising. *Journal of Political Marketing*, 13(3), 175–194.

Schaffner, B. F. (2005). Priming gender: Campaigning on women's issues in US senate elections. *American Journal of Political Science*, 49(4), 803–817. doi: 10.2307/3647698.

Theilmann, J., & Wilhite, A. (1998). Campaign tactics and the decision to attack. *The Journal of Politics*, 60(4), 1050–1062.

Thorson, S., & Rodgers, E. (2000). The interactive advertising model: How users perceive and process online ads. *Journal of Interactive Advertising*, 1(1), 41–60.

United States Election Project. (2012). Retrieved from www.electproject.org/2012.

Vogel, K. P., & Arnsdorf, I. (2016, February 8). The POLITICO 100: Billionaires dominate 2016. *Politico*. Retrieved from www.politico.com/story/2016/02/100-billionaires-2016-campaign-finance-218862.

Waldman, S. (2011, December 29). Local tv news, meet the internet. *Columbia Journalism Review*. Retrieved from www.cjr.org/united_states_project/local_tv_news_meet_the_internet.php.

Washington Post. (2012). Mad money: TV ads in the 2012 presidential campaign. Retrieved fron www.washingtonpost.com/wp-srv/special/politics/track-presidential-campaign-ads-2012/.

West, D. (2014). *Air wars: Television advertising and social media in election campaigns, 1952 to 2012* (6th ed.). Washington, DC: CQ Press.

PART IV

Airtime With No Charge and for Purchase

24

POLITICAL ADVERTISING IN AUSTRALIA

The Dominance of Television

Rodney Smith and Stephen Mills

Introduction

Australian election advertising has taken many forms since the earliest colonial contests of the 1840s. Television became part of the advertising mix after its introduction in 1956 and rose to dominance among advertising media by the early 1970s. Although television has faced a recent challenge from the Internet and new media, it remains the premier advertising medium for Australia's major political parties, as well as governments and interest groups wanting to inform and persuade voters. This chapter sets out the key features of the Australian political system that have shaped election advertising in the television era. It provides a history of the main shifts in the content and use of television advertising before evaluating the recent rise of Internet and new media campaigning. The chapter then outlines Australia's relaxed regulatory regime for election advertising and considers the effects of advertising on voters and political parties.

The Australian Political System and Political Advertising

The Australian political system has a number of distinctive features. In this section we focus on the main features that have helped to shape election advertising, particularly via television. At the outset, it must be acknowledged that Australia has a federal system, meaning that elections are regularly held for three levels of government: federal (national), state (regional) and local. Although there is some crossover between electoral campaigns at the different levels, for simplicity's sake we will focus on federal election campaigns.

Australia has a Westminster-style parliamentary system with highly disciplined and stable major parties. Most parliamentary candidates rely on party recognition rather than personal recognition for their electoral success (McAllister, 2011). Only three parties have won government over the past 75 years: the Australian Labor Party (ALP), formed in 1891; the Liberal Party (formed in 1943 but with antecedents dating to 1909) and the National Party (formerly the Country Party, dating to 1920). The Liberal and National parties always govern together in a formal coalition, usually referred to as "the Coalition."

The binary Labor versus Coalition dynamic is supported by an electoral system largely designed by the major parties, which provides for Members of the House of Representatives (lower house) to be elected from 150 single-member electoral districts using a system of preferential voting. Major party support is spread evenly enough across the country to ensure that either a Labor or Coalition candidate wins in almost every electorate. Minor parties and Independents (candidates not aligned to any party) do contest lower house seats, but overwhelmingly without success. Thus Australian election advertising primarily focuses on the major parties, and particularly on whether Labor or the Coalition parties deserve the chance to govern. The proportional representation system used to elect the 76 Senators allows minor parties the chance of winning a few seats; however, the Senate (upper house) contest is mostly treated as secondary to the contest for control of the House of Representatives and therefore government.

Compulsory voting is one distinctive feature of Australia's electoral system that has had an impact on political advertising. The requirement that all citizens enroll and vote generates high turnout by voters who do not, in other countries, normally go to the polls. This poses the challenge for political parties of gaining the votes of citizens who are politically uncommitted and in many cases uninterested but whose votes are likely to make the difference between winning and losing an election. One consequence of this is that Australian political advertising is characteristically strident, blunt and designed to attack opponents rather than portray a positive vision for government.

This negative political advertising has also been facilitated by a light-touch regulatory approach to all forms of political communication. Although this laissez-faire approach dates back to the earliest Australian elections, since the 1990s it has been bolstered by constitutional protection. Candidates on the receiving end of negative advertising have little recourse but to reply as best they can.

Finally, political advertising has been shaped by the hybrid licensing structure of Australia's broadcasting industries, with publicly funded state broadcasters (the Australian Broadcasting Corporation and Special Broadcasting Service) operating alongside privately owned broadcasters who rely on revenues derived from commercial advertising. The sophisticated commercial advertising industry with strong global connections that has developed as a result ensures that new marketing practices and techniques quickly become available to party campaign managers to adapt for use in the political contest. This in turn means that parties must raise large sums of money to try to stay ahead in the innovative political marketing contest. In part, they do this through large donations from business, trade union and other groups; however, since 1984, they have also relied on generous and steadily increasing levels of public funding.

The Emergence of Television Advertising

Television broadcasting in Australia debuted in 1956, accompanying the opening of the Olympic Games in Melbourne. Despite decades of experience in applying commercial advertising methods – in print, radio and cinema – to the electoral contest, the political parties were slow to develop a distinctive advertising role for the new visual medium (Griffen-Foley, 2003, Ch. 3). The Liberals under Prime Minister Robert Menzies were somewhat skeptical about television, while the opposition Labor Party was initially hampered by a lack of funds. The first television campaigning basically repeated material available via the press and radio. "Television," Rawson (1961, p. 121) noted of the 1958 federal election, "brought before some of the voters, with greater force and immediacy, the same images of party policy and party leadership as those put forward by the earlier propaganda media." In 1961, Labor's 10-minute documentary "Time for Decision," a compilation of newsreel footage, showed some of television's potential (Griffen-Foley, 2003, p. 107). It was not until the late 1960s, however, that either major party begin to realize the transformative potential of the medium. Labor's 1968 campaign for the South Australian state election displayed the recognizably modern features of creative, image-based advertising based on market research (Blewett & Jaensch, 1971). The party official responsible for this campaign, Mick Young, was soon appointed to mastermind Labor's national 1972 "It's Time" advertising campaign (Mills, 2014, pp. 70–88).

"It's Time" represented a breakthrough for Australian political advertising, in several respects. Where previous election campaigns had been fragmented among the various state party branches, Young was appointed national campaign director and could impose a national campaign effort, built around a single all-encompassing slogan, "It's Time," and nationally broadcast spot advertising.

"It's Time" featured a celebrity choir singing a specially written anthem, intercut with images of Labor leader Gough Whitlam and delivering, as one Labor official explained, "emotional impact not logical consideration" (cited in Blewett, 1973, p. 14). Broadcast over three months before the election campaign proper, this advertising was integrated into a year-long campaign (Blewett, 1973; Young, 1986).

The "It's Time" campaign helped return Labor to office for the first time since 1949. Learning the lessons of their defeat, the Liberal Party overhauled its organization and recruited new campaign managers and advertising consultants. Its successful 1975 election campaign featured advertisements employing high production values to combine a powerful critique of the Labor government ("Three dark years of Labor") with a more uplifting call to action ("Turn on the Lights") broadcast as a catchy song, or "jingle" (Grattan, 1977).

In 1972 and 1975, opposition parties had used television advertising effectively to promote their claim to government. But successful insurgencies have been infrequent; government has changed hands only seven times since the end of World War II. Incumbent parties also learned the techniques of television advertising and used them to devastating effect. In 1977, for example, the Coalition parties promoted their promise of tax cuts with images of a fistful of five dollar notes, in advertising that "conceded nothing to subtlety" (Lloyd, 1979, p. 257). This positive message was matched with a lavishly produced negative advertisement ("Memories"), which reminded voters of Labor's record in government. In 1980, the same government rescued its poor poll position in the final days of the campaign with another unsubtle advertisement, a scare campaign claiming Labor would introduce a "wealth tax" (Mills, 1986, pp. 101–102; Young, 2004, pp. 189–193). Political advertising thus acquired a sharper edge, a faster turnaround and multiple messages and styles. While "It's Time" had run for months, Liberal campaign director Tony Eggleton developed new advertisements frequently, sometimes daily, during the campaign, in response to events (Mills, 2014, p. 104).

The Dominance of Television

From the 1970s, television advertising quickly developed as the principal medium of electoral communication, transforming the electoral contest into an "air war" in which parties bombarded commercial television audiences around the nation with the same key themes and messages. The major parties bought the services of commercial market research and advertising agencies to provide the strategic, creative and production skills needed for television advertising campaigns. Paid political advertising carried the parties' messages directly to voters, avoiding the commentary, criticism and news agendas of journalists.

Relationships between parties and their advertising agencies have often proved problematical. Advertisers may be motivated to undertake campaign work by political loyalty or by the more self-interested prospects of commercial rewards and political influence. Advertisers have long been suspected of sometimes exerting undue influence over the policies and messages of their party client (Kaldor, 1968; Wyndham, 1968). On the other hand, retaining a political client can impinge on the agency's other commercial relationships (Dickenson, 2014). Commercial advertising success may provide insufficient guidance for mastering the dynamics of a political campaign; whereas commercial clients are often satisfied with niche positioning and market share, party clients need to win a majority of the vote. Few commercial brands suffer the kind of negative advertising that is common in election campaigns. The parties remain reliant on agencies to provide access to ever-changing commercial marketing practices, but must always use their political judgments to sieve the cutting-edge wheat from the crassly-commercial chaff. In the words of Liberal campaign director Lynton Crosby (2000, p. 67): "A political campaign is not the place for slick, glossy and too-clever-by-half corporate style advertising, which might win an award but won't win you a campaign."

Developing Relationships Between Parties and Campaign Agencies

The major parties have gradually acquired the skills necessary to direct their agencies and have increasingly exercised the prerogative to hire and fire them. In the early 1970s, Mick Young eased aside Sim Rubensohn, who had been Labor's advertising agent and fundraiser for the best part of 40 years (Goot, 2002). Rubensohn's replacement from 1975 was Malcolm Macfie, who was in turn dropped in 1987 in favor of John Singleton, the choice of Prime Minister Bob Hawke. Singleton's controversial style was strident and hard-hitting. For Labor's 1987 campaign, he produced the "Whingeing Wendy" advertisements, in which the eponymous suburban housewife demanded answers about the costs of opposition policies (Young, 2004, pp. 89–93). Despite its negativity, the advertisement complemented Labor's overall re-election strategy, exemplified by the slogan "Let's Stick Together" – an appeal for national unity through a difficult period of policy transition. Singleton also devised Labor's 1993 advertising attacking the opposition's proposed Goods and Services Tax (GST). In opposition after 1996, Labor experimented with various agencies, including the Australian arm of Saatchi & Saatchi (Young, 2004, pp. 93–95), and later the commercial marketer Neil Lawrence, who devised the "Kevin '07" advertising for Labor's successful 2007 campaign (Jackman, 2008).

The relationship between the Liberal Party and its advertisers has progressed through a similar evolution from loyalty to fluidity. In 1983, Eggleton's choice of Masius Wynn Williams (later, D'Arcy Macmanus) struggled when its campaign theme for the Liberals ("We're Not Waiting for the World") was overwhelmed by Labor's focus on new leader Bob Hawke and his promise of "Reconciliation, Recovery and Reconstruction." Masius was retained but again struggled in 1987, with a much-ridiculed campaign promoting the "Incentivation" policies of opposition leader John Howard. Masius was replaced by the local arm of the multinational George Patterson agency led by Geoff Cousins; however, this agency also struggled to create effective advertising in 1990 and 1993. From 1996, Eggleton's successor, Andrew Robb, abandoned the practice of retaining a single agency, and instead selected a team of four individuals drawn from different firms on the basis of their specific skills. This approach was reportedly cheaper and capable of devising more politically attuned advertising. The team consisted of manager and strategist Mark Pearson, creatives Ted Horton and Toby Ralph, and direct mail specialist John King. Its credits included the advertising campaign that delivered victory for Prime Minister John Howard in 1996 ("For All of Us"), the aggressive promotion of Howard's anti-asylum seeker policy in 2001 ("We will decide who comes into this country, and the circum-stances in which they come"), as well as the negative advertisements in 2004 ridiculing opposition leader Mark Latham with a learner-driver's "L Plate" (Young, 2004, pp. 309–310). This team model remains the Liberals' preferred way of contracting commercial marketing expertise. Since 2010, Labor has adopted the same approach.

In the era of television ascendancy, the parties' advertising has been strengthened by other com-mercial marketing techniques. Labor under Hawke in the 1980s and the Coalition parties under John Howard in the 1990s enjoyed intimate and long-running relationships with skilled market researchers: respectively, Rod Cameron of ANOP and Mark Textor of Crosby-Textor (Mills & Tiffen, 2012, p. 161). These market researchers became influential advisers because their quantitative survey and qualitative focus group research provided valuable insights into voter attitudes. They strongly influenced political advertising, becoming, in John Singleton's apt description of Rod Cameron, "the seeing eye dog" for campaign advertisers who would otherwise operate blindly (Lawson, 1993). Advertisements are routinely pre-tested with focus groups prior to broadcast. At a strategic level, market research provides the overall framework or theme for which specific ads are then designed as tactical and creative expressions. Market research has directed advertising away from appeals to par-tisan supporters and toward the uncommitted voters who are strategically important to the electoral contest thanks to the legal requirement of compulsory voting. The advice that Cameron provided to Labor as early as 1979 remains central to advertising strategies of both major parties:

Rhetoric is more important to the swinging voter than the details contained in policy out-looks. Sloganised epithets, which reduce complex issues to oversimplified, often distorted, catchcry positions, represent eventually the real reasons why uncommitted, often apolitical, swinging voters cast their vote.

(Quoted in Mills, 1986, p. 26)

Mark Textor used focus group research to construct two hypothetical swinging voters, "Phil" and "Jenny," who became the touchstone of the Liberal campaign in 1996. In political advertising, Labor's "Whingeing Wendy" and the Liberals' "Phil" and "Jenny" are taken to represent the demography and lifestyle of swinging voters and to articulate their concerns and attitudes (Mills, 2014, p. 178; Williams, 1997).

From the 1990s, the national focus of the "air war" was supplemented by a "ground war" approach to campaigning, in which the specific concerns of particular electorates were carefully recorded in party databases and then reflected back to those electorates via targeted mail, telephone and electronic appeals (Van Onselen & Errington, 2004). Given the indiscriminate coverage of television broadcasting in the metropolitan areas in which most Australians live, it was impossible to use television advertising in such a precisely targeted way. Outside the capital cities, however, the Liberal Party began to adapt national television advertisements to give them a more localized feel (Crosby, 2000). The Liberal Party's smaller coalition partner, the National Party, has always run its own regional television campaigns in a similar way, built round local candidates and its own leader (see, for example, Davey, 2000).

The major parties reportedly continue to allocate large sums to pay for market research, production and commercial broadcast of their television advertising. Television advertising continues to be the largest item of expenditure in parties' campaign budgets. The growing costs of television advertising in particular led to the introduction of a public funding scheme to fund campaign costs in 1984 (Tham, 2010, pp. 130–135). Parties spend much of their public funding on television advertising campaigns, while continuing to solicit donations from individuals and businesses to make up funding shortfalls. The campaign finance reporting requirements introduced as a condition of public funding in 1984 were significantly eroded in 1996; since then it has been impossible to do more than estimate party advertising budgets (Australian Government, Special Minister for State, 2008). Opacity is further increased by the murky price dynamics of the commercial broadcasting market. The unpredictable timing of national elections can create the urgent need for parties to book blocks of airtime. The resultant windfall returns to commercial broadcasters are ultimately borne by the taxpayer through the public funding regime.

Minor Party and Independent Advertising

Television advertising has been dominated by the two major parties, with most minor parties and Independents struggling to raise the funding required to produce and broadcast campaign material. Some minor parties receive free-to-air broadcast slots from the public broadcasters (see below). Since the 1950s, just three quite diverse minor parties have had a genuine television advertising presence. The first was the Democratic Labor Party (DLP), which, having split from the ALP in 1955, made a "substantial investment" in the 1958 elections, and continued to air television advertisements until its effective demise in the mid 1970s (Griffen-Foley, 2003, p. 69; Strangman, 1973, p. 82).

The Australian Greens Party, which emerged in the mid 1990s from environmental social movements and state green parties, was initially unable to afford television advertising. In the run up to the 2010 election, however, businessman Graeme Wood donated $1.6 million to the Greens with the instruction that they "run a professional advertising campaign" including "running a proper television campaign, right up to the election" (Manning, 2011). The Greens secured a record minor party vote in both the Senate and House of Representatives in that election (Bartlett, 2012).

Most recently, the mining magnate Clive Palmer formed a populist party, the Palmer United Party (PUP), to contest the 2013 federal election. On the back of heavy television advertising and other promotions, including a DVD delivered to all households in Australia, Palmer won a House of Representatives seat and three PUP candidates were elected to the Senate. PUP's "utter financial dependence" on Palmer's own wealth suggested a new form of party organization, the "plutocrat party," had arrived in Australia (Kefford & McDonnell, 2015; see also Young, 2015, p. 97).

Independent candidates in regional areas can sometimes afford basic television advertising campaigns; however, even successful Independents lack the spending power of major party candidates and consequently rely heavily on free media coverage, town hall style meetings, leaflets, posters and personal contacts (see, for example, Andren, 2003, pp. 98–113, 176–184).

The Challenge of the Internet and New Media

While Australians have been early adopters of digital technology, the development of digital election advertising has been relatively slow. The early party websites were static and text heavy, while individual candidates were mostly left to develop their own digital profiles as best they could (Chen, 2015a; Gibson & Cantijoch, 2011; Young, 2004, pp. 286–290). The 2007 election provided a turning point, with Labor integrating YouTube, Facebook and MySpace into the "Kevin07" campaign designed to promote new leader Kevin Rudd and the party's policies (Ward, 2008). By the 2010 election, the Liberal Party had caught up with Labor, producing YouTube advertisements parodying Kevin07 as "Kevin O'Lemon" and presenting new leader Julia Gillard as a puppet controlled by unseen party powerbrokers (Liberal Party of Australia, 2010a, 2010b). Both parties also made efforts to spread their marketing across a wider range of new media platforms (Chen, 2012). This multi-channeling intensified at the 2013 election, leading Chen (2015a, p. 81) to conclude that new media had "finally 'arrived' as an essential element of the contemporary electoral practices of Australian political parties."

The impact of these developments on television advertising is unclear. The parties have certainly taken new media more seriously, appointing new media managers to their central campaign teams (Chen, 2015a, pp. 82–83, 85). While their online and television advertisements are still often identical (Young, 2015, p. 101), the parties have increasingly attempted to micro-target voters with customized advertising, especially via Facebook and Google (Chen, 2015b, pp. 134–135). One impediment to a larger shift of advertising resources away from television is that it is not yet clear which new media platforms provide the most effective alternatives for parties to reach voters (Chen, 2015a, pp. 83–84).

The developing consensus among scholars is that these shifts to new media advertising confirm the "normalization hypothesis"; that is, that they have not made electoral contests between the established major parties and new competitors more even. Although the Australian Greens Party has developed a relatively strong new media presence, the resources required for sophisticated digital advertising campaigns are simply beyond the scope of most minor parties (Chen, 2015a, pp. 81–83; Gibson & McAllister, 2015).

Law and Regulation

Broadcast advertising for federal, state and local elections in Australia is predominantly governed by the Commonwealth Broadcasting Services Act 1992 (hereafter BSA). Other forms of federal election advertising are addressed in the Commonwealth Electoral Act 1918 (hereafter CEA), which deals with most aspects of federal elections. The inclusion of "postal, telegraphic, telephonic, and other like services" as a Commonwealth responsibility under section 51(v) of the Australian Constitution means that provisions of the BSA override any state or territory legislation covering election broadcast advertising. This does not apply to non-broadcast election advertising (for example, newspaper advertisements, posters and fliers), where the states and territories can pass their own laws (Orr, 2010, p. 167). Both Acts cover advertising during and outside the formal campaign period. In practice, advertisers have treated their obligations under the two Acts as equivalent.

As part of these obligations, free or paid political advertisements on radio and television, as well as paid advertisements on the Internet, must contain a spoken (and, in the case of television, written) authorization "tag" that identifies the speakers in the advertisement and the name and address of the person authorizing it (BSA Schedule 2, Part 2). The aims here, as with the similar requirements on print advertisements, posters and the like (CEA sections 328 and 328A), are to make voters aware of the source of political messages and to identify someone who can be held accountable for any legal breaches in the advertisement (AEC, 2015; Orr, 2010, pp. 174–176, 179).

The absence of "truth in political advertising" laws leaves candidates who believe that their political opponents have broadcast untruthful or defamatory advertising with few options. The Australian Electoral Commission advises candidates that it "has no role or responsibility in deciding whether political messages published or broadcast in relation to a federal election are true or untrue" (AEC, 2015, p. 1). Aggrieved candidates might initiate court proceedings under general defamation laws; however, these may not pass the test of "qualified privilege" in political discussion and would not be resolved until well after the election (Gauja, 2010, pp. 137–138). The Australian advertising industry's voluntary self-regulator, the Advertising Standards Bureau, refuses to entertain complaints about electoral advertising and advises complainants "to raise their concerns with the advertiser directly and/or with their local Member of Parliament" (n.d., p. 2).

One major difference between the treatment of broadcast and other advertising concerns is the so-called "electronic media blackout," which bans broadcasting election advertisements from midnight on the last Wednesday before polling day until the close of the polls (see BSA Schedule 2, 3A; SBA section 70C). The blackout was introduced in the Broadcasting Act 1942 (Cth) s114(4) and until 1983 it applied to broadcasting of any electoral material whatsoever. Since then, it has only applied to advertisements on television and radio (AEC, 2015, p. 10; Orr, 2010, pp. 176–177).

This blackout has been justified on two grounds: first, to give voters a period of quiet reflection before Election Day; and second, to prevent candidates from broadcasting last-minute accusations that their opponents have no opportunity to rebut. As critics point out, the restriction does not (now) prevent heavy television and radio news coverage of the final throes of the campaign, or prevent candidates from using print media or Internet advertisements to try to tarnish their opponents up to or on polling day. The blackout rests on the doubtful assumption that voters are particularly vulnerable to the seductive appeal of radio and television advertisements (Mills, 1986, pp. 177–179; Orr, 2010, pp. 176–177; Ward, 1995, p. 21).

The assumption that broadcast advertising is particularly powerful played a part in the 1991 attempt by the Labor government to outlaw commercial television and radio advertising. The ALP and the Australian Democrats (a minor party) had previously expressed concern about the growing costs of television advertising and the superficial content typically provided in short television and radio advertisements. The Liberal and National parties rejected these concerns, arguing that the volume and quality of broadcast election advertising should be a matter left to the parties, advertising agencies and commercial broadcasters (JSCEM, 1989, pp. 52–58). Labor, with the support of the Democrats in the Senate, passed the Political Broadcasts and Political Disclosures Act 1991 (Cth), which substituted blocks of free airtime allocated to parties on basis of their prior electoral support for paid broadcast advertising (Orr, 2010, p. 169; Ward, 1995, pp. 191–192; Ward & Cook, 1992).

Television networks challenged the legislation in the High Court in *ACTV* v. *Commonwealth* (1992). A majority of justices found the Act unconstitutional, arguing that it infringed the freedom of speech implied in the sections of the Australian Constitution relating to Parliament being "directly chosen by the people" (sections 7 and 24). Later cases saw the High Court refine its understanding of implied freedom of speech, a process that included a judgment in *McClure* v. *Australian Electoral*

Commission ((1999) 163 ALR 734) that free speech is not a positive right and therefore that candidates have no right to airtime (Carney, 2003, p. 179; Orr, 2010, pp. 172–173). Schedule 2 of the BSA provides that if commercial broadcasters transmit electoral matter, they "must give reasonable opportunities" for broadcasting electoral matter to all parties; however, this does not mean that they have to provide equal time, free airtime or reduced advertising rates (Orr, 2010, p. 173). The publicly funded Australian Broadcasting Corporation (ABC) does provide a measure of equitable free broadcast advertising during elections. Section 79A of the Australian Broadcasting Corporation Act 1983 (Cth) allows but does not require the ABC to provide free television and radio airtime to registered political parties. This airtime is allocated according to their parliamentary status, voter support and number of candidates (Australian Broadcasting Corporation Board, 2014). Section 70A(1) of the Special Broadcasting Service Act 1991 (Cth) allows Special Broadcasting Service to provide similar advertising opportunities.

Perhaps the most contentious lack of independent regulation of political broadcast advertising concerns official government advertising, which is "subject to minimal fetters" (Orr, 2007, p. 21). Federal government advertising typically cost under $50 million per year in the mid 1990s; however, spending rapidly doubled over the next few years and now exceeds $110 million per annum. Similar increases have occurred at state and territory levels, contributing to what some political scientists term an "Australian PR state" (Ward, 2007; Young, 2004, pp. 58–79). Much of this money is spent on television advertising (Horne, 2012, p. 21; Young, 2004, pp. 58–79; Young & Tham, 2006, pp. 66–67).

Advertising that presents straightforward information to citizens about public services has been uncontroversial; however, governments have been repeatedly criticized for campaigns promoting policy initiatives that lack cross-partisan or widespread community support. In such instances, the government of the day stands accused of using public funds to gain an unfair partisan advantage and of politicizing the public service agencies that are responsible for overseeing the campaigns. This is particularly true when the advertisements saturate the airwaves immediately before an election period, or before the policy legislation has been drafted for parliamentary consideration, or where specific funding for the advertising has not been approved by parliament (Lindell, 2007; MacDermott, 2008; Orr, 2007; Orr, 2010, pp. 175–176; Swann, 2014; Young & Tham, 2006, pp. 65–89; Young, 2007b). Since 1995, Labor and Coalition governments have both engaged in such dubious practices to promote new policies in areas such as taxation, health care, employment services, environmental policy and the treatment of asylum seekers (Orr, 2007, p. 23; Young, 2007a, pp. 194–201). On occasions, interest groups have responded to these contentious government advertising campaigns with counter advertisements, creating what Orr and Gauja (2014, p. 90) describe as a "call and response" effect for television audiences. Prominent recent cases of this phenomenon include trade union responses to advertisements for the Coalition government's "WorkChoices" industrial relations policies from 2005 to 2007 (Muir, 2010), and the mining industry's response to Labor government taxes on resource extraction in 2010 (Orr & Gauja, 2014).

Efforts by the non-government parties and other stakeholders to legislate for effective regulation of federal government advertising since the mid 1990s have been resisted by whichever party has been in government (Hawke, 2010; Horne, 2012; Young, 2007b). Since 2008, successive governments have instead developed guidelines and introduced administrative measures to try to remove the controversy without also removing their control over advertising campaigns. The third of five principles in the current Guidelines on Campaign Advertising by Australian Government Departments and Agencies states that "Campaigns should be objective and not directed at promoting party political interests," under which guideline 26 requires that "Campaigns … be presented in objective language and be free of political argument" (Department of Finance, 2014, p. 7). Proposed campaigns must be reviewed by a three-person Independent Communications Committee (ICC) (Department of Finance, 2015).

These recent measures have limitations. The ICC reviews proposed campaigns before the details regarding their wording or imagery have been developed and only attests that a proposed campaign is "capable of complying" with the Guideline principles (see Department of Finance, 2015). The advertisements that are broadcast inevitably contain an authorization tag, suggesting that they are political either in the sense of generating popular support for a contentious policy position, or by implicitly associating popular policies and programs with the party in government (Orr, 2007, pp. 24–26; Orr, 2010, p. 176). Controversies surrounding advertising campaigns under the most recent Labor and Coalition governments indicate that effective regulation of the distinction between political and government advertising has not been achieved (Knott, 2015; Swann, 2014).

Effects of Advertising on Voters

Arguably the critical question for election advertising is "Does it really work?" (Young, 2004, p. 141). Australian answers to this question usually judge advertising's persuasive effect, swaying citizens to cast their votes one way or another, rather than its participative effect, convincing citizens to participate in the poll. (Because of the compulsory voting requirement, the Australian Electoral Commission undertakes advertising to remind citizens of their obligation to vote and explain the mechanics of polling.) Further, this persuasive impact is typically measured in relation to the uncommitted, "swinging" voters, particularly those living in "marginal" electorates where the outcome has been close in previous elections (Chen, 2015b, p. 129; Young, 2004, pp. 43–57).

Thus defined, party campaign managers insist that advertising can work; apparent successes such as the Liberals' 1980 "wealth tax" and Labor's 1993 anti-GST advertisements are commonly cited (Mills, 1986, p. 153; Ward, 1995, p. 189). Yet a number of objections have been lodged against this. Ward has argued that it is "impossible to discern the particular effects of political ads" in the maelstrom of an election campaign (Ward, 1995, p. 190; see also Young, 2004, p. 142). Citing Mills (1986, p. 103), Ward also notes the view among advertisers that influencing consumers (in this case voters) requires a far longer period than a few days at the close of an election campaign (Ward, 1995, p. 189). Young (2004, pp. 144–146) and Ward (1995, p. 190) both contend that campaign advertising, particularly in its negative forms, may repel citizens rather than attracting their support and votes. Goot (2002) argues against the claim that election campaigners have successfully identified swinging voters, let alone targeted them with effective messages.

In the mid 1990s, Ward noted the lack of Australian academic research required to help resolve these competing claims (1995, p. 189). His observation remains true 20 years on. Australian political scientists have shown little inclination for the sort of experimental research used to determine the impact of advertising in countries such as the US. In the first decade of television advertising, early academic voter surveys provided some information on the impact of election advertising (Aitkin, 1982, pp. 256, 372; Hughes & Western, 1966, pp. 143–145; Rawson, 1961, pp. 170, 185–186). Nothing grew from these early suggestions, largely because a party identification model that played down campaign effects soon came to dominate explanations of voter behavior within Australian political science (Aitkin, 1982; McAllister, 2011, pp. 33–55). The series of Australian Election Study (AES) questionnaires used to understand electoral behavior at every federal election since 1987 have not included items on voters' engagement with campaign advertising on television or other media. The AES surveys suggest that at least two-fifths of Australian voters decide how to vote during election campaigns (Bean & McAllister, 2015); however, the role of television and other advertising in their decisions is unknown.

Some attention has been paid to the effects on voters of the recent rise in digital advertising. The proportion of voters using the Internet for election information has increased since the early 2000s, at the same time as reliance on other sources of media information has declined (Bean & McAllister, 2015, p. 412). Gibson and McAllister (2006, pp. 254–255) found that candidates in the 2004 federal election who had a website garnered more votes than those who did not, net of other factors. Their more nuanced exploration of the 2007 election indicated that candidates with static websites experienced no increase in their votes, whereas those who invested effort in more dynamic new media platforms to reach "niche group[s]" of voters were rewarded with small but significant increases in electoral support (Gibson & McAllister, 2011, p. 239).

Effects of Advertising on Parties

The rise and dominance of television advertising in election campaigns has had two important effects on the major political parties. The first has been to centralize power within the extra-parliamentary party organization. It is no coincidence that Mick Young's appointment as the first national campaign manager of an Australian party accompanied the first modern national television advertising campaign in 1972 (see above). The "air war" style of election campaigns required strong, simple and consistent messaging, built around well-researched themes and strategic insights, and expressed in creative ways by professional advertisers. Party head offices grew in size and strength, acquiring in-house staff specialists as well as the services of the marketing agencies. Centralization thus went hand-in-hand with professionalization, and party volunteers and amateurs found themselves largely surplus to requirements. These newly empowered head offices also experienced a ceaseless need for cash to pay for television advertising and associated campaign methods. Fund-raising from private donors and the public purse is now a constant preoccupation of contemporary Australian parties (Mills, 2014, pp. 112–128; Young & Tham, 2006).

The second effect of television advertising was to help change the dynamics of the parliamentary wing of the political parties. The party leader, rather than the frontbench or the party as a whole, is now at the center of most campaign advertising strategies. Advertisements typically focus heavily on the leader's name, face and words, allowing the viewer to see apparently authentic images of their political leaders, and further investing those leaders with authority and political significance. This personalization assisted the fortunes of prime ministers such as Hawke and Howard, who were well known figures. It also helped build the recognition of less familiar leadership aspirants – for example, Rudd's "Kevin07" campaign in 2007 (Jackman, 2008). Television advertising has also allowed parties to intensify their attacks on the qualities of their opponents' leaders, using tightly edited footage that depicts unflattering images of the leaders and/or highlights their ill-chosen words. These developments have arguably contributed to a form of "presidentialization" in Australian politics, in which leaders exercise greater power over their parliamentary party colleagues but have simultaneously become more vulnerable to removal if they are viewed as unpopular in the public opinion polls (Strangio, 2012).

Conclusion

Television advertising has proven a remarkably enduring feature of election campaigns in Australia. More than 40 years after "It's Time," and long after newspaper and radio advertising have fallen away, it has survived the fragmentation of television network audiences, the emergence of subscription (satellite and cable) television, the rise of direct mail and the advent of the Internet and social media. Indeed, the parties' continued preference for presenting their campaign messages as brief affective visual images, produced by commercial agencies driven by market research, has enabled a smooth transition from television advertising to digital campaigning through YouTube and other new media. It is likely that new forms of campaign communication and new campaign applications of digital technology will continue to evolve. But it is difficult to envisage the demise of this dominant mode of political advertising. This carries troubling implications, as television advertising has always been, and remains, more an affective and leader-centric instrument of party competition than an informative and rational aid to democratic deliberation. Given Australia's tradition of laissez-faire regulation and recent constitutional interpretations of free speech, any such concerns are unlikely to be addressed by legislative or regulatory measures.

References

Advertising Standards Bureau. (n.d.). Political and election advertising. Retrieved from https://adstandards.com. au/products-issues/political-and-election-advertising.

Aitkin, D. (1982). *Stability and change in Australian politics* (2nd ed.). Canberra: Australian National University Press.

Andren, P. (2003). *The Andren report: An independent way in Australian politics*. Melbourne: Scribe.

Australian Broadcasting Corporation Board. (2014). Allocation of free broadcast time to political parties during election periods. Retrieved from http://about.abc.net.au/wp-content/uploads/2015/01/FreeTimeElectionBroadcastsPolicySep2014POL.pdf.

Australian Electoral Commission. (2015). Electoral backgrounder: Electoral advertising. Retrieved from www.aec.gov.au/about_aec/Publications/Backgrounders/electoral-advertising.htm.

Australian Government. Special Minister for State. (2008). Electoral Reform Green Paper: Donations, Funding and Expenditure. Canberra: Australian Government.

Bartlett, A. (2012). The Greens. In M. Simms & J. Wanna (Eds.), *Julia 2010: The caretaker election*. Canberra: ANU E Press.

Bean, C., & McAllister, I. (2015). Documenting the inevitable: Voting behaviour at the 2013 Australian election. In C. Johnson & J. Wanna (with H.-A. Lee) (Eds.), *Abbott's gambit: The 2013 Australian federal election* (pp. 411–424). Canberra: ANU Press.

Blewett, N. (1973). Labor 1968–72: Planning for victory. In H. Mayer (Ed.), *Labor to power: Australia's 1972 election* (pp. 6–16). Sydney: Angus and Robertson.

Blewett, N., & Jaensch, D. (1971). *Playford to Dunstan*. Melbourne: F W Cheshire.

Carney, G. (2003). The High Court and the constitutionalism of electoral law. In G. Orr, B. Mercurio, & G. Williams (Eds.), *Realising democracy: Electoral law in Australia* (pp. 170–185). Annandale: The Federation Press.

Chen, P. (2012). The new media and the campaign. In M. Simms & J. Wanna (Eds.), *Julia 2010: The caretaker election* (pp. 65–84). Canberra: ANU Press.

Chen, P. (2015a). New media in the electoral context: The new normal. In C. Johnson & J. Wanna (with H.-A. Lee) (Eds.), *Abbott's gambit: The 2013 Australian federal election* (pp. 81–94). Canberra: ANU Press.

Chen, P. (2015b). The virtual party on the ground. In N. Miragliotta, A. Gauja, & R. Smith (Eds.), *Contemporary Australian political party organisations* (pp. 127–139). Clayton: Monash University Publishing.

Crosby, L. (2000). The Liberal Party. In M. Simms & J. Warhurst (Eds.), *Howard's agenda: The 1998 Australian election* (pp. 64–70). St Lucia: University of Queensland Press.

Davey, P. (2000). The National Party. In M. Simms & J. Warhurst (Eds.), *Howard's agenda: The 1998 Australian election* (pp. 77–81). St Lucia: University of Queensland Press.

Department of Finance (2014). Guidelines on information and advertising campaigns by non-corporate Commonwealth entities. Retrieved from www.finance.gov.au/sites/default/files/campaign-advertising-guidelines.pdf.

Department of Finance (2015). Review reports by the Independent Communications Committee on Government advertising campaigns. Retrieved from www.finance.gov.au/advertising/reports-by-independent-communications-committee/.

Dickenson, J. (2014). The politics of political advertising in Australia and Britain, 1970–1989. *Australian Journal of Politics and History*, 60(2), 241–256.

Gauja, A. (2010). *Political parties and elections: Legislating for representative democracy*. Farnham: Ashgate.

Gibson, R., & Cantijoch, M. (2011). Comparing online elections in Australia and the UK: Did 2010 finally produce "the" internet election? *Communication, Politics and Culture*, 44, 4–17.

Gibson, R., & McAllister, I. (2006). Does cyber-campaigning win votes? Online communication in the 2004 Australian election. *Journal of Elections, Public Opinion and Parties*, 16, 243–263.

Gibson, R., & McAllister, I. (2011). Do online election campaigns win votes? The 2007 Australian "YouTube" election. *Political Communication*, 28, 227–244.

Gibson, R., & McAllister, I. (2015). Normalising or equalising party competition? Assessing the impact of the web on election campaigning. *Political Studies*, 63, 529–547.

Goot, M. (2002). Rubensohn, Solomon (Sim) (1904–1979). In J. Ritchie & D. Langmore (Eds.), *Australian dictionary of biography* (Vol. 16, pp. 144–146). Melbourne: Melbourne University Press.

Grattan, M. (1977). The Liberal Party. In H. R. Penniman (Ed.), *Australia at the polls: The national elections of 1975*. Washington, DC: American Enterprise Institute for Public Policy Research.

Griffen-Foley, B. (2003). *Party games: Australian politicians and the media from war to dismissal.* Melbourne: Text Publishing.

Hawke, A. (2010). Independent review of government advertising arrangements. Retrieved from www.finance.gov.au/sites/default/files/Independent-Review-of-Government-Advertising-Arrangements.pdf.

Horne, N. (2012). The Administration of Commonwealth Government Advertising. Parliament of Australia. Parliamentary Library Background Note. Retrieved from www.aph.gov.au/About_Parliament/Parliamentary_Departments/Parliamentary_Library/pubs/BN/2011–2012/GovernmentAdvertising.

Hughes, C. A., & Western, J. H. (1966). *The Prime Minister's policy speech: A case study in televised politics.* Canberra: Australian National University Press.

Jackman, C. (2008). *Inside Kevin07.* Melbourne: Melbourne University Press.

Joint Standing Committee on Electoral Matters. (1989). Who pays the piper calls the tune: Minimising the risks of funding political campaigns. Inquiry into the conduct of the 1987 federal election and 1988 referendums. Report No. 4. Canberra: Australian Government Publishing Service.

Kaldor, A. (1968). Liberal and Labor press advertising. *Australian Quarterly,* 40(2), 40–58.

Kefford, G., & McDonnell, D. (2015). *Plutocrat parties: A comparative case study of Clive Palmer and Silvio Berlusconi's parties.* Paper presented at the Australian Political Studies Association Conference, University of Canberra.

Knott, M. (2015, March 14). Dr Karl Kruszelnicki: My role in government video does not mean I'm a Liberal Party stooge. *Sydney Morning Herald.* Retrieved from www.smh.com.au/.

Lawson, V. (1993, February 12). The spin doctors. *The Australian Financial Review.*

Liberal Party of Australia. (2010a). Labor Lemons. Retrieved from www.youtube.com/watch?v=yidl7o3hU0M.

Liberal Party of Australia. (2010b). Puppet Show Master. Retrieved from www.youtube.com/watch?v=GEnn8VQaa-g.

Lindell, G. (2007). The Combet case and the appropriation of taxpayers' funds for political advertising: An erosion of fundamental principles? *Australian Journal of Public Administration,* 66, 307–328.

Lloyd, C. (1979). A lean campaign for the media. In H. Penniman (Ed.), *The Australian national elections of 1977* (pp. 231–265). Washington, DC: American Enterprise Institute for Public Policy Research.

MacDermott, K. (2008). Marketing government: The public service and the permanent campaign. Democratic Audit of Australia Report No. 10. Canberra: Australian National University.

Manning, P. (2011, January 8). Wotif a rich man helped the Greens? *Sydney Morning Herald.*

McAllister, I. (2011). *The Australian voter: 50 years of change.* Sydney: UNSW Press.

Mills, S. (1986). *The new machine men: Polls and persuasion in Australian politics.* Ringwood: Penguin.

Mills, S. (2014). *The professionals: Strategy, money and the rise of the political campaigner in Australia.* Melbourne: Black Inc.

Mills, S., & Tiffen, R. (2012). Opinion polls and the media in Australia. In C. Holtz-Bacha & J. Strömbäck (Eds.), *Opinion polls and the media: Reflecting and shaping public opinion* (pp. 155–174). Houndmills: Palgrave Macmillan.

Muir, K. (2010). "Your rights at work" campaign: Australia's "most sophisticated campaign." *Labor History,* 51(1), 55–70.

Orr, G. (2007). Government communication and the law. In S. Young (Ed.), *Government communication in Australia* (pp. 19–35). Melbourne: Longman Cheshire.

Orr, G. (2010). *The law of politics: Elections, parties and money in Australia.* Annandale: The Federation Press.

Orr, G., & Gauja, A. (2014). Third-party campaigning and issue-advertising in Australia. *Australian Journal of Politics and History,* 60, 73–92.

Rawson, D. (1961). *Australia votes: The 1958 federal election.* Melbourne: Melbourne University Press.

Strangio, P. (2012). Prime ministerial government in Australia. In R. Smith, A. Vromen, & I. Cook (Eds.), *Contemporary politics in Australia* (pp. 226–236). Melbourne: Cambridge University Press.

Strangman, D. (1973). The DLP and the press. In H. Mayer (Ed.), *Labor to power: Australia's 1972 election* (pp. 81–83). Sydney: Angus and Robertson.

Swann, T. (2014, June 7). Rudd's irregular ad spend on people smugglers. *The Saturday Paper.* Retrieved from www.thesaturdaypaper.com.au.

Tham, J.-C. (2010). *Money and politics: The democracy we can't afford.* Sydney: UNSW Press.

Van Onselen, P., & Errington, W. (2004). Electoral databases: Big brother or democracy unbound? *Australian Journal of Political Science,* 39(2), 349–366.

Ward, I. (1995). *Politics of the media.* South Melbourne: Macmillan.

Ward, I. (2007). Mapping the Australian PR state. In S. Young (Ed.), *Government communication in Australia* (pp. 3–18). Melbourne: Longman Cheshire.

Ward, I. (2008). Kevin07. Labor's pitch to generation YouTube. *Social Alternatives,* 27, 11–15.

Ward, I., & Cook, I. (1992). Televised political advertising, media freedom, and democracy. *Social Alternatives,* 11, 21–26.

Williams, P. (1997). *The victory: The inside story of the takeover of Australia.* St Leonards: Allen & Unwin.

Wyndham, C. (1968). Labor Party advertising: The correct perspective. *Australian Quarterly*, 40(3), 19–25.

Young, M. (1986). *The build-up to 1972: The Whitlam phenomenon*. Ringwood: McPhee Gribble/Penguin Books.

Young, S. (2004). *The persuaders: Inside the hidden machine of political advertising*. North Melbourne: Pluto Press.

Young, S. (2007a). A history of government advertising in Australia. In S. Young (Ed.), *Government communication in Australia* (pp. 181–203). Melbourne: Longman Cheshire.

Young, S. (2007b). The regulation of government advertising in Australia: The politicisation of a public policy issue. *Australian Journal of Public Administration*, 66, 438–452.

Young, S. (2015). Campaign advertising and communication strategies in the election of 2013. In C. Johnson & J. Wanna (with H.-A. Lee) (Eds.), *Abbott's gambit: The 2013 Australian federal election* (pp. 95–107). Canberra: ANU Press.

Young, S., & Tham, J.-C. (2006). Political finance in Australia: A skewed and secret system. Democratic Audit of Australia Report No. 7. Canberra: Australian National University.

25

POLITICAL ADVERTISING IN CANADA

Navigating the Waters of Free and Fair Elections

Guy Lachapelle and Tristan Masson

"No doubt the most significant influence on electoral law in the post-war years was the adoption of the *Canadian Charter of Rights and Freedoms*" (Elections Canada, 2007, p. 94). For Canadians, the fundamental freedoms and democratic rights necessary for free and fair elections were only constitutionally enshrined in 1982 when Pierre E. Trudeau, the prime minister at the time, repatriated Canada's constitution from Britain. The Charter has had a far-reaching impact on Canadian life, and electoral law is no exception to its influence.

Similarly, Parliament has passed laws concerning spending and financing on six occasions: an amendment to the Canada Election Act (1970) (CEA), the Canada Expenses Act (1974), another amendment to the CEA (2000), another amendment to the CEA as well as the Income Tax Act (2004), the Federal Accountability Act (2007), another amendment to the CEA (2011), and the most recent amendment to the CEA (2014) (Elections Canada, 2015c, p. 7–9). Through these legislative changes, there has been an evolution as to how money may weave itself into the political process.

The Canadian election campaign of 2015 will be remembered for several reasons. To begin with, it was the longest election campaign on record since the 19th century (Elections Canada, 2007, p. 43). The writs of election for the 2015 election were issued by Governor General David Johnston on August 4. The ensuing campaign was one of the longest in Canadian history; only the first two election campaigns after Confederation were longer: 81 days in 1867 and 96 days in 1872. Since then, the longest campaign was 74 days, in 1926 (Canadian Press, 2015). It was also the first time since the 1979 election that a prime minister strove to remain in office into a fourth consecutive parliament. With this in mind, citizens and voters were exposed to political advertising over a longer period of time than usual, until election day on October 19. Back at the time of the Royal Commission on Electoral Reform and Party Financing (1991) or the Lortie Commission, the key concern was to reduce the cost of campaigning by reducing the length of the electoral campaign. While the last 15 years have seen different lengths of campaigns, the phenomenon of the permanent campaign has crystallized under the last government's reign (Esselment, 2014, pp. 28–29).

Because of the length of the 2015 election, the Canadian Broadcasting Corporation (CBC), the country's public broadcasting company, started a series called *Ad Hawk* to monitor election advertising during the campaign. One analyst observes that despite the belief that negative ads usually depress voters, it appears they can create the opposite effect as well (Blais, 2015). This observation was based on the higher turnout rate in 2015, a 7.4% increase according to Elections Canada and swooping victory for the Liberal Party of Canada (LPC), despite its leader, Justin Trudeau, being the brunt of negative advertising, or "attack ads."

In the same vein, it is essential to understand that political advertising is shaped by the sources and contexts of communication. Contemporary research by Small, Giasson and Marland (2014, p. 5) identifies the triangular nature of political communication in Canada. That is to say, communication travels between political institutions (e.g., political parties), news media and citizens. Likewise, Montigny (2015) notes the adaptation Canadian political parties have undergone in the digital age. Over the last few decades, there has been a decline in the electorate's party identification which, compounded with a decline in political participation, has resulted in a decline in party activism (Montigny, 2015, p. 62). This has had significant implications for election advertising since traditional elections depended on party activism. Most significantly, political parties have professionalized their campaigns by employing professional firms and by centralizing advertising strategies (Montigny, 2015, p. 65). Montigny (2015) elaborates on the implications of the twin phenomena of declining political activism and technological innovation as the latter is instrumentalized by political actors. For example, Montigny notes the outsourcing of responsibilities traditionally belonging to a party's grassroots to marketing firms. Additionally, technology makes targeted advertising more effective, but comes with the added risk of committing mistakes in the public eye, particularly on social media (Montigny, 2015, pp. 67–68).

With respect to Canada's 2015 election, this suggests that political information and messages were shaped by the digitalized media such as television and the social media. Indeed, television alone represents the lion's share of news media consumption for Canadians, with the Internet on the rise, particularly with younger generations (Keown, 2007, p. 12). One way digital media shapes political communication conforms to the *selective-exposure theory*, as Lachapelle (2015) observes: "the Internet allows citizens to select the information they want to be exposed to" (p. 151). For example, a Facebook event entitled "Stephen Harper Going Away Party" attracted roughly 447,000 virtual attendees by polling day (Drennan, 2015). This space was demonstrably opposed to the re-election of the incumbent prime minister, Stephen Harper of the Conservative Party of Canada, as one observes in the virtual conversation.

Many factors are at play in the electoral process, which gives political scientists many things to examine in the democratic exercise. Political pluralism in Canada entails that various interests will be voiced by means of political advertising. It logically follows that political advertising is not strictly reserved to registered political parties, but also to those wanting to pursue their policy interests. For this reason, we will also explore the role of *third-party* advertising in elections. To these ends, Canada's Election Act provides a set of rules to safeguard free and fair elections. We will explore some of these rules as they apply to political communication and advertising in the 2015 election in Canada.

Before moving on however, it should be noted that *Elections Canada* is a public institution which serves to promote citizens' electoral rights while administering and monitoring elections, not to mention it oversees the official polling day itself (Elections Canada, 2015h). In spite of these democratic institutions, controversies still arise and this election was no exception. Staying true to the above points, the following lines will present different provisions in the aforementioned act, and attempt to put to rest some of the controversies that have emerged in the 2015 election campaign.

Political Communication and Advertising in Canada

There are five components to Part 16 of the Canadian Election Act on communication: "Interpretation," "Election Advertising," "Election Opinion Surveys," "Broadcasting Outside of Canada" and "Political Broadcasting," with the latter requiring the most space. Concerning "Interpretation," the Act defines key terms and concepts to be used throughout the part for clarity purposes (Section 319): "election advertising," "election survey," "network," "network operator" and "primetime."

First and foremost, it is necessary to outline what constitutes political advertising in Canada. According to the CEA, section 319 defines *election advertising* as any "transmission to the public by any means … of an advertising message that promotes or opposes a registered party or the election of a candidate." In this sense, it does not include any public commentary whether this is in a speech or in an interview, personal expressions, or telephone calls. However, politicians in Canada have been crafty in their approach to connecting with the public. Just this past election, two of the three main political party leaders had published autobiographies in time for the election. Of the Liberal Party of Canada (LPC), which now forms government, Justin Trudeau published *Common Ground* one year before the 2015 election. Of the New Democratic Party (NDP), Thomas Mulcair published *The Strength of Conviction* one day before elections were called August 2. As for the incumbent Prime Minister Stephen Harper, of the Conservative Party of Canada (CPC), analysts had nine years' worth of material to work with, which converted into no less than seven published books on the former prime minister in 2015 alone.

Additionally, the Act outlines the various conditions under which ads may be publicized. This includes authorization of registered agents (section 320), prohibition against using government means of transmission (section 321), poster advertising (section 322), the blackout period (sections 323 and 324), and non-interference with transmission (section 325). Important to note, the stipulated blackout period is polling day, which applies strictly to political ads by registered parties on radio and television broadcasting, as well as the Internet, except those ads pre-dating the blackout period.

Party Financing and Spending Limits

Money in politics is another area ripe for discussion. At the start of the 2015 election, the Montréal daily newspaper *Le Devoir* reported that the Conservatives led the pack with CDN$36.6 million of ammunition for the election, with the Liberals trailing by about CDN$11 million in second (Orfali, 2015). A noteworthy point however is that the NDP had roughly doubled its fund-raising in the first and second trimester of 2015 (Orfali, 2015). Some argue that this was the strategic angle the incumbents employed for the election as it was set to more than double the average 37-day campaign (Wherry, 2015). Surely the longer the campaign and, consequently, the more money a party can spend will benefit those with superior fund-raising capacity as well as parties with hefty sums in their bank accounts. Nevertheless, Canada does have a regulatory history to minimize the influence of money in politics.

In 1974, the first limits were imposed on election expenses, public funding in the form of reimbursements were introduced, campaign contributors could receive tax credits, parties had to disclose finances, and third parties were prohibited from incurring any election expense. For the latter point, this would be contested later on in courts and would become a key component to election campaign advertising in the 21st century. However, in 1983 and 1993, when lawmakers sought to amend the CEA with respect to third parties, the courts struck these down, citing them as infringements on the freedom of expression as provided by the Canadian Charter of Rights and Freedoms (1982). Notice that the 1974 legislation expenses could not be struck down in the same vein since the aforementioned charter only came into effect eight years afterwards.

In the 2004 legislation, contributions were tightly restricted, but provisions enhanced reimbursement for eligible political entities: up from 50% to 60% for candidates, and from 22.5% to 50% for parties. In addition to these increases, the government introduced quarterly allowances to parties based on their performance in the latest elections. Briefly put, the legislation attempted to minimize the clout of private contributions and, to compensate for the financial loss, it boosted public financial support.

A few years later, legislation once again took on the issue of political finances by prohibiting contributions on behalf of corporations, trade unions and associations. Moreover, even tighter restrictions were placed on contributions to political entities than before, not to mention cash

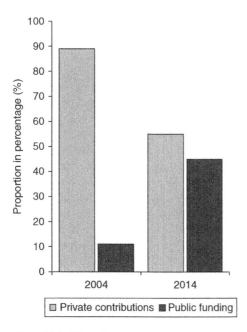

Figure 25.1 Financing sources
Source: Elections Canada, 2015c.

contributions were capped at $20. Public contributions were also modified in 2011 such that the quarterly allowances mentioned above were set to phase out completely by 2015. Finally, the most recent changes made in 2014 are manifold, but most notably, contribution limits were increased to $1,500 per year, plus higher limits to the contribution candidates can make to their own campaigns.

Given this history of regulation, it is worth looking at the changes these have had on the sources of party financing. For instance, according to Elections Canada (see Figure 25.1), the gap between private and public contributions equilibrated from 2004 to 2014 – almost reaching a 50/50 balance. Additionally, the Conservatives spent the most, whether incurred at the riding (district) level or at the party level. In fact, the Conservatives alone outspent the NDP, the Bloc Québécois and the Green Party from 2004 to 2014: CDN$179 million versus CDN$162.3 million. Another interesting data point is the NDP's difference in expenses: while expenses by candidates totaled $36.3 million, expenses by the party amounted to $69.8 million. No other party saw this kind of deviation. It may be argued this difference in spending is with the goal of expanding the NDP's reach as a viable national party. Briefly, public financing increased in proportion to private contributions for party financing in recent years, and the proportion of popular vote correlates with the expenses of parties.

Finally, regarding the 2015 election, it is important to highlight the expenses limits established for political entities. For registered political parties, the total sum was approximately CDN$54 million with the exception of the Bloc Québécois, which had a limit of $13 million (Elections Canada, 2015d). At the riding level, expense limits ranged from $169,928.60 in Egmont, Prince Edward Island, to $279,227.99 in Kootenay – Columbia, British-Columbia. However, it is important to note that in the four ridings in PEI – Canada's smallest province, both demographically and geographically – the expenses limits are lower than the rest since the province is guaranteed a minimum number of seats in the national legislature as per the Canadian Constitution. For third parties, the total expenses they may reach were $439,410.81 and $8,788.22 per riding (Elections Canada, 2015e). These limits were under heat as another strategic move by the Conservatives, as it would limit otherwise well-funded third parties like Engage Canada, according to newly-elected cabinet minister Marc Garneau (Orfali, 2015). We will consider the role of third parties in a later section.

Political Messages

Legal ramifications aside, the messages conveyed through ads are noteworthy. First, political advertising in Canada typically comes in three forms: positive, negative or comparative (which draws upon the previous two). As mentioned above, negative ads are being used more and more by political parties, and research suggests that the tone of political ads affects the cognitive reaction of viewers. Negative ads tend to engender negative thought-responses like judgment and resistance to persuasion whereas positive ads tend to do the opposite (Daignault, 2014, pp. 50–51). For example, the Conservatives and former Reform Party are known for their consistent use of negative advertising techniques. Take the image shown in Figure 25.2 for example. In this case, the Conservatives are "attacking" the leader of the NDP (note that the NDP's color is orange). Many features of this advertisement seek to reinforce the idea that Stephen Harper and the Conservative Party are the steady and safe choice, whereas the NDP would be unwise, to say the least. As the adage goes, the devil is in the details. In this fashion, a few things are worth highlighting: "risk" above Mulcair and "stability" above Harper; Mulcair is in black-and-white, while Harper is in color; Harper's image is larger; there are "x"s next to the points associated with Mulcair and checkmarks for Harper, and so on. As for the written content, Mulcair's platform is described as having fiscal gaps, higher taxes, creating higher consumer prices, and avoiding the mission against jihadism in the Middle East. In essence, this advertisement frames the contest between the two leaders in a comparative as well as negative manner. That is to say, the ad contrasts the two leaders, with Harper coming out in a favorable light.

Political parties are not the only ones to advertise during elections. For example, Elections Canada exists to promote the political rights of Canadians at times of elections and to stimulate voters to get out. This includes disseminating election information. Consider the image shown in Figure 25.3, with the polling date in large letters at the top of the ad. The ad even asks whether or not you have received your *voter information card*. This card is specially designed for elections, contains all the necessary information so that an individual may vote, and is sent to individuals prior to polling day. Finally, at the bottom of the image, the primary eligibility criteria are listed so as to avoid confusion: age,

Figure 25.2   Conservative Party attack ad

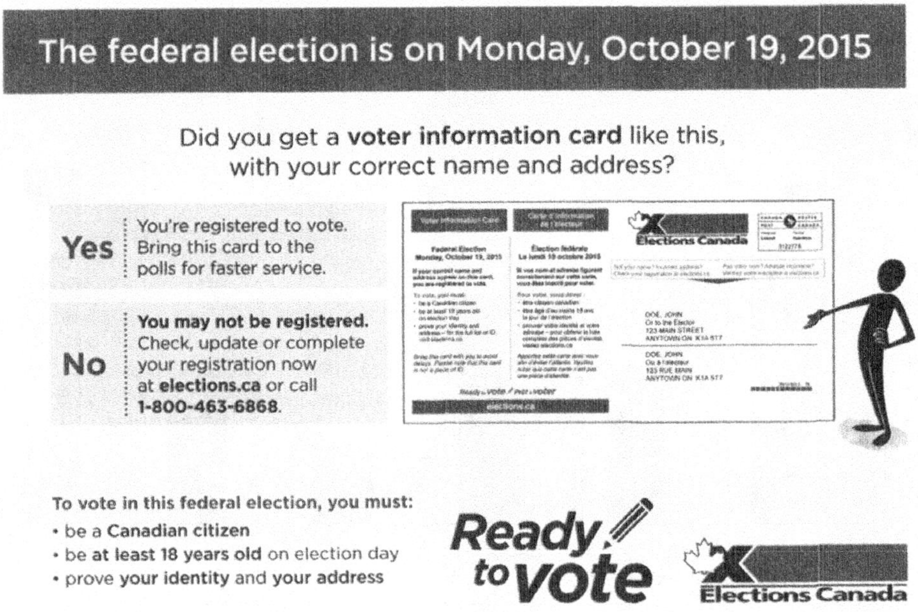

The federal election is on Monday, October 19, 2015

Did you get a **voter information card** like this, with your correct name and address?

Yes You're registered to vote. Bring this card to the polls for faster service.

No **You may not be registered.** Check, update or complete your registration now at **elections.ca** or call **1-800-463-6868**.

To vote in this federal election, you must:
• be a **Canadian citizen**
• be **at least 18 years old** on election day
• prove **your identity** and **your address**

Ready *to* vote

Elections Canada

Figure 25.3 Elections Canada ad

citizenship, proof of identity and address; in Canada, the requirements are 18 and yes to citizenship. To summarize, part of Elections Canada's tasks is to make all the relevant information available to Canadian citizens across the country in a timely manner. This usually takes the form of political advertising, not to support one party over another, but instead to encourage eligible voters to exercise their democratic right. With this in mind, we turn to the following channels of political advertising during election time: broadcasting time, social media and third-party advertising.

Broadcasting in Elections

As mentioned in the introduction to this chapter, television remains the single most important source of news for Canadians. In this respect, the CEA requires broadcasters to make 390 minutes of ad time available during prime-time hours for purchase to authorized political parties (section 335). It is important to note that this time is not sold-off to the highest bidder, as the allocation of time is divided amongst the registered political parties. This allocation is negotiated before the election campaign by a *Broadcaster Arbitrator* (section 332). This is to ensure no party has an unfair advantage over others on account of its fund-raising abilities. Additionally, the CEA prevents any one party from receiving more than half of the available advertising time (section 338). Equally interesting is the availability of free advertising time, which is guaranteed to all political parties should broadcasters allocate such free time. In this case, the CEA prohibits broadcasters to favor one party over another in this regard, which is, as with paid ad time, negotiated prior the election (section 345). Keeping these rules in mind, consider the allocation of paid broadcasting time versus free broadcasting time in the past election in Figure 25.4.

As we can see, the Conservative Party of Canada, which formed the government for the previous nine years, was allocated the most paid time as well as free time. This is because the Conservative Party had the greatest representation of seats in the House of Commons before the call for elections.

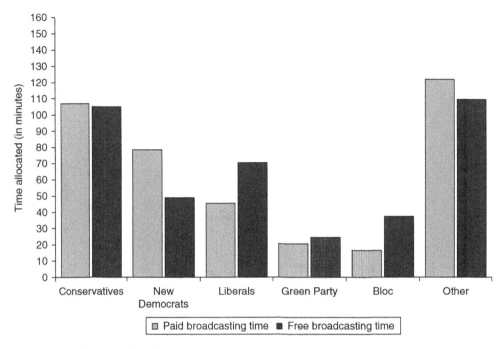

Figure 25.4 Allocation of broadcast time
Source: Elections Canada, 2015a, 2015b.

With this allocation of time, the Conservatives were able to wield influence over the "framing" of the election campaign. For example, the Conservatives launched its "Just Not Ready" advertisement campaign targeted at Justin Trudeau of the Liberal Party in the early phases of the campaign. In response, the Trudeau campaign responded with an ad entitled "Ready." Therefore, a sort of dialogue materialized through the broadcasting medium in an effort to frame important issues that affect voting such as leadership. Similarly, the New Democrats, Liberals, Greens and the Bloc Québécois were each allotted broadcasting time according to their previous representation in the House of Commons prior to the elections. This allows parties to present specific messages of their leaders, of their parties and of their platforms.

Equally notable, in Figure 25.4 it can be seen that a substantial amount of time was allocated to "other" (112 minutes of paid time as well as roughly 110 minutes of free time), which was shared between 17 political parties. Most Canadians would tell you only five or six political parties exist. Yet in keeping with the multi-party nature of Canadian parliamentary democracy, broadcast time is reserved for any registered political party. Conversely, with regard to free advertising time, the CBC was the main broadcaster on radio and television, with another private broadcaster providing free ad time as well.

Social Media

The 21st century has seen the advent of the Internet and social media as a channel for political communication with noticeable repercussions. For example, Giasson, Jansen and Koop (2014, p. 194) observe that blogging, one of the earliest forms of digital communication, has promoted political engagement. Generally, online political engagement appeals to most because it replaces the high cost of real-world participation with low-cost online engagement (Giasson et al., 2014,

p. 195). Similarly, Small (2014) has referred to the phenomenon of *e-democracy* given the interactive, unmediated and accessible nature of social media engagement (p. 92). As a result, it seems the Canadian body politic is shifting toward a *digital agora* for public debate. By 2011, it was reported that half of the population used social media and that not only was this number expanding, but the frequency at which Canadians use social media was rising (Ipsos, 2011). By the same token, as of the 2008 election all five major political parties had operating Twitter accounts (Small, 2014, p. 93). With this in mind, it should be noted that some demographic groups predict stronger online engagement, the most significant of which are younger voters. The *life-cycle effect* explains why younger generations are less interested and engaged in politics, but data suggests that the use of the Internet can be effective in reaching out to this traditionally out-of-reach slice of the electorate (Small, Jansen, Bastien, Giasson, & Koop, 2014, p. 11). With respect to the CEA, there is no section dealing explicitly with online political advertising and, thus, only the general election advertising rules mentioned above apply.

Social media activity in the 2015 election campaign set a new high for Canadians. For example, Twitter Canada reported 3,426,008 tweets using the trademark hashtag #elxn42 throughout the campaign and over 770,000 election-related tweets on polling day alone (Bogart, 2015). To give some perspective on the momentous increase this represents, the 2011 election saw only 114,000 election-related tweets on polling day, thus marking more than a sixfold increase. This digitalization has provided political advertising opportunities that were erstwhile non-existent. For example, Elections Canada partnered with Facebook to create an "I'm a voter" button which 12 million Canadians used on polling day (Bogart, 2015). As mentioned in the opening paragraphs, political parties have also seized the opportunity presented by the Internet to compensate for declining activism by developing web strategies. By creating an account for the political party, candidates and, most importantly, for party leaders, political ads have been disseminated to a growing online audience. In some cases, these ads are sponsored, but in most cases political parties simply share political ads on their account at no added cost. CBC's *Ad Hawk* examined the number of followers on Facebook and Twitter accounts used by political parties and their leaders and found that party leaders tend to garner a larger following than party accounts (McKibben, 2015). Between the parties, it is the incumbent Prime Minister Stephen Harper who had a larger Twitter following at almost 900,000 with LPC leader Justin Trudeau at a close second garnering over 700,000 followers. As for Facebook, Justin Trudeau gathered the largest followers at nearly 300,000 while Harper had 200,000. Mulcair and the NDP failed to gain as much of a social media presence as neither succeeded at passing the 200,000 threshold in online followers.

The last point we will consider on the use of social media concerns the use and effects of it on the content of political ads. Small (2014) notes that while being more democratic, *e-democracy* also tends to limit and reduce what can be transmitted (e.g., the 140-character Twitter posts) (p. 93). In spite of this, it allows political actors to draw focus onto events such as a rally or press conference, but also facilitates interactions between political actors. This last point is of importance, coupled with Montigny's suggestion that social media presence increases risk of committing mistakes in the public eye. A prime example of this would be when the Conservatives published a photo extolling the party's effort in protecting the province of British-Colombia's natural environment with a salmon soaring over crashing waves (Watters, 2015). The problem was that the photo was taken in the United Kingdom, not in Canada, and that the salmon itself was Atlantic coast salmon as opposed to Pacific coast salmon where the province is located. Social media reactions flooded the Internet over the mistake before the Conservative Party could remove it from their account. The Green Party of Canada even made corrections to the advertisement and published it on their Twitter feed (see Figure 25.5) (Green Party of Canada, 2015). Put briefly, while the Conservatives deleted the ad once the mistake was detected, it was too late to stop the bleeding. Such an episode exemplifies the risky and interactive nature of social media for political communication and ads.

Figure 25.5   Green Party Twitter response

Third-party Advertising

It is under Part 17 of the CEA that we find the regulations concerning "Third Party Election Advertising." Traditionally, political parties have been the primary vehicle for individuals to voice their interests, but another channel has emerged in the 21st century: third parties. According to Section 349 of CEA, a third party is an individual or group with a set of interests they seek to promote in the political realm. Generally speaking, third parties have no formal affiliation to registered political parties as they simply advance key policies. In Canada, such groups must be registered. For comparative purposes, third parties are similar to US super-PACs in that both represent interest groups and organizations while attempting to influence the election campaign, but Canadian third parties are limited in campaign spending, financially and geographically, and do not contribute funds to candidates (see "Party Financing and Spending Limits" above; Federal Election Commission, 2008). Historically, however, third parties have not always held the right to advertise during elections. Through several court cases in the 1990s, notably in *Libman* v. *Quebec* (1997), the Canadian judiciary

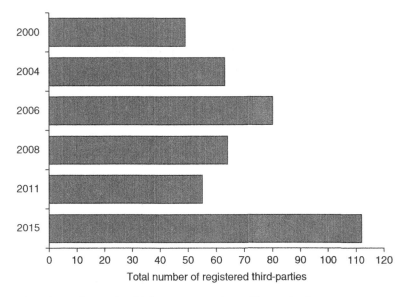

Figure 25.6 Comparing third-party registrations with past elections
Source: Elections Canada, 2015g.

recognized the right for individuals unaffiliated with political parties to promote their interests during election campaigns (Elections Canada, 2015f). The reasoning for this decision originates with the fundamental freedoms entrenched in the Canadian Charter of Rights and Freedoms. Nevertheless, third parties are limited in their spending.

The 2015 elections drew a total of 114 registered third parties (Elections Canada, 2015g). When compared to the past elections, this represents the highest participation rate on behalf of third parties (see Figure 25.6). Third parties have only been participating in elections since the 2000 campaign, but, already, as some have observed that participation tends to increase when elections are framed as elections for change (Cousineau, 2015). For example, the second election campaign that saw the most third parties, was that of 2006, in which the CPC formed government, taking over from the LPC. Likewise, the 2015 elections saw a change in government as the 2006 transition was reversed from the CPC to the LPC. Therefore, both the 2006 and 2015 elections can certainly be considered in a way as realignment elections.

To put matters briefly, third parties are a new element for electoral advertising and it is interesting to see in which elections they appear in greatest numbers, from which regions, and for what causes.

Conclusion

Overall, there are many facets of political advertising during elections in Canada. In the sections above, we described the legal interpretation of *election advertising*, as well as the constraints imposed upon political actors to keep in check the influence of money in politics; we also explored the rules concerning broadcasting. For the most part the legislation on these matters reflects the democratic character of free and fair elections. However, the appearance of the Internet in political advertising offers some contrast. Legislation does not yet single out the use of the Internet and, as a result, the *digital agora* presents lawmakers with challenging questions on the Internet's role during election times, and if and how it may undermine the integrity of free and fair elections. Lastly, the nuts and bolts of third-party advertising were presented, as these actors continue to be important come election time. It will be interesting to follow the presence of such political actors because they have been increasingly present since their entry in the 21st century.

Granted there are other areas of electoral law and political advertising that could have been addressed, which only hints at the complexity and breadth of the matter. In the final analysis, it remains important for scholars, lawmakers and citizens alike to continue to evaluate the way in which politics is communicated so that, collectively, we may safeguard the sanctity of free and fair elections. As Joseph Wearing writes on the power of democratic elections, "The simple act of voting, of marking an 'X' on a ballot, repeated twelve million times in one day, can overthrow a government without a single shot being fired" (as quoted in Elections Canada, 2007, p. xi)!

References

Blais, E. (2015, October 20). Negative ads may have spurred voter engagement. *CBC*. Retrieved from www.cbc.ca/news/politics/canada-election-2015-ad-hawk-negative-ad-voters-1.3280110 (last accessed October 20, 2015).

Bogart, N. (2015, October 20). By the numbers: How the 2015 election played out on social media. *Global News*. Retrieved from http://globalnews.ca/news/2287969/by-the-numbers-how-the-2015-federal-election-played-out-on-social-media/ (last accessed April 17, 2016).

Canada Election Act (2000, c. 9). Retrieved from the Minister of Justice at http://laws-lois.justice.gc.ca (last accessed October 5, 2015).

Canadian Press. (2015, July 29). Imminent federal election to be costliest, longest in recent Canadian history. *Toronto Sun*.

Cousineau, M. E. (2015, September 30). 85 individus et groupes d'intérêts engagé dans la campagne électorale. *CBC*. Retrieved from http://ici.radio-canada.ca/sujet/elections-canada-2015/2015/09/30/016-tiers-enregistres-elections-canada-groupes-interets.shtml (last accessed September 30, 2015).

Daignault, P. (2014). Cognitive effects of televised political advertising in Canada. In A. Marland, T. Giasson, & T. A. Small (Eds.), *Political communication in Canada: Meet the press and tweet the rest* (pp. 39–54). Vancouver: UBC Press.

Drennan, C. (2015). Hosted by "Chris Drennan." Retrieved from www.facebook.com/events/1664887353757502/ (last accessed October 24, 2015).

Elections Canada. (2007). A history of vote in Canada (2nd ed.). Ottawa: Chief Electoral Officer.

Elections Canada. (2015a). Allocation of free broadcasting time. Retrieved from www.elections.ca/content.aspx?section=abo&dir=bra/fre&document=index&lang=e (last accessed October 31, 2015).

Elections Canada. (2015b). Allocation of paid time. Retrieved from www.elections.ca/content.aspx?section=abo&dir=bra/all/2015&document=index&lang=e (last accessed October 31, 2015).

Elections Canada. (2015c). Analysis of financial trends of regulated federal political entities, 2000–2014. Retrieved from www.elections.ca/content.aspx?section=res&dir=rep/oth/aft&document=index&lang=e (last accessed November 14, 2015).

Elections Canada. (2015d). Final election expenses limits for registered political parties: 42nd general election. Retrieved from www.elections.ca/content2.aspx?section=can&dir=part/pollim&document=index&lang=e (last accessed November 14, 2015).

Elections Canada. (2015e). Limits on election advertising expenses incurred by third parties: 42nd general election. Retrieved from www.elections.ca/content2.aspx?section=thi&dir=thilim&document=index&lang=e (last accessed November 14, 2015).

Elections Canada. (2015f). Major court cases relating to the federal electoral legislation. Retrieved from www.elections.ca/content.aspx?section=res&dir=loi/court&document=index&lang=e (last accessed December 4, 2015).

Elections Canada. (2015g). Registered third parties – 42nd general election – October 19, 2015. Retrieved from www.elections.ca/content2.aspx?section=thi&dir=42ge&document=index&lang=e (last accessed October 31, 2015).

Elections Canada. (2015h). The role and structure of Elections Canada. Retrieved from http://elections.ca/content.aspx?section=abo&dir=role&document=index&lang=e (last accessed October 20, 2015).

Esselment, A. (2014). The governing party and the permanent campaign. In A. Marland, T. Giasson, & T. A. Small (Eds.), *Political communication in Canada: Meet the press and tweet the rest* (pp. 24–38). Vancouver: UBC Press.

Federal Election Commission. (2008, May). SSFs and nonconnected PACs. Retrieved from www.fec.gov/pages/brochures/ssfvnonconnected.shtml (last accessed April 25, 2016).

Giasson, T., Jansen, H., & Koop, R. (2014). Blogging, partisanship, and political participation in Canada. In A. Marland, T. Giasson, & T. A. Small (Eds.), *Political communication in Canada: Meet the press and tweet the rest* (pp. 194–211). Vancouver: UBC Press.

Green Party of Canada. (2015, August 22). Re: @CPC_HQ we fixed your graphic [Blog picture]. Retrieved from https://twitter.com/CanadianGreens/status/635139618476720128/photo/1?ref_src=twsrc%5Etfw (last accessed April 23, 2016).

Ipsos. (2011). Canada's love affair with online social networking continues. Retrieved from www.ipsos-na.com/news-polls/pressrelease.aspx?id=5286 (last accessed April 21, 2016).

Keown, L.-A. (2007). Keeping up with the times: Canadians and their news media diet. *Canadian Social Trends*, 83, 12–18. Retrieved from www5.statcan.gc.ca/olc-cel/olc.action?objId=11-008-X&objType=2&lang=en&limit=1 (last accessed October 20, 2015).

Lachapelle, G. (2015). Political parties and the Internet: Changes in society, changing politics – the case of the Parti Québécois. In G. Lachapelle & P. J. Maarek (Eds.), *Political parties in the digital age* (pp. 151–164). Berlin: de Gruyter Oldenbourg.

McKibben, K. (2015, September 6). Forget the election polls. Who's winning on social media? *CBC*. Retrieved from www.cbc.ca/news/politics/canada-election-2015-ad-hawk-social-media-analysis-1.3217076.

Montigny, E. (2015). The decline of activism in political parties: Adaptation strategies and new technologies. In G. Lachapelle & P. J. Maarek (Eds.), *Political parties in the digital age* (pp. 61–72). Berlin: de Gruyter Oldenbourg.

Orfali, P. (2015, August 1). Les coffres des conservateurs sont pleins, mais le NPD a le vent dans les voiles. *Le Devoir*. Retrieved from www.ledevoir.com/politique/canada/446540/les-coffres-des-conservateurs-sont-pleins-mais-le-npd-a-le-vent-dans-les-voiles (last accessed October 27, 2015).

Small, T. A. (2014). The not-so social network: The use of Twitter by Canada's party leaders. In A. Marland, T. Giasson, & T. A. Small (Eds.), *Political communication in Canada: Meet the press and tweet the rest* (pp. 95–109). Vancouver: UBC Press.

Small, T. A., Giasson, T., & Marland, A. (2014). The triangulation of Canadian political communication. In A. Marland, T. Giasson, & T. A. Small (Eds.), *Political communication in Canada: Meet the press and tweet the rest* (pp. 3–24). Vancouver: UBC Press.

Small, T. A., Jansen, H., Bastien, F., Giasson, T., & Koop, R. (2014). Online political activity in Canada: The hype and the facts. *Canadian Parliamentary Review*, 37(4), 9–16. Retrieved from www.revparl.ca/37/4/37n4e_14_Small.pdf (last accessed April 17, 2016).

Watters, H. (2015, August 24). Conservatives use photo of wrong type of salmon in campaign ad. *CBC*. Retrieved from www.cbc.ca/news/politics/salmon-photo-conservatives-harper-atlantic-pacific-1.3201726 (last accessed April 17, 2016).

Wherry, A. (2015, August 2). Stephen Harper's long campaign. *Maclean's*. Retrieved from www.macleans.ca/politics/stephen-harpers-long-campaign/ (last accessed October 27, 2015).

26

POLITICAL ADVERTISING IN COLOMBIA

Between the Narratives of War and Peace

Miguel García-Sánchez and Jair Alberto Arciniegas

With the end of the National Front, and later the signing of a new Constitution in 1991, Colombian democracy became a more competitive political system. At the same time, party allegiances suffered an important decline, especially among urban and young citizens (Duque, 2014). These political transformations contributed to the emergence of a volatile electorate, which is more sensitive to campaign appeals than it was in the past (Jimeno & Acevedo, 2001). As a consequence, political parties and candidates changed the way they relate with voters. Although old-fashioned ways to promote a candidate – public speeches and events – continue to be used, modern campaign techniques play a key role in electoral contests, particularly in presidential elections.

Campaign strategists have been around since the 1986 presidential election, when Jack Leslie helped Virgilio Barco win the presidency. In the last two presidential elections (2010 and 2014) foreign advisers like James Carville, J. J. Rendón, Ravi Shing, Duda Mendoça and Marcus Queiroz, as well as local advertising firms were behind the communication strategies of most presidential candidates. The professionalization of political campaigns has increased the relevance of political advertising as a mechanism of political persuasion. In 2010 each presidential campaign spent between $1.6 and $3 million in television, radio and newspaper spots, Internet content, and other advertising pieces (¿Cuánto cuesta…, 2009). Yet, beyond strategists and spending, the centrality of political advertising in contemporary Colombia can be measured through the impact of political ads on popular culture. That was the case for two television spots broadcast during the 2014 presidential campaign that gave birth to two memorable popular characters: "Mrs. Mechas" and "the mad lady with oranges."[1]

Despite the growing relevance of political advertising in presidential elections, little is known about production techniques, content and formal features of ads as most academic research consists of descriptive accounts of political strategies and campaign events. The main objective of this chapter is to present a general view of political advertising in Colombia. This balance will allow us to show that political advertising is affected by diverse factors including: regulations, international trends on campaigning, new technologies, traditions, campaign decisions, candidates' personality, and the mood of public opinion. However, beyond these factors, the evidence presented in this chapter will show that the figure of former president Álvaro Uribe, and the narratives of war and peace were the driving forces of political advertising in recent elections.

The chapter is structured in six parts. After this introduction, the next section describes the political and electoral systems. The third section summarizes regulations for political advertising. Then we turn to the research on this topic in Colombia leading into the methodology and the results of an empirical analysis of 237 television ads aired in the 2010 and 2014 presidential elections. The final section is the conclusion.

The Political and Electoral Systems in Colombia

Colombia has been recognized as one of the most stable Latin American democracies (Hartlyn & Valenzuela, 1997). For more than 50 years, electoral processes have unfolded under relatively open competition, fraud has been generally absent, and most citizens have considered winning candidates legitimate. However, for various decades Colombian democracy has co-existed with a prolonged and bloody armed conflict between the state, left-wing guerrillas, and right-wing paramilitary bands.

Contemporary democracy can be dated back to 1957, when the historic Liberal and Conservative parties signed a pact to curb political violence and re-establish democracy after a short military government. Such pact, known as the National Front, consolidated a bipartisan regime as the signing parties alternated the presidency and shared bureaucratic power for 16 years (Hartlyn, 1993). Although the National Front ended in 1974, the bipartisan regime extended for the rest of the 20th century. A new era in Colombian democracy started with the 1991 Constitution. The charter reorganized the state structure and promoted a more competitive political system.

After two decades of the constitutional change, bipartisan rule declined and new political movements emerged. Former Liberal and Conservative politicians created some of these new parties, most notably: Cambio Radical, Partido Social de Unidad Nacional and Centro Democrático. Former president Álvaro Uribe was behind the emergence of the last two movements.[2] The traditional Liberal and Conservative parties and an array of new organizations represent the center and center-right of the ideological spectrum. Leftist and independent parties also consolidated, although they capture only a minority of the vote. The coalition of left-wing politicians is known as Polo Democrático and the Green Party. In sum, today Colombia can be defined as a multi-party system in which conservative parties enjoy a strong position. Current president Juan Manuel Santos was elected for the center right Partido Social de Unidad Nacional and a coalition of parties, known as National Unity. It includes the Liberal Party and Cambio Radical, among others.

Colombia is a presidential system in which the executive is both chief of state and government. To be elected president a candidate needs to obtain an absolute majority of the votes (50% plus one). If none of the competing candidates obtains such majority, the two contestants with the largest number of ballots compete in a second round of elections. Presidents serve for a four-year term. Since this system started to be used in 1994, only one candidate, Álvaro Uribe, won the presidency in the first round of elections (2002 and 2006); in two cases the candidate who won the first round was defeated in the second ballot (Horacio Serpa in 1998 and Óscar Iván Zulaga in 2014).

Between 2004 and 2015 Colombian incumbents were able to run for re-election. Like many other Latin American presidents, Álvaro Uribe managed to reform the Constitution in 2004 to extend his presidency four more years, which he did. During his second term he tried to reform the Constitution once again so he could run for a third term. His attempt failed because a ruling of the Constitutional Court blocked it. His successor, Juan Manuel Santos, was re-elected in 2014 and during his second term he managed to eliminate re-election from the Colombian Constitution.

Two houses, the Senate and the Chamber of Representatives, compose the Colombian Congress. The Senate consists of 102 members, 100 elected in a national district and two in a special district for indigenous communities. The Chamber of Representatives consists of 166 members, 161 elected in 33 regional districts corresponding to the 32 departmental divisions plus the capital district of Bogotá. The remaining five representatives are elected in three special districts (afrocolombians, indigenous and Colombians living abroad) (Constitución Política de Colombia, 1991).

Since the electoral reform of 2003, Colombia is a proportional representation system using the D'Hondt method to allocate seats in collegiate bodies. All parties competing for Congress must present a single list but they can choose between a closed and an open list. Finally, political parties must surpass an electoral threshold to qualify for the allocation of seats (García-Sánchez & Hoskin, 2006). For the Senate, such threshold is equal to 2% of the ballots, for the Chamber of

Representatives it is 50% or 30% of the electoral quotient of the respective district.[3] These rules are meant to reduce party system fragmentation, while some intra-party competition remains (Botero, 2009).

Regulation of Political Advertising

Political advertising in Colombia is regulated by (1) the 1991 Constitution, (2) various pieces of legislation that deal with electoral processes and political parties (Law 130 of 1994, Law 996 of 2005 and Law 1475 of 2011), and (3) rulings of the National Electoral Council (Consejo Nacional Electoral, CNE). One of these regulations defines political advertising as "the group of political activities intended to call citizens to vote in favor of a particular candidate" (Law 996, 2005). This definition implies that, legally, political advertising in Colombia is understood in a very broad manner since it is not limited to ads or video clips, it may also include activities such as get-out-to vote campaigns or political rallies. In other words, the legal definition of political advertising includes both political publicity and campaign activities.

Overall, regulations on political advertising in Colombia deal with aspects such as content, periods in which parties and candidates are allowed to broadcast their advertisements, access to the media, and time on air. Compared to other Latin American countries Colombia has more rather than fewer regulations regarding campaigns and access to media (Acéves, 2009; Lauga & García, 2007).

Regarding content Colombian regulations on political advertising establish that parties and candidates are banned from using in their ads national symbols (the flag and the national emblem) and its colors, as well as other parties' logos. In addition, parties and candidates are not allowed to use, as part of their publicity, emblems of state and public institutions. The first group of restrictions, common in several Latin American countries (Lauga & García, 2007), blocks parties and candidates from presenting themselves as potential representatives of the entire nation. On the other hand, restrictions to the use of emblems of public institutions attempt to protect citizens from deceitful claims that present certain parties or candidates as having access to state benefits or resources. This is particularly important in Colombia because several politicians have tried to link their candidacies with state institutions that are in charge of distributive policies (Ocampo, 2014). Finally, negative advertisement is prohibited.[4]

Colombian law establishes that political campaigns can disseminate their publicity through the media during the 60 days prior to the first round of the presidential election. During the weeks between the first and the second round, in case a runoff election is needed, campaigns can advertise as well. Campaigns are not allowed to broadcast any advertisement 48 hours before each election. The promotion of a presidential candidate in the public sphere can begin three months before the election. Thus, campaigns can use street posters, door-to-door canvassing and political rallies to promote their candidates a month before they are allowed to broadcast television, radio and newspaper spots (Law 1475, 2011).

Legislation on political advertising grants presidential candidates free access to public and private media. It also regulates paid advertisements in radio, television and newspapers. Access to private and public media gives presidential candidates equal opportunities to present their political platforms to the citizens. During the 60 days before the election, presidential candidates have access to free space in private media consisting of one spot every weekday in prime time. The length of the free space is four minutes on radio and two minutes on television. The National Electoral Council distributes the spots among candidates using a lottery. Access to free time on public radio and television is limited to one appearance of five minutes during the first week of the campaign, and a second appearance of 10 minutes, eight days before the closing of the campaign. In addition, legislation states that presidential candidates can request up to three spaces of 60 minutes each for debating their ideas on public television stations (Law 1475, 2011). This option has not been widely used by presidential candidates since private television stations organize most presidential debates.

Candidates are allowed to buy space in television, radio and newspapers. Each presidential candidate can buy up to 10 television spots daily, starting 30 days prior to the first round of the presidential elections. For a period of two months before the election, campaigns can buy up to 25 radio spots daily of 30 seconds each. In Bogotá the number of such spots can go up to 50 each day. Campaigns are allowed to buy eight one-page ads, each day, in national newspapers (Resolución 236, 2015). Lastly, the law mandates that rates charged to candidates by private television and radio stations must be half the price of regular tariffs. Cable providers are not allowed to broadcast spots purchased by candidates on international television channels.

In sum, regulations on political advertising are very detailed as an attempt to generate a balanced field for all presidential candidates. Campaigns are limited to three months, contents are regulated, access to public and private media is granted, the duration of ads is controlled, and the number of spots campaigns can buy is limited. As we will see later, despite these efforts, there are important imbalances in access to media that are reflected in the number of spots produced by each candidate. These disparities may be linked to financial imbalances, violations of advertising regulations – especially to negative advertising (¡No mas guerra..., 2014), and different campaign strategies.

Research on Political Advertising in Colombia

Despite the relevance of television as a source of political news (Albuquerque, 2012) and its growing relevance in electoral campaigns, research on political advertising has received only scarce attention among Colombian scholars. Specifically, works that address the production, content and formal features of political ads on television are very scarce (Holtz-Bacha, Johansson, Leidenberger, Maarek, & Merkle, 2012; Kaid & Holtz-Bacha, 2008). Most contributions have analyzed political advertising and campaign communication strategies from a descriptive and interpretative perspective. Thus, in Colombia like in most Latin American countries, empirical studies on television and other media represent a minority (Lozano & Frankenberg, 2009). Research on political advertising can be organized into five groups: (1) analyses of television spots, (2) research on campaigns and politicians' communication strategies, (3) works about the effects of political advertisement on political opinion and behavior, (4) studies regarding regulations and legal aspects of campaigns, and (5) a group of academic pieces about the use of Internet as a campaign tool.

We were able to identify a couple of pieces that study political television ads. A paper by Carmona (2011) analyzed television spots aired by Santos' campaign in 2010. She concluded that most ads talked about jobs, and that Santos' commercials appealed to fear (Colombia cannot risk losing the legacy of president Uribe) and implicitly criticized his opponents. Similarly, Tamayo (2006) studied a selection of television commercials broadcast in the 2006 campaign, as well as several presidential speeches.

A second group of studies, that concentrates most of the academic production, focuses on the communication strategies of campaigns and politicians. Various authors highlight that, from the late 1980s, parties started to use modern techniques of political marketing (Jimeno & Acevedo, 2001), there was an increasing presence of campaign strategists (many of them foreign), and political campaigns appropriated the use of surveys and commercials (Acéves, 2009; Hoyos, 2014). However, despite the Americanization of Colombian campaigns, they seem to be in the intersection between modern political marketing and old propaganda (posters, mobilizations, street meetings and speeches) (Bonilla, Rincón, & Uribe, 2014).

Following this line of research, other studies have described campaign events and strategies and the content of campaign messages (Hoyos, 2014; Morgan, 2013; Richard, 2011; Tamayo, 2006; Uang, 2013). As a consequence of Álvaro Uribe's tremendous political success, some of these pieces are concerned with the former president and *Uribismo*[5] communicational style. Richard (2011) argues that the 2010 presidential campaign revolved around assuring the continuity of Uribe's legacy. Thus, three candidates defined themselves as *Uribistas* and promised to continue the president's legacy. Morgan (2013) defines *Uribismo* as "political discourse and cultural style," more specifically as the mixture of "neoliberalism, nationalism, patriarchal values, religious piety, and thuggery" (Morgan, 2013, p. 57). Bonilla et al. (2014) argue that Uribe attempted to convince citizens that he was the savior of Colombia, someone capable of founding the nation again. Patriau (2012) classifies Uribe's discourse as populist. Finally, López (2014) presents a complete analysis of Uribe's government media use, and how it allowed him to build a hegemonic narrative of politics, nation and the state.

A third group of studies deals with the effects of media and political advertisement on political opinion and behavior. For instance, considering the intensive use of Internet and social media by the Mockus campaign in 2010, there is evidence of a correlation between Internet consumption and a negative rating of Mockus' contender (Escobar, Arana, & McCann, 2014). On the other hand, Uang (2013) shows that having a civilian background and combining security with other issues determines the link between security, as a campaign flag, and electoral returns. Regarding media and political opinion, empirical studies showed a link between television consumption and approval of Uribe's government (García-Sánchez & Wills, 2011).

Another set of studies focuses on regulations and legal aspects of campaigns, including political advertising. From a comparative point of view Colombia belongs to those Latin American democracies in which campaigns and access to media are highly regulated (Acéves, 2009; Lauga & García, 2007). Regarding the link between campaign finances and media spending, data indicates that presidential campaigns spend about 40% of their resources on political advertising (Njaim, 2004), which is low compared with media spending in other Andean countries.

Finally, there is a body of research on the political use of Internet. Political campaigns in Colombia started to use web pages in the early and mid 2000s. For example, for the 2006 campaign all candidates launched a web page; however, its use and quality was very uneven. Although most pages were used as information repositories and included interactive features, only one candidate (Horacio Serpa) took full advantage of this tool by incorporating blogs and content targeted to particular audiences on his website (Tamayo, 2006). Four years later, and after the success of Obama's 2008 online campaign, Colombia witnessed its own online revolution in the 2010 presidential election (Valdez, Huerta, & Aguilar, 2011). In particular, the Green Party's candidate, Antanas Mockus, made an intensive use of Facebook, Twitter, YouTube and mailing lists, which allowed him to establish a direct and effective interaction with citizens. Results were astonishing: Mockus became the seventh world figure in Facebook, with 684,341 followers, and his Twitter account was the number one in the number of followers in Colombia (Rincón, 2011). Despite these numbers, the online phenomenon, known as the *Green Wave*, didn't succeed in the polls. The reasons: the *Green Wave* was an urban occurrence, many of Mockus' virtual followers never became actual voters, and the Mockus campaign didn't articulate a clear and convincing campaign message (Rincón, 2011). In sum, research indicates that web resources are key campaign tools, but they need to interact with other mobilizing strategies (Rincón, 2015).

An Empirical Analysis of Television Ads in the 2010 and 2014 Presidential Elections

Given that research on the production, content and formal features of political television ads is scarce, this section represents a novel contribution to the analysis of this topic in Colombia. Considering that there is no public access to television spots for elections prior to the 2010 contest, our empirical analysis will focus on the 2010 and 2014 presidential campaigns. In addition, due to the high volume of spots available for these two elections we will concentrate on the spots produced by the two candidates that made it into the second round of each election. This section presents an analysis of 372 television ads.[6] Before presenting the analytical framework used for the empirical analysis and our main results, we will briefly describe the last two presidential elections.

The 2010 and 2014 Presidential Elections

In 2010 nine politicians registered as candidates for the presidential election. This high number of contestants is relatively common in Colombia since the 1991 Constitution established a two-round system for electing the president and the consolidation of new parties.

Juan Manuel Santos, of the rightist Partido Social de Unidad Nacional, won the first round of the 2010 presidential elections with 46.7% of the votes, followed by Antanas Mockus who was supported by 21.5% of the electorate (Registraduría Nacional del Estado Civil, 2015). Santos' candidacy represented the continuity of Álvaro Uribe's government, one of the most popular administrations in recent history (Sierra, 2011).[7] Santos, the grandson of a former Colombian president, has been close to social and political power since childhood. He initiated his political career within the Liberal Party; later he abandoned this party to join Uribe's government as Minister of Defense. This post gave him national recognition due to his role combatting leftist guerrillas.

Antanas Mockus ran as the candidate of the Green Party (Partido Verde) and a coalition of independent politicians. Mockus, a Ph.D. in mathematics and former university professor, served as mayor of Bogotá in 1995 and 2001. He is widely recognized for his initiatives to transform civic culture through pedagogy and his unorthodox communication strategies (Rincón, 2015). In the 2010 campaign he embodied the opposition to a government that, despite its tremendous success in weakening guerrillas, manipulated institutions to concentrate power and harassed the opposition. Mockus' criticism of Uribe's government didn't weaken his heir, who won the balloting with almost 70% of the votes.

Despite being elected to continue Uribe's militaristic approach in the fight against the insurgency, in 2012 Santos initiated peace talks with the leftist guerrilla Fuerzas Armandas Revolucionarias de Colombia (FARC). This decision caused a breach between the incumbent and former president Uribe. In 2014 President Santos ran for re-election. His platform was reaching a peace agreement with the FARC to end the long internal conflict. Four candidates competed against the incumbent, who was defeated in the first round of the presidential elections by Óscar Iván Zuluaga (25.7% versus 29.3%, respectively). This candidate, who was a member of Congress and Minister of Finance during Uribe's tenure, represented the Centro Democrático party, a recently created organization with the aim of promoting the political agenda of Álvaro Uribe. Thus, Zuluaga embodied the opposition to Santos government and the negotiated peace. In a very close second round the incumbent, supported by 51% of the voters, defeated Zuluaga who captured 45% of ballots.

Dimensions of Analysis

Since the main characteristics of political ads in Colombia are quite unknown, we developed an analytical scheme that followed those used for other cases. In particular our instrument and its categories were inspired by Holtz-Bacha et al. (2012) and Moke (2006). However, we adjusted some attributes of our analysis to the Colombian case. Similar to the method employed for the analysis of European campaign spots, we studied television ads at two levels: formal features and content.

The analysis of formal elements starts with a description of two units of analysis: the ad and the sequence. Here, we describe the number of ads and sequences, the duration, and other formal characteristics of television spots. Then, we move our attention to the tactics used by candidates in their ads; more precisely, whether or not a candidate appears on screen, presentational formats and production techniques.

The second dimension of our analysis is content. Based on transcriptions of both the written and spoken languages of our sample of ads, we conducted a word count that allowed us to identify keywords used across the campaigns by each candidate. Subsequently, we examined slogans, and broad topics covered in the television spots. This permitted us to identify the most consistent messages and the focus of each campaign. Finally, we checked the coherence between messages, the words employed in the spots and public opinion's main concerns.

For the 2010 and 2014 campaigns we identified 372 television spots that were aired before the first and second rounds of the last two presidential elections – 89 spots in the 2010 election and 283 in the 2014 contest. Since we only studied ads produced by the two candidates that competed in the second round of each campaign, we analyzed 237 commercials (62 and 175, respectively). Our analysis didn't consider the number of times a spot was repeated throughout the campaign, therefore our results cannot clearly identify the message each candidate wanted to emphasize in his campaign. These findings only capture the general spectrum of messages that candidates presented before the public. Despite this limitation we believe our results are a good indicator of the format and content of each candidate's ads.

Formal Features

As shown in Table 26.1, Juan Manuel Santos' campaign produced the largest number of spots both in 2010 and in 2014 with 35 (39.3%) and 109 (38.5%) ads respectively. Santos' opponent in 2010, Antanas Mockus, broadcast 27 ads, which represented 30.3% of all spots produced in 2010. In 2014 Óscar Iván Zuluaga's campaign created 66 spots that were equivalent to 23.3% of all ads produced that year. It is important to highlight that ads broadcast in 2010 and in 2014 by "other candidates" represented 30.3% and 38.2%, respectively. This distribution of television commercials reflects that in spite of the existing regulations, there is an incumbent's advantage in terms of political advertisement. On the other hand, the fact that the "other candidates" represented only about one-third of all ads broadcast in each campaign suggests that a significant number of television spots were aired after the first round of the presidential elections. In other words, campaigns concentrated most of their advertisement efforts to the end of the electoral contest.

From 2010 to 2014, the number of television ads produced by all campaigns grew 218%. An analysis, by candidate, of the percentage variation of television spots indicates that from his first to his second campaign, Santos increased his spots by 211.4% (Table 26.2). On the other hand, the number of ads of Santos' opponent (Mockus in 2010 and Zuluaga in 2014) grew by 144.4%. Other candidates increased their ads by 300%. This tremendous variation in the number of ads from 2010 to 2014 can be understood considering various events. First, unlike 2010, Santos was defeated in the first round of presidential elections in 2014. The loss triggered a strong response by the incumbent's campaign that included more advertising. Second, Santos' challengers deployed very different strategies. In 2010

Table 26.1 Distribution of spots and sequences by candidate, 2010 and 2014 campaigns

Campaign – candidate	Number of spots	Distribution of spots (%)	Number of sequences
2010			
Juan Manuel Santos	35	39.3%	313
Antanas Mockus	27	30.3%	419
Other candidates	27	30.3%	N/A
Total	**89**	**100%**	**N/A**
2014			
Juan Manuel Santos	109	38.5%	1,156
Óscar Iván Zuluaga	66	23.3%	514
Other candidates	108	38.2%	N/A
Total	**283**	**100%**	**N/A**

Table 26.2 Television spots percentage variation, 2010–14 campaigns

Campaign – candidate	Percentage variation
2010–14	218.0%
Santos 2010–14	211.4%
Santos' challenger (Mockus – Zuluaga)	144.4%
Other candidates 2010–14	300.0%

Table 26.3 Television spots descriptive information, 2010–14 campaigns

	2010			2014		
	Juan Manuel Santos	Antanas Mockus	Sample	Juan Manuel Santos	Óscar Iván Zuluaga	Sample
Number of spots	35	27	62	109	66	175
Average length in seconds	5.3	47.5	49.7	42.3	70.8	52.9
Minimum length in seconds	15	20	15	15	20	15
Maximum length in seconds	213	180	213	193	355	355

the Mockus campaign relied more on social media and his activists than on television spots (Rincón, 2011). This may be the consequence of Mockus' lack of access to large financial resources (El dilema de la plata…, 2010) and that he didn't pay much attention to campaign strategists in general (¿Qué pasó con…, 2010). On the other hand, in 2014 Zuluaga deployed a more conventional strategy based on television and radio spots, in part thanks to a well-funded campaign. Finally, the increase in television spots may be also a signal of the Americanization of the electoral campaigns in Colombia (Kaid & Holtz-Bacha, 2008), which means specialized staff, targeted ads, and a varied range of stylized commercials.

In terms of time, we expect political ads to be of short duration, considering that in Colombia campaigns are less professionalized than in the US and Europe (Holtz-Bacha, 2002; Holtz-Bacha, 2014; Kaid & Holtz-Bacha, 2008); and that free time in private television stations is less generous than in other Latin American countries such as Chile and Brazil (Holtz-Bacha et al., 2012, Holtz-Bacha, 2014; Moke, 2006).

As presented in Table 26.3, television spots aired during the last two presidential elections did not differ much in length, and were significantly shorter than European ads (Holtz-Bacha et al., 2012). The average duration of spots was 49.7 seconds in 2010 and 52.9 seconds in 2014. In 2010 both Santos and Mockus produced ads of very similar duration. Four years later, there was a clear difference in terms of the length of the ads. While Santos' spots averaged 42.3 seconds, the average for Zuluaga's ads went up to 70.8 seconds. Thus, in 2014 candidates differed in terms of their use of advertisement resources. The incumbent produced several short spots whereas his challenger, Zuluaga, aired a few, but relatively long, ads.

We identified 2,402 sequences for both campaigns (Table 26.4). A sequence is an element that encloses one or several takes which integrate a continuum that is demarcated by its visual content or

Table 26.4 Sequences descriptive information, 2010–14 campaigns

	2010			2014		
	Juan Manuel Santos	Antanas Mockus	Sample	Juan Manuel Santos	Óscar Iván Zuluaga	Sample
Number of sequences	313	419	732	1156	514	1670
Average number of sequences per spot	8.9	15.5	11.8	10.6	7.8	9.5
Minimum number of sequences	2	1	1	2	1	1
Maximum number of sequences	63	69	69	80	68	80
Average length in seconds	11.4	9.3	10.5	8.1	19.8	12.5

other formal features (Holtz–Bacha et al., 2012). A total of 732 coding units were reviewed for the 2010 campaign and 1,670 for the 2014 contest. The average length of ads' sequences was 10.5 and 12.5 seconds, respectively. Despite broadcasting fewer ads than his opponent, Mockus produced the highest number of sequences of the 2010 campaign (419 coding units versus 313 sequences produced by Santos). In 2014, Santos ads accounted for 1156 sequences, more than double the number of those produced by his challenger's campaign (514).

The information about the formal features of television advertising also gives us a perspective on the "pace" of the content presented in the ads. An indicator of the ads' speed is the average number of sequences per spot. According to this measure, television ads in the 2010 campaign had a relatively faster pace than those presented in 2014 (11.8 versus 9.5) (see Table 26.4). Therefore, the duration of each sequence was slightly higher in 2014 than in 2010.[8] Table 26.4 indicates that the average duration of ad sequences in 2010 was 10.5 seconds versus 12.5 seconds in 2014. In 2010 spots had the fastest pace since candidates' spots made more segment changes and consequently spent slightly less time per subunit.

A comparison of candidates indicates that: (1) in 2010 Mockus' ads were faster than those of his contender Juan Manuel Santos; (2) from 2010 to 2014 the pace of Santos' spots increased as they had more segments and a reduction in the average segment length; (3) in 2014 Zuluaga's campaign presented ads that were significantly slower in pace than those of his opponent. This is particularly clear if we compare that the average duration of Zuluaga's segments was about two times longer (19.8 seconds) than those of the incumbent (8.1 seconds). Thus, we see important differences in ad dynamics, Mockus and Santos' (in 2014) ads being the most hectic. These campaigns presented much information that may have been difficult to follow. The lower pace of Zuluaga's ads may be connected with his effort to position himself and a clear, although complex, message. We will develop this point later.

The second broad dimension of our formal analysis of television advertising refers to presentational formats. We start distinguishing how candidates were presented to viewers. Following previous studies, ads were divided into two types according to the presence or absence of the candidate in the visuals. In the 2010 campaign 40.2% of the ads did not present the candidates either in image or audio. In 2014 the percentage of ads that did not present the candidate was 36.6%. For those ads that included the candidate, a basic question is to what extent he or she was presented as the central element or leading actor of the spot. Here it is important to mention that the mere presence of a candidate in an ad does not imply that such spot revolves around him or her.

Table 26.5 Personalized ads, 2010–14 campaigns

	Percentage of personalized ads
2010 campaign	43.5
Santos	37.1
Mockus	51.9
2014 campaign	42.9
Santos	25.7
Zuluaga	71.2

Table 26.6 Presentational formats, 2010–14 campaigns

	2010		2014	
	Juan Manuel Santos	Antanas Mockus	Juan Manuel Santos	Óscar Iván Zuluaga
Candidate present				
Packshot	30.4%	26.3%	33.6%	27.5%
Statement	14.3%	15.8%	12.1%	31.0%
Montage	14.3%	15.8%	10.7%	19.7%
Videoclip	5.4%	3.5%	8.6%	2.1%
Candidate absent				
Packshot	51.7%	38.5%	53.8%	50.0%
Animation	27.6%	23.1%	10.3%	7.1%
Testimonial (citizens or other politicians)	10.3%	23.1%	24.4%	42.9%

Note: Percentages do not add up to 100. Several formats may appear in a single ad.

Despite the centrality of individual political figures in Colombian politics, and especially in presidential elections, on average, television spots did not revolve strongly around candidates. What we can call "personalized ads" (Table 26.5) represented only 43.5% in 2010, and 42.9% in 2014, of all spots in which candidates appeared on screen. Most ads showed the candidates along with other citizens and they stressed that the success of campaign promises required the participation and ideas of the people. In other ads, candidates received support from common citizens in presenting and explaining their main proposals to the public. Óscar Iván Zuluaga represented an exception to this trend as 71.2% of his ads were personalized. Zuluaga's campaign made a tremendous effort to sell the candidate as a strong and capable leader, and someone able to represent former president Uribe's ideas and policies. Consequently, the focus of his advertisement strategy revolved around his persona.

Regardless of the presence or absence of the candidate in the visuals, the most preferred format was the packshot in which a party or campaign logo dominates the spot sequences (Holtz–Bacha et al., 2012). Between a fourth and a third of all ads that included an image or an audio of a candidate used a party or a campaign logo at the beginning and at the end of the spot. In some cases, a faded logo appeared during the entire ad. For spots without a candidate in the visuals the use of the packshot format went up to 50% (see Table 26.6).

The preference for the packshot format may be associated with the fact that both in 2010 and 2014 some of the main candidates were representing political parties that had a close connection with former president Álvaro Uribe. Considering the tremendous popularity of Uribe among Colombians, linking their names with "Uribe's party" was a way that these candidates used Uribe's popularity in their favor and showed the public that they were representing the political project of the former president. This was the case of Juan Manuel Santos in his first campaign and Óscar Iván Zuluaga in 2014. In the case of Zuluaga, along with the party logo, some of his ads included his own logo: a capital "Z" that was inspired by El Zorro's signature. Conversely, in 2010, Mockus, a candidate with a wide public recognition, used the packshot less frequently. His campaign depended more on his personality and less on the party. In fact, after Zuluaga, Mockus was the candidate with the most personalized commercials (51.9%).

Television ads in which the candidate appeared on the visuals also used the statement and the montage formats. The first format refers to the appearance of a candidate making an argument or developing some of his/her proposals. In the two campaigns analyzed, the statement format was accompanied with the presentation of written statements on screen that summarized the ideas presented by the candidate. While Santos (2010 and 2014) and Mockus used this format in less than 20% of their spots, Zuluaga made a statement in one-third of his spots. The frequent use by Zuluaga's campaign of the statement format may have been the consequence of two factors. First, he used ads to present himself as someone capable of being the president of Colombia. This was something his opponent did not need to prove since he was the incumbent. Second, Santos' campaign revolved around the somewhat abstract idea of peace. As Santos' fierce opponent, Zuluaga faced the challenge of articulating a message supporting the general idea of peace without endorsing Santos' peace talks. Consequently, Zuluaga used many of his ads to explain his criticism of the government and to appear presidential.

The montage format was used in a similar proportion as the statement setup (especially in 2010). Spots using this format were characterized by the presentation of images of iconic places and positive representations of Colombia (people, folklore, nature, etc.). These ads attempted to link candidates with ideas like prosperity, peace, equality, progress and happiness.

Along with the packshot format, television ads that didn't present a candidate in the visuals relied on animation and testimonial formats. Ads using animations showed the candidates' main proposals in a pedagogical and easy-to-understand manner. This format was used more in the 2010 campaign than in the 2014 election. Ads using the testimonial format relied on average citizens, people close to the candidates (family members), celebrities (singers, actors, athletes) and other politicians. All of these individuals made public statements about the candidate's positive qualities and the reasons why they were planning to vote for him. Mockus frequently used this format in 2010 and Zuluaga in 2014.

The final element of our analysis of television spots formats refers to production techniques. Most spots were filmed using multiple angles, although close-ups of candidates were preferred. Spots also included compilations of photographs and videos in a single sequence and the inclusion of written statements and party logos. Similarly, the use of sophisticated production techniques like split-screens, blue-screens and computer animations was evident. Most spots used background music to induce positive feelings toward candidates. When they were making a statement, ads included solemn melodies to intensify the relevance of the candidate's message. Music used in television ads varied from chants and jingles, to orchestral melodies.

Content

Slogans are an important element in any political campaign. They carry in a sentence the most appealing and ambitious proposals of candidates and they can transport voters to different scenarios. In addition, an appealing slogan can be very effective in positioning candidates' proposals (Mcguire, 2010).

In 2010 Santos' slogans talked about unity ("United with Juan Manuel," in Spanish: "*Unidos con Juan Manuel*") and the promise of jobs and better income ("Jobs and More Income: Juan Manuel," in Spanish: "*Con trabajo y más ingresos: Juan Manuel*"). In addition, both slogans attempted to highlight his first name, in an effort to bring his candidacy closer to the average citizen and to distance the candidate from a last name that in Colombia is synonymous with wealth and power.

Mockus' slogans were the popular chant "Union is Strength" (in Spanish: "*La unión hace la fuerza*"), and "If We Dream It, We Can Make It" (in Spanish: "*Si lo soñamos, lo logramos*"). Both mottos pointed to two ideas: that Mockus could win the presidential bid and the victory needed to be a collective endeavor. Mockus' slogans never went beyond these ideas, and his advertising strategy did not disseminate clear and easy-to-understand proposals.

Along with slogans, we also studied other kinds of content in television commercials. Since a single television spot may cover more than one topic, we identified the topics mentioned in each ad (and its sequences). Table 26.7 presents a count of the number of ads in which a particular topic was mentioned and the percentage that such number represents of the total number of ads. Table 26.7 displays results for spots aired by Santos and Mockus in the 2010 campaign. Content of spots was consistent with campaign mottos. Most of Santos' commercials made references to more and better jobs and higher wages (60%). This topic was followed by mentions of security (40%), and health care and education (34%). On the other hand, in the vast majority of his ads, Mockus invited people to vote (70.4%). In 59.3% of his spots this candidate presented himself as someone close to the people and capable of representing them. The third most frequent topic mentioned in Mockus' commercials was corruption (37%).

Table 26.7 Topics addressed in ads, 2010 campaign

Topic	Santos		Mockus	
	Number of ads including topic	%	Number of ads including topic	%
Change	0	0.0	3	11.1
Corruption	1	0.9	10	**37.0**
Culture and sports	3	2.6	1	3.7
Differentiated approach	5	4.3	2	7.4
Economic development	11	**31.4**	5	18.5
Education and health care	12	**34.3**	7	25.9
Family values	1	0.9	2	7.4
Human rights and law enforcement	3	2.6	9	33.3
Innovation	3	2.6	0	0.0
International affairs	1	0.9	0	0.0
Jobs and wages	21	**60.0**	1	3.7
Policy continuity	9	25.7	1	3.7
Private initiative	8	22.9	1	3.7
Security: delinquency and armed conflict	14	**40.0**	8	29.6
Social inclusion	2	1.7	1	3.7
The candidate	9	25.7	16	**59.3**
Utilities	4	3.4	0	0.0
Voting and participation	10	28.6	19	**70.4**
Total number of ads	**35**		**27**	

Note: Percentages were calculated over the total number of ads. Topics addressed more frequently by each campaign are in bold.

Figure 26.1   Most frequent words in Santos and Mockus spots

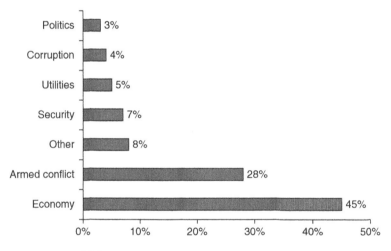

Figure 26.2   Public's main concerns, 2010
Source: The authors on the basis of data taken from AmericasBarometer – LAPOP, 2010.

Topics covered in ads were consistent with those words most frequently employed in candidates' spots. As shown in Figure 26.1 the words "jobs" and "Juan Manuel" were repeated in most of Santos' ads. In the case of Mockus' campaign the dominating words were "vote" and "Antanas Mockus."

A comparison between the leading topics of each campaign and the public's main concerns allow us to establish the extent to which campaigns responded to public opinion. Figure 26.2 displays the country's main problems according to the 2010 survey of the AmericasBarometer – LAPOP. The economy and the armed conflict were the leading concerns of Colombians that year. Thus, the content of Santos' advertising strategy was closer to the public's concerns. Conversely, Mockus' ads did not respond much to public opinion. Of the seven main problems depicted in Figure 26.2, Mockus only emphasized corruption. The closeness of Santos' messages to public opinion priorities may be an indicator that he deployed a professional campaign, which was very much concerned with producing an appealing message. Mockus' campaign was not concerned with giving to the public the message they wanted to hear. Instead, it relied on the candidate's existing image and made an effort to convince people to participate in elections and that winning the presidency was possible. Unfortunately, Mockus' campaign failed to articulate a simple and convincing message in terms of content.

Four years later, in the midst of peace negotiations between the Colombian government and the FARC, Santos' slogans revolved around peace ("Vote to Win Peace," in Spanish: "*Vota para ganar la paz*"; "In Peace We Will Do More," in Spanish: "*Con paz haremos más*"), and that the president needed more time to accomplish his mission ("We Have Done a Lot, There is Much Left to Do," in Spanish: "*Hemos hecho mucho, falta mucho por hacer*"). In his second campaign, Santos' mottos did not try to highlight his first name; he used his last name in all advertisements. His campaign focused on promoting the idea that voting for Santos was equal to voting for ending years of internal conflict.

As a fierce opponent to the Santos government and to the peace talks between the government and the FARC, Zuluaga's slogans promised a change of direction ("A New Age is About to Begin," "For a Different Colombia," in Spanish: "*Un nuevo tiempo va a comenzar*" and "*Por una Colombia distinta*"). Other slogans indicated that Zuluaga was the only candidate on the side of Colombians. Implicitly, Santos was portrayed as siding with the rebels ("Siding with Colombians," in Spanish: "*Del lado de los colombianos*"). These mottos tried to appeal to citizens who opposed negotiation with guerrillas and to those who were nostalgic for Uribe's administrations.

The content of Santos' ads aligned with his campaign slogans. Table 26.8 shows that in 74.3% of his ads the incumbent referenced the peace negotiations as the way to end the internal conflict. This topic was followed by mentions of economic development (42.4%). In a significant number of spots (40.4%), Santos' campaign invited people to vote and instructed citizens how to fill the ballot. The relevance of the voting and participation topic in Santos' advertisement strategy was probably the consequence of his defeat in the first round of the presidential elections.

Although his mottos emphasized a change of direction, some of the topics that dominated Zuluaga's ads pointed to other topics. The dominating themes of his ads were education and health care (60.6%). In 40.9% of his commercials Zuluaga remarked about the deterioration of security and, therefore, the necessity of a new direction. His communication strategy was to move the campaign away from Santos' rhetoric of peace. A third dominant topic in Zuluaga's spots was the candidate himself. In 40.9% of his ads there was an emphasis on the personal and professional qualities that made Zuluaga a suitable candidate.

Aligned with his slogans and dominating topics, the most frequent word, in Santos' TV commercials, was "peace"; followed by the words "Santos" and "president." In the case of Zuluaga, the word "president" dominated his rhetoric. This may be the consequence of Zuluaga's criticism of "the president" and Zuluaga's emphasis on his ability to be the chief executive. Thus, the dominating word was used in different contexts. Other dominating expressions were "Colombia" and "Zuluaga" (Figure 26.3).

As we can see in Figure 26.4, according to the AmericasBarometer – LAPOP survey, the main concern of Colombians in 2014 was the economy. However, none of the leading candidates fully focused on this topic. As we have discussed above, the 2014 campaign revolved around peace and a negotiated solution to the armed conflict. Thus, the content of the 2014 campaign was aligned with the second most important concern of Colombians: armed conflict. To some extent we can state that campaigns in 2014 were not very responsive to public opinion, instead they proposed their own agendas to voters.

Another component of our analysis of campaigns ads is the incidence in ads of criticisms of other candidates.[9] In 2010 none of the spots included in our sample explicitly criticized other contestants. In 2014, however, 15% of all spots studied highlighted a criticism of the other candidate. This indicates that the ban on negative advertising was not fully observed by campaigns. Beyond specific criticisms, campaigns took advantage of various scandals that made it into the media before the elections

Table 26.8 Topics addressed in ads, 2014 campaign

Topic	Santos		Zuluaga	
	Number of ads including topic	%	Number of ads including topic	%
Armed conflict and peace	81	74.3	15	22.7
Change	5	4.6	9	13.6
Corruption	2	1.8	0	0.0
Culture and sports	3	2.8	3	4.5
Delinquency	9	8.3	27	**40.9**
Differentiated approach	11	10.1	20	30.3
Economic development	46	42.2	19	28.8
Education and health care	16	14.7	40	**60.6**
Family values	11	10.1	2	3.0
Human rights and law enforcement	7	6.4	10	15.2
Innovation	5	4.6	1	1.5
International affairs	3	2.8	1	1.5
Jobs and wages	15	13.8	18	27.3
Policy continuity	11	10.1	5	7.6
Private initiative	14	12.8	11	16.7
Social inclusion	11	10.1	15	22.7
The candidate	3	2.8	27	**40.9**
Utilities	15	13.8	22	33.3
Voting and participation	44	40.4	8	12.1
Total number of ads	**109**		**66**	

Note: Percentages were calculated over the total number of ads. Topics addressed more frequently by each campaign are in bold.

Figure 26.3 Most frequent words in Santos and Zuluaga spots

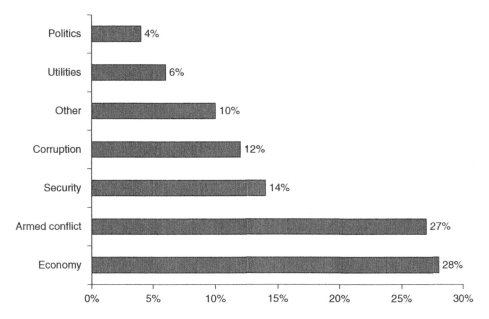

Figure 26.4 Public's main concerns, 2014
Source: The authors on the basis of data taken from AmericasBarometer – LAPOP, 2014.

to discredit their opponents. Zuluaga's campaign was accused of illegally wiretapping government officials. On the other hand, one of Santos' campaign managers was allegedly linked to a drug lord (¡No más guerra…, 2014).

Finally, memorable television spots deserve a special mention. The 2014 presidential campaign is remembered for two television spots that were aired just days before the second round of the presidential elections. Both ads became viral and are seen as crucial in explaining the electoral outcome. The first one appeared during a commercial break in the last presidential debate. This spot, known among Colombians as "Mad lady with oranges" (in Spanish: "*la loca de las naranjas*"), was a testimonial spot using an actress to present a working-class woman in her store, arguing that Colombia needed education, that the current government was doing nothing about it, and that the only candidate worth voting for was Zuluaga. In the first part of the ad the woman speaks calmly, but soon she turns outraged and at the end she throws away an orange she is holding in her hand.[10] Within hours of its broadcast, the spot triggered many reactions and went viral on social media. Commentators linked the excessive tone of this spot with the lack of moderation that Zuluaga showed at the end of the campaign. This famous spot had a boomerang effect on Zuluaga.

Days later, Santos' campaign counterattacked with a cellphone video, widely distributed through social media, known as "Mrs. Mechas." This spot was a true testimony of an 85-year-old working-class woman who explained why she was going to support Santos instead of Zuluaga. Her argument was that the current government was going to grant her family access to a house. Beyond the video's content, its success derived from its tone. Mrs. Mechas talked in a very informal, spontaneous and funny manner. She was a "true Colombian."[11] Days after this spot was distributed, Santos visited Mrs. Mechas, and a picture of him hugging her was widely distributed. Thanks to this video, Santos was able to reach the lower classes, a segment of the population that had seen Santos as elitist and distant. This single ad was so important to Santos' re-election that the president invited Mrs. Mechas to his inauguration.

Conclusion

This chapter presented an overview of political advertising in Colombia with a focus on the use of television spots in political campaigns. In this overview we considered the political and institutional contexts, the state of research on this topic, as well as an empirical analysis of television ads produced in the past two presidential elections.

There is no doubt that modern campaign techniques play a key role in presidential elections. As in other Latin American countries, political campaigns in Colombia have suffered an Americanization process. Such transformation is apparent in the increasing relevance of campaign strategists, the use of modern techniques of political marketing, the appropriation of surveys, and the production of a significant number of television spots. However, up-to-date techniques are complemented with old-fashioned campaign strategies, as streets continue to be an important location of political activism. More importantly, the effectiveness of modern campaign techniques seems to depend less on the technical sophistication of ads and more on the incorporation into political commercials of elements of the popular culture (language and aesthetics). The most popular television spots of 2014 support this claim.

Regulations indicate that Colombia is one of those Latin American countries in which political advertising is highly controlled. Such control aims to generate a balanced competition among candidates. Thus, campaigns are restricted to three months, contents of ads are regulated, access to public and private media is granted, length of ads is controlled, and the number of media spots campaigns can buy is limited. Despite these rules, the numbers presented in this chapter indicate that in 2010 and 2014 there was a significant variation in candidates' use of television commercials. The causes behind this disparity may be, among others, financial gaps and campaign strategies.

Academic studies of political advertising in Colombia are very limited. The few scholars devoted to this topic have analyzed political campaigns mostly from a descriptive and interpretative perspective. In addition, in recent years, scholars have been studying the style, discourse and communicative strategies of former president Álvaro Uribe. This interest opened a line of research evaluating the impact of Uribe on Colombian politics and on the campaign messages and strategies in the last two presidential contests. At the same time, the prominence of Uribe as a research topic has limited the development of other angles in the analysis of political advertising. Consequently, empirical works addressing the production, content and formal features of political ads in Colombia are yet to be undertaken.

Considering the research gaps in the field of political advertising in Colombia, we analyzed formal features and content of 237 television ads that were broadcast in 2010 and 2014. The analysis revealed the existence of a significant difference in the number of ads broadcast by the candidates included in this study. We also found that television spots in Colombia were significantly shorter than in Europe, probably as a consequence of high production costs, and that free time in private television stations is less generous than in other countries. Along with the differences in terms of the number of ads, candidates also diverged in the pace of their ads. Mockus and Santos in 2014 produced spots with several sequences per ad. Consequently, their spots were somewhat hectic and probably the most difficult to understand. Differences in pace may indicate a gap in professionalization of campaign staff, or simply an attempt to present as much information as possible in television spots. Surprisingly, our analysis revealed that television spots were not highly personalized. Most ads showed candidates along with other citizens, and stressed that the success of campaign promises needed people's participation and ideas. Finally, the preferred production formats were the packshot, the statement and the montage.

Regarding content of ads, this chapter showed that both in 2010 and in 2014 Álvaro Uribe played a central role in campaign narratives. In 2010 the advertising strategies of several candidates focused on the idea of being the true representative of Uribe's legacy. In 2014 Zuluaga's strategy brought Uribe back into the debate, as his ads stressed that Colombia needed to go back to the political path defined by the former president. Our analysis of campaigns' contents indicated consistency between campaign slogans, topics covered in ads, and words most frequently used in television spots. In 2010 Santos was very successful in presenting himself as the only candidate capable of continuing Uribe's policies, but he also stressed that the country needed to look forward. Thus, his campaign message emphasized economic prosperity. His communication strategy aligned with public opinion concerns. Once in government, Santos advanced his own agenda and distanced himself from his predecessor. When he ran for re-election in 2014, his campaign managed to set the agenda of the presidential election by making the issue of peace the central topic. As a result of this strategy, campaigns were less responsive to public opinion than in 2010.

The elements and evidence presented in this chapter allow us to conclude that the nature of political advertising in Colombia, like in other nations, depends on a myriad of variables that include the institutional contexts, international trends in campaigning, access to new technologies, traditions, campaign decisions, candidates' personality and the mood of public opinion. However, beyond these factors, the fluctuations of Colombian political context have played a definite effect on the direction of political advertising. In particular, the figure of Álvaro Uribe has been a key referent in recent presidential campaigns, as well as the debate between a negotiated peace and a military solution to the long internal conflict.

Notes

1 In Spanish: *"Doña Mechas"* and *"La loca de las naranjas."*
2 Uribe initiated his political career as a member of the Liberal Party, however he was elected president, in 2002, as an independent. In 2005 a group of Liberal and Conservative politicians founded Partido Social de Unidad Nacional, to promote Uribe's re-election. After abandoning his first party, Uribe created in 2013 the Centro Democrático party.
3 The proportion of the electoral quotient is contingent to the district's magnitude. The 50% applies to districts of size three or more. The 30% applies for districts of size two.
4 Before this prohibition "mudslinging" spots were common in the 1990s.
5 *Uribismo* refers to the political phenomenon that originated around the political achievements of Álvaro Uribe. Many politicians have declared their allegiance to the former president and have run for office as their followers.
6 Television ads were retrieved from the Archivo Electoral website (2015) during the months of September and October 2015.
7 Uribe served for two presidential terms, from 2002 to 2010. In 2010 a ruling of the Constitutional Court blocked Uribe's ambition of competing in a third presidential bid.
8 Although we didn't time each sequence, we divided the length of each spot by its number of sequences; this gave us a perspective on the approximated duration of each sequence.
9 Since negative advertisement is prohibited in Colombia, we focused on critiques.
10 This is the link to the ad: www.archivoelectoral.org/videos/educacion-de-calidad/12985.
11 This is the link to the video: www.youtube.com/watch?v=YGy9RBVUMPQ.

References

AmericasBarometer – LAPOP. (2010). *Muestra Nacional 2010 Colombia*. Retrieved from http://obsdemocracia.org.
AmericasBarometer – LAPOP. (2014). *Muestra Nacional 2014 Colombia*. Retrieved from http://obsdemocracia.org.
Acéves, F. de J. (2009). Elecciones, medios y publicidad política en América Latina: Los claroscuros de su regulación. *Nueva Sociedad*, 12, 33–62.
Albuquerque, A. (2012). On models and margins: Comparative media models viewed from a Brazilian perspective. In D. C. Hallin & P. Mancini (Eds.), *Comparing media systems beyond the western world* (pp. 72–95). Cambridge: Cambridge University Press.
Archivo Electoral. (2015). Retrieved from www.archivoelectoral.org/.
Bonilla, J. I., Rincón, O., & Uribe, C. (2014). Álvaro Uribe: Más patria que pueblo. Comunicación política presidencial, 2002–2010. *Revista Latinoamericana de Opinión Pública*, 5, 95–131.
Botero, F. (2009). Reforma electoral y comportamiento estratégico: Campañas electorales de candidatos al Congreso. In F. Botero & R. Macías (Eds.), *¿Juntos pero no revueltos? Partidos, candidatos y campañas en las elecciones legislativas de 2006 en Colombia* (pp. 1–9). Bogotá: Ediciones Uniandes.

Carmona, M. P. (2011). Colombia, elecciones presidenciales 2010: Análisis de los spots publicitarios para la campaña de Juan Manuel Santos. In P. R. Tarsitano & E. Goncalves (Eds.), *Publicidade no plural. Análise e reflexoes* (pp. 74–82). Sao Paulo: UMESP.

Constitución Política de Colombia. (1991). Retrieved from www.constitucioncolombia.com/.

¿Cuánto cuesta una campaña presidencial? (2009, November 26). Retrieved from http://lasillavacia.com/historia/5409.

Duque, J. (2014). Partidos y partidismo. Los partidos políticos colombianos y su enraizamiento en la sociedad. *Revista Facultad de Derecho y Ciencias Políticas*, 44, 311–347.

El dilema de la plata para los candidato (2010, March 26). Retrieved from http://lasillavacia.com/historia/8782.

Escobar, C., Arana, R., & McCann, J. (2014). Assessing candidates at home and abroad: A comparative analysis of Colombian expatriates in the 2010 presidential elections. *Latin American Politics and Society*, 56, 115–140.

García-Sánchez, M., & Hoskin, G. (2006). *La reforma política y las elecciones locales de 2003: ¿La salvación de los partidos políticos colombianos?* Bogotá: Ediciones Uniandes.

García-Sánchez, M., & Wills, L. (2011). El poder de la televisión: Medios de comunicación y aprobación presidencial en Colombia. In A. Rettberg & O. Rincón (Eds.), *Medios, democracia y poder. Una mirada comparada desde Colombia, Venezuela y Argentina* (pp. 135–158). Bogotá; Ediciones Uniandes.

Hartlyn, J. (1993). *La política del regimen de coalición. La experiencia del Frente Nacional en Colombia.* Bogotá: Ediciones Uniandes.

Hartlyn, J., & Valenzuela, A. (1997). La democracia en América Latina desde 1930. In L. Bethell (Ed.), *Historia de América Latina. 12. Política y sociedad desde 1930* (pp. 11–63). Barcelona: Cambridge University Press, Crítica.

Holtz-Bacha, C. (2002). Professionalization of political communication. *Journal of Political Marketing*, 1, 23–37.

Holtz-Bacha, C. (2014). Political advertising in international comparison. In H. Cheng (Ed.), *The handbook of international advertising research* (pp. 554–574). Malden, MA: Wiley-Blackwell.

Holtz-Bacha, C., Johansson, B., Leidenberger, J., Maarek, P., & Merkle, S. (2012). Advertising for Europe: TV ads during the 2009 European election campaign in four countries. *Nordicom*, 33, 77–92.

Hoyos, M. P. (2014). Elecciones presidenciales en Colombia (2014): Polarización electoral y periodismo espectáculo. Bogotá: Friedrich Ebert Stiftung, Working Paper 3.

Jimeno, R., & Acevedo, M. (2001). *Elecciones presidenciales 1998–2002.* Bogotá: Jimeno, Acevedo & Asociados.

Kaid, L. L., & Holtz-Bacha, C. (2008). *Encyclopedia of political communication.* Thousand Oaks, CA: Sage.

Lauga, M., & García, J. (2007). La campaña electoral: Publicidad/propaganda, periodo, prohibiciones. In D. Nohlen, D. Zovatto, J. Orozco, & J. Thompson (Eds.), *Tratado de derecho electoral comparado de América Latina* (pp. 709–743). México: FCE, Instituto Interamericano de Derechos Humanos, Universidad de Heidelberg, International IDEA, Tribunal Electoral del Poder Judicial de la Federación, Instituto Federal Electoral.

Law 996. (2005). Retrieved from www.alcaldiabogota.gov.co/sisjur/normas/Norma1.jsp?i=18232.

Law 1475. (2011). Retrieved from www.secretariasenado.gov.co/senado/basedoc/ley_1475_2011.html.

López, F. (2014). *Las ficciones del poder. Patriotismo, medios de comunicación y reorientación afectiva de los colombianos bajo Uribe Vélez (2002–2010).* Bogotá: Debate – Universidad Nacional de Colombia.

Lozano, J. C., & Frankenberg, L. (2009). Theoretical approaches and methodological strategies in Latin American empirical research on television audiences: 1992–2007. *Global Media and Communication*, 5, 1–28.

Mcguire, M. (2010). Three simple words: A rhetorical analysis of the slogan "Yes We Can." *Advances in Communication Theory and Research*, 3, 1–11.

Moke, M. (2006). Political advertising in Chile. In L. L. Kaid & C. Holtz-Bacha (Eds.), *The Sage handbook of political advertising* (pp. 145–159). Thousand Oaks, CA: Sage.

Morgan, N. (2013). Sex, soap, and society: Telenovela noir in Álvaro Uribe's Colombia. *Journal of Iberian and Latin American Studies*, 19, 53–76.

Njaim, H. (2004). Financiamiento político en los países andinos: Bolivia, Colombia, Ecuador, Perú y Venezuela. In G. Steven & D. Zovatto (Eds.), *De las normas a las buenas prácticas. El desafío del financiamiento político en América Latina* (pp. 235–271). San José: Organización de Estados Americanos, Instituto Internacional para la Democracia y la Asistencia Electoral.

¡No más guerra sucia en las elecciones! (2014). Retrieved from www.semana.com/nacion/elecciones-2014/articulo/no-mas-guerra-sucia-en-las-elecciones/386848-3.

Ocampo, G. I. (2014). *Poderes regionales, clientelismo y Estado. Etnografías del poder y la política en Córdoba, Colombia.* Bogotá: CINEP.

Patriau, E. (2012). ¡El populismo en campaña! Discursos televisivos en candidatos presidenciales de la Región Andina (2005–2006). *Colombia Internacional*, 76, 293–325.

¿Qué pasó con la ola verde? (2010, June 1). Retrieved from http://lasillavacia.com/historia/15107.

Registraduría Nacional del Estado Civil. (2015). República de Colombia. Elección Presidente y Vicepresidente – 30 de mayo de 2010. Retrieved from: www.registraduria.gov.co/elecciones_anteriores/2010PR/escrutinio.php.

Resolución 236 – Consejo Nacional Electoral. (2015). Retrieved from www.cne.gov.co/CNE/media/file/res%20236-15-presidencia.PDF.

Richard, E. (2011). *Storytelling*, narrativas de campaña. Campañas electorales para la presidencia en Colombia, 2010. *Revista Ópera*, 11, 129–145.

Rincón, O. (2011). Mucho ciberactivismo… pocos votos. Antanas Mockus y el partido Verde colombiano. *Nueva Sociedad*, 235, 74–89.

Rincón, O. (2015). Ciberpolítica.co. De Mockus a Santos, pasando por Uribe, Petro y Fajardo. In O. Rincón & C. Uribe. *De Uribe, Santos y otras especies políticas. Comunicación de gobierno en Colombia, Argentina y Brasil* (pp. 155–176). Bogotá: Ediciones Uniandes.

Sierra, L. M. (2011). *Álvaro Uribe: Un presidente de teflón. La estrategia de opinión pública que lo hizo inmune a la crisis.* M.A. Thesis, Universidad de los Andes.

Tamayo, C. A. (2006). *Mutaciones contemporáneas: Proceso electoral y medios de comunicación en Colombia 2006.* Bogotá: FESCOL, Centro de Competencia en Comunicación para América Latina.

Uang, R. (2013). Campaigning on public security in Latin America: Obstacles to success. *Latin American Politics and Society*, 55, 26–51.

Valdez, A., Huerta, D., & Aguilar, A. (2011). Las cibercampañas en América Latina: Potencialidades y limitantes. *Correspondencias y Análisis*, 1, 3–16.

27

A SERIOUS MATTER

Political Advertising in Germany

Christina Holtz-Bacha

Television in Germany was still in its infancy, when party spots appeared for the first time during the 1957 parliamentary election campaign. Household coverage amounted to only about one million television sets in the election year and slowly increased to four million in 1960 (Beyer, 2016, p. 197). So, parties seized the new opportunity for their advertising even though they could not reach but a minor part of the electorate. At that time, only one television channel (ARD) was available, a second channel (ZDF) only started in 1961. Both were organized as public service corporations, financed by a broadcasting fee and with very limited airtime to be sold for commercial advertising. Political advertising was only permitted during the last weeks of the election campaign. Airtime for electoral broadcasts was allocated for no charge and could not be purchased.

The Political and Electoral System Background

Germany features a parliamentary system which is dominated by parties. The parliament (German Bundestag) is one of two legislative bodies (chambers) on the national level. The second chamber, the Federal Council (Bundesrat), is not elected directly by the people but consists of representatives of the federal (Land) parliaments. Laws adopted in the parliament have to pass the Federal Council which occasionally provides for some tension because both chambers can have different majorities.

The chancellor is the head of the government and is elected by the parliament and not directly by the people. The chancellor selects the ministers for the government who are then appointed by the Federal President. The president is the highest ranking representative of the state, but has mainly a ceremonial function and is supposed to stand above the parties. That makes the chancellor the most influential figure in the German political system.

The parties are the central players in the system. The constitution attributes to them the task of participating in the formation of the political will of the people. Further regulation is laid down in a special Act on Political Parties. The Act also establishes the financing of the parties which is mostly based on public funding. Public funds are distributed according to the votes a party got in recent elections and the total amount of membership fees, other contributions and donations.

Germany's electoral system further adds to the influential role of the parties. It is a mixed-member proportional system giving each voter two votes. With the first vote, a party candidate in the constituency is elected, and the second vote is given to a party list. The number of seats a party gets in the parliament depends on the number of second votes thus making the party vote more important than the constituency vote. The two-vote electoral system is a regular issue in electoral advertising, either to remind voters of their meaning or because smaller parties in particular campaign for the second votes (see Holtz-Bacha, 2004).

Today, Germany features a multi-party system. Since 1949, when the first Bundestag election in the newly founded Federal Republic of Germany was held, until the 1980s, the Christian Democratic Union/Christian Social Union (CDU/CSU)[1] and the Social Democratic Party (SPD) dominated the German party landscape. Together, they regularly drew more than 80% of the votes in national elections. During the first three decades, the only other party represented in the Bundestag was the Free Democratic Party (FDP) which rarely reached two-digit results. This small party, however, enjoyed a disproportionately influential role. It was needed to form a coalition government with either one of the two big parties, which usually did not get together in a grand coalition. The situation changed in 1983 when the Greens were elected into the Bundestag for the first time. In the long run, the establishment of the Greens would allow for new coalition constellations putting an end to the FDP's role as a kingmaker for either one of the big parties. The party landscape changed again after German unification in 1990 when the successor of the former state party of the German Democratic Republic (GDR), the Party of Democratic Socialism (PDS), got elected into the Bundestag. In 2007, the party that until then had its strongest foothold in the East German states, joined forces with a group that broke away from the SPD, thus gaining ground in the West German states as well, and is now called The Left (Die Linke). The party landscape was once again scrambled when the Pirate Party was founded in 2006 and made it into some Länder parliaments but its initial success soon slowed. Instead the AfD (Alternative für Deutschland), founded in 2013 as an anti-Euro party, grew stronger, slightly missed the Bundestag 5% threshold in 2013, but got elected to the European Parliament in 2014 as well as some state parliaments. AfD developed into a populist, national-conservative party campaigning on xenophobia and against the refugee policy of the government.

Thus, since the 1990s and counting the CDU/CSU as one party, five parties have been represented in the German parliament. In the 2013 election, the FDP failed the 5% hurdle and is no longer represented in the parliament. Many other parties usually run for election but never make it over the 5% threshold.

The party receiving the majority of the votes proposes its chancellor candidate for election in the parliament. As usually neither CDU/CSU nor SPD win an absolute majority of the votes, a coalition of at least two parties is necessary in order to push a candidate through as chancellor and to form a government. Until now, the chancellor always came out of the two dominant parties, either CDU/CSU or SPD.

As neither the president nor the chancellor is elected directly by the people, the Bundestag and European parliamentary elections are the only national elections. However, due to the federal system and because the Länder parliament elections do no take place at the same time, there is always an election in sight.

The Regulatory Framework for Electoral Advertising

Since about the mid 1970s, German parties have focused their election campaigns on television. Due to the greater credibility of the programs for which the broadcasters are responsible and because the promotional character of their appearances on those programs was less obvious, politicians tried to get into the news or election related programs. On the other hand, spot advertising has the advantage of being completely in the control of the parties and did not risk any journalistic intervention. However, the amount of time available for electoral advertising was limited.

Until the mid 1980s, public service channels had a quasi-monopoly on the broadcasting market which was only then opened up for commercial stations. Over the years, the television market in particular has become extremely competitive. Whereas in 1988 German households received seven television channels on average, the number increased to 51 in 2006 and now reaches 74 (Statista,

2016). Due to the large number of channels and the fact that the programming volume is growing much more rapidly than individual viewing time, audience fragmentation has become a characteristic of the German television market. Individual channels reach a comparatively low overall audience share. The most popular channel, which in 2015 was the public service ZDF, has a share of only 12.5% (KEK, 2015). Thus, whereas in earlier times advertising on the two public service channels guaranteed a wide audience, the distribution of viewers across many channels would suggest a broad-scale advertising strategy as well. However, since the commercial channels have been opened for electoral advertising, the parties have not used this option very much.

German media law is very fragmented, which is mostly due to the fact that the legislative jurisdiction for the media lies with the 16 federal states. Whereas any ideological advertising is prohibited in the broadcast media, electoral advertising is allowed to give parties a chance to present themselves to the electorate. The right of parties to electoral advertising on public service broadcasting is laid down in the Länder laws on the nine broadcasting companies that form ARD, and in the ZDF Interstate Treaty. Electoral advertising on nationally distributed commercial television is regulated by the Interstate Broadcasting Treaty, regional and local commercial broadcasters are subject to the regulation of Länder media laws. These are rather general regulations that determine the right of the parties to airtime for their electoral advertising during parliamentary, European parliamentary and Länder parliamentary election campaigns. Usually, the relevant paragraphs refer to the German Act on Political Parties regarding equal treatment of all parties running for election. In addition, some of the laws emphasize the right of the broadcasting companies to reject party spots if they are obviously not electoral advertising or violate general laws. These general regulations provided the basis for a common practice of making airtime available during election campaigns. Over the years, many complaints about the allocation practices and rejections of individual spots were brought to court and to the Federal Constitutional Court in particular. Their decisions generated further interpretation of the right to electoral advertising on television and radio.

Due to Germany's electoral system, only parties and not individual candidates can get broadcast time for their electoral advertising. Each party registered for an election has the right to obtain free airtime on the two public television channels. In accordance with regulation for other public services provided for parties, the equal opportunity rule is the guiding principle for the allocation of advertising time on television. Nevertheless, a system of graded allocation is applied, with smaller parties getting less time (fewer spots) than the larger ones. This has been the subject of several cases submitted to the Federal Constitutional Court which, however, approved the graded allocation system. To allow for a certain repetition effect, which is regarded as a necessary condition for reaching audience attention, the minimum number of television spots per party was set to two (per public channel).

The number of spots an individual party may broadcast is calculated according to the number of votes it got in earlier elections and according to its expected success in the upcoming election. According to the public service provision mentioned above, allocation roughly follows an 8-4-2 rule: The two big parties, Christian Democratic Union (CDU) and the Social Democratic Party (SPD), receive eight time slots per public channel, adding up to 16 for each party. The other parties that are also represented in the parliament get four slots and all others get two.

Since the election of 1998, the maximum length for the individual spot to be broadcast in these time slots was fixed at 90 seconds. Until then, since the 1960s, airtime for each spot had been 150 seconds. The large number of campaigning parties, which each have the right to obtain at least two time slots, causes a capacity problem for the public stations. For instance, 30 parties were running for the parliamentary election in 2013. Thus, public channels have to set aside a large amount of airtime for electoral advertising. This and the fact that they are obliged by law to broadcast the party spots and thus content that they cannot influence are the main reasons why electoral advertising is not very popular with the public stations. In addition, they fear being perceived as the producers of the spots. Therefore, they do everything to make clear that the parties are responsible for the contents and to dissociate themselves from the advertising (see Holtz-Bacha, 2003). Immediately before the spots are shown on German television – on public as well as on commercial channels – an off-camera speaker announces that electoral advertising is coming up and emphasizes that the parties are responsible for the contents and the broadcasters are obliged by law to carry the party spots. Of course, these announcements are not in the interest of the parties because they weaken the surprise effect of the advertising and could almost be an invitation for viewers to switch to another channel. In addition to this, the television stations put the spots in a frame during their entire length with a permanent insert saying "electoral advertising" to point out that responsibility for the contents lies with the parties.

In addition to free allocation of airtime by public service channels, parties may purchase airtime on commercial television. Parties only have to pay the prime costs, which in recent elections was around 50% of the rates for commercial advertisers. Nevertheless, only few parties indeed go on commercial television. Whereas Christian Democrats and Social Democrats regularly buy advertising time on several commercial channels, even the smaller parliamentary parties do not invest in additional television advertising and if they do, much less than their big competitors. As advertising on commercial channels has the advantage of parties being allowed to choose the broadcast time, the surrounding program and thus address specific target groups, relinquishing this opportunity only means that the smaller parties cannot afford to purchase airtime.

The public channels schedule the broadcast time of the spots. According to an earlier court decision, the spots have to be on air when a substantive number of viewers can be reached. Therefore, spots are broadcast in the evening, with the earliest aired around 6 p.m. and the latest at about 11 p.m. On the public channels, the party spots are not part of the advertising blocs and also not credited against the maximum allowable amount of advertising.

Party spots do not have their "own" audience. Instead they profit from the previous or following program. Spots broadcast before or right after the news or, even better, before or after a soccer match or any other popular program reach the highest audience ratings. As the broadcast time for a specific spot is assigned at random, the lucky slot is also at random. The random assignment of time slots also leads to viewers being caught by the spots and the specific party by chance. This procedure plays into the hands of the smaller and unknown parties which thus may reach an audience that otherwise would not have come across their advertising.

During the election campaign in 2013, the best ratings for individual spots on public television exceeded three million viewers and were reached by spots broadcast around the evening newscasts. On commercial television, the audience shares for CDU and SPD spots tended to be somewhat higher. Peaks of more than four million viewers appeared around the German adaptation of "Who wants to be a millionaire?" (Arbeitsgemeinschaft Fernsehforschung, 2013a, 2013b, 2013c, 2013d).

The production of the television spots is the responsibility of the parties, which usually commission advertising agencies. The broadcasters can refuse spots only if they obviously do not contain electoral advertising or contravene criminal law as for instance through incitement of hatred and violence. However, the broadcasters do not have to determine whether a spot is in accordance with the Basic Law (constitution) which would be established by the Federal Constitutional Court. In general, if there are controversial cases, the courts mostly rule in favor of the incriminated party on the grounds of giving them an opportunity to present their platform to the public and let voters decide for themselves whether they like the party's ideas or not.

Most controversies were caused by right-wing extremist propaganda. When extreme right parties got stronger in Germany in the early 1990s and in order to avoid having to broadcast their oftentimes xenophobic spots, some public broadcasters started a discussion about the spots and proposed to change the broadcasting laws in order to eliminate the obligation of electoral advertising altogether. Across all parties, politicians were divided in their stance on the broadcasters' push because the abolishment of the right to free airtime during election campaigns would have been to their own disadvantage. Eventually the debate petered out but may be revived in view of the recent rise of right-wing thought and xenophobia on the political scene.

German Party Spots 1957 until 2013

In Germany, research into party advertising took off in the early 1990s. Until then, only a few studies were available that examined different aspects of the spots (for an overview cf. Holtz-Bacha, 2000, 2006). The establishment of commercial broadcasting and the possibility of purchasing airtime made electoral advertising on television and radio a more interesting campaign instrument than before and research followed suit. The European parliamentary elections that were held as direct elections for the first time in 1979, provided additional research opportunities and also a unique setting for cross-country comparisons (Kaid et al., 2011; Rafter, Novelli, & Holtz-Bacha, 2016). Most of the studies on electoral spots presented content analyses and focused on television. A recent study (Brück, 2014) analyzed the contents of electoral spots on radio and their agenda setting potential. Podschuweit (2012) examined the interplay of media reporting and party advertising and the effects of different constellations on voting intention. However, research into effects is still greatly needed.

The following part presents findings from a long-term content analysis of the German party spots shown on television since their introduction in the 1957 parliamentary election until the most recent election which was held in 2013. The spots from 16 campaigns altogether were analyzed on the basis of the same codebook which was only partially updated for the most recent campaigns but only in the form of supplementary categories in order to maintain comparability over time.

In contrast to most US studies and according to a concept developed first by Lessinger (1997; see also Holtz-Bacha, 2006) this analysis mostly refers to sequences as coding units and not to the whole spot. Each spot was coded on two different levels. In the first step, structural data were coded for the whole spot, in the second step, formats and contents of the spots were coded according to spot sequences or scenes (for a more extensive description, see Holtz-Bacha, 2000). Adopted from film theory, a spot sequence is defined as a unit containing one or multiple takes (separated by cuts or superimpositions) that constitute a continuum connected to a unit by several criteria. These criteria either refer to the content (e.g., a continuum of location, time, action, the constellation of actors, or the topic) or to the formal features (e.g., a continuum of sound, music, narrator). A sequence changes if the content and/or formal brackets change and another action and/or constellation of figures and/or another topic and/or other formal features dominate. One sequence is always separated from another sequence through a cut or a superimposition, but any cut is not necessarily the beginning of a new sequence. The coding unit is closely connected to presentational style or format. Formats are visual strategies as for instance montages, video clips, candidate statements or interviews. A change of format always implies the beginning of a new sequence or scene but the beginning of a new sequence does not necessarily imply a change of format. "Format" here is exclusively used as a formal category and the content of the spot is coded independently.

The data refer to 557 spots with altogether 2,703 sequences from 16 Bundestag election campaigns. All in all, the longitudinal analysis yields only a few continuous trends in the form of linear or almost linear increases or declines. Instead, ups and downs over the years speak for varying "fashions," as for instance individual formats disappearing and being revived again, and the influence of the specific constellation of each campaign.

Over the years, the average length of the spots became shorter. This is mostly explained by the decision of the public broadcasters to cut the time allotted for individual spots. In the early years of electoral advertising on television, the parties received 5- and even 10-minute slots. In the 1960s, airtime was shortened to 150 seconds and again in 1998 to 90 seconds which has remained the same since then. Another reason for the decline in average spot length is the opening of commercial television for electoral advertising where parties have to pay for airtime and therefore prefer shorter spots. So, if the average length of the individual spots went down from 201 seconds in 1957 to 81 seconds in 2013, this development mostly reflects the allocation policy of the broadcasters. In addition, as only few parties go on commercial television and this analysis only includes different spots and no repetitions, the average length is still very much determined by the amount of time available on public television.

Formats (production techniques) are differentiated according to the presence of a candidate and provide a rough indicator for personalization. Of 2,679 sequences for which a format could be identified, 69% did not present a candidate-focused format. All in all, this finding speaks against electoral advertising being much personalized. In part, it is also an effect of the methodological procedure considering the fact that German electoral spots usually combine a number of formats and sequences and, if at all, only some of them show a candidate. If the unit of analysis were the whole spot, any appearance of a candidate, independent of its length, would point to personalization.

Figure 27.1 displays the share of sequences with formats that do not show a candidate. The most common formats without candidates are montages and packshots. A montage is produced by dissolving several pictures or scenes into each other. In political advertising, montages often show beautiful landscapes (mountains, rivers, coastlines, lush green pastures, romantic villages) or famous buildings (Reichstag, Brandenburg Gate). As such, montages are used to target voters at an emotional level and convey a feel-good atmosphere. Between 1957 and 2013, this format appeared in 31% of all sequences without a candidate.

A packshot is a format adopted from commercial advertising. It contains pictures of the advertised product and is usually combined with a slogan or the brand name. Packshots mostly appear at the end of a commercial and serve to solidify the name of the product and the advertiser with the viewers. In the same way, in political advertising packshots are sequences dominated by the party logo employed to reinforce the party name and to remind viewers of who is responsible for the advertising and to be associated with the ideas expressed in the spot. Packshots were used in 26% of the sequences. Signal shots, ranking third here, serve as structuring elements and usually consist of one picture only. They are used to separate one format from the next. Testimonials, another format adopted from commercial advertising, were coded in this context as citizens and not party representatives speaking in favor of a party. Over the years, they appeared in 11% of the spot sequences and thus belong to the standard repertoire of formats in electoral advertising.

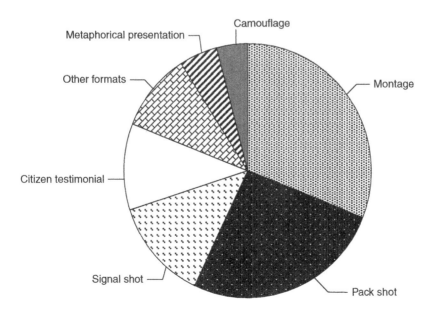

Figure 27.1   Formats of spots without candidates 1957–2013 (n = 1,844)

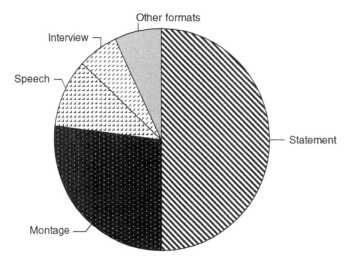

Figure 27.2 Formats of spots with candidates 1957–2013 (n = 835)

The candidate statement is probably the format most often associated with electoral audiovisual advertising. All sequences, with and without appearances of politicians, taken together, candidate statements (15%) rank third behind montages (22%) and packshots (18%). This order once again reflects the more issue-oriented advertising in the party-dominated electoral system. It comes as no surprise, however, that statements are the most frequently used format among the sequences including a party representative (Figure 27.2). It accounts for 50% of the sequences. Summing up to 27% of the sequences, montages, showing candidates carrying out their official duties, rank second. Clippings from candidate speeches are used in 10% of the sequences whereas the obviously staged formats such as interviews or candidates in conversation with citizens are of minor importance.

The personalization of election campaigns, particularly in party-oriented political systems, has been one of the major research issues in the field of political communication in recent decades. Due to divergent definitions and operationalizations findings are heterogeneous and differ across countries. The analysis of electoral advertising provides information about the personalization strategies of the campaigners. As the dataset used here covers 16 election campaigns from more than 50 years, it is also possible to assess the development over time.

This study used several indicators to fathom the personalization process. The differentiation of formats and sequences with or without politicians, as shown in Figures 27.1 and 27.2, provided a first impression of the relevance of personalization in the electoral advertising. In addition, Figure 27.3 presents the development across the 16 campaigns.

Over the years, sequences without the appearance of a politician dominate advertising. Only in two campaigns, 1961 and 1972, sequences showing a politician outweigh the formats without a party representative. In addition, there is no linear trend towards the increased employment of formats focusing on a candidate and a personalized strategy. However, it has to be kept in mind here that these findings are based on the spots of all parties. With more than 20 parties running for election, this includes many small contenders with mostly unknown candidates which cannot be used for personalized campaigning. The case should be different for the parties that are represented in the parliament and even more so if they participate in the government. Their top politicians and particularly if they are ministers of the government usually have a certain degree of recognition and therefore lend themselves for their party's advertising. That applies all the more for the chancellor candidates. Until today, only the two big parties, Christian Democrats and Social Democrats, had a chance to win the chancellorship and were the only ones[2] to actually nominate chancellor

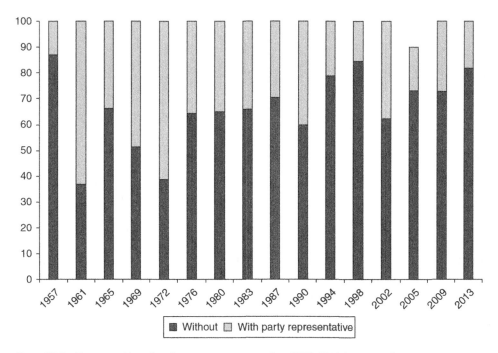

Figure 27.3 Formats with and without party representatives 1957–2013 (n = 2,679)

candidates. As a consequence, their campaigns have taken on the character of a duel between the incumbent chancellor and the competitor which intensified even more with the introduction of one-on-one television debates in 2002. The two major parties, CDU and SPD, account for 46% of the sequences. If these are taken out, the ratio of formats with and without a party representative is 29 to 71% for all other parties. With an overall ratio of 27 to 73% the CDU advertising is just a little bit less personalized, whereas the SPD shows a ratio of 38 to 62% and thus displays a much stronger focus on their party personnel.

In its operationalization of personalization, this study does not follow the "image versus issue" dichotomy used in previous research and in the candidate-oriented political system of the US in particular. Instead, this analysis considers that issue-focused formats are also employed for shaping a candidate's image and associating a candidate's name with a certain policy area. Following the argument of Shyles (1986) who suggested "a difference in the meaning of 'image' when used to refer to graphic methods or presenting candidates (visual display), versus character attributes of candidates" (p. 115), this study distinguishes whether candidates simply appear in the visuals or whether they are actually made the topic of the spot. Thus, a distinction is made between a candidate appearing in the advertising and for instance talking about their political goals or the candidate being made the topic for instance in a testimonial where others praise the contender's character and personal traits. The latter is perceived as a stronger indicator of personalization as opposed to a politician just appearing in the visuals or talking about the party platform.

Using this distinction, Figures 27.4 and 27.5 show if and in which role the chancellor candidates of the two big parties appeared in their party's advertising. Christian Democrats (CDU) and Social Democrats (SPD) have the most prominent candidates because at least one of these parties has always been part and senior partner of the outgoing coalition government. If there is a trend towards personalization in political communication, it should first be apparent in the case of the chancellor candidates. Figure 27.4 presents the findings for the appearance of the Christian Democratic chancellor candidates in their spots, Figure 27.5 shows the correspondent findings for the SPD chancellor

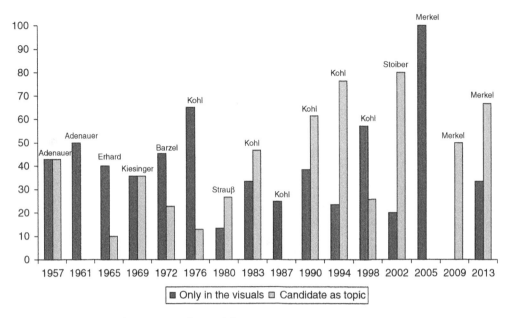

Figure 27.4 Presence of CDU chancellor candidates

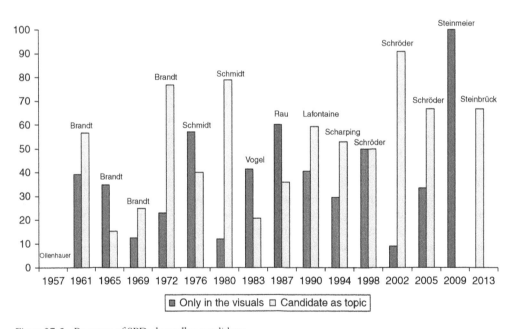

Figure 27.5 Presence of SPD chancellor candidates

candidates. The dark columns stand for the percentage of sequences that show the party's chancellor candidate in the visuals only. The light columns represent the percentage of sequences in which the party's chancellor candidate is the topic. The percentages for both variables have been calculated on the basis of all sequences that show a politician of the respective party. For instance, in 1957 the spots produced by the Christian Democrats comprised 12 sequences, five of them did not show a party representative. The CDU's then chancellor candidate Konrad Adenauer appeared in the visuals of three sequences that showed a CDU politician and was made the topic of the advertising in another three sequences.

All in all, the findings do not speak for any continuous trend towards personalization, neither in the visual appearances nor as topic of the advertising. The same is true for the SPD spots (Figure 27.5). However, the SPD advertising again displays a higher degree of personalization than the CDU spots. If the chancellor candidate is present in the advertising, they are also more often made the topic in the SPD than in the CDU spots.

Of particular interest here are the findings for those chancellor candidates that ran in more than one election. In the case of the CDU, Helmut Kohl was the party's chancellor candidate in six campaigns, in five of them he was the incumbent. Over the years, the party focused the election advertising on Kohl to very different degrees. The same holds for Angela Merkel who ran in three campaigns, two as incumbent. In the case of the SPD, advertising with Willy Brandt, who ran in four campaigns but in only one as incumbent, featured the candidate to an extent that changed considerably from one election to the other.

The ups and downs in the extent to which the parties focus their advertising on the chancellor candidates and particularly the differences in the spots for the same chancellor candidate suggest that personalization is obviously dependent on various factors and strategic decisions. In general, the Social Democrats are more prone to put their chancellor candidate at the center of the television advertising than the Christian Democrats. In addition to the political climate altogether and who is the opponent, the popularity of a candidate within the party and in the electorate seems to be an influential factor. The SPD advertising with and for Willy Brandt is a good example in this respect. When he ran for the first time in 1961, he was 47 years old and appeared young compared to the 85-year-old incumbent chancellor Adenauer. One spot showed him with his family and engaged in leisure activities with his young sons. He was also portrayed as a humble man in spite of being a top-ranking politician. At that time Brandt was the Governing Mayor of Berlin which provided him with an advantage to react when the Berlin Wall was built in the middle of the 1961 election campaign. After Brandt had become chancellor in 1969 he was controversial because of his policy towards the East ("Ostpolitik") but his reputation rose again after he had been awarded the Nobel Peace Price in 1971. On the part of the CDU, the case of Kohl is similar. He ran for the first time in 1976 when he only just entered the national political scene and had to be made known to the wider electorate. When he ran again in 1983, he already was the incumbent because he had been elected chancellor after a constructive vote of no confidence against chancellor Helmut Schmidt (SPD) in 1982. Even as an incumbent, Kohl was not equally present in all campaigns. His party almost banned him from its advertising in 1987. When his popularity rose again after achieving German unification in 1990, the party focused its campaign on Kohl for the first all-German election and tried to exploit his role as the "father" of unification once again in 1994.

An instructive case in point is the advertising with Angela Merkel. When she challenged Gerhard Schröder in 2005, her party relied on a bleak spot that attacked the previous red-green (SPD/Greens) government. Merkel only appeared at the end of the spot promising to make things better and to serve the country. Her appearance and only the hint of a smile gave the impression that she did not feel quite comfortable in this role. Four years later, the CDU spot completely focused on Merkel who seemed to have accepted that candidates are an important part of a party's campaign strategy. Known for her reticence regarding her private life, it was surprising to hear Merkel speak about her political career, her feelings when the Berlin Wall came down and during the 2006 soccer world championship, which took place in Germany and was dubbed "a summer fairytale." In 2013, when Merkel ran for the third time, she was one of the most popular politicians in Germany and had achieved a pivotal role in EU politics. Once again, the CDU produced a spot completely focusing on her. Dressed in a bright red jacket and in a presidential demeanor, Merkel was speaking the whole time while the camera went unusually close to her face revealing "the traces of power" (Medick & Wittrock, 2013) and thus provided an impression of intimacy with the chancellor.

German electoral advertising is predominantly a serious matter. Over the years, humor appeared in 6% of the sequences only. If it is used, humor is mostly employed in reference to opponents (37%) or related to issues (31%). Recently, some of the smaller parties that run without any prospect to overcome the 5% hurdle, used their broadcast time for making fun of the political business altogether. However, because these spots differ from the common patterns of electoral advertising, they usually attract a disproportionate amount of attention in the public and thus draw an ever bigger audience since they can also be watched on the parties' websites or appear on YouTube.

Overall, if a candidate appears in the spot, the setting is mostly formal, either indoors (46%) or outdoors (20%). The findings for the most recent election campaigns seem to indicate a trend toward more informal appearances. In 2009, 41% of the sequences showed formal and institutional settings and another 41% presented the candidates in an informal ambiance leaving 18% for a combination of diverse settings. Four years later, 39% of the sequences presented formal settings, whereas 59% showed the candidates in an informal environment. Nevertheless, candidates overwhelmingly are dressed in business-like attire. In 83% of the sequences, candidates were dressed formally in suits or lady's costumes, shirts and ties and only in 15% they appeared more casual.

Candidates rarely appear in private environments. Altogether, the spots contain only few private scenes. In fact, if candidates are shown in private settings, it is usually part of a broader strategy designed to make the candidate better known or to convey a softer image of otherwise wooden and aloof politicians. Over the years, there is no trend towards privatization of electoral advertising in the sense of providing glimpses into the private life of the candidates.

Policy issues addressed in the advertising, vary from one election to the other. There are only few topics that are present in every campaign. Their ups and downs in particular reflect the specific economic situation at the time of the election.

Considering the fact that the spots are party advertising, it does not come as a surprise that references to the campaign dominate the issues in almost all election years (Figure 27.6). Campaign related issues comprise calls to vote, either in general or for a specific party, explanations of the electoral

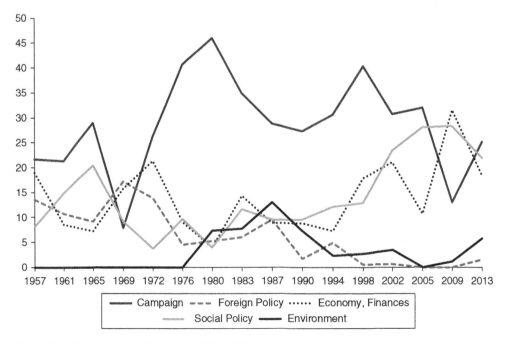

Figure 27.6 Issues addressed in the spot, 1957–2013

system and the relevance of the two votes, or commitments to a specific coalition. Over all campaigns, almost one quarter of the sequences in which issues are addressed, refer to the campaign in one way or the other. Figure 27.6 displays only those issues that reached at least an overall average of 3%. In addition to campaign related topics, only four policy areas make it over this threshold. Social policy and the economy are the two areas that are represented in all campaigns. The former is usually regarded as being owned by the Social Democrats whereas competence for the latter is attributed to the Christian Democrats. The increase of references to social policy since the mid 1990s reflects the growing preoccupation with unemployment, the curve for economic and financial issues rose sharply with the start of the financial crisis in 2008. Environmental issues only came up with the growth of the Greens and other parties taking up the topic in answer to the rise of the new policy area but in recent campaigns it has been superseded by other issues. The relevance of foreign policy as a campaign issue has decreased since the end of the Cold War and the fall of the Berlin Wall.

Conclusion

In addition to electoral posters, television spots are among those campaign instruments that German voters usually recollect first when asked where they saw or heard something about the ongoing election campaign. Even though attention does not stand for voting intention, it is an important precondition for an advertising effect on the vote.

Nevertheless, in the most recent election campaigns, the two major parties in particular have given the impression that they invest in television advertising routinely but do not attach much importance to this campaign instrument. They only produce one or two different spots for their slots on public television and use a shortened version for commercial television. The lack of commitment to television spots seems to indicate that the major parties no longer attach much value to this kind of advertising. This development may be due the broadcasters' dissociation strategy with announcements, disclaimer and inserts that emphasize the character of the spots as advertising and almost function as a warning to viewers. The waning interest of the larger parties in television advertising may have also been boosted by the availability of the social network sites and thus new campaign instruments that also allow parties to address voters directly. However, because the public broadcasters are obliged to allocate broadcast time at no charge, television advertising remains a great opportunity for the smaller and often unknown parties to reach an audience that they would never draw with any other campaign event.

Long-term analysis of the television spots does not reveal any continuous development in form and content. Instead, what is addressed and who appears in the spots is very much dependent on the political and economic situation during the campaign and on the personality of the candidate and their standing in the party. Even though personalization is deemed to be a characteristic of modern campaigning, even in parliamentary and party-oriented systems, it does not appear as a significant feature of the self-presentation of German parties in their television advertising.

Notes

1   The CSU only runs in the southern state of Bavaria, whereas the CDU only runs in the other 15 states. In the national parliament, CDU and CSU form a single parliamentary group referred to as CDU/CSU.
2   There was one exception in 2002 when the FDP nominated their party leader as chancellor candidate which had tactical reasons.

References

Arbeitsgemeinschaft Fernsehforschung. (2013a). *Fernsehzuschauerforschung in Deutschland. Basisinformationen Fernsehnutzung. 35. Kalenderwoche 2013, 26.08.-01.09.2013.* Frankfurt am Main: AGF.
Arbeitsgemeinschaft Fernsehforschung. (2013b). *Fernsehzuschauerforschung in Deutschland. Basisinformationen Fernsehnutzung. 36. Kalenderwoche 2013, 02.09.-08.09.2013.* Frankfurt am Main: AGF.

Arbeitsgemeinschaft Fernsehforschung. (2013c). *Fernsehzuschauerforschung in Deutschland. Basisinformationen Fernsehnutzung. 37. Kalenderwoche 2013, 09.09.-15.09.2013.* Frankfurt am Main: AGF.

Arbeitsgemeinschaft Fernsehforschung. (2013d). *Fernsehzuschauerforschung in Deutschland. Basisinformationen Fernsehnutzung. 38. Kalenderwoche 2013, 16.09.-22.09.2013.* Frankfurt am Main: AGF.

Beyer, A. (2016). Die Geschichte des Fernsehens in Deutschland. In O. Altendorfer & L. Hilmer (Eds.), *Medienmanagement. Band 2: Medienpraxis – Mediengeschichte – Medienordnung* (pp. 195–211). Wiesbaden: Springer VS.

Brück, P. (2014). *Wahlwerbung im Radio.* Wiesbaden: Springer VS.

Holtz-Bacha, C. (2000). *Wahlwerbung als politische Kultur. Parteienspots im Fernsehen 1957–1998.* Wiesbaden: Westdeutscher Verlag.

Holtz-Bacha, C. (2003, May). *To the advantage of the big parties but they seem to lose interest: TV advertising during the 2002 German national election campaign.* Paper presented at the annual conference of the International Communication Association, San Diego, CA.

Holtz-Bacha, C. (2004). Germany: The "German Model" and its intricacies. In J. Roper, C. Holtz-Bacha, & G. Mazzoleni, *The politics of representation: Election campaigning and proportional representation* (pp. 9–27). New York, NY: Peter Lang.

Holtz-Bacha, C. (2006). Political advertising in Germany. In L. L. Kaid & C. Holtz-Bacha (Eds.), *The Sage handbook of political advertising* (pp. 163–180). Thousand Oaks, CA: Sage.

Kaid, L. L., Adam, S., Maier, M., Balzer, M., Berganza, R., Jalali, C., Negrine, R., Raycheva, L., Róka J., Schuck, A. R. T., Stetka V., & de Vreese, C. (2011). Televised advertising in the 2009 European Parliamentary Elections: Comparing campaign strategies and videostyles. In M. Maier, J. Strömbäck, & L. L. Kaid (Eds.), *Political communication in European parliamentary elections* (pp. 91–110). Farnham: Ashgate.

KEK. (2015). Zuschaueranteile. Retrieved from www.kek-online.de/medienkonzentration/zuschaueranteile.html#c4337.

Lessinger, E.-M. (1997). *Politische Information oder Stimmenfang? Eine explorative Studie zum Kommunikationsstil in Wahlwerbespots der Bundestagswahlen von 1976 bis 1994.* Bochum: Unpublished Master's Thesis.

Medick, V., & Wittrock, P. (2013). Wahlwerbespots von CDU und SPD: 90 Sekunden Merkel, 9 Sekunden Steinbrück. Retrieved from www.spiegel.de/politik/deutschland/wahlwerbespots-cdu-setzt-auf-merkel-die-spd-aufs-volk-a-918066.html.

Podschuweit, N. (2012). *Warum Wahlwerbung schaden kann. Wirkung von Parteienwerbung im Kontext der Medienberichterstattung.* Konstanz: UVK.

Rafter, K., Novelli, E., & Holtz-Bacha, C. (2016). "More European but more negative": Political advertising in the 2014 European Parliament elections. In C. Holtz-Bacha (Ed.), *Europawahlkampf 2014. Internationale Studien zur Rolle der Medien* (pp. 35–56). Wiesbaden: Springer VS.

Shyles, L. (1986). The televised political spot advertisement: Its structure, content, and role in the political system. In L. L. Kaid, D. Nimmo, & K. R. Sanders (Eds.), *New perspectives on political advertising* (pp. 107–138). Carbondale, IL: Southern Illinois University Press.

Statista. (2016). Anzahl der durchschnittlich pro Haushalt empfangbaren TV-Sender in Deutschland in den Jahren 1988 bis 2015 (jeweils 1. Januar). Retrieved from http://de.statista.com/statistik/daten/studie/160407/umfrage/frei-empfangbare-tv-sender-in-deutschland-seit-1988/.

28

JAPANESE POLITICAL ADVERTISING IN A CHANGING MEDIA AND ELECTORAL ENVIRONMENT

Jinah Lee

Introduction

Japan is characterized as having a unique political culture due to its long period of single-party dominance. The Liberal Democratic Party (LDP) has dominated the Japanese political scene as a single party or as part of a ruling coalition for most of the postwar period. Its long-term dominance for 38 consecutive years is often called "the 1955 regime," a party system with the LDP as the ruling party and the Japan Socialist Party in opposition until the 1993 general election. Although the political situation has been extremely fluid since then, the LDP remains the party in power as the head of the ruling coalition.

This situation has certainly affected the political process and electoral culture of Japan. Its long-term dominance has led to the inheritance of a support base. Owing to name recognition as part of a political family with strong support based on a constituency and financial resources, hereditary candidates have had a huge advantage in electoral competition on the whole. It is generally said that Sanban (meaning the three "bans") comprises primary political resources for running for election in the Japanese political arena, namely Jiban (constituency), Kanban (reputation) and Kaban (campaigning funds), all of which have benefited hereditary candidates.

As a result of the long period of political dominance, deep-rooted corruption spread, particularly among the powerful factions within the LDP, which triggered the end of the 1955 regime. The LDP could no longer turn to personal campaign channels and societies in support of politicians, and they started to use the appeal of party images to voters using mass-media channels.

The changing media and electoral environment also brought about the transformation of political advertising in Japan. Japan lagged behind in terms of online campaigning. The revision of the election law in 2013 finally enabled parties and candidates to run online campaigns during the election period, and there were three national elections in 2013, 2014 and 2016 under the revised law. This chapter seeks to investigate the dynamic relationship between political development and political advertising in Japan, focusing on the role of the LDP in the process.

The Political and Electoral Environment

The political system of Japan is a parliamentary representative democracy having an emperor as the symbolic head of state and a prime minister as the head of government who is elected by the Designation Election of the Prime Minister in the National Diet. The National Diet of

Japan comprises the House of Representatives (the lower house) and the House of Councillors (the upper house). The Public Offices Election Law regulates Japanese elections. The House of Representatives has 475 members who are elected every four years, 295 seats in single-seat constituencies and 180 seats by proportional representation. The 242 members of the House of Councillors are elected for a six-year term, and 121 – one half of its members – are elected every three years. Seventy-three seats are filled by a single non-transferable vote based on prefectures and 48 by proportional representation on a nationwide basis. Local elections for office in prefectures, cities and villages take place every four years. Each Election Administration Committee on a prefectural or municipal base administers the elections under the supervision of the Central Election Committee.

The history of postwar democracy via Japanese politics can be roughly divided into four phases according to a history of the LDP on its website (Liberal Democratic Party, n.d.): the periods of preparation, property, maturity and coalition. During the period of "preparation," the LDP was established in 1955 by the merger of two conservative parties – the Liberal Party and the Democratic Party – following the allied occupation of Japan from 1945 to 1952. The LDP won the following elections and formed a majority government. In the 1960s, Japan entered a new era of "property" by promoting economic growth. The LDP enjoyed a long period of dominance that might be called the period of the "maturity" of democracy in Japan. However, the LDP lost in the 1993 general election, which ended the 1955 regime as mentioned previously, but then returned to power in 1994 as part of a ruling coalition. The Democratic Party of Japan (DPJ) won a landslide victory in the 2009 general election due to the distrust of the LDP which was triggered by a pension scandal involving the mishandling of pension records by the Social Insurance Agency. The LDP regained control of the government in the 2012 general election due partly to the deep disappointment among Japanese voters about the DPJ after Japan's 2011 earthquakes, and the LDP still functions as the governing party as part of a "coalition" with Komeito.

Factionalism is one of the main characteristics of the Japanese party system. Voters view the faction system unfavorably due to the political corruption and faction struggles that are entailed. Although the factionalism of the LDP has declined over recent decades, they still play an important role in the party's operations including the party presidency and the allocating of official posts within the party and government, as well as in elections by recruiting members and providing their candidates with campaign funds and resources (Köllnera, 2004).

The Media Environment and Political Communication Channels

Terrestrial broadcasting in Japan comprises a dual broadcasting system that consists of a public broadcaster, the NHK (Nippon Hoso Kyokai), and commercial broadcasters such as Nipon Hoso, TBS, Fuji TV and TV Asahi. While people are able to access the NHK's channels, including General TV and Education TV nationwide, the number of commercial television channels differs according to region, with an average of 7.8 commercial television channels including direct broadcasting satellite (DBS) and cable channels, according to the NHK Broadcasting Culture Research Institute (2015). The BCRI survey reveals, as of June 2015, that the average daily television viewing time per head is 3 hours 38 minutes, with 56 minutes for NHK and 2 hours 41 minutes for commercial television channels, with elderly people tending to view the NHK for longer than the younger generation, regardless of gender.

The leading national daily papers include the *Asahi Shimbun*, the *Mainichi Shimbun*, the *Yomiuri Shimbun*, the *Sankei Shimbun* and the *Nikkei Shimbun* (an economics paper). Newspaper reach rate is as much as 77.7% as of 2015 (The Japan Newspapers Publishers and Editors Association, 2015), and the *Yomiuri Shimbun* has the largest daily circulation, accounting for around 10 million per day supported by a home delivery system (Yomiuri Shimbun, 2015). There are also *Tokyo Shimbun* in Kanto and Chubu and *Chunichi Shimbun* in Tokai, owned by the Chunichi Company, *Hokkaido Shimbun* in Hokkaido, *Nishinippon Shimbun* in Kyushu, *Kahoku Shimpo* in Tohoku and *Chuogoku Shimbun* in Chogoku comprising the main regional papers. There exists a strong capital relationship between newspaper, commercial radio and television networks.

Japanese voters still tend to rely on traditional media such as television (63.2%) and newspapers (23.2%) rather than the Internet (7.2%) for political and electoral information, according to a recent survey by the Association for Promoting a Fair Election (2015). However, online and social media deeply impressed Japanese people after the 3/11 disaster of Japan by playing a significant role in mobilizing people and organizing antinuclear protests (Takeshita, Saito, & Inaba, 2014). The number of social media users is gradually increasing according to a recent survey of the Ministry of Internal Affairs and Communications (2015). Taken together, it is expected that online and social media will function as important political campaign channels in the near future.

It is generally considered that *Asahi* and *Mainichi* are liberal whereas *Yomiuri* and *Sankei* are conservative (Akuto, 1996). Their viewer characteristics and reporting styles are generally considered to be quite different, depending on the broadcaster. Elderly people have a tendency to rely on the NHK, as mentioned above. Meanwhile, the NHK's news is quite "descriptive," focusing on facts, while commercial stations tend to be "interpretive" and "entertainment-oriented" (Saito & Takeshita, 2009, pp. 390–391). Taniguchi (2002) has revealed that NHK News 10 primarily reported straight news whereas the News Station of TV Asahi, focused on interpretive news in the coverage of the 2000 general election. Moreover, the News Station emphasized a strategic frame that focused on the win-lose aspects of the campaign and a negative portrayal of politicians, and viewing News Station increased political cynicism (Taniguchi, 2002). Likewise, Saito (2008) has shown that television news viewing was associated with political inefficacy among non-NHK news viewers.

The History and Development of Political Advertising

Previous studies have divided the development of political advertising into several phases according to changes in the media and the social and electoral systems (e.g., Schafferer & Kawakami, 2006; Tak, 2006). Based on previous studies, Lee (2011) investigated the historical development of Japanese political advertising in terms of five eras, namely "the emergence of political advertising" (1881–1924), "the embarkation of political advertising" (1925–the end of the war), "the revival of political advertising" (1945–68), "the development of political advertising" (1969–93) and "the turning point of political advertising" (since 1994). This chapter would like to add "the Internet age of political advertising" (since 2013) as the sixth era.

The first era is "the emergence of political advertising" (1881–1924). Modern political parties were formed in the 1880s, and political parties attacked Meiji government policies and announced their political gatherings in their party newspapers (Schafferer & Kawakami, 2006). According to Yamamoto (1972), recommendation ads can be viewed as the first election ads in Japan, and the number of political ads increased, including ads against false propaganda, the announcement of the founding of parties and political gatherings, recommendation ads by party presidents and executives, and self-recommendation ads since the first general election in 1890.

The second era can be regarded as "the embarkation of political advertising" (1925–the end of the war). During the early period of elections, the right to vote had been restricted according to the residential area, property requirements and gender. The vote was extended to male adults in the 1928 election after the revision of the election law in 1925. As door-to-door campaigns were banned and there was no limit to the number and the posting area of posters, whole towns were filled with the campaign posters of the two major parties, the Association of Political Friends and the Constitutional Association (Umeda, 2001). During the 1930s, the government launched an "election purification campaign" to control political parties and strengthened regulation over party activities and ads (Yamamoto, 1972). The military government gained power and all political parties were dissolved before the war.

The third era is "the revival of political advertising" (1945–68). After the end of the war, political parties were re-established and the first election in postwar Japan was held in 1946. The election was also the first with universal male and female adult suffrage in Japan. During the 1950s, competition among LDP candidates in the same constituency became intense, and societies in support of individual candidates gradually become an important campaign channel (Schafferer & Kawakami, 2006).

The LDP succeeded in presenting its image of bringing prosperity to Japan through slogans such as "Double national income" of the Ikeda Cabinet during the 1960s (Alexey, 2007). Ikeda himself appeared on the first Japanese party spot, saying "I do not tell a lie ... Leave the economy entirely to Ikeda" (Takase, 2005). The 1960s can be described as the beginning of image politics in Japan. It is worth noting two celebrities elected in the 1960s: Ryokichi Minobe, who hosted television shows as an economist and who won the 1967 Tokyo mayoral election, and Shintaro Ishihara, a popular author who won a huge victory in the 1968 House of Councillors election (Schafferer & Kawakami, 2006).

The fourth era is called "the development of political advertising" (1969–93). In the 1969 general election, Japan entered a new phase of election campaigning. The 1968 US presidential campaign affected Japanese political advertising in many respects, such as using professional political consultants and running political spots, and election broadcasts started in 1969 as well (Kawamura, 2001).

From the 1970s onwards, the LDP lost seats in elections due to repeated political corruption scandals. Particularly, as a result of the Recruit scandal in 1988, a bribery and corruption scandal by governing politicians and Recruit Co., the LDP struggled in the 1989 House of Councillors election. A number of women candidates from the Japan Socialist Party (JSP) were elected under the leadership of Takako Doi, the first female party leader in Japan. The image of a woman as an agent of change coupled with an emphasis on social issues worked to their advantage. The media called the popularity and victory of women candidates in the election "the Madonna boom" (Iwai, 1993). The JSP aired party spots in which Doi appeared focusing on consumption tax issues and political corruption.

During the early 1990s, election campaigns involving a flurry of new political parties gained the attention of voters who had become deeply disappointed with the established parties (Kawakami, 1998), and the Hosokawa coalition government, the first non-LDP government, was established following the 1993 general election.

The fifth era is "the turning point of political advertising" (1994–2012). As Akuto (1996) has pointed out, personal connections and organizations were important while the effect of the media was limited in Japan for a long time, and newspapers were more important in Japan by comparison with US election campaigns. The end of the LDP's single-party dominance coupled with electoral reform and social changes in the early 1990s meant that the LDP and other parties could no longer rely on traditional election campaigning based on a strong support base (Holden, 1999). In the 1996 general election, the first election under the single-seat constituencies and proportional representation system, party spots increased, and negative campaigning by the LDP and the then New Frontier Party received attention (Kawakami, 2002). The LDP also used emotional and patriotic appeals to build a new image of the LDP in party spots in the 1996 election.

The tenure of Junichiro Koizumi as prime minister from 2001 to 2006 can be characterized as the age of tele-politics in Japan (Saito & Takeshita, 2009). He enjoyed huge popularity as a result of his personal character and media strategy, which saw Koizumi's *Cabinet Mail Magazine* set the world record by acquiring 1.82 million subscriptions in two weeks compared to the 780,000 subscriptions to its inaugural issue (Schafferer & Kawakami, 2006). The LDP won a landslide victory in the 2005 general election, which Koizumi had called to privatize the Japanese post office. In this election, so-called "assassins" – his handpicked candidates – were elected in competition with his own party's members who opposed the postal reforms. This dramatic situation gained media interest as the so-called "Koizumi Theater" (Saito & Takeshita, 2009). Koizumi himself appeared on LDP spots like a celebrity. Advertising expenses for the election also surged during this period. Taking the 2001 House of Councillors election as an example, the LDP and other parties spent large amounts of money on political advertising, doubling that spent in the 1996 election (Schafferer & Kawakami, 2006).

The sixth era is "the Internet age of political advertising" (2013–present). Although parties and politicians have used online media in their political activities, they were prohibited from setting up and updating their websites and social media during the official election period immediately preceding the election. The 2013 revised election law finally allowed parties and candidates to campaign online. Parties and candidates competed by making use of online campaign channels and social media in the 2013, 2014 and 2016 elections. Online campaigns have gained attention from the expectation that it can open up a new way of election campaigning, including lowering campaign costs. However, with regard to online ads, the dominant parties such as the LDP nevertheless spent huge amounts of money on online campaigning during the 2013 House of Councillors election (Lee, 2014).

While the number of party spots on television is gradually decreasing, a number of online party ads are available on party websites and party channels on video sharing sites such as YouTube and Japanese Niconico. In the 2014 and 2016 elections, a number of parties decided to go online instead of running party spots on television. It is considered that the high cost of television party spots and a trend of people turning away from watching television to using the Internet might be the primary reasons.

Political Activities Versus Electoral Campaigns: The Regulation of Political Advertising

Election campaigns in Japan are very short and intensive. Pre-election campaigning before notice of candidacy is strictly regulated, and campaigning is permitted only during the official election period: 12 days for the House of Representative election and 17 days for the House of Councillors election. The Public Offices Election Law strictly distinguishes between political activities and election campaigns. Political parties are emphasized over candidates during the election campaign, and the regulations governing election campaigns favor official party candidates in comparison with independent candidates.

In addition to free, supervised newspaper and election broadcasts on NHK and commercial stations, parties can run paid newspaper and television ads on commercial stations at any time to carry out political activities. Since party spots are not electoral, it is not permitted to ask for a vote. However, the spots tend to concentrate around the election period. Commercial broadcasters generally refrain from airing party spots on election day, while the parties run paid newspaper ads on election day, such as "Changing government" by the DPJ (opposition party) and "Protecting Japan" by the LDP (ruling party) on election day 2009 (Lee, 2011).

A series of political reforms in the 1990s coupled with the view of the then Ministry of Home Affairs that parties could run political spots as a part of political activities resulted in an increase of party spots from the 1990s onwards (Kawakami, 2002). Individual candidates cannot run paid television ads, but politicians as party leaders or executives can appear on the party spots to appeal to the party supporters. While the quantity of supervised newspaper ads and election broadcasts are allocated to parties on a proportional basis, there is no limit to the quantity and amount of money for paid party spots.

Candidates are also given free, supervised ad space in newspapers and election broadcast time for the introduction of their personal careers and their own short speeches. However, candidates are not permitted to buy space in newspapers or time on television. Supervised newspaper ads and election broadcast time are allocated according to the election type. Unlike the US and some other countries, interest groups and individuals are not permitted to buy broadcast time on television to support parties or candidates.

The length and expression of supervised newspaper ads are highly limited. Furthermore, as election broadcasts have been intensely regulated, including the length of time available and the style, and as they air early in the morning or late at night, candidates' television appearances have not gained the voters' attention. The revision of the Public Offices Election Law in 2000 allowed parties to bring their own video to the studio. There were arguments both for and against the revision: while the new style of election broadcasts is able to catch voters' attention, it might bring about the commercialization of election broadcasts by focusing on superficial image rather than the discussion of issues and political visions (Takase, 2005).

There are also election bulletins and electoral posters as supervised campaign channels. The election bulletins that the Election Administration issues for elections include each candidate's information. Both the party and the candidate can be put on posters at public notice boards during the election period. Coupled with the parties' and candidates' posters, campaign cars running through towns, candidates' wayside speeches and the distribution of handbills near stations are common scenes during the election period in Japan, all of which are strictly restricted and predetermined by election law.

As regards online campaigns, even though parties and candidates have their own online and social media for political activities, online campaigning was not permitted during the official election period. The revision of the Public Offices Election Law in 2013 allowed parties and candidates to use the Internet for their election campaigning, including running online party ads during the election period. However, political parties and official candidates are emphasized over independent candidates online, as with the traditional mass media. Political parties are permitted to run banner ads linked to the parties' websites that they introduce official candidates. However, independent candidates are not able to run online political ads.

The Content and Appeals of Political Advertising

This chapter investigates the content of political advertising in Japan following the fifth era in the development of Japanese political advertising both quantitatively and qualitatively. Lee (2011) analyzed political advertising using 222 party spots from 1989 to 2008. Lately, there has been a decreasing trend in the number of party spots, while a number of online party ads have gained voter's attention. Thus, instead of adding party spots for recent elections to the data, this chapter investigates the content of political advertising on television and the Internet from 2009 to 2016 qualitatively.

Issues, Images, Negativity and Appeals

Issue ads are referred to as ads that "focus on general issue concerns or policy positions, such as the economy, taxes, foreign policy concerns, social welfare topics, and other such concerns" (Kaid, 2006, p. 41), while image ads are "related to the personal characteristics or qualities of a candidate, to his or her background, experience, previous personal actions, character, and so on" (Kaid, 2006, p. 41). Lee (2011) analyzed whether issue or image are emphasized in ads instead of indicating the ad-type as issue or image. Issues were emphasized in 51.4% and image in 45.5% of party spots. With regard to political and social issues that were emphasized in party spots, 22.5% of party ads emphasized social security, followed by reform (18%), economic issues (17.6%), tax (13.5%), education and childcare (9%), employment (5.4%), the constitution (5%) and environmental issues (3.6%).

According to Kaid and Johnston (1991), negative ads are considered to be ads that "focus on criticisms of the opponent" (p. 53), whereas positive ads "focus on the 'good' characteristics, accomplishments or issue positions of the sponsoring candidate" (p. 53). Lee (2011) investigated as to whether ads contain negativity instead of determining negative or positive ads, with negative expressions categorized according to two types – explicit and implicit – considering Japanese indirect forms of expression (Benedetto, Tamate, & Chandran, 1992; Lee, 2007). Explicit negative expressions were defined as "those in which opponent party itself, party leader or members are criticized directly" (Lee, 2011, p. 38), while implicit expressions were defined as "those in which negative incidents such as the opponent party's scandal, policy and issues are criticized so that people can easily associate it with the opponent party, party leader and members" (Lee, 2011, p. 38), even though such things are not mentioned directly in the ads.

The results showed that negative expressions were less dominant in Japan, and that explicit ones were less often utilized. Only 21.6% of party spots contained negativity, including explicit and implicit expressions, and the ads with explicit negative expressions accounted for only 1.8%. In fact, the Public Offices Election Law in Japan regulates negative campaign, and there have been several cases where television stations declined to air negative expressions or else required the party to change the content based on the election law or their own television codes (Kawakami, 2002). These included DPJ (opposition party) spots that attacked the LDP (ruling party) on the huge expenditure on public works, and the Social Democratic Party (opposition party) spots that attacked Koizumi's popularity in the 2001 House of Councillors election.

As an early negative campaign in Japan, the LDP ran opinion ads in *Sankei Shimbun* that directly attacked the Japanese Communist Party (JCP) in 1973. The JCP sued *Sankei Shimbun* in the courts, seeking the right of rebuttal, but the Supreme Court dismissed the case in 1987 (Yamamoto, 1972). Negative campaigns between the LDP and the New Frontier Party (NFP) in the 1996 general election also received considerable media coverage and voters' attention (Kawakami, 1998). A major campaign issue was the increase in the consumption tax rate, and the LDP attacked the NFP on the discrepancies among its leaders and executives over the tax rate in newspaper ads, "How much is the rate, actually?" The NFP also launched a counterattack ad, involving "Squeezing the public" with the visual of squeezing lemons. While the LDP did not run the ad on television, the NFP brought the negative campaign to television with a vivid image and narration.

According to Kaid and Holtz-Bacha (2006), logical appeal is characterized by "factual information and examples and often offer statistical data to substantiate their points" (p. 450), whereas emotional appeal relies on "language and images to try to evoke feelings or emotions such as happiness, patriotism, anger, or pride" (p. 450). Source-credibility appeal refers to "good character to make their appeals, including information about the qualifications, integrity, and trustworthiness of the candidate or of someone speaking on behalf of the candidate or party" (p. 450). Lee (2011) revealed that source-credibility appeal accounted for as much as 74.3%, which tends to be emphasized in Asian political advertising, followed by emotional appeal (47.7%) and logical appeal (23%).

LDP Versus Non-LDP

Lee (2011) also compares the content and appeal of LDP and non-LDP party spots to investigate Japanese political traits (Table 28.1). Regarding issues and image, LDP ads concentrated on image while non-LDP ads focused on issues. The party spots of non-LDP parties contained more negative expressions than those of the LDP. The LDP relied on source-credibility and emotional appeal more than non-LDP parties based on its long dominance as the ruling party. For instance, the LDP primarily used emotional source-credibility ads with patriotic expressions to convey the new image of the LDP in the mid 1990s. Former Prime Minister Ryutaro Hashimoto promoted a new LDP in the spots, with slogans such as "JAPAN DREAM" and "Open. New LDP."

With regard to issue presentation, as indicated in Table 28.2, the LDP has emphasized reform whereas non-LDP parties mentioned tax and employment more than the LDP. Constitutional issues were slightly more emphasized in non-LDP ads. These results might come from the political positions of both sides. The revision of Article 9 of the Japanese Constitution has been an important issue in Japanese politics. The LDP is trying to revise the constitution stipulating the self-defense force, which has been criticized as contradicting the no-war clause. The non-LDP parties, especially the

Table 28.1 Content of political spots by party (%)

Content and appeal	LDP	Non-LDP
Ad emphasis		
Issue	44.3	54.6
Image	54.3	41.4
Negativity		
Explicit + implicit	11.4	26.3
Explicit	0.0	2.6
Appeal		
Logical	27.1	21.1
Emotional	61.4	41.4
Source credibility	82.9	70.4
Party leader		
Party leader appearance	77.1	75.7
Mentioned party leader's name	35.7	11.2
Others		
Patriotism	31.4	12.5
Humor	12.9	28.9

Source: Adapted from research on party spots for 1989 through to 2008 (Lee, 2011).

Table 28.2 Issues of political spots by party (%)

Issues	LDP	Non-LDP
Economy	15.7	18.4
Reform	27.1	13.8
Employment	1.4	7.2
Tax	1.4	19.1
Social security	20.0	23.7
Education/childcare	14.3	6.6
Environmental issues	5.7	2.6
Constitution	2.9	5.9
Others	2.9	4.6

Source: Adapted from research on party spots for 1989 through to 2008 (Lee, 2011).

Japanese Communist Party and the Japan Socialist Party, the current Social Democratic Party, have been appealing to Japanese voters by attacking the right wing position of LDP in the ads.

Party leaders appeared in 85% of party spots during the 2000s as compared to 63.9% in the 1990s. There was no difference between the LDP and non-LDP parties, but the mention of the party leader's name was more frequent with the LDP. In particular, the LDP's leader almost automatically holds the post of prime minister concurrently; hence, his celebrity might lead to more frequent appearances on party spots. During the late 1990s, the LDP expressed its manifesto as "Hashimoto Vision" on the spots, named after its party leader and former Prime Minister Ryutaro Hashimoto. There was also a somewhat unique series of spots at the time in which citizens called him a nickname, Hashiryu when watching him on television. Former Prime Minister Koizumi's "I'm Koizumi" series in the 2003 House of Representatives election might be the most famous commercial of these personalized types. During the early 2000s, against the background of high levels of distrust in politics, Koizumi appealed to the Japanese people by asserting "Destroy the LDP", which succeeded in presenting him as a challenger to the LDP for political reform (Alexey, 2007). He appeared in a series of LDP spots, such as "I'm Koizumi," and the LDP spots gradually turned into personalized Koizumi spots. The Komeito party even used a pun of the party leader's name in its samurai-style commercial series. Taken together, these suggest that parties have come to rely on the party leader's personal charisma and popularity.

Patriotic appeal – another popular appeal in political advertising – has also characterized the difference between the LDP and non-LDP parties. Verbal expressions that rouse patriotism, such as "Japan Again" and "Japanese Power," have often been used in recent times: 12.5% in the 1990s and 22.9% in the 2000s used patriotic appeal. The long Japanese recession might be a factor in the increasing use of these expressions. As the conservative, ruling party, the LDP has often used patriotic expressions in ads compared to non-LDP parties.

Lee (2011) also attempted to categorize party spots using cluster analysis, and showed that the LDP (38.6%) relied on future-oriented image ads compared to non-LDP parties (28.3%), whereas non-LDP (42.1%) centered on economy-oriented issue ads rather than LDP parties (30.0%). There was no difference between the LDP (31.4%) and non-LDP parties (29.6%) in regard to social security-oriented issue ads.

The Content of Political Advertising on Television and the Internet: 2009 to 2016

The change in government with the DPJ in 2009 is one of the most significant changes that Japan has experienced. The LDP and the DPJ have together comprised the Japanese political arena since the late 2000s, which also led to changes to Japanese political advertising. This chapter investigates the content of political advertising following 2009, focusing on the LDP's and the DPJ's campaigns.

The LDP struggled in the 2007 House of Councillors election due to the pension scandal, and most parties concentrated on issue ads using logical appeals (Lee, 2011). In the next general election, 2009, the LDP was put in a more difficult situation and ran an explicitly negative online campaign for the first time by attacking the change of government campaign of the DPJ (Lee, 2011, 2014). The LDP contended that the change in government would bring about a "retreat of the regime" and "economic recession" through a series called "Non-stop recovery." The closer that election day came, the more negative the ads became. The LDP produced three animated online ads: "Propose," "Ramen" and "Bure four (Four flip-floppers)." The LDP attacked the DPJ's "unfounded confidence" that a man who looks just like Yukio Hatoyama – the then-leader of the DPJ – could promise unrealizable plans to a woman on the "Propose." The LDP also attacked the inconsistent policies of the DPJ on the "Ramen" ad. The same man was portrayed as changing the way of cooking ramen one after another at the request of customers. Lastly, the LDP attacked the changeable and inconsistent political views and policies of four DPJ leaders and executives on a "Bure four" ad, asserting "Can you leave the future of Japan to the Bure four?" By comparison, the LDP and Komeito appealed "Protect" people's lives and "Responsibility" as the ruling coalition on television spots. The LDP contended that "We have a definite policy and a good reason" to reassure voters on a "Declare to Japan" series of spots.

The 2010 House of Councillors election was an interim appraisal of the DPJ government, and it ran positive spots emphasizing the meaning of government change. The LDP ran the "Ichiban" (Japan is the best) series to appeal to the pride of the Japanese people and patriotism, focusing on the fields that Japan has been strong and the hope to become one of the happiest nations once again. The LDP returned to power as a result of the 2012 general election. In the election, this time, the DPJ attacked the LDP by asserting the "lost 20 years were undecided years" on the spots. Shinzo Abe, who was prime minister from 2006 to 2007, also returned to LDP as president just before the election, and he appealed "Get Japan back" on the spots. "Get Japan back" implied that the DPJ had brought about an unstable situation, and the only the LDP would get Japan back to previous prosperous eras. The LDP employed the slogan "Get Japan back" both on television and in Internet ads in the 2013 House of Councillors election again. During this period, the number of party spots dropped and some of the parties ran their political advertising only on the Internet.

The 2013 House of Councillors election – the first Internet election in Japan – was an interim appraisal of the LDP government. The LDP made extensive use of online advertising. A traffic analysis of party websites from July 1–21, 2013 showed that 12% of LDP website visitors came from online ads, including banner ads (Values, 2013). In addition, the LDP made full use of listing ads, ad exchanges and ad networks, and 45.9% of its website visitors came from organic searches and 17.5% via other websites, such as Facebook and Twitter, which was far higher than for other parties (Values, 2013). However, the content of the online ads was limited to the introduction of candidates and the announcement of campaign speeches (Sankei Shimbun, 2013).

The 2014 general election was dubbed "Abenomics dissolution," in which Prime Minister Abe asked voters to appraise his economic policy. Abe focused on "Abenomics" on television and online ads, asserting "Economy recovery – there is no alternative." As it was a relatively sudden dissolution and campaign, the election campaign did not capture voters' attention.

The 2016 House of Councillors election was the first election that 18- and 19-year-olds could vote in, and LDP tried to appeal to young voters using online ads.

The Reception and Effects of Political Advertising

The Japanese "Internet Election" and Political Advertising

In a survey conducted after the 2014 general election – the first general election after the online campaign was introduced – APFE (Association for Promoting a Fair Election, 2015) analyzed voters' exposure to campaign channels, including newspaper and television advertising, based on a nationwide random sample of 2,029 voters. Among 23 election campaign channels, the candidate poster (51.1%) was top, and election broadcasts on television by parties (41.1%) and election broadcasts on television by candidates (40.7%) were viewed by more than 40% of voters. Election bulletins (38.9%), candidate newspaper ads (34.1%), candidate handbills (31.1%), party handbills and posters (30.9%) and party newspaper ads (30.6%) accounted for more than 30% of voters, and party spots were viewed by 28.5% of voters. With regard to which election campaign channel was useful, election broadcasts on television by parties (19.4%) was evaluated as the most useful. Election broadcasts on television by candidates (17.6%), election bulletins (17.1%) and candidate newspaper ads (14.7%) were each more than 10%. Only 3.3% named party spots as useful as a campaign channel. There was a significant difference between exposure and perceptions of usefulness of political advertising such as candidate posters (view rate: 51.1%; usefulness rate: 10.1%), candidate newspaper ads (34.1%; 14.7%), party newspaper ads (30.6%; 11.2%) and party spots (28.5%; 3.3%). Likewise, Lee (2011) indicates differences in the responses to party spots and election broadcasts due to credibility of election broadcasts on television and paid-party spots.

With regard to online campaigns, APFE (Association for Promoting a Fair Election, 2014, 2015) investigated the extent to which voters engaged in the online campaign of the 2013 and 2014 election. Most respondents did not engage with the online campaign (2013: 74.0%; 2014: 81.5%). Less than 10% of respondents viewed websites, blogs and social media by party or candidate (8.5%; 7.6%). Similarly, only 10.2% answered that they used the Internet as a reference when voting in the 2013 election (Sankei Shimbun, 2013). Overall, the effects of the online campaign were very limited in the 2013 and 2014 election.

Reactions to Political Spots

In an experiment concerning reactions to party spots and their effects among undergraduate students, Lee (2011) indicated five dimensions of reaction to party spots using factor analysis: "entertainment," "ambiguity," "negativity," "reliability" and "informativeness." The study analyzed the effects of ad perceptions on variables such as attitude toward the ad, desirability as party spots, attention to party spots, new hooks of party spots, possibility of realization of visions expressed on the party spots and third-person perception using multiple regression analysis. The results showed that reliability and informativeness were positively associated with desirability of party spots. Entertainment and informativeness affected attention towards the party spots, and entertainment and informativeness were positively related with the news hooks of the party spots. Negativity was conversely related to the possibility of the realization of visions expressed in the party spots and third-person perceptions, suggesting that negative ads are likely to affect negative political attitudes.

The effects of the reaction to party spots on recall were further examined. Recall data were categorized into "central information recall," such as policy, political visions, and the party president, and "peripheral information recall." The results showed that informativeness was positively associated with central information recall, whereas entertainment was related to peripheral information recall. Informativeness was negatively related with recall errors. Lee (2011) showed that humor is another characteristic of Japanese party spots with non-LDP parties (28.9%) using more humor than the LDP (12.9%). Taken together with the results, humor and entertainment-oriented expression are likely to distract people from issues and visions on party spots.

Discussion

The role of electoral advertising for candidates and politicians is limited in Japanese politics as a campaign channel, due primarily to stringent and extensive restrictions under election law that has sought lower costs and fairer elections since the 1950s. Usaki (1990) has argued that these restrictions are contrary to democracy and political freedom. The deregulation of online campaigning in 2013 was a big move towards changing the long history of restrictions on election campaigns. It was highly anticipated that online campaigns would increase political participation. However, voter turnout was 52.61%, a decrease of 5.31% from the previous House of Councillors election in 2010, which recorded the third lowest after the 1992 and 1995 House of Councillors elections. The 2014 general election also marked a new postwar low of 52.66% (Ministry of Internal Affairs and Communications, 2016).

There exists a substantial disparity between large parties and small- and medium-sized parties in terms of political advertising. Pervasive cynical attitudes and criticism of party spots centered on the fact that party subsidies from taxpayer's money primarily cover costs for political activities and election campaigns. In a survey conducted on the third-person effect of political news and advertising, it was revealed the smallest third-person perceptions were for party websites and the greatest for party spots (Lee, 2009). The perception that others are more susceptible to party spots and that "they" can affect politics might diminish people's political participation.

Gender is another important aspect that it is necessary to discuss regarding the issues of political advertising. Political resources such as Sanban – mentioned previously – have disadvantaged women, and political advertising might become an important tool for campaigning for women candidates. Women candidates with a high media profile focused on issues that have been viewed as equally male and female issues through the use of Twitter in the 2013 House of Councillors election (Lee & Lee, 2015). By comparison, in an analysis of newspaper ads in the 2005 general election and the 2007

House of Councillors election, Lee (2011) indicated that male candidates emphasized the economy and political reform slightly more than female candidates, whereas female candidates focused on childcare, education and social security. Owing to the low representation of women in Japan, it is necessary to rely on gender framing, which means that gender cues still serve as a major political resource in Japan.

Finally, there have been arguments both for and against the lowering of the voting age, and the minimum voting age was finally lowered from 20 to 18 with the revision of the election law in June 2015. This will lead parties and candidates to look for ways of appealing to the younger generation, which in turn might change the style of election campaigns. A recent poll suggested that voters (38.3% of respondents) anticipate that online campaigning would increase voter turnout among young voters (Association for Promoting…, 2014). Will the changing electoral system and online campaigning invigorate political discourse and encourage political participation? This requires ongoing research into the question.

References

Akuto, H. (1996). Media in election campaigning in Japan and the United States. In S. J. Pharr & E. S. Krauss (Eds.), *Media and politics in Japan* (pp. 313–337). Honolulu, HI: University of Hawaii Press.

Alexey, A. (2007). Perspectives of political marketing in Japanese political arena. *The Journal of the Study of Modern Society and Culture*, 39, 125–141.

Association for Promoting a Fair Election. (2014). Dai 23 kai sangiingiin tujyo senkyo zenkoku ishiki chosa. [National attitudinal survey on the 23rd House of Councillors election]. Retrieved from www.akaruisenkyo. or.jp/wp/wp-content/uploads/2011/07/23sanin111.pdf.

Association for Promoting a Fair Election. (2015). Dai 47 kai shugiingiin sosenkyo zenkoku ishiki chosa. [National attitudinal survey on the 47th House of Representatives election]. Retrieved from www.akaruisen-kyo.or.jp/wp/wp-content/uploads/2011/10/47syuishikicyosa-1.pdf.

Benedetto, C. A., Tamate, M., & Chandran, R. (1992). Developing creative advertising strategy for the Japanese marketplace. *Journal of Advertising Research*, 32, 39–48.

Holden, T. J. M. (1999). Commercialized politics: Japan's new mass-mediated reality. *Japanese Studies*, 19(1), 33–47.

Iwai, T. (1993). The Madonna boom: Women in the Japanese diet. *Journal of Japanese Studies*, 19, 103–120.

The Japan Newspapers Publishers and Editors Association. (2015). 2015 nen zenkoku media sesshoku hyoka chosa gaiyou [2015 national media access and evaluation survey overview]. Retrieved from www.pressnet.or.jp/ adarc/data/research/pdf/2015media/gaiyou_web_2015.pdf.

Kaid, L. L. (2006). Political advertising in the United States. In L. L. Kaid & C. Holtz-Bacha (Eds.), *The Sage handbook of political advertising* (pp. 37–61). Thousand Oaks, CA: Sage.

Kaid, L. L., & Holtz-Bacha, C. (2006). Television advertising and democratic systems around the world. In L. L. Kaid & C. Holtz-Bacha (Eds.), *The Sage handbook of political advertising* (pp. 445–457). Thousand Oaks, CA: Sage.

Kaid, L. L., & Johnston, A. (1991). Negative versus positive television advertising in US presidential campaigns, 1960–1988. *Journal of Communication*, 41(3), 53–64.

Kawakami, K. (1998). Nihon ni okeru media politikkus: 1996nen sosenkyo ni okeru media no eikyo [Media politics in Japan: Media effects in 1996 general election]. *Senkyo Kenkyu*, 13, 100–109.

Kawakami, K. (2002). Seiji kokoku no situteki henyo – akauntabiriti heno turu he [Qualitative change of political advertising: Towards a tool of accountability]. *Bulletin of Nikkei Advertising Research Institute*, 201, 41–46.

Kawamura, N. (2001). Gendai nihon no senkyo kyanpen kokokushi – soseiki [Election campaigning and advertising in modern Japan: The early period]. *The Journal of the Study of Modern Society and Culture*, 21, 1–18.

Köllnera, P. (2004). Factionalism in Japanese political parties revisited or how do factions in the LDP and the DPJ differ? *Japan Forum*, 16(1), 87–109.

Lee, J. (2007, July). *Verbal expressions in Japanese political advertising: A content analysis of newspaper and television political advertising.* Paper presented at the 50th Annual Conference of International Association for Media and Communication Research (IAMCR).

Lee, J. (2009, July). *Third-person effects of political news and advertising.* Paper presented at the 52nd Annual Conference of International Association for Media and Communication Research (IAMCR).

Lee, J. (2011). *Seiji kokoku no Kenkyu [The content and reception of political advertising in Japan].* Tokyo: Shinyosha.

Lee, J. (2014). Tayokasuru media kankyo ni okeru seiji kokoku [Political advertising in a changing media environment]. The Japanese Society of Mass Communication, *Mass Communication Research*, 85, 23–39.

Lee, J., & Lee, K. (2015). Overcoming gendered images: Japanese women politicians' self-presentation on Twitter. Mita Philosophy Society, *Philosophy*, 135, 91–109.

Liberal Democratic Party. (n.d.). A history of the Liberal Democratic Party. Retrieved from www.jimin.jp/english/about-ldp/history/index.html.

Ministry of Internal Affairs and Communications. (2015). Heisei 27 nen ban jyoho tsushin hakusho [2015 White paper on information and communications in Japan]. Retrieved from www.soumu.go.jp/johotsusintokei/whitepaper/ja/h27/pdf/index.html.

Ministry of Internal Affairs and Communications. (2016). Kokusei senkyo ni okeru tohyoritu no suii [Trend on voter turnout in a parliamentary election]. Retrieved from www.soumu.go.jp/senkyo/senkyo_s/news/sonota/ritu/index.html.

NHK Broadcasting Culture Research Institute. (2015). Present situation regarding television viewing and radio listening: A summary of the results of nationwide survey on individual audience ratings conducted by NHK in June 2015. Retrieved from www.nhk.or.jp/bunken/english/reports/pdf/report_15091501.pdf.

Saito, S. (2008). Television and political alienation: Does television news induce political cynicism and inefficacy in Japan? *International Journal of Japanese Sociology*, 17(1), 101–113.

Saito, S., & Takeshita, T. (2009). The media coverage of election campaigns and its effects in Japan. In J. Strömbäck & L. L. Kaid (Eds.), *The handbook of election news coverage around the world* (pp. 385–402). New York, NY: Routledge.

Sankei Shimbun. (2013, July 22). Netto senkyo, yukensha hiyayaka sankoni shita wazuka 1wari [Internet election, only 10% as reference]. Retrieved from www.sankei.com/politics/news/130722/plt1307220052-n1.html.

Schafferer, C., & Kawakami, K. (2006). Electoral campaigning in Japan. In C. Schafferer (Ed.), *Election campaigning in East and Southeast Asia: Globalization of political marketing* (pp. 11–28). Burlington, VT: Ashgate.

Tak, J. (2006). Political advertising in Japan, South Korea, and Taiwan. In L. L. Kaid & C. Holtz-Bacha (Eds.), *The Sage handbook of political advertising* (pp. 285–305). Thousand Oaks, CA: Sage.

Takase, J. (2005). *Jyoho seijigaku kogi [Lectures on the study of information and politics]*. Tokyo: Shinhyoron.

Takeshita, T., Saito, S., & Inaba, T. (2014). Social media and political participation in Japan. In L. Willnat & A. Aw (Eds.), *Social media, culture and politics in Asia* (pp. 127–142). New York, NY: Peter Lang.

Taniguchi, M. (2002). Masu media [Mass media]. In A. Fukuda & M. Taniguchi (Eds.), *Demokurashi no seijigaku [Politics of democracy]* (pp. 269–286). Tokyo: University of Tokyo Press.

Umeda, S. (2001). *Posuta no shakaishi [The social history of poster]*. Tokyo: Hituzi shobou.

Usaki, M. (1990). Restrictions on political campaigns in Japan. *Law and Contemporary Problems*, 53(2), 133–156.

Values. (2013, July 26). Saninsen netto yu-za- kodo bunseki [An analysis of behavior of net users in the House of Councillors election]. Retrieved from www.valuesccg.com/topics/detail/id=33.

Yamamoto, T. (1972). *Shimbun ni miru seiji kokoku no rekishi [The history of political advertising in the newspaper]*. Tokyo: Asahi Shimbun Publications.

Yomiuri Shimbun. (2015). Media data 2016–2017. Retrieved from http://adv.yomiuri.co.jp/m-data/english/download/ymd_2016-2017.pdf.

29

POLITICAL ADVERTISING IN THE NETHERLANDS

(Still) Little Ado About (Almost) Nothing

Rens Vliegenthart and Sanne Kruikemeier

Introduction

Political campaigning has changed fundamentally in the Netherlands in the past decades. As many other countries, it is argued that the Netherlands has moved into an era of "media logic," with high levels of campaign professionalization, volatile voters and new opportunities to reach the electorate through online media. Given the fact that more voters change (last minute) voting preferences and the availability of new communication channels, it is remarkable, to put it mildly, that political marketing, in terms of advertising, has remained relatively limited. There might be multiple explanations for this, and part of it might also be regarded as a "silence before the storm." Here, we explore those explanations that are grounded in institutional, judicial and cultural arrangements.

In this chapter, we first introduce the political and electoral system of the Netherlands. This context, characterized by proportional representation, coalition formation and consensus seeking, offers a partial explanation for the limited presence of political advertising. Second, we discuss the historical development of political advertising in the Netherlands. Based on an analysis of campaign posters, we discuss the main changes that have taken place since World War II. Furthermore, we introduce a particular characteristic of the Dutch system: advertising time on public television that has been distributed freely to political parties. We also discuss some examples of recent activities by political parties in this realm – mainly some first examples of negative campaigning, personalization and targeting. Third, we provide an overview of the regulations for political advertising and show that parties in principle do not face many formal constraints on employing this kind of campaign tool. They are, however, limited in terms of financial resources constraining their opportunities to buy for example airtime on national television. In the final section, we discuss the limited research that exists on the reception and effects of political advertising in the Dutch context.

The chapter sketches a picture of a country that has so far, at least when it comes to political advertising, not been "Americanized." Part of the explanation lies in the "muting" effect of the political system that does not yield "head-to-head" races where political ads might be most effective. Furthermore, due to the abundance of free media attention, many political parties do not need other sources of communication very much. In addition, there still exists a general unease with the professionalized political campaign and related developments such as the rise of spin doctors and political ads. The context, however, offers fertile ground to expand its use of political ads: a highly volatile electorate results in political campaigns where something can be gained (or lost), regulations offer limited constraints and the omnipresence of Dutch citizens on social media provides a clear channel for personalized and targeted communication. It remains questionable, however, whether such an expansion will yield the desired outcomes by users: the research into political advertising in the Dutch context so far suggests only limited effects, but this might be different in a context where it is more heavily and consistently used.

The Dutch Political and Electoral System

The Netherlands has a bicameral parliamentary system. Officially being a monarchy, the power of the king is largely ceremonial. The Senate (*Eerste Kamer*), consisting of 75 members, is elected indirectly by regional representatives after provincial elections. The main chamber is the *Tweede Kamer*, which is elected directly. Proportional representation is at the heart of the Dutch political system. There are no electoral thresholds, and any party that is able to gain enough votes to obtain at least one of the 150 seats (i.e. 0.67% of the total votes) gets its place in Parliament. During the previous elections in 2012, 10 parties were elected. The system of proportional representation results in a situation in which after each election parties enter into government negotiations and coalition formation takes place. Typically, governments have majority support in parliament and consist of two or three parties. The consensus-seeking behavior typically extends beyond the formal political realm and all kind of institutional arrangements exist to involve stakeholders (e.g., employers organizations and labor unions) in decision-making processes.

Elections take place using open party lists. In principle, the list order determines which candidates are elected in parliament. Additionally, candidates can move up in the list order if they obtain a certain threshold of preferential votes – equaling 25% of the votes necessary for one seat. This threshold is considerably lower than it was in the past and has resulted in a personalized election campaign.

Members of government are not members of parliament. If the government loses its majority support in parliament, it typically calls for new elections. This happened on several occasions in the past 12 years. The past decades, since 1989, have also shown both a large increase in electoral volatility (as much as between 15 and 31 seats changing parties in every single election between 1994 and 2012) and the rise of various new parties, mainly at the right side of the political spectrum, with several of them gaining substantial numbers of votes: Lijst Pim Fortuyn with 26 seats in 2002 and Geert Wilders' Partij voor de Vrijheid with 24 seats in 2010 (Andeweg & Irwin, 2014).

Historical Overview of Political Advertising in the Netherlands

As in many other Western countries, political campaigns have changed substantially in the Dutch situation in the past decades. A useful distinction to map those changes is the three-stage model of political communication as introduced by Kees Brants and Philip van Praag (2006).

Political Logic

The first stage they identify is that of the *party logic*, which was in place in the Netherlands after World War II until approximately the mid 1960s. It was characterized by a pillarized society and a consociational democracy (Lijphart, 1975). The society was clearly divided and organized ("pillarized") along religious and ideological cleavages. Interaction between people belonging to different pillars hardly took place, except at the level of political elites. Political parties were very powerful political institutions and had also substantial influence and power over media (mainly newspapers and radio broadcasts) in their own pillar. It was not uncommon that political leaders were part of the editorial board of newspapers and coverage in individual outlets was highly favorable toward the party with the same denomination. These newspapers were the main source of information for the large majority of citizens and reached very high circulation numbers. The electorate was characterized by high stability, with only small changes in composition of the parliament over time. This stability was also reflected in the election campaigns. They were relatively short and directed toward mobilizing their own electorate. Outside of the main party communication channels and free media, parties used little other formal campaign channels to reach their voters, except for campaign posters. These posters have been used for over a century in the Dutch context and offer an interesting and insightful image of the changes that have taken place in the past decades. An analysis of all posters used in parliamentary election campaigns since World War II is provided by Vliegenthart (2012a). For the era of *political logic*, the analysis reveals that posters combine a relative strong emphasis on visual representations of ideology (and religion) with textual references to the party leader. This indicates the importance of both ideological aspects as well as the familiarity of voters with the political leaders belonging to their own pillar.

Public Logic

The second era Brants and Van Praag identify is that of a *public logic*, running from the end of the 1960s until the early 1990s. It was characterized by fundamental changes in society, with processes of secularization, individualization and depillarization. Also the media quickly underwent professionalization and the rise of television fundamentally altered the media landscape. While the television broadcasting system remained structured by broadcasting organizations that all represented one of the initial pillars, viewers did not stick to broadcasts belonging to their "own" organization. Political parties lost their central position and solid basis of support, with several new parties being successful in gaining a stable place in parliament (e.g., the social-liberal party D66). Journalists approached politicians more critically, but still with some distance and respect. They were, perhaps somewhat idealistically, considered to work in the interest of the general public and aimed to inform the public adequately. Other means of campaigning occurred, most notably television debates made their entry in the Dutch political scene relatively early (in 1963, Vliegenthart, 2012b). Furthermore, the government also assigned broadcast time to political parties on Dutch television. They already received some free airtime on public radio and with the rise of the television, they were also allocated time slots in 1959, and more regularly since 1962 (Aalbers, 2014). The "political party broadcasts" were 10 minutes long and initially broadcast right after the main news broadcast and during halftime of the European soccer matches, therefore attracting a substantial audience. This changed quickly after the broadcasts were rescheduled to other time slots and the length was limited after 1989, initially to five and later on to two minutes, but there was no change in the low viewing numbers (Aalbers, 2014).

The changes that took place during the era of public logic are also reflected in campaign posters: they became more professional (i.e., in design and the use of the party's logo) and more frequently had a picture of the political leader on them. This latter observation is in line with the increasing importance of visualization associated with the rise of television.

Media Logic

The third era that Brants and Van Praag distinguish is that of *media logic*, which is argued to have begun in the 1990s and is still in place. It is characterized by a further professionalization of political campaigns, a situation where media establish the informal "rules of the political game" and the disappearance of boundaries between politics and entertainment (i.e., the rise of "infotainment," Brants, 1998), with for example politicians appearing in all kind of entertainment shows. The pressures of commercialization arguably resulted in coverage that is less substantial and more focused on persons and the horse race (though empirical evidence for personalization is mixed, see Vliegenthart, Boomgaarden, & Boumans, 2011; Kleinnijenhuis, Takens, & Oegema, 2009). Television gained even more prominence and is the main source of information about politics. Other types of programs, such as (late night) talk shows offer a mixture of politics and entertainment (infotainment, see Brants, 1998). Among voters, we saw a strong increase in volatility, with considerable shifts and the rise of various new, mainly far-right, political parties.

Since the end of the 1990s, the Internet became a factor of importance. Political parties started to use websites as a means of communication and now use it as a means to communicate (through text, but also visuals and videos) and interact with potential voters. In the past years, politicians became increasingly active on social media sites, such as (initially) Hyves, Facebook and Twitter. We see those developments also reflected in the campaign posters that remain, though being an "old-fashioned" communication channel, widely visible and frequently used. They have become even more professionalized, with a stronger match between visual and text, and an ever more prominent place for the party leader.

Recent Examples in Dutch Political Advertising

In this section, we discuss some of the recent examples that can be considered prototypical for the changed media environment in which political communication nowadays takes place. Several characteristics have been mentioned as central features of the current "mediatized" constellation (see Strömbäck, 2008). These include, among others, personalization and negativity (or negative campaigning, see Walter & Vliegenthart, 2010). Furthermore, the search for "authenticity" (Donsbach & Jandura, 2003) can be regarded as an important struggle in a situation that is dominated by a media logic and the omnipresence of strategy framing. We illustrate the presence of these three aspects in three recent videos, the first two being purposefully edited for an election campaign, a third one going "viral" on the Internet without having that purpose.

Campaign Videos

The first example is a clip called "Roos" which could be found on the website of the liberal-conservative party VVD during the weeks before the municipality elections.[1] It has been labelled a "breakthrough" in campaign culture by one of the national newspapers (De Fijter, 2006). "Roos" refers to "rose," the symbol of the Labor Party, PvdA, and shows an animation of a rose that loses one petal after the other, not being able to provide a clear stance on some of the major political issues municipalities faced back then. It was clearly designed to provide an image of the PvdA as a flip-flopping party with no clear stance and changing opinions on key issues. It can be regarded as one of the first clear examples of negative campaigning in the Dutch context, with its simplicity contributing to the clarity of the message.

The second example is the television clip for the 2012 parliamentary elections by the PvdA, focusing on its party leader, Diederik Samsom.[2] It is a highly personalized video that shows his disabled 10-year-old daughter, one of Samsom's main motivations to be a politician and make the country better. It can be regarded as a clear example of a specific form of personalization, namely privatization (Van Santen & Van Zoonen, 2010). While Van Santen and Van Zoonen argue that personalization and privatization are not new in the Dutch context and have already been present for decades, it is one of the first times that a politician so clearly "uses" his family to put forward a political message. The specific clip mentioned here received considerable media attention and was discussed elaborately for its potential effectiveness. Again, however, it is important to keep in mind that this video clip only reaches a limited part of the electorate, especially compared to general media coverage and, for example, election campaign broadcasts (Vliegenthart, 2012b).

A third example is not a campaign spot, but a clip that does show the potential of the Internet when it comes to political messages. This clip was a small part of a debate on refugees held in parliament in October 2015. Far-right politician Geert Wilders was mentioning a list of incidents that involved asylum seekers, but was interrupted by the leader of the Greens, Jesse Klaver, who took over and came with a list of extreme-right violent acts against and intimidation of asylum seekers. Klaver explicitly stated that he would not blame Wilders for those actions, but that in a similar vein not all asylum seekers should be blamed for the incidents that involved one or a few asylum seekers. This message was not intended for campaign purposes, was not broadcast on the official YouTube channel of the Greens, but was posted only on Facebook and within a week reached 1.4 million views. In comparison, the much-discussed clip with Diederik Samsom's family only had 150,000 views on YouTube over more than three years (Bellemakers, 2015). It shows that new media have a great potential and can reach large audiences, but also that it is, to a large extent, unpredictable when this will happen and that party strategists have only limited steering options.

Micro-targeting

Also the practice of micro-targeting has gained some ground in the Netherlands during recent years. Again often discussed as an "Americanization" of politics, the idea of targeting specific (groups of) voters during election campaigns is a practice that also started to be used by Dutch political parties, though so far only to a limited extent. The Christian Democratic party CDA is ahead in this respect. During the 2012 parliamentary election campaign, it used a system that combined data from the Dutch statistical office, research on lifestyles conducted by an independent research company and its own member administration to decide where more traditional forms of campaigning (e.g., canvassing, sending letters) should be concentrated. Political parties also target specific groups online. PvdA, for example, uses Facebook ads for specific groups – based, for example, on age and place of residence. Additionally, they use the opportunity to advertise on Facebook pages of friends of those who shared official party messages. Finally, a specific online means of social targeting mentioned by political parties is ads via Google search. If an Internet user searches for certain keywords (political issues, but also names of competing parties for example) an ad for the PvdA appears as the first option in the search results.

It is clear that Dutch political parties only just started to explore the possibilities of micro-targeting. Again, they are seriously constrained by campaign budgets. The Dutch Labor Party, for example, spent, €2.1 million on the campaign for parliamentary elections in 2012. Only €150,000 was spent on online campaigning, which included a whole range of activities and products. Also privacy regulations make it more difficult in the Netherlands to employ the full possibilities of data mining strategies (Nieuwboer, 2012).

Regulation of Political Advertising

Political parties and candidates try to persuade voters in many different ways. Political actors adopt an extensive marketing mix to inform citizens, discuss policy issues and convince voters to vote for them. In the previous section, we mentioned a variety of forms in which parties reach potential voters, many of those using media. As media play a central role in how citizens are informed and persuaded, it is important to discuss the regulations that "control" the extent to which political parties use media to influence their electorate. Compared to other countries, in the Netherlands, political actors enjoy a lot of freedom in choosing how they distribute their messages. Still, political parties and candidates have to follow certain rules when they organize their political campaigns.

The current regulations focus almost solely on (public) broadcasting media. It is important to note that no formal rules exist regarding the *content* of media coverage. In other words, the current regulations do not apply to the political issues or actors themselves, but they do apply to, for instance, the distribution of airtime on public broadcasting channels. As we mentioned in the previous paragraph, the allocation of free airtime ("airtime for political parties") is an important aspect of the Dutch system. According to the Dutch media law, the Dutch Media Authority gives political parties that have a seat in the parliament (house of representatives and senate) free airtime. Political parties present themselves during the airtime – which lasts a few minutes – to citizens, give information, invite citizens to become members, and persuade citizens to vote for them. Although the broadcasts enjoyed large audiences in the 1960s, they were never popular. As argued earlier, nowadays, the programs do not have a large audience anymore which is mainly due to the abundant choice of broadcasters and programming decisions (Aalbers, 2014). The Minister of Education, Culture and Science decides upon the amount of airtime. During elections, the Dutch Media Authority also allocates airtime to political parties that participate in national and European elections. Using a lottery, the Dutch Media Authority selects the order of the broadcasts (Commissariaat voor de Media, 2015; Wet- en regelgeving, 2015).

Turning toward political advertising more specifically, some rules are important here. Both public and commercial broadcasters are not permitted to obtain sponsoring for broadcasting political information. Since 1998, Dutch political parties can buy commercial airtime (Mediaredactie, 1997). The cost of buying (commercial) airtime is nonetheless very expensive; especially because of the small budgets parties have for each election (Jacobs & Spierings, 2016). Therefore, outside of election campaigns, parties do not buy airtime on a regular basis mainly due to the lack of financial resources. Even during election campaigns, political parties rarely buy commercial airtime (Parlement, 2015).

Today, no formal regulations apply to online media and social media. This might be surprising, as social media advertising (such as promoted Facebook posts that appear in users' timelines or buying ads on GoogleAd) and online micro-targeting (i.e., targeting specific users with political advertisements based on their online surf behavior or background characteristics) become more popular among and used by political parties (Strömbäck & Kiousis, 2014).

Spending and Efforts of Political Parties

In the Netherlands, election campaigns are amongst the "cheapest" in the world. All costs that political parties have are – in general – funded from their total budget. To get some insight in the total spending of political parties, it is thus important to take a closer look at the entire budget of political parties. Political parties are funded in many different ways, via internal revenues, such as membership fees and salary payments of representatives, and external revenues, such as donations and (governmental) funding.

With regard to the internal revenues, membership fees are the most important source of income. Half of the total budget is based on the membership fees. This is quite high compared to other European countries. In those countries, on average, only a quarter of the total budget consists of membership fees. Another important source of income is the salary payments of representatives (i.e., party tax). In general, around 10% of the total income of representatives must be handed over to the party, and mostly left-wing parties, such as the Labor Party and the Greens, ask (or require) their representatives to give up a part of their salary. However, the Socialist Party is an exception to this rule and asks its representatives to hand in their entire salaries. In turn, the representatives receive a middle or average income as payment. The last internal sources of income are fund-raising activities, such as organizing events (Parlement, 2015).

With regard to external sources, the Netherlands has a specific regulation that provides governmental funding for political parties that have a seat in the parliament. The total budget is €15 million for each year (Stuiveling & Van Schoten, 2011). The funding amounts are quite low compared to other countries. The amount depends partly on internal funding (such as the number of paying party members), but also on whether or not the party has a scientific bureau and a youth organization. The Netherlands is reluctant to regulate the donations and other private sources of funding of political parties, which often leads to serious discussion. In general, donations more than approximately €4,500 that are not from individuals must be included in party annual financial reports. This is a fairly high amount compared to other countries (Stuiveling & Van Schoten, 2011).

Turning to specific financial resources – especially for election campaigns – of parties, it should be noted that the budgets are quite small as well. For the last two elections, the two largest parties in the Netherlands (the Conservative-Liberal and Labor Party) had a total budget of around €2 million, while another party (the Social Liberals party, D66) had a much smaller budget – about €900,000. Around 60% of that budget is spent on advertising, broadcast and social media. The other 40% is spent on employees, conference expenses, merchandising and printing.

Turning to social media, political parties recognize the opportunities that online platforms bring. Research by Jacobs and Spierings (2016) shows several important insights into the resources used for online campaigns. In general, politicians in the Netherlands are often enthusiastic about online and social media, because it is inexpensive and many citizens can be reached at once. However, resources are still necessary to provide a more professional online campaign, for instance by hiring a (full-time) social media team, buying software to analyze online media, being aware of tweets from journalists, answering immediate questions, offering training from consultants or to enhance the quality of online messages (e.g., including info-graphics; Jacobs & Spierings, 2016). The parties in the Netherlands are also more likely to deploy a more professional social media team, for the simple reason that they have more resources. The Conservative-Liberal Party, for instance, bought sponsored stories to generate more "likes" on Facebook. Yet, these paid "ads" are far more expensive than unsponsored ads. Also the small Christian Party invested in Facebook to "boost a message." Smaller but more active parties have fewer resources to invest in social media, but they do invest in paid social-media managers, staff and web care teams. However, interestingly, they do so only during election campaigns. In addition, some smaller parties have volunteers that also helped with the online campaign. Some smaller parties, which are often more traditional, decide not to invest in online campaigning at all, because of their limited resources (Jacobs & Spierings, 2016).

Research into Content, Reception and Effects of Mediatized Information

In the Netherlands, political advertising comes in many forms, such as advertising in traditional media, online media and other channels that are used for campaigning, for instance campaign posters (Vliegenthart, 2012a). Political parties still use free airtime on public broadcast television, although they know that these programs are not popular. Politicians perceive online media as very important, although less important than newspapers (Weber Shandwick, 2014). Effects of all kinds of communication have been studied in the Dutch context. Unfortunately, but maybe also not surprisingly, research into actual campaign ads has been relatively limited, first because of their limited audiences (on television) and for online ads also because of the relative novelty of the phenomenon. In this section, we briefly discuss studies that looked into the content and effects of a wide variety of mediatized online information, which also might give an indication of the potential impact of sponsored and targeted ads.

First of all, research shows that the content of the free airtime broadcasts did not change that much over the course of time (Klinkenberg, Willemsen, & Hermans, 2006). Klinkenberg et al. found that the only notable persuasive strategies that *did* change were personalization and dramatization. The broadcasts showed an increased focus on the politician as a private person. For example, party broadcasts were more often about the politicians' personal characteristics instead of their records as politicians. There is an increased focus on the emotional aspects of political issues. Most changes took place at the end of the 1980s. Klinkenberg et al. believe that this can be explained by the arrival of commercial television, as political parties tried to compete with an abundance of new media channels. The reason why *not* many strategies changed might be the relative big role and stable format of the free airtime broadcasts and the rather limited use of paid ads on commercial television (due to limited financial resources). Lastly, the political system in the Netherlands may hinder the use of more confrontational strategies such as the use of a conflict strategy. As parties do not want to be excluded from possible involvement or inclusion in the government, a conflict strategy is in many instances not a good idea.

Compared to traditional advertising on television, in recent years, online campaigning became very popular. This might be caused by the fact that offline campaigning (via traditional media) is too expensive for Dutch political parties. Besides, in the Netherlands, almost every Dutch citizen has Internet access, which makes the threshold for using online media for advertising much lower. In a direct way, a large audience can be reached. Political parties seized this opportunity and today they often engage in communication with their electorate online – especially during elections – and almost every politician (even at local levels) uses online media to communicate with citizens. They mainly use social networking sites, such as Facebook and Twitter, and party websites. Also email seems to be quite frequently used during elections (Kruikemeier & Van de Pol, 2015). Blogs, personal websites and YouTube are less popular. This latter finding is confirmed by Walter and Van Praag (2012), who found that YouTube did not mobilize the audience. Instead, it is mainly used to broadcast advertisements. The ads did not enjoy large audiences and did not influence both online and traditional media. Furthermore, they found that "short, comparative ads that contain the party leader, that are uploaded early on in the campaign, that stem from small or wining parties and that have numerous links on external websites are likely to reach more viewers" (p. 443). So the general conclusion is that online, and social media in particular, foster personalized communication, because politicians have their own profiles on these social networking sites and are more visible in online YouTube ads (Kruikemeier, 2014).

Another important tool, which is very popular in the Netherlands, is Voting Advice Applications (VAAs, Van de Pol, Holleman, Kamoen, Krouwel, & De Vreese, 2014). VAAs are online "applications [that] assist voters in the electoral decision by comparing their policy preferences with the programmatic stances of political parties and/or candidates" (Marschall & Garzia, 2014, p. 1). Around one-third of the population consults a VAA during an election (Kruikemeier, Van Noort, Vliegenthart, & De Vreese, 2014a). Research shows that VAAs can increase citizens' intention to go out and vote (Kruikemeier, Van Noort, Vliegenthart, & De Vreese, 2014b). The most popular VAAs are principally developed independently (i.e., *Stemwijzer* and *Kieskompas*), with financial resources from the Dutch government or developed by Dutch universities. Parties have limited to no power to strategically influence VAAs. However, they do try to do so (Krouwel, Vitiello, & Wall, 2012). For instance, a spin doctor from the Christian Democratic Party tried to manipulate a statement from a VAA, by not providing the party position according to its manifesto, but by giving the most popular answer. This instance led to a debate in the Netherlands about the quality of VAAs (Krouwel et al., 2012).

Another important campaign activity, at least according to (local) candidates, that involves political advertising, is distributing folders and other promotion materials (such as campaign gadgets) on the street. Municipalities make market stalls available and volunteers and party leaders are present. The folders (that often contain a summary of views and positions of the parties) are also delivered to people's homes. Especially during local elections, parties engage in creative activities such as distributing rain covers for bike seats (Rosema & Boedeltje, 2011).

Lastly, campaign posters are also popular, especially during election campaigns. Municipalities decide which locations are available for posters, by placing specific boards at different locations. Specifically during local elections, but also during national elections, the municipalities make specific rules about the sizes of the posters and where to place them, which parties seem – to some extent – to follow (Rosema & Boedeltje, 2011). Research shows that since World War II, campaign posters did change over time, as we also discussed in the section on the three stages of political communication. For instance, posters more often include a party logo and a picture of the party leader, showing no clear evidence of increased personalization. Over the last 60 years, posters refer less to ideology in the visuals, but references to ideology were more often present in the text. Interestingly, a focus on negativity was – in general and in line with YouTube videos – not present on the posters (Vliegenthart, 2012a).

Research examining the effects of political advertising is scarce, because it is, in general, difficult to measure the effectiveness of political marketing (Van Steenburg, 2015). However, turning to the literature on the use of online media during online campaigns, there are some interesting findings. Research shows that typical online communication styles used on social media by political candidates and parties can be successful. For instance, politicians' interactive communication style on social media makes citizens more likely to feel involved in politics. Interactive communication includes starting and responding to conversations, but also the use of interactive features on, for instance, websites (Kruikemeier, Van Noort, Vliegenthart, & De Vreese, 2013). This interactive communication can result in a greater number of preferential votes (Kruikemeier, 2014). Also a more personalized communication style (e.g., communication that stems from an individual politician, instead of the party) is likely to instigate political involvement among citizens (Kruikemeier et al., 2013). This is also in line with the research above focusing on the effectiveness of YouTube, that shows that those videos are more successful if they contain the party leader and links are included (Walter & Van Praag, 2012). So, we can observe a general trend toward more personalized communication in an online media environment, which is also, in light of the positive effect of personalization, maybe not that surprising.

Some anecdotal evidence additionally suggests that online political micro-targeting might be not that successful in the Dutch context. Research shows that Dutch citizens are more negative toward micro-blogging practices, such as promoted tweets, as these tweets activate citizens' knowledge that they are being persuaded (Boerman & Kruikemeier, 2014). As there is a widespread normative belief among citizens that political actors should not buy advertising or engage in such persuasion tactics, this could explain why Dutch citizens are more negative toward these practices.

Conclusion

Politics in general, and campaigning in general, has changed fundamentally during previous periods. On the one hand, voters were said to be adrift, with many of them changing voting preferences from one election to the other and deciding only at the last minute whom to vote for. On the other hand, political parties try to get a grip and even profit from this new insecure situation by professionalizing their campaigns and relying on new means of communication. It might be appealing to focus on the dynamics here and argue that turbulence and insecurity are the most outstanding characteristics of the current situation. Remarkably enough, however, we find considerable stability when it comes to political advertising. Due to the limited resources political parties have, they hardly expanded their traditional forms of political ads. The most well-known ones are still those that are broadcast on public television. Television ads may be well-known, but they are also poorly watched and often criticized for being unprofessional (Aalbers, 2014). Political parties commonly still use traditional campaign posters and distribute flyers door-to-door or at weekly markets. In that sense, there is a remarkable parallel between advertising and media coverage of Dutch politics. Fundamental changes are often discussed, but stability is greater than often assumed (Kleinnijenhuis et al., 2009; Vliegenthart, 2012a), with content, for example, still being substantive and not increasingly personalized for the past two decades.

There is a set of reasons that can account for this stability in political advertising. First of all, the system of proportional representation and coalition governments might restrain the use of political advertising. As we know from the US context, political ads are often negative and target political opponents (Lau, Sigelman, & Rovner, 2007). In the Dutch context, it is often unclear who the main opponent is and the main opponent is likely to be also the one to negotiate about a joint coalition after the elections. Keeping relationships good might be an important consideration to not use political ads and not to "go negative." Second, the limited financial resources seriously constrain political parties in their campaigns. For national campaigns, the largest political parties have a budget of around €2 million, for which they have to organize a wide range of activities. They use some of the money for research and new forms of advertisements, such as micro-targeting, but to a very limited extent. Third, political advertising still has a somewhat negative connotation among Dutch politicians and citizens, being associated with a focus on persuasion and negativity, rather than content (Vliegenthart, 2012b).

Of course, this does not mean that the Netherlands is at a standstill. When it comes, for example, to employing the opportunities of social media, Dutch politicians are active, being among the early adopters and frequent users of Twitter. Also political advertising increasingly takes place over the Internet. In recent election campaigns (and also somewhat outside that), political parties have started to use micro-targeting strategies, both online and offline. The question is whether or not these activities will increase in the future. Though hard to predict, one can at least argue that there are relatively few legal constraints. Political parties face relatively few legal hurdles when it comes to advertising, though for micro-targeting and data mining somewhat strict privacy regulations do exist. Also, in the general political culture, we have witnessed a shift in focus, with a greater emphasis on the political horse race (Vliegenthart, 2012b) and an increased emphasis on which party will become the largest and is thus most likely to deliver the prime minister (as reflected in, for example, the "prime ministerial debate" organized by the main commercial broadcaster, RTL, during recent election campaigns). This yields a situation in which it is easier for political parties to identify a clear opponent and use political advertising in the mix of communication efforts directed toward "winning" the race. In the long run, it might be mainly an issue of attracting enough financial resources to finance such a strategy. The fact that political parties have almost continuously struggled with their finances in the past decades suggests that this might remain a serious constraint in the future as well.

Notes

1 www.youtube.com/watch?v=hQcN4w0_VqU.
2 www.youtube.com/watch?v=Js-3Tyljx30.

References

Aalbers, J. (2014). Het mysterieuze voortbestaan van de zendtijd politieke partijen. *Tijdschrift Voor Mediageschiedenis*, 16(2), 61–74.

Andeweg, R. B., & Irwin, G. A. (2014). *Governance and politics of the Netherlands*. Basingstoke: Palgrave Macmillan.

Bellemakers, H. (2015). Hoe Jesse Klaver van GroenLinks viral gaat. Retrieved from http://bkbcampaignwatch.nl/hoe-jesse-klaver-van-groenlinks-viral-gaat/.

Boerman, S. C., & Kruikemeier, S. (2014). *Sponsored by: The effects of disclosing sponsored tweets on persuasion knowledge and source evaluations*. Paper presented at the 5th European Communication Conference (ECREA), Lisbon, Portugal.

Brants, K. (1998). Who's afraid of infotainment? *European Journal of Communication*, 13(3), 315–335.

Brants, K., & Van Praag, P. (2006). Signs of media logic half a century of political communication in the Netherlands. *Javnost – the Public*, 13(1), 25–40.

Commissariaat voor de Media. (2015). Zendtijd politieke partijen. Retrieved from www.cvdm.nl/praktisch/zendtijd-politieke-partijen/.

De Fijter, N. (2006, February 16). VVD doorbreekt campagnecultuur. *Trouw*, pp. 4–5.

Donsbach, W., & Jandura, O. (2003). Chances and effects of authenticity candidates of the German federal election in TV news. *The International Journal of Press/Politics*, 8(1), 49–65.

Jacobs, K., & Spierings, N. (2016). *Social media, parties, and political inequalities*. Basingstoke: Palgrave Macmillan.

Kleinnijenhuis, J., Takens, J., & Oegema, D. (2009). Personalisering van de politiek. In G. Voerman (Ed.), *Jaarboek documentatiecentrum politieke partijen 2007* (pp. 1010–128). Groningen: Documentatiecentrum Nederlandse Politieke Partijen.

Klinkenberg, I., Willemsen, A., & Hermans, L. (2006). De Nederlandse politieke televisiespot van 1963 tot 2003: Het gebruik van persuasieve strategieën. *Tijdschrift Voor Communicatiewetenschap*, 34(3), 282–295.

Krouwel, A., Vitiello, T., & Wall, M. (2012). Voting advice applications as campaign actors: Mapping VAAs' interactions with parties, media and voters. In D. Garzia & S. Marschall (Eds.), *Matching voters with parties and candidates: Voting advice applications in comparative perspective* (pp. 67–78). Colchester: ECPR Press.

Kruikemeier, S. (2014). How political candidates use Twitter and the impact on votes. *Computers in Human Behavior*, 34, 131–139.

Kruikemeier, S., & Van de Pol, J. (2015). Online campagnevoeren. In D. Kok (Ed.), *Open Gemeenten – de sociale media-almanak voor gemeenten 2015* (pp. 217–221).

Kruikemeier, S., Van Noort, G., Vliegenthart, R., & De Vreese, C. H. (2013). Getting closer: The effects of personalized and interactive online political communication. *European Journal of Communication*, 28(1), 53–66.

Kruikemeier, S., Van Noort, G., Vliegenthart, R., & De Vreese, C. H. (2014a). Nieuwe media, een politieke belofte? Politiek internetgebruik tijdens de verkiezingscampagne. In P. Van Praag, & K. Brants (Eds.), *Media, macht en politiek. De verkiezingscampagne van 2012*. Diemen: ABM.

Kruikemeier, S., Van Noort, G., Vliegenthart, R., & De Vreese, C. H. (2014b). Unraveling the effects of active and passive forms of political internet use: Does it affect citizens' political involvement? *New Media & Society*, 16(6), 903–920.

Lau, R. R., Sigelman, L., & Rovner, I. B. (2007). The effects of negative political campaigns: A meta-analytic reassessment. *Journal of Politics*, 69(4), 1176–1209.

Lijphart, A. (1975). *The politics of accommodation: Pluralism and democracy in the Netherlands*. Berkeley, CA: University of California Press.

Marschall, S., & Garzia, D. (2014). *Voting advice applications in a comparative perspective: An introduction*. Colchester: ECPR Press.

Mediaredactie (1997, November 7). Partijen staan niet te trappelen in verkiezingstijd zendtijd te kopen. *Trouw*, p. 9.

Nieuwboer, D. J. (2012, November 3). Nederlanders kopen liever een billboard. *De Volkskrant*, p. 8.

Parlement. (2015). Partijfinanciering. Retrieved from www.parlement.com/id/vhnnmt7l6hu4/partijfinanciering.

Rosema, M., & Boedeltje, M. (2011). *Gemeenteraadsverkiezingen 2010: Een blik achter de schermen*. Enschede: Universiteit Twente.

Strömbäck, J. (2008). Four phases of mediatization: An analysis of the mediatization of politics. *The International Journal of Press/Politics*, 13(3), 228–246.

Strömbäck, J., & Kiousis, S. (2014). Strategic political communication in election campaigns. In C. Reinemann (Ed.), *Political communication* (pp. 109–128). Berlin: Walter de Gruyter.

Stuiveling, S. J., & Van Schoten, E. M. A. (2011). *Financiering politieke partijen*. Den Haag: Algemene Rekenkamer.

Van de Pol, J., Holleman, B., Kamoen, N., Krouwel, A., & De Vreese, C. (2014). Beyond young, highly educated males: A typology of VAA users. *Journal of Information Technology & Politics*, 11(4), 397–411.

Van Santen, R., & Van Zoonen, L. (2010). The personal in political television biographies. *Biography*, 33(1), 46–67. doi:10.1353/bio.0.0157.

Van Steenburg, E. (2015). Areas of research in political advertising: A review and research agenda. *International Journal of Advertising*, 34(2), 195–231.

Vliegenthart, R. (2012a). The professionalization of political communication? A longitudinal analysis of dutch election campaign posters. *American Behavioral Scientist*, 56(2), 135–150.

Vliegenthart, R. (2012b). *U kletst uit uw nek: Over de relatie tussen politiek, media en de kiezer*. Amsterdam: Bert Bakker.

Vliegenthart, R., Boomgaarden, H. G., & Boumans, J. W. (2011). Changes in political news coverage: Personalization, conflict and negativity in British and Dutch newspapers. In K. Brants, & K. Voltmer (Eds.), *Challenging the primacy of politics* (pp. 92–110). Basingstoke: Palgrave Macmillan.

Walter, A. S., & Van Praag, P. (2012). Een gemiste kans? De rol van YouTube in de verkiezingscampagne van 2010. *Res Publica*, 54(4), 443–464.

Walter, A. S., & Vliegenthart, R. (2010). Negative campaigning across different communication channels: Different ball games? *The International Journal of Press/Politics*, 15(4), 441–461.

Weber Shandwick. (2014). *Twitter en de tweede kamer*. Den Haag: Weber Shandwick.

Wet- en regelgeving. (2015). Mediawet. Retrieved from http://wetten.overheid.nl/BWBR0025028/Hoofdstuk6/Titel61/Afdeling611/Artikel61/geldigheidsdatum_25-07-2011.

30

TOWARDS PROFESSIONALIZATION AND AMERICANIZATION

Audiovisual Political Advertising in Poland (1989–2015)

Bogusława Dobek-Ostrowska

Introduction

Analysis of the development of electoral campaigns and political advertising in democratic Poland perfectly parallels the three phases of the evolution of the US campaign environment – the newspaper age (premodern era), the television age (modern era) and the digital age (postmodern era) (Farrell, Kolodny, & Medvic, 2001). The main difference between the US and Poland is the amount of time it took for those stages to evolve. In the US, it took about two centuries, in Poland – just over two decades.

More than 10 years ago, political advertising was, on the one hand, a celebrated but, on the other one, a reviled form of political communication (Kaid, 2004, p. 155). Political ads remain one of the most important ways of gaining potential voters. Television ads play a huge role in all kinds of democratic models – the American Exceptionalism, the mature "West European mass party" countries and the "new democracies" in East and Central Europe, Asia and Latin America (Farrell et al., 2001). Television advertising plays an important role in commercial broadcasting systems, public television systems, and in dual systems of public and commercial advertising. Poland was then classified by Kaid and Holtz-Bacha (2006) as an example of an "evolving democracy" (Cwalina & Falkowski, 2006) together with Hungary, Russia, Bulgaria and the Czech Republic. Is this statement still true today?

A quarter of a century of experience with democratic procedures deeply reinforced democracy in this state. Poles voted 25 times in six presidential, nine parliamentary, seven local and three European parliamentary elections. Voter turnout suggests that two kinds of elections have developed, first-order elections in the case of presidential, parliamentary and local ones, and second-order elections in the case of the European parliamentary elections (see Figure 30.1). Political parties and the political system needed about five to six years after the collapse of communism to consolidate. This phase ended with the passing of the new Constitution in 1997. The alternation of power, which is a typical phenomenon of democracy, began to work.

A stable media system and press freedom standards are other important pillars responsible for the quality of democracy. Thanks to the Law of Broadcasting Media adopted in 1992, a dual system of public and commercial political advertising was introduced. The public broadcaster TVP SA and the

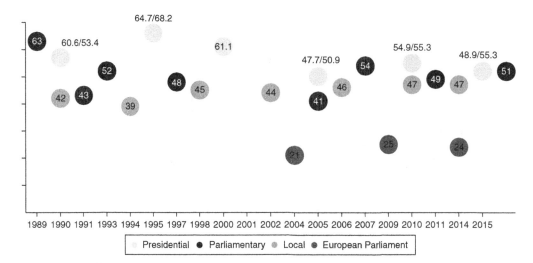

Figure 30.1   Electoral participation in Poland from 1989 to 2015 (in %). Results are given for the first and second rounds of presidential elections
Source: Author on the basis of data from the National Electoral Commission (PKW).

first commercial station TV Polsat began to operate in 1994. The new regulation was the road to the development of television political ads and this option was first tested during the presidential election in 1995. In a short time, audiovisual electoral broadcasts and spots produced for television by parties, candidates or non-affiliated independent groups, obtained a dominant position. Television was the main distributor of all political ads for the next two decades. It is still the main channel of advertising, but its position in the structure of advertising expenses has slowly, but continually, eroded. In 2005, costs of television ads were the highest (about 141 million euros, about 53% of the overall advertising market) and the cost of Internet ads the lowest (6 million euros, 2.5%). Within just one year, Internet ads income increased by 55% and held a share of 3.7% of the overall market (Dobek-Ostrowska, 2007, p. 392). Over the past five years, the leading position of television has been slowly limited by the Internet. In 2012, the market share of television dropped to 49% while the participation of Internet ads rose to 17.5%. Among all media only Internet expenditures are still rising. The rate was +10.7% in the case of Internet and +2.6% for television ads in 2014 (Rynek reklamowy…, 2015). Additionally, the expenses for all online ads in this rose more than 7% in 2014 in comparison with 2013. Significant changes were noted in the case of mobile (+122%) and social media (+33%) (Raport AdEx…, 2015). This tendency is reflected in the structure of advertising expenses of political actors.

Besides the political experience of society and development of the media market, a deep change in the demographic structure of the recipients forms in the political advertising market. An average viewer of traditional television is 50 years old (more than 55% of the Polish population), lives in the countryside (54%) and is a pensioner (about 40%) (Kozielski, 2014, p. 9). We should add that the Polish society is growing old, people who are more than 60 years old constitute ca. 18% of the population, and non-employed citizens aged 45 or more, about 24% (Rozwój…, 2013). In the case of this older group of the Polish population, television is the main source of information about the world and politics, what is more, they are the most disciplined voters. For this reason, distribution of electoral television spots is one of the most important electoral tasks for political actors. But, on the other hand, about 40% of the Poles are 18 to 44 years old. They are active and use several platforms – the computer, tablet or mobile (Kozielski, 2014, p. 10).

The intensive social and technological changes observed over the last decade in Poland significantly influence the electoral communication policies of political actors. Two different categories of media consumers have appeared among these two generations of voters over the past few years. Young people aged 35–40 are active and do not have enough time to watch television. They learn about politics from the Internet and social media, and they constantly use their cell phones or tablets. But young voters are not reliable voters. They are not much interested in politics and their voter participation is significantly lower than that of the older generation (Cześnik, 2009, p. 17). Poles aged 45 years and older spend a lot of time watching television, which is also caused by a decrease in readership and a drastic limitation of newspaper distribution in the last decade – from 1.5 million copies of daily newspapers in 2005 to 450,000 in 2012 (Nakłady…, 2013). This generation is the smallest group of users of new communication technologies. Generally, it is not only a result of lack of money in their family budget but, above all, they do not have any or very limited experience with the new media and the skills indispensable to using them.

How does this differentiation of the Polish media market work in the political context? The most important variables exerting influence on voter participation (apart from a citizen's sense of obligation, which is the first one) are education and age. According to empirical research from the decade of 1997 to 2007 (Cześnik, 2009, pp. 17–22) showed that 78% of the Poles with higher education voted in four elections which took place during this time period. In 1997, the average turnout of voters under 45 years old was 50% and older than 65 years old, 65%. Ten years later it was 60% for the younger and 75% for the older generation. Additionally, pensioners were the most frequent participants in all parliamentary elections during this period. This sociological image of the Poles cannot be insignificant for the "ads policy" of electoral committees.

Pre-modern Chaotic Phase of Political Ads in the 1990s

The first phase of democratic transition in Poland after the collapse of communism in 1989 was an eventful period. It was a time of very deep political, economic and social transformations. The Polish parliament needed a few years to introduce new laws and the Constitution (1997). The first Broadcasting Act was accepted at the end of 1992 and it began to operate in 1993. On the basis of this regulation, a dual system of public and commercial broadcasting was developed, as for instance in Germany and Italy. The party system is one of the solid pillars of European democratic political regimes. The formation process of the stable party system took about one decade in Poland.

The semi-democratic parliamentary election in 1989 paved the way for democracy in Poland. There were 111 parties and political organizations that took part in the ballot in the first fully free parliamentary election in 1991, and 29 of them entered parliament. Apart from two parties which were linked with the former regime, all the others were new organizations based on anti-communist political opposition. In the 1993 election, candidates from 16 parties, which were on the ballot were elected. A weak party system resulted in political instability. The situation changed thanks to a new party law accepted by parliament a few months before the election in 1997. Then only six committees entered the Sejm and post-Solidarity parties were able to form a stable parliamentary majority, which made it possible for them to govern until the end of their term of office. Additionally, two presidential campaigns took place in this first premodern phase (Farrell et al., 2001). The legend of the Polish Solidarity opposition movement, Lech Wałęsa, won in 1990, and 41-year-old Kwaśniewski, the leader of the post-communist left, won in 1995.

There were some common features typical of this period. The committees did not have any, or very little, experience in campaigning and in garnering financial support. Professional personnel responsible for the party's or the candidate's communications did not exist then. For this reason, they were rather amateurish and spontaneous campaigns, sometimes chaotic, with a predominance of posters and print ads. However, the Law on the Election of the President (1990) guaranteed free time for election committees on public television 15 days before election day.

In the case of the presidential election in 1995, broadcasting of video ads was limited to the free time on public broadcasting, which was guaranteed by law. There were 14 blocks in TVP1, six on TVP2, and two on TVP Polonia. Among the 81 spots, a positive focus characterized 93% of them, emotional messages (67%) dominated over logical (21%) and source credibility (12%). The introspective style format was typical of 36% and the documentary style format of 32%. More ads were dedicated to issues (56%) than to image (30%).

Overall, television played a marginal role in the campaign process in the first years of political transformation. On the one hand, the video advertising was unprofessional, long and boring, which provoked a negative reaction from the viewers. On the other hand, thanks to changes in this period, when political actors exercised their political skills and gained experience, video ads became an inseparable part of political communication and election campaigns. The Polish political market developed dynamically, and at the end of the 1990s, Poles lived in a different "era," where television became the dominant channel of political communication.

Dominance of Professional Television Ads in the 21st Century

The main political actors needed about one decade to enter a new phase of campaign professionalization. It was possible thanks to intensive development of the television system, marketing and advertising agencies. Poland joined the group of states with dual public and commercial systems.

The dominance of broadcasting in keeping voters informed about politics has been highlighted by many scholars. The most important characteristics of this phase are the reduced length of party election broadcasts, the dominance of issue advertising and cultivation of nonpolitical and promotional styles (Scammell & Langer, 2006, p. 75). Other features have been described, such as the Americanization of campaign style, such as in Brazil and many other new democracies (Porto, 2006, pp. 133–134), also "telepolitics," personalization and "carnivalization" as a "kind of gala carnival, complete with balloons, signs, performers, singing, and dancing" (Caspi & Leshem, 2006, p. 123). Many empirical studies showed a significant impact of television on political communication. It was "the most important medium to use in keeping voters informed about politics" as in Italy (Mazzoleni, 2006, p. 253). This trend triggered and intensified the development of political consultants and professional agencies producing television spots. Did the features typical of many countries come to Poland too?

We noted a significant growth in the amount of time spent on broadcasting paid spots in public and private channels from 2005 to 2007 for all of the largest parties (Civic Platform from 73.8 to 164.9 hours, Law and Justice from 47.4 to 161.8 hours, the left party/coalition from 60.8 to 188.6 hours, the peasant party 21.1 to 157.3 hours) (Informacja…, 2005; Parlamentarna…, 2007). These data confirm that television ads played the most important role in campaign communication for each party and candidates in the 21st century.

The presidential campaign in 2000 was the first one to be fully televised. There were three important candidates – the incumbent president Kwaśniewski, the representative of the left party, Krzaklewski (post-solidarity party AWS), and Olechowski (conservative party). The very popular incumbent president Kwaśniewski was the winner with 54% of votes in the first round, which has happened in Poland only once since 1989. Television was the main channel of political communication in this campaign. Television spots played a significant role, not only in the presidential campaign of 2000, but also one year later in the parliamentary election. The role of television is further corroborated by the amount of money that candidates spent on video spots in both campaigns. At that time a 15-second video clip on the main public and private national channels cost about €10,000, in contrast to print ads in local newspapers – about €500, and national radio stations – about €1,250 (Walecki, 2001, p. 162).

The observation that candidates who are behind in the polls attack more than those who are ahead (Benoit, 2007, p. 69) was confirmed. The video clips of Kwaśniewski were rather bland because he was sure to be a winner. His main opponent, Krzaklewski, was the most active and determined in this campaign. He decided to polarize the political scene and destroy the myth of Kwaśniewski as "the president of all Poles." In fact, his was the first aggressive campaign. The last two weeks before the voting day were filled by short and negative television ads paid for by Krzaklewski's team and directed against Kwaśniewski. They were technically professional spots produced by advertising agencies. Election results showed that this extremely negative kind of political communication was not accepted by the voters. Krzaklewski, who spent the most money on television ads, took third position in the vote.

The presidential campaign in 2000 and the parliamentary election campaign in 2001 marked the end of an era when the main characteristic in politics was animosities based on a sharp distinction between post-communist and post-Solidarity movements resulting from their different historical backgrounds.

The next presidential and parliamentary elections were held in 2005. Because both campaigns took place at the same time, it was sometimes difficult to separate the campaigns' messages. Fifteen years after the first presidential democratic election, the party system solidified. In contrast to the left party (SLD), which had four years of discredited government, the parties with oppositional roots – center/liberal Civic Platform (PO) and conservative Law and Justice (PiS), strongly reinforced their position on the political scene. After 10 years of Kwaśniewski's presidency, the left party did not have a candidate who could fight the opposition. In fact, the 2005 elections started a new period in political competition. The main line of political opposition ran, not between the left and the right, but between the right (conservative PiS) and the center (liberal PO). The left party was pushed to the margins of the political scene. This structure of competition, which formed in the middle of the first decade of the 21st century, and has worked until today, was exceptional in the new democracies of Central and Eastern Europe.

Some critical and empirical research dedicated to the campaigns after 2011 supports the view that it was a period of domination of televised ads. A stronger adaptation of professional political marketing strategies was evident (Adamik-Szysiak, 2012, p. 220). Kaczynskis' party Law and Justice cooperated with the SPC House of Media. The Media Insight Polska worked for Civic Platform and Tusk. The left coalition Left and Democrats (LiD) was linked with the media house Media Concept in 2007. It was the time of traditional *politicos*, strategists and tacticians (Farrell et al., 2001), who were often members of political parties and they were close to their leaders. Some of the political operatives had experience in US campaigns of the 21st century. In 2005 and 2007, and also in 2010, the Law and Justice Party offered professional "American-style" campaigns. "Telepolitics" and "carnivalization" of official party meetings, conventions, etc. (Caspi & Leshem, 2006, p. 123) became standard practice (Porto, 2006, pp. 133–134). Apart from the free time on public television guaranteed to each registered party, public and private channels were usually used for distribution of paid video ads. This kind of campaign provoked a rapid increase in costs.

The campaign of the two main candidates in 2010 was more expensive than in 2005 (see Table 30.1). In 2005, Lech Kaczyński, the Law and Justice candidate spent about €76,000 more on television spots than Donald Tusk, his opponent from Civic Platform. In 2010, the cost of Jarosław Kaczyński's television ads was ca. €133,000 higher than his brother's. In 2010 twice as much money (20%) was allocated from the campaign's total budget as in 2005 (10%). The lowest amount of money was spent on television ads by Donald Tusk in 2005 (about 7%), and more for Komorowski's spots (above 15%). The Civic Platform candidates spent less money on television ads than the Law and Justice contenders.

The same tendency could be observed for the parliamentary elections in 2005 and 2007. The costs of the television spots of Law and Justice in both campaigns were significantly higher than of the other parties (see Table 30.2) – €2.6 versus €1.7 million in 2005 and €2.2 versus €1.9 million in 2007.

Analyses of the costs of the presidential and parliamentary elections in the 2000s shows that a high budget dedicated to television spots cannot guarantee success. Although Law and Justice had the most professional campaigns in 2005, 2007 and 2010, the highest budget for television ads, and, in 2010,

Table 30.1 Costs of presidential campaign in 2005 and 2010 (in million euros)

The main candidates		Year of election	Total cost of campaign	Costs of television ads	Cost of television ads as % of total cost of campaign
PiS	Lech Kaczyński	2005	3.4	0.338	10.03
	Jarosław Kaczyński	2010	3.6 ↑	0.729	19.98 ↑
PO	Donald Tusk	2005	3.6	0.262	7.35
	Bronisław Komorowski	2010	3.9 ↑	0.596	15.5 ↑

Source: Own calculation on the basis of data from the State Electoral Commission (PKW) (Komunikat…, 2006b; Komunikat…, 2010).

Table 30.2 Costs of parliamentary campaign in 2005 and 2007 (in million euros)

The main party/coalition	Total cost of campaign		Cost of television ads		Cost of television ads as % of total cost of campaign	
	2005	2007	2005	2007	2005	2007
Law and Justice PiS	7.5	7.1	2.7	2.3	35	32
Civic Platform PO	6.8	7.4 ↑	1.8	1.9 ↑	26	27
The left party/coalition SLD/LiD	6.4	6.5 ↑	0.6	1.3 ↑	10	20
Peasant party PSL	2.4	1.5	0.7	1.5 ↑	29	21

Source: Own calculation on the basis of data from the State Electoral Commission (PKW) (Komunikat…, 2006a; Komunikat…, 2008).

Jarosław Kaczyński spent twice as much money on television clips as the opponent, the party and its candidate lost the battle, just like in the case of Krzaklewski in 2000.

The content analysis of video clips in 2005, 2007 and 2010 had a lot of features typical of American television advertisements. They were shorter and more dynamic in comparison with the 1990s. A short message needs special tactics, because each second has to be used effectively. As Tuman noted, a televised clip is a composite of visual image and text, voice-over narration, musical score and color choice (2008, p. 235). In this context, identification and personal imagery take precedence over a superiority over issues.

In the 21st century, the new practice was adopted in Poland. The candidates were often shown in close-up, and their faces took up the whole screen. In 2005, there were head shots in 41% of Tusk's clips and 24% of Lech Kaczyński's spots. The number rose significantly in 2010, when headshots were presented in 70% of Komorowski's and 44% of Jarosław Kaczyński's ads (Adamiak-Szysiak, 2012, p. 121). This same trick was quite popular in parliamentary ads in 2007, 2011 and later. "Talking head" ads also appeared at that time. Tusk's talking head took 45% of the time of his ads in 2005 and 42% in 2007, in contrast to Jarosław Kaczyński – where a talking head took only 5.5% in 2005 and 22% of the time in 2007. But other "speaking leaders" filled from 9% to 52% of the clip time in 2007 and 2011 campaigns (Adamiak-Szysiak, 2012, p. 210).

Polish political consultants, who studied election techniques in the US, recommended television spots as "cinema vérité," "documentary," "testimonial" or "people in the street" ads. In fact, almost each electoral committee produced those types of clips.

Many spots presented candidates not only in formal situations, but also in informal ones. In 2005, the main candidates in the presidential election decided to reveal facts from their private lives. They

Table 30.3 Negative ads in parliamentary campaigns (% of all negative ads/% of ads with a negative fragment)

Party/coalition	2005	2007	2009 (EU election)
Law and Justice PiS	30/10	45/11 ↑	75/6
Civic Platform PO	0/38	62/2 ↑	17/17
Left party SLD/coalition LiD	0/34	50/11 ↑	40/20
Peasant party PSL	0/20	0/13	0/0

Source: Data from Adamik-Szysiak (2012, p. 134).

presented their family members, and in this way, they introduced the "family picture" style to Polish political ads, which was very popular in the 2007 and 2010 campaigns. In general, a family picture has become a stable element of electoral ads.

Superiority of image over issue encourages candidates to make negative comparisons and contrasts with opponents in Poland. As in American ads, authors of Polish political clips willingly used negative emotions. They frequently exposed pictures of neglected and hungry children, old, poor and ill people, pathological situations and occurrences. Negative ads are typical of contemporary democratic campaigns, above all in the US, but also in some Western European countries. Negative presentation of political opponents and aggressive criticism of them, started at the beginning of the 2000s and systematically increased over the next decades (see Table 30.3). In the case of Law and Justice, there were 15% more fully negative clips in 2007 and 45% more in 2009 in comparison with the parliamentary election in 2005. Additionally, 10% of all the ads in 2005 and 11% in 2007 contained attacks on political opponents. The data show that negative spots were dominant in the 2007 parliamentary campaign. In the case of Law and Justice, fully 45% of the ads were negative and 11% more contained attacks. Civic Platform produced 62% fully negative ads and 2% of ads with negative attacks, and the left party/coalition – 50% and 11% of ads, respectively. Negativity was much greater than in former campaigns (Adamik-Szysiak, 2012, p. 134).

One of the main functions of negative messages is the "we–they" dichotomy between candidates: we have a good program and offer better solutions to society, we are better leaders and more effective than other candidates. Most candidates and parties often used fear in their message. On the one hand, they terrified voters into thinking that voting for their opponents would have negative economic and social consequences, such as an increase in prices, reduction in salaries, problems with health care, social services and others. On the other hand, they attacked their opponents personally in a brutal way and accused them of lack of honesty, corruption, abuse of alcohol and public money, etc. However, the Polish experience with negative advertising shows that it was rather a deceptive way to appeal to voters. In many cases, candidates and committees that directed toxic and hostile ads against their opponents did not win, such as Krzaklewski in 2000 or Law and Justice in 2007.

Television ads were the most popular ads in presidential and parliamentary campaigns in the 2000s. Many studies of local elections confirm that the channel was too expensive in these kinds of campaigns and the main role was played instead by outdoor advertising, posters and flyers.

Television ads played a marginal role in the European Parliament campaigns. Poles were not interested in these elections. The low voter turnout (2004 – 21%, 2005 – 25% and 2014 – 24%) confirms that they were second-order elections (see Figure 30.1). The first campaign to the EP in 2004 passed without a special engagement by political parties. It was a new experience for Polish voters. Civic Platform spent more than €1 million for two hours of television ads on public and private channels, which was more than the Law and Justice Party (about €812,000 for 2.9 hours). Other parties allocated a small part of their budget, such as the peasant party PSL (€319,000 for 1 hour).

The main function of these ads was "image" (74%), followed by "motivation" (13%) and attack (13%). Polish topics (85%) dominated over European ones. A mixed argument was the most frequent one (56%), followed by emotional (29%) and rational (16%) (Mazur, 2010, pp. 146–147). Jacuński and Wiszniowski (2011, p. 92) selected 30 television spots and analyzed their content. They noted that the majority of issues were typical of national elections. About 43% of spots dealt with the economy, 23% with social issues, 20% with international relations, 20% with the Polish constitution and 20% with agriculture. The main parties expressed positive or balanced opinions about the European Union and European integration.

Post-modern Campaign on the Internet

The 2010 presidential and 2011 parliamentary campaigns were the first ones when social media was used on a wider scale but did not threaten or weaken the primary position of television. Less than 50% of the population used the Internet then.

The 2010 presidential campaign was overshadowed by the Smolensk air disaster which killed President Lech Kaczyński. For this reason, television spots were soft and positive. The main candidates avoided aggressive tones, attacks and criticism. Jarosław Kaczyński and Bronisław Komorowski showed mostly biographical and documentary spots. They spoke about their family roots, parents and youth, their activity in the oppositional Solidarity Movement in the communist period. Television was still the main channel of ads distribution, but websites of parties and candidates and YouTube were also used for broadcasting electoral spots.

One year later, in the 2011 parliamentary election, the Poles who voted (31%) and those who did not vote (22%) often looked for information on the Internet. They searched for news about the candidates on the news websites (19%), the social media (13%), the websites of parties (9%) and of candidates (9%). Television news programs (63%), the printed press (38%) and television and radio spots (31%) were the main source of information about the candidates (Batorski, Nagraba, Zając, & Zbieranek, 2012, p. 69). Twenty-six percent of the respondents to a survey indicated that the Internet was their main source of information (Roguska & Zbieranek, 2011). So, at the beginning of the decade, the traditional media retained their priority in political communication and television was the first channel of electoral advertising. The popularity of the candidates' and parties' websites rose significantly in 2011: 48% of the candidates at the top of electoral party lists, 26% of the candidates for the Sejm and 46% of the candidates for the Senate had personal websites (Batorski et al., 2012, p. 22). The same spots were distributed via television and on the party or candidates' websites. It was also possible to watch them on YouTube. A spot of the peasant party PSL, "Man is the most important" (Człowiek…, 2011) was the most popular (more than 220,000 visits). The second most popular spot was the ad of Palikot's Movement, "Do not wake up too late" (Nie budź…, 2011), which was viewed more than 100,000 times. The spots of the main parties – Civic Platform and Law and Justice – had about 50,000 visitors each. One very popular clip of the left party SLD candidate had a few thousand visitors. The most popular spots presented the typical style of "carnivalization" with the participation of singing and dancing politicians. But the popularity of those spots was not reflected in the result of the vote. Both parties lost votes in comparison to the previous election.

The social networks were used in a rather limited way in the presidential election in 2010, but its role grew one year later. Many patterns, which were introduced in Obama's campaign in 2008, were repeated in Poland three years later. Facebook was used by 47%, blogs by 19%, Twitter by 12% of candidates. Facebook was the first channel of activity for 48% of candidates to the Sejm and 42% to the Senate. Almost 60% of the Civic Platform candidates were active on Facebook. Alternative social media played a marginal role. The party of Palikot, which took the third position in the vote (10%), was the most active on Facebook with more than 68,000 fans, and the winner in this campaign, Civic Platform, had about half that amount (33,000). The other parties had much fewer fans (Batorski et al., 2012, pp. 25–27).

It was a phase of full "internetization" of political campaigns in Poland. It was the crucial time for the creation of a "technological duopoly" of Polish voters. Young Poles use only, or mainly, new communication technologies. If they watch television, they do it in a different way. They watch television and use a computer (62%), a mobile (52%) or a tablet (26%) at the same time. About half of them (42%) look for more information about issues presented on television, and 83% of Polish Internet users were multiscreeners in 2014 (Kozielski, 2014, pp. 10–12).

This technological background helps to understand how the idea of political ads in Poland has evolved and changed thoroughly from dominant paid ads in the traditional media, above all on television, to ads distributed free of charge on the Internet and the social media. The same advertisings were distributed via all accessible channels, also by smartphones and tablets.

The EP and local elections in 2014 were a kind of "warm-up" for political actors. They tested their popularity, but also technical and professional skills and possibilities before the most important battle for voters in 2015. Each committee distributed their video spots doubly by television and the Internet. Smaller committees and many candidates preferred websites and social media because they were cheaper. The ruling party, Civic Platform, produced some positive spots and boasted of its political and economic success. Law and Justice, after a long time in opposition, strongly criticized and attacked the ruling party.

The result of the presidential election in May 2015 was a great surprise for Poles. President Bronisław Komorowski was one of the most popular politicians. A popularity rating of over 60% according to different surveys lulled Komorowski and his team into a false sense of security. Additionally, Law and Justice's presidential candidate was not a well-known politician. An awakening came too late after the first round when Duda received more votes. The intensification of Komorowski's campaign in the second round did not change the trend, and he lost the election.

It was the first fully postmodern and mature Internet campaign. It arrived in Poland seven years after Obama's success in 2008. As a representative of the young generation, Duda was open to the new technologies. He has been a user of the Internet and social networks for a long time and he has built his position thanks to them. He has become a well-recognized personage in a short time. But this case shows that the number of fans on Facebook did not automatically translate into election results. The leaders of those rankings lost the election, and Komorowski, who used both media intensively, did not win either.

The social media were the primary tools among the younger generation. Television was still the leading channel for the older generation. Those same video ads were distributed in all accessible technological ways, on television and the Internet.

Positive "image" ads were dominant in the first round, afterwards, they attacked opponents. They showed programs of rivals as a social and economic catastrophe. YouTube was full of extremely negative ads, which were produced by different individual authors not officially linked with the candidates.

In July 2015, 69% of Poles indicated television and 37% the Internet as their source of information about the candidates. The increase was 10% more in the case of television and 23% for the Internet in comparison with the 2011 parliamentary election (Odbiór…, 2015, pp. 1–2).

Poles voted a few months later in the parliamentary election, but the style developed in the previous one was continued, only the actors changed. Finally, alternation of power, typical of democracy, took place not only in the Presidential Palace, but also in the parliament. Conservative Law and Justice led an effective campaign, well-designed by professional agencies and realized by traditional *politicos* – deeply involved members of the party. Liberal Civic Platform made many mistakes and it lost the support of many voters. As a ruling party it was attacked by all of the other parties. Television ads were one of the most important elements of this strategy and a spot of Law and Justice, "Ewa and Friends" (Ewa…, 2015) was one of the most drastic examples. The competitors produced mainly negative and emotional spots. Positive and rational messages were in the minority. In this group, social and economic issues dominated. The parties proposed new programs dedicated to education, family, health and employment policies, tax systems and propositions for agriculture. Law and Justice produced a series of spots each of which explicated one topic in a simple way so that an average voter could understand it. Those issue ads were placed, above all, on the party's campaign website. Civic Platform produced some negative, emotional spots against Law and Justice and attacked its leaders Jarosław Kaczyński and Beata Szydło. Apart from them, this party also distributed positive personal ads which promoted Ewa Kopacz, and issued ads dedicated to the party's program. Other parties also produced ads but they had much smaller campaign budgets at their disposal and only a few of them were distributed via television, as they mostly used the Internet and YouTube.

In summary, easier access to the new tools was reflected in political communication. Poles voted seven times since 2010: once in the European Parliament (2014), twice in local (2010, 2014), presidential (2010, 2015) and parliamentary elections (2011, 2015). The analysis of political ads shows that television ads were systematically moved to the Internet and the difference between ads distributed by those two media was blurred. Many commentators and politicians agreed with the opinion that the campaigns in 2015 were crucial for the Polish political scene, as they changed its structure and character. They showed clearly "two Polands" composed of two categories of citizens – older television viewers and younger Internet users. In a fact, this same political messages reached those generations but thanks to another medium.

Conclusion

In a short time, Poland has come a long way from an unprofessional to professional political advertising market. Citizens had to learn democratic standards. Political actors found out how to use the traditional and new media efficiently in communication with voters. The gap which existed between Poland and full democracies in Europe was vast both in the technical aspect of communication and in the political culture of politicians and voters at the beginning of the transformation. But in Central and Eastern Europe time "has passed" more quickly than in other parts of the world. Electoral campaigns with audiovisual advertisements underwent a deep evolution in three phases after the collapse of communism. The first premodern phase in the 1990s was still unprofessional with the predominance of ads in the print media, posters and flyers. Television and audiovisual spots played a secondary role. The pattern changed completely in the 2000s when television was the first channel of political communication and thanks to television ads had a preferential position. This phase can be called a televised one. The third postmodern period of development of television ads was very dynamic in Poland. The parties' and candidates' websites were also well recognized at that time but the real technological revolution happened in the 2010s with the implementation of the social media. They radically changed political communication, electoral campaigns and spots. On the one hand, thanks to easy access to the new technologies, political actors and voters have learned how to use them effectively and put them into political practice. This technology encouraged individual politicians and committees to produce many more clips than in the previous periods. Their publication on websites and distribution via the social networks was cheaper and accessible not only to the main actors but also to small parties. On the other hand, the marketing, public relations and advertisement market in Poland was well developed, just as in Western Europe. Many specialists and professional agencies appeared then and they supported political actors. But television was also in use. The committee staffs had to reach all generations of voters. Only the parallel distribution of spots via television and the Internet guaranteed effective communication. The younger generation uses the Internet and the social media, the older generation draws its knowledge about politics from television. Additionally, technological development obliterates borders and distinctions between typical video spots of political actors and their public relations activity on the Internet and the social media. It also allows users to play not only the role of a receiver but also of message senders. They can comment and add their opinions to political discourse.

A content analysis showed that negative spots appeared more often than positive ones. The conclusion made by Kaid and Holtz-Bacha (2006, p. 454) can be repeated in the case of Polish video ads that election committees more frequently relied on emotional than logical appeals. More clips concentrated on the candidates' image and non-programmatic elements than on issues and programs. In general, the style and climate of Polish spots were close to American patterns, and Americanization is a visible feature of Polish campaigns. There is no doubt that video ads are one of the most important kinds of campaign messages.

References

Adamik-Szysiak, M. (2012). *Telewizyjna reklama polityczna w Polsce w latach 2005–2010 [TV political advertising in Poland 2005–2010]*. Lublin: Wydawnictwo UMCS.

Batorski, D., Nagraba, M., Zając. J. M., & Zbieranek, J. (2012). *Internet w kampanii wyborczej 2011 [Internet in the 2011 campaign]*. Warszawa: Fundacja Instytut Spraw Publicznych.

Benoit, W. (2007). *Communication in political campaigns*. New York, NY: Peter Lang.

Caspi, D., & Leshem B. (2006). From electoral propaganda to poltical advertising in Israel. In L. L. Kaid & C. Holtz-Bacha (Eds.), *The Sage handbook of international political advertising* (pp. 109–129). Thousand Oaks, CA: Sage.

Cwalina, W., & Falkowski, A. (2006). *Marketing polityczny*. Gdańsk: Gdańskie Wydawnictwo Psychologiczne.

Cześnik, M. (2009). *Partycypacja wyborcza Polaków [Electoral participation of Poles]*. Warsaw: The Institute of Public Affairs.

Człowiek jest najważniejszy [Man is the most important]. (2011, August 25). Retrieved from www.youtube.com/watch?v=hrHYXMvoBao.

Dobek-Ostrowska, B. (2007). *Komunikowanie polityczne i publiczne [Political and public communication]*. Warszawa: WN PWN.

Ewa i przyjaciele [Ewa and Friends]. (2015, October 13). Retrieved from www.youtube.com/ watch?v=mLnoep JzBzs.

Farrell, D. M., Kolodny, R., & Medvic, S. K. (2001). Parties and campaign professionals in a digital age: Political consultants in the United States and their counterparts overseas. *The International Journal of Press/Politics*, 6(4),11–30. doi: 10.1177/108118001129172314.

Grabiec, P. (2015, May 18). *Oto nowy raport dotyczący dostępu do Internetu w Polsce [This is a new report dedicated to Internet access in Poland]*. Retrieved from www.spidersweb.pl/2015/05/dostep-do-internetu-w-polsce.html.

Informacja o wydatkach i wykorzystaniu czasu antenowego w radiu i telewizji na emisję płatnych ogłoszeń wyborczych zleconych przez Komitety Wyborcze w trakcie kampanii wyborczej do Sejmu i Senatu Rzeczpospolitej Polskiej w 2005 roku [Information about costs and use of a paid time for advertising in radio and TV of Electoral Committees during the electoral campaign to Sejm and Senate in Poland in 2005]. (2005, December 10). Retrieved from www.krrit.gov.pl/Data/Files/_public/pliki/publikacje/biuletyn/nr_06_10_12.pdf.

Jacuński, M., & Wiszniowski, R. (2011). Telewizyjna reklama polityczna w kampanii do Parlamentu Europejskiego w 2009 roku. [TV political advertising in the 2009 European Parliamentary election]. In B. Dobek-Ostrowska & K. Majdecka (Eds.), *Studia empiryczne nad komunikowaniem politycznym w Polsce [Empirical studies in political communication in Poland]* (pp. 85–98). Wrocław: WUWr.

Kaid, L. L. (2004). Political advertising. In L. L. Kaid (Ed.), *Political communication research* (pp. 155–202). Mahwah, NJ: Lawrence Erlbaum.

Kaid, L. L., & Holtz-Bacha, C. (2006). Television advertising and democratic systems around the world. In L. L. Kaid & C. Holtz-Bacha (Eds.), *The Sage handbook of political advertising* (pp. 445–457). Thousand Oaks, CA: Sage.

Komunikat Państwowej Komisji Wyborczej z dnia 16 stycznia 2006 r [Report of State Electoral Commission from January 16, 2006]. (2006a, January 16). Retrieved from http://pkw.gov.pl/wybory-do-sejmu-rp-i-do-senatu-rp-2005/.html.

Komunikat Państwowej Komisji Wyborczej z dnia 30 stycznia 2006 r [Report of State Electoral Commission from January 30, 2006]. (2006b, January 30). Retrieved from http://pkw.gov.pl/wybory-prezydenta-rp-2005/.html.

Komunikat Państwowej Komisji Wyborczej z dnia 30 stycznia 2008 r [Report of State Electoral Commission from January 30, 2008]. (2008, January 30). Retrieved from http://pkw.gov.pl/wybory-do-sejmu-rp-i-do-senatu-rp-2007/.html.

Komunikat Państwowej Komisji Wyborczej z dnia 11 października 2010 r [Report of State Electoral Commission from October 11, 2010]. (2010, October 11). Retrieved from http://pkw.gov.pl/2010–22877/.html.

Kozielski, M. (2014, September). Content is king. *Press. Wydanie specjalne*, 9, 4–14.

Mazur, M. (2005). Negatywna telewizyjna reklama polityczna. Doświadczenia amerykańskie i polskie [Negative TV political ads]. In B. Dobek-Ostrowska (Ed.), *Kampania wyborcza: Marketingowe aspekty komunikowania politycznego [Electoral campaign: The marketing aspects of political communication]* (pp. 77–95). Wrocław: WUWr.

Mazur, M. (2010). Who will care about the Polish interests? In M. Kolczyński (Ed.), *The picture of the European Parliament elections (2009)* (pp. 136–152). Katowice: WNiA.

Mazzoleni, G. (2006). TV political advertising in Italy: When politicians are afraid. In L. L. Kaid & C. Holtz-Bacha (Eds.), *The Sage handbook of political advertising* (pp. 241–258). Thousand Oaks, CA: Sage.

Nakłady gazet 2005–2012 [Edition of newspapers 2005–2012]. (2013, February 14). Retrieved from www.iwp. pl/rynek_prasy.php.

Nie budź się za poźno [Do not wake up too late]. (2011, September 16). Retrieved from www.youtube.com/ watch?v=6sSqs3jwtWA.

Odbiór kampanii wyborczej i aktywność polityczna w internecie [Reception of electoral campaign and political activity in internet]. (2015, July). Retrieved from www.cbos.pl/SPISKOM.POL/2015/K_098_ 15.PDF.

Parlamentarna kampania wyborcza w 2007 roku [Parliamentary election campaign in 2007]. (2007, November 5). Retrieved from www.krrit.gov.pl/Data/Files/_public/Portals/0/kontrola/program/kampania_parlamen-tarna_2007.pdf.

Porto, M. P. (2006). Political advertising and democracy in Brazil. In L. L. Kaid & C. Holtz-Bacha (Eds.), *The Sage handbook of political advertising* (pp. 129–143). Thousand Oaks, CA: Sage.

Prejs, A. (2015, April 16). Kampania prezydencka w social media. [Presidential campaign in the social media]. Retrieved from http://blog.sotrender.com/pl/2015/04/kampania-prezydencka-w-social-media/#close.

Raport AdEx 2014 – wydatki na reklamę online w roku 2014 [Report of AdEx 2014 – expenses for ads on the internet in 2014]. (2015, April 1). Retrieved from http://iab.org.pl/badania-i-publikacje/ raport- adex-2014-wydatki-na-reklame-online-w-roku-2014/.

Roguska, B., & Zbieranek, J. (2011). *Wiedza i opinie Polaków o prawie wyborczym i mechanizmach kampanii [Knowledge and opinion of Poles about election law and mechanism of campaign]*. Warszawa: ISP.

Rozwój demograficzny Polski 2012 [Demographic development of Poland in 2012]. (2013, January 31). Retrieved from www.egospodarka.pl/art/galeria/90411,Ludnosc-wedlug-ekonomicznych-grup-wieku-w-wybranych-latach,14,39,1.html.

Rynek reklamowy w Polsce wzrośnie [Ads market in Poland grows]. (2015, September 16). Retrieved from www.wirtualnemedia.pl/artykul/rynek-reklamowy-w-polsce-wzrosnie-o-2-4-proc-dzieki-internetowi-telewizji-i-radiu-globalnie-zyska-4-proc.

Scammell, M., & Langer, I. (2006). Political advertising in the United Kingdom. In L. L. Kaid & C. Holtz-Bacha (Eds.), *The Sage handbook of political advertising* (pp. 65–82). Thousand Oaks, CA: Sage.

Tuman, J. S. (2008). *Political communication in American campaigns*. Thousand Oaks, CA: Sage.

Walecki, M. (2001). Finansowanie kampanii wyborczej [Financing of electoral campaigns]. In S. Wilkos & W. Ferenc (Eds.), *Kampania wyborcza [Electoral campaign]* (pp. 143–168). Warszawa: Wydawnictwo Sejmowe.

31

THE RISE OF TELEVISION ADVERTISING IN A TRADITIONAL CAMPAIGN ENVIRONMENT

The Case of South Africa

Robert Mattes and Ian Glenn

Introduction

Voters learn about politics through a range of "information intermediaries" including personal discussants, social organizations, news media and political parties (Gunther, Beck, Magalhaes, & Moreno, 2016; Gunther, Montero, & Puhle, 2006). However, political advertising is one of the ways that political parties can communicate directly with voters free of the screens or biases provided by those other intermediaries. As a "fourth wave" democracy (Berg-Schlosser, 2009; Dorenspleet, 2000; McFaul, 2002), South Africa has traversed, in a relatively short period, the span from a total prohibition of television campaign advertising in its first three democratic elections (1994, 1999 and 2004) to an environment in its most recent elections (2009 and 2014) in which political parties are allowed to purchase advertising time on both private and public television networks, and where the public broadcaster is also required to provide free advertising time. Thus, South Africa provides a laboratory in which to understand effects of political advertising in a new democracy.

Prohibition: 1994 to 2008

The relatively recent arrival of television advertising to South Africa's electoral environment has nothing to do with that society's ability to design, produce or broadcast such advertisements. Indeed, South Africa's advertising industry is sophisticated and displays an unusual degree of humor and satire, and regularly receives international awards. Rather, the absence of television electoral advertising was a result of decisions made in the run-up to the country's first democratic election in 1994, and continued by the newly created Independent Communications Authority of South Africa (ICASA). Television advertising was explicitly banned, according to South African media scholar Ruth Teer-Tomaselli (2006), on the grounds that its cost made it less equitable than radio, and that it was seen by the regulators to be particularly persuasive. Instead, political parties were allowed to present their views through two-minute "public election broadcasts" on South African Broadcasting Corporation *radio* stations, distributed on "equitable" rather than an "equal" basis (Teer-Tomaselli, 2006), meaning that time was allocated on the basis of a formula that took into account each party's legislative representation and the number of candidates it was currently fielding (Davis, 2005; Teer-Tomaselli, 2006). Parties were also permitted to buy any amount of additional advertising time on radio, or space in newspapers (Teer-Tomaselli, 2006). Political parties have used and continue to use billboards and posters on a widespread basis. Ironically, while South Africa's electoral system of closed party-list proportional representations is dominated by parties, its parliamentary system grants unusual powers to the chief executive (called a "President") around whom parties center their election campaigns. The effect is best exemplified in the typical photograph on posters and billboards of the presidential candidate who heads the party list.

However, given the huge electoral advantages the African National Congress (ANC) has enjoyed over its competitors, stemming from its successful struggle to bring an end to the *apartheid* regime, and the ANC's continuing electoral alliance with the Congress of South African Trade Unions (COSATU), the prohibition of television advertising was far from a neutral, public-spirited decision. Television election campaign advertising is one of the quickest ways that an opposition party, particularly a new one, can reach a large number of voters, build a distinctive image in voters' minds, and present a case for why they offer voters a preferable alternative to the governing party. But an electoral environment without television advertising leaves political parties, especially new and/or small parties, with the options of paying for advertisements on radio or in newspapers (with print being particularly expensive), or contacting voters directly in order to present their cases.

While the South African state has provided public funds to political parties since 1997, the lion's share of this money (90%) is allocated to national party organizations based on their *current* national and provincial legislative representation. The remainder (10%) of the fund is divided across the county's provincial legislatures, depending on their size, and given equally to each party represented in that assembly. The net effect is that the electorally dominant ANC receives the great proportion of public funds. If public funding is meant to support multi-party democracy by creating a level playing field on which voters are able to choose from a range of alternatives, this is hardly the way to achieve this.

Public funds, moreover, cover only a small share of all campaign expenses. In 1999, for example, the country's parties collectively spent an estimated R300 to R500 million on their election campaigns, but received only R53 million from the public purse. Thus, parties have to look to private donors to make up this massive shortfall. While South Africa's political parties are not required to disclose the funds received from private sources, it is widely believed that the ANC (due to its control over public policy and state contracts) and the largest opposition party, the Democratic Alliance (DA) (due to its historical links with the business community) receive far more private donations than any other political party. Certainly, only the ANC and to a lesser extent DA are able to employ professional, permanent staff for things like fund-raising, market research, policy development or publicity. In the 2004 campaign, these two parties dominated the rest across all forms of advertising media, with the ANC outpacing the DA in spending on paid outdoor advertising (such as billboards, murals and ads on taxis) by R12 million to just R200,000, and in print advertising by R3.8 million to R800,000. Yet the DA actually purchased more radio time than the ANC by R5.9 million to R4.8 million. Other opposition parties were largely restricted to a heavy reliance on street-side posters which contain only very simple messages and captions (Davis, 2005).

In terms of direct contacting, the ANC's electoral alliance with COSATU has given it the ability to deploy union officials to canvass voters and transport them to the polls on Election Day. For example, the 2015 South African National Election Study (Centre for Social Science Research, 2015) found that the ANC directly contacted 29% of the electorate in the 2014 campaign, more than twice the number of its main competitors, the DA (14%) and the new entry Economic Freedom Fighters (EFF) (8%), and at least three-quarters of those ANC contacts (21%) were in-person visits.

The Advent and Use of Television Campaign Advertising: 2009 to 2014

The rules governing South Africa's campaign environment shifted abruptly in 2008. Following the September 2008 removal of Thabo Mbeki as president by the ANC, several high-profile

ANC officials and former union leaders led a breakaway group to register a new political party, the Congress of the People (COPE), to challenge the ANC in the upcoming 2009 election. While Mbeki proclaimed his loyalty to the ANC, the new party was believed by many to have Mbeki's support if not advice and direction. With little warning, South Africa's Independent Communications Authority – whose Board and chief operating officer had been appointed by Mbeki – issued new regulations in late 2008 that would clearly advantage a new start-up party such as COPE. As in other national media systems dominated by public broadcasters (Holtz-Bacha, 2014), all television broadcasting license holders were now required to provide four two-minute time slots every day for "public election broadcasts" during the designated campaign period (a move that was strongly opposed by the SABC on the grounds that it could not afford the time).[1] And in contrast to the formula for allocating multi-party funding (which favored large parties like the ANC), airtime would be allocated proportionally based only on the current number of *candidates* fielded by a party (rather than by its number of currently elected legislative representatives) (Independent Communications Authority of South Africa, 2009). Perhaps as important, the new regulations also enabled political parties to purchase commercial television airtime for partisan "political advertisements." Therefore, as long as they were able to field a full slate of candidates, opposition parties were provided with the possibility of reaching a national audience and cutting into the ANC's huge advantage in direct, explicit face-to-face party campaigning, meetings and rallies (as well as its ability to make more implicit, indirect partisan contacts through government officials, or government events such as openings of housing or infrastructure projects) (Booysen, 2014; Schulz-Herzenberg, 2014).

By 2014, however, with a Board and senior leadership, now dominated by officials appointed by President Jacob Zuma, ICASA changed the formula for allocating free airtime to include both the number of candidates *and* the size of current parliamentary representation. And where the 2009 regulations allowed parties to recycle their free airtime advertisements in commercial spots, the 2014 rules stipulated that content broadcast in free time could not be re-used in commercial slots (Duncan, 2014; Independent Communications Authority of South Africa, 2014a). Both rule changes had the effect of diluting the access of small parliamentary parties as well as new start-up parties.

Assessing the Impact of Television Campaign Advertising

Extent of Television Advertising

The first issue to consider is timing. The new regulations on television advertising were only promulgated in late 2008. This gave political parties little warning in advance of the upcoming April 2009 election. And in both 2009 and 2014, free airtime spots could only be allocated once the South African Independent Electoral Commission had verified each party's slate of candidates. Thus, political parties were only able to air their advertisements in the final weeks of the campaign. Furthermore, while the airtime was free, parties still had to find people to design and produce the ads, and pay them for their services. Thus, in 2009, political parties used just 40 of the 84 free two-minute spots made available by the SABC (Schreiner & Mattes, 2012). And in 2014, while 19 parties made use of free radio time, just 12 made use of free television time (Duncan, 2014). However, because parties were able to purchase additional commercial slots, a total of 368 advertisements were aired on television between mid-February and Election Day 2009 (Schreiner & Mattes, 2012). But as a result of the rule changes from 2009 to 2014 described above, the total number of advertisements aired in 2014 actually declined from 368 to 259 (Independent Communications Authority of South Africa, 2014b; Schreiner & Mattes, 2012). And while 12 parties made use of the "party election broadcasts" spots in 2014, only seven parties paid for additional political advertising slots (Duncan, 2014).

Content of Television Advertisements

Most South Africans could probably recall dozens of humorous or serious local television advertisements produced by sophisticated advertising agencies, powerful political cartoons such as those by internationally acclaimed Jonathan Shapiro, or even the political caricatures images provided by the South African equivalent of Spitting Image, ZaNews. Yet most people would struggle to recall even one or two television or radio advertisements for a political party. One reason that political advertising has been so tame is that while South African advertising is often humorous, negative or comparative advertising has not been permitted as a result of a kind of "gentleman's agreement" between members of the Advertising Standards Authority. South African media have tended to see their role as providing balance. Talk show hosts, for example, usually play a centralizing or balancing role rather than the tendentious and partisan role common in the US. Thus, it may be that parties concluded that advertisements which seem nasty or negative were out of touch with prevailing cultural norms.

The ANC has certainly had a deliberate strategy of positive campaigning. As various commentators like Tom Lodge (2005) and Antony Butler (2009) have pointed out, its campaign advertising – developed by Ogilvy SA – has been professional, but uncontroversial, featuring high definition images and focusing on its own achievements, rather than criticizing other political parties (also see Ranchod, 2013; Sindane, 2014). According to Butler (2009, p. 65) it has been in the ANC's interest "to keep the temperature of these campaigns low, in order to starve opposition parties of the media coverage and controversy they required to mobilize recalcitrant core voters. The liberation movement could rely on citizens' quite limited knowledge of what opposition parties represent and why they should be deserving of attention."

The ANC's R8.1 million (Schreiner & Mattes, 2012) 2009 television campaign spots featured testimonials by a number of ordinary people corresponding to key ANC target constituencies, each talking about how their everyday lives had been affected by Nelson Mandela, the ANC and the transformation it had brought, but also ended with presidential candidate Jacob Zuma pronouncing a few standard campaign slogans (Ranchod, 2013; Zvomuya, 2009). However, their 2014 R17.9 million (Sarakinsky, 2014) television campaign saw a sharply reduced emphasis on the incumbent Zuma, given his scandal-plagued first term in office, and played powerfully on the notion of a society in which things had improved steadily for black South Africans. It invoked, to use a phrase from Henry James, the "commonplace prosperity" of many black South Africans with improved standards of living and access to better housing, water and electricity as justification of ANC government over two decades.

The main opposition DA's 2014 television campaign, assisted by American pollster Stanley Greenberg (who had worked for the ANC in the 1990s) and advertising agency Saatchi & Abel, spent R13 million on television (three times as much as the R4.1 million it spent in 2009) (Sarakinsky, 2014; Schreiner & Mattes, 2012), and included a series of "Know Your DA" spots to try and overcome its regnant image as a party for whites and other minorities. One spot showed party leader Helen Zille looking through her scrapbook to highlight her anti-*apartheid* credentials as a young crusading journalist who had helped expose the police's murder of Steve Biko in the 1970s. More controversially (see below), other ads used Mmusi Maimane, the new, young black leader of its large Gauteng region (Johannesburg and Pretoria) and adopted a much more aggressive approach aimed at black voters, under the slogan of "Ayisafani iANC" ("The ANC, it is not the same"). Maimane, speaking to himself in a mirror, argued that the ANC, under Zuma, had reversed the gains achieved under the country's first two presidents, Nelson Mandela and Thabo Mbeki (Chiumbu & Ciaglia, 2015; Jolobe, 2014, pp. 64–65). The new 2014 opposition entry, the Economic Freedom Fighters, led by the firebrand, former leader of the ANC Youth League Julius Malema, produced a spot that highlighted the brutality used by the South African police in an infamous, violent 2012 confrontation with striking miners at Marikana. However, as we will see below, this advertisement never saw the light of day on broadcast television.

We have already seen the extent to which smaller, less well-resourced opposition parties were unable to take full advantage of the free "public election broadcasts." Yet the advertisements that they did manage to produce have often been amateurish and put together by people with little grasp of how to communicate political messages. For instance, another widely anticipated 2014 start-up party, Agang, led by Mamphela Ramphele, former partner of Steve Biko, university president, and vice president of the World Bank, ran an ad that featured Ramphele who adopted a tone of severe disapproval of government expenditure on Zuma's private home, but resorted to catch-phrases that many of her audience probably did not understand, i.e., "This is a poster-child for corruption in the ANC."

State Regulation of Content

Another important dimension of South Africa's regulatory environment is the prohibition of any ad which violates the Constitution or other electoral legislation, or is "calculated, or that in the ordinary course is likely to provoke or incite any unlawful, illegal or criminal act, or that may be perceived as condoning or lending support to any such act" (Independent Communications Authority of South Africa, 2009, pp. 7, 9). These provisions were invoked on at least two occasions in 2014 when the public broadcaster, the SABC, refused to air DA and EFF advertisements.

The SABC contended that the visual screen statement at the end of the EFF advertisement, "Destroy e-tolls physically," combined with footage of police pointing guns, and reference to police killings, all constituted an incitement to violence, and also (along with references to government corruption) constituted the publication of false information. An ICASA tribunal subsequently agreed that the ad could be perceived as condoning or supporting illegal acts (ICASA, 2014b, p. 31). And seizing on the DA ad's assertion that "We've seen a police force killing our own people," the SABC argued that the spot, which showed video of police violence against citizens, was likely to incite violence, provided false information, violated advertising industry standards, and contained a personal attack on the president. After a legal response by the DA, the SABC agreed to air the ad and postpone further proceedings indefinitely. But a few days later, the South African Police Service lodged its own complaint and an ICASA tribunal sided with the police (Chiumbu & Ciaglia, 2015; ICASA, 2014b, pp. 30–34). An amended version of the ad was finally aired, but only after all references to police killings were removed.

Both the ICASA regulation and the actions of the SABC have received severe criticism from South African media scholars. Chiumbu and Ciaglia (2015) argue that the ICASA regulations are constitutionally questionable, and Duncan (2014, p. 146) has called them "overbroad," going further than the South African Constitution, which excludes only the incitement to imminent violence as a form of protected speech, concluding that "the censorious nature of ICASA's regulations suggests they were not designed to facilitate electoral competition, which requires minimal restrictions on freedom of expression to ensure a thorough airing of political differences."

Chiumbu and Ciaglia (2015, p. 149) conclude that the action of the SABC "undermines freedom of expression and the credibility of both the SABC and ICASA" (Chiumbu & Ciaglia, 2015, p. 149). And Schulz-Herzenberg (2014, p. 6) has argued that the SABC's decision "hindered the EFF's and DA's ability to reach a national audience in the crucial weeks before the election." In some ways, the banning was self-defeating: after the SABC's refusal to air the DA ad, it was viewed by nearly a half a million people on YouTube in less than a day (Jolobe, 2014). But the SABC's actions clearly blocked both ads from a wider viewership, particularly among poorer South Africans without digital access.

Assessing the Impact of Television Campaign Advertising in South Africa

Exposure to Party Advertisements?

As suggested at the top of this chapter, voters learn about politics through a range of "information intermediaries" including personal discussants, social organizations, news media and political parties (Gunther et al., 2006, 2016). While political parties try to communicate to voters indirectly via those other intermediaries, they also attempt to communicate to voters directly: to those who work in their campaigns, who attend their rallies, and who they contact through various forms of traditional canvassing. They also use political advertisements, however, to make direct appeals to voters over the heads of those other intermediaries. Thus, the first potential impact of the advent of television broadcast advertising in South Africa might be that it has expanded the reach of South Africa's political parties, enabling them to make direct, unmediated contact with a far wider audience of voters.

In order to examine this, and other potential impacts, we turn to data from the South African National Election Project, a series of post-election surveys carried out, initially by the Institute for Democracy in South Africa (1994 and 1999) and then by the University of Cape Town (2004, 2009, 2014).[2] Subsequent to ICASA's abrupt change of regulations of political advertising in 2008, we added a series of questions in the 2009 and 2015 surveys. After asking respondents about the frequency with which they used television, radio, newspapers and social media to follow the election campaign, we asked them whether they remembered seeing, hearing or reading any party election advertisements, and then which specific parties.

To what extent did television advertising expand the ability of political parties to take their appeals directly to the voters, compared to more traditional methods of direct contacting and attending rallies? In 2004, the South African National Election Study (SANES) found that more than one-third of all potential voters had either worked for a party campaign (5%), attended a party rally (23%) or were contacted by a party (26%), with a total of 38% of the electorate taking part in at least one of these activities (Centre for Social Science Research, 2004). As the ANC faced greater competition from the DA, as well as from splinter parties COPE (in 2009) and the EFF (in 2014), the intensity of its traditional campaigning increased, eventually coming into contact with 44% of all voters by 2014 (see Table 31.1). However, taking the number of people exposed to any form of campaign advertising (print, radio or television), fully seven-in-ten (71% in 2009 and 70% in 2014) voters were contacted by a party, or exposed to at least one form of political advertising.

However, television advertising played an especially important role in this regard as the number of voters exposed to a television advertisement significantly outpaced other formats. While there was a decline in the number of people who either read or heard a newspaper or radio ad between 2009 (45%) and 2014 (35%), the number of people exposed to a television ad increased over the same period from 42% to 48%. Four-in-ten voters (42%) recalled seeing a television advertisement in 2009, increasing to 48% in 2014 (see Table 31.2). Thus, access to television significantly expanded the reach

Table 31.1 Did television advertising expand parties' unmediated contact with voters?

	2004 (%)	2009 (%)	2014 (%)
Work for political party	5	4	4
Attend party rally	23	31	28
Contacted by party	26	23	35
Worked, or attended, or contacted by party	38	40	44
Worked, or attended, or contacted, or read, heard or saw any advertisement	–	71	70

Source: South African National Election Study (Centre for Social Science Research, 2004, 2009, 2015).

Table 31.2 Total campaign advertisements read, heard, watched

	2009	2014
Internet/social media	1	2
Newspapers	30	7
Radio	31	33
Read or hear any advertisement	46	35
Television	42	48
See, or read or hear any advertisement	59	57

Source: South African National Election Study (Centre for Social Science Research, 2009, 2015).

of the campaign to a larger slice of the electorate than would have been achieved by strategies based only on radio and print.

A second potential impact of the advent of television advertising in South Africa would be to not only expand the exposure of voters to unmediated partisan messages, but also level the playing field, or at least reduce the gap in terms of direct access to voters between the electorally dominant ANC and opposition parties. The SANES data suggest that this is indeed the case (see Table 31.3). In 2014, the ANC held a 3:1 advantage over the closest opposition party, DA, in terms of the numbers of people who saw one of their newspaper advertisements, and a 2.6:1 advantage in the numbers who heard their radio spots. In terms of television, however, the ANC held just a 1.8:1 advantage.

A third potential impact might be that television ads have helped parties reach beyond their traditional support bases. We know that parties across the world, especially those that rely on traditional campaign methods, tend to focus on turning out their "base" supporters, rather than convert independent voters – especially in countries with polarized, party (rather than candidate) based systems like South Africa (Karp, 2012). Thus, we anticipate television advertising to have also reached a far higher proportion of non-partisan voters. The data in Table 31.4 not only show the same declining advantages of the ANC over all opposition parties collectively when one moves from traditional campaigning or print and newspaper advertisements (1.4:1) to television (1.1:1). They also demonstrate that almost four-in-ten (38%) independent voters recall seeing a campaign television ad, compared to just one-quarter of non-partisans who recall hearing a radio or reading a newspaper ad, or being contacted in traditional canvassing methods.

Accordingly, a fourth potential impact of television ads, particularly relevant to South Africa's unique history, may be that it has enabled political parties to reach across racial lines. South African newspapers and radio stations historically have been targeted at specific linguistic, and thus racial, audiences. Thus, we expect to find that television advertising reduced the racial distance between South Africa's political parties. Since 1994, few black voters have ever voted for a political party that cannot trace its roots in some way to the country's liberation movement, and few whites have voted for a party that did not trace its roots to the old apartheid political system, with colored and Indian voters somewhere in between, though far less likely to vote for parties linked to the liberation struggle.

Table 31.5 breaks down the identity of those who recall seeing different types of ANC and DA ads by race. The results demonstrate, indeed, that television has exposed many more white, colored and Indian voters to ANC messages, and black voters to DA messages, than either radio or print advertising. Where less than one-tenth of white, colored or Indian voters heard or read an ANC ad on radio or newspapers, one-quarter saw one of its television ads. Conversely, television has given the historically "white" DA far more exposure to black voters. While less than one-in-ten black voters heard or read a DA ad, 17% saw one of their television advertisements. Thus, television

Table 31.3 Television advertisements: whose advertisements were seen (compared to other methods)?

	2009	2014
Television		
African National Congress (ANC)	38	35
Democratic Alliance (DA)	23	19
Congress of the People (COPE)	19	3
Independent Democrats (ID)	7	–
Inkatha Freedom Party (IFP)	5	1
Economic Freedom Fighters (EFF)	–	5
Other parties	12	3
Radio		
African National Congress (ANC)	29	26
Democratic Alliance (DA)	12	10
Congress of the People (COPE)	10	2
Independent Democrats (ID)	3	–
Inkatha Freedom Party (IFP)	6	1
Economic Freedom Fighters (EFF)	–	3
Other parties	4	3
Newspapers		
African National Congress (ANC)	27	6
Democratic Alliance (DA)	16	2
Congress of the People (COPE)	13	1
Independent Democrats (ID)	5	–
Inkatha Freedom Party (IFP)	7	<1
Economic Freedom Fighters (EFF)	–	1
Other parties	–	1

Source: South African National Election Study (Centre for Social Science Research, 2009, 2015).

Table 31.4 Unmediated exposure to political parties

	2009			2014		
	ANC	Opposition	Non-partisan	ANC	Opposition	Non-partisan
Work, rally or contact	46	46	23	61	44	27
Radio or newspaper ad	51	45	37	46	33	25
See TV advertisement	45	39	37	56	51	38

Source: South African National Election Study (Centre for Social Science Research, 2009, 2015).

advertising helped move South Africa's electoral environment closer to the ideal of a common, national conversation.

A fifth and final potential impact of television advertising may have been to engage more voters in the electoral process, convince them to turnout and vote, and ultimately enhance their attitudes toward the electoral process. As can be seen in Figure 31.1, voter turnout and campaign interest plunged in the period between South Africa's 1994 founding election of Nelson Mandela and the 2004 re-election of Thabo Mbeki. Significantly, television advertising was banned during this period. However, once television advertising was introduced, voter turnout stabilized. And while general

Table 31.5 Did television advertising expand intra-racial contact?

	2009		2014	
	Black	White, colored, Indian	Black	White, colored, Indian
ANC newspaper ads	25	31	6	4
ANC radio ads	32	19	31	7
ANC television ads	39	37	37	27
DA newspaper ads	11	31	1	4
DA radio ads	10	18	8	14
DA television ads	21	30	17	24

Source: South African National Election Study (Centre for Social Science Research, 2009, 2015).

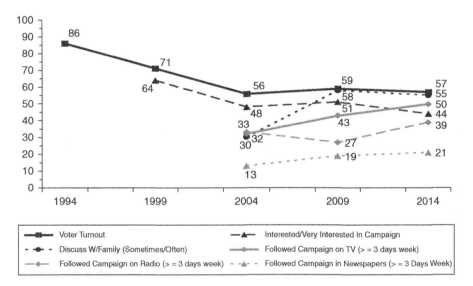

Figure 31.1 Election campaign engagement, 1999–2014

campaign interest continued to decrease, the frequency with which South Africans discussed the campaign, and followed the campaign through various news media, increased significantly. Is this mere coincidence, or is there any evidence that television advertising had a discernible impact on the engagement of South African voters with the political system?

Before we attempt to assess the impact of exposure to television campaign ads, we first assess the extent to which those who saw an ad also differed on other demographic or cognitive variables, variables that might themselves affect campaign engagement (see Table 31.6). As indicated previously, during the 2014 campaign, 48% of all citizens recalled seeing a partisan advertisement. While there were no significant differences according to gender or race, urbanized (52%), educated (high school graduates, 52%), older respondents (those aged 66 to 75, 54%), were slightly more likely to have seen an advertisement. In terms of partisanship, those who identified with any political party, in general (54%), and the ANC, in particular (56%) saw an ad. But the largest impacts occurred with respect to news media use (79% of those who watched television campaign news on a "daily" basis saw an ad) and interest in politics (61% of those who were "very interested in politics" saw an ad).

Table 31.6 Who saw television advertisements?

	2014	
	Percent	*Coefficients*
All respondents	48	
Campaign TV use (daily)	79	0.529★★★
Interest in politics ("very interested")	61	0.204★★★
Party identification (ANC)	56	0.166★★★
Partisanship (identifier)	54	0.161★★★
Age (66 to 75)	54	0.052★★
High school graduates	52	0.086★★★
Residential location (urban)	52	0.118★★★
Race (blacks)	49	NS
Gender (men)	49	NS

Notes: Cells in the "Coefficient" column display Kendall's Tau B coefficients (with exception of nominal variables, in which case the coefficient is Cramer's V).
★★ $p \le .01$, ★★★ $p \le .001$.

Source: South African National Election Study (Centre for Social Science Research, 2015).

Thus, in order to assess the possible impact of exposure to television campaign advertising on election campaign engagement, we estimate a series of logistic regression models that control for respondents' gender, urban–rural status, race, age, level of education, partisanship, level of interest in politics, and frequency of news media use during the election campaign. And to isolate the precise impact of television ads, we also control for whether the respondent read a print ad or heard a radio ad.

While the effects of exposure were not consistent across all variables tested, the results in Table 31.7 demonstrate several important results. In terms of campaign knowledge, those who were exposed to a television advertisement were better able to provide interviewers with the name of the leader of the official opposition party (DA leader Helen Zille) and to tell interviewers whether they had a favorable or unfavorable view of the DA. Indeed, the impact on the ability to rate the DA was substantial: those who had seen a television ad were more than three times as able to provide a rating (positive or negative) of the DA than those who had not. There were no such impacts, however, with regard to the ability to provide ratings of the governing ANC, or the start-up EFF.

And with regard to campaign discussion, respondents who had seen a campaign television ad were about 50% more likely to have discussed the campaign with family members, though no effect exists for other forms of campaign discussion (neighbors, friends or co-workers). Probably the most important finding, however, is that respondents exposed to a television campaign ad were 70% more likely to have voted in 2014. Again, it is important to note that this finding obtains even after controlling for key demographic characteristics such as gender, urban residence, age and race, as well as other cognitive covariates such as levels of education, news media use, and interest in politics, or exposure to other types of ads.

There is no evidence that television advertising affected respondents' voting decisions. We examined whether those who had seen a television ad were any more likely to have considered voting for a different party than the one they ultimately supported, decided their vote later in the campaign, voted for a party other than the one with which they identified (defection), or voted for different parties at the national and provincial level (ticket splitting). In each case, the coefficient for exposure to television advertisement was not statistically significant.

Finally, we examined whether exposure to television ads affected how people viewed the larger electoral process. Because having voted usually produces more positive views of the electoral process,

Table 31.7 Estimated effects of television advertising exposure on campaign engagement

	Logistic Regression Coefficient	Exp (b)	Nagelkerke R^2	N
Campaign knowledge				
Knows name of DA leader	0.326*	1.385	0.100	1,296
Able to rate ANC	NS	NS	0.398	1,296
Able to rate DA	1.271**	3.563	0.229	1,296
Able to rate EFF	NS	NS	0.181	1,296
Campaign engagement				
Interest in campaign	NS	NS	0.634	1,296
Campaign discussion (family)	0.445**	1.560	0.288	1,274
Campaign discussion (friends)	NS	NS	0.301	1,276
Campaign discussion (neighbors)	NS	NS	0.192	1,260
Campaign discussion (co-workers)	NS	NS	0.165	959
Persuades others to vote for specific party	NS	NS	0.286	1,296
Turnout	0.538***	1.713	0.317	1,296
Partisan choice				
Considered voting for another party	NS	NS	0.069	946
Date of voting decision	NS	NS	0.050	946
Defect from party identification	NS	NS	0.264	782
Split ticket voting (national vs. provincial vote)	NS	NS	0.251	948
Attitudes toward voting and election				
Who is in power matters	NS	NS	0.071	1,296
Vote matters	0.473**	1.605	0.119	1,296
Election free and fair	0.539***	1.714	0.158	1,296
Election results accurate	NS	NS	0.173	1,296

Notes: The first and second columns display the logistic regression coefficient and the odds ratio for television campaign ad exposure, after controlling for gender, urban–rural status, race, age, level of education, partisanship, level of interest in politics, frequency of campaign news media, and exposure to print and radio advertisements (not shown).

* $p \le .05$, ** $p \le .01$, *** $p \le .001$.

Source: South African National Election Study (Centre for Social Science Research, 2015).

and because we have already found that television ads appear to increase voter turnout, we added an additional control for whether or not one had voted. Even after taking this into consideration, we find that those who were exposed to a television ad were 60% more likely to think that their vote mattered, and 70% more likely to say that the election process was free and fair.

Conclusion

Television campaign advertising has come only recently to South African electoral politics. However, since its introduction in 2009, the evidence reviewed in this chapter demonstrates that television has expanded the ability of that country's political parties to make direct, unmediated contact with substantially larger audiences of potential voters. It has also improved their ability to go beyond traditional support bases, and take their messages to independent, non-partisan voters, and particularly important for South Africa, to take their message across traditional racial cleavages.

Finally, it appears that the use of television campaign advertising in 2009 helped to staunch the rapid decline in voter interest and participation witnessed between 1994 and 2004. While we cannot make definitive causal conclusions, the data suggest that across all key demographic categories, and across all levels of education, interest and news media use, those voters who were exposed to television ads were more likely to know something about the country's main opposition party, discuss the campaign with family members, and turn out to vote. In turn, those who had seen an ad were also more likely to agree that their vote matters, and see the recent election as free and fair.

Notes

1   In 2004, the private broadcaster, e-tv, invited parties to produce and submit short party election broadcasts that they broadcast during their news bulletins (Teer-Tomaselli, 2006). However, this channel had a relatively small footprint compared to the state broadcaster, so the effect was likely minimal.
2   The 2004, 2009 and 2014 surveys were also carried out as part of the international Comparative National Elections Project (see Gunther et al., 2006, 2016).

References

Berg-Schlosser, D. (2009). Long waves and conjunctures of democratization. In C. Haerpfer, P. Bernhagen, R. Inglehart, & C. Welzel (Eds.), *Democratization* (pp. 55–73). Oxford: Oxford University Press.

Booysen, S. (2014, May 4). Why ANC will stroll to an easy victory. *Sunday Independent*, p. 17.

Butler, A. (2009). The ANC's national election campaign of 2009: Siyanqoba! In R. Southall & J. Daniel (Eds.), *Zunami! The 2009 South African elections* (pp. 65–84). Johannesburg: Jacana.

Centre for Social Science Research. (2004). South African National Election Study. Cape Town: University of Cape Town.

Centre for Social Science Research. (2009). South African National Election Study. Cape Town: University of Cape Town.

Centre for Social Science Research. (2015). South African National Election Study. Cape Town: University of Cape Town.

Chiumbu, S., & Ciaglia, A. (2015). Public servant or censor? The South African Broadcasting Corporation in the era of political television advertising. *Journal of African Elections*, 14(1), 149–170.

Davis, G. (2005). Media coverage in election 2004: Were some parties more equal than others? In J. Piombo & L. Nijzink (Eds.), *Electoral politics in South Africa: Assessing the first democratic decade* (pp. 232–249). New York, NY: Palgrave Macmillan.

Doreenspleet, R. (2000). Reassessing the three waves of democratization. *World Politics*, 52(3), 385–406.

Duncan, J. (2014). The South African media and the 2014 elections: Competition without diversity. In C. Schulz-Herzenberg & R. Southall (Eds.), *Election 2014 South Africa: The campaigns, results and future prospects* (pp. 133–154). Johannesburg: Jacana.

Gunther, R., Beck, P. A., Magalhaes, P., & Moreno, A. (Eds.). (2016). *Voting in old and new democracies*. London: Routledge.

Gunther, R., Montero, J. R., & Puhle, H.-J. (Eds.). (2006). *Democracy, intermediation and voting on four continents*. Oxford: Oxford University Press.

Holtz-Bacha, C. (2014). Political advertising in international comparison. In H. Cheng (Ed.), *The handbook of international advertising research* (pp. 554–574). Malden, MA: Wiley-Blackwell.

Independent Communications Authority of South Africa. (2009, March 3). Regulations on party election broadcasts, political advertisements, the equitable treatment of political parties by broadcasting licensees and related matters. *Government Gazette*, 525(31980), 3–11.

Independent Communications Authority of South Africa. (2014a, February 17). Regulations on party election broadcasts, political advertisements, the equitable treatment of political parties by broadcasting licensees and related matters. *Government Gazette*, 584(37350), 18–26.

Independent Communications Authority of South Africa. (2014b, November 17). Report on coverage of 2014 national and provincial elections. *Government Gazette*, 593(38212), 3–47.

Jolobe, Z. (2014). The Democratic Alliance election campaign: "Ayisafani"? In C. Schulz-Herzenberg & R. Southall (Eds.), *Election 2014 South Africa: The campaigns, results and future prospects* (pp. 57–71). Johannesburg: Jacana.

Karp, J. (2012). Electoral systems, party mobilization and political engagement. *Australian Journal of Political Science*, 47(1), 71–89.

Lodge, T. (2005). The African National Congress: There is no party like it; Ayikho Efana Nayo. In J. Piombo & L. Nijzink (Eds), *Electoral politics in South Africa: Assessing the first democratic decade* (pp. 109–128). New York, NY: Palgrave Macmillan,

McFaul, M. (2002). The fourth wave of democracy and dictatorship: Noncooperative transitions in the postcommunist world. *World Politics*, 54(2), 212–244.

Ranchod, R. (2013). *A kind of magic: The political marketing of the ANC*. Jacana: Johannesburg.

Sarakinsky, I. (2014). Party political finance and multi-party democracy in South Africa's 2014 election. *South Africa Election Updates*, 9 (pp. 3–9). Johannesburg: Electoral Institute for Democracy in Africa.

Schreiner, W., & Mattes, R. (2012). The possibilities of election campaigns as sites of political advocacy: South Africa in comparative perspective. In H. Thuynsma (Ed.), *Public opinion and interest group politics: South Africa's missing links?* (pp. 154–172). Pretoria: Africa Institute of South Africa.

Schulz-Herzenberg, C. (2014, August). The South African 2014 national and provincial elections: The integrity of the electoral process. Institute for Security Affairs. *Policy Brief*, 62.

Sindane, S. (2014). The commodification of political advertising on television during the 2009 general elections in South Africa. *Global Media Journal: African Edition*, 8(1), 1–29.

Teer-Tomaselli, R. (2006). Political advertising in South Africa. In L. L. Kaid & C. Holtz-Bacha (Eds.), *The Sage handbook of political advertising* (pp. 429–442). Thousand Oaks, CA: Sage.

Zvomuya, P. (2009, February 27 to March 5). ANC takes flight. *Mail and Guardian*, p. 9.

PART V

Conclusion

32

CONCLUSION

Democracy and Political Advertising

Marion R. Just

Attitudes toward political advertising in the public and even among scholars are ambiguous (Kaid, 2004). Ads are often seen as a necessary evil rather than a public good. The main concern is that ads appeal primarily to emotions rather than rational thought (Brader, 2006). Because of the threat of emotions in politics, this volume shows that many political systems regulate political advertising to limit the public's exposure to ads.

Democracy and Political Advertising

On the positive side, ads are accepted as a way to provide the public with "low cost" political information. Anthony Downs described the paradox of voting, namely that for most people gathering information to correlate their votes with their interests is not worth the benefit of rational voting. Downs assumes that people have many other priorities in their lives that limit the amount of time that they can devote to discovering information and making independent judgments about how to vote. In addition, people in many walks of life do not have the educational tools, personal contacts or information base that would lower the cost of obtaining information about complex topics. In his analysis of the role of political parties, E. E. Schattschneider argued that strong political parties are an essential heuristic for people to make electoral choices (1975). Sam Popkin (1991) maintained that voters necessarily employ shortcuts including potent symbols to help them decide where their interests lie. Because the information in ads is often presented in an entertaining way and may be encountered in the pursuit of other goals (such as amusement), political ads reduce the cost of information to voters while improving the chances that their votes will correlate with their interests.

Some researchers have argued that even if ads have a strong emotional component, the distinction between reason and emotion is a false dichotomy. Emotions result from experience with choices people made in the past – what is called "experiential reasoning." People are often unaware that what seems like rational decision-making automatically involves their emotions (Crigler & Just, 2012; Epstein, 2014). Daniel Kahneman (2013) has argued that people employ a dual system for thinking. Even what appears to be rational thinking involves emotional biases that are baked into the brain by evolutionary processes. Because advertising engages people in the political process, even though it employs emotional reasoning, advertising is tolerated in most systems.

In addition to political engagement, the democratic concept of freedom of speech supports the right of political parties and candidates to persuade voters to support them in electoral contests. The experience of several systems described in this book with strictly policy-oriented rational presentation of each party or candidate's point of view is that most of the television audience finds these party presentations incredibly boring. In fact, in several instances the parties have relinquished much of the time available to them for these televised presentations in order to better engage the public.

The public shares academics' concerns about political advertising. They associate advertising with commercial product ads and do not want their leaders sold to them "like soap." They report in focus groups that they do not like to have their emotions manipulated (Just et al., 1996, p. 162). As several chapters in this volume have shown, when asked what influences their votes, citizens generally mention some other kind of political communication before mentioning ads. Ads are not a socially desirable answer to the question because people think mentioning ads would show that they are easily manipulated. They are likely therefore to say that other people are influenced by ads, or that party election broadcasts or political debates are the source of their information. The audiences for the PEBs and debates, however, do not support those explanations.

Advertising is belittled compared to more verbose political statements because they cannot contain extensive argument. The most essential ads in political posters contain merely the name of the party and a picture or symbol. It is interesting that in political systems that prohibit television advertising (see Chapter 1) political posters are retained. It is possible, in fact, for a system to practice multi-party campaigns and elections in an essentially illiterate society by merely employing symbols on the ballot, as in parts of India. The question of the brevity of political ads is one of the areas where the mismatch between democratic theory of an informed electorate meets the actual motivations of the political actors.

Information and Persuasion

One egregious mismatch concerns turnout. Political candidates are motivated to suppress turnout of supporters of their competitors. Therefore they will attempt to attribute blame and impugn the reputations of the candidates or parties with whom they compete. In the US, in order to control costs, political actors generally air ads only in states where the candidates are competitive. As a result, during a great part of the campaign, television ads show the opposition in the most unfavorable light in order to persuade opposition voters to stay home. If left to their own devices, political opponents may be motivated to depress participation in order to win elections, as they do in the US. Some researchers have argued that trading attack ads will depress turnout all around, but the evidence is mixed. Negative ads appear to have different effects by gender – women are put off by attacks and men are excited by them (Fridkin & Kenney, 2011).

Advertising encompasses both negative and positive persuasion, but it is important to keep in mind that persuasion and not information is the goal, even though the products may overlap. This is the primary divergence between political motivation and the theory of an informed electorate. Advertising is inherently biased, informing only to the extent that it suits the goals of the sponsors. Depending on the practitioners and the relevant political regulations, advertisers may avoid outright lies, but even that is not guaranteed. Fact-checking organizations are always busy during election campaigns as candidates and parties bend the truth to their own purposes (Politifact.com, FactCheck. org in the US, for example).[1]

As a form of persuasive speech, therefore, ads do not need to be accurate or factual. Parties and candidates express bias and that bias means that some essential facts are modified or omitted to strengthen the internal consistency of the argument. By incorporating persuasive speech into campaign communication, political systems are contradicting the essential element of rational decision-making. The marketplace or the adversarial courtroom provide models in which persuasive speech can be incorporated into rational outcomes. The prosecutorial American and British models of the courtroom lie in the belief that after hearing the pro and con arguments a judge or jury will reach an appropriate decision. In the marketplace, the better product will outsell the poorer product. To apply those models to politics, however, requires an assumption of the equality of the presentation.

Americans, for example, are generally aware that the better-funded side in a trial has the best chance of hiring the most experienced and qualified attorney or barrister to make the case, and justice suffers for it. Likewise the best product is not always the most popular. A case in point is the Beta video system – a better engineered product than VHS that went on to maintain a place among professionals but lost out to public preferences. The great champion of freedom of the press, Benjamin Franklin, believed that "When Truth and Error have fair play, the former is always an overmatch for the latter." It is difficult, however, to have lived in modern society and believe that to be the case.

Journalists generally fact-check political ads as they do other political communication. An attempt to counter biased information that was popular for a few years in the US was the "Ad Watch" introduced by Kathleen Hall Jamieson as a means to counter what she found was widespread deception in political advertising (Jamieson, 1993). The Ad Watch recommended a specific "grammar" for critiques of ads that would limit the free advertising of deceptive ads presented on television news.

The grammar consisted of a using some visual device to alert the viewer that the ad was not part of the news (usually by showing the ad video in a box that looked like a television screen), accompanied by specific claims marked or stamped FALSE. The broadcasting company CNN was supported by foundation grants to employ ad watch grammar in the 1992 US presidential campaign. The format is still used in a few outlets including WiscTV and some US newspapers. Print ad watches presented special boxes with the the full text of the ads along with statements about the truth or falsehood in the ads. The *New York Times'* ad watches also included journalists' expert opinions about the effectiveness of the ads. The *Times* eventually decided to integrate ad coverage with campaign news without a separate format. Critics of the formal ad watch argued that it exacerbated political cynicism by portraying all politicians as liars and that the one-time news ad watch was no match for multiple exposures to political advertisements. Some researchers showed that the ad watch grammar could not defeat the impact of the ad if people were interested in the content (Just et al., 1996).

Advertising Effects

Results from experimental studies finds that people are actually much better at remembering information from ads than from debates (Just, Crigler, & Wallach, 1990). After watching candidate debates with unfamiliar candidates, viewers cannot remember who said what, but the same viewers remember the name of the candidate that advertised his position on an issue.

The reason that ads are more memorable is that an "ad buy" assures that people in a media market will actually see the ad preferably five times to ensure memorability. Systems that limit ads try to ensure the opposite, i.e., that ads will not be memorable, either by allowing television ads at times of day when the audience is scarce or by limiting the number of minutes devoted to advertising. In nations with a more laissez-faire approach, such as the US or Australia, advertisers know that people will remember some contents of an ad or party slogans by repetition, even if they do not agree with the position itself.

There is a limit to the persuasive effects of ads. Partisans will automatically "counter-argue" against messages of ads of a known opponent. According to John Zaller's RAS model of communication, audiences must not only receive a message (e.g., view an ad on television), they must also accept it before it becomes available for "sampling" in a public opinion survey (Zaller, 1992). Once partisans identify an ad for an opposing political party or group, they suspend belief. Of course not every member of the advertising audience has a strong loyalty to a party or candidate. For that reason, ads are considered to be most effective when viewed by voters who are undecided or uninterested in politics.

Political advertising employs other techniques to avoid "counter-arguing," such as surprise, humor or story-telling. Humor can disarm partisans because people are happy to be entertained. An ad may tell a story and engage viewers before surprising viewers with a partisan communication. A classic example of the unexpected message is the "Bear in the Woods" ad for President Reagan in the 1984 campaign (see Chapter 23, in this volume). The ad begins by showing the woods and an announcer asks whether or not there is a bear in the woods. When first shown the ad focus group members did not know that they were watching a political ad. Some even thought that the topic was protecting forests. They were surprised to hear the announcer ask "isn't it smart to be as strong as the bear … if there is a bear?" followed by the identification of the sponsoring candidate (www.youtube.com/watch?v=NpwdcmjBgNA).

In addition to narratives, some political ads use high production values and cinematic techniques to draw in the audience in ways that that are not offensive, boring or annoying. For example, in 2012 Diederik Samsom, a Dutch party leader, told the story of his handicapped daughter in his political message (www.youtube.com/watch?v=Js-3Tyljx30, see Chapter 29, in this volume). It is important to keep in mind that the most persuasive effects of political ads are fleeting – usually a few days (Gerber, Gimpel, Green, & Shaw, 2011). These short-lived effects do not make the impact of advertising negligible. The authors of the study believe that ads mostly prime the audience to highlight particular issues. Some people, usually those most uninvolved in politics, do not make up their minds until the last days or week of the campaign. These uninvolved voters are the most vulnerable to persuasion and the late timing of ad placement may put the ad within the window of strong effects. Negative attacks launched in the last few days and blanketing the airwaves may not afford the target any opportunity to respond. Unanswered attacks can be devastating (as was the case in the US 2004 Bush/Kerry presidential campaign). As we have seen, many nations forbid advertising in the last few days before voters go to the polls (as in Argentina) in order to prevent a last-minute attack strategy from affecting the outcome of an election.

There is evidence that some people are more immune to advertising in general, not only when it is from an opposing party or candidate. In some cultures, such as those of Scandinavia, the public believes that advertising is manipulative and resists television ads because of that view. For example, television advertising was not permitted in Sweden until 2005. In eschewing US style advertising spots many nations have permitted Party Election Broadcasts or Public Service Broadcasts of various lengths on both public and private outlets.

Typically, Party Election Broadcasts, especially when they are heralded by an announcement about the upcoming content, result in audiences turning the channel or otherwise avoiding what is often regarded as an invitation to boredom. These announcements are required in order to alert the audience that the material is not unbiased information and does not carry the imprimatur of the broadcaster or the government. This free air time, however, notably provides parties with a more level playing field than advertising centric systems. In the US, access to advertising platforms system is based on the party or candidate's ability to pay (even when the rates are somewhat lower than commercial rates). The divergence between advertising centric systems and party election broadcast modes has narrowed with the emergence of Internet technology.

Online Advertising

The Internet provides an opportunity for all kinds of campaign communication and in particular for videos. Dedicated video-sharing platforms, such as YouTube, have provided a venue not only for ads but also for speeches, conventions and campaign events. Beginning in the 2008 presidential campaign, YouTube sponsored one of the US presidential debates with questions from viewers uploaded to the site. Campaign videos can now be accessed on mobile devices such as smartphones and tablets, giving them a wide audience. The Internet, with its websites, blogs, Facebook, Twitter, Periscope and Snapchat, has transformed campaign communication and to some extent has leveled the playing field without external regulation. The cost of Internet access is essentially close to zero, so that smaller, minor parties and individual candidates can establish some kind of presence without paying for staff or airtime. As such, the Internet has become a major competitor to television with the added benefit of open access.

Of course, there are costs involved in using Internet channels. By using the video cameras on most smartphones, some kind of access is almost universally available. The challenge on the Internet is to make the presentation sufficiently interesting/attractive that users will be motivated to choose that site, blog, Facebook post, tweet or video over innumerable others. While almost any small political party can make a video, high production values distinguish the more well-funded players. A candidate or party that produces television ads has almost no additional cost to uploading its ads to a video-sharing website, but smaller parties do not have that capacity and therefore eschew Internet video as well. The better funded campaigners generally fund the production of videos made especially for the Internet. In the US, candidates and parties are expected to spend about $1 billion on online advertising according to research by Borrell Associates (Lapowsky, 2015). In the US, spending is expected to rise to three times that amount by the presidential election year of 2020. Other nations will surely see proportional increases as well.

Ads specifically produced for the Internet differ from television ads in a number of ways. They are often longer than the 30 seconds length that has become standard in the US and different versions of the same ad appear at various times online. Internet ads are geared mostly to supporters. Unlike television, where political ads appear unbidden and are sometimes unavoidable, ads online are viewed primarily when people search for them. The online ad audience can find ads on candidate websites or on YouTube. The people who are most likely to engage in that search are supporters (Crigler, Just, Hume, Mills, & Hevron, 2011).[2]

Because the audience for Internet ads is segmented by party support, the ads likewise are expressions of support for a candidate or party. A study of the first US presidential YouTube election found that unlike the Obama television spots, his online ads were overwhelmingly positive (Crigler et al., 2011). Surprisingly, however, Republicans posted a large number of negative ads attacking Obama. The research question is what do supporters want to see. In some cases attacking the opposition can be precisely the kind of message that appeals to party supporters. As time goes on and the Internet platform expands, it is likely that Internet ads will look more like television ads, both in production value and tone. Because Internet ads are mostly unregulated, they may also change the culture surrounding political advertising in general (see Chapter 22, this volume).

A significant new element of Internet ads is that the line between the audience and content producers has been erased. YouTube was founded for video sharing, not for top-down communication. It is still a platform where members of the audience can originate content. In the 2008 US presidential campaign one of the most popular online ads was produced by musicians who set an Obama speech to music, "Yes, I Can" (www.youtube.com/watch?v=74mKVwC799k). The ad was produced at various lengths and went "viral" (i.e., was shared across the Internet). Although the production values were modest, the musicians who took part included some of the most popular performers and the ad had the feel of a music video.

Ad developers all hope that they will get the "viral" effect where millions share the video on social media sites. Some audience originated ads are parodies of actual ads and some are produced from scratch. The team of JibJab produced one of the most widely watched viral videos parodying the George Bush and John Kerry 2004 campaign ("This Land is Your Land"). Some comedians such as Sarah Silverman ("The Big Shlep") or celebrities such as Paris Hilton have produced videos during election campaigns promoting specific candidates (mostly Democrats). The field, however, is rife with individuals getting into the act by producing their own YouTube videos. Audience-produced ads are a lively addition to the Italian political scene as well (see Chapter 13, this volume).

New distribution networks have emerged on Facebook and Twitter for distributing videos both from parties and candidates as well as unofficial producers. Facebook and Twitter now include live streaming, which means that all kinds of political news can move on social networks other than YouTube. These new Internet venues are mostly unregulated and accessed inexpensively. There is an increasingly wider audience for online advertising. Younger members of the audience get their election news primarily on the Internet – two-thirds of 18- to 29-year-olds in the US (Gottfried & Shearer, 2016; Pew Research Center, 2016). As time goes on, the majority of the citizens will also prefer these platforms. With the open Internet, political restrictions make little sense. For all of these reasons, the future of political advertising is going online.

Notes

1   The American website Politifact now has a global edition that fact-checks international politics.
2   Facebook's Newsfeed more resembles the television experience, but that is a relatively new phenomenon. Facebook is now in the process of reducing third-party news because consumers prefer to hear from people they know in their news feeds. People may encounter opposing ads on Facebook sent by connections who disagree with their views.

References

Brader, T. (2006). *Campaigning for hearts and minds: How emotional appeals in political ads work*. Chicago: University of Chicago Press.

Crigler, A., & Just, M. (2012). Measuring affect, emotion and mood in political communication. In H. Semetko & M. Scammell (Eds.), *The Sage handbook of political communication* (pp. 211–224). London: Sage.

Crigler, A., Just, M., Hume, L., Mills, J., & Hevron, P. (2011). YouTube and TV advertising campaigns: Obama vs. McCain in 2008. In R. L. Fox & J. M. Ramos (Eds.), *i-Politics: Campaigns, elections, and governing in the new media era* (pp. 211–224). Cambridge: Cambridge University Press.

Epstein, S. (2014). *Cognitive-experiential theory: An integrative theory of personality*. Oxford: Oxford University Press.

Fridkin, K. L., & Kenney, P. (2011). Variability in citizens' reactions to different types of negative campaigns. *American Journal of Political Science*, 55(2), 307–325. doi: 10.1111/j.1540-5907.2010.00494.x.

Gerber, A. S., Gimpel, J. G., Green, D. P., & Shaw, D. (2011). How large and long-lasting are the persuasive effects of televised campaign ads? Results from a randomized field experiment. *American Political Science Review*, 105(1), 135–150.

Gottfried, J., & Shearer, E. (2016, May 26). News use across social media platforms 2016. *Pew Research Center*. Retrieved from www.journalism.org/2016/05/26/news-use-across-social-media-platforms-2016/.

Jamieson, K. H. (1993). *Dirty politics: Deception, distraction and democracy*. New York, NY: Oxford University Press.

Just, M., Crigler, A., Alger D., Cook, T., Kern, M., & West, D. (1996). *Crosstalk: Citizens, candidates, and the media in a presidential campaign*. Chicago: University of Chicago Press.

Just, M., Crigler, A., & Wallach, L. (1990). Thirty seconds or thirty minutes: What viewers learn from spot advertisements and candidate debates. *Journal of Communication*, 40(3), 120–133.

Kahneman, D. (2013). *Thinking fast and slow*. New York, NY: Farrar, Straus and Giroux PB.

Kaid, L. L. (2004). Political advertising. In L. L. Kaid (Ed.), *Handbook of political communication research* (pp. 155–202). Mahwah, NJ: Lawrence Erlbaum.

Lapowsky, I. (2015, August). Political ad spending on line is about to explode. *Wired*. Retrieved from www.wired.com/2015/08/digital-politcal-ads-2016/.

Pew Research Center. (2016). The modern news consumer, 6. Young adults. Retrieved from www.journalism.org/2016/07/07/young-adults/.

Popkin, S. (1991). *The reasoning voter: Communication and persuasion in presidential campaigns*. Chicago: University of Chicago Press.

Schattschneider, E. E. (1975). *The semisovereign people: A realist's view of democracy in America* (revised edition with David Adamany). Independence, KY: Cengage Publishing.

Zaller, J. (1992). *The nature and origins of mass opinion*. Cambridge: Cambridge University Press.

INDEX